Resurrection

Resurrection:
New Testament Witness and Contemporary Reflection

PHEME PERKINS

Geoffrey Chapman
London

A Geoffrey Chapman book published by
Cassell Ltd
1 Vincent Square, London SW1P 2PN

Published in the United States of America by Doubleday & Company, Inc.
First published in Great Britain 1985

ISBN 0 225 66418 6

Library of Congress Cataloging in Publication Data

Perkins, Pheme.
  Resurrection: New Testament witness and contemporary reflection.

  Bibliography: p. 453.
  Includes index.
  1. Resurrection—Biblical teaching. 2. Jesus Christ—Resurrection.
3. Bible. N.T.—Criticism, interpretation, etc. I. Title.
BS2545.R47P47   1984   232'.5

Library of Congress Catalog Card Number: 83-25473

Printed and bound in Great Britain at
The Camelot Press Limited, Southampton

Contents

Abbreviations

CBQ	Catholic Biblical Quarterly
CBQMS	Catholic Biblical Quarterly Monograph Series
c. Cel.	*Contra Celsum*
CD	Cairo (Genizah text of the) Damascus (Document)
CG	Cairo Gnostic (Codices = Nag Hammadi Library)
2 Clem	Second Clement
Com. In Jo.	Commentary on John
Conf. Ling.	On the Confusion of Tongues
Congr.	On Mating with the Preliminary Studies
Daim. Soc.	On the Daimon of Socrates
Def. Or.	On the Decline of Oracles
EBib	Études Bibliques
Ebr.	On Drunkenness
Ep.	*Epistles*
ETL	*Ephemerides theologicae lovanienses*
ETR	*Études théologique et religieuses*
EvT	*Evangelische Theologie*
ExpTim	*Expository Times*
De Fac. Lun.	On the Face in the Moon
Fug.	On Flight and Finding
Gig.	On the Giants
Greg	*Gregorianum*
Heres	Who Is the Heir of Divine Things?
HeyJ	*Heythrop Journal*
HNT	Handbuch zum Neuen Testament
HR	*History of Religions*
HSM	Harvard Semitic Monographs
HTR	*Harvard Theological Review*
HTS	Harvard Theological Studies
Int	*Interpretation*
JBL	*Journal of Biblical Literature*
JEH	*Journal of Ecclesiastical History*
JR	*Journal of Religion*

JTS	*Journal of Theological Studies*
Jub.	Jubilees
LAB	Book of Biblical Antiquities
Lat.	Latin
Leg.	*Legatio*
Leg. All.	Allegorical Interpretation of Genesis
LXX	Septuagint
IV Macc.	Fourth Maccabees
m. San	mishnah Sanhedrin
Mut	On the Change of Names
NHLE	*Nag Hammadi Library in English* (ed J. M. Robinson)
NHS	Nag Hammadi Studies
NRT	*La nouvelle revue théologique*
NovT	*Novum Testamentum*
NTS	*New Testament Studies*
Opif.	On the Account of the World's Creation Given by Moses
Or.	*Oratio*
Paed.	Paedagogus
Pleas. Life Imposs.	On the Impossibility of the Pleasant Life
Pram.	On Rewards and Punishments
Ps. Sol.	Psalms of Solomon
1 QApGen	Genesis Apocryphon from Cave 1
QD	Quaestiones disputatae
QGen	Questions and Answers on Genesis
1 QH	Hôdāyôt (Thanksgiving Hymns) from Cave 1
1 QM	Milhāmah (War Scroll)
1 QS	Serek hayyahad (Rule of the Community; Manual of Discipline)
RAC	*Reallexikon für Antike und Christentum*
RB	*Revue biblique*
Rep.	Res publica
De Res.	*On the Resurrection*

Res. Car.	*On the Resurrection of the Flesh*
Res. Mort.	*On the Resurrection of the Dead*
RSR	*Recherches de science religieuse*
Sacr.	*On the Sacrifices of Cain and Abel*
StANT	Studien zum Alten und Neuen Testaments
SBLDS	Society of Biblical Literature Dissertation Series
SBS	Stuttgarter biblische Beiträge
SBT	Studies in Biblical Theology
SC	Sources chrétiennes
Sib. Or.	Sibylline Oracles
SNTSMS	Studiorum Novi Testamenti Societas Monograph Series
Sobr.	*On Sobriety*
Spec. Leg.	On the Special Laws
Strom.	Stromateis
Suppl.	Supplicatio
T. Abr.	Testament of Abraham
T. 12 Patr.	Testaments of the Twelve Patriarchs
T. Ben.	Testament of Benjamin
T. Jud.	Testament of Judah
T. Levi	Testament of Levi
T. Sim.	Testament of Simeon
T. Zeb.	Testament of Zebulun
THKNT	Theologisches Handkommentar zum Neuen Testament
TQ	*Theologische Quartalschrift*
Tral.	*Epistle to the Trallians*
Tusc. Disp.	Tuscan Disputations
TZ	*Theologische Zeitschrift*
VC	*Vigiliae christianae*
Virt.	Philo, *On Virtue*
Vit. Con.	On the Contemplative Life
WMANT	Wissenschaftliche Monographien zum Alten und Neuen Testament
ZKT	*Zeitschrift für katholische Theologie*
ZNW	*Zeitschrift für die neutestamentliche Wissenschaft*
ZTK	*Zeitschrift für Theologie und Kirche*

Resurrection

ONE

The Resurrection Question

RESURRECTION AS FOUNDATION

Most Christians would agree that they believe in "resurrection." When resurrection language is combined with the related symbols of exaltation, resurrection can be found almost everywhere in the New Testament.[1] The early Christian kerygma stands or falls with the resurrection, since exaltation forms the foundation of the confession that Jesus is Lord.[2] Resurrection also appears as the presupposition for the emergence of the Christian group as a new community. That community's claim that God's salvation has been revealed in the cross and resurrection of Jesus will also lead to new formulations about God.[3]

Most Christians probably imagine resurrection more as a miraculous return from the dead than as the foundation of their community or of other beliefs that they hold about Jesus. The resurrection narratives that conclude the gospel accounts of Jesus' life are treated simply as accounts of "what happened." Yet they, too, are eloquent

testimony to the creative relationship between resurrection and the
foundations of Christian life and belief: the exaltation of Jesus to
universal lordship; the diffusion of the Spirit of God in a new community; the understanding of the coming of Jesus as fulfillment of the
promises of the Scriptures; and the apostolic mission of the Christian
community to the world.[4]

Resurrection is presented as the culmination of the Biblical story of
human captivity and God's deliverance. It is not merely an assertion
in the creed but pervades Christian speech in the New Testament.
One might even go so far as to say that it is the condition for the
emergence of Christian speech itself.[5] The foundational character of
resurrection speech has led to an awkward inability to explore the
boundaries of resurrection as a category in Christian theology.
J. Cameron illustrates this difficulty from a lecture in which a theologian asserted, "The resurrection narratives are logically odd." The
speaker meant to claim by his assertion that one could not ask
whether the resurrection accounts were true or false. Such sentences
may act as "signposts" to tell nonbelievers and historical critics to
"keep out." But it is difficult to perceive them as adequate accounts
of what the New Testament authors meant in speaking of resurrection.[6] Rather, it would seem that twentieth-century Christians must
explore the "truth" of resurrection as the founding language of their
tradition. Such exploration cannot stop with asserting that some symbols or concepts are "untouchable." It must ask, instead, what space
such speech can occupy in the linguistic world of the twentieth-
century Christian. This question is not simply destructive meddling
on the part of exegetes and theologians. It urges itself upon us from a
Christian life and speech that have lost contact with the illuminating
power of resurrection symbolism.[7] One need not surround resurrection with "do not touch" signs born of an apologetic instinct to bolster
the foundations. Instead, one must acknowledge that the challenge
of a twentieth-century understanding of resurrection embraces several levels of reflection:

1. Exegetical, historical analysis of the first-century affirmation of
resurrection seeks to recover what might have been meant by such
language in its originating context. With all the difficulties that attach
to recovering "what was meant," the methods and hypotheses of
exegetical analysis still provide our primary route to understanding
the language of the Biblical text. They are particularly necessary for
symbols, metaphors, and concepts that, like resurrection, can be
shown to have lost their original network of understanding.

2. Theological or reflective clarification seeks to explain in discursive terms what Christians mean by their use of resurrection language. Since resurrection emerges from the levels of symbol and story, even the first- and second-century authors found themselves called upon to explain what affirmations or consequences should or should not follow from belief in resurrection. The task is even more pressing for twentieth-century Christians, who require such reflective speech as a way back to the roots of their tradition.

3. Reflective clarification may also go beyond the believing community in its quest to situate resurrection in the larger world of human discourse. Does such a perception of things contribute, for example, to the root problems of scientific or philosophical understanding?

Clearly, such a project of clarification can hardly be accomplished in a single book. Each of these tasks has its own literature, methods, and conflicting schools of thought. Since its author is an exegete by training, this book will focus on the first task. But the exegetical and historical task is not pursued merely with the intention of adding yet another stone to the pile of exegetical studies. Rather, our hope is to further the digestion of the mass of exegetical results by the larger community. We will follow the resurrection traditions into the debates of the second century, since they largely set the tone for what later generations of Christians would take from the insights and formulations of the first century. The final two chapters will sketch the state of resurrection in some quarters of contemporary philosophy and theology. These chapters do not pretend to cover those fields, but they reflect what appear to an exegete looking in to be characteristic approaches.

SURVEYING THE NEW TESTAMENT

The New Testament itself raises questions that have divided exegetes. One finds two types of resurrection affirmation, that of the kerygmatic formula (e.g., 1 Cor 15:3–7; Rm 4:25) and that of the narratives that conclude the gospel accounts. Although the formulae are the oldest witnesses to resurrection belief, one cannot simply derive the later narratives from the earlier formulae.[8] The narratives themselves contain as many points of divergence as they do of similarity. They cannot be treated as fragments of a single account. The gaps that the narrative traditions present cannot be filled in by some additional facts. At the level of the gospel narrative, each account may be viewed as an integral conclusion to the story of Jesus as presented by the evangelist. Differences at this level indicate apologetic concerns and show the development of early Christian reflection on resurrection.[9] Nevertheless, it remains a constant temptation of interpreters to create a synthetic account that will "unify" this diversity. The narrative traditions can also be divided. Some center on the finding of the empty tomb; others, on appearances of Jesus to his disciples. The kerygmatic traditions of 1 Cor 15:3-7 refer to appearances but not to the tomb. Each of the three streams of tradition —kerygma, appearance, tomb—has come down to us in a context of further interpretation. In Mark and Luke the finding of the empty tomb provides the occasion for the kerygmatic announcement of the resurrection by an angel. Matthew and John, on the other hand, know traditions that combine the empty tomb and an appearance of Jesus.

Since even our earliest resurrection traditions show signs of development, exegetes attempt to relate those developments to the history of the earliest communities. The hermeneutical problem is that of tracing the situations in which various traditions interact as they develop. The New Testament text is not perceived as a fixed source of dogmas and universal symbols. Rather, it witnesses to a process of development, interpretation, and reinterpretation.[10]

Further complexity is introduced by the traditions of Jesus' exaltation (e.g., Phil 2:9; Eph 4:10; 1 Tim 3:16). The traditions of exaltation and resurrection are independent. One cannot be deduced from the other.[11] The independence of exaltation traditions suggests that certain Christian beliefs are not dependent on resurrection as a necessary condition, though it may be a sufficient condition for their appearance. Thus, one learns the following from this distinction:

a. It is possible to speak of Jesus' return to the Father without resurrection language.

b. The sending of the Spirit is more closely tied to Jesus' exaltation than to resurrection.

c. Resurrection is not a necessary prelude to exaltation. In many traditions the One manifested as risen is already exalted.

d. Exaltation serves just as well as resurrection to relativize death.[12]

Exaltation language, Schillebeeckx argues, is most easily suited to the expectation that Jesus is to return at the parousia. The parousia will represent the cosmic demonstration of his lordship. Thus, it is possible to construe the original Easter experience as one in which the risen/exalted Jesus is to return soon and bring the Reign of God and vindication of the righteous. In the parousia pattern of understanding, the conquest of death is still tied to that impending judgment. However, the tomb and appearance traditions reflect a point at which the conquest of death is perceived as an important resurrection theme.[13]

Resurrection anticipates the eschatological victory over death. This element of victory should never be lost, whatever interpretation one gives the varied New Testament formulae.[14] But can one say that "present and available to faith" and "eschatological victory over death" are really reducible to a single affirmation? Should one presume that the various ancient formulae are really about a single core that could be articulated in equivalent formulae? Rather, it would appear that the genuine diversity of the New Testament witness already suggests that resurrection functions as a much more comprehensive symbol to draw together a number of perceptions, experiences, and insights. Further, one must also ask whether or not one finds substantive changes within the New Testament traditions themselves, changes that can only be described as "meaning something different" from what is understood elsewhere in the New Testament. H. Kee finds clear evidence of such changes. Future expectation in passages like 1 Cor 15:52 expects resurrection as a promise fulfilled at the end of the age. Passages like 1 Tim 1:17 and 1 Pt 1:4, on the other hand, look toward an immortal inheritance kept in heaven. Resurrection language is transformed as one moves beyond the apocalyptic dualism of awakening those who sleep in the dust (cf. Dan 12:2) into an environment of hellenistic, ontological dualism. The opponents of Mk 12:18–23 mock a literalist vision of resurrection as resumption of life with all its relationships. Jesus' answer in Mk 12:24–27 has already accepted a hellenized spiritualizing of resurrection. Paul is forced to come up with language about "spiritual body" and imperishability to counter the opposing soteriology at Corinth (1 Cor 15:35–50). In so doing, however, he has adopted a set of categories that are not really appropriate to the earlier views of resurrection. Though the pastoral epistles use resurrection in formulae from an earlier period or as a slogan against opposing eschatologies (e.g., 2 Tim 2:8, 18), they really imagine Jesus quite simply as an immortal being.[15] Similarly, N. Frye has observed that even though Christians placed resurrection of the body in their creed, that belief had no discernible effect on their development of a body/soul dichotomy.[16] These developments make it clear that no single, unified picture of resurrection is presented in the tradition. Exegetes must always take pains to avoid creating a false unity out of genuine diversity.

INTERPRETING THE APOCALYPTIC CODE

Increasing interest in the social sciences has led exegetes to reformulate their approach to the development of tradition. Theological concepts and symbols are not viewed in a vacuum. They are seen to emerge from, and in turn shape, the experiences of the community that uses them. One must ask, therefore, What situations gave rise to resurrection symbolism? What functions did it fulfill in the community? How did it function in contexts other than the originating one?[17] Thus, one sees in the New Testament an ongoing process by which a religious community interprets and constructs its world in symbol.[18]

Resurrection symbolism emerges during Maccabean times within the larger context of apocalyptic symbols. These symbols portray God's impending judgment of a world that is dominated by the powers of evil. Only a small group of elect righteous know the truth about the heavenly world and the coming judgment. Scholars have argued that apocalyptic emerges in response to crisis. The previous pictures of the world that defined order and value collapsed and left their adherents in an uncharted chaos. Apocalyptic traditions meet the crisis by retrieving archaic mythic symbols in which they are able to describe the evils of the present world, the divine victory over evil, and the subsequent condition of paradisaical bliss, which represents the reestablishment of cosmic order.[19]

Further, apocalyptic wisdom does not seek to show humanity how it might be harmoniously integrated into the processes of this world, since there is a sharp discontinuity between this world and the order of divine salvation.[20] Within this apocalyptic schema, resurrection emerges as a mode of transcending death whereby humans participate in the heavenly sphere of reality. 1 En. 93, for example, describes the seer's translation into that heavenly world.[21] But this translation presumes such a discontinuity between the present world and the divine that one cannot presume that resurrection emerges from the mythic context of a cyclic renewal of nature. The apocalyptic visions all presume a radical new creation to follow upon the divine victory. The question about resurrection as the return to life of a physical body that belongs to the present order of creation can only arise when resurrection is stripped of its original context of discourse within the apocalyptic code.

The New Testament shows that resurrection is quickly divorced from its originating context. This separation is in part due to the spread of Christianity among the urban population outside Palestine. Even the Jewish community of those cities looked upon Roman imperial power as beneficent (as in Rom 13:1–7) and not as the embodiment of evil shortly to be overthrown by divine intervention. The Christian image of resurrection, because a new age was seen as having begun with Jesus, also initiated a metaphoric shift within the symbolic patterns of the apocalyptic code. For Jewish apocalyptic the mythic story of the divine victory over evil and the renewal of creation is located in the future, at the parousia. Whether the first Christians were entirely conscious of the shift or not, their attachment of resurrection symbolism to Jesus collapsed that scheme. With the resurrection of Jesus, the Christian story discovers that the transcendence of death by resurrection does not bring the time of ordinary experience to an end. Consequently, one finds Christians combining the apocalyptic code of a divine victory at the parousia with the belief that the victory over death has been accomplished. Frye points to shifts in our perception of language and its function that make it even more difficult for contemporary Christians to appreciate the metaphoric traditions of the Bible. The Bible still uses the metaphoric traditions of epic poetry and myth. Such language does not draw clear distinctions between subject and object. It emphasizes the realm of feeling in which subject and object are linked by a common energy. Even words that seem abstract to us, like soul, mind, courage, emotion, and thought, were perceived as concrete. They function as the subjects of concrete action and are given physical descriptions. Descriptions of the gods identified the personalities of the divine with aspects of nature. Operations of the mind are controlled by "power words," formulas that focus mental activity.[22]

Many of the features of this stage of language are still operative in the New Testament. Indeed, the short kerygmatic formulae and acclamations like *"Marana tha"* (Aramaic: "Come, Lord") and "Jesus is Lord," as well as the short resurrection formulae, function to "focus the mind" within the setting of the community ritual, as Frye suggests. However, the New Testament is also influenced by the shift that was initiated with the Platonic revolution in human consciousness. This revolution originates with an intellectual elite. They discover that reflection makes it possible to separate subject and object. Words no longer function as magical formulae. Instead, they are perceived as outward expressions of inner thoughts, of ideas. Emotions are distinguished from abstract concepts. The Socratic discovery also provided another way to transcend death. It recognizes the superior power of thought in the face of death, since it can command feeling and can penetrate to a transcendent order. Properly employed, language can create a verbal imitation of that reality that lies beyond itself. This vision of reality requires that one move beyond a world dominated by a plurality of gods to that philosophic monotheism in which the individual attains immortality through identification with the transcendent, divine reality, with the good. The mind cannot be controlled by magic formulae. It must be disciplined by dialectic to assent only to properly constructed verbal argument.[23]

When we look back at these traditions, we do so from the perspective of yet a third shift in language. Language is understood as descriptive of this world. Symbolic language does not represent another reality but a tool for the manipulation of the material cosmos, which is the foundation of the modern sense of what is real. Frye points out that religious terms and words about "god" are dysfunctional in contemporary speech not so much because of a lack of willingness to believe but because there is no situation in which they must be used by a person who is to deal successfully with the commonly held views of reality.[24]

These three shifts in language have also brought with them shifts in the perception of the soul and in the understanding of the function of narrative. These changes, too, make it difficult for us to relate to resurrection language and to its context. In the first stage, soul is imagined as a plurality of psychic forces that disintegrate at death. In the second, the human senses the division between the body, our connection with material creation and mortality, and the soul, which returns to the transcendent if it is not too heavily dependent on the material world. In the third period, "soul" has no place. It is replaced by "mind," which is seen as an instrument to be used in interaction with the world. Frye observes that the expression "immortality of the mind" does not carry with it the same sense of conviction as immortality of the soul.[25]

Our own immersion in the modern mode of discourse makes it difficult to appreciate the images of direct, personal, divine action and presence that are so comfortably part of the first type of discourse as anything less than something of a "fairy tale." Thus, our task is to recover a way into the reality of that earlier world of discourse. One such route was through the use of sociological categories to understand the situation in which the apocalyptic symbolism of resurrection arose. The bizarre mythic images of evil and divine victory appear to reflect an experience of social disintegration in which the divine order no longer appears to be operative in the world as directly experienced. Our ability to exegete such implicit codes will always be limited when we are dealing with a culture as removed in time from ours as that of the New Testament, since the textual remains from that time are fragmentary and scattered.

THE CREATION OF MEANING

The pursuit of a text's symbolic codes also seeks to illuminate the new meanings created by metaphor. The Christian shift to "resurrection of Jesus" created something different in the apocalyptic scenario, since its orientation toward the future victory over death could no longer remain simply future. P. Ricoeur has argued that metaphor is our most potent weapon for gaining new insight into reality through redescription. The power of metaphor lies in its suspension of the patterns of literal reference. Thus, one must reject the theories of metaphor that treat it as a substitution for something else. Similarly, one cannot accept any treatment of metaphor that implicitly assumes that what is said metaphorically could be said as well without metaphor.[26] The creation of new meaning requires an earlier linguistic code against which it emerges.

For resurrection, this linguistic code is formed out of complex, symbolic descriptions of the world and its story. We will frequently find resurrection language closely associated with perceptions about God as Creator. As contemporary speakers, we may find ourselves in some difficulty when we seek to move beyond describing the original use and probable intent of such language to its significance for us. Our difficulty stems in part from the poverty of modern poetics. We think of mastering an inanimate material world through techniques and power, but we are less conscious of a need for a poetic, symbolic description of the world that would render it a human place. Thus, even the archetypal symbols that form part of the rites and customs with which we celebrate resurrection at Easter have often degenerated into excuses for religious sentiment and nostalgia. They do not carry the power of revelation.[27] One of the most anachronistic elements in modern theology is its treatment of the natural world. This anachronism is in part due to the lack of a poetic rooted in the scientific transformation of nature, which could present that transformation to a human imagination. Wilder argues that the insecurity that results from the lack of a religious vision of the cosmos is evident in the pseudosciences of the twentieth century. From the "tao of physics," astrology, and apocalyptic science fiction to the ecological mystique, people construct partial cosmologies and images to fill the void.[28]

This pseudoapocalyptic vision often informs our attempts to understand the apocalyptic of the first century. We presume that it represented the same chaotic flight from a reality whose intelligibility has become too fragmented for most people such as we find in our own world. Thus, Christians face the task of engaging more than the ideas that people form. They must also address those unconscious axioms and inherited symbolics that inform our behavior. A. Wilder points out that there is never any "naked spirituality." Images, metaphors, and the attitudes toward life that are conveyed by them count for everything.[29]

The symbolic structure of resurrection language may often appear to be a roadblock to its appropriation. Wilder tells of a conference at which a speaker claimed to accept God and morality but to have "disaffection of the Doctrine of the Resurrection." Resurrection was felt to be too massively involved in the ancient structures of imagination and thinking to be "demythologized."[30] We have already seen that on the exegetical level resurrection symbolism is too complex to admit of being "demythologized" as a concept expressed in a sentence or two. Wilder points to the need for "testing" our social dreams and myths.[31] Our culture also operates with its myths. Nor, Wilder argues, is the human psyche dead to the message of older symbolics. The psyche does not change with the same rapidity at that level as does the so-called innovation in our scientific and technological culture.[32] The symbolics of resurrection cannot be transformed into a miracle cure for the crucifixion.[33] Christians who transform Easter into a "Band-Aid" for Good Friday fail to perceive that the "myth" of resurrection belongs to a much larger story, the story of God's dealing with Israel and, through her, with humanity. The renewal of creation and the coming of the rule of God belong to the context of resurrection speech. The temporal shift in the Christian use of resurrection requires a combination of narrative and expressions of epiphany as well.

Wilder suggests that there are three dimensions to the resurrection event: the psychic, the cosmic, and the moral. The narratives struggle to say how the world has ended or changed in light of the risen Lord. They use the genres of divine epiphany and apocalyptic language of cosmic restoration to express this perception. But a contemporary expression of that resurrection transformation of the world might be found in quite different genres. The poesis of resurrection should be appropriate to the modern imagination.[34] Thus, Wilder points to the metamorphosis in Delmore Schwartz's poem "Starlight Intuition Pierced the Twelve" as an evocation of the dimensions of the original myth. The poem uses the modern genre of a dramatic monologue for the metamorphosis genre. As the disciples and the glorified Jesus gaze on one another, the whole world is changed. Thus, the poem evokes the world-transforming power of resurrection.

Liberation theologies also seek to find the liberating power of the resurrection symbol. They find in the cross an affirmation of divine solidarity with the oppressed and victims of the world. This affirmation depends on the transcending of the cross in resurrection. T. Driver argues that the vision of God participating in the world of human suffering implies a God who changes. That change also implies that the risen Christ changes and is not frozen in the past. Vindication language tends to freeze the cross/resurrection in the past event. Driver challenges theologians to find resurrection as a true historical event in which Christ lives today with the liberating power of our future.[35] The liberation of Christ from the dead, Driver argues, should imply that he is free to approach us now in the present/future in forms that we cannot foretell.[36] T. Driver's process hermeneutic seeks to explode fixed theological categories and symbols from the perspective of that "open future," which is the common theological translation of the eschatological symbolism of the New Testament. Even if we could establish facts about resurrection as a past historical event, they would not prove anything about faith or carry the meaning of resurrection as "event" in this dynamic relationship between God and the world.[37]

Driver's proposal, in effect, finds in resurrection and Biblical eschatology a completely open future. New meaning may come to humanity in its living with God that is not at all bound by those past meanings embedded in a tradition. Most theologians are uncomfortable with such a radical proposal. They would prefer to look to the dynamics of symbol and reflection to understand the way in which Christians may live out of their tradition. Symbols are related to the world of human feeling. They are polyvalent. They even persist in combining contradictory meanings. By doing so, they play an important role in mediating the tensions, conflicts, and contradictions of human life. In the process of interpretation we become conscious to ourselves. That consciousness requires a step away from the symbol. It requires the ability to transfer the elemental meanings of the image to the realm of linguistic meaning.[38] Ricoeur comments, "A symbol is a double-meaning linguistic expression that requires an interpretation, and interpretation is a work of understanding that aims at deciphering symbols."[39] These observations make it clear that one should not presume to separate the "experience of resurrection" from its symbolic nexus too easily. Yet the process of interpretation will seemingly always create a new linguistic form in place of the expression one seeks to understand. Reflection also implies a judgment upon our present world, as well as pressing upon us the question of the reality to which the symbols point.[40] We will encounter acute difficulties in attempting to relate the symbols and metaphors of resurrection to reality as it is understood in our own world. Yet we cannot be satisfied with the presumption that one gains no more from the New Testament than information about what people believed in the past. The theological task remains one of articulating meaning in a conceptual framework that is not bound to a single sociocultural horizon.[41] Thus, our reflection does not seek to create a religious experience of encounter with the risen Lord. It seeks understanding of the symbols, metaphors and reflection on them found in the Christian tradition.

THEOLOGICAL QUESTIONS

We have already raised a number of theological questions in our survey of the various quests to understand the meaning of resurrection. Theological reflection requires a certain distance and generalization that loses something of the rich diversity and immediacy of the metaphoric world. Nevertheless, the task of theological reflection cannot be avoided by appealing to some other mode of understanding the tradition. Christianity makes a claim for salvation in Jesus that does not clearly address the modern questions of well-being in our psychological and technological world. Theologians must use all the exegetical and interpretive methods available to show that belief in Jesus as the definitive saving reality of God gives the final purpose to human life in their own time.[42]

Nor should one expect that a single theological picture will do justice to the rich elements of the image of Jesus that come to us from the tradition. A theology of Jesus as saving reality might focus on Jesus as inspiration for Christian living, or it might take up the Easter message of Jesus' presence to be celebrated in Christian liturgy. Those who look for a "this worldly" Christianity may find Jesus an inspiring model for living quite apart from membership in a church community as such. Others may find that the message of the presence of the crucified and risen Lord operating through his disciples requires a strong image of church and intense involvement with the structures of Christian community. Similarly, concern for the oppressed born out of the identification of God and the rejected of the earth could manifest itself in a struggle for justice quite without any translation of the eschatological categories of the first century. Others may insist that in the celebration of the exalted Lord's presence Christians find the Spirit as a pledge of eternal life. One interpretation looks to the life and message of Jesus as a cause that is affirmed and universalized through the resurrection. Another looks to the ecclesial, church-founding dimensions of the resurrection traditions, to the affirmation of resurrection within the worship of the believing community.

W. M. Thompson, for example, emphasizes the kerygmatic presentation of the risen Christ with its liturgical, communal, and eschatological embodiment as the central element in the transforming power of the great symbols of Christianity.[43] H. Küng, on the other hand, begins with the confrontational image of Jesus embedded in the gospel narratives. Jesus' claims can only be tied together with his "God forsaken death" in the affirmation of resurrection.[44] Though the diversity of traditions and the varied implications of resurrection symbolism make it impossible to construct a single, unitary account of resurrection, the theologian must seek to articulate some more unified account of resurrection than that given on the narrative or symbolic level. Without such unification, the issues of generalization and transportability into new horizons could not be addressed. Küng proposes a series of central claims that emerge in connection with all the diverse traditions.[45]

1. Resurrection cannot be described as a historical event in the ordinary sense of the word. There were no human witnesses to resurrection itself. The New Testament consistently presents resurrection as an eschatological act of God, as part of the final transformation of the world. That perspective also implies that resurrection is more than vindication of a particular person, Jesus of Nazareth. Thus, Küng finds Christology implied in the very affirmation of Jesus' resurrection. God's salvation is involved in Jesus in such a way that after Easter Jesus becomes the norm for the relationship between humanity and God.[46]

2. Speaking of resurrection as an "eschatological event" distinguishes it from miraculous intervention in the natural order, such as the revival of a corpse or a near-death experience. It also implies that

resurrection is an event for Jesus, not merely a change of awareness on the part of the disciples. As "eschatological," resurrection implies that Jesus is not the same as the other righteous people who have died.

3. The variety of traditions and types of witnesses makes it impossible to reduce resurrection to the projection of the disciples' need to recover the "heady intimacy" of their fellowship with Jesus.

4. Finally, "eschatological event" implies that the "bodily" reality involved is discontinuous with the material reality we experience. One might even say discontinuous with our experience of bodily death such as we might discover it through medical studies. As a "new act of God" resurrection should not be considered a variant of some universal, philosophic speculation about human survival. But it should also not be taken as binding Christians to the specific anthropologies or cosmologies of the apocalyptic code in which resurrection originated.[47]

The theological task of articulating the significance of resurrection for twentieth-century Christians still remains to be undertaken. We shall return to explicit efforts to make such a translation in our concluding chapters. As C. F. Evans has observed, resurrection is so central to the New Testament and so concealed and expanded in varied layers of tradition that the difficulty is not whether one should believe in resurrection but in knowing what it is that is being proposed for belief.[48] Consequently, we must now wade into the details of the tradition.

NOTES

1. C. F. Evans, *Resurrection and the New Testament* (SBT ser. 2, no. 12; London: SCM, 1970). 1. Resurrection language appears in all the New Testament writings except 2 Thess, Tit, Phlm, 3 Jn, 2 Pt, Jude, and Jas.
2. J. Fitzmyer, "Nouveau Testament et Christologie: Questions actuelles," *Nouvelle Revue Théologique* 103 (1981), 191. "Ne pas admettre la résurrection de Jésus, c'est ne pas être chrétien."
3. Evans, op. cit., 2; on the importance of the events of salvation in Jesus (cross/resurrection for Paul) for the formulation of a specifi-

cally Christian perception of God, see L. Keck, *Paul and His Letters* (Philadelphia: Fortress, 1979), 119.

4. Evans, op. cit., 132.

5. N. Frye *(The Great Code. The Bible and Literature* [New York: Harcourt Brace Jovanovich, 1982], 171f., 193f.) sees the whole Bible as a mythic cycle about the rule of God. It originates with the Exodus as the archetype of all Biblical events. For the New Testament, resurrection emerges as that archetypal event and hence can be seen as its antitype of the Exodus.

6. J. M. Cameron, "The Idea of Christendom," *The Autonomy of Religious Belief* (ed. F. Crossan; Notre Dame: Notre Dame University, 1981), 8f.

7. J. Guitton ("Epistémologie de la résurrection. Concepts préalables et programme de recherches," *Resurrexit* [ed. E. Dhanis; Rome: Libreria Editrice Vaticana, 1974], 108–24) has pointed out that the needed exploration would require the cooperative effort of philosophy and science, since only certain understandings of bodily reality would be compatible with the confession of resurrection. Guitton's actual proposal is not very satisfactory. Taking a clue from Teilhard de Chardin, he suggests that humans were originally body *(sōma)* animated by soul *(psychē)*. Humanity entered its final phase through the spirit *(pneuma)*. This description comes close to being a twentieth-century version of the tripartite anthropology rejected by Paul in 1 Cor 15 and common in Gnostic writings.

8. See the extensive discussion of the problems of theories that have sought to demonstrate the development of the kerygmatic formulae into resurrection narrative by J. E. Alsup, *The Post-Resurrection Appearance Stories of the Gospel Tradition. A History-of-Tradition Analysis* (Calwer theologishe Monographien 5; London: SPCK, 1975), 23–29.

9. Evans, op. cit., 128–29; against the attempts to order the appearances according to a single scheme, see also Fitzmyer, op. cit., 193: "Les récits de la résurrection avec toute leur diversité, sont à considerer comme des essais réalisés pour nous présenter les détails complémentaires des informations qui concernent des apparitions du Christ ressuscité et qui sont conservées dans les proclamations fondamentales comme 1 Co 15,3–7." Fitzmyer suggests that we must presume the complementarity of the details of the various accounts, since they do refer back to the same event of resurrection.

10. J. M. Robinson, in H. Koester and J. M. Robinson, *Trajectories through Early Christianity* (Philadelphia: Fortress, 1971), 2–31.

Robinson's attempt to reconstruct such a trajectory for the resurrection itself appears to be too simply divided into dualistic categories that provide a neat schema for the concurrent development of resurrection traditions and the interpretation of Jesus' sayings in the direction of Gnostic heresy, on the one hand, and second-century orthodoxy, on the other:

Heretical	Orthodox
A. 1 Corinthian opponents denied future resurrection; debated interpretation of Jesus' sayings	A. Paul: eschatological reservation
B. 2 Timothy (and Polycarp) opponents; baptismal resurrection	B. Colossians/Ephesians: "are raised, enthroned" with Christ; Tit 3:5; 2 Timothy; Jn 3:3, 5, regeneration; safe categories
C. Gnostics: sayings as postresurrection wisdom, Gos. Thom., Dial. Sav., Thom. Cont.; Gnostics add ascent soul to resurrection; Gos. Phil 90 attacks those who say that we die and then rise	C. Regeneration as orthodoxy; development of a general view of resurrection; Polycarp 7.1, first clear tie between sayings interpretation and resurrection

Robinson ties the debate over the meaning of resurrection in the life of the Christian to the history of the transmission of the sayings of the Lord (op. cit., 30–46). The crossing lines of influence are more complex than this dualistic scheme suggests.

11. R. E. Brown, *The Virginal Conception and Bodily Resurrection of Jesus* (New York: Paulist, 1973), 74.

12. E. Schillebeeckx, *Jesus* (New York: Seabury, 1979), 533–38.

13. Ibid., 538f. Schillebeeckx also points to the strength of parousia language and perception of the present as "just before" the end in Paul's own thematizing of resurrection. Robinson (see note 10), points to the importance of this Pauline eschatological reservation in countering the tendency to deduce from the presence of the Spirit that Christians have already attained the perfection to which salvation points.

14. Schillebeeckx, op. cit., 75. Brown suggests that there is no victory language in the New Testament that is really clear of the assertion of resurrection.

15. H. C. Kee, *Christian Origins in Sociological Perspective* (Philadelphia: Westminster, 1980), 46–48. On the spiritualizing of the resurrection implicit in the Markan controversy story (12:18–27), see also J. R. Donahue, "A Neglected Factor in the Theology of Mark," *Journal of Biblical Literature* 101 (1982), 575–78. Don-

ahue comments, "Resurrection is not return from the grave, but enduring life hidden in the power of God."

16. Frye, op. cit., 20. Frye points to the development of a body/soul dichotomy as the inevitable result of the movement to abstract, conceptual language.

17. G. W. E. Nickelsburg, *Resurrection, Immortality, and Eternal Life in Intertestamental Judaism* (Harvard Theological Studies xxvi; Cambridge: Harvard, 1972), 11.

18. W. Meeks, *The First Urban Christians* (New Haven: Yale University, 1983), 1–8.

19. P. Hanson, "Old Testament Apocalyptic Reexamined," *Interpretation* 25 (1971), 455.

20. See the extensive discussion of this issue by J. Collins, "Cosmos and Salvation: Jewish Wisdom and Apocalyptic in the Hellenistic Age," *History of Religion* 17 (1977), 121–42.

21. See J. J. Collins, "Apocalyptic Eschatology and the Transcendence of Death," *Catholic Biblical Quarterly* 36 (1974), 21–43. Though 1 En. 93 describes the resurrected as being transported bodily into the sphere of life, one must be wary of presuming that the empty tomb would automatically imply that Jesus had been raised or that all Jewish images of resurrection implied translation of a physical body into the heavenly sphere.

22. Frye, op. cit., 5–7.

23. Ibid., 7–12.

24. Ibid., 14–18.

25. Ibid., 19.

26. P. Ricoeur, *The Rule of Metaphor* (Toronto: University of Toronto, 1977), 6f., 20, 65f.

27. A. Wilder, *Theopoetic. Theology and the Religious Imagination* (Philadelphia: Fortress, 1976), 3f.

28. Ibid., 3f. Wilder observes that the shadow side of the scientific and technological culture in which we live is a mentality composed of magic and mythology. He suggests that that distorted mythology requires the corrective of the Biblical perception of creation to order the way in which we imagine the world (p. 6). It had best be pointed out that Wilder's call for a Biblical image of creation has nothing to do with the fundamentalist rejection of science in the name of creation. See also the call for a renewal of cosmology among theologians, philosophers, and scientists in S. Toulmin's *Return to Cosmology* (Berkeley: California, 1982), 257.

29. Wilder, op. cit., 29, 66.

30. Ibid., 89.

31. Ibid., 74. Wilder also cautions against those modern critics who would seek to separate a so-called existential language from Jesus' parables and sayings without acknowledging that those same parables and sayings are embedded in a wider symbolics of myth and apocalyptic. Jesus inherited that symbolic and made use of it as a horizon for his speech (pp. 76–78). Despite Wilder's caution, his student E. Breech has used modern literature and philosophic concepts to perform just such an operation on the sayings and parables of Jesus in his *The Silence of Jesus* (Philadelphia: Fortress, 1983). Moderns would, it appears, most easily translate the New Testament into their own poetic idiom rather than dialogue with the troublesome idioms of the Bible.

32. Wilder, op. cit., 93; E. Brann *(The Paradoxes of Education in a Republic* [Chicago: University of Chicago, 1979], 3f.) argues that we mistake the accumulation of information for change. There is, in fact, little change in American culture; Toulmin (op. cit., 21–71) criticizes the scientific mythologies created around entropy and evolution. For an attempt to use the perspective of analysis to describe the impact of Biblical symbols on the human psyche, see W. Rollins, *Jung and the Bible* (Atlanta: John Knox, 1983), 56–127. As in Jung's own work, one finds resurrection assimilated to a broad range of patterns of regeneration.

33. Wilder, op. cit., 95.

34. Ibid., 95–96.

35. T. Driver, *Christ in a Changing World: Toward an Ethical Christology* (New York: Crossroad, 1981), 3f.

36. Ibid., 11.

37. Ibid., 8.

38. B. Lonergan, *Method in Theology* (New York: Herder, 1972), 66f.

39. P. Ricoeur, *Freud and Philosophy* (New Haven: Yale University, 1970), 9.

40. The relationship between reality and speech encourages movement beyond speech to extralinguistic reality. Hermeneutics seeks to regulate the transition from the structure of a work to the world and to interpret the display of the world to which the work refers by virtue of its arrangement. In doing so, the difference between metaphor and speculative discourse must still be respected, though speculative discourse requires the semantic dynamics of metaphor as its own condition of possibility. See Ricoeur, *Rule of Metaphor,* 220; and idem, *Hermeneutics and the Human Sciences* (Cambridge: Cambridge University, 1981), 111–13.

41. One can understand the horizon as the structured result of past

human achievements, which both condition and limit further development. The horizon is structured because learning is a process of organic growth out of structure. The boundaries of such structures set limits to our capacities for assimilation. Thus, Lonergan sketches three types of horizon: (1) complementary, such as one finds in the instance of different specialists engaged in a study of the communal world; (2) genetic, that is, genetically successive stages of development that are related in such a way that the later stage presupposes the earlier ones; and (3) dialectic, that is, what is intelligible, true, and good in one horizon may be unintelligible, false, or evil in another. Therefore, a person holding one view must reject those formulated against the other horizon. See Lonergan, *Method,* 236–37. Lonergan, *Insight* (New York: Philosophical Library, 1957), 562–67.

42. Schillebeeckx, op. cit., 19–38.
43. W. M. Thompson, *Jesus, Lord and Savior: A Theopathic Christology* (New York: Paulist, 1980), 15, 33. Thompson undertakes the task of describing the experiential correlate behind the symbols of Christianity from the perspective of theories of the transformation of human consciousness.
44. H. Küng, *On Being a Christian* (Garden City, N.Y.: Doubleday, 1976), 343.
45. Ibid., 344–61.
46. Ibid., 384.
47. Ibid., 365f. Küng insists that one can speak of the personal identity of Jesus in a new existence with God and leave the question of anthropology open. However, the "body" metaphor does suggest that not all doctrines of postmortem survival would be acceptable explications of what is meant by resurrection.
48. Evans, op. cit., 130.

TWO

Resurrection and Immortality in Judaism

Resurrection symbolism first appears in the context of the apocalypse in Dan 12. It does not appear as a major theme in the Jewish apocalypses known to us. Resurrection occurs as a minor motif in the larger scenario of judgment.[1] As a minor stage prop to judgment scenes, resurrection language is quite variable. Many popular treatments of resurrection often presume that it reflects a "Jewish" view of the unity of the human person over against a Greek dualism of soul and body.[2] We have already seen that the so-called unitary person reflects a metaphoric stage of language and consciousness over against the development of philosophical conceptualization. Further studies of textual and archaeological evidence have shown that there is no peculiarly Jewish view of the person in the period under discussion.[3] On the fringes of the Hebrew Scriptures one also finds images of continuity in Sheol, of ghosts and shadows called to life, and the conviction that Yahweh has power over life and death. The assumption of figures like Enoch (Gen 5:24) and Elijah (2 Ki 2:11), as well as the psalmist's words of intense communion with God, all provide a foundation for the later development of traditions of postmortem survival. Jewish apocalyptic writings contain images of Sheol as the land of shades and oblivion (1 En. 102.6–8, 11; 2 Apoc. Bar. 10.6–12.4) which are indistinguishable from the Sheol of Greek traditions.[4] Though the Greeks clearly distinguished the body that was buried from the psyche that went elsewhere, one finds both literary and ceremonial evidence for the notion that in addition to the body in the grave, another might undergo quite physical punishment. The Greeks feared that the dead would lose their intelligence. Any hopes for survival were focused on the possibility of memory. If the dead can remember who they are and what they did, then they are partially themselves.[5] This preoccupation of Greek poetry and art finds itself transformed and given new scope by philosophical traditions of the soul's immortality.

What would appear peculiar in the Jewish descriptions of Sheol is their preoccupation with judgment and punishment. One finds rather complex systems of compartmentalization (e.g., 1 En. 22). Sometimes Sheol is pictured as a complex "holding place" until the judgment. The righteous are separated in "treasuries." Judgment merely intensifies the torments already suffered by the wicked (e.g., 2 Apoc. Bar. 36.11).[6]

One can also find Greek terminology in the Jewish writings of this period. 2 Macc 7:9 combines resurrection, eternal life, and resuscitation. The word *anabiōsis* (come to life again) appears in Plato's *Phaedo* (71c) where it refers to the soul's entry into a new body. Both Dan 12:2–3 and Wis 3:7 attribute astral immortality to the souls of the righteous. Such images of immortality may also be reflected in the visions of the righteous as those who dwell with the angelic hosts in 1 QH 3.19–23; 11.9–14 (or 1 En. 102.5; 103.3–4; 104.6).[7] Josephus attributes Pythagorean language about transmigration of souls to the Pharisees.[8] Archaeological evidence from the first century C.E. also shows a wide diversity in tombstone formulae with no significant difference in the percentage of references to immortality over resurrection between inscriptions from the Diaspora and those from Palestine.[9] In his survey of the contents of Jewish apocalypses J. J. Collins has found only two, the Apocalypse of Weeks (1 En. 93; 91.12–17) and T. Levi 2–5, that fail to contain some form of personal immortality. The Apocalypse of Weeks is concerned with the judgment of the nation as a whole. One would expect the importance of individual afterlife to be moderated in political apocalypses that are primarily concerned with the fate of the nation. Resurrection appears as the primary mode of eschatology in Dan 7–12; the Animal Apocalypse (1 En. 89.70–77; 90.17), 2 En., 2 Apoc. Bar., and 4 Ezra. Each is a composite writing that is more interested in historical surveys than in the heavenly journeys of a seer. This concern with *ex eventu* surveys of history makes the temporal dimension of transcendence more important than the spatial (earth/heaven) one.[10] These observations lend further weight to the suggestion that unlike some of the other forms of transcendence, resurrection emerged in response to particular crises in the fate of the nation. The most consistent context for resurrection remains that of a judgment to establish divine justice. However, there is no well-defined doctrine or symbolism of resurrection. Nor is there a consistent anthropology in the writings of this period. One can only be certain of a continuity in personal identity and of the radical reversal of the conditions of this world.

VINDICATION OF THE RIGHTEOUS

The circles of the pious who were responsible for the Daniel apocalypse clearly see resurrection as the crowning vindication for their piety and fidelity:

> At that time, Michael, the great prince who has charge of your people, shall arise. There will be a time of great trouble unlike any that has been since the nation began until that time; but, at that time, your people will be delivered, everyone whose name is found written in the book.
> Many of those who sleep in the dust of the earth will awake; some to everlasting life; some to shame and everlasting contempt.
> And the wise shall shine like the brightness of the firmament; those who turn many to righteousness, like the stars forever and ever.   (Dan 12:1–3)

This passage appears to limit resurrection to the best and the worst among the people during the persecution of Antiochus IV, that is, to the "wise" and to those who were apostates. The Son of Man vision in Dan 7:27 describes Israel's exaltation to share angelic dominion. The picture of the "wise" shining like the stars in 12:2 appeals to the same tradition.[11] Michael serves as Israel's angelic defender, here apparently in a judicial capacity, against the angelic forces behind the imperial powers.[12]

Scholars have found several parallels between this passage and the servant material of Third Isaiah. Like the suffering servant, the wise *(maskilim)* "justify" the many, submit to death, and are then exalted.[13] The metaphor of sleep and waking for the restoration of Israel comes from another eschatological passage in Isaiah (26:19a). Those who are condemned awake to everlasting contempt. The word *deara'on* (abhorrence) also appears in Is 66:24 for the sin of hellenizing. The exaltation of the righteous recalls the exaltation of the suffering servant in Is 52:13.[14] We have in the resurrection image of Daniel what appears to be a clear example of the development of a new metaphor out of an older code, that of the suffering servant. The image of resurrection is not the only shift in language. Sleeping and awakening had been used for the restoration of the nation before. But this passage moves from the horizontal dimension of changes in the nation's historical fate to the vertical one. The solution to the dilemma faced by the righteous is no longer found in Israel's triumph over the nations of the earth. Instead, it belongs to a completely new order of reality.[15] Here the judgment does not concern nations but individuals within Israel. The astral imagery suggests that the "wise" have been admitted to the heavenly host.[16] However, this vision of individual judgment is not universalized. It only refers to particular persons in the crisis.

As. Mos. 10 and Jub. 23 use images of judgment and exaltation to describe what will follow upon the same crisis. As. Mos. 10 no longer mentions the "wise" in its vision of cosmic restoration:

Then His kingdom will appear in all creation. Then Satan will be no more, and sorrow will depart with him. Then the hands of the angel, who has been appointed chief, will be filled, and he will immediately avenge them of their enemies. For the Heavenly One will rise from his royal throne. He will go forth from His holy dwelling with indignation and wrath on account of His sons. The earth will tremble and be shaken to its extremities. The high mountains will be made low and they will be shaken and fall. The horns of the sun will be broken and it will be turned into darkness. The moon will not give light, and will be turned completely into blood. The circle of stars will be disturbed; the sea will retreat into the abyss; the fountains of waters will fail, and the rivers will dry up.
For the Most High will arise, the one Eternal God. He will appear to punish the Gentiles. He will destroy all their idols.

Then, you, O Israel, will be happy. You will mount on the neck
and wings of the Eagle. They will be ended, and God will exalt
you. He will cause you to approach the heaven of the stars in
their dwelling. You will look from on high and see your enemies
in Gehenna. You will recognize them and rejoice. You will give
thanks and praise your creator.[17]

Many phrases from this passage recall the Isaiah tradition: "sorrow
shall depart" (v. 1; Is 35:10); "go forth . . . His dwelling" (v. 3; Is
26:21; 63:15); "mountains . . . low" (v. 4; Is 40:4). Daniel applied
exaltation to the special situation of the "wise." Here there is no
distinction made among those in Israel. Rather, the enemies appear
simply as the Gentiles.[18]

The political message of As. Mos. 10 appears to be related to that of
Daniel, which advocates passive resistance to Antiochus. The vision
of Yahweh's coming in vengeance draws upon the imagery of the
divine warrior, but for As. Mos. that coming supports a stance of
nonviolent resistance. The author has tied this picture of divine vengeance to the story of the martyrdom of Taxo in chapter 9. The cry
for vengeance of the innocent sufferers aided by angelic intercession
is met with divine judgment.[19] 2 Macc 7 uses resurrection as an
expectation of vindication for those who have actually been
martyred. This vision of judgment/salvation sees the vindication of
the innocent as God's exaltation of all of Israel and the destruction of
her enemies. It is not directly concerned with the fate of the martyrs.
At this point in the development of the tradition one cannot be
entirely sure that the metaphors of heavenly exaltation and cosmic
destruction are used of a new dimension of salvation. They may yet
have carried expectations of a concrete earthly victory by Israel
under the leadership of the pious. The "God alone" stance of the
writing carries an implicit critique of the military and political poli-
cies of the Maccabean leadership.

Jub. 23.26–31 comes from the same period. It envisages the time of
salvation in which Satan will be destroyed and righteousness will
prevail:

In those days, children will begin to study the Law and seek the
commandments and return to the path of righteousness . . .
There will be no old people nor person full of days,[20] for all will
be like children and young people . . . At that time, the Lord
will arise and heal His servants. They will rise up and see great
peace and drive out their adversaries. The righteous will see and
give thanks and rejoice forever and ever. They will see all their

judgments and their curses on their enemies. Their bones will rest in the earth, and their spirits will have much joy. They will know that it is the Lord who executes judgment and shows mercy to hundreds and thousands, to all who love Him.

This passage has been overinterpreted by those seeking doctrines of resurrection in Maccabean Judaism. There is no resurrection of the righteous to see their vindication. Nor does the passage push a doctrine of the immortality of the soul.[21] The body rests peacefully in the grave. The rejoicing soul reflects the simple assurance of divine justice and the peace of the righteous dead. G. Nickelsburg has reconstructed a common pattern of vindication and exaltation of the righteous behind these traditions. This pattern has been developed out of Isaiah material. The servant of Is 50:7–9 appeals to his adversary to stand trial with him in the presence of God. The judgment scene pattern can be found in Dan 12, As. Mos. 10, Jub. 23, T. Jud. 20.25, 1 En. 104, 4 Ez 7, and Rev 12:20–22.[22] This pattern has four elements:

1. Witnesses. The good and evil angel. The evil angel is defeated.
2. Book of life or deeds.
3. Postmortem judgment of the evil or of both good and evil.
4. Description of the consequence: vindication of the righteous and condemnation of the wicked; exaltation or ascent of the righteous to heaven.

Daniel is the only example from the earliest group of texts to associate resurrection with the vindication scene. However, resurrection or judgment quickly becomes generalized. Traditions from T. 12 Patr. show a dual perspective. Some speak of universal judgment. Others suggest that resurrection applies only to a specific group like the *maskilim* of Daniel. T. Jud. 25.4 speaks of the pious rising, while T. Zeb. 10.2 and T. Ben. 10.2 speak of a resurrection of the patriarchs in order to rule over the renewed Israel.[23]

The traditions in T. Jud. 25, T. Ben. 10, T. Zeb. 10, and T. Sim. 6 all allude to resurrection. They appear to be dependent on Dan 12:2 (cf. T. Ben. 10.8; T. Jud. 25.4). Nickelsburg suggests that T. Jud. 25 is part of a judgment scene that includes T. Jud. 20.1, 4f.[24] It begins with a catalog of blessings on the twelve tribes.[25] This catalog is attached to the affirmation that the patriarchs will arise along with Abraham, Isaac, and Jacob. After the destruction of Satan, a second "resurrection" will restore those who have suffered for the Lord's sake:

Those who have died in grief will rise in joy. Those who were impoverished for the Lord's sake will be made rich. Those who were put to death for the Lord's sake will be made alive.

This eschatological reversal is part of the rejoicing of a renewed Israel. It belongs to an established confessional pattern:[26]

1. God is the one who makes alive.
2. Gathering the tribes of Israel.
3. Elimination of the power of evil.
4. Salvation for the righteous; punishment for the wicked.
5. Description of eschatological joy and fullness.
6. The nation glorifies God.

This pattern does not require resurrection per se. It appears in T. Jud. 25 as a reversal of fate for a particular group, those who have "died in grief" and those who have been put to death "for the Lord's sake." They are enabled to participate in the renewed Israel by their resurrection.

T. Ben. 10.5–10 also has an order of resurrection that runs ancient patriarchs, the twelve patriarchs, and then others. The passage creates additional difficulties for interpreters, since it contains a description of the judgment of Israel through the Gentiles that is without parallel elsewhere in T. 12 Patr.[27] The section that alludes to a general judgment clearly refers to Dan 12:2:

Then we will all be changed, some into glory and some into shame. For the Lord judges Israel first for the unrighteousness which they have committed, and then He will judge all the Gentiles, and will convict Israel through chosen Gentiles just as he convicted Esau through the Midianites, who loved their brothers.

Salvation and judgment of the Gentiles may reflect Is 52:10. This passage has apparently universalized the resurrection of Daniel to apply to all, or at least all in Israel, who are to be judged. T. Zeb. 10.2–3 preserves another fragment of this tradition. Zebulun consoles his children with the promise that he will rise again and rule in the midst of his tribe, that is, those who keep the commandments of the Lord. The wicked will be destroyed by the Lord.

T. Sim. 6.3–7 belongs to a complex passage that has been extensively edited by Christians. After the divine victory over the evil spirits the patriarch "will arise in joy, and bless the Most High because of His marvelous works." Thus, the general pattern of the resurrection traditions in T. 12 Patr. continues to be one of judgment as eschatological renewal. The joyous Israel will be reestablished on earth, headed by the risen patriarch.[28] In comparison with the other eschatological themes in T. 12 Patr., resurrection is quite minor. The most common use of the motif is in connection with the patriarchs of Israel, who return to rule over those who make up the renewed Israel. Some passages also suggest that resurrection might be a more general reward for the righteous. T. Ben. is the only one that suggests that resurrection might have been tied to a general judgment. T. Ben. uses the Daniel traditions from which the resurrection image originated. Therefore, the Danielic picture of the resurrection as attached to the judgment of particular groups, the wise and the apostates, may have been generalized at an early period. At the same time, T. 12 Patr. is not as concerned with exaltation to the heavens as Daniel and As. Mos. 10. Its images of eschatological joy and renewal are situated in Israel and could easily describe a transformation of Israel as an earthly community. The difference between these two traditions suggests that resurrection language could be used without the implications of heavenly exaltation or transformation into angelic existence. T. 12 Patr. suggests that resurrection perhaps carried with it the image of the restoration of the community as it should have existed. Hence, the return of the patriarchs, or the *maskilim,* to rule over such a community reflects the final establishment of the true community of the righteous.

As. Mos. 10 presented its vision of resurrection and judgment as the divine response to the martyrdom of Taxo and his sons. Resurrection also appears in the traditions of the martyrs in 2 Maccabees. The parallel accounts in 1 Maccabees (2:15–28; 49–68) do not contain resurrection.[29] There Judas's military action (8:3) is the divine response to the plea for vengeance. The mother's speech reflects the piety of the hasidic exegesis of Third Isaiah. God as cosmic creator guarantees the restoration of her sons to life (7:22f., 28). This piety of restored life is the sense in which resurrection appears in 7:9, 14, 23. The only explicit reference to bodily resurrection occurs in 7:11. The martyr points to his hands and declares his hope to get them back again. This reference is clearly dictated by the metaphoric possibilities of the martyrdom story. It is not the theoretical development of the exegetical tradition.

The traditions in IV Macc. are dominated by the philosophical image of the immortal soul conquering the passions. The martyr's detachment proves the "wisdom" of Judaism, since it enables reason to dominate the passions. The martyr's soul will pass directly to eternal life, to incorruption (7:3; 9:22; 13:17; 16:25; 17:18f.).

This presentation of Judaism as enabling people to become truly wise has no place for resurrection or for expression of vindication, of Jewish exaltation over Gentile enemies. Nickelsburg reads the stories of 2 Maccabees in light of another genre, the story of the wise Jewish sage at the court of a foreign king.[30] Dan 3 and 6 and the story of Susanna show an important shift in Maccabean times. Originally, the wisdom tale stressed the cleverness by which the Jewish sage succeeded at a foreign court and overcame his or her enemies. In these later stories, however, cleverness has been replaced by righteousness, obedience to the Torah. That obedience is the cause of the suffering that the hero undergoes. When the righteous person finally triumphs over his or her enemies at court, faithfulness to the Torah is vindicated.

Initially, vindication implied escape from the threat of death. However, the tale was transposed in light of the apocalyptic traditions of a cosmic victory of Yahweh. Then the earthly monarch's court is no longer the scene of triumph but the heavenly divine court. Or the political implications may be completely dissolved, as they are in Wis 2:4–5:14. There one finds the story of heavenly exaltation/vindication as a portrayal of the fate of the righteous person in an evil world.[31] The tale concludes when the righteous one, exalted in the heavenly court, is seen by his persecutors, who have also died (4:20–5:14). Wisdom combines this picture of exaltation with immortality. The righteous attain the immortality that God intended humans to have from the beginning.[32]

The apocalyptic images of the second century B.C.E. had combined the Isaiah traditions of the vindication of Israel's persecuted leaders and the vision of an impending divine judgment against Israel's enemies. The Enoch traditions provide further examples of this pattern of vindication and judgment. In 1 En. 62.1–63.2, the nations are gathered before the "elect one," the Son of Man. The wicked confess their sinfulness and are destined for Sheol. The righteous, on the other hand, will rise to a glorious life with the Son of Man. They are clothed with "garments of glory," "garments of life," which never pass away. Whether this passage presumes that the glorious dwelling place is heavenly or earthly is more difficult to determine. The use of the image "Son of Man" from Dan 7 suggests heavenly exaltation. On the other hand, glorified life on a transfigured earth seems to be the primary image in the 1 Enoch tradition. Resurrection of the dead as part of the transformation of the earth that takes place with the enthronement of God's elect is described in 1 En. 51:1–5. Other elements of the Enoch traditions concern themselves with the coming of judgment.[33]

1 En. 108.10–15 takes the image of the suffering righteous, persecuted and trampled by the wicked, and describes their glorious exaltation in God's presence. This exaltation is presented as the reward
deserved by the righteous for the deeds that did not receive any
reward while they were living. As in Wis 2–5, the sinners lament
when they see the exaltation that is the reward of righteousness. This
passage is not directly concerned with resurrection. It has generalized the themes of enthronement and transformation into angelic
light. "I will bring forth in shining light those who have loved my
Holy Name, and I will seat each on the throne of his honor, and they
shall be resplendent forever" (1 En. 108.12–13).

1 En. 102–104 develops the judgment scene imagery even further.
These Enoch traditions serve a didactic purpose. The reader is
warned not to compromise righteousness or piety by association with
the wicked no matter how wealthy they may be. The problem to
which this exhortation responds concerns the pain that appears to
accompany the life of piety. Righteousness does not receive the reward that the tradition promised. This evaluation parallels that in
Wis 2. The wicked look at the pious and see such a life as worthless
(Wis 2:6–11; 1 En. 102.1–10). The righteous are helpless before their
oppressors (Wis 2:18–20; 1 En. 102.10–11). The righteous live lives of
misfortune, it appears. Their pleas for justice and vindication go
unheeded. But they are assured by the author that what appears is
not the truth. Their deeds are all recorded and will be rewarded.
Their spirits will not perish, so they need not fear what is said about
them in this life (1 En. 103.3–4). They will shine and rejoice like the
angels in heaven, thus reversing the ills and afflictions of their present life. Divine judgment will prove to be their vindication (1 En.
104.1–5). Thus, the seer brings the vision to its conclusion with a
paraenetic injunction: "Therefore, you righteous ones, do not be
afraid when you see the wicked grow strong and prosper. Do not join
in their ways, but keep far from their violence, for you will become
companions of the hosts of heaven" (1 En. 104.5f.). Another strand of
the Enoch tradition involved the visions of the seer on heavenly
journeys through the heavens. On these journeys, he saw the places
of punishment for the wicked and the special storage places for the
righteous. Even the wicked may be "pre-sorted." Those who are
punished in this life are said to have an easier time than those who
have escaped entirely (1 En. 22.9–13). Further, resurrection of the
wicked is said to make it possible for them to receive punishment (1
En. 22.11). These traditions appear to reflect a speculative concern
with issues of postmortem rewards and punishment.

Nickelsburg suggests that the primary function of the eschatology of 1 Enoch is to assure the righteous that their salvation is already secured in heaven.[34] This certain translation into angelic glory comes close to the imagery of the Dead Sea Scrolls. The community is described as following the way of life, or the angel of light, while others follow the way of death, or the angel of darkness. This "two ways" theology generates a perception of the community as the place in which one possesses knowledge of God, salvation, and participation in angelic glory.[35]

Thus, it is clear that in the two centuries before Christ, which saw the full-blown development of the religious language that would be typical of the first century C.E., concern with the vindication of the righteous engendered new religious language. These metaphors of vindication and judgment drew on traditions of divine holy war, on the visions of Daniel, and on the suffering servant of Isaiah. Resurrection is a rather small part of larger scenarios of judgment. Often, exaltation to heavenly or angelic glory provided the centerpiece for apocalyptic reversal of fortunes. But it also remained possible to envisage a renewed earth on which the righteous might dwell. Much of this speculation remains at the level of the imagination. We see little concern to systematize eschatological speculation. Nor are the occasional images of resurrection the source of much speculation. The various postmortem treasuries of the Enoch journeys perhaps evidence some reflective systematization. They at least reflect a desire to inflict proportionate punishments on the wicked. The earlier expressions of divine punishment originated in a period of religious persecution. They addressed the injustice of the persecution and the problem of apostasy. Such examples hardly required the careful weighing of whether a particular evildoer had been punished in this life or not. Even the generalization of the vindication/exaltation tradition in 1 Enoch presumes that the righteous are persecuted. This time by the rich. The author seeks to warn his audience that they should not be taken in by the apparent success of the rich. They should never think that righteousness is not rewarded or that their pleas are not heard.

FIRST-CENTURY JUDAISM

The traditions that originated in Maccabean times continued to be influential in the first century C.E. We also find the philosophic traditions of immortality in the writings of Philo of Alexandria. The destruction of Jerusalem in 70 C.E. forms the background for two apocalyptic writings, IV Ezra and 2 Bar. Once again, the older traditions of apocalyptic prophecy are revived to address the new crisis. But both writings show considerably more evidence of speculative reflection on the problems they confront. Israel's suffering seems disproportionate to any wickedness she might have committed. God's continued failure to come with the expected judgment and vindication presses on the mind and heart of the seer.

IV Ez 7:31–43 describes a time of primeval silence prior to the divine re-creation of the world. The dead are restored for judgment before the throne of God. Both Gehenna and Paradise are revealed so that the wicked see what is in store for them as well as the glorious paradise that they might have enjoyed. IV Ezra appropriates the language of restoration from Isaiah as well as the Son of Man traditions from Daniel.[36] The parallel between the new creation at the end of time and the primordial creation enables the author to mix imagery from the heaven/Gehenna tradition with the image of a renewed earth as the dwelling place for the righteous. One also finds traditions of heavenly journey in which the postmortem judgment of the souls of the wicked is revealed. In short, IV Ezra presents a compendium of eschatological speculation and metaphors.[37] The Adam traditions of IV Ez 7:11–16 proclaim that immortality is the reward for those who have followed the narrow way of righteousness. The seer also learns that those who survive the trials of the messianic age will see God's salvation. Those who were thought not to have died like Enoch would appear, and the evil spirit would be blotted out of the hearts of those who remained on earth (IV Ez 6:25–29). Resurrection is not an explicit theme of many of these revelations. G. Stemberger has identified a formula in IV Ez 7:32 that has parallels in 1 En. 51.1 and 2 Bar. 21.23f.:

> The earth shall restore those who sleep in her,
> and the dust those who rest in it,
> and the chambers those entrusted to them.
>
> (IV Ez 7:32)

> In those days, the earth will also give back what has been entrusted to it,
> and Sheol will give back what it has received,
> and hell will give back what it owes.
>
> (1 En. 51.1)

And let Sheol be sealed so that from this time on it may
not receive the dead,
and let the treasuries of souls restore those enclosed
in them.

(2 Bar. 21.23f.)

2 Bar. sets the formula in the context of an intercessory prayer for
the coming of divine judgment. This judgment is no longer invoked
as the response to a particular evil. Instead, the angel of death—once
the angelic power behind the nation's enemies—is to be destroyed. 2
Bar. 42.7 introduces a variant of the formula with a reference to the
two ways, corruption and life. The earth will be required to restore
those who belong to life. 2 Bar. 30.2–5 associates this formula with the
system of heavenly storage places that provide for preliminary judgment prior to the end.[38] This formula appears in Rev 20:13 without
the reference to storage places and in LAB 3.10.[39] Thus, it appears to
have been a well-known "shorthand" for the restoration of the dead
at the judgment.

IV Ezra's resurrection imagery is dominated by the radical new
creation after all is reduced to the primordial silence. However, one
also finds stellar motifs promised those who practice self-discipline (7,
78, 97, 113f., 125a; cf. Dan 12:3). The "new creation" after the destruction of the old also appears as the prelude to judgment and new
life for the righteous in Sib. Or. IV 176–90[40]:

When everything has finally been reduced to dust and ashes and
God has put out the giant fire just as He kindled it, then God
Himself will refashion the bones and ashes of humans and raise
up mortals as they were before. Then the judgment will come in
which God Himself will pass sentence, judging the world again.
A heap of earth and murky Tartarus and the black recesses of
hell will cover those who have sinned with deeds of impiety
again. But all who are righteous will live again on earth when
God gives breath and life and grace to the righteous. Then all
will see themselves, seeing the lovely and pleasant sunlight.
Thrice blessed the person who lives until that time.

The tragedy of the war with Rome drives IV Ezra and 2 Bar. to
turn to all of the eschatological images and traditions known to them.
IV Ezra looks at the universality of Adam's sin (3:7–36; 4:30; 7:11–88)
and sees that Israel could never extricate herself from the universal
history of sin. Yet the Law stands as the standard by which all human

actions, both of individuals and nations, are to be judged.[41] The tradition of storage caverns in 7:75–101 answers the pressing problem of the fate of various souls after death—especially as the immediate end of the world and judgment seems difficult to sustain. The scholastic questioning of the tradition in these writings shows that metaphoric affirmation of eschatological faith was not felt to be sufficient. The strain on traditional affirmations of faith was such that at least one group raised the objections to the level of consciousness and sought arguments to aid their reaffirmation of the traditional beliefs and images.

2 Bar. 49–51 contains one of the few examples of reflective treatment of resurrection of the body. The seer is assured that the dead will be raised as they were committed to the earth. In that way those still living will recognize the truth behind the teaching on eternal life:

> For certainly the earth will then restore the dead. It will not change their form, but just as it received them, so it will restore them. And as I delivered them to it, so it will raise them. For then it will be necessary to demonstrate to the living that the dead come to life again and that the departed have returned. And, when they have each recognized those whom they know now, then judgment will grow strong, and the things spoken of before will come about.   (2 Bar. 50.2–4)

In earlier judgment scenes recognition occurred in heaven or in the storage place of the souls. In the conclusion to this section the wicked lament their sins when they see the righteous transformed into angelic glory. Thus, bodily resurrection is now a prelude. It is distinguished from the real destiny of the righteous, their transformation into angelic glory (2 Bar. 51.1–6), which is followed by their entry into the glories of Paradise and their place before the divine throne. Indeed, the author promises that the transformed excellence or glory of the righteous will surpass that of the angels (2 Bar. 51.8–13). Thus, 2 Bar. has synthesized the various metaphors of the earlier eschatological traditions. It presumes that each metaphor can be fitted into a sequence of events before or after the judgment. This effort at synthesis, like the scholastic dialogues of IV Ezra, suggests that the old metaphors have lost some of their power to speak directly of people's experience. They are now the object of reflective speculation.

The pressure toward apologetic and reflective organization in IV Ezra and 2 Bar. represents increasing concern for the fate of the righteous as individuals over against the collectivity. We find 2 Bar. concerned with recognition of individuals by those who had known them. The earlier symbols, even when referred to specific groups like the *maskilim,* had operated out of the conviction that the most pressing questions concerned the destiny of the nation. Or when the nation as a whole was seen to be split, the destiny of that group within the nation that represented its tradition and true relationship with God, the righteous. IV Ezra still refers to these historical experiences. But their lesson of defeat and sinfulness leads to the conclusion that the sinfulness that has been with humanity since Adam makes widespread obedience to the Torah impossible. Vindication is also collective, though IV Ezra persists in reminding God, and the reader, that the righteous are a distinct minority. Within these traditions the development of degrees of postmortem punishment reflects the further tendency to seek judgment proportionate to the particular acts of definite individuals. The recognition scene in 2 Bar. also makes this concern for individuality clear.

However, the concern for individuality is better served in the traditions that focus on the immortality of the soul. Wis 2–5 combined the older images of divine vindication and judgment with that understanding of the human being. The body represents the individual's link to the material, perishable world, while the soul is the source of the divine image and natural immortality.[42] Wisdom paves the way for one combination of the two traditions: immortality of the soul and exaltation. Other writings collect eschatological expressions with little effort to synthesize them. One example of such a collection is found in Pseudo-Phocylides 99–115.[43] This writer protests the practice of dissection of the human body that was a hallmark of the Alexandrian medical school in this period (l. 102).[44] The exhortation to avoid immoderate grief reminds the reader that the body belongs to the dust, while the soul is created in the image of God (ll. 106–108).[45] In the same context, one finds the older language of return out of the earth and heavenly exaltation:

> For, in fact, we hope that the remains of the departed will soon come to light again out of the earth. And afterward, they will become gods.   (ll. 103–104)

The author probably saw this expression as a variant of the immortality language. It grounds the protest against the practice of dissection that comes immediately before it. The argument for immortality is the only one to which the author gives exegetical support.

Other examples of the combination of immortality and exaltation

language can be found in the propaganda of hellenistic Judaism. Job
uses it to describe the glorious destiny of the person who is converted
out of the "death of idolatry" (4.9). Job's wife sees the glory of the
children of heaven and knows that she will rise (40.4). Job is taken up
to heaven in a chariot like that of Elijah (52.2ff.).[46]

Conversion to Judaism and the promise of immortality are linked
in *Joseph and Aseneth*. The proselyte is given a meal that consists of
the bread of life or immortality (15.3–4). Resurrection or being gathered up into Paradise is symbolized by the food given (16.6–8).[47]
Joseph refuses to kiss Aseneth because lips that have blessed the
living God, eaten the blessed bread of life, and drunk the cup of
immortality should not touch a strange woman who blesses idols and
eats from their table (8.5). *Joseph and Aseneth* has thoroughly assimilated the vocabulary of immortality and incorruptibility.[48] It forms
part of the appeal for conversion to Judaism.

Passages in Josephus also develop the language of immortality.
Some are said to believe that death separates the soul from the body
(Bel. 3.362). Our earthly bodies are made of perishable stuff, while
our souls are "deathless" and thus like the divine (Bel. 3.372).[49] According to Bel. 2.163, the Pharisaic belief in resurrection could be
understood as the postmortem wandering of the soul. One finds
diversity of views in the Psalms of Solomon, which are also thought to
reflect the views of the Pharisees. Ps. Sol. 3.3–12 refers to the final
destruction of the sinners as their death. The "resurrection of the
righteous" in vv. 11–12 could refer simply to the soul. T. Abr. shows
further development toward the individualization of eschatology.
The soul alone survives death and is immediately judged.[50] Early
rabbinic traditions debate the significance of Ezek 37:1–14 for resurrection. The passage raises the question of the relationship between
human remains and the resurrected body. For the school of Shammai
the bones form the basis for the continuity in identity. The Hillelites,
on the other hand, use Job 10:10–12 to demonstrate that the resurrected body is an entirely new one. M. San. 10.1a includes those who
do not believe in resurrection among those who have no share in the
life to come. There resurrection is based on Is 60:21. However, it is
not clear what is intended by the expression "deny the resurrection."[51] M. San. 90b–92a contains elements that might have formed
part of Pharisaic debate with the Sadducees: (a) Where is resurrection found in the Torah? (b) How do the dead rise? (c) What ought one
to believe?[52] It appears that defense of resurrection was found in the
combination of Ezekiel and Isaiah. These debates suggest that resurrection no longer carries the original overtones of persecution and
vindication of the righteous. It merely reflects one *topos* among sev-

eral that can be believed about the final destiny of humans. Belief in resurrection might also serve to distinguish schools of interpretation. Consequently, its inclusion in the list of things to be believed if one is to inherit the age to come reflects the consolidation of Pharisaic teaching authority at the end of the first century C.E. However, that inclusion did not make resurrection a pressing issue. It continues to be lightly represented in the surviving texts.

The most consistent argument for the immortality of the individual soul is found in Philo of Alexandria. The body is mortal, simply. However, Philo does not wish to use the philosophic tradition to imply that souls have a natural right to immortality. Rather, immortality is infused by God into those souls whose knowledge unifies them with Him (Opif. 135: Spec. Leg. 1.345). Immortality depends on attaining virtue. For the virtuous person death is the moment at which the soul is released (Vit. Con. 13; Opif. 77; Gig. 14). Philo is less clear about the fate of the wicked. It appears that they pass out of existence (Leg. All. 1.107f.; Congr. 57; Pram. 60). Philo also uses some of the language of astral immortality in speaking of the soul as composed of the same stuff as the stars (Sacr. 5; Gig. 61).

This view of immortality is grounded in interpretation of Genesis. The dual creation of Gen 1:27 and 2:7 was taken as evidence of a dual anthropology: the earthly human, made up of body and soul, and the heavenly human, the mind or spirit, that inhabits the body. Immortality requires that the soul overcome the hindrance of the body by attaining union with the divine through its practice of virtue.[53] Genesis makes this distinction by speaking first of an incorruptible, heavenly *anthrōpos* (Greek, human being) that is created in the image of God (Gen 1:27) and then of the "moulded," earthly one (Gen 2:7). The earthly *anthrōpos* is caught between the heavenly mind and its quest for union with God and the pull of the body with its passions. In itself, the body is simply corruptible and will perish. This natural death, Philo argues, has no particular significance. But the soul, which is the subject of moral instruction, could die if it did not attain virtue (Leg. All. 1.88–89).

Philo frequently speaks of two types of *anthrōpos*. The first, "the one who was made," rests in Paradise, secure in the practice of virtue. The second, "the one who was moulded," is the subject of commands and moral instruction (Leg. All. 1.92).

When Philo comes to the death promised those who eat from the tree of knowledge, he points out that the act of eating was not followed by physical death. Therefore, he argues, the death to which Scripture refers must mean death of the soul through loss of virtue:

It is for this reason that God says not only "die" but "die the death", not pointing to the death common to us all, but to that special death which is the soul becoming entombed in passions and evils of all kinds. This death is almost the opposite of the death which awaits us all. The latter is separation of combatants who had been pitted against one another, i.e., body and soul. In the former, on the other hand, the worse, that is, the body, overcomes the better, the soul. Whenever Moses speaks of "dying the death", he means this penalty-death, not that which takes place in the course of nature . . . The penalty-death takes place when the soul dies to the life of virtue and is alive only to that of evil . . . now when we are alive, the soul is dead and has been entombed in the body as a sepulchre; whereas should we die, the soul lives from then on its own proper life and is released from the body.   (Leg. All. 1.105–107)

For Philo the mind of Gen 1:26f. is the place of the divine image. One should not suppose that the "image" corresponds to anything bodily:

. . . nothing earth born is more like God than a human being. Let no one present the likeness as one to a bodily form; for neither is God in human form nor is the human body Godlike. No, the word "image" is used to refer to the mind, the ruling element of the soul, for the mind of each of those who successively came into being was moulded according to the archetype of a single mind, the mind of the universe . . . and since images do not always correspond to their archetype and pattern, but in many cases are unlike it, the writer brought out his meaning further by adding the words "after the likeness" to "after the image" thus showing that an accurate cast bearing a true impression was intended.   (Opif. 69–71)

The immortalizing transformation of the human person through wisdom has no place for the body. The latter is mortal and, worse, associated with the passions that imprison the soul. At the same time, the limitations of this individualized description of immortality are also clear. The wise person remains stable in virtue and contemplation of the divine, but there is no place here for the masses of people. There is no place here for the national and corporate symbols of persecution and vindication of the righteous. Only the wise person is rightly called noble, wealthy, honorable, free, king.[54] This elitist vision of the philosopher's immortality will not address many of the

concerns that engendered apocalyptic symbols of vindication, exaltation, and resurrection.

M. Hengel notes that the burning question of theodicy gave rise to
the concern for resurrection in hasidic circles.[55] Resurrection
emerges as an interpretation of Dan 12:2 in particular groups, along
with the exegesis of the suffering-servant passages of Isaiah. These
traditions are primarily interested in the imagery of judgment, exaltation, and vindication. Resurrection of itself appears as a secondary
theme. It may appear as part of the restoration of Israel, as part of the
new creation, or as part of a scene of heavenly exaltation to dwell
with the angels. For the early tradition the direct, physical interpretation of resurrection appeared in the imagery of the body of the
martyr that was to be restored. Descriptions of living on the renewed
earth also presuppose that there is something "bodily" about that
new existence, though the definition of bodily under those conditions
is not specified. Resurrection as angelic existence is more easily converted to exaltation or equated with the philosophic language of
immortality, as Wisdom shows. The ease with which the metaphors
could slide into one another is often obscured by modern attempts to
categorize a rigid boundary between resurrection on the one hand
and immortality of the soul on the other. We have seen that many, if
not most, texts combine eschatological metaphors.[56]

The particular imagery one finds in a text is more likely to be
dictated by the other images that surround it than by concerns for a
dogmatic position about life after death. The primary focus of much
of the metaphoric language in these traditions appears to be the
renewal of life that transcends and overturns the tensions and evils of
this world. The writings in which we do find speculative approaches
to resurrection seek to reassure the reader about the truth of the
inherited tradition. Resurrection can, then, be taken as an item independent of its earlier context in scenes of judgment and vindication.
It can be individualized and give rise to questions about the appropriate judgment of individual souls or their fate after death. At the
most generalized level it no longer addresses itself even to the appro-
priateness of rewarding those righteous who have suffered evil in
their life for righteousness' sake. We have seen that in 2 Bar. the
systematization of resurrection led to its relocation as a prelude to
the real eschatological event of judgment. It provides for recognition
of those who are to be judged. This shift may reflect growing skepticism about the traditional eschatology of the judgment scene.[57] 2
Bar. promises that those who have died without having seen the
messianic age will do so.[58] Thus, the work maintains the solidarity of
the community of the righteous in the face of continued eschatologi-

cal disappointment. In both 2 Bar. and IV Ezra the questioning of the eschatological metaphors has moved to a new level of discourse. Affirmation of the tradition in collective and symbolic visions clearly does not suffice. Reasons must be given. The peculiarities of the tradition must be defended. In the early rabbinic traditions an exegetical base for the affirmation of resurrection is found in Ezekiel and Isaiah. There one finds the emergence of a further question: what is the relationship between the body that is buried and the resurrected or transformed body of the new age? A similar question emerges out of the encounter between the resurrection metaphors and a wisdom spirituality closer to Philo's conception of the immortalizing of the soul in 1 Cor 15. But all such questions reflect analysis and dogmatizing of what was originally a visionary affirmation of the tradition of righteousness and divine judgment. Taken outside the larger context of the vision and metaphor, resurrection begins to appear a somewhat peculiar doctrine. It also shows that the fluidity of metaphors for eschatological vindication could not, even in the first century, be pinned down in the conceptual framework of "eschatological doctrine."

SOME GRECO-ROMAN VIEWS

This section will not enter into the complex debate over the varied cults and their implications for pagan beliefs about the afterlife in any detail. Resurrection was not the creation of such pagan speculation. However, a survey of the non-Jewish images and understandings of the postmortem fate of the individual will indicate those perceptions and images with which a person in the first or second century might have understood the Christian message. At the same time, one must not lose sight of the possibility that the Christian metaphors about resurrection did not fit well within this horizon, that Christian emphasis on resurrection and judgment was "something new" for the pagan convert.

In the later period, Christian art represented the ascent of Christ along the same lines as those employed for the *apotheosis* of the emperor.[59] During the funeral proceedings the emperor's body and effigy were cremated. Some, seeking to curry favor with the *dives* Caesar, might claim that they had seen the soul of the deceased emperor ascend.[60] The earliest representation of the heavenly ascent of the emperor appears on the arch of Titus where the eagle bears

the divinized emperor aloft. The iconography of imperial divinization was not well established until the reign of Hadrian. Then one
finds an established tradition of temple and altar for the *divus,* which
implied granting the emperor a cult by which he continued to be
present among humans through the memory of his deeds. The eagle
or the chariot or the winged genius of the emperor is regularly shown
bearing him aloft on imperial coinage.[61]

Elements of the iconography of heavenly ascent appear on individual tombstones, and in a more general sense this imagery could be
seen to crystallize the rather nebulous hopes for immortality held by
individuals.[62] One could argue that a similar process has occurred
with the Jewish resurrection imagery. The stellar exaltation of a
specific group of leaders, the *maskilim,* becomes the focus for general developments in the expectations for the righteous of the community as a group and then as a prelude to universal judgment. This
transition is more natural in the context of the Jewish community,
since its social structure did not separate an individual teacher from
the rest of the community with the sharp class pyramid typical of the
imperial order.

Cicero's *Dream of Scipio,* like its Jewish counterparts, uses an eschatological vision of the future to respond to the crises of the first
century B.C.E.[63] Those political and religious traditions that depended on the integrity of the local community, its class structure,
and vision of the virtuous life were placed under severe strain by the
sweep of imperial conquest. Though Cicero participates in the
changes that are overtaking the world at quite a different level from
the writers of apocalypses, he nevertheless acknowledges the disloca-
tions that are following in its wake. As was typical of those cast into
the turbulent lives and deaths engendered by the "new politics,"
Cicero sought in philosophic reflection a way of understanding the
tradition now that the old Roman virtues and the *cursus honorum* no
longer functioned as an integrating pattern of life. Faced with the
danger that his class would flee public life, Cicero sustains in the
Dream the view that only those who benefit the city have hope of
immortality (Rep. 6.13).

This promise encourages Scipio to hold to his course of service to
the state despite the grim prediction (6.12) that he would lose his life
through the treachery of members of his own family. Scipio's question about the fate of his ancestors introduces a discourse on the life
of the soul independent of the body: "Surely all those who have
escaped from the bondage of the body as from a prison are alive; but
that so-called 'life' of yours is really death" (6.14). Scipio asks to hasten
to the place in which his ancestors are alive. He is told that he must

remain with his duty to the state, since the soul's descent from the stars binds it to that duty (6.15–16).

Scipio is then shown the celestial spheres. This vision points out the smallness of the earth and the insignificance of the empire. Like the heavenly journeys in the Enoch tradition, this vision includes a brief course in astronomical wisdom. At the same time, it teaches the insignificance of human affairs over against the magnitude of nature's power and of celestial time (6.15–22). Thus, the young Scipio is inoculated against the human vanity that might tempt one destined for fame and public life (6.23). The true self is not the body but the inner divinity, which is immortal:

> Strive on, indeed, and be sure that it is not your self that is immortal but only your body. For the man revealed by your outward form is not your self. The spirit is the true self; not the physical shape which can be pointed to with a finger. Know, then, that you are a god, if a god is that which lives, feels, remembers and foresees, and which rules, governs and moves the body over which it is set, just as the supreme god above us rules the universe. And, just as the supreme god moves the universe, which is partly mortal, so the immortal spirit moves the frail body.   (6.24)

This comparison of the soul's rule over the body with that of god over the universe was a philosophic *topos*. It is followed by a scientific account of the first unmoved cause. This account provides the final argument for the immortality of the soul:

> Now that it is clear that what is self-moved is eternal who can deny that this is the nature of spirit? For whatever is moved by an external impulse is spiritless; but whatever possesses spirit is moved by its own inner impulse, for that is the peculiar nature and characteristic of spirit. And, since spirit is the only self-moving force, it surely has no beginning and is immortal. Therefore, use it in the noblest pursuits! And the noblest tasks are those undertaken in defense of your native land. A spirit occupied and trained in such activities will have a swifter flight to this, its true home and permanent dwelling place. This flight will be even swifter if, while still confined in the body, it looks out and by contemplating what lies outside itself, becomes detached from the body as much as possible. For the spirits of those given to sensual pleasures have become like slaves. And the spirits of those who violated the laws of gods and men at the instigation of

these desires which are subservient to pleasure—their spirits after leaving the body fly about close to the earth and do not return to this place except after many ages of torture.   (6.25)

The tradition of astral immortality moves in two directions. The dialogue begins with the older tradition in which only the souls of leaders received astral immortality. This immortality is presented as compensation for the failure of that form of immortality that most concerned the ancients, the presence attained through the memory of one's deeds among men. This immortality was captured in the funeral ritual with the mask of the family ancestors and the ceremonial *laudatio funebris*. [64] Part of the breakup of the old certainties is reflected in the somber statements about the forgetfulness of humanity. The memories of men are short in connection with the aeons of time. Scipio faces treachery from within the family, which was most charged with such memory. Consequently, the astral immortality for the leaders of the people is to serve as true immortality in the face of the untrustworthy character of human relationships and human glory.

The combination of the astral immortality of the leaders with the philosophic tradition of immortality and astronomical lore has altered the conclusion of the document. Those who attain virtue—not simply the illustrious political leaders—through dissociating the soul from the body and its passions achieve astral immortality. The "self-mover" argument for the nature of the soul compels the conclusion that even the souls of the wicked must be immortal. Consequently, they must undergo punishment and purgation in the sublunar spheres before they can return to the astral region that is the source of all that is self-moved. This democratization of immortality, not limited to the offspring of old families bound to their traditions of community leadership and service, will provide a new source of energy for the imperial period. The *Dream of Scipio* itself seeks to uphold the older vision of the virtuous ruling families at the same time as it shows the destruction of the old order. In its way this apocalypse is as much a response to dangerous political times as the Maccabean apocalypses were. The young must be encouraged to continue to uphold the vision of the good and public service that had motivated their ancestors. Philosophic and cosmological speculation is used to provide a comprehensive vision of the true reality of the earth and human vanity. This vision is to unmask the false views of the masses that might have led the young Scipio to flee the dangers of public life. Thus, this dialogue is not seeking to answer the question of the soul's survival out of a simple pleasure in philosophic dogmatism. The question is more pressing: Can the ideal of public service that had shaped the ethos of the aristocracy under the old republic with its feel for family honor and tradition hold out in the imperial age? What happens when the new opportunities for ambition make it impossible to trust even one's own family?

Just as resurrection was not a universal concern among Jews, so immortality was not a pervasive one among pagans. R. MacMullen argues that the common view that the widespread growth of religious cults was fueled by a concern for personal immortality has little to support it. He examines two types of evidence: that from the cults themselves and that from the Christian apologists. Lucius's initiation claims that the hero has blessedness and is reborn "in a certain way." It does not say reborn *"in aeternam."* Indeed, the blessedness experienced by the hero refers directly to rewards in the present life that are brought about by service to the goddess. Similarly, the rituals of passing through the heavens in Mithraism are not clearly aimed at postmortem immortality but at enjoying divine power or protection in this life. Even the "dying/rising" vegetation cults did not address the afterlife. The Attis cult does not appear to have had a resurrection of the god until the second century. Rather, the bull sacrifice was thought to extend one's earthly life in a state of ritual purity for a number of years. Thus, the best one can get from these cults is a vague idea of ritual purity that would make for an agreeable afterlife.[65]

Seneca's letters present either the disembodied existence of the Stoic Logos that lies at the heart of life or annihilation as the only two plausible accounts of what happens to a person who dies.[66] No one should have any desire to return to what is bodily, since the body is the source of all the ills we experience:

> Behold, this clogging burden of a body to which nature has chained me! "I shall die," you say. You mean to say, "I shall cease to run the risk of sickness; I shall cease to run the risk of imprisonment; I shall cease to run the risk of death." . . . Death either annihilates us or strips us bare. If we are then released, what remains is the better part after the burden has been removed. If we are annihilated, nothing remains; good and bad alike are removed.   (Ep. 24.18)

The Stoic doctrine of the return of all things proves that the principle of life comes back. Death is merely an interruption in the process of cosmic return (Ep. 36.10–11).

For Seneca, then, the order of the universe according to the dictates of Stoic physics provides the tranquillity with which to face death. He considers the old stories of punishments in Hades fit only for children.

Though one might be tempted to argue that Seneca's conversion to philosophy sets him apart from the majority, who continue to fear the gods and death, it is difficult to show that concern for immortality was an important feature of popular piety. The masses are said to fear the gods, on the one hand, and to enjoy the pleasant festivals made possible by religion, on the other. The motivating forces of popular religious belief are pleasure and relief from the anxieties of this life. Plutarch's defense of the piety of common people against the "atheistic" arguments of the Epicureans has nothing to do with the possibilities of immortality (Pleas. Life Imposs. *Moralia* 1101D–1102B). Even the philosopher's piety is one that can expect prosperity and favors from the gods. "All things belong to the gods, as Diogenes said. Among friends all property is common. Good men are friends of the gods and it cannot be that one dear to the gods should fail to prosper or that the temperate and upright man should fail to be dear to the gods" *(Mor.* 1102F).

The second-century satirist Lucian argues that the Christian convictions about immortality rest on a false indifference to things of this world. That indifference makes the Christians vulnerable to religious frauds like Peregrinus:

> The poor wretches have convinced themselves first and foremost that they are going to be immortal and live forever. As a result, they despise death and are even willing, most of them, to give themselves into custody. Furthermore, their first lawgiver persuaded them that they are all brothers after they have transgressed once and for all by denying the Greek gods and worshipping that crucified sophist, himself and living under his laws. Therefore, they despise all things indiscriminately and consider them common property, receiving such doctrines by tradition without any real evidence. So if any charlatan or trickster able to profit by such occasions comes among them, he quickly acquires sudden wealth by imposing on simple people.   (Peregrinus 1)

Christianity's pagan critics generally viewed resurrection as misunderstood metempsychosis at best. At worst, it seemed ridiculous. Minucius Felix reports the following mockery of the Christian views of judgment and resurrection:

And they are not satisfied with this lunatic notion (= end of the world). They embellish and embroider it with old wives tales. After death, ashes and cinders, they tell us they are born again. They all believe their own lies with such unaccountable confidence that you might think they had already come to life again! Look at their double delirium, their twofold madness. They solemnly proclaim that the heavens and constellations will perish even though we leave them just as we find them. And, they firmly pledge themselves eternity when they are dead and gone though we perish just as we were once born. I presume this is supposed to explain why they reject funeral pyres and condemn cremation. But, of course, every body, whether taken from the flames or not, is eventually reduced to earth . . . Led astray by this ridiculous idea, they promise themselves, since they are the just, an everlasting life of bliss after death and the rest of humanity, being the wicked, perpetual punishment.   (Octavian 11.2–5)

Thus, there are stories of punishment in Hades based on Homer, philosophic doctrines of the survival of the soul, and images of astral immortality abroad in paganism. But the general pagan view seems to have been to take death as one finds it. It is an event that cannot be escaped and whose outcome is uncertain, though it probably leads to annihilation. At any rate, one's postmortem state is of little concern. The Stoic vision of a disembodied divine spark or soul leaving the body at death is not likely to galvanize strong personal feelings. That view, like the immortality in the *Dream of Scipio,* is a philosopher's view and one of those convictions that "one may hold without remembering that one holds it."[67] No one would care much about an eternal life that did not apply to the person but only to a divine spark. Similarly, the Savior language used of gods and goddesses did not refer to the soul and its eternity but to health, prosperity, pleasure, or some other good that was directly experienced in this life. Thus, MacMullen concludes, no pagan cult promised an afterlife for the worshiper as he knew and felt himself to be. The preaching of resurrection may well have been—as it seems to have been known by Christianity's second-century opponents—a distinctive feature of the Christian group. We cannot assume that resurrection answers a longing already being expressed in pagan society. Indeed, MacMullen cautions, we must be careful not to attribute to the first three centuries social or spiritual needs that were in fact created by Christianity.[68] Given the marginal status of resurrection and immortality in

Judaism as well as paganism, we must agree with this caution. Resurrection comes into prominence in Christianity. And it may well be that Christianity has created a hope and expectation rather than responded to a widely held pattern of belief or practice.

NOTES

1. C. F. Evans, *Resurrection and the New Testament* (SBT ser. 2, no. 12; London: SCM, 1970), 16–17.
2. D. S. Russell, *The Method and Message of Jewish Apocalyptic* (Philadelphia: Westminster, 1964), 353–56.
3. H. C. C. Cavallin, *Life After Death: Paul's Argument for the Resurrection of the Dead in 1 Cor 15. Part I: An Enquiry into the Jewish Background* (Lund: Gleerup, 1974), 15f., 23–24. Resurrection emerges during a period of intense hellenization under Antiochus IV. We cannot say with certainty how much the linguistic and conceptual changes embodied in Greek thought may have contributed to its emergence.
4. For a survey of the treatment of Sheol in apocalyptic, see Russell, op. cit., 357; for the Greek tradition, see E. Vermule, *Aspects of Death in Early Greek Art* (Berkeley: University of California, 1979), 7–41.
5. Ibid., 8f., 27–29.
6. Russell, op. cit., 357–66.
7. D. Winston, *The Wisdom of Solomon* (AnBi 43; Garden City, N.Y.: Doubleday, 1979), 30–32. Winston dates Wisdom of Solomon in the first century A.D., since he claims that it has been influenced by Alexandrian middle Platonism and a loss of optimism about the possibilities of cultural accommodation.
8. A. E. Harvey, *Jesus and the Constraints of History* (Philadelphia: Westminster, 1982), 150f. One finds *metabainein* (War 2.163) and *ek peritropes* (Contra Apion 2.218; War 3.374).
9. See the discussion of the tombstone evidence in E. M. Meyers and J. F. Strange, *Archaeology, the Rabbis and Early Christianity* (Nashville: Abingdon, 1981), 85–102; and U. Fischer, *Eschatologie und Jenseitserwartung im Hellenistichen Diasporajudentum* (BZNW 44; Berlin: Walter de Gruyter, 1978), 230–35.
10. J. J. Collins, "Jewish Apocalypses," *Semeia* 14 (1979), 25f., 33–36.

11. J. J. Collins, *The Apocalyptic Vision of the Book of Daniel* (Harvard Semitic Monograph 16; Missoula, Mont.: Scholars, 1977), 143. Collins goes on to suggest that "holy ones" is a title for humans because of the association of angels and humans in the eschatological community.

12. G. Nickelsburg, *Resurrection, Immortality, and Eternal Life in Intertestamental Judaism* (HTS xxvi; Cambridge: Harvard University, 1972), 11–16. Michael's appearance in T. Levi 5.6f. and T. Dan 6.1–5 may represent an early exegesis of this passage. He also appears to plead the cause of the righteous in the Animal Apocalypse.

13. Is 52:13 speaks of the servant as "causing others to understand," *yaskil*. This is the prophecy that Daniel saw fulfilled by the *maskilim*.

14. Collins, *Vision*, 170f.; Nickelsburg, op. cit., 17–20.

15. Collins, *Vision*, 172f. Collins finds this perception that salvation must come from the "heavenly dimension" to be the cornerstone of apocalyptic visions of reality.

16. Ibid., 173. Collins takes Dan 11:35 to mean that not all of the *maskilim* will die but that they will "be changed" to the astral state. Whether this presumption can be found in Daniel or not remains disputed. However, it is the interpretation that Paul gave to the resurrection in 1 Cor 15:51f., where he claims to be revealing an apocalyptic "mystery." Other scholars question the ástral imagery found in this passage. They suggest that Daniel is only speaking figuratively of a time when the wise will participate in the instruction of a renewed Israel (see Nickelsburg, op. cit., 26).

17. On the early date for As. Mos. 10, see Nickelsburg, op. cit., 43–45; Collins, *Vision*, 199. The writing in its present form comes from the last years of the pre-Christian era, but its core derives from the time of Antiochus IV. This core consists in 8:1–5, a description of Antiochus's persecution; 9:5–7, the martyrdom of Taxo, with the implication that the blood of the martyrs is avenged; 10:1, 8–10, the appearance of the Kingdom of God.

18. Nickelsburg, op. cit., 82–84. Nickelsburg speaks of the exaltation tradition here as "secondary democratization." Judgment at the hands of the angel is not directly tied to exaltation, but the results of that judgment are presumed. Therefore, it is possible that the resurrection motif of Daniel is a special creation of the Danielic school's concern with wisdom.

19. Collins, *Vision*, 200. The tradition of Holy War from Deut 32:35–43 is taken to mean that vengeance belongs only to God in this

pacifist stance. On the role of angelic mediators in furthering the cry for vengeance, see D. C. Carlson, "Vengeance and Angelic Mediation in *Testament of Moses* 9 and 10," *Journal of Biblical Literature* 101 (1982), 89–93.

20. Following the reconstruction of J. C. VanderKam, *Textual and Historical Studies in the Book of Jubilees* (Missoula, Mont.: Scholars, 1977), 270.

21. Against Evans's claim (op. cit., 17) that this passage shows the influence of a doctrine of immortality of the soul, see Cavallin, op. cit., 37f. Nickelsburg (op. cit., 31–33) makes too much of a possible contradiction between the passage's vision of earthly peace and the peaceful rest of the dead. The two are commonly associated and might even be said to belong to the most archaic human images of the future of the dead.

22. Nickelsburg, op. cit., 25–27, 38.

23. Some interpreters suggest that the eschatological traditions in T. 12 Patr. represent stages of editing. Later Christian editing of the work also requires caution in dealing with some of the eschatological passages in the book. E. Becker, *Untersuchungen zur Entstehungsgeschichte der Testamente der zwölf Patriarchen* (Leiden: Brill, 1970), 325f., 373–76, 403f. Some images of messianic salvation appear to have been influenced by the later Christian views as T. Levi 18.9–14 and T. Dan 5.11ff. Cavallin (op. cit., 53–56) rightly rejects the attempt to harmonize T. 12 Patr. into a single eschatology that one finds in G. Stemberger, *Der Leib der Auferstehung* (AnaBib 36; Rome: Biblical Institute Press, 1972), 69. See also the discussion of the eschatology of T. 12 Patr. in Hultgård, *L'eschatologie des Testaments des Douze Patriarches* (Acta Universitatis Upsalensis. Historia Religionum 6; Stockholm: Almqvist & Wiksell, 1977), 253–59.

24. Nickelsburg, op. cit., 35–37.

25. The catalog of blessings on the twelve tribes by heaven and earth may be a later addition. Related traditions occur elsewhere in T. 12 Patr. but there is no repetition of this list. See the discussions in M. de Jonge, *The Testaments of the Twelve Patriarchs* (Assen: Van Gorcum, 1953), 95; E. Becker, "Testamente der zwölf Patriarchen," *Jüdische Schriften aus hellenistisch-römischer Zeit* (ed. W. G. Kummel: Gütersloh: Mohn, 1974); and Hultgård, (op. cit., 235–38). Hultgård suggests (pp. 238f.) that this catalog may have been derived from astrological speculation tied to the twelve patriarchs.

26. Hultgård, op. cit., 241f. He bases this pattern on 1 Q IV, address to Zion and Judah; 11 Q apoc Psalm B; 1 En. 10 and Tob. 13.

27. Ibid., 233. The text provides no indication of whether the Gentiles who will condemn Israel are raised in order to be judged or are merely those alive at the time. The condemnation of Israel is presented as Haggada on Gen 27:41ff., which is not attested elsewhere. The LXX changed the passage to reflect the negative vision of the Midianites in Numbers 25. This passage may imply that Midianite "love of brothers" created the group that "feared the Lord" (see Hultgård, 233f.).

28. The special place given to the patriarchs is paralleled in Mt 8:11f./Lk 13:27–29, IV Macc. 7.19 and 16.25 (Hultgård, op. cit., 261). I would agree with Hultgård (op. cit., 261f.) that T. Asher 1.3 and 6.4–6 are about the soul at death and derive from the two-spirits tradition. Since they come from a different tradition, these expressions cannot be taken as directly opposed to the resurrection sections of T. 12 Patr. (pace Becker [1970], 368; Cavallin, op. cit., 55; and Nickelsburg, op. cit., 173).

29. Nickelsburg, op. cit., 98–102. Stemberger (op. cit., 23f.) reads resurrection into the offering for the dead in 2 Macc 12:43. It seems more likely that the context is the sacral imagery of priestly/angelic mediation. The document is not offering the kind of information about the relationship between body and soul that Stemberger seeks to extract from it.

30. Nickelsburg, op. cit., 48–57. Examples of the wisdom story are Joseph in Gen 37:3–42:22, Ahikar, chapters 3–8, and Mordechai in Esther 3:1–14; 6:1–11; 7:10; 8:1–8; 9:4ff.; 10:3.

31. Ibid., 58–62.

32. Ibid., 87–89; Winston (op. cit., 30f.; 60f.), who dates Wisdom in the first century C.E., thinks that it is possible that the author follows Philo in claiming that only souls are immortal (for Philo, see QGen 1.16; Opif. 150; Conf. Ling. 149). Cavallin (op. cit., 126–31) notes that the allusion to Isaiah in Wis 5:1ff. creates the appearance that the author is speaking of resurrection when all that is at stake is cosmic vindication.

33. The similitudes reinterpret the Son of Man figure with Enoch as the judge. They also combine the servant and the transcendent Son of Man. 1 En. 46.1–8 describes the Son of Man taking the throne from the Ancient of Days as the occasion for the condemnation of the wicked. In 1 En. 47, the prayer of the righteous for vengeance is part of the judgment scene. That prayer is answered when the hidden Son of Man is named prior to delivering the wicked into the hands of the Elect One in chapter 48. Nickelsburg (op. cit., 85f.) sees the naming scene as a further development of the Isaianic exaltation traditions.

34. Nickelsburg, "The Apocalyptic Message of *1 Enoch* 92–105," *Catholic Biblical Quarterly* 39 (1977), 323–26.
35. As in 1 QH 3.19–23; 7.22–25; 1 QSa 2.3–10; Nickelsburg, op. cit., 156–67; Collins, *Vision*, 177f.; Cavallin, op. cit., 60–65.
36. Nickelsburg, *Resurrection*, 38. He provides a table that includes all the elements of the judgment scene (op. cit., 138–40). For parallels between IV Ez 7:26–30 and Second Isaiah, see J. M. Myers, *I and II Esdras* (AnBi 42; Garden City, N.Y.: Doubleday, 1974), 253. For the exegesis of Daniel in IV Ezra, see Stemberger, op. cit., 79–82.
37. Cavallin (op. cit., 80–84) rightly insists that IV Ezra is a complex mixture of eschatological imagery that cannot be harmonized. IV Ez 7:21 refers to a preliminary judgment of Israel prior to the coming of the messianic kingdom and the judgment of all people (Myers, op. cit., 253).
38. Stemberger, op. cit., 88–95; Cavallin, op. cit., 86f.
39. Cavallin, op. cit., 75–79. This tradition includes the heavenly glorification of the patriarchs (4.11) and the exaltation to the stars of those who fight for the people (33.5). For the caverns of souls, see 15.5; 32.13; 23.13. See also the discussion in Stemberger, op. cit., 99–109. LAB, like the other writings of this period, uses a variety of metaphors that cannot be harmonized or reduced to a single anthropology.
40. Nickelsburg, op. cit., 140f. Cavallin (op. cit., 148f.) suggests that this section is dependent on Ezek 37:1–14.
41. Myers, op. cit., 124–26. For further treatments of the theology of IV Ezra, see E. Breech, "These Fragments I Have Shored Against My Ruins: The Form and Function of IV Ezra," *Journal of Biblical Literature* 92 (1973), 267–74; and A. L. Thompson, *Responsibility for Evil in the Theodicy of IV Ezra* (SBLDS 29; Missoula, Mont.: Scholars, 1977).
42. On the immortalizing transformation inherent in the Greek discovery of the soul, see E. Voeglin, *The Ecumenic Age* (Baton Rouge: Louisiana State University, 1974), 214–38. Voeglin thinks that this fundamental Platonic insight was destroyed by the dogmatic traditions of Stoic and Philonic philosophy. However, it is precisely in the "dogmatic philosophies" of the hellenistic period that it becomes available to the wider range of persons. This wider availability also derives from the creation of a new, "middle class" reading public through the traditions of hellenistic education. See M. Grant, *From Alexander to Cleopatra: The Hellenistic World* (New York: Scribners, 1982), 138f.

43. See the text and commentary in P. W. Van der Horst, *The Sentences of Pseudo-Phocylides* (SVTP iv; Leiden: Brill, 1978), 185–96; see also Cavallin, op. cit., 151–53; U. Fischer, op. cit., 131–34. Van der Horst argues for a date sometime between 30 B.C.E. and 36 C.E. on the grounds that the openness to hellenistic culture would have been uncharacteristic of any Alexandrian Jew writing after the pogroms that marked the reign of Caligula.

44. Van der Horst, op. cit., 81–83; Fischer (op. cit., 108f.) insists that since the author is not an advocate of bodily resurrection, the passage cannot be taken as a reference to the practice of dissection.

45. This passage grounds its anthropology in the exegesis of Genesis; see Cavallin, op. cit., 152f.; Fischer, op. cit., 136f.; Van der Horst, op. cit., 190–92.

46. Cavallin, op. cit., 160–62.

47. Ibid., 155–58.

48. M. Philonenko, *Joseph et Aseneth* (SPVS 13; Leiden: Brill, 1968), 155. See *athanasia* in Wis 3:4; 4:1, 8–13, 17; 15:3; IV Mac. 14.5; 16.3; *aphtharsia,* Wis 2:23; 6:19; IV Mac. 9.22.

49. Fischer, op. cit., 145.

50. See A 7: B 13; A 1: B 4; A 20: B 14; Cavallin, op. cit., 96f.

51. Cavallin, op. cit., 171–78.

52. Ibid., 178–80.

53. See the discussion of Philo in B. Pearson, *The Pneumatikos Psychikos Terminology in 1 Corinthians* (SBLDS 12; Missoula, Mont.: Scholars, 1973), 17–21; R. A. Horsley, "How Can Some of You Say that There Is No Resurrection of the Dead? Spiritual Elitism in Corinth," *Novum Testamentum* 20 (1978), 216–25.

54. The terms have their origin in popular Cynic-Stoic preaching but were thoroughly at home in hellenistic Judaism; see, for example, Wis 6:20; 7:8, 11; 8:3, 5, 10, 14, 18; Virt. 174; Sobr. 55–57. Horsley (op. cit., 210f.) points to the negative effect of this doctrine of the "wise person" as glorious and wellborn in Corinth.

55. M. Hengel, *Judaism and Hellenism* (Philadelphia: Fortress, 1974), 196–202. Hengel overemphasizes the influence of Iranian vegetation deities and Greek Orphic sources in contributing to the rise of resurrection imagery. We have seen that resurrection has important structural differences from both the cyclic vegetation myths and the Orphic speculation, since it does not concern itself with patterns of return whether of nature or of the soul.

56. In addition to the passages cited above, *Adam and Eve* contains a vision of universal resurrection on the last day, 13.3b, 6; 51.2;

immortality of the soul, 43.1 (Latin translation); and Adam's restoration to his lost glory, 39.2. Apoc. Abr. 13 has Abraham's exaltation to an angelic throne, though it is not clear whether a resurrected body is implied; chapter 31 refers to judgment and the trumpet but does not contain a judgment scene.

57. This tradition may have intended to limit participation in the reward of glory as a response to the numbers who would have died before the judgment. P. Bogaert *(Apocalypse de Baruch* [SC 144; Paris: Éditions du Cerf, 1969], 419–22) argues that 2 Bar. maintains the traditional view of judgment as the collective victory of Israel rather than as a personal or moral judgment. He presumes that after 70 C.E. resurrection was without viable opposition as an eschatological view, since it had been imposed by the anathema of m. San 10.1.

58. Bogaert (ibid.) contrasts this view with IV Ez 7:29–31, which still presumes that only those who happen to be living at the time are privileged to witness the messianic age.

59. Plates 26–36 in S. G. MacCormack, *Art and Ceremony in Late Antiquity* (Berkeley: University of California, 1981). The fourth-century examples in Plates 35 and 36 show the parallelism between the emperor and Christ. Plate 35 pictures Constantine's imperial chariot being aided into heaven by the hand of God. Plate 36 shows Christ mounting on the clouds with the aid of a similar hand of God.

60. Dio 56.46f., 59.11, and the satire of the imperial *apotheosis* in Seneca's "Pumpkinification of Claudius." See also K. Hopkins, *Conquerors and Slaves* (Cambridge: Cambridge University, 1978), 203.

61. Ibid., 99–100, 214–15.

62. MacCormack, op. cit., 98.

63. See the discussion of the dream of Scipio as a pagan example of the apocalypse genre in H. Attridge, "Greek and Latin Apocalypses," *Semeia* 14 (1979), 163.

64. MacCormack, op. cit., 96–97.

65. R. MacMullen, *Paganism in the Roman Empire* (New Haven: Yale University, 1981), 133.

66. Ibid., 56.

67. Ibid., 56.

68. Ibid., 136f.

THREE

Resurrection and the Life of Jesus

Christian proclamation of the resurrection attaches the metaphoric language of resurrection to the life of a particular individual, Jesus of Nazareth. The claim is not that Jesus will be resurrected with the righteous in the last day but that he has been raised by God. Many of the other elements attached to resurrection in Jewish traditions remain as much a part of the imagined future as they always were. Jesus' resurrection did not usher in the final judgment of humanity. Nor could one point to the death of Jesus as a publicly acclaimed martyrdom on behalf of the Torah. The connection between resurrection and vindication of the righteous sufferer does require that one regard the life of Jesus from a certain point of view to be sure. The assertion that the life of Jesus culminates in resurrection presumes a relationship of piety between Jesus and God and that his death be viewed as the sort of deliberate act of evil and injustice that would be met with divine vindication. None of these perspectives would of itself explain the prominence of resurrection imagery in the

New Testament. Consequently, some exegetes argue that the emphasis on resurrection metaphors must be grounded in the teaching or life of Jesus himself. In fact, one might argue that exaltation would be a more natural image to use for Jesus' place with God, since it would not involve the possibility of a counterclaim that none of the other eschatological predictions such as resurrection of the patriarchs, triumph over enemies, divine judgment, had occurred. In this chapter, we will examine the various links that are proposed between resurrection and the life of Jesus from sayings and healing miracles to the early kerygmatic formulae and traditions behind the gospel accounts.

SAYINGS OF JESUS

The difficulty would be solved if Jesus' teaching had explicitly concerned itself with resurrection. Even within the gospels themselves we find evidence of the early Christian teachers' attaching explicit indications of resurrection to sayings of Jesus that had a more general orientation.

Luke 16:19–31

The parable of the rich man and Lazarus provides an example of this process. The initial story uses the imagery of the judgment scene in a striking reversal of the fate of rich and poor. It presumes a postmortem judgment and describes both the rich and the regions of heaven/hell in language very close to the preaching of 1 Enoch.[1] At the same time, the story is not cast as one of cosmic judgment but along the lines of a wisdom tale or folk story. The rich, who oppress the poor, will not repent, since they are deaf to the message of Moses and the prophets. However, the poor can take heart from this story, since their fate will be like that of Lazarus. The final verse of the story as it is transmitted in Luke has shifted from such a general statement of disbelief to a statement about the failure to repent when Jesus is preached as having been raised from the dead: "If they do not hear Moses and the prophets, neither will they be convinced if someone should rise from the dead" (v. 31). This conclusion points to the opposition encountered by the Christian preaching of Jesus' resurrection. It also points to another element that we find in the early resurrection kerygma, the claim that Jesus' death and resurrection fulfills Moses and the prophets. The parable itself operates within the metaphoric world of judgment scenes in the wisdom tradition. The early Christian missionaries found it a telling comment on their own experience of preaching the gospel. Of itself, the parable was not concerned with teaching about afterlife. It made use of a popular image of judgment and reversal to comment on the obstacles to repentance in this life.

Matthew 12:39–42/Luke 11:29–32

The sayings on the sign of Jonah from the Q tradition also illustrate the reinterpretation of Jesus' teaching from the perspective of resurrection. In Q, the saying was part of a prophetic testimony against the evils of an unbelieving generation. Such preaching sought to encourage repentance in light of the Kingdom of God.[2] Lk 11:30 reflects the original version of the saying in question: "For as Jonah became a sign to the men of Nineveh so will the Son of Man be to this generation." Mt 12:40 has modified the saying so that the sign provided by the Son of Man is the resurrection: "For as Jonah was three days and three nights in the belly of the whale, so will the Son of Man be three days and three nights in the heart of the earth." This interpretation is made possible by the "three days" that formed the part of the early Christian preaching about the resurrection. It provided a link to the story of Jonah as an analogy for resurrection. Once that link has been made, the resurrection becomes the sign of judgment against the evil generation.

Luke 14:12–14

This collection of sayings attached to the saying about "places at table" (Lk 14:8–11) concludes with a beatitude. The blessing on those who invite the poor, who cannot repay, to table presumes the common pattern of eschatological reversal. Resurrection here belongs to the context of reward for the righteous at the judgment just as it does in the Enoch traditions. The saying "And you will be blessed because they cannot repay you. You will be repaid in the resurrection of the just" (v. 14) presumes that the audience shares this common tradition. They know that "resurrection of the just" refers to the time of divine judgment. Similar concern for teaching generosity appears in the sayings on love of enemies in Lk 6:35–36. Lk 14:14 has attached expectation of reward "in the resurrection" to the preaching of generosity.

Mark 12:18–27/Matthew 22:23–33/Luke 20:27–38

The only direct discussion of resurrection in Jesus' sayings occurs in the controversy story in Mk 12:18–27. The Lukan version of the story has expanded the section on not marrying with an apocalyptic saying that contrasts those who belong to the present age and those who belong to the new age (vv. 34–35). This passage belongs to the traditions of "two ways" paraenesis. Among the Essenes, such traditions spoke of those who belong to the elect realizing the images of future salvation in the present. Consequently, the saying may have originated without the reference to resurrection as a paraenetic contrast between the children of this age and the children of the age to come. The former marry; the latter do not.

The pronouncement story itself is resolved with the first saying, which grounds its claim in another common image of resurrection: resurrection as translation into angelic glory. The continuation of the Markan passage has all the earmarks of a later addition. Mark introduces it with the expression "concerning the dead, that they are raised." This introduction, along with the following, "Do you not know in the book of Moses, at the bush how he said . . . ," turns what follows into a piece of scholastic elaboration or teaching about resurrection. It suggests the type of objection to resurrection that one finds in 1 Cor 15:12. J. R. Donahue sees this whole section of Mark as a carefully constructed catechesis based on the monotheistic affirmation of the one God as God of the living. Mark apparently wishes to advocate a spiritual concept of resurrection rooted in the power of God. He wishes to deny any crudely materialistic images of resurrection such as that suggested by the Sadducees or the false view of Herod that Jesus is John the Baptist returned (6:14b, 16).[3] J. R. Donahue points to Wisdom and IV Macc. as the closest parallels to the theology of divine transcendence in this section of Mark. Within the context of that theology, "God of the living" must refer to continued life with God and not to resurrection as some future return to the body.[4]

Luke's version has expanded the phrase "are like angels in heaven" by incorporating it into an explanatory sentence, "for they cannot die anymore because they are equal to angels and are sons of God, being sons of the resurrection" (v. 36). This explanation has put together several metaphors, the unusual "sons of the resurrection," which had been attached to the apocalyptic paraenesis about marriage in Luke; becoming like angels, which appears to have been the story's original understanding of resurrection; and the combination of "sons" of God and immortality, grounded in the wisdom tradition. When one abstracts from the obvious explanatory developments of these sayings, one finds that the use of resurrection in the sayings of Jesus is similar to that of his Jewish contemporaries. It appears occasionally but is not a major topic of discussion. Nor can one presume that Jesus makes any significant contribution to or elaboration of these common modes of speaking.[5] Once resurrection is an established theme of Christian preaching, the evangelists must take some pains to provide explanations for it.

These examples also suggest that had there been more teaching about resurrection preserved in the Jesus tradition, it would have found its way into the gospel narratives. Explanations of that symbolism were required even in the first century. The paucity of resurrection language in the teaching of Jesus, then, and its use in ways that are apparently typical of other Jewish speakers of the period make it impossible to explain the centrality of resurrection in later Christian preaching by appeal to the teaching of Jesus.

HEALING MIRACLES

Some interpreters point to the stories of healing in which Jesus restores a dead person to life as the foundation for later Christian emphasis on resurrection. Like the sayings material, these stories show signs of editing and of development in early Christian catechesis. These stories also reflect specific concerns with the fate of those Christians who had died.

Luke 7:11–17

Though this story has overtones of Elijah's healing of the widow's son (1 Ki 17:17–24), it does not appear to have been based on that story.[6] Luke situates it between the story of the healing of the centurion's son and the coming of the messengers from John the Baptist. The question posed by the messengers of John the Baptist focuses attention on these stories as healing miracles. They form the content of what the disciples of John the Baptist have heard about Jesus.[7] The acclamation of the crowd in 7:16 invokes the prophet Christology as the key to the significance of the miracle. Luke has apparently expanded that acclamation with the additional phrase "God has visited his people."[8] The primitive association of the miracle with a Christology of Jesus as the great prophet has already been made subservient to the more prevalent view of Jesus as Lord by the substitution of *ho Kyrios* (the Lord) for Jesus in v. 13.[9] All of these interpretations tie the miracle story to christological developments in which Jesus is perceived as the fulfillment of messianic prophecies.

Mark 5:21–24a, 35–43/Luke 8:40–42a, 49–56/ Matthew 9:18–19, 23–26

Verse 21ab may have originally introduced the story of the woman with a hemorrhage, while Mark added v. 21c to introduce the healing of Jarius's daughter and then had to provide the crowds for the story of the woman in v. 24. Verse 43a reflects the Markan concern for secrecy. The story of the woman may have been associated with the healing of Jarius's daughter in Mark's source. Jesus is presented as a powerful healer who can cure chronic illness and restore life to the dead.[10] Matthew has abridged Mark considerably. Both stories are reduced to the essentials of the miracle performed. They illustrate the faith in Jesus that moves the recipients of the miracle. Luke has smoothed out details in Mark's account by abridging and rearranging it. At the same time, he omits the "magic formula" by which the cure is effected in Mark (5:41) and emphasizes instead the importance of Jarius's faith in making the healing possible.[11]

Rochais proposes that the pre-Markan tradition saw the story as closely tied to resurrection. He divides the story into four scenes: (1) 5:22–24a, the request; (2) 5:33–37, announcement of the girl's death; (3) 5:38–40a, Jesus' arrival and meeting with the crowd; and (4) 40b–43, the miracle and its effects.[12] Scenes 1 and 4 represent the primitive Christology of Jesus as the powerful prophet who frees people from suffering and death.

Scenes 2 and 3 already represent development in the direction of community catechesis. Christians are being instructed in how to respond to death. First, the father is told, "Do not fear, only believe" (v. 36). Then, the crowd is told that the girl is not dead but only sleeping (v. 39). These instructions reflect Christian teaching about how one is to react to the death of fellow Christians. We find such teaching in Paul's instructions to the Thessalonians in 1 Thess 4:13f.[13] The Christian has hope in the face of death, which those outside do not.

G. Rochais also suggests that the confession of faith in the story is grounded in the early resurrection kerygma. This type of preaching appears in the stories of the women at the tomb. They are told, "Do not fear" (Mk 16:6). Mary Magdelene is asked, "Why are you weeping?" (Jn 20:15). The injunction not to fear originally belongs to the apocalyptic vocabulary of the appearance of an angelic revealer.[14] However, the question in Jn 20:15 is not directly derived from such stories. Therefore, Rochais concludes that all three examples are indebted to early Christian catechesis. They sought to spell out the implications of belief in the resurrection of Jesus for the Christian attitude toward the death of fellow Christians before the messianic age.

John 11:1–46

Similar catechetical concerns are part of the tradition of the raising of Lazarus. The Johannine tradition appears to have developed a healing miracle similar to the story of Jarius's daughter.[15] Rochais suggests that the original story presented Jesus as the one whose healing fulfilled the servant predictions and the psalmist's confidence in God:[16]

. . . to make those bound come out, and those who dwell therein out of prison . . .   (Is 42:7, LXX)

. . . saying to those in chains, come out, and to those in darkness, come into light . . .   (Is 49:8f., LXX)

You will not abandon my soul to Sheol. You will not permit your holy one to see corruption.   (Ps 16:10, LXX)

Rochais thinks that the "four days" motif was not merely a way of making the power of Jesus even more extraordinary. Rather, he argues, it reflects the concern to reassure Christians about the fate of those who have died.[17] The same concerns can be found in the dialogue between Jesus and his disciples in Jn 11:11–14. The peculiarly Johannine understanding of the resurrection appears in the dialogue with Martha, which refers back to sayings in Jn 5:24, 25, 28. The eschatological associations of resurrection are recast by the gospel's perception that the judgment that leads to eternal life comes in the encounter with Jesus (5:24).[18] This conviction is grounded in the christological assertion that Jesus is the Son to whom the Father has given life (5:26). Lazarus's emergence from the tomb fulfills the promise that the voice of the Son of Man would summon the dead from the tombs (5:25, 27–29). The future-oriented Son of Man saying in 5:27–29 reflects the conviction that the judgment would be accompanied by the resurrection of the dead, "those who have done good deeds to resurrection of life, those who have done evil to resurrection of judgment."[19] The Fourth Gospel presents these promises as realized in the presence of the Son of Man.[20] This shift has made one's faith in Jesus as Son the key to eternal life.

The stories of Jesus' bringing the dead back to life show clear signs of development. The healing miracles were not immediately associated with resurrection. These stories apparently had a catechetical use in instructing Christians about the fate of those who have died. This instruction promised the Christians that they had no cause to weep over the dead, as others did. Jesus' resurrection might be invoked as further evidence for this different Christian hope, which could be seen as special to the salvation that has come through Jesus. The Fourth Gospel makes christological affirmation the center of the whole story.

CHRISTOLOGICAL SAYINGS

The final group of sayings are those that refer to Jesus directly. In addition to the explicit reference to Jesus' resurrection, we also find traditions from Daniel and the suffering servant attached to the life of Jesus.

John 2:19–22

In the Johannine version of the disturbance at the temple, resurrection appears as the explanation of Jesus' temple saying. The story of the cleansing of the temple has been combined with a saying about its destruction, which is also attributed to Jesus (Mk 13:2; 14:58; 15:29; Ac 6:14). Jn 2:19 has been formulated as a direct attack on the community's Jewish opponents. They, the plural "you," are the ones responsible for the destruction of the temple. Mk 13:2 is a prophetic saying that the temple will be destroyed. Mk 14:58 uses the prediction as the content of a false accusation against Jesus. The mockery in Mk 15:29 refers back to the first part of that false accusation. Thus, these sayings make the "threat" to destroy the temple the centerpiece of the saying. The second half of the saying in Mk 14:58 refers to Jesus' raising up a temple not made with hands in "three days."

The expression "three days" is problematic. It could have come into the saying from the "three days" of the resurrection kerygma. Or it could simply be an expression for the short interval prior to fulfillment of the apocalyptic expectation that a new temple would be established in the messianic age.[21] Jn 2:22 explicitly interprets the "three days" in the saying as a reference to Jesus' resurrection. This interpretation suggests that the saying was not initially understood as a resurrection saying but as an apocalyptic prophecy about the temple. The heavenly temple, "not made with hands," will replace the earthly temple.[22] The temple saying points toward the tradition of apocalyptic preaching as the larger context for early use of resurrection language. Scholars continue to be divided over the extent to which such expectations can be traced back to Jesus' own teaching. J. Jeremias argues, for example, that the "three days" of Mk 14:58 was originally prophetic. It showed that for Jesus there was no distinction between resurrection, the judgment at the end of the age, and the building of the new temple. The saying reflected the conviction that the triumph of God would soon follow his ministry.[23] Jesus' own teaching did not separate resurrection out from its apocalyptic matrix. Consequently, Jesus cannot be said to have explicitly taught about resurrection. However, Jeremias does suggest that Jesus used traditions from the suffering servant and Zech 13:7b to interpret his own fate along the lines of the suffering to be expected by God's eschatological messenger. This suggestion has been challenged on the grounds that the servant of Isaiah was not understood to die as atonement for the people. The Maccabean martyr traditions provided the possibility of seeing the suffering of the righteous as a death that led God to turn and save his people. But the initiative lies with God. Atoning death is not a project that can be adopted beforehand by an individual.[24]

These cautions do not rule out the possibility that Jesus' own teaching did employ the language of hasidic piety. The temple episode contains elements of such piety. Is 56:7 is used in 1 Macc 7:37. G. W. E. Nickelsburg suggests that the Maccabees passage shows that hasidic circles read Isaiah as a guide to their own situation.[25] Another sign of the continued influence of these traditions in the teaching of Jesus can be found in Jesus' teaching of nonviolent resistance. Josephus's examples of nonviolent resistance are founded on the expectation that God will come to vindicate the righteous ones. The crowd at Caesarea responds to Pilate's threat by baring their necks on the ground (Bel. 2.9.1–3; Ant. 18.3.1).

Since Jesus' preaching of the rule of God does not appear to have been a call for zealot-style resistance, it is likely that he shared the piety of this stream of the hasidim.[26] The most dominant image from Daniel in the teaching of Jesus is that of the Son of Man from Dan 7:9–14. Jesus also speaks of the future coming of the Kingdom in terms of an eternal fellowship with God. Thus, the language of corporate vindication of the righteous would appear to be part of Jesus' preaching.[27] It is more difficult to argue that Jesus clearly taught that he personally would be vindicated or exalted like the *maskilim* of Dan 12. P. Grelot argues that such traditions did not exist. If they had, the universal perplexity over Jesus' fate that appears in the passion and resurrection traditions would not make sense.[28]

Son of Man Sayings

Scholarly debate over whether or not Jesus could have used the expression "Son of Man" of himself or of another figure shows no signs of reaching a consensus. On the one hand, the expression was not clearly understood by later Christians and rapidly ceased to function as a meaningful title. On the other, there is no clear evidence that "Son of Man" had a titular usage in Judaism or that it referred to a supernatural figure who would come at the end of the age. In Jewish Aramaic the expression "one like a Son of Man" from Dan 7:13 is generic. It means "human likeness" and is not a title.[29] Nor does first-century Aramaic provide any grounds for the claim that the expression could be used to refer to an individual or as a surrogate for "I." J. A. Fitzmyer concludes that without the peculiar alteration between third-person "Son of Man" and first-person "I" in the Jesus tradition, scholars would never even have suggested such a usage.[30] Thus, linguistic considerations appear to rule out two common proposals. They rule out the view that "Son of Man" is a Greek misunderstanding of an Aramaic idiom for "I." And they rule out the proposal that Jesus could have spoken of "the Son of Man" as a messianic figure who would come to vindicate himself and his mission.[31]

The use of "Son of Man" in first-century Judaism is limited to traditions that are interpreting Daniel. The only similarities between the New Testament and the Similitudes of Enoch occur in Matthew and John. Mt 19:28 and 25:31f. present the Son of Man seated on the heavenly throne. The enthronement of the Son of Man is a prominent feature in 1 En. (45.3; 55.4; 61.8; 62.5). Jn 5:27 speaks of God's having given the exercise of judgment over to the Son of Man. Similarly, God is said to turn over judgment in 1 En. 69.27.[32] The form in which Son of Man is put in the mouth of Jesus is different from the form used for the other christological titles. The other titles appear in sentences in which Jesus is directly equated with the figure, prophet (Ac 3:22f.), Son of God (Ac 9:20), and Messiah (Mk 8:29).[33] Nor do we find any hint in the other sayings of Jesus that his mission must somehow be completed by another figure. Instead, Jesus speaks of the decisive inbreaking of the kingdom of God with his ministry.[34]

Either Jesus is responsible for an interpretation of Dan 7:13 that applied to his own mission, or the Son of Man sayings are all developed by early Christians after the resurrection to express Jesus' heavenly exaltation. The Son of Man sayings preserved in the tradition alternate between using "I" (= Jesus) and Son of Man. Their dependence on Daniel is evident in the associated motifs of clouds and coming with angelic powers.[35] Thus, the metaphor is not being used in a collective sense to refer to all the righteous. Either Jesus has created this individualizing use of Son of Man to refer to his own vindication, or the early Christians have coined it to refer to Jesus' vindication and the parousia.[36]

C. F. D. Moule suggests that Jesus placed himself in the center of a vindicated, martyr people of God.[37] The exaltation scene in Dan 7 represents divine judgment in favor of the persecuted. However, it is only a short step from that scene to the conviction that judgment is handed over to the Son of Man (Mt 19:28/Lk 22:28–30). Indeed, the comment in 1 Cor 6:2f. that the righteous are to judge the angels shows that the expression of collective judgment also occurred in early Christian circles. Rev 20:4 quotes Daniel in presenting the saints who "reign with" Christ.[38] The alternative to grounding the exegesis of Dan 7 in the preaching of Jesus is to provide an account of its emergence in the preaching of the early community. The most detailed approach to that problem has been offered by N. Perrin. He agrees that Jesus expressed a general confidence that his ministry would be vindicated by God. Jesus also saw that individuals would find their place in judgment determined by their response to the preaching of the Kingdom. The sayings comparing Jesus' generation to that of Jonah represent an elaboration of that authentic tradition. It is characteristic of Jesus' preaching to summon the hearer to repent in light of the nearness of the Kingdom of God. The Jonah sayings belong to that tradition of preaching.[39] Perrin suggests that in Mt 24:26f./Lk 17:23f. one finds the later substitution of the expression "coming of the Son of Man in his day" for an original reference to the Kingdom of God.[40]

Such substitutions require a shift in the way in which Daniel is understood. The focus has to move from the image of the Son of Man ascending to the heavenly throne as a sign of vindication to the Son of Man coming. The latter is quite different from the exaltation/ascent that belongs to the metaphor initially. Moule has tried to make the transition by focusing on the element of appearance to one's enemies that is characteristic of the Jewish judgment scenes as we have seen. Vindication required that the exalted one be shown to those on earth. He moves from this "showing forth" in the heavenly court to the parousia. The Enoch traditions still maintain that the exaltation and manifestation of the Son of Man take place on the heavenly throne in judgment. Some early Christian traditions also maintain this primary location of exaltation in heaven. Stephen's vision in Ac 7:56 represents Jesus at the right hand of God, for example.

Perrin concludes that the introduction of Son of Man into the gospel tradition reflects a process of exegetical interpretation of the resurrection. The citation of Daniel in Mk 13:26 and 14:62 has turned the clouds of the Daniel passage into the means of transport for the Son of Man. The reference to his "coming with the clouds" shows that the saying envisages Christ as having ascended to heaven already. Perrin suggests that the tradition of Christ's exaltation to the right hand of God must be based on a passage different from the parousia reference in Daniel. The tradition of Christ at the right hand of God is apparent in Ac 7:56 and Mk 14:62. It derives from Ps 110:1.[41] Mk 14:62 carries the connotations of the earlier exaltation traditions. Jesus, on trial at the hands of his enemies, threatens them with heavenly vindication. Thus, the saying forms part of a tradition in which the persecuted righteous will be exalted to the right hand of God and thus prove that the false charges of his enemies were impious.[42]

Perrin argues that the hypothesis that all the Son of Man sayings are the result of early Christian exegetical traditions makes it possible to understand the peculiarity of the image in the New Testament. Son of Man is always applied to Jesus, since Dan 7:13f. was applied only to his ascension into the heavenly court. The apparent reference to the coming Son of Man as future vindicator in Mk 8:38 is likely to be a secondary development from the type of expression found in Lk 12:8f. There Jesus uses the theological passive to express his certainty that God will vindicate his mission. The earliest version of the saying would probably have run, "Everyone who acknowledges me before human beings will be acknowledged before the angels of God." Once early Christians had come to speak of Jesus as Son of Man and to envisage his role in judgment, the Markan elaboration would naturally follow.[43]

This approach to resolving the problems of the use of Son of Man imagery in the sayings of Jesus makes it clear that such developments presuppose an understanding of Jesus' resurrection as heavenly exaltation. While Jesus certainly expressed confidence that his ministry would be vindicated by God, one cannot show that he is responsible for any sayings in which Son of Man is applied to himself. We are still left with a metaphor that held little interest in Jewish exegesis of the period. Fitzmyer reminds us that the "missing link" between the Daniel traditions and the synoptic Son of Man sayings has not yet been discovered.[44] Nickelsburg has proposed that the Enoch traditions were preserved and circulated in upper Galilee. He finds geographical clues in 1 En. 12–16 that suggest that locale. It would also provide an alternative to the temple of Jerusalem as the "sacred place." Nickelsburg observes that the vision in T. Levi 2–7 is associated with Northern Israel. There the eschatological High Priest receives his call. The second vision takes place at the ancient sanctuary of Bethel (T. Levi 7.4–8.19; see also Jub. 32.1). Consequently, this region of Galilee appears to have been considered a place of divine revelation.[45] Nickelsburg proposes that the commissioning of Peter at Caesarea Philippi (Mt 16:13–19) belongs to this visionary tradition. He argues that the commissioning vision was originally one of the risen Jesus. The original story had Peter as the only one to see and respond to the Christophany.[46] If visionary Enoch traditions influenced early development of the Petrine tradition, then one might also ask if the early development of Son of Man traditions is to be attributed to the same source. Unlike 1 En 12–16 and T. Levi 2–7, which appear at Qumran, the Son of Man speculation may reflect a later development of the tradition. The Similitudes of Enoch also show an individualizing of the Son of Man metaphor in attaching it to the seer Enoch. There the exaltation of the seer into heaven appears to provide the metaphoric link. On the Christian side, the vision of the risen Jesus in Galilee is apparently interpreted through the Son of Man image. The two developments may have been contemporaneous. In seeking a source for the early Christian development of the Son of Man traditions, the sectarian Enoch speculations of upper Galilee appear to be a likely environment. However, the peculiarity of the Christian use of these traditions appears to call for the resurrection visions of Jesus as a necessary catalyst. This tradition would envisage resurrection as Jesus' exaltation to the right hand of God. It may also have been tied to the tradition of a resurrection vision of Peter in Galilee. It does not seem possible to move behind this level of the tradition to any certainty about Jesus' own teaching. Grelot suggests that the best one can presume is that Jesus was familiar with imagery like the resurrection/vindication of Dan 12:1–3, but the tradition as it has come down to us suggests that he is more concerned with developing the image of the Kingdom of God than that of future vindication.[47]

Since the eschatological horizon of exaltation and vindication is still associated with the resurrection of Jesus, one should not, Grelot warns, presume that resurrection can be reduced to a single historical event. It still represents the transition from this world to the world to come.[48] The concurrent emergence of resurrection language and sayings that give expression to the authority of Jesus and his relationship to God represents one set of convictions that must be part of the peculiarly Christian language of resurrection.

RESURRECTION AS THE CONCLUSION OF JESUS' LIFE

Many people would immediately think of the stories of Jesus' empty tomb as the central content of Christian preaching about Easter. Yet our oldest example of an early Christian witness to resurrection, the formula that Paul reports in 1 Cor 15:3–5a, does not say anything about the tomb. Instead, we find a tradition that focuses on the experience of having seen the Lord. We have seen that many of the metaphors about resurrection in the New Testament period did not concern themselves with the question of what happened to the body that had been buried. Since there is no clearly defined connection between the body that is buried and the resurrected person, one cannot proceed on the hypothesis that the conviction that Jesus had been raised, founded on the vision of the Lord, would of itself produce stories about the empty tomb. Nor, on the other hand, can one insist that if a tomb containing the body of Jesus were to be found by archaeologists, the Christian proclamation of Jesus as the one who has been raised and exalted by God would be destroyed and with it the Christian claims about Jesus' place in salvation.[49]

Finding a person's tomb empty would not in itself have led to the conclusion that the person had been raised, since resurrection was associated with the imagery of final judgment and the end of the world. Thus, it is equally difficult to presume that the tomb tradition by itself could have generated the preaching about having seen the Lord. However, the combination of an early tradition of appearances of the Lord and the conviction that Jesus' tomb was empty would help to explain the significance of resurrection in the Christian message about Jesus. We have seen that exaltation metaphors might serve just as well to express a conviction about divine vindication. But, though not necessarily tied to the body that had been buried, resurrection did carry with it some sense of bodily transformation. Therefore, the discovery of the empty tomb might provide a catalyst for the Christian development of resurrection images.[50]

Jeremias tries to reconcile the divergence in the various resurrection traditions by constructing a sequence of events that might have lain behind the later accounts. He insists that one cannot pick either the appearance tradition or the tomb tradition as more original and make all diversity later development.[51] Rather, he suggests, one should try to find the most likely combination of events that would fit the earliest recoverable strata in each tradition. He finds the following elements as "given":

1. "On the third day" is associated with resurrection in both traditions.

2. Appearances, especially that to Peter, are fundamental to the tradition.

3. The appearance stories in the gospels are attached to two locations: Jerusalem (Lk 24, Jn 20, and the appearance to Magdalene at the tomb in Mt 28) and Galilee (promised in Mk 16, Mt 28, and Jn 21). The kerygma tradition of 1 Cor 15:3–5a does not attach any geographical indicator to the appearance.

4. 1 Cor 15:3–5a and some of the gospels imply that there was a temporal spread of appearances as well as geographical.

5. In all the gospels (not 1 Cor 15), the Easter events are set in motion by the women's discovery of the empty tomb.

6. The event was a mystery, a puzzle to the disciples.

Jeremias, then, attempts to construct an account that will embody all of these features.[52] He acknowledges that a high degree of uncertainty must always attend such a reconstruction, especially since it represents an attempt to harmonize apparently conflicting witnesses. However, he argues, reconstruction of a series of events behind the resurrection tradition is preferable to treatments that limit the "something happened" to Peter's vision of the Lord, for example, and then presume that all of the rest of the resurrection traditions are no more than narrative explications of the faith generated by that event.[53]

Resurrection also has another peculiar characteristic. Quite unlike Elijah's assumption into heaven, for example, or even some of the pagan stories of the *apotheosis* of the emperor in which the hero is viewed by those on earth being taken into heaven, the resurrection itself is not witnessed.[54] Ac 1:6–11 will later give verbal representation to the theme of Jesus' being taken up. However, that verbal representation presupposes the distinction between resurrection and ascension into heaven. It introduces the period of forty days between the two, even though Lk 24:51 presumes that Easter itself is Jesus' ascent into heaven, as does the tradition in Jn 20:17. Jesus' appearance in Ac 7:56 occurs from heaven.[55]

Jeremias argues that his skeleton of resurrection events carries with it a high degree of probability. Each element has features that are not explicable on the presupposition that they had simply been elaborations of some earlier tradition.

1. Scholars have not been able to find any strong evidence for use of a prophetic text to generate the detail of "on the third day." Yet it appears in all the traditions. Therefore, one should presume the most likely origin to be the fact that the resurrection events began on the third day after the crucifixion.[56]

2. All the gospel accounts report these events to have been set in motion by the women. P. Benoit suggests that Jn 20:1–2 is the earliest version of that tradition. If so, then the simplest account suffices: Magdalene went to the tomb to mourn, found it empty, and returned to tell the disciples. No visions of angels or of Jesus are presupposed.[57]

3. Lk 24:12 suggests that an early tradition held that Peter had then visited the tomb alone, found it empty, and left without any idea of what had happened.

4. The angelophany at the tomb, followed by the vision of the risen Lord, has all the elements of a commissioning by the risen Lord. It is later reduced to a special mission to the apostles.

5. Lk 24:34 and 1 Cor 15:5 both hold that Peter was the first to see the Lord. Neither the appearance to Peter nor the appearance to James, the brother of the Lord (1 Cor 15:7), are the subject of any narrative tradition in the New Testament. Matthew feels the lack of such an account and consequently omits Peter's name from the commission to the women in Mk 16:7.[58]

6. Peter's vision was followed by a series of other christophanies of which Paul's may have been the last, as he claims (1 Cor 15:8).

Jeremias finds four types of development in the resurrection traditions:[59]

1. The Christophany traditions quickly generate the need to say what the angel's message was. This message often appears in the form of the early kerygma.

2. Various apologetic themes are brought in to answer objections that had been directed at Christians from outside. The body was not stolen by the disciples because the tomb was guarded (Mt 27:62–67). That view was merely a malicious rumor spread by the embarrassed authorities (Mt 28:11–15). The visions were not hallucinations. Their reality is demonstrated by manifestations of the physical character of the resurrected one (Lk 24:39, 41–43; Jn:20, 27). The Johannine version demonstrates that the one who appeared to the disciples was indeed the crucified by pointing to the marks of crucifixion.

3. Addition of traditions that had developed within the community. The baptismal formula is mandated by the risen Lord in Mt 28:19. Certain elements of the Christian calendar are linked to resurrection, especially the day of commemoration of the Lord (Jn 20:26; Ac 2:1ff.). The obligation to evangelize "the nations" is grounded in the commissioning of the risen Lord along with some particular traditions from various communities (Mt 28:16–20; Lk 24:44–49; Ac 1:4–8; Jn 20:21–23).

4. Finally, there are those elements that Jeremias attributes to "narrative style of the period." These elements include recognition themes (as Lk 24:14–35) and such descriptive accounts as in the opening of the tomb by the angel (Mt 28:2–4). Despite the widespread assertion in the New Testament that resurrection is "according to Scripture" (1 Cor 15:4; Ac 2:23; Lk 24:27, 44f.), one finds little use of Old Testament citations in connection with resurrection. This scarcity stands in striking contrast to the passion of Jesus in which the "according to Scripture" is amply demonstrated. The common scripture texts are those associated with exaltation and enthronement like Ps 110:1; Ps 2:7; Is 55:3; Ps 118:22.

This brief survey indicates the complexity of moving behind the explicit statements about resurrection in the New Testament. The various versions of the tradition are quite different and, on occasion, even at odds with one another. It appears that a group, perhaps not as neatly ordered as in Jeremias, of events constitute Jesus' resurrection.

1 CORINTHIANS 15:3–5

Scholars generally agree that the formula in 1 Cor 15:3–5 embodies a pre-Pauline tradition. Consequently, it is our earliest example of resurrection proclamation. Paul does not seek to provide deductive proof of resurrection from the kerygma. The formula in 1 Cor 15:3–5 is followed by a list of witnesses to resurrection. Exegetes disagree about the origins of the later material. But all the various explanations have two points in common: (a) v. 3b marks the beginning of the formula, and (b) from v. 8 onward Paul is speaking of his own case. Most would also agree that the list in vv. 6–7 is an addition to the formula.[60] Some scholars have also argued that the material in vv. 3–5 represents a collection of statements that were not originally unified. We would agree with the view that holds that the use of *"hoti"* to introduce each item is not a sign of independent origin for what follows but a technique of listing the items.[61]

J. Murphy-O'Connor has argued for the unity of the section by pointing out that Paul uses *hoti* differently in passages like 1 Cor 8:4. There it separates two slogans, both of which are held by his opponents. Further, if the section were not a unity before Paul adopted it, then v. 4 would be an unusually short "that he was buried *(hoti etaphthē)."*[62] Paul may have introduced *hoti* into his repetition of the formula, but the formula itself represents an earlier unit of tradition:

(that) Christ died for our sins, according to the Scriptures;
(that) he was buried;
(that) he was raised on the third day, according to the Scriptures;
(that) he appeared to Cephas, then to the twelve.

Murphy-O'Connor thinks that v. 7 contains an additional piece of early appearance tradition: "then he appeared to James, then to the apostles."[63] Others have proposed that Paul created v. 7 in imitation of v. 5.[64] But Murphy-O'Connor has pointed out that v. 7 does not appear to be Paul's. Paul does not engage in such imitations elsewhere, and one would expect him to have used *"epeita eita"* to begin the second clauses, as in vv. 23b–24, rather than *"eita."*[65] The tradition understands "apostles" as a group different from the "twelve." This tradition reflects the view that resurrection appearances represented apostolic commissioning. The congruence between that function and Paul's own defense of his right to be an apostle (cf. Gal 1:11–

12) leads some to see the whole as a Pauline creation out of the simpler tradition of an appearance to James. The list of other witnesses also includes reference to "five hundred brethren." The use of the expression "brethren" appears to be typically Pauline,[66] but the reference would appear to be to an earlier tradition, since the five hundred play no role elsewhere in the New Testament. It suggests that resurrection appearances may have been more general than their restriction to reconstituting the group of the twelve and commissioning for mission would indicate.

The formula in vv. 3b–5 parallels the phrases about crucifixion and burial with those about resurrection. Later narrative traditions will describe Jesus' appearance(s) to the twelve. But there is no narrative of an appearance to Peter, though some think that a resurrection appearance to Peter may have been the source of the Transfiguration account. "On the third day" represents a common element in both the kerygmatic accounts and the stories of the empty tomb. The origin of the "on the third day" formula is still disputed. The first clause of our formula does not make it clear whether the expression "according to the Scriptures" is meant to refer to "died for our sins" or "on the third day." If it refers to the whole sentence, then the formula simply recalls a widespread use of Old Testament materials to demonstrate the necessity of Jesus' death. If it refers only to "on the third day," then one has a more difficult time discovering the origins of the reference.

Many exegetes feel, however, that the grammatical structure of the passage forces one to conclude that "according to the Scriptures" refers specifically to the third-day traditions.[67] The only direct association between "third day" and the Old Testament occurs in the application of Jon 2:1 in Mt 12:40. However, Matthew depends on the prior development of the resurrection traditions. Thus, we should say that the Jonah passage represents Matthew's attempt to answer the same question that faces us: what Old Testament passage could be meant by the proclamation that "on the third day" is according to the Scriptures? It also shows that there was no widespread tradition that gave the answer to that question at the time Matthew wrote.

Scholars usually point to Hos 6:2, where Yahweh promises salvation "on the third day," as a possible Old Testament reference. However, explicit citation of Hos 6:2 is not part of the apologetic use of the Old Testament. E. L. Bode argues that "on the third day" is not a direct reference to the finding of the empty tomb. The tomb stories contain the expression "on the first day of the week" (Mk 16:2; Mt 28:1; Lk 24:1; Jn 20:1, 19f.).[68] The variable use of "on the third day" expressions suggests that the evangelists did not understand it to have been a formulaic part of the Easter preaching. Lk 24:7, for example, lo-cates the "third day" as part of the passion prediction (9:22–24; 19:31–33). Lk 24:21 speaks of the dashing of the disciples' hopes with the reference to the "third day since . . ." the crucifixion. Lk 24:46 and Mt 27:63f. use it in a formula that predicts the Messiah. The formula "on the third day" does appear to have been part of the proclamation of Jesus' resurrection (see Ac 10:40). Lk 24:46 shows that it was also traditionally tied to fulfillment of the Scriptures in such formulae. Since the formula is not clearly a chronological refer-ence or a reference to a specific Old Testament passage, scholars have sought to find another source for its early appearance. They suggest that Jewish midrashic traditions had come to associate events of salvation with "the third day." Gen 22:4 showed Abraham's arrival at Moriah to have occurred "on the third day," and this event of salvation was associated with others of similar character like the prophecy in Hos 6:2.[69] But since these traditions are not used in the New Testament, the use of an early Jewish midrashic tradition must be considered tentative. Neither in Paul's treatment of resurrection nor in the kergymatic speeches of Acts do we find references to the stories of the empty tomb or of Jesus' appearances. Paul's own discus-sion of resurrection in 1 Cor 15:12–58 describes it as transformation of our mortal bodies into a "spiritual body." Paul never speaks either of the empty tomb or of the resurrection appearances in making this argument. He is concerned only with arguing from the metaphorical premises of the apocalyptic vision of a new creation. The New Testa-ment use of "resurrection," an image for the end-time reward of the righteous, of an individual is already a departure from customary uses of imagery, as we have seen. As a result, one cannot predict what other transformations the language of resurrection will undergo. The move toward spiritual transformation of the body in order to enable it to share the fate of the individual such as we find in Paul is only one possible expansion of the imagery.[70] It is possible, for example, that some of the appearance traditions were seen as "from heaven." Ac 7:56 provides an example of such a vision, as do the cryptic refer-ences that Paul makes to his own experience (Gal 1:12). But it is the very fact that the connection between appearances and "empty tomb" is so tenuous that gives the tomb stories their claim to an equally ancient tradition. If resurrection does not automatically im-ply an empty tomb, then the argument that the tomb traditions were fabricated to provide "proof" for the resurrection kerygma cannot be sustained. Bode suggests that since the tomb accounts themselves tend to introduce more and more elements of the appearance traditions, one must presume that the relationship went in the other direction. The introduction of the appearances into the tomb traditions was an "apologetic" for the tomb stories.[71] By themselves, the stories of the empty tomb do not prove anything. Consequently, they must be combined with kerygmatic traditions and appearance stories in order to be a significant part of the Christian kerygma.

THE EMPTY TOMB

The divergence of detail surrounding the stories of the tomb suggests that there was no unified tradition about the empty tomb in early Christianity. Chart One presents the details of the four accounts of the Empty Tomb.

Chart One
Empty Tomb Traditions

	Mt 28:1–8	Mk 16:1–8	Lk 24:1–12	Jn 20:1–13
TIME	after the Sabbath	when the Sabbath had passed	(on the Sabbath they rested, 23:56)	
	toward dawn	very early	at early dawn	early
	first day of the week	first day of the week	first day of the week	first day of the week
		when sun had risen		while still dark
NAMES	Mary Magdalene	Mary Magdalene	Mary Magdalene	Mary Magdalene
	the other Mary	Mary, mother of James	Joanna	
		Salome	Mary, mother of James and the other women	
PLACE	grave *(taphos)*	tomb *(mnēma)*	tomb *(mnēma)*	tomb *(mnēmeion)*
PURPOSE	to see the grave	to annoint him		
BROUGHT		spices	spices they had prepared (23:56, spices and ointments)	
THINKING		who will roll away the stone		
STONE	angel had rolled it back; was sitting on it	stone was rolled back	rolled away from the tomb	stone taken away from the tomb

	Mt 28:1–8	Mk 16:1–8	Lk 24:1–12	Jn 20:1–13
OTHER **DETAILS**	great earth-quake angel's descent	it was very large		
ENTRY		entering the tomb	when they went in	stooped to look in
FOUND			no body	[grave clothes; napkin by itself]
REACTION			they were per-plexed	[beloved disciple: faith] thinks body has been moved
ANGEL(S)	seated on the stone	young man on the right	two men stood by them	two angels sitting where body had been
DESCRIBED	appearance: lightning clothes: white as snow	white robe	dazzling clothes	dressed in white
REACTION(S)	guards trembled for fear be-came like dead men	were amazed	were fright-ened, bowed faces to ground	
MESSAGE	(to women) Do not be afraid I know you seek Jesus, the cru-cified, he is not here, for he has been raised, as he said	Do not be amazed you seek Jesus of Nazareth, the crucified he has been raised he is not here	 Why do you seek the liv-ing with the dead he is not here but has been raised (lacking in some mss.) remember how he said to you when he was still in Gali-lee, that the Son of Man must be deliv-ered into the hands of sin-ful men, and be crucified, and on the third day rise	Why are you weeping? (Mary) I seek my Lord, and I do not know where they laid him [Jn 20:9, they did not yet know the Scripture that it was nec-essary for him to be raised from the dead]
	go quickly and tell his disci-ples he has risen from the dead, and be-hold, he is go-ing before you to Gali-lee; there you will see him, Lo I have told you.	go tell his disci-ples and Pe-ter he is going be-fore you to Galilee; there you will see him, as he told you.		[Jn 20:17, but go to my brethren and say to them, I am ascending to my Father and your Father, to my God, and your God]

	Mt 28:1–8	Mk 16:1–8	Lk 24:1–12 [and they remembered his words]	Jn 20:1–13
DEPARTURE	and they left the tomb quickly	and they went out and fled from the tomb	and returning from the tomb	so she ran
	with fear and great joy	for trembling and amazement had seized them		
	they ran to tell his disciples	they said nothing to anyone	they told all these things to the eleven and the rest	went to Simon Peter and the other disciple whom Jesus loved
		for they were afraid		
REPORT			(24:10c) told this to the apostles	said to them, "They have taken the Lord, from the tomb and I do not know where they have laid him."
				(20:18) Mary Magdalene went and said to the disciples, "I have seen the Lord," and told them that he had said these things to her.
			but these words seemed to them an idle tale, and they did not believe them.	

At almost every point, the accounts go in separate directions. It is impossible to harmonize them in such a way as to produce a single, simpler tradition that has then been redacted by the narrators.[72] It is necessary to assess each instance of divergence and the particular context within which it occurs in order to see whether it might be an independent development of tradition or the redactional work of the evangelist.

Some scholars have argued that the tomb traditions developed out of the practice of early Christian worship at the site, possibly at Easter. Some see the angel pointing to the place of burial as part of this cultic celebration.[73] Unlike the kerygmatic formula of 1 Cor 15:3b–5, which is "placeless" and hence appropriate to the churches in the hellenistic period, the tomb traditions are focused on a particular locale. However, there is no evidence for early veneration of Jesus' tomb. Had the tomb tradition originated in a solemn liturgical setting, one would expect more homogeneity than we find in the stories. Therefore, it is more likely that the tomb traditions were in existence before they were used as etiological legends to explain the annual or the weekly commemoration of Jesus' resurrection.[74]

Other theories that make the empty tomb accounts entirely derivative have proved equally unsatisfactory. It is possible to identify some elements of the stories as narrative expansion, as in Matthew's defense against the claim that the disciples stole the body. Others simply represent developments in narrative imagery. But since the story of the empty tomb is not presupposed by the kerygmatic traditions, one cannot presume that it would have been created to advance that preaching. Nor would the presence of women as witnesses have been likely in a story that was entirely fabricated. In comparison with the apocryphal stories of later centuries, the tomb stories show little elaboration of miraculous detail. In comparison with developments in New Testament materials, they do not show extensive influences from Old Testament passages. Hence, we must presume that the story is early and that there was no clear evidence to controvert it. Either the location of Jesus' tomb was not known, or the place that was so venerated was empty.[75]

The nucleus behind the tomb traditions appears to be in the discovery of Jesus' empty tomb by some women disciples, who then left perplexed. The nucleus of the tomb story probably did not include an angelophany, since the angel's message reflects the kerygmatic preaching of resurrection and thus requires an understanding of the significance of the empty tomb gained from the appearance traditions.[76] Finding the tomb empty was not the source of early Christian belief that Jesus had been raised. Jeremias has also pointed to the persistent use of recognition motifs in the appearance stories. On the one hand, these motifs fit a characteristic style of storytelling. On the other, they continue the oldest stratum of the tomb story: recollection of the mysterious puzzle created by the events of Easter.[77]

We cannot presume to reach the direct experience of those who became convinced that Jesus had been raised, since our earliest sources are quite reticent in that regard. From Paul we may presume that it is a spiritual experience that carried with it the conviction of a revelatory encounter with God. Paul sees himself to have been commissioned as much as one of the Old Testament prophets had been. But details in the appearance traditions, such as the emphasis on the "bodily" element in Luke and John, suggest later polemic against the possibility that such experiences had been hallucinatory. Such demonstrations would not necessarily have been part of the original experience. Jeremias seeks to draw a distinction between the resurrection of Jesus and other experiences in which God was felt to have acted in Israel's history. Jesus is exalted into the glory of the "new age." He is not merely translated to heaven or exalted as the suffering righteous One in Wisdom. Thus, the disciples' immediate experience of resurrection is not that of a "mighty act of God" in the course of history but of the dawn of the new age.[78]

THE GALILEAN APPEARANCE TRADITION

Another tradition has Jesus appear to his disciples in Galilee (Mk 16:7). Many scholars think that stories now located in the life of Jesus —the Transfiguration and the calling of the disciples by the sea of Galilee—originally belonged to the resurrection tradition. Some interpreters even think that these stories may preserve features of the primitive appearance stories that were lost in the later transmission.

The Transfiguration (Mark 9:2–8 par.)

Those who point to the Transfiguration as a resurrection story that was retrojected back to the life of Jesus emphasize its vision of Jesus' heavenly status. They also point to the connection between the Transfiguration and resurrection that is made in Mk 9:9–10.[79] A number of details that are often taken to show that the Transfiguration story is a transposed resurrection account have been interpreted by other scholars to show quite the opposite. J. E. Alsup points out that the gospel traditions attach "light imagery" to angels, not the risen Jesus. Ōphthē (appeared) applies only to the two heavenly figures, Moses and Elijah, and not to Jesus.[80] The cloud is not taken from the Danielic ascent of the Son of Man. Coupled with the divine voice, the cloud can only refer to the presence of God. The high mountain does not have to be the mountain of the Galilean appearance. Indeed, only Matthew locates that appearance on a mountain. Mountains are a natural place of epiphany, but there are other nonresurrection mountains in the Jesus tradition (Mt 5:1–2; Mk 3:13–19/Mt 14:23). Advocates of the resurrection interpretation of this passage point to the Transfiguration of Jesus' clothes as a sign of his divine glory.[81] However, one may also invoke apocalyptic traditions in which such clothes are a sign of heavenly being.[82] 2 Pt 1:16–21 provides an additional source for the Transfiguration tradition. Studies of that account show that it was not understood as a resurrection account by 2 Peter.[83] The differences between this account and that in the synoptic tradition suggest that it may even be independent of the gospel accounts. It takes place on "the holy mountain" (Mark, "a high mountain"). Those with Peter are unnamed. The glory comes to Jesus as a result of the heavenly voice rather than forming the initial theophany into which the voice is set. God is described as having glory—an indication that the author of 2 Peter interpreted the cloud as the divine presence. Peter is described as "eye-witness" who hears what transpires. The elements of confusion found in the gospel tradition are absent in this account. Thus, Peter is pictured as the recipient of divine revelation. J. Neyrey's analysis of the function of this account shows that the author understood the story as evidence of the Second Coming. This interpretation is further evident in the Ethiopic *Apocalypse of Peter.*[84]

In that work, the glory of the transfigured Jesus shows the glory that he will have at the parousia. That of Moses and Elijah prefigures the glory that awaits those who are saved. Thus there are two elements in this parousia interpretation of the Transfiguration: the future paradise of humans and the parousia of the Lord. These two elements are not explicitly referred to in 2 Peter, but the function of the story is similar. The author is arguing against those who scoff at the Christian teaching of the parousia (3:1f.). They are apparently claiming that the parousia is a humanly concocted story. In answer to such objections, the author argues that God is the author of true prophecy. Peter is the recipient of such prophecy. The "heaven sent" word that he has in mind as the prophecy is the Transfiguration.[85] Chart Two contains the gospel accounts of the Transfiguration.

Chart Two
The Transfiguration

Mt 17:1–8	Mk 9:2–8	Lk 9:28–36
And after six days Jesus took with him Peter and James and John his brother and led them up a high mountain apart.	And after six days Jesus took with him Peter and James and John, and led them up a high mountain apart by themselves.	Now about eight days after these sayings he took with him Peter and John and James and went up on the mountain to pray.

Mt 17:1-8	Mk 9:2-8	Lk 9:28-36
And he was transfigured before them and his face shone like the sun,	And he was transfigured before them,	And as he was praying, the appearance of his countenance was altered,
and his garments became white as light.	and his garments became glistening, white as no fuller on earth could bleach them.	and his raiment became dazzling white.
And behold, there appeared to them Moses and Elijah talking with him.	And there appeared to them Elijah with Moses; and they were talking to Jesus.	And behold two men talked with him, Moses and Elijah, who appeared in glory and spoke of his departure, which he was to accomplish at Jerusalem. Now Peter and those who were with him were heavy with sleep but kept awake, and they saw his glory and the two men who stood with him. And as the men were parting from him,
And Peter said to Jesus, Lord it is well that we are here; if you wish, I will make three booths here one for you and one for Moses and one for Elijah,	And Peter said to Jesus, Master it is well that we are here; let us make there booths, one for you and one for Moses and one for Elijah, for he did not know what to say, for they were exceedingly afraid.	Peter said to Jesus, Master it is well that we are here; let us make three booths, one for you and one for Moses and one for Elijah—not knowing what he said.
He was still speaking when a bright cloud overshadowed them,	And a cloud overshadowed them,	And as he said this a cloud came and overshadowed them; and they were afraid as they entered the cloud.
and a voice from the cloud said: This is my beloved Son with whom I am well-pleased: listen to him. When the disciples heard this, they fell on their faces and were filled with awe. But Jesus came and touched them saying "Rise and have no fear" And when they lifted up their eyes, they saw no one but Jesus only.	and a voice came out of the cloud, This is my beloved son, listen to him.	And a voice came out of the cloud, saying, This is my beloved Son, my chosen; listen to him.
	And suddenly, looking around they no longer saw any one with them, only Jesus.	And when the voice had spoken, Jesus was found alone

Both Matthew and Luke are dependent on the Markan story. They have added some new material to Mark and curtailed his account in other places.[86] Both accounts have made it clear that the "fear" of the disciples in the Markan version is to be understood as awe in the presence of the divine. The Matthean disciples behave as at an angelic theophany when they hear the divine voice. In Luke they are overcome with fear as they actually enter the cloud that represents the divine presence (9:35).[87]

R. J. Dillon makes the connection between the Transfiguration and resurrection by arguing that Lk 24:4–7 formed the basis for Luke's expansion of the Transfiguration story. The conversation between heavenly figures that is hidden from the sleeping disciples is said to show that the destiny of the Messiah can only be perceived when Easter unlocks its secret.[88] However, he acknowledges that for Luke, Jesus' *analempsis* (taking up) and *episodos* (entrance) are best understood as references to the whole complex of passion through ascension by which Jesus returns to the Father. Hence, they cannot be limited to the resurrection as such.[89] Luke's addition of *doxa* (glory) may represent his own understanding of the Transfiguration as a hint of the coming resurrection.[90] Both Luke and Matthew make the christological significance of the heavenly revelation clear by expanding the "Son" title. As in the Markan source, this identification of Jesus as Son takes the reader back to the baptismal scene in which Jesus' identity is first proclaimed. For Luke that link has special significance. It concludes the ministry that had begun under the Spirit as Jesus turns toward his divinely appointed destiny in Jerusalem.[91] The title Son in this context is not merely a messianic designation. "Son" does not appear in a messianic sense in the Old Testament. Nor has it been found in Palestinian Jewish literature of the period. Consequently, it is better understood as a Christian development. The title makes it clear that Jesus is not a Moses redivivus or Elijah.[92]

Luke has added the reference to "glory" in v. 32. It looks toward the resurrected Jesus of Lk 24:26. It is Luke, and not Mark or his tradition, who has created the connection between Transfiguration and the resurrection through his image of Jesus' *exodos*. Further elements of Luke's redaction are evident in the implicit connection between the glory of the Transfiguration and Yahweh's glory in the story of Moses' and Elijah's journey to Horeb. Moses and Elijah represent the Israel that is passing.[93] Lukan reshaping of the incident shows that it was not perceived primarily as a resurrection account. The link to the glory of the resurrection serves to complete the sequence that began with the first announcement of the passion.

When we turn to Matthew's editing of the material, it is possible that the saying about Peter as rock that Matthew inserts into the Markan account of Peter's confession should be tied to the resurrection. But the saying has the characteristics of a saying that had circulated independently. Perhaps it represented the verbalization of the commissioning of Peter by the risen Jesus. It did not, however, carry with it the descriptive elements of an appearance story. Matthew has given the saying a place in his narrative of Peter's confession. However, locating a saying attributed to the risen Jesus within a story from the life of Jesus does not turn the whole episode into a resurrection scene.[94]

Nickelsburg has recently attempted to attach narrative significance to Peter's commissioning by tying it to the story of the Transfiguration. Nickelsburg suggests that Peter's commissioning in Mt 16:13–19 depends on a pre-Matthean tradition in which Peter's denial is reversed. Peter is commissioned to fill the role of the messianic High Priest. The Transfiguration, he goes on to suggest, should be taken as based on Peter's vision of the risen Lord. The Christophany to Peter is set in a traditional site for revelation in Upper Galilee.[95] However, the evidence for this tradition is tendentious and would appear to represent later elaboration rather than the original intent of the Transfiguration account. One objection raised against treating the incident as one that occurred during Jesus' life is the dissonance between such a striking revelation of divine approval and the events of the passion in which the disciples all flee.[96] None of the explanations clarifies the historical background of this story. V. Taylor suggests some experience that led to the insight of the confession in Mk 8:29 as the best one can do to explain the emergence of the Transfiguration story. But as Fitzmyer points out, one is still left with the puzzling phenomenon of Peter's denial. Therefore, he concludes that we cannot make a historical assessment of what sort of incident in the life of Jesus was involved in the Transfiguration. However, we should not write the story off as imaginative fiction even though we can no longer recover its historical contours. Further, it appears that the connections between this story and the resurrection are posterior to the development of resurrection appearance traditions. The evangelists have created the links between this story and the resurrection. They have not disguised a resurrection tradition of which they no longer approve.[97]

The Calling of Disciples (Luke 5:1–11)

Lk 5:1–11 has also been taken as example of a resurrection story that found its way back into the life of Jesus. This story does have parallels in both the calling of the disciples of Mk 1:16–20 and the resurrection appearance by the Sea of Galilee in John 21:1–8. Chart Three illustrates the parallels to this story.

Chart Three
The Calling of the Disciples

Luke 5:1–11
While the people pressed upon him to hear the word of God,

he was standing by the Lake of Gennesaret. (v. 1)

And he saw two boats by the lake, but the fishermen had gone out of them and were washing their nets. (v. 2)

Getting into one of the boats, which was Simon's, he asked him to put out a little from the land, and he sat down and taught the people from the boat. (v. 3)

Parallels

And passing along by the Sea of Galilee (Mk 1:16),

he saw Simon and Andrew the brother of Simon casting a net in the sea, for they were fishermen (Mk 1:16)

And when he had ceased speaking, he said to Simon, "Put out into the deep and let down your nets for a catch." And Simon answered, "Master, we have worked all night and took nothing. (vv. 4–5ab)

Simon Peter said to them, "I am going fishing." They said to him, "We will go with you." They went out and got into the boat; but that night they caught nothing. Just as day was breaking, Jesus stood on the beach; yet the disciples did not know that it was Jesus. (Jn 21:3–4)

Jesus said to them, "Children, have you any fish?" They answered, "No." He said, "Cast the net on the right side of the boat and you will find some." (Jn 21:5–6a)

But at your word I will let down the nets." (v. 5c)

And when they had done this, they enclosed a great school of fish; and as their nets were breaking. (v. 6)

they beckoned to their partners in the other boat, to come and help them, and they came and filled both boats so that they began to sink. (v. 7)

So they cast it, and now they were not able to haul it in, for the quantity of fish. (Jn 21:6b)

But the other disciples came in the boat,

dragging the net full of fish, for they were not far from the land, (Jn 21:8ab)

But when Simon Peter saw it, he fell down at Jesus' knees saying, "Depart from me, Lord, for I am a sinful man," (v. 8)

When Simon Peter heard that it was the Lord, he put on his clothes, for he was stripped for work, and lept into the sea. (Jn 21:7b)

Luke 5:1-11	Parallels
For he was astonished, and all that were with him at the catch of fish they had taken. (v. 9)	So Simon Peter went and hauled the net ashore, full of large fish, a hundred and fifty three of them. (Jn 21:11)

and so also were James and John, sons of Zebedee, who were partners with Simon (v. 10a)	And going on a little further he saw James the son of Zebedee and John his brother who were in their boat mending the nets. (Mk 1:19)
And Jesus said to Simon, "Do not be afraid; from now on you will be catching men." (v. 10b)	And Jesus said to them, "Follow me and I will make you fishers of men." (Mk 1:17)
And when they had brought their boats to land, they left everything and followed him. (v. 11)	And immediately they left their nets and followed him. (Mk 1:18) And immediately he called them; and they left their father, Zebedee, in the boat with the hired servants and followed him. (Mk 1:20)

Fitzmyer's analysis of the story suggests that Luke does not see it as connected to resurrection. He argues that Luke has recast the Markan story of the calling of Peter in order to accommodate it to a story of the miraculous catch of fish derived from his special material. He has directed the story toward the saying "You shall be fishers of men." Thus, he has shifted attention away from the miracle and turned the episode into a pronouncement story.[98]

The central part of the story parallels the story in Jn 21. The same chapter of John does have a tradition of the reversal of Peter's denial (Jn 21:15–17), but it is not part of this episode. In that tradition, Peter is commissioned as shepherd of Jesus' sheep.[99] Those who think that the Lukan story was originally a postresurrection appearance point out that Peter's reaction, "Depart from me, Lord, for I am a sinful person," would seem to be more appropriate to the postresurrection context than to the miracle tradition. Astonishment would, they contend, be the appropriate reaction for the latter. However, the story appears to be based on earlier material in which both the John and Luke develop a synoptic type of tradition.[100]

The Johannine tradition as we have it has been extensively reshaped. The commissioning of Peter is a separate episode, and the elements of recognition in the resurrection scene have been reshaped to incorporate the Beloved Disciple (Jn 21:7a). The story is perplexing in that the disciples who have already been commissioned by the risen Lord in Jerusalem (Jn 20:19–23) appear to have returned to fishing as though nothing had happened. The final redactor acknowledges the difficulty by calling the story the third postresurrection appearance (Jn 21:14). Thus, the story has clearly had an

independent history. It could have circulated as an account of the
first resurrection appearance to the disciples who had returned home
to Galilee.[101] Other exegetes insist that one must separate the elements of commissioning in the story from those of a miraculous catch
of fish. It is the combination of the two traditions, they argue, that has
created the anomalies in the story. The story is a nature miracle that
must have originally been part of the other stories of Jesus' demonstration of his divine power such as the walking on water.[102] The
story of Jesus as a "divine man" may have been reused to provide a
setting for the tradition of Jesus' postresurrection commissioning of
the disciples in Galilee, precisely because there was a tradition of
Jesus' appearance to his disciples there that lacked a narrative embodiment. Early Christian preaching clearly set the resurrection at
the end of the life of Jesus. It was the crucial symbol of the place Jesus
occupied in the story of salvation. We have seen that the expectation
of resurrection as it emerges in the New Testament cannot be said to
have been grounded simply in Jesus' own preaching. Jesus' preaching can best be seen as contributing the expectation that God was
inaugurating the new age and the confidence in divine vindication
that are important prerequisites for the development of resurrection
language. We have also seen that it is not reasonable to presume an
overly subjective account of resurrection that would presume to
trace it all back to the single conviction that despite the disaster of
the crucifixion Jesus' cause continued. Nor, on the other hand, can
one find evidence to support the elaborate attempts that have been
made to provide a naturalist account of the emergence of resurrection preaching. Since the empty tomb tradition would not have
served to prove that Jesus had been raised in the first century, we can
presume that it has a base in early tradition. Once the appearance
traditions are connected with the stories of the empty tomb, then
resurrection can explain why Jesus' tomb was empty. We have seen
that the tomb story never had any value as proof of resurrection in
the kerygmatic tradition. Instead, it emerges at the point at which
the written gospel seeks to narrate the events of the life of Jesus as
part of the account of those final days. Though there may have been
traditions about the tomb prior to Mark, one should ask if it is not his
move to narrate the life of Jesus that gives that tradition its place in
the tradition. Mark then locates the proclamation of Jesus' resurrection at an angelophany at the tomb. We will turn to more detailed
investigation of the New Testament understanding of resurrection in
the following chapters. It is clear that the significance that is attached
to it in Christianity cannot be founded in its Jewish background. Nor
does the conviction that Jesus had been raised prove to be simply

equivalent to claiming that Jesus had been vindicated like any other righteous hero. Instead, it will serve to focus the most distinctive Christian claims about salvation in the New Testament period. It will prove to be the symbol of the insistence that this salvation cannot be found anywhere except in Jesus.

NOTES

1. G. W. E. Nickelsburg, "Riches, the Rich and God's Judgment in 1 En. 92–105 and the Gospel according to Luke," *New Testament Studies* 25 (1979), 324–44.
2. R. A. Edwards, *A Theology of Q* (Philadelphia: Fortress, 1976), 41, 50f., 113f.
3. J. R. Donahue, "A Neglected Factor in the Theology of Mark," *Journal of Biblical Literature* 101 (1982), 575–78.
4. Donahue, ibid., 569.
5. G. Rochais, *Les Récits de résurrection des morts* (SNTSMS 40; Cambridge: Cambridge University, 1980), 167–76. Rochais makes it clear that there is no necessary connection between resurrection and the various images of Messiah in the Judaism of Jesus' time. However, he still speaks of Jesus' sharing Pharisaic belief in resurrection (ibid., 185) as though that were a well-defined complex of teaching.
6. See the chart in Rochais, ibid., 8–13. For a treatment of Luke's use of Jesus/Elijah parallels, see Rochais, ibid., 32–35. P. J. Achtemeier ("The Lucan Perspective on the Miracles of Jesus: A Preliminary Sketch," *JBL* 94 [1975], 561f.) does not think that Luke has carried out a consistent policy of making Jesus equivalent to Elijah, though the comparison is introduced in 4:25–27.
7. Rochais (op. cit., 30) points to the accompanying crowd, the compassion of Jesus for the mother, the reaction of amazement, and spreading word of the miracle about as typically Lukan features. See also Achtemeier, op. cit., 552, 557.
8. Rochais, op. cit., 35; Achtemeier, op. cit., 561.
9. Rochais, op. cit., 35.
10. See P. J. Achtemeier, "Toward the Isolation of Pre-Markan Miracle Catenae," *Journal of Biblical Literature* 89 (1970), 276–79.
11. Rochais, op. cit., 88–96. Rochais observes that the invitation to

Jarius's house, Jesus' compassion, and the miracle as response to
Jesus' word are all characteristic of Luke (pp. 74, 79, 83). The
miracles are evidence that the time of salvation has arrived
(ibid., 87). See also Achtemeier, "Catenae," 279; and idem, "Lucan Perspective," 549, 557.

12. Rochais, op. cit., 55.
13. Rochais, op. cit., 72f., 111.
14. Ibid., 73.
15. See the chart with the parallels between the two stories in
Rochais, op. cit., 123f.
16. Ibid., 125–32.
17. Ibid., 136.
18. See J. Blank, *Krisis* (Freiburg: Herder, 1964), 109–82.
19. Though both Son of Man and resurrection occur in Daniel, the
Son of Man image is more directly tied with exaltation than
with resurrection. See the discussions of the Son of Man traditions in N. Perrin, *Rediscovering the Teaching of Jesus* (New
York: Harper & Row, 1967), 165–97; C. Rowland, *The Open
Heaven* (New York: Crossroad, 1982), 178–88.
20. See the discussion of the Johannine Son of Man sayings in R.
Schnackenburg, *The Gospel According to St. John. Vol. 1:
Chaps. 1–4* (New York: Herder, 1968), 529–42.
21. See D. E. Nineham, *The Gospel of St. Mark* (Baltimore: Penguin, 1967), 406f.; R. Pesch, *Das Markusevangelium II. Teil.
Kommentar zu Kap. 8, 27–16, 20* (HTKNT II/2; Freiburg:
Herder, 1977), 433–35; V. Taylor, *The Gospel According to St.
Mark* (New York: St. Martin's, 1952), 566.
22. This prophetic saying belongs to the renewal of apocalyptic
expectation that appears to have been generated by the Roman
destruction of the temple. Mark seeks to both console his audience and to counter the excesses of such speculation; see Donahue (op. cit., 563). This section of Mark is critical of the temple
cult (ibid., 570, note 21).
23. J. Jeremias *(New Testament Theology. Vol. 1: The Proclamation
of Jesus* [New York: Scribners, 1971], 285–86) points out that
one never finds resurrection and parousia side by side as two
separate events in the sayings attributed to Jesus.
24. The atonement is based on a particular understanding of the
Maccabean martyrs. Their death was regarded by God as lifting
the curse created by the sins of the people from the land. See
the discussion in S. K. Williams *(Jesus' Death as a Saving Event.
The Background and Origin of a Concept* [HDR 2; Missoula,
Mont.: Scholars, 1975], 178f.). That the initiative lies with the

action of God after the death of the martyrs to regard that death as atonement makes it difficult to agree with those who claim that Jesus claimed that his death would be vicarious. For an attempt to argue the latter case, see J. C. O'Neill, "Did Jesus Teach that His Death Would be Vicarious as Well as Typical," *Suffering and Martyrdom in the New Testament: Studies Presented to G. M. Styler* (eds. W. Horbury and B. McNeil; Cambridge: Cambridge University, 1981), 9–27.

25. G. W. E. Nickelsburg, *Resurrection, Immortality, and Eternal Life in Intertestamental Judaism* (HTS xxvi; Cambridge: Harvard University, 1972), 21.

26. See the discussion in J. J. Collins, *The Apocalyptic Vision of the Book of Daniel* (HSM 16; Missoula, Mont.: Scholars, 1977), 215–18. A similar ethos appears in Rm 12:19–20 and Rev 13:10. Speaking of the "kingdom" or the "rule" of God has overtones beyond a simple victory in the political order, but one still presumes that the rule of God is to be applied to this world and its relationships. It is not a symbol of a heavenly existence detached from the affairs of this world any more than the symbols of Daniel refer to a world apart from this one.

27. P. Grelot ("The Resurrection of Jesus: Its Biblical and Jewish Background," *The Resurrection and Modern Biblical Thought* [ed. P. DeSurgy; New York/Cleveland: Corpus, 1970], 12–15) understands Dan 12:1–3 as an individualizing of the collective image of vindication in Dan 7:9–14, since it singles out a particular group of leaders in the community for exaltation.

28. Ibid., 24.

29. See J. A. Fitzmyer, "The New Testament Title 'Son of Man' Philologically Considered," *A Wandering Aramean: Aramaic Essays* (Missoula, Mont.: Scholars, 1979), 143–60.

30. Ibid., 153f.

31. See also the argument against the view that there was a noncollective use of Son of Man in J. D. G. Dunn, *Christology in the Making* (Philadelphia: Westminster, 1980), 68–74. Dunn argues that one cannot presume that the Son of Man is to be identified with Michael in Daniel.

32. Ibid., 77f.; Perrin, op. cit., 166–73.

33. Also Mk 6:15; 8:28; Mt 11:3. Compare the expression "You are the Son of Man" in 1 En. 71.114 (Dunn, op. cit., 85).

34. Dunn, loc. cit.; see Mt 11:5/Lk 7:22f.; Mt 13:16f./Lk 10:23f.; Mt 12:40f./Lk 11:31f.; Lk 12:54–56.

35. Ibid., 66–67. For the alteration of "I" and Son of Man, see Mt 5:11/Lk 6:22; Mt 10:32/Lk 12:8; Mk 8:27/Mt 16:3. The clearest

use of Dan 7:13f. appears in Mk 13:26; 14:62; and 8:38. In addition, it appears in four Q passages: Mt 19:28/Lk 22:30; Mt 24:27/Lk 17:24; Mt 24:44/Lk 12:40; and in the following sayings, which only appear in Matthew or Luke: Mt 10:23; 13:41; 16:28; 24:39; 25:31; Lk 12:8; 17:22, 30; 18:8; 21:36.

36. Ibid., 86–88.

37. C. F. D. Moule, *The Origins of Christology* (Cambridge: Cambridge University, 1977), 18–21.

38. Ibid., 19–22. Moule argues that the New Testament use of Son of Man in sayings referring to the presence of Jesus as Son of Man, to his suffering, and to his parousia must be based in Jesus' own way of speaking since it belongs neither to Judaism nor to later Christian preaching. One must be somewhat cautious about the second half of that assertion. Achtemeier has suggested that Mark deliberately exploited Son of Man as a symbol for the paradoxical reality of Jesus' suffering messiahship ("He Taught Them Many Things: Reflections on Markan Christology," *CBQ* 42 [1980], 480f.). Similarly, the Fourth Gospel uses Son of Man in its controversy discourses to point to a christological perception beyond the views that Jesus' opponents should have reached on the basis of their understanding of Moses.

39. See Lk 17:26f./Mt 24:37–41. Matthew has intensified the parousia reference (Perrin, op. cit., 197).

40. Ibid., 195–96. Other developments of the tradition may be found in Matthew's version of the exhortation not to follow false preachers with the Q saying about the day of the Son of Man; Mt 24:26–28/Lk 17:23–24. In Matthew's version, the lightning in the sky flashes from east to west; cf. 2 Bar. 53.9.

41. Perrin, op. cit., 173–80. Perrin thinks that Ac 7:56 provides an important clue to the development of Son of Man as an early Christian exegetical tradition. It shows that Son of Man was not always placed on the lips of Jesus and consequently that the gospel use of the expression only on the lips of Jesus cannot be taken as a clue to its derivation from the teaching of Jesus himself. The visionary context of the saying suggests that the application of Son of Man to Jesus might have had its origins in early Christian prophecy (ibid., 180). On the general connection between early prophecy, the sayings tradition, and the presence of the risen Lord, see the study of M. E. Boring, *Sayings of the Risen Jesus* (SNTSMS 46; Cambridge: Cambridge University, 1982). Boring argues that it was the tendency of the prophetic traditions that underlie Q to place all sayings of Jesus in the mouth of the risen Lord (op. cit., 167–68).

42. See the discussion of the use of the trial/vindication seen in the Markan passion narrative by G. W. E. Nickelsburg, "The Genre and Function of the Markan Passion Narrative," *Harvard Theological Review* 73 (1980), 153–84.

43. Ibid., 185–91. Perrin rejects the earlier tendency to regard the saying in Mk 8:38 as more original than its Lukan parallel by noting that it lacks the reference to "coming with clouds" that is distinctive of the exegetical references to Daniel. (See a similar observation in Fitzmyer [op. cit., 153] that the New Testament marks its use of the Daniel tradition with references to elements surrounding the Son of Man in the vision.) Consequently, Son of Man has been introduced into Mark at a point at which the reference has acquired independent status in early Christian speech.

44. Fitzmyer, op. cit., 154.

45. G. W. E. Nickelsburg, "Enoch, Levi and Peter: Recipients of Revelation in Upper Galilee," *Journal of Biblical Literature* 100 (1981), 575–90.

46. Nickelsburg (ibid., 590–99) sees the scene with the high priest in Acts 4 as the reversal of Peter's denial. Other links between the Enoch and Petrine traditions are found in the Petrine letters. Compare the punishment of the disobedient angels in 1 Pt 3:19–20 and 2 Pt 2:4–5 with the punishment of the watchers in 1 En. 12–16 (op. cit., 599–600).

47. Grelot, op. cit., 21.

48. Grelot, op. cit., 26.

49. K. Schubert, "Die Entwicklung der Auferstehungslehre von der nachexilischen bis zur frührabbinische Zeit," *Biblische Zeitschrift* n.f. 6 (1962), 177–214; idem, "Auferstehung Jesu im Lichte der Religionsgeschichte des Judentums," in E. Dhanis, ed., *Resurrexit. Actes du symposium international sur la résurrection de Jésus* (Rome: Libreria Editrice Vaticana, 1974), 217–19.

50. E. Schillebeeckx *(Jesus* [New York: Seabury, 1979], 73) rightly emphasizes the necessity to presume some continuity between the historical memories of Jesus, the disciples' experiences with Jesus, and the Easter events as the point of departure for the early Christian kerygma. He later argues *(Christ* [New York: Crossroad, 1981], 826–29) that the gospel was constructed out of three sequences, each of which further advanced an earlier perception of "God at work," even if the authors were not conscious of the development explicitly: (1) the life of Jesus as determining one's ultimate relationship to the rule of God; (2)

the passion, centering on the suffering of Christ and the apparent failure of his mission; (3) tomb and appearance stories as the culminating experience of the presence of God in Jesus. Looking backward from that point shows the apparent failure of the passion to have been a lie.

51. See J. Jeremias, "Die älteste Schicht der Osterüberlieferung," in E. Dhanis, ed., *Resurrexit*, 185–96.

52. Jeremias, ibid., 188–93; idem, *Theology*, 303–308.

53. Such a simple reduction is implied in W. Marxsen's view, since the faith of the twelve is finally reduced to the single experience of Peter, which led him to reconstitute the group of disciples. Whether or not there were further appearances does not matter, since the reestablishment of the group of disciples and the conviction that Jesus' mission continued are the center of the Easter event. The appearance stories provide us with no access to the originating experience of Peter beyond the fact that he had believed (W. Marxsen, *The Resurrection of Jesus of Nazareth* [Philadelphia: Fortress, 1970], 92–97). Paul's use of "he appeared" in 1 Cor 15:8 is seen as simply an assimilation of his own experience of God's bringing him to faith in Jesus to the language of apostolic appearance traditions. Paul never uses his own experience as proof of the resurrection, even in 1 Cor 15:14 (op. cit., 105–110). Marxsen is correct to emphasize the fact that the Easter discovery of faith involves acknowledgment that one stands in continuity with the faith Jesus called forth before Easter. This conjunction is the aim of all of the gospel narratives (op. cit., 127).

54. Only the second-century *Gospel of Peter* tried to remedy this deficiency by providing an account of the actual resurrection. All the guards see Jesus emerging from the tomb: "they saw three men come out of the tomb and two of them holding up the other and a cross following them. The heads of the two reached to heaven, but that of the one whom they were leading by the hand passed beyond the heavens" *(Gospel of Peter,* 39–40; see E. Hennecke and W. Schneemelcher, *New Testament Apocrypha. Vol. 1* [Philadelphia: Westminster, 1963], 186).

55. See E. Haenchen, *The Acts of the Apostles* (Philadelphia: Westminster, 1971), 292.

56. Jeremias, "Schicht," 189.

57. P. Benoit, "Marie Madeleine et les disciples au tombeau selon Jean 20, 1–18," *Judentum, Urchristentum, Kirche* (BZNW 26; ed. W. Eltester; Berlin: Töpelmann, 1964, 2nd ed.), 141–52.

58. Jeremias, *Theology*, 307. We doubt that there ever was an ac-

count of an appearance to Peter in the early tradition. Jeremias presumes that it was suppressed by radical Palestinian Jewish Christians who opposed Peter's universalism (as in Gal 2:12b; Ac 11:2).

59. Jeremias, ibid., 302–303.
60. See K. Lehmann, *Auferweckt am dritten Tag nach der Schrift* (Quaestiones Disputatae 38; Freiburg: Herder, 1968), 17–26. See J. Murphy-O'Connor, "Tradition and Redaction in 1 Cor 15:3–7," *Catholic Biblical Quarterly* 43 (1981), 582–83.
61. So R. H. Fuller, *The Formation of the Resurrection Narratives* (New York: Macmillan, 1971), 11–16. See J. Kremer, *Das älteste Zeugnis von der Auferstehung Christi: Eine bibeltheologische Studie zur Aussage und Bedeutung von 1 Kor 15, 1–11* (SBS 17; Stuttgart: Katholisches Bibelwerk, 1967), 27.
62. Murphy-O'Connor, op. cit., 534.
63. Ibid., 585; see also the discussion of this passage in U. Wilckens, *Die Missionsreden der Apostelgeschichte* (WMANT 5; Neukirchen: Neukirchener, 1961), 74.
64. As is argued by K. Wengst, *Christologische Formeln und Lieder des Urchristentums* (Gütersloh: Gerd Mohn, 1972), 94.
65. Murphy-O'Connor (op. cit., 587) is willing to grant that "he was seen" *(ōphthē)* may not have been the original verb in this passage. Paul could have introduced the verb in vv. 6 and 8 to describe his own experience and thereby establish that it was the same as that of the twelve.
66. Murphy-O'Connor (loc. cit.) points out that "more than" *(hoi pleiones)* is typically Pauline. He uses it in Phil 1:14. The use of "remain" in a phrase like this is also typical of Paul, as in Phil 1:25, and "fall asleep" is always used by Paul with the sense of "to die."
67. See E. L. Bode, *The First Easter Morning: The Gospel Accounts of the Women's Visit to the Tomb of Jesus* (Rome: Biblical Institute Press, 1970), 116f.
68. Ibid., 113f., 118; and Lehmann, op. cit., 159.
69. See the citation of the Midrash Gen Rabbah in Strack-Billerbeck 1.747, 790; Bode, op. cit., 119–25; Lehmann, op. cit., 206–208.
70. Bode, op. cit., 98f.
71. Bode, op. cit., 104.
72. Bode, op. cit., 6–17. Bode argues (p. 15) that the stories with the purpose of the visit as anointing in Mark and Luke reflect a separate tradition from that in Matthew.
73. G. Schille, "Das Leiden des Herrn: Die evangelische Passions-

tradition und ihr Sitz im Leben," *Zeitschrift für Theologie und Kirche* 52 (1955), 195–99. W. Nauck, "Die Bedeutung des leeren Grabes für den Glauben an den Auferstandenen," *Zeitschrift für Neutestamentliche Wissenschaft* 47 (1956), 262. Luke is said to have changed the words of the angel's proclamation, since Gentile Christians would not have been interested in the place. See L. Schenke, *Auferstehungsverkündigung und leeres Grab* (SBS 33; Stuttgart: Katholisches Bibelwerk, 1969, 2nd ed.), 89–94.

74. Bode, op. cit., 130–45.
75. Bode, op. cit., 155–65.
76. Bode, op. cit., 166–75. Bode points out (p. 170) that while the reference to Galilee could refer to an actual appearance tradition, it might also point to the significance of Galilee in Mark's gospel. H. C. Kee *(Community of the New Age* [Philadelphia: Westminster, 1977], 100–5) argues that Mark's geographical inaccuracies show an origin in Galilee itself to be impossible. Therefore, he suggests that the Markan community was located in southern Syria.
77. Jeremias, "Schicht," 188.
78. Jeremias, *Theology,* 310. Jeremias (p. 311) points to the pre-Pauline tradition in 1 Cor 15:7b–8 as evidence that early Christians thought they stood in the time of salvation.
79. See C. E. Carlston, "Transfiguration and Resurrection," *Journal of Biblical Literature* 80 (1961), 233–40. Carlston's arguments do not rely on the evidence of second-century Gnostic material as the carrier of this primitive resurrection material. The case has been argued using the Gnostic material by J. M. Robinson (see H. Koester and J. M. Robinson, *Trajectories Through Early Christianity* [Philadelphia: Fortress, 1971], 48f.). Robinson argues that the Transfiguration is not different in form from the appearance to Stephen or to Paul in Acts. Both presume that the risen Lord appears from heaven in glory or light. The physical canons of later apologetic that were linked to Luke's scheme of a forty-day resurrection period made it impossible for such luminous appearance stories to be preserved as resurrection traditions except in heterodox circles. J. M. Robinson, "Jesus: From Easter to Valentinus (or to the Apostles' Creed)," *Journal of Biblical Literature* 101 (1982), 5–37.
80. J. E. Alsup, *The Post-Resurrection Appearance Stories of the Gospel Tradition. A History-of-Tradition Analysis* (Calwer theologische Monographien 5; London: SPCK: 1975), 141–43; so also R. H. Stein, "Is the Transfiguration (Mk 9:2–8) a Misplaced

Resurrection Account?" *Journal of Biblical Literature* 95 (1976), 80–82.

81. Carlston, op. cit., 235. The glory of resurrection is emphasized outside the narrative traditions in such passages as Ac 7:55; 9:3; 22:6, 9, 11; 26:13; 1 Cor 15:8, 40; 1 Pt 1:11; 1 Tim 3:16; and Heb 2:9.

82. Such as Rev 4:4; 7:9; 1 En. 62.15–16; 2 En. 22.8. However one accounts for its origins, the Transfiguration story is unusual. Carlston (ibid., 234) points out that it is the only example of a miracle being done to rather than by Jesus. It also differs from the resurrection stories in which Jesus is mistaken for a human being.

83. Stein, op. cit., 88–99. See also the discussion of the apologetic purpose of this section of 2 Peter by J. Neyrey, "The Apologetic Use of the Transfiguration in 2 Peter 1:16–21," *Catholic Biblical Quarterly* 42 (1980), 504–19.

84. Neyrey, ibid., 509–14. See 512, note 34 for the argument against those who think that the *Apocalypse of Peter* is a resurrection appearance and use that argument to bolster their case for the resurrection origins of the synoptic Transfiguration accounts.

85. Ibid., 514–19.

86. See J. A. Fitzmyer, *The Gospel According to Luke I–IX* (AnBi 28; Garden City, N.Y.: Doubleday, 1981), 791–804. Fitzmyer argues against the view that the story is a transposed resurrection account (ibid., 796).

87. Fitzmyer (ibid., 802) points to the apocalyptic use of fear in the vision of Dan 10:7.

88. R. J. Dillon, *From Eye-Witnesses to Ministers of the Word: Tradition and Composition in Luke 24* (Rome: Biblical Institute Press, 1978), 20–24.

89. Fitzmyer, *Luke,* 800.

90. Ibid., 794.

91. Ibid., 793.

92. Ibid., 793; see also the discussion of the Son of God title in M. Hengel, *The Son of God* (Philadelphia: Fortress, 1976), 57–66.

93. Ibid., 794f.

94. Fuller, op. cit., 165–67.

95. Nickelsburg, "Enoch," 590–600.

96. Carlston, op. cit., 233; and see the summary of the various hypotheses in Taylor, op. cit., 386–88.

97. Taylor, op. cit., 388; Fitzmyer, *Luke,* 796.

98. Fitzmyer, *Luke,* 560–62; on the Johannine story, see R. E.

Brown, *The Gospel According to John XIII–XXI* (AnBi 29A; Garden City, N.Y.: Doubleday, 1970), 1090.

99. R. E. Brown, *The Epistles of John* (AnBi 30; Garden City, N.Y.: Doubleday, 1982), 110–12. Brown thinks that this redaction of chapter 21 represents the accommodation of Johannine Christians to Petrine authority after the period of crisis evidence in the Johannine letters. They are willing to acknowledge the need from Petrine authority.

100. Fitzmyer, *Luke,* 87–88.

101. Fitzmyer *(Luke,* 561) thinks that while there may be some form of postresurrection tradition behind this story, Luke no longer understood the story as such.

102. Fuller, op. cit., 160f.

FOUR

Resurrection in the Gospels: Mark and Matthew

We have seen that it is difficult to establish a historical nucleus to the resurrection traditions. Nevertheless, such a nucleus must be presupposed in order to understand the explosive development of a way of understanding Jesus and his fate that cannot be said to have been established in either Judaism or the explicit teaching of Jesus.[1] Resurrection plays such a formative role in the early Christian preaching that we would hardly expect the Easter message to remain without any narrative embodiment. Any study of these stories quickly finds that it must deal with both their relationship to pregospel traditions and each gospel's understanding of the place of resurrection in the story of Jesus and his disciples. The gospels tell us much less about the historical events surrounding the resurrection than they do about the legacy of faith in Jesus as the risen One that has shaped the traditions that have come down to us.

We have seen that the relationship between the appearance stories and the resurrection kerygma remains a central question. The keryg-

matic proclamation of 1 Cor 15:3–5 is not a summary of a resurrection narrative. Nor are the narratives simply imaginative expansion
of the kerygma. Although it is generally agreed that the evangelists
have used pregospel tradition in their accounts, the nature of that
tradition is hotly disputed.[2] One of the biggest questions raised about
the resurrection stories is the question of their genre. Some interpreters think that they follow the conventions of angelophanies;
others, that they are primarily legends. Still others seek to construct a
genre of commissioning story that underlies these materials. An alternative to seeking an established genre for these stories is to adopt
the classification proposed by C. H. Dodd. Dodd attempts to set up an
inductive typology of the resurrection stories by asking what the
common patterns in the stories themselves are. He divides them into
the "concise" type of appearance represented in Mt 28:8–10; 16–20
and Jn 20:19–21 and the "circumstantial type." The latter, such as
one finds in the Emmaus story of Lk 24 and in Jn 21, develop details
within the resurrection story. The failure of the "concise" type to
hold against such expansion suggests to some that it does not represent a genre that operated to shape the way in which resurrection
stories were narrated in the same way that the genres of the form
critics appear to do.[3] Consequently, others have attempted to find a
storytelling genre that is familiar to the evangelists and hence gov-
erns their narration of events.[4] If one asks of analysis only statements
whose claims will meet the standards of a scientific history of "what
happened to whom, when, and how did they interpret and respond
to those events," the resurrection appearance stories have little to
tell us.[5] We have seen that resurrection belongs to a sequence of
images that point toward the culmination of all things.[6] Many of the
elements from the Jewish tradition find their way into the stories of
Jesus' resurrection.

MARK 16:1–8

Mark does not contain any story about the appearance of the risen
Jesus. Its story of the empty tomb is not associated with an appearance of Jesus. This section presents several problems: Is it independent of the Markan passion narrative? What is the function of the
angelic announcement in v. 7? What is the significance of the wom-
en's flight in v. 8, and can one find behind this passage a *Vorlage* that
Mark has edited?

Mark 16:1–8 and Pre-Markan Tradition

The three passion predictions earlier in the gospel concluded with the announcement of the resurrection of Jesus (8:31; 9:9, 31; 10:34). The passion as a whole comes to its end with the announcement of the resurrection of Jesus in his open, empty grave. The passage as it stands is closely related to its context as the conclusion of the passion narrative. R. Pesch points to the following connections between the tomb story and the burial account that precedes it in Mk 15:42–47: (1) time (15:42; 16:1); (2) comment about the purchase of the necessary herbs (15:46; 16:1); (3) notice about the burial (15:46f.; 16:6); (4) use of the terms *mnēma* and *mnēmeion* for the tomb (15:46; 16:2, 3, 5, 8); (5) the stone (15:46; 16:3, 4); (6) the women see where Jesus is laid (15:47; 16:4), and (7) the list of names (15:47; 16:1).[7] Other commentators would hold these parallels to be the marks of careful editing rather than the example of a non-Markan source throughout the last chapters of the gospel.[8] They see the list of names and the angelic kerygma in 16:7 as clear examples of secondary expansion. Whoever is responsible for the connections, the tomb story clearly forms a part of the Markan passion narrative as it is now composed.

The attempts to reconstruct pre-Markan tradition behind this story can be separated into two groups: those who argue for an original that did not have an angelophany[9] and those who think that the angel's appearance was part of the Markan *Vorlage.*[10] For those who see the primary element in any resurrection story as its relationship to apocalyptic, the angelic appearance becomes the key to the whole passage.[11]

The argument for pre-Markan tradition seems stronger than that which holds that the story is entirely a Markan creation.[12] Large-scale features in the two sections give this impression: the tomb and burial scenes do not in fact "match." The names of the women are not the same. The Markan introduction to the tomb story is overloaded with temporal markers. The words of the angel in v. 7 clearly represent the preaching of the early church and are not an interpretation of the tomb itself.[13]

J. Kremer concludes that the most likely *Vorlage* had the women go to the tomb, find the angelic messenger there, and flee (1b, 2a and b, 5, 6, 8a).[14] J. Delorme observes that while early kerygmatic summaries connect crucifixion and resurrection, that connection is not part of the passion narrative. Nor is the burial in Mk 15:46 incomplete. Any pre-Markan source must be isolated with regard to the tomb pericope alone.[15] Though the details of various reconstructions vary, there is general agreement that the kerygmatic summary in v. 7 must have been added to the existing story. The simplest hypothesis is to assume that Mark added it on the basis of Jesus' saying in 14:28.[16] Nevertheless, the summary appears to have an independent origin in an earlier tradition. It probably stems from a tradition something like that of 1 Cor 15:5. Thus, agreeing that Mark has inserted the verse into the story does not imply that he is responsible for having composed it.[17]

Verse 1: *And when the Sabbath was over, Maria Magdalene and Maria the (mother of) James and Salome bought aromatic spices so that they could go and anoint him.*

The temporal expression *diagenomenou tou sabbatou* refers to the evening after sunset, the official end of the Sabbath. Since Mark has brought the events of the burial to a close on the eve of the Sabbath (15:42), it would seem likely that this expression is his resumption of the story.[18] The second element of the passage is the list of the names of the women. Some scholars think that it was inserted into a story that originally had only "some women" finding the tomb, as is the case with the summary in Lk 24:22–23.[19] Others argue that the presence of three different lists in Mark (15:40, 47; 16:1) shows that each pericope had names attached to it in the tradition. They suggest that Mark moved the names from the original introduction to the story in the previous verse to this position.[20]

The names of the women in the parallels to Mk 15:40 (Mt 27:56; variant, Jn 19:25) also change. The Lukan tradition simply has "women who had accompanied him from Galilee" (Lk 23:49). Lukan readers might supply a list of names from Lk 8:3, where we find: Mary Magdalene; Johanna, wife of Chuza; and Susanna. In the parallel to Mk 15:47, Luke preserves the expression "women who had accompanied him from Galilee" (Lk 23:55), while Matthew has Mary Magdalene and "the other Mary" (Mt 27:61). Mary Magdalene "and the other Mary" appear in Matthew's parallel to Mk 16.1 as well (Mt 28.1). Luke has continued the indefinite use of "some women," and John has the singular Mary Magdalene, who is in any case the only stable figure in the collection of names. It seems to us most likely that the pre-Markan stories of burial and finding the tomb contained different names for the companion(s) of Mary Magdalene and that Mark is responsible for the list at 15:40 in an attempt to harmonize the two traditions. It is somewhat more difficult to say whether or not all names should be seen as secondary to a tradition without them or as additions to the single figure of Mary Magdalene.[21]

The final element in this passage is the purchase of the spices for anointing, which parallels the purchase made by Joseph in 15:46.[22] The real question is the relationship between this text and the anointing of Jesus in view of his death in Mk 14:3–9. Both Kremer and Pesch connect anointing and Markan composition. Jesus has already been anointed. There will be no body to anoint, since he has not remained in the grave.[23] R. Mahoney, on the other hand, suggests that the very awkwardness of the motif attests to its pre-Markan character. He suggests that Mark has moved the purpose clause *"hina . . . haleipsosin auton"* from its attachment to the end of v. 2. In that way he is able both to show the women starting their preparations as soon as the Sabbath is over and to explain why they waited so long to anoint Jesus.[24]

Thus, with all the qualifications, it still seems possible to argue that v. 1 is a combination of Markan composition and tradition. Mark has provided the temporal introduction and the clause about the women purchasing the aromatics. In so doing, he may have reformulated the original introduction to the story by moving the names of the women and their intention to this verse from the following one. Or he may have supplied both from other traditions. But the lack of consistency between the names and anointing and the earlier references to both in the gospel makes it seem unlikely that the evangelist has simply composed this verse out of whole cloth.

Verse 2: *And very early on the first day after the Sabbath they came to the tomb, after the sun had risen.*

The second verse piles up temporal indicators. Commentators are divided over the significance of the concluding specification about the sun having risen. Since Mark tends to use a "double step" technique in which the second phrase qualifies the first, it seems likely that the concluding expression is his.[25] Pesch points to the use of *"proi ennucha lian"* in Mk 1:35 as an indication that the expression *"lian proi"* is Markan.[26] Only the second reference to the "day after the Sabbath" remains a problem. It is a Semitic expression, which Mark has probably retained from his source.[27] If one accepts Mahoney's suggestion that the purpose clause that now concludes the first verse originally ended the second, then one may see that Mark has created a two-step time sequence by modifying the beginning and end of this verse. The initial story would have had a simpler introduction in which the women come to the tomb to anoint Jesus on the day after the Sabbath.

Verse 3: *And they were saying to each other: who will roll the stone away from the door of the tomb for us?*

This verse sets the stage for the next, which concludes by assuring the reader that the stone was "very large."[28] The last clause also refers the reader back to the sealing of the tomb in 15:46. The quest for a helper evokes a primitive narrative technique that will point to the true helper, the angel, in a way that the women do not expect.[29] Thus, the details of the moving aside of a great stone are most appropriate to the "legendary" elaboration of the story at the oral stage of the tradition.

Verse 4: *And looking up, they saw that the stone had been rolled away—which was very large.*

The brief sentence heightens the reader's expectation for the miraculous event in the next verse. The passive form of the verb and the notice about the size of the stone all make the suggestion, which will be explicit in Mt 28:2, that the angel is responsible for its removal.

Verse 5: *And when they entered the tomb they saw a young man seated on the right wearing a white garment and they were astounded.*

With v. 5 we come to the more problematic areas of interpreting this passage and its tradition. The first concerns the identification of the "young man" seated in the tomb. Some scholars identify this *"neaniskos"* with the *neaniskos* who flees by leaving his *"sindon"* (linen cloth) at the arrest of Jesus in 14:51–52. This view is often coupled with another that presumes that the "young man" is the type of the baptized initiate. Such interpretations of Mark draw heavily on the Pauline traditions of baptism as dying and rising with Christ (e.g., Rm 6:3–5; Col 2:11f.; 3:1–3; Eph 2:4–6).[30]

There are several difficulties with this interpretation. The young man in 14:51–52 is in flight and not sharing the death of Jesus. We do not have evidence for disrobing as baptismal ritual until the second century A.D.[31] The most likely interpretation sees the young man as an angel. The white garment is part of his angelic status. The designation "young man" also applies to angels in Jewish writing of the period. The reaction of amazement is typical in angelophanies.[32] The phrasing of the passage also contains typical Markan themes of fear and amazement, which run throughout the gospel. The verb *ekthambesthai* (to be greatly surprised or alarmed; see 9:15; 14:33) reflects the typical reaction to the miraculous as an epiphany of the divine in Mark's narrative (see 6:49 and 9:6).[33]

Verse 6: *He said to them: Do not be afraid. You seek Jesus the Nazarene the crucified. He has been raised, he is not here. See the place where they placed him.*

The reassurance "do not fear" belongs to the genre of angelophany and hence belongs to the epiphany elements in the pre-Markan tradition. The angel's message, like the earlier indications of place, is overloaded. The designation *"Nazarenos"* appears to be peculiarly Markan (1:24; 10:47; 14:67); elsewhere in the New Testament one finds forms of *"Nazoraios/-an."*[34] The identification of Jesus as "the Nazarene" clearly does not provide information for the women. With the epithet "the crucified," we find ourselves in the realm of the early kerygmatic formulae.

The closest parallel to the whole expression here is Ac 4:10: "in the name of Jesus Christ, the Nazarite, whom you crucified; whom God raised from the dead."

The angel's message begins by reminding Christian readers of the kerygma that they have been familiar with in preaching since the beginning. It cannot be taken as a historical record, since the crucified/risen parallel does not address the situation of the women but that of the reader. Such a parallel between the character and reader is characteristic of Mark.[35] Only after the kerygmatic proclamation of the resurrection does the angel point to the fact that the tomb is empty.

Those who reconstruct a dawn ceremony at the tomb of Jesus read this passage as the dramatic climax of the ceremony. The pilgrims are shown the empty tomb with the announcement "Behold he is not here. See where they laid him."[36] However, it is difficult to make the case for such an early celebration. Further, the story does not focus on the women's viewing the emptiness of the tomb. Scholars are divided over whether Mark has worked with a story that simply dealt with the women's finding the tomb empty and departing perplexed or whether there was some form of kerygmatic announcement tied to the story. It seems to us that the story used by Mark did contain kerygmatic elements. Mark adapted it to provide the suitable conclusion to the threefold passion predictions of his gospel (e.g., 8:32–33).[37]

Verse 7: *But go tell his disciples and Peter that he goes before you into Galilee. You will see him there. As he told you.*

Most interpreters see this verse as a secondary insertion into the narrative. However, it may include pre-Markan elements. Several problems attend the interpretation of this verse. Some scholars have tried to insist that the "seeing of Jesus in Galilee" can only refer to the parousia and does not apply to the resurrection at all. Thus, the promise fulfilled by the passage is the parousia expectation of the returning Son of Man and the judgment oracle of the Sanhedrin trial in Mk 14:62.[38]

However, several elements in the passage itself do not lend themselves to a parousia interpretation. None of the vocabulary of the glory associated with the parousia appears here. Nor do we have clear evidence that Mark associated Galilee with the parousia, as this hypothesis presumes. Galilee functions as a theological symbol in Mark as the place of Jesus' ministry prior to the fatal confrontation with the Jerusalem authorities. Otherwise, it appears in association with the tradition that the risen Jesus appeared there. Those who favor a parousia interpretation point to the use of *opsesthē* in the parousia predictions of Mk 13:36 and 14:62. However, the same verb also occurs in connection with resurrection traditions as in 1 Cor 9:1; Mt 28:17; and Jn 20:18, 23, 29. The special reference to Peter in v. 7 also points in the direction of Peter's role as witness to the resurrection (1 Cor 15:5).[39]

The exact relationship between this passage and Mk 14:28 is disputed. Mahoney points out that in the former a verb is used *(proadzein)*, which means to assemble physically and lead the disciples. Indeed, R. H. Fuller points to its awkwardness in comparison with v. 6, which would appear to imply that Jesus is already in heaven. However, as E. L. Bode points out, one can hardly avoid the presumption that Mark does suppose that the verb designates activity of Jesus in both a temporal and spatial sense. In 6:45, it refers to the disciples' going before Jesus to the other side of the lake; in 11:9, to the crowd's going before Jesus at the entry into Jerusalem. The only instance in which it is used of Jesus is Mk 10:32, where Jesus is going before his frightened disciples to Jerusalem. There it introduces the final prediction of the passion. Thus, the verb fits into passion tradition as a reversal of that journey. Its presence in Mk 16:7 may indicate a sense of Galilee as the place of mission, as Fuller has suggested.[40] Not all scholars think that this passage and the one in Mk 14:27f. to which it refers are entirely Markan composition. Mk 14:28 follows a citation from Zech 13:7. This passage appears to have been traditionally associated with the flight of the disciples, since it appears in Jn 16:32 quite independent of any Markan influence. The question is whether or not Mk 14:28 represents some form of pre-Markan Easter tradition. In its present form, the verse appears to be a comment by the evangelist. Mk 16:7 would, then, be an attempt to reconcile the Jerusalem tomb tradition with the tradition of Jesus' appearance in Galilee.[41]

A further question arises about the special insertion of Peter alongside the reference to the disciples in this verse. Minimally, that reference may be taken as a reference to the priority of the Petrine tradition, much as one finds in 1 Cor 15:5. However, some interpreters suggest that the reference to Peter in this verse, combined with the allusion to the *proagein* of Mk 10:32 and the scattering of the disciples in 14:28, indicate restoration of the disciples and of Peter after his betrayal.[42] If there is pre-Markan tradition behind vv. 14:28 and 16:7, then it is in the restoration of the disciples. However, one may also argue that the element of restoration is a feature of Markan redaction. Mark has shaped the picture of the disciples during the ministry as one of increasing inability to comprehend Jesus. This lack of comprehension is particularly evident in their reactions to the passion predictions.[43] But restoration as the Markan intention of the passage as a whole conflicts with the insertion of the angelic command. The women do not obey the command. They flee.

Verse 8: *And, going out, they fled from the tomb, for trembling and astonishment seized them; and they said nothing to anyone, for they were afraid.*

The overloading of this verse suggests that Mark has expanded an earlier source. Some of the elements of fear may have been traditional, since fear is associated with the genre of angelic epiphany. Thus, many exegetes suggest that the women's fearful flight from the tomb in v. 8a represents the conclusion to the tomb story in Mark's source.[44]

The passage has been expanded by the use of words for fear that occur elsewhere in Mark. The primary parallels are to the final clause in the passage: "for they were afraid." The word *tromos* (trembling) does not appear elsewhere in Mark. Where it is used in the New Testament, it is part of the combination "fear and trembling." That expression is often used in paraenetic contexts to speak of how persons should conduct themselves.[45] The word *ekstasis* (amazement) appears in Mk 5:42 as the crowd's reaction to a healing miracle. In contrast to these rare words, the use of the words for fear, *phobos* (n.)

and *phobeisthai* (v.), in connection with disciples is frequent in Mark. They indicate inadequate responses to Jesus. Mk 4:41 uses them to describe the disciples' reaction to the calming of the sea in a phrase that is similar to the crowd response in 5:42.

In 9:6, Mark attributes Peter's statement about making three tents to fear. The motif of fear appears in connection with the second and third passion predictions. In 9:32, the disciples do not understand what Jesus has said, "and they were afraid to ask him." In 10:32, alluded to in 16:7, the disciples are following Jesus on the journey to Jerusalem in fear. Mark consistently uses "they were afraid" for the disciples' failure to understand or react appropriately to Jesus' words. The conclusion to v. 8 applies this perspective to the women's reaction to the events at the tomb.

Since the women are here treated as Mark treats the disciples in the rest of the narrative, their flight cannot be explained as Mark's attempt to deny them status as witnesses to the resurrection kerygma.[46] It is sometimes argued that Mark has simply inserted the women's silence in order to explain why the tomb tradition was not part of the earlier resurrection kerygma. However, it seems to us that the whole pattern of the passage fits Mark's image of discipleship. The other "fear" passages either include things that the disciples say but are inappropriate, or they have the disciples not speaking or asking Jesus about what they do not understand because of their fear. This passage falls into the second category, the combination of fear and silence. Mark is not concerned about their disobedience to an angel or even about whether or not the women are witness to the resurrection. Rather, he has them repeat the pattern that has been previously established in the stories of the disciples. Thus, Mark appears to have taken an earlier tradition about the finding of the empty tomb that ended with their flight. He has incorporated that motif into a larger pattern of disciple stories. Far from indicating that the women are in some way inferior to the disciples, Mark's redaction makes them equal to Jesus' other disciples.

This passage forms an *inclusio* with the story of the journey to Jerusalem. It completes the Markan narrative. At the same time, the return to Galilee, the place in which Jesus' mission began, hints at a restoration. Despite their failure, Jesus' disciples will still be his witnesses.[47] But the ending of the gospel also carries a warning in its incompleteness. One must not repeat the pattern established by the disciples and the women. As the warnings scattered throughout the second half of the gospel show, Mark still reckons with the possibility of failure on the part of Jesus' disciples. Of course, his readers know that the disciples did become witnesses to the Lord, that they did overcome their fear, and that some had even been martyred. But the warning must remain in place for the Markan community in its time of trial. There will be no resolution of that paradox of suffering until the return of the glorified Son of Man.[48]

The divine promise, whose fulfillment is proclaimed in resurrection, continues to be the same for the Markan Christians as for the disciples. The faith and assurance that God vindicates them in their sufferings remains hidden. Thus, Mark has not turned the story of the empty tomb into a demonstration of the resurrection, just as he has not emphasized the resurrection itself as an event. Rather, the story is only understood in light of the faith that the narrator and his readers have on the basis of the kerygma. Mark makes it clear that all Christians believe through hearing the proclamation that the Lord is raised.

T. E. Boomershine views the final passion prediction of Mk 10:33-34 as providing the structure for the entire conclusion of the gospel. In fulfillment of that prophecy, we find Jesus: (1) handed over to arrest (14:26-52); (2) condemned to death by the Sanhedrin (14:53-72); (3) turned over to Pilate (= the Gentiles), (15:1-20); (4) crucified (15:21-47); and (5) raised (16:1-8). With the exception of the trial before Pilate, which does emphasize the fulfillment of the prophecy, each of the sections ends with the response by Jesus' followers: (1) flight; (2) denial; (3) women are witness to crucifixion; (4) women flee and are silent. The narrative demands both a negative judgment on the women's flight and a certain sympathy created by the narrative distance from which one sees these events. Jesus' prophecies of denial (Mk 14:26-31) establish the point of view that the reader is to take. The theological pattern of the suffering Messiah and his followers is directed toward the community's own response to such a dilemma. Thus, Boomershine argues, one can see the shock of Mk 16:8 as a negative example. It is to purge the fear that is associated with preaching the gospel in the Markan community.[49]

The restraint of the Markan story makes it evident that the empty tomb itself is ambiguous and that it is not immediately viewed as evidence for resurrection. The discipleship motif in this passage suggests a tie to the resurrection traditions of commissioning. The appearance stories will have the risen Lord commission the disciples. Here the angelic command commissions the women, and they react in a way that is consistent with what we have seen of Mark's portrayal of the disciples throughout the gospel. Like the resurrection itself, the reversal of that situation in a restoration to fellowship and understanding is only barely hinted at in the Markan story. This complex interlocking of the story of the tomb with other Markan themes makes it difficult to reconstruct the shape and purpose of the material that Mark used for his story, though the overloaded construction of certain verses seems a clear indication that he did have such material to use. That material seems to be ancient, not a later legendary creation. Nor does it appear to us that it has been formed in the kind of liturgical setting that is sometimes proposed. We will see in the more expanded narratives of the other gospels various ways in which the tomb traditions are integrated into a tradition of resurrection as Jesus' appearances to his disciples.

MATTHEW

Matthew has adapted Mark's story of the empty tomb by combining it with an apologetic legend about the posting of the guard at the tomb. That legend had the emptiness of the tomb reported to the Jewish authorities (Mt 27:62–66; 28:11–15). The story serves to counter the suspicion that Jesus' disciples had removed the body from the tomb. This legend is further developed in the *Gospel of Peter* where the guards become witnesses to Jesus' emergence from the tomb. Matthew also differs from Mark in including appearance stories after the account of the empty tomb. The women see Jesus as they leave the tomb (28:9–10), and the gospel concludes with a commissioning appearance in Galilee (28:16–20). When compared with the more lengthy appearance stories in Luke and John, the Matthean ones are still quite undeveloped. They focus on the commissioning of disciples by the risen Lord.

The brevity and restraint of Matthew's appearance stories distinguishes them from those in Luke and John. They remain centered on the double theme of recognition and mission. Although each gospel handles the commissioning of the disciples differently, there is always a strong awareness that "sending" lies at the basis of the appearance stories.[50]

The elements of recognition and commission are prior to the apologetic motifs that have been introduced into Matthew's account. He uses the sealing of the tomb and the placing of the body in a new grave to counter the charge that the body had been stolen. Such apologetic arguments may belong to pre-Matthean tradition. J. Meier suggests that in Matthew they have been given a further function. They make it clear that nothing can hinder Jesus' resurrection.[51] That motif may also be developed in the apocalyptic overtones that

Matthew adds to the story of Jesus' crucifixion. We have seen that resurrection motifs in Judaism appear in the context of the apocalyptic vindication of the righteous. Mt 27:51b–53 contains a proleptic resurrection of the righteous at the hour of the crucifixion. Though the earthquake and other heavenly signs are typical apocalyptic features, the Matthean episode appears to be based on Ez 37. The earthquake in Mt 27:51 is parallel to the great noise of the assembling of the bones in Ez 37:7. The other three elements—the opening of the graves, the rising of the dead, and the procession into the city—all reflect the oracle in Ez 37:12. The original prophecy spoke of the return home of exiled Israel. For Matthew it is a messianic prophecy realized in the person of Jesus.[52] The connection of this passage with Ezekiel should serve as warning against two false concerns. The first is undue speculation about those who were said to have been raised at the moment of crucifixion. Matthew acknowledges the awkwardness of this story by having them raised at the crucifixion but not appear in the city until after Jesus' resurrection. It would be false to presume that the image of the "resurrection of the Just" here somehow contradicts the expectation that the resurrection of Christians lies in the future. The second false concern would be to turn the image of fulfilled prophecy into some sort of additional evidence for the resurrection of Jesus. The soteriology of this section of Matthew makes it clear that the turning point of the ages is the crucifixion, not the moment of resurrection. The crucifixion and its signs are witnessed by humans. The moment of Jesus' resurrection is not. Thus, D. Senior speaks of an "implicit soteriology" in the turning point of salvation history reflected in Matthew's description of the crucifixion.[53]

The use of apocalyptic images to present the passion of Jesus as a central soteriological event also brings out the apocalyptic context of the image of resurrection. The shift of the aeons with Jesus' death includes the resurrection of the righteous. Their vindication implies that the "messianic age" is now open with the death of Jesus. By portraying the crucifixion as an eschatological event, Matthew makes it clear that what follows must also fulfill the apocalyptic promises of salvation. Thus, what follows about resurrection must be understood as the culmination of God's dealing with the people, Israel. The resurrection of Jesus is more than the vindication of an individual righteous sufferer. It is the climax of the fulfillment of the promises of salvation.

Matthew also announces the shift in the ages by presenting the torn curtain of the temple. The cult characteristic of the old age is past (27:51–53). Matthew then changes the acknowledgment of the crucified as Son of God from being the confession of the single centurion, as it is in Mk 15:39, to being an acknowledgment by the centurion and all of those with him (Mt 27:54). While the Markan centurion makes his confession upon seeing Jesus breathe his last, the confession in Matthew depends on the fear engendered by the earthquake and the other signs that accompany the death of Jesus. Meier suggests that this acclamation also reflects the entry of the Gentiles into the people of God. Those who had mocked Jesus are now the first to confess that he is Son of God.[54] But this confession also reflects Matthew's understanding of the resurrection. He centers the appearance story on the universal exaltation of the risen One as Son of God. The calling of the nations is the focus of the commission given in Matthew's understanding of the appearance in Galilee.[55]

MATTHEW 28:1-10

Matthew's account of the events at the tomb includes a revision of the Markan story (28:1–8) and an appearance of Jesus to the women (vv. 9–10). The revision of Mark includes additional legendary and apologetic material in vv. 2–4. One also finds additional miraculous elements in the passage, which tend toward the type of narration of the resurrection that one finds in the *Gospel of Peter.*[56] Some of these details continue the apologetic defense against the charge that Jesus' disciples stole the body.[57]

Verse 1:

Matthew	Mark
Now after the Sabbath,	*And when the Sabbath was past,*
toward dawn on the first day of the week,	*Mary Magdalene, and Mary the mother of James, and Salome, brought spices to go and anoint him.*
Mary Magdalene and the other Mary went to see the sepulchre.	*And very early on the first day of the week they went to the tomb, when the sun had risen.*

Matthew has shortened Mark's introduction to the story. The formal sealing of the tomb and the posting of the guard make it impossible for him to retain the anointing of the body as a motive for their visit.

Consequently, Matthew has supplied another purpose, "they went to see the tomb," in v. 1b. He has also removed the discrepancies between the various Markan lists of the names of the women. The two women in his account are those named as disciples in 27:56, Mary Magdalene and the "other Mary," that is, the mother of the sons of Zebedee. They are present at the burial in Mt 27:61. Some scholars tie their visit to a later rabbinic tradition that held that a tomb should be watched for three days.[58] Matthew has also edited the Markan introduction to create a consistent pattern of temporal references.

Verse 2:

Matthew	Mark
And behold there was a great earthquake, for an angel of the Lord came down from heaven and came and rolled back the stone and sat on it.	*and looking up they saw that the stone was rolled back, for it was very large.* *. . . they saw a young man seated on the right.*

With this verse Matthew departs from Mark and returns to the apocalyptic images that were introduced into the crucifixion scene. The descent of the "angel of the Lord", the earthquake, the rolling away of the stone, all recall apocalyptic images. The earthquake refers directly back to the imagery of the crucifixion. At the same time, the quake and the opening of the tomb are not the moment of resurrection as they will become in the *Gospel of Peter.* [59] The elements of apocalyptic point forward to the appearance of the glorified Jesus in vv. 9–10.[60] Mark's account left the reader to conclude that the young man in the tomb was an angel and was responsible for removing the stone. Matthew has the women see the angelic visitation. He omits all reference to their concern about who will roll the stone back (Mk 16:3). Instead of being inside the tomb, the angel is seated on the stone. This shift also reflects the apologetic context of the narrative. The tomb is never open without witnesses. It was never left unguarded. Its being open is an act of God attested to by witnesses.

Verses 3 and 4:

Matthew	Mark
His appearance was like lightning,	
and his garments white as snow	*dressed in a white robe*
Out of fear of him, the guards trembled,	*and they were amazed*
and became like dead men.	

These verses continue the apocalyptic elements from the previous verse. The description of the angel follows typical patterns (as in Dan 10:6; 7:9; 1 En. 71.1). Fear is the expected consequence of such a visitation. The guards fall to the ground as though they were dead. Matthew has linked them to those who had seen the apocalyptic signs of the crucifixion by using the same word in 28:4, *terountes,* as he had for the associates of the centurion in 27:54. Thus, these details make it clear that the power of God has been responsible for all the events that have occurred. It has frustrated the human attempts to keep the crucified in the tomb. Later, the guards are responsible for spreading the story that the disciples had stolen the body (28:11–15). The lack of apocalyptic signs or angelic glory make the women's fear in the Markan story somewhat unclear. Matthew leaves no doubt that fear is the appropriate response to the signs that have occurred.

Verses 5–7:

Matthew	Mark
The angel said to the women, do not be afraid, for I know you seek Jesus who was crucified. He is not here, for he is risen as he said; Come, see the place where he lay. Then go quickly and tell his disciples, that he has risen from the dead, and behold, he is going before you to Galilee, there you will see him. Lo I have told you.	*He said to them do not be amazed. you seek Jesus of Nazareth who was crucified. He has risen; he is not here. see the place where they laid him. But go tell his disciples and Peter that he is going before you to Galilee, there you will see him as he told you.*

The angel's words to the women reformulate those in Mark. Matthew omits the destination "of Nazareth." This omission may be merely stylistic unless it was also absent from Matthew's source. He retains the Markan "Jesus of Nazareth" at 26:71 in dependence on Mk 14:67.[61] Just as Matthew made the figure at the tomb unmistakably an angel, so he attributes to the angel knowledge of the women's errand. He shifts the announcement of resurrection to the beginning of the angel's message. Thus, he makes it clear that Jesus is not in the tomb because he has been raised. With the earlier apologetic emphasis on the posting of the guard at the tomb, there can be no other explanation for the absence of Jesus' body. Matthew also sets the announcement of resurrection with the expression "as he said." That phrase, so troublesome in Mark's use of it for Jesus' going before the disciples to Galilee, now clearly refers back to the resurrection predictions (Mt 16:21; 17:23; 20:19). The priority of the message that Jesus has been raised is also evident in the commission to the women. They are to go quickly and announce that Jesus has risen. Thus, they are primarily messengers of the resurrection.[62]

This shift of emphasis makes the meeting in Galilee dependent on the angel's word rather than on Jesus' promise. However, Matthew has retained the promise of a meeting in Galilee in 26:32. Consequently, Bode thinks that the angelic "I have told you" should be seen as a prophetic speech pattern referring to Yahweh. However, one can just as easily presume that Matthew has shifted emphasis onto the angel because he has used the "as he told you" to emphasize the resurrection of Jesus. Further, if one takes the saying about Galilee as prophecy of the place where the risen Jesus appears, then the appearance to the women becomes awkward. Jesus himself is about to confirm the message that is to be taken to the disciples.[63]

Verse 8:

Matthew	Mark
And they departed quickly from the tomb with fear and great joy, and ran to tell his disciples.	*And they went out and fled from the tomb, for trembling and astonishment came on them and they told no one anything for they were afraid.*

Matthew is able to transform Mark's conclusion, since the element of fear belongs only to the angelic theophany. Otherwise, the women respond as those commissioned to announce the resurrection might be expected to do. They run away from the tomb because the angel had told them to go quickly.

Verses 9 and 10: *Jesus met them and said, "Hail!" They came; took hold of his feet and worshipped him. Then Jesus said to them, "Do not fear; go and tell my brothers to go to Galilee and there they will see me."*

The appearance of the risen Lord, which concludes Matthew's version of the tomb story, does not add anything to the angelic message. Since the story does not require any information beyond that in Mark, some scholars think that the whole may be a Matthean composition.[64] Unlike other appearance stories, including the appearance to Mary Magdalene at the tomb in John, this story lacks the element of nonrecognition. The women know immediately that it is Jesus and respond appropriately by worshiping him. The Johannine story (Jn 20:14–18) also has the Lord prohibit Mary from touching him, since he has not yet ascended to the Father. The typically Johannine character of that concern suggests that the evangelist may have modified a tradition in which the response to the appearance was to fall down in worship. Matthew also has the traditional element of reassurance that belongs to the angelophany traditions in the "do not fear." Therefore, it seems probable that Matthew reflects a tradition already in existence about an appearance of Jesus near the tomb. The Johannine version is an elaboration of an independent version of that tradition. Matthew may be responsible for the lack of "nonrecognition." The women react here exactly as the disciples do in Mt 28:17. They worship the Lord. In the latter instance, Matthew has preserved an element of nonrecognition by attaching "some doubted" to the notice of the disciples worshiping the Lord.[65]

The story provides a transition from Jerusalem to Galilee. At the same time, it shows that Matthew was aware of both Jerusalem and Galilee traditions about appearances of the risen Lord. The Johannine material shows the same double awareness. When the angel instructed the women to deliver the message, he sent them to Jesus' "disciples." Jesus now sends them to "my brothers." Some scholars have suggested that the shift is meant to indicate a new status that the disciples are to have as witnesses to Jesus, as the ones who will bring the nations to discipleship.[66] Again, the Johannine tradition contains a possible parallel. The farewell discourses, which often appear to be spoken by the glorified rather than the earthly Jesus, contain an explicit shift from the name "servants" to "friends" (15:11–17). This shift is occasioned by Jesus' impending death and glorification. It depends on their keeping what he has taught, loving one another, and bearing fruit. Thus, it is possible that the same tradition from which Matthew derives the story of the appearance at the tomb contained the tradition of a shift in the relationship between Jesus and his followers signified by a change in name.

This story, like the others of the risen Jesus, points beyond itself. The women must continue with the commission that they had received from the angel. Matthew interrupts the culmination of their mission with the story of the bribery of the guards (28:11–15). On the narrative level, that story fills in the time between the appearance to the women and that in Galilee. It also brings the apologetic motifs interwoven into the story to their conclusion. The false stories that are being circulated cannot hinder the true message about the Lord.

MATTHEW 28:16–20

Scholars have made various attempts to attach a genre to this section
of Matthew. Some have suggested that it belongs to a genre of divine
epiphanies. Some have pointed to the stories in which a hero is
translated into heaven, as in the case of Apollonius of Tyana.[67] Others
have attempted to find the Gattung of the passage in stories of the
calling of the Old Testament prophets. Commissioning during the
course of a theophany or angelophany is closer to the function of this
appearance story than are the hellenistic models. This story is not
concerned with the miraculous or heavenly existence of the hero. It
is focused on the mission that the risen Lord entrusts to his disciples.[68] However, Matthew's differences from each of the proposed
type of story are at least as great as his similarities. Consequently, it is
difficult to argue that he has taken over a well-established form of
story here.[69]

Others look at the patterns of Matthean composition in the passage.[70] The passage consists of a narrative framework (28:16–18a) and
three sayings (28:18b; 19–20a; 20b). Commentators are divided over
whether or not there is independent material in the sayings. Some
argue that Matthew has composed the entire section.[71] Whatever
traditional material Matthew may have employed, the story as we
have it has been thoroughly recast by the evangelist. The appearance
itself does not appear to be taken from a pre-Matthean source. Indeed, if Matthew is entirely responsible for the narrative introduction, then the story cannot be said to supply any information about
the appearance to the eleven beyond the fact of an appearance such
as we find in the kerygma of 1 Cor 15:5. Matthew need not be
dependent on a tradition like 1 Cor 15:5. He could have inferred the
existence of such an appearance from Mk 16:7.

We have seen that Matthew omitted "and Peter" from the angel's
instruction to the women. Matthew gives Peter primacy in the gospel
as spokesperson for the disciples, as guardian of Jesus' interpretation
of the Law, and as representative of the typical disciple, but he does
not place Peter above the others. He is firmly anchored within the
circle of disciples to whom the ministry of the post-Easter church is
entrusted.[72] One may even wonder if some scholars have gone too
far in pushing 1 Cor 15:5 to imply that the primacy Peter enjoyed

among the disciples was based on his rallying the others after his vision of the risen Lord.[73]

Matthew is unlike the appearance traditions of Luke and John in its restraint. There are no supernatural elements associated with Jesus' appearance or his actions. He does not appear and disappear suddenly or walk through closed doors. Those who see him do not report any peculiar sensations, as they do in Lk 24:32, for example. This restraint leads R. H. Fuller to argue that Matthew did not know any narrative tradition of Jesus' appearance. He composed his account from a "list type" of tradition. The three sayings can all be formulated on the basis of parallels elsewhere in the Jesus tradition.[74] Thus, even at a relatively late period, resurrection as an appearance of Jesus is not the conclusion to the life of Jesus. The emphasis remains on the resurrection as kerygma—as preached within the community.

Verses 16 and 17: *The eleven disciples went to Galilee to the mountain which Jesus had commanded them. And seeing him, they worshiped (him), but some doubted.*

Matthew has given his readers an account of the death of Judas (27:7–10). Here he corrects the tradition that the appearance was to "the twelve" by referring to the correct number of the remaining disciples as "the eleven." Since none of the predictions of resurrection refer to a mountain, Matthew has probably provided the location as well. Mountains appear several times in the Matthean narrative (4:8; 5:1; 8:11; 14:23; 15:29; 17:1, 9). However, the expression "which Jesus had commanded them" does not appear elsewhere in Matthew. Therefore, even scholars who think that Matthew has composed most of the episode presume that it reflects some form of pre-Matthean tradition.[75] The concluding phrase, "some doubted," also creates difficulties as Matthean composition. The verb for doubt, *distazo*, only occurs here and in Jesus' rebuke to the doubting disciples in Mt 14:31. There it appears coupled with the typically Matthean phrase "of little faith," *oligopiste*. Little faith is clearly a Matthean expression. It is always corrected—at least in part—by the teaching of Jesus that follows. J. D. Kingsbury points out that in 14:33, for example, we find the disciples worshiping Jesus and confessing that he is truly the Son of God.[76] While the phrase about those who doubted appears somewhat out of place, the combination of doubt and worship could be said to be Matthean. Further evidence of Matthew's composition is detected in the use of the verb *idon* plus an accusative or a dependent clause for the activity of seeing. This usage is characteristic of Matthew. The resurrection predictions, on the other hand, have the verb *opsesthai* for seeing. In short, there is very little evidence for non-Matthean language in this passage. Matthew does not seem to be dependent on a narrative of Jesus' appearance to his disciples. Instead, the introduction to the episode is cast in the general mold of other stories in the gospel that show the wavering uncertainty of Jesus' obedient followers.[77] Just as Mark has cast the women at the tomb in the mold of his picture of the disciples, so Matthew has continued a typical pattern.

Verse 18: *Jesus came and said to them, "All authority in heaven and on earth has been given to me."*

The introduction to the first saying is typical of Matthean composition. However, the saying itself appears to be derived from pre-Matthean tradition. Some interpreters see it as a reflection of Mt 11:27.[78] But there are no direct verbal parallels between the two. Mt 11:27 has "all things" *(panta)* and "delivered" *(paredothē)* and no mention of heaven and earth. Those who would claim that Matthew has used the earlier Q saying to formulate this one must explain why Matthew does not use *exousia* (authority) for the work of Jesus as Lord. The heaven/earth contrast would also appear to derive from pre-Matthean tradition. Other scholars trace the formulation of this passage back to the Son of Man image in Dan 7:14 (LXX). It provides the image of an everlasting authority over the nations of the earth. It also refers to the recognition of that authority by "all the peoples *(panta ta ethnē)."* Concern with extending Jesus' message to *panta ta ethnē* occurs in the next saying of this passage. Therefore, this saying, as well as the motifs of all the peoples and everlasting presence in the next verses, would appear to be associated with the tradition that identified the risen Jesus with the exalted Son of Man.[79] The resurrection/exaltation has reversed any limits to Jesus' authority. Matthew emphasizes the significance of that tradition for the disciples in the following verses. Though it is originally a christological claim about the risen Lord, it will become the foundation of Matthew's understanding of the post-Easter community.

Verses 19–20a: *Go, then, and make disciples of all the peoples, baptising them in the name of the Father, the Son and the Holy Spirit, teaching them to keep all the things which I have commanded you.*

The three commands that make up the commission to the disciples remove limitations that had existed during the ministry of Jesus. The limitation to Israel (10:5–6; 15:24) is replaced by the mission to "all the peoples." Circumcision as the sign of belonging is replaced by baptism. The Torah is replaced by what Jesus had taught.[80] This passage is the earliest example of a triadic baptismal formula, which was more commonly carried out "in the name of Jesus." In placing Jesus on the same plane as the Father and the Holy Spirit, this formula goes beyond the usual christological images of the gospel. The association of baptism and resurrection must also be traditional (cf. Ac 2:38).[81] Scholars are divided over the range of meaning that should be given to the expression "all the peoples." Most interpreters presume that Matthew is using the word *ethnē* (peoples) to mean the Gentiles as opposed to the Jews. Therefore, this commission represents a definite command to move beyond the confines of Judaism. This position is strengthened by S. Brown's analysis of Matthew. He argues that the gospel has been composed to defend the mission to the Gentiles. He sees the Matthean church at an impasse. It must decide whether to continue with a failing mission to convert Israel or to expand its efforts toward the Gentiles. Matthew is arguing for the latter.[82] Thus, this formulation of the resurrection commission is designed to invoke the authority of the exalted Lord in legitimating the move toward Gentile mission. Meier, on the other hand, argues that Matthew does not use the expression *ethnē* with the sense of Gentiles as opposed to Jews. He points to the general sense that it has in the Daniel passage, all the nations or peoples of the earth whether Jew or Gentile.[83] Other scholars dispute that view. They point to parallels in the judgment scenes of Jewish apocalypses in which *ethnē* (the nations) clearly refers to the judgment of the Gentiles. Thus, they argue the context of this passage would presume that sense of the word.[84]

Whichever view one takes about the significance of *ethnē*, the commission does mandate a universal mission. The expression "make disciples" is typically Matthean (13:52; 27:57). This mission is grounded in the universal sovereignty attributed to the risen and exalted Jesus. It seems likely that the pre-Matthean tradition associated resurrection with Jesus' exaltation to a universal sovereignty over all the nations, using the expression *ethnē* in the general sense that Meier suggests. However, we have already seen that Matthew adds apocalyptic images to the crucifixion scene so that it represents the turn in the ages. Those scholars who argue that *ethnē* in its present context refers to the Gentiles are invoking another apocalyptic motif, the coming of the Gentiles, whether in conversion or judgment after the messianic visitation of Israel. Matthew's understanding of that tradition would appear to be reflected in this passage.

Jesus' exaltation to universal lordship mandates his disciples' preaching to all the peoples, that is, it includes the Gentiles.

Verse 20b: *And lo, I am with you always until the end of the age.*

This pericope, and the gospel as a whole, concludes with a saying of reassurance. It recalls the elements of permanent authority that we found in Dan 7:14. The abiding rule of the Son of Man is expressed in Jesus' permanent presence with his disciples. The connection between this promise and the Son of Man tradition leads some interpreters to describe it as a "proleptic parousia." Jesus' presence answers the dilemma created by the delay in the parousia. Thus, Meier suggests that this passage represents the answer to the oracle at the Sanhedrin trial (27:64) that Jesus' opponents would see the Son of Man enthroned.[85] The Lukan and Johannine traditions have similar promises of abiding presence. For Luke, the Holy Spirit fills that role in the community; for John, it is Jesus' presence in the Paraclete. Matthew's gospel contains two other promises of abiding divine presence: the Emmanuel prophecy in Mt 1:23 and the presence of Jesus to the assembled community in Mt 18:20.[86] The initial setting of such traditions appears to have been the assembly for worship. These assemblies also appear to have been the occasion for Christian prophecy in which the prophet speaks the Word of the exalted Lord.[87] This saying, as well as the pre-Matthean form of the previous commissioning, may have originated in such a context. It reflects the liturgical tradition embodied in the *"Marana tha"* ("Come, Lord") prayer (1 Cor 16:22; Rev 22:20). The presence of the Lord in the Christian assembly is seen as an anticipation of his future coming.

This pericope is not an appearance story as such. There is no description of the risen Jesus. Nor do we find any indication of the departure of the revealer. From the standpoint of Matthew's narrative Jesus is now permanently present to the community. That presence is grounded in traditions of Christian apocalyptic and prophecy that see the resurrection as Jesus' exaltation over the nations. That exaltation is the culmination of the turning point in the story of salvation that Matthew presents as beginning at the crucifixion. However, the allusions to Daniel in the sayings are the only apocalyptic images in this story. They are not attached to the narrative context of the story that speaks only of Jesus without any associated apocalyptic images. If the three logia originated in the words of early Christian prophets, then the Daniel allusions probably belong to their pre-Matthean form. Matthew has combined and adapted the sayings to provide the final commissioning as conclusion to the story of Jesus.

Jesus' authority and teaching are to be extended to all the nations through the mission of his disciples. That expansion is grounded in his entry into messianic glory.

In both instances in which Matthew speaks of appearances, then, he does not presuppose any narrative of such appearances. The details that he supplies could often be his own additions on the basis of narrative presuppositions that are evident elsewhere in the gospel: an angelophany or a Christophany occasions an element of fear (14:27, 30); the reaction of the disciple to such an event is a composite of doubt and worship (14:31, 33). Jesus appears as the One whose presence reassures his disciples. Matthew's appearance stories are formed by the sayings that provide their content. The appearance to the women at the tomb repeats their angelic commission and thus also refers back to the kerygma. The appearance to the disciples also represents a commission, this time one of preaching to the nations. It is formed of a series of three sayings. The first is a different form of the kerygma in which what follows on Jesus' death is his exaltation as Son of Man. Exaltation provides the cosmic sovereignty by which the teaching of Jesus is to be expanded to all the nations through the mission of the disciples that is to continue until the end of the age.

Neither Matthew nor Mark associate any narrative with the resurrection as such. This lack of narrative might appear to be in tension with the element of "seeing the Lord" implied in the resurrection kerygma and in promises like that of Mk 16:7. It is sometimes held, as we have seen, that the visionary elements of the resurrection traditions have been repressed and relocated in the earthly life of Jesus; that the Transfiguration represents such a resurrection vision. However, if we take the *Sitz im Leben* of inspired prophecy in the assembly seriously, we must reevaluate our own presuppositions about the primacy of the visionary as access to reality. W. Kelber has recently argued that the writing of Mark's gospel represents a radical discontinuity in the religious world of early Christianity. It reflects a shift out of the world of oral communication, immediacy, and prophetic presence to the world of textuality in which one becomes aware of the distance between oneself and the subject about which one speaks. Only in that world does the crucifixion achieve its central character as a paradox. Only through the distancing mediation of text can we see the disciples as something less than heroic, as struggling believers in a crucified Son of Man. For the oral modes of religious consciousness, on the other hand, the Lord is present as risen, exalted in the powerful words of the Christian prophets and the other signs of the Spirit's power, such as healing, active through Jesus' disciples.[88]

The transition to textuality brings with it a fundamental shift in the consciousness of the "real." For those whose perceptions are shaped by texts, the real is represented by the world of visual objects. For those whose perceptions are shaped by the experiences of an oral world, the real is represented by what is heard. The Lord is risen and present because he speaks. This perception accords with the early traditions of resurrection that we find in the New Testament. They are auditory and not visionary. The speaking, whether in prophecy or in kerygmatic proclamation, is what counts. This observation does not deny that visionary elements are associated with the proclamation of resurrection. But it suggests that those elements were not of primary significance in establishing the reality of the resurrection and hence were not transmitted as part of the message from the beginning. What counts is the testimony that the Lord is risen and that what has been heard is the divine Word of commissioning and presence. The conclusion of the Markan gospel is more ambiguous in this regard than that of Matthew, since Mark ends with a striking image of Jesus' absence and only the promise of a renewed presence. We have seen that the mode of that renewal is itself ambiguous, since it might refer to the parousia rather than to a manifestation of the risen Lord. Matthew, on the other hand, resolves the Markan ambiguity in favor of the presence that is mediated through the Word of Jesus. At the same time, he appears to envisage that word as the one set down in the gospel and interpreted by the disciples rather than as Jesus' continued speech through Christian prophets.

The study of Mark and Matthew, then, suggests three sources of primitive resurrection traditions behind the gospel narratives. One finds the kerygmatic tradition like that reflected in 1 Cor 15:3–5. One finds an old tradition about the finding of Jesus' empty tomb by some women disciples. This tradition is interpreted by the resurrection kerygma. And one finds Christian prophets who speak in the name of the Lord, proclaiming his messianic exaltation. Matthew's narrative shows the tendency to "fill out" the narrative with details and images drawn from apocalyptic descriptions of judgment. However, such images have not been applied to the description of the risen Lord. He continues to appear simply as the one about whom the story has just been told, as Jesus.

NOTES

1. See R. Mahoney, *Two Disciples at the Tomb. The Background and Message of Jn. 20.1–10* (Theologie und Wirklichkeit 6; Frankfort: Peter Lang, 1974), 158–60. Mahoney rejects the view that one can recover a historical nucleus to the tomb story. He sees the passage as an "independent legendary apophthegm." While Mahoney may have identified the best form critical category for the story as it has come down to us, he does not attend to the anomalous character of resurrection language in connection with the life of a single individual. Consequently, even the historian is pressed to ask what sort of events may have led to the use of such language.

2. For an extensive survey of the attempts to reconstruct a *Vorlage* for Mk 16:1–8, see F. Neirynck, "Marc 16, 1–8 tradition et rédaction," *Ephimerides Theologicae Lovanienses* 56 (1980), 56–88.

3. C. H. Dodd, "The Appearances of the Risen Christ: An Essay in Form Criticism of the Gospels," *Studies in the Gospels* (R. H. Lightfoot volume; D. E. Nineham, ed.; Oxford: Oxford University, 1957), 9–35.

4. Thus, one might insist that the description of the form of the stories must proceed from comparison with story types known to the tellers and not by induction from the texts themselves. This approach is taken by B. Hubbard *(The Matthean Redaction of a Primitive Apostolic Commissioning* [Missoula, Mont.: Scholars, 1974]) in using Old Testament commissioning stories to reconstruct a commissioning genre behind the Matthean appearance story.

5. H. Grass, *Ostergeschehen und Osterberichte* (Göttingen: Vandenhoeck & Ruprecht, 1970, 4th ed.). J. E. Alsup *(The Post-Resurrection Appearance Stories of the Gospel Tradition. A History-of-Tradition Analysis* [Calwer theologishe Monographien 5; London: SPCK, 1975], 32–36) criticizes Grass for assuming that a "light appearance" is the type of appearance to Paul and is normative for the tradition generally. He points to the "human appearance" as an equally ancient type. The same priority is accorded to the "light appearance" in J. M. Robinson, "Jesus:

From Easter to Valentinus (or to the Apostles' Creed)," *JBL* 101 (1982), 5–37. Alsup's emphasis on the "human appearance" must also be taken in relation to the narrative context in which these stories occur. They reflect the culmination of the story of a human being as they are presently used in the gospel. Thus, quite without presupposing any desire of the evangelists to oppose a "gnosticizing" light type of story (as Robinson does, for example), the "human appearance" story could be seen to develop with the gospel genre.

6. Wilckens ("The Tradition History of the Resurrection of Jesus," *The Significance of the Message of the Resurrection for Faith in Jesus Christ* [ed. C. F. D. Moule; SBT ser. 2, no. 8; London: SCM, 1968], 69) thinks that the form of vision known to the disciples was dictated by the apocalyptic traditions with which they were familiar. This prior knowledge was fundamental to their understanding of the experience as the revelation of a hidden eschatological mystery. However, the appearance stories do not present us with the full trappings of such an apocalyptic scene. Neither the angel nor Jesus function as an apocalyptic revealer. They do not reveal any secret teaching. Both these functions are supplied in the second-century Gnostic elaboration on the revelation genre.

7. R. Pesch, *Das Markusevangelium. II Teil. Kommentar zu Kap. 8, 27–16, 20* (HTKNT II/2; Freiburg: Herder, 1977), 518–20. Earlier materials in the passion narrative that are picked up in the tomb story are: (a) list of women, 15:40/16:1; (b) indication of time, early *(proi)*, 15:1, 25, 33f.; 14:7; (c) use of the verb *theoreō* (to see), 15:40; (d) the expression Nazarene, 10:47; 14:67/16:6; (e) "the crucified," 15:13–15, 20, 24, 25, 27; 14:28/16:6; (f) the angel, 14:28/16:7; (g) flight of the disciples, 10:32; 16:8. See also U. Wilckens, *Auferstehung. Das biblische Auferstehungszeugnis untersucht und erklärt* (Themen der Theologie, 4; Stuttgart/Berlin: Krenz, 1970), 59–64. Mahoney (op. cit., 142) does not find these parallels significant.

8. See A. Lindemann, "Die Osterbotschaft des Markus. Zur Theologischen Interpretation von Mk 16.1–8," *New Testament Studies* 26 (1979/80), 301f.

9. See the summary of the arguments about vv. 5 and 6 in Neirynck (op. cit., 56–62).

10. Ibid., 62–64; and on the position of the angel within the theophany, 72–75.

11. The apocalyptic elements in the scene are more evident in Matthew's version; see the list in Pesch (op. cit., 521–24). Pesch notes

that the elements of apocalyptic make this story different from other parts of the passion tradition, which are more directly narrative. It is the apocalyptic elements that give the story its character as "legend." Those who emphasize the apocalyptic background to the tomb story lay great emphasis on the angelophany; see Neirynck (op. cit., 76–83).

12. J. D. Crossan ("Empty Tomb and Absent Lord (Mark 16:1–8)," *The Passion in Mark* [ed. W. Kelber; Philadelphia: Fortress, 1976], 136–45) points to the inability of scholars to reach any consensus about a pre-Markan passion narrative as evidence that such a tradition is lacking. T. E. Boomershine ("Mark 16:8 and the Apostolic Commission," *Journal of Biblical Literature* 100 [1981], 226, note 4) points to the lack of unambiguous signs of history of development in this passage.

13. Pesch (op. cit., 520) acknowledges these arguments by introducing his discussion of the passage with an elaborate argument that aims to show that the temporal arrangements in it are merely a way of indicating that something new is occurring. Literary analyses have pointed to double time markers as a feature of Mark's narrative technique. D. Rhoads and D. Michie *(Mark as Story* [Philadelphia: Fortress, 1982], 47f.) identify this feature as part of a "two step" progression technique that is typical of Mark. The second step is always a clarification of the first. Though one can argue that this passage does fit that pattern, one is still left with the problem of the pileup of temporal markers in this passage.

14. J. Kremer, "Zur Diskussion über 'das leere Grab,' " *Resurrexit. Actes du symposium international sur la résurrection de Jésus* (ed. E. Dhanis; Rome: Libreria Editrice Vaticana, 1974), 152–54.

15. J. Delorme, "The Resurrection and Jesus' Tomb: Mark 16, 1–8 in the Gospel Tradition," *The Resurrection and Modern Biblical Thought* (ed. P. De Surgy; New York/Cleveland: Corpus, 1970), 83–85. Delorme suggests that varied influences were mediated through the tradition of the preaching of the community and contributed to shaping these traditions.

16. Kremer, op. cit., 151. Also Delorme, op. cit., 81. Pesch (op. cit., 540) does not agree with this analysis.

17. R. H. Fuller, *The Formation of the Resurrection Narratives* (New York: Macmillan, 1971), 61, 67f.; Lindemann, op. cit., 308f.

18. R. Mahoney, *Two Disciples at the Tomb. The Background and Message of Jn 20.1–10* (Theologie und Wirklichkeit 6; Frankfort: Peter Lang, 1974), 143. Pesch (op. cit., 529), who does not think that this feature is redactional.

19. See Fuller, op. cit., 56. Fuller suggests that the earliest tradition

may have had Mary Magdalene alone as the one who discovers the tomb. See also P. Benoit, "Marie Madeleine et les disciples au tombeau selon Jean 20, 1–18," *Judentum, Urchristentum, Kirche* (BZNW 26; ed. W. Eltester; Festschrift für J. Jeremias; Berlin: Töpelmann, 1964, 2nd ed.), 150f.; R. E. Brown *(The Gospel According to John XIII–XXI* [AnBi 29A; Garden City, N.Y.: Doubleday, 1970], 999) thinks that the Johannine tradition had several women come to the tomb. He points to the plural verb in v. 2 as further confirmation for that view.

20. Mahoney, op. cit., 144; he is following L. Schenke, *Auferstehungsverkundigung und leeres Grab. Eine traditionsgeschichtliche Untersuchung von Mk 16, 1–8* (SBS 33; Stuttgart: Katholisches Bibelwerke: 1969, 2nd ed.), 28, 36.

21. See Mahoney, op. cit., 105–109. If the original tradition gave no names, then one might adopt the view held by Wilckens that the names have been added in v. 1 and that they have deliberately been changed from those in 15:47 in order to separate this episode from the burial (ibid., 57f.).

22. Mahoney, op. cit., 144. Mahoney correctly challenges Schenke's view (op. cit., 35–37) that the anointing has been introduced in order to complete the burial because 15:46 had not mentioned anointing. He points out that there is no indication that something is amiss in the passage itself.

23. Kremer, op. cit., 152; Pesch (op. cit., 530), who thinks that the whole section is tradition, finds the anointing subservient to the preaching of the resurrection of Jesus.

24. Mahoney, op. cit., 144.

25. See the catalog of opinions in E. L. Bode, *The First Easter Morning: The Gospel Accounts of the Women's Visit to the Tomb of Jesus* (Rome: Biblical Institute Press, 1970), 6–11. Bode (p. 11) thinks that the phrase specifies "very early." We see no reason to think that the expression refers to dawn services held at the tomb, as Schenke suggests (op. cit., 62f.), or that "sun" is symbolic of Jesus, as Kremer *(Osterbotschaft,* 16) holds. See also the reservations expressed by Pesch, op. cit., 531; J. Kremer, "Zur Diskussion über 'das leere Grab,'" in E. Dhanis, ed., *Resurrexit,* 152. Mahoney (op. cit., 146) finds it impossible to decide whether both expressions belong to Mark or to pre-Markan tradition.

26. Pesch, op. cit., 530.

27. Kremer, "Diskussion," 152.

28. Hence, some scholars like Kremer ("Diskussion," 153) excise both from the original story. Others suggest that the original lacked the angelic theophany in vv. 5–7 but did contain the

miraculous opening of the tomb and the women leaving perplexed; see F. Schnider and W. Sterner, *Die Ostergeschichten der Evangelien* (Schriften zur Katechetik, 13; Munich: Kösel, 1970), 22–29. Mahoney (op. cit., 146f.) argues that the whole section is constructed to lead up to the greater discovery in v. 5.

29. Pesch, op. cit., 531. The irony of the search for a "helper" works better as an element of Mark's narrative technique. Mark consistently portrays the ironic reversal of the expectations of the actors. Thus, the reader comes to participate in the narrator's perspective; see the discussion of irony in D. Rhoads and D. Michie, *Mark as Story* (Philadelphia: Fortress, 1982), 59–61.

30. R. Scroggs and K. J. Groff, "Baptism in Mark: Dying and Rising with Christ," *Journal of Biblical Literature* 92 (1973), 540–43.

31. Pesch, op. cit., 532; Bode, op. cit., 26; M. Gourgues, "À propos du symbolisme christologique et baptismal de Marc 16.5," *New Testament Studies* 27 (1980/81), 672–78.

32. For angels as young men see 2 Macc 3:26, 33–34; Josephus, *Ant.* v. 8.2. White clothing as a sign of angelic status appears in Dan 7:9; Rev. 3:4f., as well as in the Markan Transfiguration story, (9:3); see Bode, op. cit., 27; Pesch, op. cit., 532; Mahoney, op. cit., 149; V. Taylor, *The Gospel According to St. Mark* (New York: St. Martin's, 1952), 606.

33. Pesch, op. cit., 532; see the study of this motif in R. H. Lightfoot, *The Gospel Message of St. Mark* (Oxford: Oxford University, 1950), 86–88.

34. Delorme, op. cit., 86; Bode, op. cit., 29.

35. L. Schenke, op. cit., 74; Taylor, op. cit., 607; Mahoney, op. cit., 149, note 38.

36. This view has also been advanced by G. Schille, "Das Leiden des Herrn: Die evangelische Passionstradition und ihr Sitz im Leben," *Zeitschrift für Theologie und Kirche* 52 (1955), 161–205. If the tradition belonged to an annual festival held only in Jerusalem, one would not expect the elements of commissioning or even an appearance of Jesus. Those who defend the veneration of Jesus' tomb as the *Sitz im Leben* for this tradition point to the interest in the tombs of the patriarchs and of the Maccabean martyrs. For the Maccabees at Modin, see Josephus *Ant.* 13.21; for Herod's monument built near that of David, *Ant.* 16.16. The existence of another monument over that of the patriarchs at Hebron (Josephus, *War* 4.532) suggests that the tombs of the patriarchs were important places of veneration, as does the Q logion in Lk 11:47–48/Mt 23:29–31. On the tomb as the place of veneration, see also IV Macc. 17.8–10.

37. Lindemann (loc. cit.) suggests that 5b and 6a were the original elements of the story that led to the conclusion in v. 8.
38. T. Weeden, *Mark. Traditions in Conflict* (Philadelphia: Fortress, 1971), 111–16. N. Q. Hamilton ("Resurrection Tradition and the Composition of Mark," *Journal of Biblical Literature* 84 [1965], 415–21) reverses the view of the parousia character of v. 7. He suggests that Mark wishes to counter false expectations of the parousia that had been raised by the resurrection, and so he constructed the story to focus on Jesus' absence. Verse 7 establishes the continuity between the ministry of Jesus and the passion/resurrection.
39. Fuller, op. cit., 60–69; Bode, op. cit., 31–36.
40. Bode (op. cit., 310) rightly emphasizes the parallel with Mk 10:32 in the use of *proagein*. See also Mahoney, op. cit., 154f.; Fuller, op. cit., 61. On Galilee as the place of mission in Mark, see Fuller, op. cit., 58–60, 67f.
41. Delorme, op. cit., 92. Fuller (op. cit., 66) points out that this reference need only be to a kerygmatic tradition. There is no indication that appearance stories as such are involved; see also Pesch, op. cit., 534.
42. Fuller, op. cit., 69; Bode, op. cit., 31; Rhoads and Michie, op. cit., 99.
43. Rhoads and Michie, op. cit., 122–29.
44. Bode, op. cit., 37; Pesch, op. cit., 535; Lindemann, op. cit., 31; Schenke, op. cit., 47.
45. E.g., 1 Cor 2:3; Phil 2:12; Eph 6:5.
46. See Pesch, op. cit., 535; Lightfoot (op. cit., 92) rejects the suggestion that Mark had any ulterior motive in presenting the women as silent. For the theories that the flight and silence of the women represent repression of their original function as witnesses to the resurrection, see Neirynck, op. cit., 72. Grass (op. cit., 22) solves the problem by referring to the view that women were not competent witnesses in antiquity.
47. Pesch, op. cit., 540; Fuller, op. cit., 69; Bode, op. cit., 48; Evans, op. cit., 81; see also T. E. Boomershine and G. L. Bartholomew, "The Narrative Technique of Mk 16:8," *Journal of Biblical Literature* 100 (1981), 214–22; and R. Tannehill, "The Gospel of Mark as Narrative Christology," *Semeia* 16 (1979) 83f.
48. Rhoads and Michie (op. cit., 99) argue that Mark deliberately leaves an aborted message at the end to warn Christians that when the Kingdom is established in power, they will be judged in terms of their behavior.

49. Boomershine, "Commission," 231–38. Boomershine argues that the women flee because of what the commission implies.

50. Alsup, op. cit., 212–13; X. Leon-Dufour, "The Appearances of the Risen Lord and Hermeneutics," *The Resurrection and Modern Biblical Thought* (ed. P. De Surgy; New York/Cleveland: Corpus, 1970), 123f.

51. J. Meier, *The Vision of Matthew* (New York: Paulist, 1979), 207.

52. D. Senior, "The Death of Jesus and the Resurrection of the Holy Ones (Mt 27:51–53)," *Catholic Biblical Quarterly* 38 (1976), 320–26. Pesch's account of the pre-Markan passion narrative presumes that the "deep structure" of the story of the righteous sufferer would have demanded that the story conclude with an element of resurrection and consequently that the tomb story belonged to that pre-Markan tradition. We have already seen that the connection between the two traditions does not work as well as Pesch's thesis requires. Matthew, on the other hand, does give indications that he is consciously using the apocalyptic pattern of vindication. Further, his additions to the passion narrative of Mark suggest that he did not find that tradition already represented in Mark. See also C. F. Evans, *Resurrection and the New Testament* (SBT ser. 2, no. 12; London: SCM, 1970), 82; Meier, op. cit., 205; Bode, op. cit., 51.

53. Senior, op. cit., 326–28. Senior argues (p. 321) that this passage is not a transposed resurrection epiphany. It was not created to provide proof for Jesus' resurrection.

54. Meier, op. cit., 205.

55. J. D. Kingsbury, "The Composition and Christology of Mt 28:16–20," *Journal of Biblical Literature* 93 (1974), 580–83.

56. See Grass, op. cit., 22–27. In the *Gospel of Peter* (ix, 35ff.), the quake and the opening of the tomb occur in the middle of the night. Matthew has them coincide with the women's arrival in the early morning.

57. Fuller (op. cit., 72–73) observes that the accusation "deceiver" in vv. 63f. was not directed against the historical Jesus. Therefore, the opposition that inspired this apologetic must be aimed at early Christian preaching of Jesus as Messiah. The request for guards shows that the original story was of a friendly burial; otherwise, there would have been no need to make a request that the tomb be guarded. This polemic presumes that the allegation of fraud in the tomb story would silence claims that Christians make for Jesus. Thus, it suggests that the empty tomb had come to play a role in the kerygma.

58. T. R. W. Longstaff ("The Women at the Tomb," *New Testament*

Studies 27 [1980/81], 278–81) refers to Semahot 8.1, though he admits that the date of the passage is disputed. He argues that the regulation is early because it presumes cave burial and the presence of lamps in the tombs, both features of first-century C.E. burials. Therefore, he argues, the women are fulfilling an obligation that would be familiar to Matthew's Jewish audience. Their visit on the third day would confirm the death of Jesus. Longstaff goes beyond any textual evidence to assert that Matthew created this scene as an ironic counterpart to a guard over the tomb that would prohibit the women from fulfilling their pious obligations—a guard set by those who should be most concerned to see such an obligation fulfilled.

59. The angel of the Lord appears only here and in the infancy narratives (Bode, op. cit., 50). *Gospel of Peter* turns the rolling away of the stone into the moment at which Jesus emerges from the tomb (Evans, op. cit., 82; Meier, op. cit., 208).

60. See. H. W. Bartsch, *Das Auferstehungszeugnis. Sein historisches und sein theologisches Problem* (Hamburg: Herbert Reich, 1965), 12.

61. Matthew explicitly attaches the epithet "Nazaraios" to the prophecy from Is 11:1 in 2:23. These are the only references to Jesus' origins as from Nazareth in Mt. The expression appears more frequently in Acts. It is part of the kerygmatic speeches (2:22; 3:6; 4:10; 6:14). One of the appearances to Paul has Jesus identify himself as *"Iēsou Christou tou Nazoraiou"* Ac 22:8. And it is used as a designation of Jesus in Ac 26:9. Thus, the expression may have belonged to some forms of the kerygma.

62. Bode, op. cit., 53–54; Fuller, op. cit., 77; Evans, op. cit., 83–87.

63. Bode, op. cit., 53f. The angel omits the reference to Peter. Fuller (op. cit., 76) suggests that Matthew did not know any story of an appearance to Peter apart from that to the eleven.

64. See F. Neirynck, "Les femmes au tombeau," *New Testament Studies* 15 (1968/69), 170–90.

65. Bode (op. cit., 55f.) sees this tradition as both a doublet of the angelic announcement and as a confirmation of it. Fuller (op. cit., 78f.) argues for dependence on pre-Matthean tradition on the basis of the Johannine parallels. See also Grass, op. cit., 27f., on this point.

66. W. Trilling, *Das Wahre Israel* (Munich: Kösel, 1964), 29–31.

67. See Alsup, op. cit., 214–39.

68. Hubbard (op. cit., 91–103) argues that the following pattern underlies this section: introduction (v. 16); confrontation (v. 17a); reaction (v. 17b); commission (vv. 19–20a); reassurance (v. 20b).

Alsup (op. cit., 239–65) presents a variant on the suggestion that Old Testament theophany and commissioning traditions are behind the appearance stories.

69. See the discussion in J. Meier, *Matthew* (Wilmington: Glazier, 1980), 416–23. Meier agrees that the best description one could give of the overall genre of the passage lies in the direction of Old Testament theophany traditions. The story of the opening of the tomb uses some elements from apocalyptic visions of the divine theophany.

70. H. Schieber, "Konzentrik im Matthäusschluss. Ein form- und gattungskritischer Versuch zu Mt 28, 16–20," *Kairos* 19 (1977), 286–307. Schieber sees a concentric pattern typical of Matthean composition (cf. Mt 6:25–34; 19:16–22) in this passage: A = 18b; B = 19a; C = 19b; B' = 20a; A' = 20b. The case for Matthean composition of the whole pericope on the basis of Mt 11:27 has been argued by J. Lange, *Das Erscheinen des Auferstandenen im Evangelium nach Matthäus. Eine traditions- und redactionsgeschichtliche Untersuchung zu Mt 28, 16–20* (Würzburg: Echter, 1973).

71. Interpreters who argue in favor of traditional material behind this passage point to independent logia in 18b, 19–20a, and 20b. See G. Bornkamm, "Der Auferstandene und der Irdische. Mt 28, 16–20," *Zeit und Geschichte* (ed. E. Dinkler; Tübingen: J. C. B. Mohr, 1964), 173; Grass, op. cit., 30–31; Meier, *Matthew*, 407f. Evans argues (op. cit., 90) that the passage is almost entirely Matthew's composition, since it lacks significant non-Matthean vocabulary. The emphasis on Jesus' teaching is also characteristic of the evangelist. J. D. Kingsbury (op. cit., 573–79) also thinks that the language and style of the whole section speak against any use of tradition here.

72. See the detailed argument of J. D. Kingsbury, "The Figure of Peter in Matthew's Gospel as a Theological Problem," *Journal of Biblical Literature* 98 (1979), 72–74.

73. It is equally difficult to draw clear distinctions between the missionary and church-founding appearance traditions. Fuller (op. cit., 80) tries to use the distinction to argue for Matthew's independence of 1 Cor 15:5. He considers the latter a church-founding tradition and hence not the source for the mission-inaugurating appearance in Mt 28. However, we do not know how the appearance to Peter functioned. Paul's image of resurrection calling as the basis for apostleship may be as true of the Petrine experience as of his own.

74. Fuller, op. cit., 81f.

75. Kingsbury, "Composition," 575–79; Meier, op. cit., 409.
76. Kingsbury, "Composition," 581; Meier, loc. cit.; C. H. Giblin, "Structural and Thematic Correlations in the Matthean Burial and Resurrection Narratives," *New Testament Studies* 21 (1974/75), 406–20.
77. Meier, *Vision*. Mt 14:31–33 makes a similar correction of Matthew's Markan source. The Markan disciples (6:52) are said to have "hardened hearts," which Matthew changes to being of "little faith."
78. Kingsbury, "Composition," 581. Kingsbury denies all ties with Son of Man imagery in this passage, since he wishes to see it as the conclusion of the Son of God Christology that he finds as the structuring principle in Matthew.
79. Fuller (op. cit., 83) points out that Matthew's own Christology is that of the "Son" and not the Son of Man. If the saying is an allusion to the Son of Man, then it must derive from pre-Matthean tradition.
80. Use of a baptismal formula would fit with other elements of liturgical editing in Matthew's gospel (e.g., Mt 6:9–13). See G. Strecker *(Der Weg der Gerechtigkeit* [Göttingen: Vandenhoeck & Ruprecht, 1971], 208–14), who thinks that this passage is a catena of traditional logia.
81. Meier, *Vision*, 213. In addition the link between forgiveness and resurrection found in Lk 24:47 and Jn 20:23 fits most naturally into the baptismal context; Fuller, op. cit., 85–87.
82. S. Brown, "The Matthean Community and the Gentile Mission," *Novum Testamentum* 22 (1980), 193–221.
83. J. Meier, "Nations or Gentiles in Matthew 28:19," *Catholic Biblical Quarterly* 39 (1977), 94–102. See the opposing view defended by D. A. Hare and D. J. Harrington, "Make Disciples of All the Gentiles (Matthew 28:19)," *Catholic Biblical Quarterly* 37 (1975), 359–69. We find S. Brown's redaction critical study of the gospel as a whole decisive in terms of establishing Matthew's understanding of *ethnē* to be "Gentiles."
84. Evans, op. cit., 91f.
85. Meier, *Vision*, 192; 215 note 206.
86. Meier, *Vision*, 216; Kingsbury, "Composition," 581; Fuller, op. cit., 89f.
87. M. E. Boring, *Sayings of the Risen Jesus* (SNTS Monograph Ser. 46; Cambridge: Cambridge University, 1982), 195–229.
88. W. Kelber, *The Oral and the Written Gospel* (Philadelphia: Fortress, 1983), 44–80.

FIVE

Resurrection in the Gospels: Luke and John

Both Luke and John move well beyond the concise treatment of resurrection that we find in Matthew. Both develop a tradition of appearances in Jerusalem. Jn 21 also contains a Galilean appearance that we have seen contains parallels to the story of the calling of the disciples in Lk 5:1–11. Both traditions also have an appearance to the disciples at a meal (Lk 24:36–43; Jn 20:19–23). Recognition of Jesus in the breaking of the bread at Emmaus (Lk 24:41–42) has been compared to the meal recognition in the fish of Jn 21:9–14. Such parallels suggest a common development of tradition behind the stories as they have come to the evangelist.[1] Each author has further developed these traditions so that they fit his understanding of resurrection and the ongoing life of the community.

These resurrection stories also reflect the developing christological traditions of their various communities. We have seen such development in the Matthean picture of Jesus' authoritative rule and teaching. Both Luke and John are conscious of the need to understand how this absent Jesus remains present to the community. They both emphasize a tradition that linked resurrection to the opening up of the Old Testament prophecies to christological interpretation. After the resurrection it becomes possible to understand Jesus as the fulfillment of those promises. This understanding extends the presence of Jesus back to the past promises of salvation as well as forward to the experience of the community.

Narrating resurrection appearances leads both evangelists to a more physical description of the risen One. The bodily identification of the risen Christ with the crucified Jesus is demonstrated. Some scholars think that it was necessary to distinguish resurrection from the *apotheosis* of semidivine figures like Hercules or the emperor.[2] Others argue that the Lukan emphasis on the physical reality of the risen One has its grounding in his narrative. He has presented the life of Jesus as the tragedy of an innocent victim. By showing the resurrection in solid, bodily form, Luke assures his reader that divine goodness has triumphed.[3] The ascension images in Luke appear to use as models those stories in which the hero is snatched up into heaven. Such figures included Enoch and Elijah in the Old Testament (Gen 5:24; 2 Ki 2:9–11; 1 Macc 2:58; Deut 34:5f., Moses). Apocalyptic revelations had the seers snatched up to heaven for their revelations—often prior to the death of the seer. Paul speaks of Christians who are alive at the Second Coming being "snatched up" to meet the Lord (1 Thess 4:17). In the hellenistic world there were similar stories of people being snatched up and then even appearing later to their followers. Chariton's novel *Chaerea et Callirohe*, iii, has the heroine snatched from her tomb. The philosopher Apollonius of Tyana is also said to have been snatched up to heaven. Similarly, legend held that the companions of Romulus returned to the city rejoicing after witnessing his *apotheosis*. In addition, as we have seen, such images were often used of the deceased emperor. Thus, the general image of Jesus' being taken up into heaven would be familiar to a wide variety of readers. Luke has probably used the story of Elijah (2 Ki 2:7–10) as the basis for the details of ascension. These details provide the elements of narrative, which have been used to expand a more primitive tradition of exaltation.[4] Since, as we have seen, the resurrection traditions do not appear to have been embodied in narrative form from the beginning, the evangelists must find other resources to present the resurrection as story. John concludes the story of Thomas's meeting with the risen Lord with a benediction on those who have believed without seeing (Jn 20:29). One might say that the narrative impulse evident in the Lukan and Johannine tradition seeks to provide those who have not seen with images by which they can envisage the reality of Jesus' resurrection. Even in these traditions, one does not lose sight of the resurrection kerygma.

LUKE

Lk 24 has been the subject of extensive redaction-critical analysis.[5] Some of Luke's material appears to derive from traditions that were close to those that developed independently into the Johannine sources. Though it is not possible to attribute every non-Markan motif to Lukan redaction, it is difficult to determine the extent of the tradition that Luke has used.

Lk 24 can be divided into four sections: (a) the story of the women at the tomb, which ends with Peter's visit to the tomb to check it (vv. 1–12); (b) the story of the disciples on the road to Emmaus, which culminates in their learning that the Lord had also appeared to Peter (vv. 13–35); (c) the appearance of the Lord to his disciples at a meal, which culminates in the commissioning (vv. 36–49); and (d) the ascent into heaven (vv. 50–52). J. Dillon has also pointed to a redactional pattern that runs throughout this chapter: what happens in the narrative is always elucidated by words (vv. 2–3 by 5–7; vv. 19–24 by 25–27; vv. 36–43 by 44–49). These comments indicate how Luke wishes the reader to understand the progress of the resurrection events.[6]

LUKE 24:1–12

The story of the women at the tomb falls into three parts: (a) the account of finding the tomb (vv. 1–8); (b) the women reporting to others (vv. 9–11); and (c) Peter's visit to check the tomb (v. 12). Some interpreters think that all the differences between Luke and earlier traditions are due to the evangelist's rewriting of Mark. Others insist that Luke must have been working with other traditions in addition to Mark.[7] We find the arguments for an independent pre-Lukan tradition more plausible.

Luke 24:1–8

Luke departs from both Markan and Johannine traditions in the account of the finding of the tomb. Luke had Mark as one of the sources for this story. But Luke's version differs in its description of the revealers, two angels rather than a young man; the angelic message, a recollection of the passion predictions; and the reaction of the women—they deliver the message to the twelve disciples. Some of these changes are also evident in Matthew. In both, the women react with a gesture appropriate to the angelic theophany, worship; in both, they are clearly presented as fulfilling the mission given them. Luke has them actually deliver the message, while Mt 28:11 implies that they did so. However, Matthew is much closer to Markan wording in his account of the angelic commission to the women than Luke. Jn 20:1–2 presents the sequence of events in a much more abbreviated form, without any angelic commission. Mary Magdalene arrives at the tomb, finds the stone rolled away, and immediately runs to tell the beloved disciple and Peter that someone has taken the Lord from the tomb.

Verse 1

But on the first day of the week, at early dawn, they went to the tomb taking the spices which they had prepared.

See Luke 23:55–56: The women who had come with him from Galilee followed, and saw the tomb and how his body was laid; then they returned, and prepared spices and ointments. On the Sabbath they rested according to the commandment.

Luke has created a single episode of the burial and the empty tomb by involving the women in the burial itself. Their visit resumes burial rites that were interrupted by the Sabbath (23:56).

Verses 2–5a: *And they found the stone rolled away from the tomb, but when they went in they did not find the body. While they were perplexed about this, behold, two men stood by them in dazzling apparel; and as they were frightened and bowed their faces to the ground, . . .*

Luke may have omitted the Markan suggestion that the women were concerned about moving the stone because he presumes that they would have been able to enter the tomb to continue the burial process. Or one may take that omission along with the variant tradition of the angelophany to be part of the pre-Lukan tradition that is behind this version of the story.[8] Luke differs from all of the other gospels in having the women actually enter the tomb and find the body missing prior to their vision of the angelic messengers. One might argue that the Johannine tradition presupposes that Mary had entered the tomb, since her message to Peter is that the body has been taken. Luke's combination of the burial tradition and the women's visit to the tomb makes their entry an obvious initial step in the story. Consequently, one cannot decide the issue of Lukan redaction and pre-Lukan source simply on the basis of this detail.

The psychologizing note that the women were perplexed is repeated in the disbelief that greets their report (v. 11). Mary's report in Jn 20:2 also carries this element of perplexed suspicion. She presumes that the body has been removed from the tomb. Luke's burial scene has prepared the reader for the emphasis on the body of Jesus by its attention to the necessary preparation of the body for burial. Dillon argues that Luke is also the one who transformed the single young man of Mark into the two men seen by the women. However, most commentators prefer the suggestion that the doubling of the angels is pre-Lukan, since Jn 20:12 has Mary see two angels dressed in white in the tomb, marking the spot where the body had lain.[9]

The description of how the angels are dressed provides another hint of pre-Lukan tradition. Mark speaks of the young man as dressed in white *(leukos)*. Luke has the same word when he speaks of the Transfiguration (9:29) and of the two men who speak to the disciples at the ascension (Ac 1:10). Here, on the other hand, they are described as in dazzling clothing *(esthete astraptouse)*. The closest Luke comes to this expression is the "white clothing" of Ac 1:10. Luke does not use dazzling in connection with angelic figures. He uses *exastrapton* for Jesus' garment at the Transfiguration (9:29) and *periestrapsen* for the light that accompanies Paul's vision of the Lord (Ac 9:3; 22:6f.). However, the form of the angel at the tomb is described as *astrape* in Mt 28:3. Fear is a typical element of angelophanies. It accompanies those in the Lukan infancy narratives (1:12f., 29f.; 2:9f.) and in all of the synoptic tomb stories.[10] Lk 24:5a describes the women as prostrating themselves on the ground. This description may reflect a more primitive tradition than the version in Mt 28:4b where the guards fall to the ground as though they are dead. Mt 17:6 adds prostration to the Transfiguration story. When Luke adds "falling to the ground" to the story of Paul's vision in Acts (9:4; 22:7; 26:14), he does not include the expression "bowing the face to the ground." This difference suggests that he is dependent on an earlier source for this account.

Verses 5b–7: . . . *the men said to them, "Why are you seeking the living among the dead? Remember how he told you while he was still in Galilee, that the Son of Man must be delivered into the hands of sinful people, and be crucified, and on the third day rise."*

In Mark the angel had acknowledged that the women were seeking the crucified; here the angels' question implies a rebuke. The women seek Jesus where he cannot be found.[11] The contrast between dead and living is central to Luke's perception of resurrection. Luke summarizes the angelic message with "he lives" (24:24). Jesus is present as living during the forty days (Ac 1:3). Paul preaches the resurrection as an announcement of Jesus' being alive in Ac 25:19. Like Mt 28:6, Lk 24:6 transposes the order of the "he is not here" and the affirmation that Jesus has been raised. The announcement of resurrection becomes the interpretation of the empty tomb. Like Matthew, Luke implies that resurrection belongs to prophecy that Jesus' disciples are to remember. But unlike Matthew's "he has been raised, as he said," Luke calls upon the women to remember what Jesus had told them while they were in Galilee. Jn 2:22 uses "remember" as a technical term for the postresurrection interpretation of Jesus' words in the light of Old Testament prophecies. Luke's tradition may have contained a similar technical use of "remember." Luke locates all of the resurrection appearances in Jerusalem. Consequently, Galilee is transformed into the place where Jesus had predicted his passion and resurrection. Luke does not preserve any of the Markan traditions about Jesus appearing in Galilee or the disciples fleeing there. The first passion prediction occurs as Jesus' Galilean ministry is ending (9:22). The Lukan Transfiguration story that follows this first passion prediction emphasizes Jesus' departure at Jerusalem (9:31). The resurrection concludes that departure into glory (24:26).[12] Another tie between this passage and the period of the Galilean ministry was established when Luke included women (8:2f.) among the disciples who had followed Jesus there. He has made it clear that the same women are the ones who witnessed the crucifixion and the burial and now complete their mission by witnessing to the truth about the tomb.[13]

The Lukan passion predictions mix traditional formulae with Lukan editing. The angel's words in 24:7 summarize that tradition. As in Lk 18:31, the disciples must come to learn that what has happened is in accord with Scripture. Luke will emphasize the necessity of suffering as the condition for the Messiah's entry into glory (vv. 26; 44–46). The summary may not be entirely Luke's composition. It has the peculiar element of speaking of Jesus' being handed over to "sinful people." A similar expression appears in the Gethsemane episode in Mk 14:41 and its parallel in Mt 24:45 but is lacking in Luke.[14] The expression "on the third day" is unique to the Lukan resurrection narrative. It appears in all of the Lukan references to the passion that speak of the resurrection (9:22; 18:33; 24:46). This section of the gospel locates all of the events connected with Easter on the third day (23:54, 56b; 24:1, 6, 13, 21b, 37, 46). Thus, it appears to be introduced by Luke as a temporal marker linking various episodes together.[15]

Verse 8: *And they remembered his words, . . .*

Verse 8 insists that the women do remember what they had heard from Jesus in Galilee. Consequently, it is difficult to accept Dillon's view that the protagonists throughout the chapter are without genuine faith in the resurrection until the actual appearance of the risen Lord.[16] This verse affirms the resurrection kerygma as the source of faith in the risen Jesus. Guillaume tries to argue that the angelic announcement in Lk 24:7 no longer refers to that kerygma. He thinks that resurrection proclamation can depend only on what one has heard from the risen Lord.[17] We find such "unkerygmatic" readings of these verses highly improbable. The angels' message suits the established traditions of passion and resurrection preaching in the Lukan community. The women hear the angels' words and remember what Jesus had said, just as the evangelist expects his readers to do. To presume that the women have some inadequate faith or that the angels are not recalling the kerygma dissolves the obvious links that Luke has established between this passage and the rest of the gospel.

Luke 24:9–11

The next section in the tomb story shows the women carrying out the mission they have been given. Luke has apparently composed v. 9 to serve as a transition between the angels' message and the delivery of the message. Unlike the Matthean and Johannine traditions, Luke does not have any account of a Christophany in the vicinity of the tomb.

Verses 9–11: *. . . and returning from the tomb, they told all these things to the eleven and all the rest. Now it was Mary Magdalene and Joanna and Mary, the mother of James, and the other women with them who told this to the apostles, but these words seemed to them an idle tale and they did not believe them.*

These verses show that Luke has expanded the tradition of those involved in the original circle of disciples to include a larger group of women and of "the rest" who had followed Jesus from Galilee. This larger group will also be the witnesses to Jesus' resurrection. Luke also makes it clear that the women's witness was in accord with their mission. They told the eleven and the others "all these things."[18]

However, the announcement leaves the other disciples of Jesus in the same state of perplexity that the women had when they encountered the angel. Thus, Luke paves the way for the rest of the chapter in which their perplexity will be lifted. The parallel tradition in Jn 20:2 has Mary Magdalene report to Peter and the Beloved Disciple. Her report there reflects a state of perplexity, since the fact of the resurrection has not yet been revealed. Luke must designate the response as disbelief, since the women's message is not simply that Jesus' body has vanished from the tomb but includes the kerygmatic formula used by the angel. Lukan editing of this story to fit it with the burial story apparently led Luke to remove the list of the names of the women from the beginning. It is now inserted at the end and appears to combine Mk 16:1 and the list of women disciples from Galilee in Lk 8:2f.[19] Disbelief is not intended to indicate that the women's testimony had failed. Luke alludes back to it in the Emmaus episode (24:22–23) where the reliability of their report is confirmed. Thus, their testimony provides one of the elements that moves the narrative toward its culmination.

Verse 12: *But Peter rose and ran to the tomb; stooping and looking in he saw the linen cloths by themselves; and he went home wondering what had happened.*

This verse is missing in some ancient manuscripts, but some account of a confirmation of the women's story is required by Lk 24:24. Therefore, we presume that it is original. This motif also continues the parallelism in sequence between the Lukan and Johannine traditions. Mary's report is followed by Peter (and the Beloved Disciple) visiting the tomb. Though John has inserted the Beloved Disciple as the prototypical believer, it is clear that his tradition also ended in disbelief. Jn 20:9 makes another element in the tradition clearer: this disbelief is correlated with a lack of understanding of the scriptural testimony to Jesus. Although Luke has only Peter visit the tomb, it may be that there was a tradition that more than one disciple had gone to check the tomb, as Luke presumes in 24:24. The emphasis on Peter fits the tradition that Peter was the first recipient of an appearance of the risen Lord. However, Luke does not apparently have any account of such an appearance. The shorter, Lukan narrative would appear to be closer to the type of tradition that developed into the more elaborate Johannine story. The explicit motif of the fulfillment of Scripture appears to be one sign of the divergence of the pre-Lukan and pre-Johannine traditions.[20]

Both the Lukan and the Johannine stories lack the element of commissioning that is typical of the other stories, whether merely angelic commissioning, as in Mark, or both angelic commissioning and that of the risen Lord, as in Matthew. The report of the women to Peter and the other disciples is presented as a spontaneous action rather than as divine mandate. Luke may have presumed that such commissioning is implied in the angel's use of a kerygmatic formula. But the Johannine story does not even have an angelophany. Mary goes to Peter because she is perplexed. Since the element of commissioning appears to be attached to the resurrection kerygma, the existence of tomb traditions in which it is not present indicates that the tomb traditions developed independently of the resurrection traditions.

LUKE 24:13–35

Lack of parallel traditions makes redaction-critical analysis of the Emmaus story difficult. The names Cleopas and Emmaus would appear to be based on tradition. The reference to a resurrection appearance to Peter certainly is traditional, and it is likely that recognition at meal was also an established part of the pre-Lukan tradition (24:28–32).[21]

The recognition scene is preceded by a lengthy dialogue between two disciples and a stranger. The first section of the dialogue summarizes the events of the passion. It carries the reader through the inspection of the tomb by some of Jesus' disciples (vv. 13–24). The transition between these events and the meal scene is made by the stranger's interpretation of the Scriptures so that they show the necessity of messianic suffering (vv. 25–27). The meal scene itself is followed by the disciples' return to the others, where they learn of the appearance to Simon (vv. 33–35). As was the case with the story of the women at the tomb, the disciples report their experience. Their claim to have recognized Jesus in the breaking of bread introduces the next element in the narrative. Jesus immediately appears to the disciples assembled for a meal. Thus, the Emmaus episode has been shaped into a transition between the events of the passion and discovery of the tomb and the appearance tradition. The Emmaus story is different from the other resurrection appearances in that the Lord disappears at the moment of recognition. It focuses on two important elements in the life of the community: the understanding of the passion and resurrection of Jesus as fulfillment of Scripture and the presence of the Messiah, who has thus entered his glory in the meal.[22]

Luke 24:13–24

Verse 21a provides a natural transition to the stranger's interpretation of Scripture. Verses 21b–24 provide a summary of the previous narrative. This summary includes the emphasis on the "third day," the angelic message as the assertion "he lives," and reference to the women's report and a visit by the disciples to the tomb. The summary of the passion in vv. 19d–20 resembles summaries in Acts (2:22–23; 10:37–39).

Verses 13–16: *That very day two of them were going to a village named Emmaus, about sixty stadia from Jerusalem, and talking with each other about all the things that had happened. While they were talking and discussing together, Jesus, himself, drew near and went with them. But their eyes were kept from recognizing him.*

This story begins with two disciples on a journey *(poreuesthai)*. Journey is a typical feature of Lukan narrative. It ties the passage to the larger setting of the journey by which Jesus moves toward the passion (13:33; 18:31–33). Verse 16 invokes the recognition theme that provides the dynamic for the entire story (vv. 31 and 35). Recognition is a fundamental element in appearance traditions. However, the expansion of that motif in this story suggests to some interpreters that Luke conceives the episode along the lines of a folktale of hospitality to strangers. The examples of Abraham's and Lot's hospitality (Gen 18:1–8; 19:1–3) serve as general examples of the virtue of hospitality (e.g., Heb 13:2).[23] But the formulation of v. 16 goes beyond the disguised divine visitor of folklore. Luke uses the passive voice: "their eyes were kept from seeing." The passive makes God the cause of their failure to recognize Jesus. It implies that God will also be the one to lift the veil from their understanding.

Verses 17–21a: *And he said to them, "What is this conversation you are holding with each other as you walk?" And they stood still and looked sad. Then one of them, named Cleopas, answered him, "Are you the only visitor to Jerusalem who does not know the things that have happened there in these days?" And he said to them, "What things?" And they said to him, "About Jesus of Nazareth, who was a prophet mighty in deed and word before God and all the people. And how our chief priests and rulers delivered him up to be condemned to death, and crucified him. But we had hoped that he was the one to redeem Israel."*

The first part of the report summarizes the events of the passion. Dialogue is a typical feature of Lukan narrative. This scene has been compared with the dialogue between Philip and the Ethiopian in Ac 8:26–39. A stranger appears on the scene who questions the traveler. Christological instruction based on Scripture, a sacramental act, and the mysterious disappearance of the stranger conclude the episode.[24] The image of Jesus as the Mosaic prophet in v. 19b is reflected in the Pentecost sermon in Acts (2:22, 36, 38). Acts agrees that his mission includes word (Ac 2:22) and deed (Ac 10:38). Luke frequently emphasizes the public character of Jesus' activity. What he says and does is known to all. It is also typical of the Lukan passion narrative to hold the leaders of the people responsible for Jesus' death.

Although the passage as a whole is Lukan composition, it does echo earlier traditions. The *paredoken* (handed over) of v. 20 is reminiscent of earlier traditions found in Mark. R. H. Fuller points out that it embodies one of the oldest interpretations of the passion, the human "no" of the crucifixion that is met by the divine affirmation of the resurrection. The older formulas use "killed" *(apokteinein)*. Luke has apparently changed the verb here and in v. 7 to "crucified." The persistent allusions to the preaching of the passion and resurrection of Jesus in the story contribute to its irony. The disciples have heard the prophecies of what was to befall Jesus at Jerusalem, but they do not yet see that those events are unfolding all around them.[25]

Verse 21 recalls the early Christology of Jesus as the prophet-Messiah, who is to renew Israel. A similar prophet Christology also appears in Ac 3:12–14 and 7:2–53. The traditions on which Luke appears to draw in formulating this dialogue do not constitute a narrative in themselves but appear to reflect familiar traditions of Christian preaching. Luke is the one who has provided the framework that links such traditions together in a story.

Verses 21b–24: *Yes, and besides all this, it is now the third day since this happened. Moreover, some women of our company amazed us. They were at the tomb early in the morning and did not find his body; and they came back saying that they had even seen a vision of angels at the tomb, who said that he was alive. Some of those who were with us went to the tomb and found it just as the women had said; but him they did not see.*

The only difference between the summary and the stories that Luke has just told lies in speaking of several disciples rather than just Peter going to the tomb and emphasizing the fact that they did not see Jesus there. Either Luke does not know the tradition of appearances near the tomb such as we find in Matthew and John, or he wishes to emphasize only the appearance to the disciples. The disciples, he may wish to imply, have the false expectation that the "living Jesus" is a resuscitated corpse who is to be found near the tomb. They do not recognize that Jesus has entered his glory.[26]

Verses 25–27: *And he said to them, "O foolish ones, and slow of heart to believe all that the prophets have said! Was it not necessary that the Christ should suffer these things and enter into his glory?" And beginning with Moses and all the prophets, he interpreted to them in all the scriptures the things about himself.*

Jesus' reply emphasizes the divine darkening of the disciples' heart. What they are told is formulated in Lukan terms. He is the only one who explicitly speaks of the *"Christos"* (Messiah) as suffering (also Ac 3:18; 17:3; 26:23). *Christos* cannot be substituted for the suffering servant of Is 52:13–53:12.[27] We have seen that Luke has already introduced the ideas of prophetic fulfillment and divine necessity into the narrative in the words of the angels to the women at the tomb.

The motif of a postresurrection understanding of the Scriptures in reference to Jesus' passion is hardly unique to Luke.[28] The announcement that the prophecies have been fulfilled recurs in the conclusion of the next section. Both refer to Scripture and the prophets and insist on the necessity of the Messiah's suffering (vv. 25f. and 44). Both sections speak of the consequence of that messianic suffering as entry into glory (vv. 26 and 46). Both speak of opening the disciples' understanding to what is contained in the Scriptures (vv. 27 and 45). Thus, the dialogue with the stranger on the road to Emmaus foreshadows the instruction to be given the eleven. This instruction presupposes the kerygmatic traditions of the early community.[29] The pattern of this dialogue between the risen Jesus and the disciples reappears in the kerygma of Acts (Ac 2:22–26; 3:13–26; 4:8–12; 5:29–32; 10:36–43; 13:17–24).[30] The Lukan reader would have no difficulty in seeing that the preaching of the church was a reflection of the Easter instruction of the Lord himself.

Verses 28–32: *So they drew near to the village to which they were going. He appeared to be going further, but they persuaded him saying, "Stay with us for it is near evening, and the day is now almost gone." So he went in to stay with them. When he was at table with them, he took the bread and blessed and broke it and gave it to them and they recognized him; and he vanished from their sight. They said to each other, "Did our hearts not burn within us while he talked to us on the road; while he opened to us the Scriptures?"*

The recognition theme appears somewhat out of place after the dialogue, since the interpretation of the Scriptures would seem to have indicated the stranger's identity. Since the culminating Easter event is an appearance of the Lord at a meal, this episode has a proleptic character. From the angels' recalling the words of the Lord to the stranger's interpretation of Scripture to the distinctive act of breaking bread, the chapter has been building toward its appearance scene.

Meals play an important role in the Lukan narrative. Luke's description of the feeding of the multitude begins by shifting the Markan "teach" to "speak about the kingdom of God" (9:11). The same expression occurs in the summary of the forty days' teaching in Ac 1:3f. This teaching provides the introduction to a feeding miracle in which Jesus' actions parallel those performed here. They are taken from Mark and shape the account of Jesus' actions at the Last Supper, taking, blessing, breaking, and giving bread (cf. Mk 14:22; Mt 26:26). The Lukan account of the supper replaces the expression for blessing, *eulogesas,* with giving thanks, *eucharistesas* (22:19). Both expressions appear to belong to early eucharistic formulae.[31] The Lukan reader would have no difficulty identifying Jesus as the One who performs these actions. One may also point to the extensive use of meals as places of instruction in Luke. The Last Supper looks forward to the passion and thus indicates the necessity to follow the suffering Messiah (22:7–20, 24–38). Jesus is frequently presented as present at meals during which he instructs those present (5:29f.; 33–35; 11:37;

10:38–42; 14:1; 6:21a; 12:37; 14:14). Dillon points to the association of meals and missionary instruction in Acts as another important factor in the development of the Lukan meal traditions (e.g., Ac 27:34).[32] Ac 1:3 makes meal fellowship one of the characteristics of Jesus' association with his disciples during the forty days. This story, then, dramatizes the rich associations of meals in the Lukan tradition. These meals tie together Jesus' earthly ministry, the period of the resurrected One's appearances to the disciples, and the eucharistic experiences of Lukan Christians.

Luke does not appear to have created the story of Jesus' making himself known to disciples at a meal. Elements of such a story appear in the recognition of Jesus in Jn 21:9, 12, 13. The two traditions have developed quite differently. Here Jesus is pictured reclining as the house guest of Cleopas. In Jn 21, Jesus is a stranger on the shore who has prepared a meal for his disciples. Luke emphasizes hospitality in the instructions for missionaries (10:5–7). Thus, the Emmaus story may have had another significance in the Lukan community in that it reflected the hospitality that the Christian was to show wandering missionaries.[33] The risen Jesus is about to turn over his mission to his disciples. The kerygmatic instruction associated with this episode also represents the content of their preaching about him.

Verses 33–35: *And they rose at that same hour and returned to Jerusalem; and they found the eleven gathered together and those who were with them, who said, "The Lord has risen indeed and appeared to Simon!" Then they told what had happened on the road, and how he was known to them in the breaking of the bread.*

Once again, a message about the risen Lord is reported to the eleven and those with them. It suggests that all of Jesus' disciples are gathered for the final appearance. The use of "Simon" for Peter suggests that the formula in v. 34, "he appeared to Simon," is traditional. Luke has not previously spoken of Peter as Simon. This announcement interrupts the expected sequence in which the disciples should report their experience. The insertion of the proclamation that the Lord is risen and has appeared to Simon sets the kerygmatic announcement of the resurrection in the first place. The Emmaus story is not about the first resurrection appearance, after all. It prepares the way for the final example of Jesus' appearance to the disciples at a meal. There they will be commissioned to take that message out to the world.

LUKE 24:36–49

The appearance of Jesus at the meal falls into two sections: (a) the appearance itself (vv. 36–43) and (b) the words about the fulfillment of Scripture and commissioning of the disciples (vv. 44–49). The fulfillment theme occurs in the kerygmatic formula of 1 Cor 15:3–5. It does not appear in other stories of resurrection appearances, however. Therefore, Luke appears to have introduced this theme. The story of a meal appearance has parallels in Jn 20:19–23, which suggests that Luke has reworked traditional material.[34] The extensive development in the second half of the story as well as its integration into the chapter as a whole lead J.-M. Guillaume to suggest that John has preserved the more primitive outline of this tradition.[35]

Verses 36–43: *As they were saying this, Jesus, himself, stood among them and said to them, "Peace be to you." But they were startled and frightened and supposed that they saw a ghost. And he said to them, "Why are you troubled and why are questions arising in your hearts? See my hands and feet—that I am he. Touch me and see. A ghost does not have flesh and bones as you see that I have." And as he said this, he showed them his hands and feet. But they still did not believe out of joy and they were amazed, so he said to them, "Do you have some meat there?" They gave him a piece of broiled fish. And taking it, he ate it in their presence.*

Luke's story of the finding of the tomb emphasized that Jesus' body could not be found in the tomb. His account of the resurrection appearance of Jesus is equally concerned with the demonstration that Jesus' resurrection is bodily and not an apparition. This appears to be independent of the Emmaus tradition, which had presumed that the Lord was able to manipulate physical objects and appeared as a human being, not a ghost. Elements of bodily proof are also typical of the Johannine stories.

Several peculiarities in the Lukan account are explained if the evangelist is reworking an earlier tradition. The connection between joy and unbelieving amazement that leads to the final demonstration of Jesus' reality in eating some of the fish is particularly awkward. The general format of appearance stories would suggest Jesus' appearance and greeting, such as the "peace be with you" of the Johannine version; doubt or disquiet among the disciples, followed by reassur-

ance, such as we find in Mt 28:17; and a reaction of joy on the part of
the disciples, such as we find in John. The pre-Lukan tradition may
have further developed the motif of doubt around the theme of the
bodily reality of Jesus. John has attached that theme to Thomas and
embodied it in a separate meal appearance.[36]

The Johannine tradition of a meal by the Sea of Galilee has Jesus
give the disciples fish and bread. Some commentators think that this
detail in the Lukan story indicates a tradition that originated in
Galilee. The bread is now part of the meal as recognition scene in the
Emmaus story. Only vv. 33 and 47 situate this meal tradition in
Jerusalem. Without them, the story could have been located anywhere.

Suspicion that the risen Lord is a ghost may also be part of the pre-
Lukan tradition. The Johannine narrative makes Jesus' peculiar entry into the room explicit by emphasizing the locked doors. Luke
simply has Jesus appear in the middle of the disciples. The closest
parallel to such a suspicion occurs in the Markan story of Jesus' walking on the water (6:45–52). The disciples are thrown into confusion
because they think they are seeing a ghost. Luke does not have this
story. If this tradition was at one time set by the Sea of Galilee, then
the fear of seeing a ghost may be tied to that setting. The walking on
water story follows the story of the miraculous feeding of five thou-
sand in Mk 6:30–44, which does occur in Luke and which is one of the
traditions invoked by the Emmaus story.

Interpreters are divided over the function of the elaborate demonstration of Jesus' bodily reality in the Lukan story. Some think that
Luke is already confronted with a naive docetism that denied the
bodily character of resurrection. Luke's entire account of the Easter
events presents the resurrection as an event that affects Jesus' body.
Dillon suggests that we should not presume, however, that these
emphases are directed against docetism, though they may later serve
as weapons against it. He proposes that the self-identification "I am
he" is the center of the passage. It makes the identification of the
risen Lord with the earthly Jesus explicit. Thus, it shows that the path
from Galilee to suffering and entry into glory at Jerusalem is being
completed.[37]

This story also makes elements that were present in the Emmaus
story explicit. The Johannine parallels and the conclusion of the Emmaus story picture Jesus as the One who gives the disciples bread—as
was the case during the feeding and Last Supper stories that they
invoke. But the Lukan stories also represent Jesus as the One who
receives hospitality and food from the disciples. In the Emmaus
tradition that shift evokes the folklore traditions of unwittingly enter-
taining the divine visitor. The resulting benediction is Jesus' self-

revelation to the disciples. Dillon thinks that both of these stories have been shaped by the missionary traditions of the Lukan community. Jesus stands in the place of the missionary who receives hospitality. Mk 9:41 and Mt 10:40–42 preserve sayings that promise reward to the person who offers hospitality to the disciple-missionary. These sayings are not preserved in Luke. Ac 10:41f. associates the disciples' eating and drinking with the risen Lord and their commission to evangelize.[38]

The focus on the kerygma forms the second section of the Lukan story. The appearance is not simply an apologetic demonstration of Jesus' bodily reality as in the separate story of an appearance to Thomas in Jn 20:24–29. Luke has expanded the traditional commissioning sayings of the resurrection appearances with the affirmation of the kerygma, which has been a guiding thread in Luke's construction of this chapter.

Verses 44–46: *He said to them, "These are my words which I spoke to you while I was still with you, that it was necessary that everything written in the law of Moses, the prophets and the psalms about me be fulfiled." Then he opened their minds to understand the Scriptures. And he said to them, "Thus it is written, the messiah will suffer and rise from the dead on the third day . . ."*

These verses recapitulate the themes that have been introduced in the previous stories. The understanding that the disciples gain after the resurrection was already given in the teaching of Jesus during his ministry (24:6–8); the suffering and resurrection of the Messiah on the third day is founded in the divine plan set forth in Scripture (24:25–27). Each example in the chapter has been more explicit. The women were reminded that Jesus had predicted the death and resurrection of the Son of Man while he was in Galilee (v. 7). The disciples on the road to Emmaus are told that Moses and the prophets had predicted that the Messiah would have to suffer and so enter his glory (vv. 25–27). Now all of Jesus' disciples—including the earlier groups —are told that Jesus had previously taught them that Moses, the prophets, and the psalms had predicted the suffering of the Messiah and his resurrection from the dead on the third day (vv. 44–46). This passage sums up the previous two passages. It adds the psalms, a common source of early Christian proof texts, to the testimony of Moses, the prophets, and Jesus. The psalm quotations in the sermons of Acts represent the type of proof familiar to Luke's readers: (a) Ps 118:2 in Ac 4:11; (b) Ps 16:8–11 in Ac 2:25–29; 13:35; (c) Ps 110:1 in Ac 2:34f.; (d) Ps 2:1f. in Ac 4:25f.; (e) Ps 2:7 in Ac 13:33. These citations

typically describe God's triumph over human rebellion and wickedness.[39] The collection of psalm texts in the sermons of Acts demonstrates the rejection of the Messiah (cornerstone; Ac 4:11); the implication of hostile Gentiles in his death (Ac 4:25); the resurrection as
exaltation of Jesus to messianic authority as Son with the subjection of
his enemies (Ac 2:34; 13:33); and the divine promise of delivering his
holy One from corruption (2:25–29; 13:35). The last, based on Psalm
16:8–11, is the closest Luke can come to proof for the resurrection as
it is envisaged here. The other proof texts for resurrection that are
more common in the New Testament, Ps 110:1 and Ps 2:1, 7, are
based on the traditions of resurrection as exaltation. Nothing in this
tradition reflects the "on the third day" tradition. Luke has exploited
the traditional designation of the time of resurrection to tie the
events of this chapter together. The same speeches in Acts contain
citations from the Law and the prophets. Ac 3:22, for example, invokes the prophet of Deut 18:15–16 to describe Jesus, while Ac 3:23
warns against rejecting the prophet on the basis of Deut 18:19 and
Lev 23:29. We have seen that Cleopas referred to Jesus as "a prophet
mighty in deed before God and all the people" (Lk 24:19). Since
Luke has explicitly identified Jesus as "the prophet," he may have the
Deuteronomy text in mind when he speaks of the Law of Moses.
Certainly the use of quotations in the kerygmatic speeches of Acts
reflects the type of demonstration from Scriptures that Luke is
grounding in the instruction of the risen Lord.

However, Luke does not wish to suggest that this process of interpretation represents a new development in the postresurrection
community. We have seen that the Markan tradition of a prophecy of
Jesus' future appearance in Galilee becomes a reference back to
Jesus' teaching in Galilee in Lk 24:5–7. Once again, this passage
identifies Jesus' previous teaching as the content of what is being
recalled in this use of the prophets. In a passage that might represent
a tradition similar to that presumed by Luke, Jn 14:26 promises that
the Holy Spirit/Paraclete will teach the disciples all things and cause
them to remember everything Jesus has said to them. Lk 24:7f.
presents remembering Jesus' teaching as the basis of the angels' call
to faith.

Verses 47–49: . . . *and for repentance and forgiveness of sins to
be preached in his name to all the nations—beginning from Jerusalem. You are witnesses of these things. And behold I am sending the
promise of my Father upon you. Remain in the city until you are
clothed with power from on high.*

The story now shifts to the commissioning of the disciples as witnesses to Jesus. Once again, the overall formulation is unmistakably Lukan, but the passage has elements in common with the commissioning in the other appearance traditions. Luke shares the elements of forgiveness of sins and the bestowal of the Spirit with the Johannine tradition. The expression "to all the nations" recalls the commission in Mt 28:19. Other elements in the passage are unmistakably Lukan. Jerusalem is singled out as the place from which the message is to go forth. Unlike the Johannine parallel in which Jesus bestows the Spirit at Easter, Luke has Jesus promise the future coming of the Spirit at Pentecost (also Ac 1:5). Luke frequently uses "in the name of Jesus" for the power whereby the missionary continues the presence of Jesus. He also characteristically describes the disciples as Jesus' witnesses and associates witnessing with the power of the name of Jesus.[40] It is difficult to determine whether Luke is using the term "witnesses" in the limited sense that it has later in Ac 1:8, 22, in which the eleven are the ones who receive the commission. Some scholars presume that they are the only ones included in this commissioning.[41] Others point out that throughout the passion narrative the group around Jesus is a much larger group than the twelve. Ac 1:21f. presumes that there is such a larger group from which a "witness" can be selected to take Judas' place. This expanded group is the group gathered for the meal at which Jesus appears. Therefore, the commission to witness is more reasonably presumed to be the entire group of those who have followed Jesus from Galilee. Since that group explicitly includes a number of women disciples of Jesus, they should also be presumed to be included in this commissioning. Their inclusion reflects the important role of women as missionaries in the earliest period, as attested to in both the Pauline letters and in Acts.[42] Their role may also be grounded in the presumption that the women are witnesses to the resurrection and have, as in the case of the women at the tomb, been entrusted with the kerygmatic proclamation.[43]

Both the Lukan and Johannine traditions agree that the missionary activity of the disciples is linked to the bestowal of the Spirit. The missionary traditions embodied in the sayings traditions of the synoptic gospels also link the disciples' mission with a gift of divine power (exousia) (see Mt 10:16; Mk 6:7; Lk 9:2). Luke must shift the bestowal of the Spirit from the Easter appearance in order to accommodate the chronology of passion, resurrection, ascension, and Pentecost as separate events that forms the basis of his narrative.

LUKE 24:50–53

The final verses of the chapter appear to violate the neat chronological scheme that links the gospel with the opening of Acts, since Jesus
is pictured as ascending on Easter. Verse 49 points the reader toward
Pentecost as the next significant event in the story. Yet the opening
chapter of Acts presupposes a period of resurrection appearances
that covers forty days between Easter and Pentecost. However,
Luke's summaries of that period in Ac 1:3–5 and Ac 10:41–43 show
that he envisages a continuation of the same sort of appearance
tradition that he has described in Lk 24. It is unlikely that Luke had
any further traditions about resurrection appearances beyond those
that he has used in the conclusion to the gospel. We have seen that
the tradition presupposes that Jesus' appearances continued over an
indefinite period of time after Easter (1 Cor 15:3–7). Luke fills that
period with the Easter traditions as he understands them.

Verses 50–53: *He led them out to the vicinity of Bethany and
lifting up his hands, blessed them. And while he was blessing them
he parted from them and was taken up into heaven. And after they
worshiped him, they returned to Jerusalem with great joy, and were
always in the temple blessing God.*

The Lukan images of the ascension represent Jesus' being taken up
into heaven as the culmination of Jesus' departure to glory, which
was to be accomplished at Jerusalem. Both passages appear to be
Luke's own composition.[44] Stories of individuals being snatched up
into heaven can be found in all sectors of the hellenistic world. Luke
has adopted this common pattern to provide the image for Jesus'
departure into heaven, though he has not copied any particular ascension story in detail.[45]

The earlier resurrection traditions see the return of Jesus to
heaven as exaltation. They did not require any imagery for the bodily
translation of the exalted righteous person into heaven. Luke reflects
these traditions of exaltation in Acts (see 2:33–36; 5:30–31). But, as we
have seen, the Lukan narrative is preoccupied with the bodily reality
of the risen One. Consequently, the only images available to describe
Jesus' departure to heaven are those of ascension. At the same time,
Luke also knows that the risen Jesus appears from glory. Thus, we are
left with the peculiar combination of Jesus' departure from the disci-

ples on Easter as an ascension and the ascension in the opening chapter of Acts. The introduction to the ascension story in Acts recalls the Easter stories: (a) Ac 1:3 refers to Lk 24:42f.; (b) Ac 1:4 refers to Lk 24:50–52. The two angels who rebuke the disciples as they are staring after the ascending Jesus refer to the two angels whom the women encounter in the tomb. The story of Jesus' being taken from the disciples in the gospel does not use the imagery of Jesus' being taken up on clouds. Instead, Luke evokes a liturgical posture of blessing, which is followed by the response of worship.[46] We have seen that Mt 28:17 pictured the disciples worshiping the risen Lord. It is possible that Luke has adopted such a tradition. The allusion to worship also provides the transition into the conclusion of the gospel in which the disciples are blessing God in the temple. With Jesus' passage into heaven, the journey of the gospel from Galilee through the suffering of the passion to glory at Jerusalem is complete.

JOHN

In some cases, the Johannine tradition appears to reflect an earlier form of a tradition than that found in Luke. But frequently the judgment about which form of a story is likely to be older is difficult to make. Some scholars think, for example, that the account in Jn 20:1–2 in which Mary Magdalene visits the tomb alone, finds it open/empty, and rushes off to report the matter to the disciples represents the historical core of the tomb tradition. There is no angelophany, no appearance of the risen Lord. Both elements appear upon Mary's subsequent visit to the tomb (Jn 20:11–18). Others think the appearance by the Sea of Galilee in Jn 21:1–14 reflects the original story of the Lord's appearance to Peter. This tradition has been scattered throughout the synoptics in incidents during the life of Jesus: (a) walking on water (Mt 14:28–33); (b) Peter as foundation of the church (Mt 16:16b–19); (c) the miraculous catch of fish (Lk 5:1–11).

Both Luke and John are conscious of the perspective from which they narrate the events of Jesus' life. It is a perspective shaped by the "remembering" of the scriptural traditions applied to Jesus in light of the resurrection. John makes this perspective the central one throughout his entire gospel. He attributes this activity of remembering to the Paraclete/Holy Spirit, whom Jesus promises to send the disciples after his glorification (Jn 14:26; 16:14; see also 12:16). The gift of the Spirit, the bestowal of peace, and the commissioning of the disciples to the same mission on which the Father sent Jesus form the core of the tradition of Jesus' appearance at a meal in Jn 20:19–23. At the same time, the evangelist has spelled out all of these themes in greater detail in the Farewell Discourses (Jn 13:31–17:26). Thus, the Johannine tradition has gone beyond the Lukan perception that the message as well as the mission of the community is grounded in the earthly teaching of Jesus and has explicitly embodied the postresurrection perspective in the Farewell Discourses. The ambiguity of the Johannine dialogues is clearly evident in Jn 17. Jesus speaks as One who is about to be glorified (17:5) and is no longer in the world (17:13f.). John insists that the crucifixion is the moment of Jesus' glorification (13:1, 31f.). These images are closely related to the understanding of resurrection as exaltation and glorification. Jesus regains the glory that he enjoys as the only begotten of the Father. Thus, Johannine Christology transforms the pattern of the exaltation of the suffering righteous by insisting on the unity of Jesus and the Father. C. K. Barrett speaks of this process of recasting earlier traditions as "critical acceptance."[47]

John 11:20–27

The dialogue between Martha and Jesus in the story of Lazarus exemplifies such a recasting of tradition. Through an ironic twist, the miracle becomes the cause of Jesus' death. The bearer of life-giving revelation is killed for giving life. In the exchange between Martha and Jesus the evangelist presents the significance of the miracle as proof that the hope of resurrection is actualized in Jesus. The dialogue begins with a confession of faith that Jesus could return Lazarus to life (vv. 21–22). Martha believes that her brother will be raised "in the resurrection on the last day" (v. 24). Not only does such a confession suit the belief of many pious Jews of the time of Jesus; it also represented the common belief in resurrection among Christians of John's day.[48]

Jesus' reply to Martha's statement follows a typical narrative pattern in the Fourth Gospel. Jesus is equated with the expectations and symbols of the tradition. Belief in Jesus, not merely belief in resurrection, is the key to eternal life. Martha's reply focuses on this christological claim: Jesus is the Son of God, the One who comes into the world. This understanding of Jesus transforms traditional Christian expectations. This passage recalls the earlier affirmation that one's response to Jesus was the hour of judgment, of life or death (Jn 5:24). The Johannine community retained the earlier traditions, like that in

Jn 5:17c–29, which affirmed that Jesus comes in judgment as the Son of Man. Lazarus's emergence from the tomb at Jesus' call demonstrates the summons that the Son of Man issues to all those in the tombs. Matthew contained a legend about the righteous emerging from their tombs with the crucifixion and resurrection of Jesus as a demonstration of the cosmic eschatological power that has now been made available in Jesus. The Johannine story goes back to the period just before Jesus' glorification on the cross to demonstrate that such power is available in Jesus. In so doing, the evangelist implicitly corrects those traditions in which the resurrection is the condition for Jesus' entry into the glory of divine sonship. For John, Jesus has always possessed this glory.[49]

A primary concern in the Johannine resurrection accounts is the transformation of the traditional beliefs in resurrection given the new christological insights of the gospel. To what extent does the perception that Jesus and the Father and later Jesus and the Father or the Paraclete and the community are one make the tradition of resurrection as future exaltation and vindication unimportant? Jn 16:7–11 proclaims that Jesus' vindication and the condemnation of an unbelieving world come to the community with the Paraclete after Jesus' return to the Father. This return is already part of the experience of the community and is the gospel's primary interest. The diversity of resurrection traditions known to the Johannine community is evident in the two chapters devoted to such material. Even though chapter 21 is widely considered a later addition to the gospel, the traditions upon which it draws appear to have been circulating within the community. The Fourth Gospel contains the traditions of three and perhaps four different appearances of the risen Lord: (a) the appearance to Mary Magdalene near the tomb; (b) the appearance to the disciples at a meal on Easter evening; (c) a Galilean appearance to Peter; and (d) possibly, an additional appearance to the "twelve" at a meal in Galilee. In addition, the evangelist has created a second appearance at a meal in Jerusalem from the tradition of doubt about the reality of the risen Lord.

JOHN 20:1–18

Jn 20:1–18 falls into three scenes: (a) Mary's discovery of the empty tomb and her report to Peter (vv. 1–2); (b) Peter's and the Beloved Disciple's visit to the tomb (vv. 3–10); (c) Jesus' appearance to Mary

near the tomb (vv. 11–18). The final two sections clearly show the
influence of Johannine theology. The Beloved Disciple believes simply by seeing the grave clothes lying in the tomb. Thus, he stands in
the place of the angel who interprets the empty tomb by proclaiming
the Easter kerygma in the other traditions.[50] When he appears to
Mary, Jesus proclaims his resurrection as his ascent back to the Father. This ascent represents the culmination of Jesus' hour, the time
of his glorification from the cross.

Verses 1–2: *On the first day of the week, Mary Magdalene came to
the tomb early in the morning while it was still dark, and saw the
stone taken away from the tomb. Therefore, she ran to Simon Peter
and the other disciples whom Jesus loved and said to them, "They
have taken the Lord and we do not know where they have laid him."*

Awkward points in the passage suggest that the evangelist has sum-
marized an earlier tradition. Though Mary is said to visit the tomb
alone (v. 1), her report speaks of "we" (v. 2). John has corrected this
inconsistency in 20:13. P. Minear thinks that John shifts to "we"
whenever he wishes to set the position of the Johannine Christians
over against that of their Jewish opponents (as in Jn 1:14; 3:11).[51] This
view requires that one specify the charge to which the evangelist is
responding.

Most commentators agree that Mary's report contains the implicit
view that Jesus' body was removed from the tomb. Mt 28:13–15
shows that this suspicion was leveled at Christians by Jewish opponents. The importance of v. 2b is underlined by its repetition in the
section (vv. 13 and 15). Minear points out that John uses the ambiguous "they" to refer to the Jews in the passion and burial narratives
(19:7, 31). Fear of the Jews is introduced into the meal scene as the
reason the disciples are locked in a room (20:19, 26). Therefore, the
suspicion voiced in Mary's words is that the authorities have removed
the body as an act of hostility.[52]

The Matthean tradition has the women's visit to the tomb followed
immediately by an appearance of Jesus near the tomb. Jn 20:11 takes
up the tradition of such a Christophany. However, this passage and
the Lukan tradition suggest that there was a tradition about the
finding of the empty tomb that did not contain any elements of such
an appearance.[53] John has used the expression in v. 2b to link the two
stories together (vv. 13 and 15). Minear suggests that the question
"Why are you weeping?" reminds the Johannine reader of the emphasis on Jesus' departure that was typical of the Farewell Discourses
(see Jn 14:1, 18; 16:20–22). Jesus' first announcements of departure

were directed against opponents whose failure to believe would find
them condemned when they could no longer find him (7:11, 33f.;
8:21). Jesus' followers are promised that they will be where he is
(12:26), a promise to which the Farewell Discourses return as they
seek to console the disciples, who will grieve until they see Jesus
again.[54] The dynamic of grief and consolation was an important element in Luke's account of the disciples on the road to Emmaus. John
has made Mary the dramatic focus of the disciples' plight. Her grief
will be lifted when she encounters the Lord.

Verses 3–10: *Then Peter and the other disciple went out and came
to the tomb. They both ran and the other disciple ran faster than
Peter and came to the tomb first. Bending down he saw the grave
clothes lying there but did not go in. Then Simon Peter came following him, and he went in to the tomb and saw the grave clothes lying
there and the cloth which was over his head not lying with the grave
clothes but rolled up in a place by itself. Then the other disciple, who
arrived first at the tomb, came in and saw and believed. For they did
not yet know the Scripture that it was necessary for him to rise from
the dead. Then the disciples went back to their homes again.*

This account is considerably more expansive than Lk 24:12. But it
shares with the Lukan tradition the view that Peter visited the tomb
after the women's report and that the disciples could not understand
the events surrounding the tomb because they did not know the
scriptural prophecy that Jesus would rise from the dead. It is possible
that the narrative in John is a late development. Nothing contained
in it requires tradition beyond the notice that Peter had visited the
tomb, the story of the women's visit, and the special Johannine traditions about the Beloved Disciple.[55] Lk 24:24 speaks of several disciples visiting the tomb rather than just Peter. Jn 20:3 may be based on
a tradition in which Peter goes to the tomb accompanied by an
unnamed disciple. The Beloved Disciple is introduced in Jn 20:2. As
in the case of the Magdalene story, the passage is inconsistently
edited. Jn 20:3 has Peter go out (singular verb), while the second verb
is a plural referring to Peter and the Beloved Disciple. The tradition
behind this section, then, has Peter (possibly with an unnamed companion) go to the tomb, see the grave wrappings, and return without
any understanding of what has happened (vv. 3, 6–7, and 10).[56]

Verses 4 and 5 have an awkward scene in which the Beloved
Disciple arrives ahead of Peter but delays entering. Various hypothe-
ses about the significance of the delay have been advanced. R. E.
Brown insists that since the two are always friends in John, it cannot

imply hostility between them. Therefore, he presumes that the early arrival of the Beloved Disciple is a sign of his greater love for Jesus.[57] It is also necessary to delay the Beloved Disciple's entry into the tomb in order to make his "saw and believed" the climax of the story.

The Lukan and Johannine traditions agree that Peter did not see Jesus at the tomb (vv. 6–7; Lk 24:12). John introduces another motif that is not paralleled in other tomb stories: the grave clothes remained in the tomb. This theme is different from the other examples of the tomb in which the angels are found in or near the tomb. Mary will see angels when she enters the tomb (v. 12). Some exegetes think that John has formulated this detail in order to contrast the resurrection with the Lazarus story. At the conclusion to that story, Lazarus still had to be released from the wrappings (11:44). The neat arrangement of the burial clothes may also serve as a sign that the body had not been stolen. The other tomb stories interpret the significance of the empty tomb by the angel's proclamation of the resurrection kerygma. This account lacks any trace of the resurrection kerygma. However, it is implied in the reaction of the Beloved Disciple in v. 8. He sees and believes. This reaction is repeated in the story of Jesus' appearance by the sea. The Beloved Disciple immediately recognizes the Lord (21:7). Such belief is contrasted with Thomas's demands for visible proof of the bodily reality of the risen Lord later in the chapter. The evangelist pronounces those who do not see and yet believe blessed (20:29). However, the exemplary faith of the Beloved Disciple plays no role in the rest of the chapter. We have seen a related ambiguity in Luke. The women recall the words that Jesus had previously spoken to his followers (24:8), yet the events of the empty tomb remain shrouded in mystery until the appearances of the risen Lord.

Verses 11–18: *But Mary stood weeping outside the tomb, and as she wept she stooped to look into the tomb, and she saw two angels sitting where the body of Jesus had lain, one at the head and one at the feet. They said to her, "Why are you weeping?" She said to them, "Because they have taken away my Lord and I do not know where they have laid him." Saying this, she turned around and saw Jesus standing there; but she did not know that it was Jesus. Jesus said to her, "Woman, why are you weeping? Whom are you seeking?" Thinking that he was the gardener, she said to him, "Sir if you have carried him away, tell me where you have laid him and I will take him away." Jesus said to her, "Mary." She turned and said to him in Hebrew, "Rabboni" (which means teacher). Jesus said to her, "Do not hold me, for I have not yet ascended to the Father; but go to my*

brothers and say to them, I am ascending to my Father and your
Father, to my God and your God." Mary Magdalene went and said to
the disciples, "I have seen the Lord"; and she told them that he had
said these things to her.

This tradition contains some parallels to the Christophany of Mt
28:9f. There is a duplication between the words of the angel and
those of the Lord, though here only the Lord gives Mary the message
to carry the resurrection kerygma back to his disciples. Since the
Lukan tradition and the earlier Johannine tradition suggest a visit to
the tomb that was independent of any Christophany, Brown thinks
that this section has combined pieces of two earlier traditions. Verses
11–13 are a truncated report of a visit to the tomb in which the
women encounter an angel. Verses 14–18 are the Johannine elaboration of a tradition in which the risen Jesus had appeared to Mary
Magdalene outside the tomb. It is possible that the oldest tradition
only spoke of the woman (or Mary) seeing the Lord and that Matthew
and John have each formulated an independent dialogue to suit the
story.[58] R. Schnackenburg points out that the evangelist has also
reworked v. 12. The angels now mark the head and feet of the absent
body. Presumably, they are seated in the positions where Peter had
seen the grave clothes. The absence of any reaction of fear makes it
unlikely that John thought of the story as an angelophany. The angels' question "Why are you weeping?" resembles the Lukan "What
are you seeking?" (Lk 24:4).[59] The encounter in the tomb has been
truncated so that the story moves on to its real focus, the encounter
with the risen Lord. The initial dialogue and nonrecognition parallel
the opening of the Emmaus story and are probably traditional. However, the recognition at hearing Jesus call her name reflects the
Johannine theme that Jesus' "own" hear his voice and respond
(10:3f.). Jesus' words to Mary form the focus of the passage:

Do not touch me, for I have not yet ascended to the Father.
Go to my brothers and tell them, I am ascending to my Father and
your Father, to my God and your God.

As is the case in other versions of the tomb story, the woman is
commissioned to take a message to Jesus' disciples. Like Mark, this
message concerns where Jesus is going; like Matthew, it embodies
the resurrection kerygma—Jesus is going back to his Father. This
formulation reflects the Johannine understanding of Jesus' hour, his
crucifixion and glorification, as return to the Father from whom he
came.

Commentators frequently take the opening command not to cling

to Jesus as an indication that she has misunderstood Jesus' promise to
return to his disciples (14:18–19; 16:22) to imply that Jesus is to be
physically present with his disciples rather than present through the
Spirit.[60] This interpretation undoubtedly captures one level of meaning in the context of the Fourth Gospel. However, the parallel between this episode and Mt 28:9 suggests another level of interpretation. The original point of Mary's action may have been an act of
worship like that in Matthew. A further indication of the relationship
between this passage and the earlier Matthean tradition lies in the
use of the expression "my brothers." It not only appears here in John
but is also found in Mt 28:10.[61] At the level of the evangelist's redaction an act of worship is prohibited because Jesus' return to the
Father is not yet completed.

The message sent to the disciples is typical of the Johannine kerygma. John understands the crucifixion as Jesus' return to the Father
(12:32–33). The theme of Jesus' ascent or return to the Father dominates references to the crucifixion in the Johannine discourses (3:13;
6:62; 7:33; 13:1, 3; 14:4, 28; 16:5, 17, 28; 17:13). The message to the
disciples does not contain any of the traditional expressions of the
resurrection kerygma such as we find in the other gospels. Nor does it
promise them an encounter with the risen Lord. Instead, it announces that the glorification promised in the Johannine passion
narrative is now completed. Therefore, fulfillment of the promises
made in the Farewell Discourses is at hand. Jesus' passing from the
world to the Father means his permanent presence to the community in the Spirit. Mary's words to the disciples, "I have seen the
Lord," are repeated in the disciples' proclamation to Thomas (v. 25).
Thus, the significance of the tomb stories in the Johannine narrative
is not tied to the faith of the disciples as much as it is to the christological affirmation about Jesus' return to the Father from whom he came.
Jesus is indeed not where those who belong to the world can find
him. He has returned to the Father.

JOHN 20:19–29

Both Luke and John have the meal appearance preceded by reference to another one. In Lk 24:34, we find, "The Lord has risen indeed
and appeared to Simon," and in Jn 20:18, Mary's announcement, "I
have seen the Lord." Brown has suggested that John has deliberately
replaced a reference to Peter with the tradition known in the Johan-

nine community that Mary was the first person to see the risen Lord. This replacement is an acknowledgment of her equality with Jesus' other disciples as a witness to the resurrection.[62] In John as in Luke, the apostolic kerygma precedes the appearance to the disciples as a group. Johannine editing is evident in v. 20. Since the evangelist has created a separate story in which Jesus demonstrates the physical reality of his risen body, there is no reason for Jesus to point to the wounds of the crucifixion. This passage also poses the same question as the Lukan story about the persons covered by Jesus' commissioning. Some might presume on the basis of the reference to Thomas as "one of the twelve" in v. 24 that only that group is intended. However, the Fourth Gospel does not use "the twelve" as a designation for its group of Jesus' disciples. The expression probably represents pre-Johannine tradition.

Verses 19–23: *On the evening of that day, the first day of the week, with the doors where the disciples were shut out of fear of the Jews, Jesus came and stood among them and said to them, "Peace be with you." When he had said this, he showed them his hands and his side. The disciples rejoiced when they saw the Lord. Jesus said to them again, "Peace be with you. As the Father has sent me so I send you." And when he had said this, he breathed on them, and said to them, "Receive the Holy Spirit. If you forgive anyone's sins, they are forgiven; if you retain anyone's sins, they are retained."*

The indication of evening as the time of the meal appears to be traditional. John has added the motif of fear of the Jews to the introduction of the story, since the Johannine community continued to experience persecution by Jews as a threat to its own existence (Jn 16:2). The original story may have included closed doors to emphasize Jesus' miraculous appearance among the disciples. The Lukan story simply had Jesus appear in their midst (Lk 24:36). Both stories also have the opening greeting "Peace be to you" (Lk 24:37; Jn 20:19). In Luke an element of doubt follows immediately; we have seen that this doubt may have provoked the demonstration of Jesus' hands and side that remains in Jn 20:20. Rejoicing is also part of the traditional story (Mt 28:8; the women leave the tomb rejoicing; Lk 24:41; attributes the disciples' disbelief to their joy; Lk 24:54; has them return to Jerusalem rejoicing). But within the Johannine context it also represents the fulfillment of Jesus' promise that after their sorrow his disciples would rejoice (e.g., 16:20–22). John has avoided the awkwardness of combining joy at the fulfillment of the eschatological promise of rejoicing and doubt by placing the burden for the

latter on a disciple who is not present, Thomas. The physical signs of
Jesus' hands and side refer the reader back to the crucifixion scene.
Though John does not use the kerygmatic formula about the crucified as risen, Jesus' appearance here may be seen to demonstrate that
reality.

As in the other traditions of Jesus' appearance to disciples, the
central element of the story lies in the words of commissioning. This
commissioning has already been embodied in the Farewell Discourses (13:20; 17:18).[63] One can only guess which elements in this
commissioning are derived from pre-Johannine tradition. Certainly
the sending formula, while a major element in the Christology of the
Fourth Gospel, would appear to reflect an earlier tradition. The logion about forgiving or binding sins in v. 23 also represents an early
tradition (cf. Mt 16:19; 18:18). Verse 21 contains two parts: the gift of
peace and the commissioning saying. Both appear to be traditional
elements in the resurrection appearance tradition. The Johannine
formulation of the commission makes its relationship to the earlier
type in which the disciples are to evangelize ambiguous. Schnackenburg observes that this formula does not appear to be based on
missionary language but is addressed to all disciples.[64] Jn 17:20 adds
to the commissioning "all who will believe through them." This addition might suggest that the Johannine tradition did attach missionary
overtones to the formula. However, it also suggests that "sending" is
not limited to the eleven. It describes the position of every disciple.

The bestowing of the Spirit is not attached to the other appearance
traditions, though Luke's narrative ends with the promise of the
coming of the Spirit. Jn 7:39 and 16:7 promise that the disciples will
receive the Spirit when Jesus has been glorified. Verse 17 had an-
nounced that glorification to be taking place. Thus, it is possible to see
this element as the evangelist's addition to the tradition.[65] On the
other hand, Schnackenburg thinks that this motif was part of the pre-
Johannine tradition about forgiveness of sin. He points to the combination of the Spirit and eschatological forgiveness of sin in the Old
Testament (Ez 36:25, 27) and the Dead Sea Scrolls (1 QS 3.7; 4.20f.). It
is also part of the association of forgiveness and baptism in the New
Testament (Ac 2:38; Tit 3:5; 1 Pt 1:23; 2:1f.; 1 Jn 3:5; 1 Cor 6:11). Since
the next verse uses quite un-Johannine language in speaking of forgiveness of sin, Schnackenburg holds that the conferring of the Spirit
was also traditional.[66] The saying about forgiveness in v. 23 is quite
different from the treatment of sin elsewhere in the gospel. There sin
is failure to believe in Jesus as the One sent by the Father. 1 John
shows (1:9 and 2:19) that the Johannine community had a tradition
about forgiveness of sins. The formula implies an action on the part of

the community that is to be upheld in the judgment. Those scholars who think that Mt 16:19 was originally part of the tradition of Peter's vision of the risen Lord would find that an additional parallel to the pre-Johannine tradition here. Forgiveness may be implied in the instruction to baptize in Mt 28:19, and it is at the center of the commission in Lk 24:47. Thus, it would seem preferable to see forgiveness here as having the implication that one is to bring new members into the community rather than giving it the ecclesial interpretation of Mt 18:19 in which it concerns how the community deals with the sinfulness of its members.[67]

Verses 24–29: *Now Thomas, one of the twelve called the twin, was not with them when Jesus came. So the other disciples told him, "We have seen the Lord." But he said to them, "Unless I see in his hands the print of the nails, and place my finger in the mark of the nails and place my hand in his side, I will not believe." Eight days later, his disciples were again in the house, and Thomas was with them. The doors were shut, but Jesus came and stood among them, and said, "Peace be with you." Then he said to Thomas, "Put your finger here, and see my hands; and put out your hand and place it in my side; do not be disbelieving but believing." Thomas answered him, "My Lord and my God!" Jesus said to him, "Have you believed because you have seen me? Blessed are those who have not seen and yet believe."*

This story dramatizes the motif of doubt that was part of the pre-Johannine tradition. The incident appears to have been created by the evangelist. Verse 25 repeats the words of v. 20, and v. 26 is a paraphrase of the description of Jesus' appearance in v. 19. Verses 24 and 25 come as something of a surprise, since there was no previous indication that one of the disciples had been missing.[68]

Thomas's confession of faith is characteristic of John's Christology. The christological confession of Jesus' unity with the Father is repeated throughout the gospel (e.g., 1:49; 4:42; 6:69; 9:37f.; 11:27; 16:30; 20:17). Such confessions of belief may well have been part of the liturgical tradition of the Johannine community. Jn 14:9f. insisted that to see Jesus is to see the Father. Thomas now sees the crucified and glorified Jesus as Lord and God. The episode concludes with a macarism that looks toward future believers. From now on, faith in Jesus is to be based on Jesus' presence in the Spirit. Despite what later Christians might feel, such faith is not inferior to that of those who have seen the Lord.[69]

This striking christological confession brings the story of Jesus to a close. Like Matthew but unlike Luke, John never describes the departure of the risen Jesus. He may intend to convey the same impression that the concluding logion of Matthew makes explicit: Jesus is not absent. He remains with the disciples forever.

JOHN 21:1–14

The chapter is divided into an account of a resurrection appearance by the Sea of Galilee (vv. 1–14) and a collection of sayings of the risen Jesus about Peter and the Beloved Disciple. Schnackenburg does not think that the evangelist was responsible for the composition of the chapter. Not only does it presume the death of the gospel's author (vv. 23–24), but the disparate collection lacks the integrating perspective typical of the evangelist. These traditions have not been reinterpreted in light of the gospel's Christology.[70]

Verses 1 and 14 link this chapter to the previous one. Jn 21:1a mentions Jesus' previous appearance to the disciples. Verse 14 ends the appearance story with a numbering that identifies it as the third appearance of Jesus to the disciples after his resurrection. Verse 2 uses the name "Simon" for Peter, as in Jn 20:6. Thomas is also designated "twin" *(didymos)* as in Jn 20:25. The Johannine character of this tradition is also evident in the explicit inclusion of Nathanael as one of the group. The dominant figure in this chapter is Peter. Even the sayings about the Beloved Disciple in the concluding section of the chapter are provoked by Peter's question (vv. 20–21). The emphasis on Petrine motifs, the commissioning of Peter as shepherd, and the eucharistic overtones of the meal attached to the appearance by the sea suggest that the chapter is written out of the ecclesial concerns of the Johannine community.[71]

The first section of the chapter appears to contain two separate traditions. The first, the appearance by the Sea of Galilee, is often compared to the story of the calling of Peter in Lk 5:1–11. It is thought to reflect the appearance of the Lord to Peter. The miraculous catch of fish suggests Peter's commissioning as a missionary apostle. Other elements in this Petrine tradition, which are sometimes taken to be derived from postresurrection stories, are the walking on water (Mt 14:28–33) and the announcement that Peter is the cornerstone of the new community (Mt 16:16b–19).[72] The second element in this chapter appears to be a recognition of the risen Lord in a meal.

As in the earlier story of Peter's visit to the tomb, the figure of the

Beloved Disciple is suddenly introduced into this appearance story. He is not mentioned in the list of disciples given in v. 2. Yet he suddenly appears in v. 7 and—as at the tomb—immediately recognizes the truth about resurrection. He hails the stranger on the shore as the Lord. Schnackenburg thinks that the role played by the Beloved Disciple in the tomb visit (Jn 20:8) is the basis for his introduction here.[73] Just as he saw the disposition of the grave clothes and believed, so he sees the bursting nets and knows that it is the Lord. The Lukan story of a miraculous catch parallels the abundance of fish with the ensuing mission. This parallel suggests that the large number of fish is intended to represent either the size or the universality of the mission.[74] Given that interpretation, the miraculous catch stands in the place of commissioning the disciples to evangelize in other stories of resurrection appearances.

Fish also belong to the tradition of a postresurrection meal, which is interlocked with the story of the miraculous catch (vv. 9b, 12, and 13). Jesus' action in preparing the food and giving it to the disciples recalls the Johannine picture of the feeding of the crowd with its eucharistic overtones in Jn 6:11. Such overtones are also present in the Emmaus story (Lk 24:30f.) and the meal appearance in Lk 24:35.

Unlike the stories in the previous chapter, these stories do not allude to the Farewell Discourse symbolism. The choice of these traditions appears to be due to their focus on Peter. These stories only take on overtones of universal mission or eucharistic recognition when they are read in light of the type of resurrection traditions we have already studied. From the Emmaus tradition one sees the possibility that the meal scene was originally one in which the risen Lord was recognized in the meal. From the miraculous catch in Lk 5:1–11, one sees the possibility that the large catch should be tied to the commission to evangelize. The specifically Johannine references to the names of disciples and the insertion of the Beloved Disciple into this story show that the traditions had circulated in the Johannine communities. But they have not been recast to reflect the peculiar theology of the evangelist. It is not possible to decide whether the miraculous catch of fish should be seen as a resurrection tradition that Luke has retrojected into his gospel or whether it is a miracle tradition from the life of Jesus that the Johannine community has linked to the tradition of a Galilean appearance of the Lord. Just as the evangelist has supplied an additional Jerusalem appearance to incorporate the tradition of Thomas's doubt, so the community may have used a miracle associated with the calling of the disciples to fill out the Galilean tradition. Certainly the introduction to the story gives no indication that the disciples had had experience of the risen Lord.

They are merely pursuing their customary occupation of fishing. If we reverse the view that the miraculous catch was a postresurrection event retrojected into the life of Jesus and see it as an incident from the life of Jesus used to fill in where narrative was lacking, then we could say that the Johannine tradition has only one resurrection story, Jesus' appearance to his disciples at a meal.

JOHN 21:15–24

Verses 15–17 commission Peter as the shepherd of Jesus' sheep. Verses 18–23 concern the fate of Peter and the Beloved Disciple. The editor may have connected the two themes with reference to Peter, since Jn 10:11 sets up the model of the good shepherd as the one who lays down his life for the sheep.[75] Verse 24 identifies the Beloved Disciples as the source of the Johannine traditions about Jesus.[76] By explaining Peter's special position as shepherd and the fates of the two heroes of the tradition, the author of the chapter has moved his readers from the period of Jesus' resurrection appearances to the postapostolic period in which they now live.

His readers are those who believe without having seen and who must be assured that the testimony about Jesus that they have received is reliable (v. 25). This emphasis takes on added importance if one follows Brown's suggestion that the chapter was edited after the period of schism and controversy over the true interpretation of the Johannine tradition that we find in the Johannine Epistles.[77] The future direction of the Johannine community itself is at stake. Concerns for the future of the community in the earlier resurrection traditions are subsumed under the confidence in the presence of the Lord. But the schism that split the Johannine community had shown that even claims to the same presence and the Spirit did not guarantee the unity of the community or the interpretation given it by later generations. Thus, this formulation of the commissioning tradition shows an unusual, inner ecclesial tone.[78]

Verses 15–17: *When they had finished breakfast, Jesus said to Simon Peter, "Simon, son of John, do you love me more than these?" He said to him, "Yes, Lord; you know that I love you." He said to him, "Feed my lambs." A second time, he said to him, "Simon, son of John, do you love me?" He said to him, "Yes, Lord, you know that I love you." He said to him, "Tend my sheep." He said to him a third time,*

"Simon, son of John, do you love me?" And he said to him, "Lord, you know everything; you know that I love you." Jesus said to him, "Feed my sheep."

This brief dialogue is cast in a repetitious pattern: Peter is asked about his love for Jesus; he gives an affirmative—even if increasingly irritated—answer and is then commissioned as the one to take charge of Jesus' sheep. The initial question "Do you love me more than these?" perhaps recalls Peter's vow that he would give his life for Jesus in Jn 13:37. The threefold pattern permits Peter to rehabilitate himself after the threefold denial, which had demonstrated the failure of that vow (Jn 18:17, 25, 26). In Jn 18:25, Peter actually denies that he is a disciple of Jesus.[79] Jesus is presented as the ideal shepherd in Jn 10. He fulfills the Ezekiel prophecies that God will shepherd the people Israel. The Dead Sea Scrolls use "shepherd" as a designation for the guardian or overseer of the community. This commission makes Peter shepherd of Jesus' sheep. It does not establish a relationship of superiority by which he commands the other disciples.[80] The traditions preserved in this chapter do not answer the question of what is meant by the command "Tend my sheep." If one presumes that the tradition originated in the missionary commissioning of Peter, then the reference might be to the "other sheep" of Jn 10:16. But even that passage has its exegetical difficulties. Most commentaries on the Fourth Gospel presume that it refers to expanding the message to the Gentiles, as symbolized in the Greeks coming to Jesus in Jn 12:20. If so, the tradition would make Peter responsible for the expansion of the mission "to the nations." It would be a commissioning like that addressed to the eleven in Mt 28:19.

However, if one presumes that the postresurrection commissioning of Peter is related to overseeing the Christian community, as in the saying of Mt 16:18f., then tending the sheep refers to those "other sheep" who are the Christians who do not belong to the Johannine fold. When their hero Peter is contrasted with the Johannine hero, the Beloved Disciple, his faith and love for Jesus are shown to be inferior. Brown suggests that the crucial issue separating the Johannine and apostolic Christians was christological. Perhaps, he speculates, the delayed confession of Jesus' divinity made by Thomas was intended to express the evangelist's hope that such Christians would come to accept the understanding of Jesus found in the Johannine community. The two groups are also divided in their ecclesiology. For the Johannine community, Jesus shepherds the sheep directly. No human shepherds intervene between the Lord and the community.[81] The schism of the Epistles period had shown that this

form of leadership was difficult to sustain. Therefore, Brown suggests
that the Johannine Christians were seeking accommodation with
those from the Petrine churches. Acknowledgment of Peter's love
for Jesus and his commission by the risen Lord to "feed the sheep"
would make it possible for Johannine Christians to accept patterns of
authority developed in other churches. At the same time, the positive acknowledgment of Peter might remove suspicion of Johannine
Christians from the other communities.[82] These new concerns represent the effort of the Johannine community at the end of the first and
beginning of the second century to refocus its self-understanding in
relationship to the apostolic Christians and their forms of community
leadership. It is difficult to go behind these reformulated images to
the earlier stages of this tradition. It may have originated with a quite
different understanding of the commission of Peter, who was remembered as instrumental in the conversion of the Gentiles (Gal 2:9,
Ac 10–11).[83]

Verses 18–23: *"Truly, truly I say to you, when you were young, you
girded yourself and walked where you wanted; but when you are old
you will stretch out your hands and another will gird you and carry
you where you do not wish to go." (This was said to show by what
death he would glorify God.) Peter turned and saw the disciple
whom Jesus loved, who had lain on his breast at the supper and had
said, "Lord who is it that is going to betray you." When Peter saw
him, he said to Jesus, "Lord, what about this man?" Jesus said to him,
"If it is my will that he remain until I come, what is it to you? Follow
me!" The saying spread abroad among the brothers that this disciple
was not to die, yet Jesus did not say to him that he was not to die, but
"If it is my will that he remain until I come, what is it to you?"*

The final verses are clearly secondary reflection on the fate of both
Peter and the Beloved Disciple. This reflection is based on sayings
attributed to Jesus. In Mk 10:39 and parallels, Jesus is pictured as
predicting that the sons of Zebedee will drink the cup of martyrdom.
Other passages in both the synoptics (Mk 13:10–13) and John (16:2)
predict death as part of the trials that are to come to Jesus' disciples.
Mt 10:10–20 associates such trials with the command to evangelize.
Verses 18–19 appear to embody a proverb that points toward persecution, though it does not directly refer to death. The author, writing
after the fact, presumes that it is about Peter's martyrdom. He also
immediately subordinates the theme of martyrdom to the demand
that one "follow Jesus." Peter's rehabilitation means that he will be
Jesus' disciple to the death.[84]

The editor of the chapter has made a rather awkward transition between the saying about Peter to another piece of tradition about the Beloved Disciple. He introduces the Beloved Disciple with an elaborate reference back to the special relationship between the Beloved Disciple and Jesus in the Johannine supper account (13:23–25). Peter's question is not aimed at suggesting hostility between the two. The introduction has been composed in order to make the transition to the traditional saying in v. 22 and the author's correction in v. 23 possible.[85] It has been suggested that the saying was originally attached to an anonymous, long-lived disciple. The redactor has made it a statement about the Beloved Disciple.[86] Our closest parallel to the type of logion here is the synoptic promise that some of Jesus' company will not die before the coming of the kingdom (Mk 9:1).[87] This additional piece of tradition would appear to set the Beloved Disciple and Peter on an equal level.

The peculiar feature of this explanation is that it does not invoke the uniquely Johannine solution to the problems presented by the death of the Beloved Disciple, the presence of the Paraclete in the community. This omission is another example of the lack of theological elaboration in this chapter.[88] The author appears to have incorporated primitive sayings into the resurrection traditions to meet new problems in the Johannine community.

In both the Johannine and the Lukan traditions, we have seen a process of extensive reshaping of earlier traditions about Jesus' resurrection. Both use appearance stories to carry a message about the identity of the Christian community and the source of its traditions. The Johannine tradition has developed some themes, like that of the bodily reality of the risen Lord, differently from the Lukan tradition. In chapter 20 much of the development of the resurrection tradition can be traced to the specific emphases of Johannine Christology. Such developments do not suggest idle speculation about the risen Lord and his appearances. The analysis of these chapters has suggested a diversity of resurrection traditions and stories, some of which may have undergone several shifts in emphasis or function prior to their embodiment in the evangelist's narrative. Both the Lukan and Johannine traditions see the appearance and commissioning of the risen Lord as closely related to the meals of Jesus with his disciples. For the Fourth Gospel, this link is most strongly embodied in the resurrection perspective from which the discourses at the Last Supper are given. For Luke, the recognition at Emmaus serves to make the connection. These stories also suggest that the experiences that the early Christian communities had in following the risen Lord, whom they knew to be present to them, provided crucial elements in the way in which the evangelists imagined the first encounter(s) between Jesus and his disciples.

NOTES

1. See J.-M. Guillaume, *Luc interprète des anciennes traditions sur la résurrection de Jésus* (EBib; Paris: Gabalda, 1979), 15–30.
2. C. F. D. Moule, *The Origins of Christology* (Cambridge: Cambridge University, 1977), 99f.
3. J. L. Houlden, *Patterns of Faith* (Philadelphia: Fortress, 1977), 42.
4. See R. H. Fuller, *The Formation of the Resurrection Narratives* (New York: Macmillan, 1971), 127–29; G. Lohfink, *Die Himmelfahrt Jesu: Untersuchungen zu den Himmelfahrts- und Erhöhungstexten bei Lukas* (StANT 26; Munich: Kösel, 1971), 55–58; 186f.; Schillebeeckx *(Jesus* [New York: Seabury, 1979], 340–43) has adopted this explanation. He argues that it does not represent mythologizing of the Jesus story but reflects the same process that the theologian follows in trying to find categories in which to explain what has happened in Jesus. Luke has taken a Christian datum and made it intelligible to his audience by using a widely available literary model.
5. Guillaume, op. cit.; R. J. Dillon, *From Eye-Witnesses to Ministers of the Word. Tradition and Composition in Luke 24* (Rome: Biblical Institute Press, 1978), and the analysis of the Emmaus traditions by J. Wanke, ". . . wie sie ihn beim Brotbrechen erkannten. Zur Auslegung der Emmauserzählung Lk 24, 13–35," *Biblische Zeitschrift* 18 (1974), 180–92.
6. Dillon, op. cit., 20.
7. Dillon consistently holds to Lukan redaction of Mark as the only necessary hypothesis (op. cit., 5–17). Fuller, on the other hand, argues that Luke has edited an independent tradition while keeping his eye on Mark (op. cit., 95). Guillaume (op. cit., 50) strengthens the case for a pre-Lukan tradition that was independent of Mark by pointing to elements in Luke that appear to stand midway between the Markan tradition and the Johannine tradition.

8. Dillon (op. cit., 16f.) thinks that Luke has omitted the perplexity over the removal of the stone in order to focus the entire episode on the discovery that the tomb is empty.

9. Dillon (op. cit., 20–23) points to several parallels in narrative technique between this story and the Lukan editing of the Transfiguration. The Transfiguration refers to a conversation between Jesus and two figures about his impending departure, an expression that includes both crucifixion and ascension (9:30f.). The two are dressed in white, as are the two men who address the disciples after the ascension (Ac 1:10).

10. E. L. Bode, *The First Easter Morning: The Gospel Accounts of the Women's Visit to the Tomb of Jesus* (Rome: Biblical Institute Press, 1970), 59f.; Dillon, op. cit., 26f.

11. Fuller, op. cit., 97.

12. Guillaume (op. cit., 37–41) emphasizes the parallels between the Lukan Transfiguration and this section: 24:4/9:29f., 39; 24:3/9:36; 24:9/9:36. On the Lukan understanding of the ministry of Jesus as a way that culminates in the Messiah's transit to glory, see Fitzmyer, op. cit., 169f.; 194.

13. Guillaume, op. cit., 47–50.

14. Fuller, op. cit., 98f.; Bode, op. cit., 62f. Dillon (op. cit., 38–45) holds that Luke has no sense of Son of Man as part of a resurrection as exaltation tradition. He is using a traditional expression about the passion. The title appropriate to the risen One in Luke is *"Christos"* (vv. 26 and 46). Son of Man, he argues, belongs to the period of concealment that is not over until the risen Lord appears.

15. Bode, op. cit., 64; Dillon, op. cit., 47f.

16. For pre-Lukan tradition, see Bode, op. cit., 67. Dillion (op. cit., 51) bases his case for the inadequacy of their faith on the consistent use of words *(rhēmata)* for the passion predictions that are always misunderstood and to the explicit references to new understanding in vv. 31 and 45.

17. Guillaume, op. cit., 35f.

18. Dillon, op. cit., 53–56. Bode (op. cit., 67) emphasizes the integrity of the women's witness.

19. Dillon, op. cit., 56–58. Dillon thinks that the presence of two witnesses from the list of followers in Galilee adds to the credibility of the women as witnesses and hence increases the tension in the story between their testimony and the disbelief of the apostolic leaders of the community.

20. Fuller, op. cit., 102f.; P. Benoit, "Marie Madeleine et les disciples au tombeau selon Jean 20, 1–18," *Judentum, Urchristentum,*

Kirche (BZNW 46; Fest. J. Jeremias; ed. W. Eltester; Berlin:
Töpelmann, 1964, 2nd ed.), 142–44; idem, *The Passion and Res-
urrection of Jesus Christ* (New York: Sheed & Ward, 1969), 289.
Fuller and Benoit argue for two independent traditions that
diverged from a common source. H. Grass *(Ostergeschehen und
Osterberichte* [Göttingen: Vandenhoeck & Ruprecht, 1964, 3rd
ed. (1956)], 34) has tried to argue that Luke is summarizing a
Johannine tradition, which was without the elements of belief.
See also Dillon, op. cit., 58–65; Bode, op. cit., 69f.; Guillaume, op.
cit., 59.

21. See H. D. Betz, "Ursprung und Wesen des christlichen Glaubens
nach der Emmauslegende (Lk 24, 13–32)," *Zeitschrift für Theologie und Kirche* 66 (1969), 7–21.

22. Betz, op. cit., 16–20; Dillon (op. cit., 83) argues that it also accounts for the alteration between the eleven and the wider
circle of disciples that is a persistent feature in the transitional
chapters of Luke-Acts.

23. Fuller, op. cit., 106.

24. Fuller, op. cit., 110.

25. Fuller, op. cit., 111; on the irony of v. 20, see Dillon, op. cit., 128.

26. Dillon (op. cit., 109) emphasizes the irony of this recital. Those
reporting the events are completely ignorant of their significance, though the reader knows that these are the culmination
of the story of salvation.

27. J. Fitzmyer, *The Gospel According to Luke I–IX* (AnBi 28; Garden City, N.Y.: Doubleday, 1981), 200.

28. Fuller (op. cit., 111) points to the motif of fulfillment of Scripture
as one of the indications that Luke is using material from earlier
traditions. Dillon (op. cit., 132f.) claims that the reproach here
and that given the women by the angel are intended to be
identical. He thinks that Luke means to show that even Scripture does not lead to faith. Faith can only be the gift of the risen
One. However, we would insist that there is a distinction between the "they remembered" attributed to the women and the
"hardheartedness" attributed to the disciples on the road. The
women have come to faith in Jesus because they remember his
teaching. The disciples on the road must have it repeated for
them.

29. Guillaume (op. cit., 120f.) suggests that the parallels between vv.
25–27 and vv. 44–46 are intended to show that the kerygmatic
instruction of the community derives from the risen One, himself.

30. See the detailed charts in Guillaume, op. cit., 122–27.

31. Fitzmyer, op. cit., 766–68.
32. Guillaume, op. cit., 147–57; Dillon, op. cit., 105–12; 149.
33. Dillon, op. cit., 150–53.
34. See A. George, "The Accounts of the Appearances to the Eleven from Luke 24, 36–53," in E. Dhanis, ed., *Resurrexit. Actes du symposium international sur la résurrection de Jésus* (Rome: Libreria Editrice Vaticana, 1974), 52–73. George notes that although one cannot establish a single story, Luke, John, and Matthew all appear to know a tradition in which there is only one appearance to the disciples gathered as a group. Matthew and Luke emphasize the passion and resurrection as the turning point in the history of salvation. All three traditions connect the Easter revelation of Jesus' lordship with the commissioning of the disciples to undertake a mission of preaching.
35. Guillaume, op. cit., 170–201. Guillaume thinks that it is impossible to decide whether the parallels between Luke and elements of the Johannine tradition are based on a written source or oral traditions.
36. Fuller, op. cit., 115; Dillon, op. cit., 186–92. Fuller contrasts this concern over the physical reality of the risen body with Paul's images of a "spiritual body" that is not "flesh and blood" in 1 Cor 15:35–50. However, one should avoid pushing the contrast, since as we shall see, the traditions and problems addressed in 1 Corinthians are quite different from those involved in Luke. The suspicions to which Luke responds appear to be generated once the resurrection comes to be narrated as appearance. The disciples are suspected of "seeing things."
37. Dillon, op. cit., 193–95.
38. Ibid., 187–89.
39. Ibid., 205–206.
40. Dillon, op. cit., 210–12. Dillon (op. cit., 213–25) points out that Jerusalem is the city in which the prophets and hence the prophet Jesus is destined to die (Lk 13:31–34; 18:31). This function is continued when the death of the first martyr, Stephen, initiates the actual spread of the gospel to the Gentiles (Ac 8:1–4).
41. Fuller, op. cit., 118.
42. See E. S. Fiorenza, *In Memory of Her. A Feminist Theological Reconstruction of Christian Origins* (New York: Crossroad, 1983), 160–204; A. Weiser, "Die Rolle der Frau in der urchristlichen Mission," *Die Frau im Urchristentum* (eds. G. Dautzenberg, H. Merklein, and K. Muller; Freiburg: Herder, 1983), 158–81.

43. See H. Ritt, "Die Frauen und die Osterbotschaft. Synopse der Grabesgeschichten (Mk 16, 1–8; Mt 27, 62–28, 15; Lk 24, 1–12; Joh 20, 1–18)," in *Frau im Urchristentum*, op. cit., 117–33. The Fourth Gospel has explicit missionary roles for women in the story of the Samaritan woman and in its positioning of Mary Magdalene in the role of the first recipient of a vision of the risen Jesus. See R. E. Brown, *The Community of the Beloved Disciple* (New York: Paulist, 1979), 187–92.

44. Dillon, op. cit., 170–72; Fuller, op. cit., 120–23. Guillaume (op. cit., 228–48) goes into a detailed literary analysis to show that Luke is responsible for both stories of Jesus' going up into heaven.

45. Guillaume, op. cit., 250–61.

46. Dillon (op. cit., 179–80) points to the raising of the hands as the Levitical gesture of blessing (Lev 9:22; Sir 50:20). Worship (ibid., 220–23) is the high point of the entire passage.

47. C. K. Barrett, *The Gospel According to St. John* (Philadelphia: Westminster, 1978, rev. ed.), 562.

48. Barrett, ibid., 395. Barrett notes that John does not usually use *anastasis* as a term for resurrection. It appears with Jesus as the subject who raises the believer in Jn 6:39f., 44, 54. It appears with other traditional terms in Jn 5:29, a passage that also contains John's favorite eschatological term "life." John generally prefers to use the verb *egeirein* for resurrection.

49. As in Rom 1:4; Ac 2:32, 36; 5:31; 13:33; Brown, op. cit., 86 note 161.

50. P. Minear, "We Don't Know Where . . . Jn 20:2," *Interpretation* 30 (1976), 125–39.

52. Minear, op. cit., 126. Minear goes on to propose that John is deliberately answering the charge that Jesus cannot be the Mosaic prophet by paralleling Moses' unknown burial place with the fact that the body of Jesus is not even here (ibid., 137f.). John is deliberately using this detail as the summary for the controversy themes over "where" Jesus is going when he speaks of the world not being able to find him (Jn 8:22–23; 7:35f.; op. cit., 133–37). John answers the question about "where" Jesus goes in two ways: he goes to the Father, and he dwells in the community.

53. See Benoit, op. cit., 141–50. Benoit argues that the original tradition was contained in 11a and 14b–18 and that Mt 28:9f. is dependent on an early version of the pre-Johannine tradition.

54. Minear, op. cit., 133–34.

55. R. Mahoney, *Two Disciples at the Tomb. The Background and Message of Jn 20.1–10* (Theologie und Wirklichkeit 6; Frankfort: Peter Lang, 1974), 194–202; 214–27.

56. R. E. Brown, *The Gospel According to John XIII–XXI* (AnBi 29A; Garden City, N.Y.: Doubleday, 1970), 995f.
57. Brown, *John* II, 1004–1008; Mahoney, op. cit., 250; Bode, op. cit., 76. We agree with the view of Brown and Schnackenburg that v. 8 is intended to be an example of true faith. Bode and Mahoney see no further significance in the sequence of verses than the need to end the story with v. 9.
58. Brown *(John* II, 1002–1004) thinks that on the basis of comparison with the late ending of Mark (Mk 16:9–11), one must conclude that the appearance to Mary Magdalene alone is earlier than that to a group such as we find in Matthew.
59. R. Schnackenburg, *Das Johannesevangelium III. Kap. 13–21* (HTKNT IV/3; Freiburg: Herder, 1975), 372–73.
60. Brown, *John* II, 1011–13.
61. Schnackenburg, op. cit., 376f.
62. Brown, *Community,* 189–92. Though Brown falls into speaking of Mary's role as "quasi-apostolic," he himself acknowledges that apostleship within the Johannine tradition falls outside the pattern of the "twelve apostles" common in other sectors of Christianity (op. cit., 81–88). Therefore, by Johannine standards Mary's role is no more "quasi-apostolic" than that of the other Johannine disciples.
63. D. B. Woll, *Johannine Christianity in Conflict: Authority, Rank and Succession in the First Farewell Discourse* (SBL Dissertation Ser. 60; Chicago: Scholars, 1981), 85f. However, his identification of the power to forgive sins with the logion about answered prayer in Jn 14:12f. is less persuasive. Barrett, op. cit., 568f.; Brown, *John* II, 1029, 1036. Schnackenburg (op. cit., 384) speaks of the earlier scenes of commissioning as "indirect." However, that characteristic only refers to the fact that John is clear that the disciples do not take up their commission until after the return to the Father.
64. Schnackenburg, op. cit., 385. Against views like that of C. F. Evans *(Resurrection and the New Testament* [SBT ser. 2, no. 12; London: SCM, 1970], 124f.), who presumes that John is directing the disciples to undertake a world mission here. Such a direction may, of course, have been the intent of John's sources.
65. Brown, *John* II, 1030.
66. Schnackenburg, op. cit., 386.
67. So Brown, *John* II, 1039–44, against C. H. Dodd, *Historical Tradition in the Fourth Gospel* (Cambridge: Cambridge University, 1963), 348. The context of Christian initiation is fundamental to the traditions about forgiveness of sin in 1 John; see Brown, *The*

Epistles of John (AnBi 30; Garden City, N.Y.: Doubleday, 1982), 242–45. Schnackenburg (op. cit., 389) notes that the language of binding and losing here is closely related to that in 1 Jn 1:7–9 and 5:16.

68. Brown, *John* II, 1032; Schnackenburg, op. cit., 390. Schnackenburg (op. cit., 395) points to a similarity in construction between this scene and the Nathanael episode: a person who expresses doubt about the claims made for Jesus is brought to belief through a personal encounter with him.

69. Schnackenburg, op. cit., 395–98; Brown *(John* II, 1049f.) rightly rejects the view that John intends to present some deep opposition between the two groups.

70. Schnackenburg, op. cit., 407.

71. Ibid., 409; Brown, *John* II, 1078–82. Brown's most recent work on the Johannine material *(Epistles,* 110–12) relates this final chapter to the reconciliation of Johannine and Petrine Christians. It is the final chapter in the story of the Johannine community as it is preserved in the Johannine literature. The schism of the Epistles period had made it evident that Johannine Christians could only preserve their tradition by making common cause with those of the Petrine communities. At the same time, the Johannine Christians wish to secure a place for the unique, high Christology of their tradition. Brown thinks that the redaction of Jn 21 was intended to remove suspicion on both sides.

72. Brown, *John* II, 1085–92. Brown thinks that the miraculous catch story is a retrojection of a postresurrection tradition, since he cannot think of any reason for putting a story from the period of Jesus' life into the resurrection period (ibid., 1091). We have already discussed the alternative view, which we find more plausible. Lack of an account to which to attach the tradition of an appearance to Peter led to using a story from the life of Jesus to create a plausible account of that event.

73. Schnackenburg, op. cit., 423.

74. Ibid., 426f.; Brown, *John* II, 1096f. Brown also thinks that the fact that the net does not tear is symbolic. He compares hauling in the net with the Father's drawing people to Jesus in Jn 6:11; 12:30.

75. So Schnackenburg, op. cit., 363.

76. Even if one distinguishes the evangelist from the Beloved Disciple (as Brown, *Epistles,* 95–97), this material cannot be attributed to either one. The concern for a reliable witness (v. 24) and the copying of the conclusion to the gospel (v. 25) both suggest a later date. If the author is writing after the period of the Epistles,

then the concern for the reliable witness contained in the gospel may be directed against the secessionist interpretation of the Johannine tradition. Verse 25 would appear to be a defense of the editor's addition of material to the gospel. Brown (*John* II, 1129f.) also notes that true witness in the gospel is not linked to human testimony—unlike the concern for human witness in the Lukan material. Jesus is and gave the true witness (5:31–32). The Paraclete now continues that function (15:26). This emphasis may have been dropped when it gave rise to inordinate claims of authority on the part of some members of the community; see Woll, op. cit.

77. Brown, *Epistles*, 110–12.

78. Schnackenburg (op. cit., 429) is critical of Brown's (*John* II, 1111–13) emphasis on the connection between the catch of fish and mission based on the example of Lk 5:8–10. He questions whether there is any missionary commission in the Johannine stories. At the level of the redaction of the chapter, the missionary emphasis, if there was one earlier in the tradition, has taken a back seat to ecclesial concerns.

79. Denial that one is a disciple of Jesus was a particularly serious offense in the situation of persecution through which the Johannine community had come (Brown, *Community*, 84). Perhaps the traditions of Peter's rehabilitation had developed out of a concern to encourage Johannine Christians who had denied Jesus.

80. CD 13.9–10; Brown, *John* II, 1114–16.

81. Brown, *Community*, 82–87.

82. Brown, *Epistles*, 159–62. Brown argues that the Johannine group was absorbed into the apostolic churches and hence disappears as a separate entity in the second century. The secessionist group, on the other hand, moved into the developing Gnostic groups.

83. Brown, *Community*, 81, note 153.

84. Schnackenburg, op. cit., 429–35; Brown, *John* II, 1112–13.

85. Schnackenburg, op. cit., 440–42; Brown, op. cit., 1118–22.

86. So Mahoney, op. cit., 294ff. Mahoney thinks that the Beloved Disciple serves only to embody literary perspectives. The later editor has then identified that figure with the source of the community's tradition.

87. Schnackenburg, op. cit., 441f. Schnackenburg agrees that the saying was circulating independently and unattached to any figure in particular. Brown (*John* II, 1118) points out that the

necessity to correct the saying suggests that it did not come attached to this context.

88. This "falling off" from the gospel's high Christology and realized eschatology is also typical of the understanding of the Johannine tradition represented in the Epistles. See Brown, *Epistles*, 25–30. The author has recovered "older" strata in the tradition to argue against the schismatics (ibid., 97–100).

SIX

Resurrection as Apostolic Commission

The stories of resurrection contained a number of earlier traditions. Each of these traditions reflected a different situation in which resurrection language was used by early Christians. The next three chapters will pursue three of them to see how they are used elsewhere in the New Testament. The material from the Pauline letters brings us back to traditions several decades older than those in the synoptic gospels. We will see that resurrection proved to be a symbol that integrated a number of early Christian concerns. Thus, it has been considerably expanded over the rather "thin" and limited associations that we observed in Jewish material of the New Testament period. Elaboration of resurrection symbolism beyond the ecstatic conviction of divine vindication was fundamental to the early community's self-understanding. It formed the basis of its claim to be living out of a new reality. Resurrection as such was not a public event. Nor did it usher in the judgment and messianic age on the cosmic scale pictured in Jewish writings of the time. But the community experienced the presence of Jesus in the Spirit and felt itself to be living out of that new reality. It is also clear that the various developments of the resurrection symbol cannot be placed on a straight line moving logically out from one point to the next. The resurrection stories and the early kerygma in 1 Cor 15:3–5 suggest that the kernel of this new reality was established in the commissioning of specific individuals. The leaders of the Jerusalem church, Peter and James, for example, represent persons who based their authority within the community on a commission by the Lord.[1] Though elements of commissioning appear in several resurrection stories, resurrection appearances of themselves did not legitimate an individual's leadership. Paul speaks of an appearance to "more than 500 brothers" (1 Cor 15:6), which can hardly represent commissioning as leaders or apostles.[2] The recognition story on the road to Emmaus also lacks the element of commissioning. The importance of the appearances to the women has been the subject of more intense debate than the previous two examples of appearances that do not appear to be commissioning. On the one hand, they could have simply been discoverers that the tomb was empty. On the other hand, the prominence of Mary Magdalene in the tradition is easier to explain if one assumes that some form of commissioning appearance was associated with her from the beginning.[3] Our most explicit connections between encountering the risen Lord and apostolic calling are made by Paul. Both his own testimony and the narrative elaboration of Paul's call in Acts present it as the fruit of his vision of the Lord.

RESURRECTION AND PAUL'S DEFENSE OF HIS APOSTLESHIP

Paul's statements about his apostolic authority as grounded in a commission of the risen Lord are always found in situations in which he is pressed to defend his preaching of the gospel. It is frequently difficult to spell out the exact nature of the accusations that he is answering.

Galatians opens with a rhetorical statement of the charge against the apostle (Gal 1:6–9). The attack has been mounted against Paul by others—apparently outsiders to the Galatian church—who are suggesting that Paul's Gentile converts must adopt at least minimal prescriptions of the Law. They have apparently suggested that Paul's preaching of salvation through faith outside the Law represented his personal perversion of the gospel. They may also have accused him of insubordination toward the authorities in Jerusalem who were apostles before him and who exercised some supervision over the Gentile mission that Paul had joined at Antioch.[4]

Galatians 1:1

Paul, apostle not from human beings nor through human beings but through Jesus Christ and God the Father who raised him from the dead.

The greeting of the letter emphasizes the connection between apostolic authority and resurrection. Paul's more usual formulae are a simple "apostle of Christ Jesus" (1 Cor 1:1; 2 Cor 1:1) or, in the case of Romans, an expanded form, "slave of Christ Jesus, called to be an apostle, set apart for the gospel of God" (Rom 1:1). The opening of Galatians, however, has been expanded with an extensive defense of the divine source of Paul's commission. It is not based on human authority.[5] The double denial of a human source for Paul's apostleship is followed by a double reference to its divine origin: Jesus Christ and God, the Father, who raised him from the dead. Thus, the risen Lord is the foundation of Paul's authority. The clause "who raised him from the dead" occurs frequently in Paul's letters. It is a formula proclaiming the resurrection independent of a statement about the crucifixion (Rm 4:24; 8:11; 10:9; 1 Cor 6:14; 15:15; 2 Cor 4:14; 1 Thess 1:10). However, this is the only example of the formula in Galatians. Galatians does not mention resurrection outside the opening verses.

H. D. Betz thinks that this section of the letter corresponds to an apology directed toward outsiders. He compares it with the Socratic appeal to the Delphic oracle as the cause of Socrates' mission for which he is standing trial.[6] Betz's suggestion clarifies the possible impact of Paul's formula on an audience that was accustomed to the *topoi* of philosophic rhetoric. The passage is not concerned about the resurrection as such. Rather, it exploits the contrast between actions pursued out of human motives or on the basis of human authority and those undertaken as a result of divine election. A person cannot be condemned for obeying God, a point that Paul will emphasize in v. 10. That verse suggests that perhaps Paul's opponents had accused him of "pleasing human beings" when he preached freedom from the Law. Verses 11–24 have Paul defending his message in the same terms that he defended his apostolic authority. For him, the legitimacy of the apostle is integrally bound up with the gospel that he serves.[7] Verse 12 insists that a "revelation of Jesus Christ" is the source of Paul's gospel, not human teaching. The section begins with the strong affirmation "I want you to know," an expression Paul uses in situations in which he is insisting upon a fundamental principle (1 Cor 15:1; 2 Cor 8:1; 1 Cor 12:3). Verse 16 suggests that the genitive in the expression "of Jesus Christ" refers to Jesus Christ as the content of the revelation rather than as its source. Paul follows Gal 1:12 with the account of his past life and calling. He implies that his devotion to Judaism would not lead him to preach salvation without the Law short of some divine intervention. Paul was neither ignorant of the Law nor unsuccessful in keeping it.

Paul introduces the reference to the revelation of Jesus by speaking of his calling as having been set aside from his mother's womb. This motif is derived from the calling of the prophets in Is 49:1–6 and Jer 1:4–5. It shows that Paul saw his experience as a calling like that of the Old Testament prophet. Thus, it is continuous with his life of zealous service to God and not a rejection of it. Paul says that God revealed his Son "so that I might preach him among the Gentiles." Like the prophet, Paul is entrusted with a specific message to a specific group. Paul goes on to insist that he did not consult with any human being (v. 16c) and did not go to the authorities in Jerusalem (v. 17) but set out directly to preach. The rest of the section describes the visits Paul later made to Jerusalem in such a way as to emphasize his independence from the Jerusalem apostles (vv. 18–24).

The expression "revealed his Son in me" has caused exegetical problems. The allusion to the revelation of God's Son may imply as its content something like the cross and resurrection creed that appears so frequently in Paul. The questions are raised by the use of "in me" instead of "to me." Elsewhere (1 Cor 9:1 and 15:8) Paul uses expressions about seeing the Lord that suggest some sort of external vision. Betz proposes to solve the problem by pointing out that Paul did not have a fixed vocabulary in which to describe his encounter with the risen Lord. The best clue for what he means by "in me" lies in what he says about Christ and the Spirit in Gal 2:20 and 4:6. The vision is an ecstatic experience equivalent to other experiences of the Spirit.[8] Thus, the references to resurrection in this section do not convey any information about the experience as such. They belong to the rhetorical context of a defense of one's independence from human authority. They seek to show that Paul's gospel and apostleship are founded in divine choice and not in some authority that he has derived "secondhand" by the commissioning of the Jerusalem authorities or any other human beings. The most we can say about the resurrection experience itself is that it was an ecstatic experience such as early Christians commonly attributed to the Spirit.

1 Corinthians

Paul's other references to apostleship and seeing the Lord occur in 1 Corinthians in contexts in which Paul is explicitly comparing himself with the other apostles, especially Peter. Once again, Paul wishes to establish the equality of his claim and theirs. He also emphasizes his independence. 1 Cor 9:1–11 responds to accusations that appear to have been leveled at Paul's missionary praxis.

What appears to be at stake are Paul's freedom and rights as an apostle. These have been questioned by those who see his working for a living as a violation of the charismatic style of radical dependence on the community in which one preaches that was the norm for other apostles. Paul admits that the apostolic right to support from the community was even extended to the families of apostles. The passage reflects an intense debate over the appropriate mode of support for apostles in the early church. This debate was intensified by the contrast between Paul's style of founding communities and the tradition of wandering preachers and charismatics, which went back to the ministry of Jesus. The wandering preacher sought hospitality and sympathizers among those in the towns and villages visited.[9] Paul is not claiming that his modification of that apostolic style derives from having seen the Lord. Indeed, he does not even make having seen the Lord the full evidence for his apostolic status.[10] Rather, he insists that the very existence of the Corinthian community is the decisive proof of his apostleship. They are the strongest evidence that he has to bring against his opponents. If they were to deny their connection with the apostle, the Corinthians would have to deny their own reality as Christians. Once again, the passage does not tell us anything about Paul's experience of resurrection as such. But it does suggest that "having seen the Lord" formed part of Paul's preaching in the churches that he founded. Paul can presume that the Corinthians know what he is speaking about. He is not presenting it as a new piece of information for the purposes of debate.

1 Corinthians 15:8–11

Paul's final mention of his vision is attached to the credal passage in 1 Cor 15:3–7. Paul has added traditions about other appearances of the Lord to the short kerygmatic formula in 1 Cor 15:3–5. The additional listing of witnesses culminated in Paul's own assertion of his apostolic authority in vv. 8–10 and the insistence that all the apostles preach the same kerygma in v. 11.[11] Paul uses "was seen" *(ōphthē)* for each clause in the attached tradition. His own *ōphthē* then corresponds with that of the traditional lists of resurrection witnesses. J. Murphy-O'Connor suggests that Paul has created v. 7 as a transition to his own experience because he needs to emphasize the connection between being an apostle and seeing the Lord. He has marked the emphasis on the word apostle by adding "all" to it. The logic of Paul's construction is clearer if one presumes that he is deliberately trying to extend *apostolos* beyond the circle of the twelve. Peter, the twelve, and James are all presented as called directly by Christ. Paul uses James as a transitional figure. His calling and apostleship show that the commission extended beyond the circle of the twelve from the beginning. This passage is similar to the defense of Paul's apostleship in Gal 1:15–17. It contains the same combination of birth metaphor, emphasis on divine grace, and apostolic call that one finds in the earlier passage.[12] Clearly, Paul can expect that a claim to have had the same experience of the risen Lord as the other apostles will carry part of the argument for his authority. However, just as in 1 Cor 9:1f., it is not the whole story. Paul points immediately to the fruits of his apostolic labor as evidence of the grace of God working through him (v. 10). The way in which Paul uses resurrection to defend his contested claim to apostolic authority suggests that the connection between resurrection commission and apostleship was not a Pauline invention. It had been established by others before him.

The arrangement of the credal materials in this passage and Paul's preoccupation with his independence from Jerusalem in Galatians suggest that the original tradition was associated with the twelve and with James.[13] But Paul does not suppose that appeal to having seen the Lord is sufficient to maintain his apostolic authority. He consistently refers to the results of his calling in the churches that came into being as a result of the grace given him. Thus, we must be cautious about assuming that apostolic legitimation was automatically attached to having "seen the Lord." Paul's case suggests that it is necessary to look carefully at the way in which the connection is made in each case.

PAUL'S CONVERSION IN ACTS

In contrast to the reticence of the Pauline letters in describing the experience of encountering the risen Lord, Acts has no less than three accounts of Paul's conversion (9:1–19; 22:4–16; 26:12–18). The differences in the three Acts accounts of Paul's conversion and their divergence from Paul's own silence on the matter have spawned a number of theories about the genre of Luke's account and the extent to which he has taken a free hand in composing the stories.[14]

C. Hedrick's detailed comparison of the three Lukan accounts has shown that the opening sections of each one are strikingly similar:

a. Paul is approaching Damascus carrying letters from authorities (9:1–3a; 22:4–6a; 26:13–14a).

b. A light flashes around him, and he falls to the ground (9:3b–4a; 22:6b–7a; 26:13–14a, which includes Paul's companions).

c. Voice that says, "Saul, Saul why do you persecute me?" (9:4b and c; 22:7b and c). Ac 26:14b adds, "In Hebrew" and v. 14c adds, "It hurts to kick against the goads."

d. Paul's question: "Who are you?" (9:5a; 22:8a; 26:15a).

e. Answer: "I am Jesus whom you are persecuting." (9:5b; 22:8b adds "of Nazareth"; 26:15b).

After this point the three narratives diverge considerably.[15] The commissioning element in Ac 9:1–19 is contained in the Lukan redaction in vv. 13–16. Without it, we have a healing narrative. The commission itself has only a minor place in the rest of the narrative. It gets Ananias to go to Paul. The action in v. 17 makes no reference to the commissioning. Therefore, Hedrick concludes that Luke has probably added commissioning to this story to harmonize it with the two accounts that follow. The statement in Ac 9:15–16 is the only one that mentions Jewish and Gentile missions. Its formulation appears to deliberately go back to Ac 1:8.

This commissioning marks the decisive turning point between the Jewish mission in Jerusalem and that to the Gentiles. The other stories of Paul's conversion follow the rejection of the Jewish mission in Ac 13:44–52. They are more directly centered on the Christophany.[16]

In Ac 22:4–16, the miraculous elements so prominent in the first version are passed over. Instead of concluding with Paul's being cured, it ends with the commission of vv. 14–15.

The baptism that follows in v. 16 is Paul's first public witness in fulfillment of the Lord's command. It is not related in any way to Paul's being healed. Luke presents the bright light and the voice as a vision of the Lord, the just One. This vision is confirmed by a second vision immediately following, which—contrary to Paul's own claims in Gal 1:11–23—takes place in the temple in Jerusalem (Ac 22:17–21). Jesus warns Paul to leave Jerusalem because a persecution is about to break out. Sending Paul out among the Gentiles is represented as the Lord's strategy for protecting his apostle. From the point of view of the narrative in Acts that strategy is over. Paul is speaking of his conversion while he is defending himself in Jerusalem against those who wish to kill him. Hedrick argues that Luke is presuming a reader who knows the story in chapter 9. He has created this account to fit the trial scene in which it is set.[17] The final account (26:12–18) is all commissioning. Rather than have the commission delivered by Ananias, it comes directly from the Lord. This commission contains elements that are not part of the earlier versions (vv. 16–18).

Paul then opens the defense in which this account figures by arguing that it is obedience to divine command that has led to the hostility against him. Hedrick argues that Luke has deliberately waited to provide a direct report of what was said on the road to Damascus until this final trial scene.[18] The three accounts of Paul's conversion are, like the Lukan resurrection stories, tailored to their setting in Acts. But Luke has probably used some earlier sources about Paul. The basic story with which Luke worked appears to have been a legend about Paul's miraculous conversion. The account in Ac 22 may have been based on a different story of Paul's conversion. While the first story retains the legendary and miraculous flavor of the conversion of the former persecutor, the second appears to have been shaped to vindicate the Christian mission to the Gentiles. Luke has made it part of Paul's defense before fanatical Jews. For them, Ananias's esteem among those in Damascus shows that becoming a Christian did not turn a person against the Jewish community. Paul himself visits the holy temple in Jerusalem immediately after his conversion. And in a vision in the temple—a deliberate invocation of the calling of Isaiah?—Paul learns that the mission to the Gentiles is God's response to the hostility that Paul encounters among the Jews. The defense before the Gentiles in the final chapter is designed to show the divine nature of Paul's commission to preach among the Gentiles by contrasting his early behavior as a fierce persecutor of Christians with his obedience to divine will. Thus, each account of Paul's commissioning carries a Lukan theme: the divine inspiration of the mission to the Gentiles. The first story refers back to the final instructions of the Lord to the twelve in Ac 1:8. The second and third stories show that the subsequent mission followed persecution. They establish the Lukan pattern of Jewish rejection followed by mission to the Gentiles. The final scene also shows that God has been involved from the beginning.

RESURRECTION AND MISSION

The connection between resurrection and mission was not unique to Paul. Mt 28:19 associates mission with the resurrection commission to the disciples as a group. The Johannine tradition had the glorified Jesus pass on his commission as "one sent by God" to the community. The Pauline material reflects some ambiguity in the understanding of resurrection and apostolic authority. B. Holmberg has argued that Paul was indeed "subordinate to" those at Jerusalem.[19] His activity as a member of the Antioch church places him within the sphere of their authority. At the time Paul writes Galatians, Paul is no longer willing to acknowledge his dependence on Jerusalem. We see him attempting to establish his independence from that circle.[20] The resurrection vision as the foundation of a claim to independent, divine origin for Paul's mission may have taken on a significance in this context that it did not have earlier.[21] However, there is clearly another factor in Paul's argument, the success of his mission. J. D. G. Dunn suggests that that argument was persuasive, since the Jerusalem authorities had previously acknowledged it in their acceptance of Paul's work.[22] Thus, the resurrection commission does not bear the whole weight of Paul's claim to apostolic authority or of his claim to independence from Jerusalem.

The process of shifting patterns of apostolic legitimation in the Pauline letters leads one to ask whether the association of resurrection appearance and mission is the result of developments within the Christian movement itself. Though the disciples were clearly involved in preaching the gospel to fellow Jews from the beginning, such activity may not have been as closely connected with the resurrection commissioning as legitimation for such activity as now appears to be the case. Perhaps, for example, that initial impulse to evangelization was more akin to the dynamic preserved in the traditions of the women at the tomb. One must go and tell those who had followed Jesus, "He has been raised," that is, a message directed at those who had been followers of or sympathizers with Jesus during his life. The proclamation of God's vindication and exaltation of Jesus would be a fundamental key to the disciples' message about him. We have evidence of the resurrection as legitimation for a particular missionary approach in Matthew. There, as we have seen, it is possible to see a pattern of development in which a community that had been concentrated on mission to the Jews turned toward a mission to the Gentiles. S. Brown has pointed out that there was no clear warrant to be found in the teaching of Jesus for such a shift. The expectation that the Gentiles would turn to God when they witnessed the messianic repentance of Israel did not suggest that human efforts would be required to bring in the Gentiles. Mt 8:11-12 preserves a tradition that holds that the Kingdom of God will come even if Israel remains unrepentant. The traditions of Peter's turn to the Gentile mission in Ac 10:9-16 (and 11:5-10) present it as a decisive shift well after the mission to Israel. They also associate it with a new divine initiative reflected in Peter's vision about clean and unclean, not as the consequence of resurrection commissioning. The conversion of Gentiles to Judaism itself was quite different from what we find in Christianity. The Jewish appeal to them was not cast in eschatological categories (as in 1 Thess 1:9-10). It used a philosophical apologetic; nor did it presuppose a pattern of traveling missionaries. Proselytes, attracted by Jewish apologetic, probably attended the Jewish synagogues in which the wandering missionaries preached. These missionaries may well have claimed that the risen Messiah had sent them to preach to Israel.[23]

S. Brown has suggested that the rather un-Lukan view expressed in Ac 15:13f. that God has made himself another people alongside Israel was the initial interpretation of the Gentile conversions as a divine *fait accompli*. The agreement between Paul and the Jerusalem authorities merely permitted separate missions. It did not solve the sociological or theological problems attendant upon relationships between the two groups. Paul clearly expects that Jerusalem should accept Gentiles, who have not also adopted Judaism, as one Israel with the Jews. His failure to gain practical recognition for that view in the dispute over table fellowship between Jewish Christians and non-Jewish converts, who were not circumcised (Gal 2:11-14), with Peter at Antioch seems to have provoked his shift to an independent posture. It may also have provoked the Jerusalem decree preserved in Ac 15:23-29, which represents the conditions under which Jerusalem would accept Gentiles.[24] The question of the Gentile mission appears to have been under debate in Matthew's community. Matthew has included a veiled reference to the expansion of the mission to the Gentiles in 13:38 by making the field the world and not the ethnic group Israel. Reference to the nations in Mt 24:14 also points toward that mission. But Peter, Matthew's authority in the teaching of the community, is not represented as the source of Gentile mission. For some, accepting Gentiles would mean a definitive end to a relationship with Judaism that they would have preferred not to break (23:2f.). Matthew hopes to persuade his readers that the mission is part of the inevitable plan of God. He has deliberately concluded the gospel with a commission from the risen Lord that makes the mandate unmistakable.[25] One may still wonder at the omission of Peter from the explicit command in Mk 16:7. Should the rock upon which Jesus builds not be singled out for special commissioning as well? Could Matthew not be aware of the role played by Peter in establishing the Gentile mission elsewhere?

COMMISSIONING THE COMMUNITY: THE JOHANNINE TRADITION

The Johannine community had been forced out of its ties with Judaism when Christians were excommunicated from the synagogue. R. E. Brown suggests that the separation led to the type of active engagement in the mission to the Gentiles, which S. Brown has seen as the issue facing the Matthean community. As a result of the crisis the community consolidated around elements of sectarian identity: they constituted the small group of elect in a hostile world. Their position was identical with that of Jesus, who had been rejected by "his own" (15:18–16:4a). This parallel is reflected in the use of an Old Testament proof text, which elsewhere belongs to the tradition of passion apologetic, to the world's hatred toward Jesus, his Father, and, a fortiori, the disciples who now stand in his place (Jn 15:25). This description of the world may indicate that the once-promising Gentile mission is meeting rejection and even persecution.[26]

Some scholars wonder if one should attribute commissioning to mission to the Johannine traditions.[27] Persecution has caused the community to turn inward. Though the traditions in the Fourth Gospel give evidence of missionary efforts directed at Jews, Samaritans, and Gentiles, the community now lives in an uneasy relationship with the world. Its commissioning emphasizes the necessity for the community to repeat the pattern set in Jesus' mission. Consequently, one could argue that the renewal of the community's relationship with Jesus and the Father described by the Farewell Discourses, the indwelling presence of the Spirit, or the vindicating testimony of the Paraclete are the most important gains from the resurrection commission. Both the gift of the Spirit and forgiveness of sins can be understood—as they were among the Essenes—to describe life inside a community of the elect rather than a commission to evangelize those outside.

THE UNIVERSAL MISSION IN ACTS

The examples of Matthew and John suggest communities in which the systematic turn toward evangelizing the Gentiles is associated with the increased Jewish hostility toward Christianity in the years after the Jewish War. For Matthew, the commissioning of the risen Lord served as a powerful symbol to legitimate that shift. For John, on the other hand, the symbol is more ambiguous. While the community has not lost its sense of a commission to witness, continued hostility seems to have evoked a more inner-directed sense of unity with the divine presence. Both evidence shifts in the understanding of resurrection commission, which suggest that it was not univocally perceived to be the legitimation of apostolic mission.

The Lukan traditions, however, continue the patterns evident in the Pauline mission, one in which extensive missionary activity among the Gentiles had been accepted much earlier. We have seen that the traditions in Luke-Acts not only attach the pattern of missionary expansion from Jew to Gentile to the resurrection traditions, but they expand those traditions into a sequence of events from Easter to Pentecost. In addition, Luke associates key shifts in the mission with other visions, like that of Peter, which have nothing to do with resurrection appearances. Those stories suggest that there were other legends about the turn toward the Gentile mission that did not involve resurrection. Similarly, the Lukan understanding of the missionary commission attached to resurrection also appears to be a reflection of subsequent developments. Lk 24:47 makes that commission the first announcement of the program in Acts: "and you will preach repentance and forgiveness of sins in his name to all the nations, beginning from Jerusalem." The second version of this commissioning, the ascension story, follows the same pattern that C. Hedrick has detected in Luke's use of stories about Paul's conversion. The same commission is repeated in a framework whose changes in detail are dictated by the new setting. The instruction to wait in Jerusalem for the Spirit is the center of the story. The Old Testament basis for the promise of the Spirit will not be introduced until the Pentecost speech in Ac 2:17. Here Luke refers back to the saying about baptism with the Spirit, which his gospel had attributed to John

the Baptist (Lk 3:16/Mt 3:11). Since the summary of Jesus' postresurrection activity in Ac 1:3 spoke of Jesus' teaching the disciples about
the kingdom, the reference back to a saying from the period of Jesus'
ministry is appropriate to the context. The same saying will appear
again in the debate over the baptism of Cornelius (Ac 11:16). There it
is directly attributed to the Lord. Scholars think that in the earlier
period Christian prophets spoke directly in the name of the Lord.
Thus, it is possible that this story derives from an older tradition in
which the mission to the Gentiles was legitimated by the application
of a saying of the Lord. That saying may indeed have been felt to
have been spoken by the risen Lord, but it is not grounded in a
special apostolic commissioning in an Easter appearance.

Jesus' promise of the eschatological outpouring of the Spirit in Ac
1:6 provokes the question about when the eschatological renewal of
Israel would occur. The question is turned aside as knowledge that
God has reserved to himself. Luke has taken a saying that appears in
the apocalyptic discourse of Mark (Mk 13:32/Mt 24:36) as the basis
for this reply. The promise of the Spirit is no longer linked to the
parousia but to the initiation of the community's mission to the
world.[28] This shift also implies that the Kingdom of God is not to be
limited to a renewed Israel. It is to be realized in the universal
mission that is to be undertaken under the guidance of the Spirit.[29]

This passage also shifts slightly the terms of the commissioning in
Lk 24:48. There Luke spoke of Jesus' commissioning his followers to
be his "witnesses." In Acts, the "witnesses" appear to be limited to
the apostles (1:8, 22; 2:32; 3:15; 5:32; 10:39, 41; 13:31). Luke does use
"witness" in the two scenes that present Paul's commissioning to
preach to the Gentiles (22:15; 26:16). Thus, Luke is able to reserve
"apostle," Paul's own term for his status, to the twelve and use the
related term "witness" along with the parallel phrasing of the mission charge to bring Paul's activity into the plan of salvation presented by the risen Lord.[30] Luke includes Jesus' resurrection as the
subject about which the witness testifies before the Jews and Gentiles. E. Haenchen suggests that Luke puts resurrection in this position because he understands it to provide the link between Christianity and Judaism. Its decisive place is indicated in the concern for the
life of the risen Lord with the disciple/witnesses at the beginning of
Acts.[31] Peter and John must testify about the resurrection before the
Council in Ac 4:20.[32] The apostles give their powerful testimony to
the resurrection in the founding days of the community (4:33). Luke
summarizes the apostolic testimony to resurrection in Ac 10:40–43.

Luke has created this summary to present those in Cornelius's
house with a summary of the story as it has developed in Acts. The

Pentecost experience of those Gentiles follows the story (vv. 44–48).
Thus, the opening of Acts has been repeated in miniature at the
beginning of the mission to the Gentiles. That mission is brought
under the commission of the risen Lord to witness to him and is
confirmed by the bestowal of the Spirit. Paul's speech to the Jews at
Pisidian Antioch establishes the pattern of Jewish rejection followed
by Gentile acceptance (vv. 46–47). It includes a lengthy argument
defending the resurrection (vv. 30–37). The argument is based first of
all on the testimony of Jesus' disciples and second on the evidence
that Scripture is fulfilled in Jesus.

The testimony to resurrection in Acts treats resurrection as part of
the content of apostolic preaching. It is not merely the affirmation of
Jesus' exaltation and vindication by God, though that pattern clearly
belongs to Lukan traditions. Luke views divine vindication through
the imagery set by the scheme of divine response to the human
rejection implied in the crucifixion of Jesus. The connection between
resurrection and mission is found in the perception of the apostles as
Jesus' witnesses before the world. Their testimony fulfills the divine
plan to spread the message of salvation from Jerusalem to Rome.

THE COMMISSIONING OF PETER

Peter figures prominently in the resurrection traditions. While Peter's preeminence in the circle of the apostles is associated with his
having seen the Lord, the commission that may have followed from
that claim is less clear. There are no traditions in which Peter is
pictured as encountering the risen Lord. Sayings like Lk 22:34 and Jn
21:18–19 include an element of rehabilitation of Peter. They reflect
Peter's authority in the community and may represent another form
of legitimation based on resurrection traditions.

What we can learn from the New Testament directly about Peter's
role is considerably less clear than is sometimes supposed. Gal 1:18f.
speaks of Peter as head of the apostolic circle in Jerusalem. Dunn
argues that Paul's use of the verb *historēsai* (visit) about his visit to
Jerusalem implies a visit with the purpose of gaining information.
Presumably, Paul is admitting to having visited Peter to gain information—presumably about Jesus. The second visit is also described in
such a way that the apostle admits that the confirmation of the Jerusalem apostles was important (Gal 2:2) even if Paul is not dependent on
Jerusalem for his message and its truth.[33] An adverse decision could

presumably have affected the missionary activity of the apostle. Had they been unwilling to acknowledge Paul's preaching to the Gentiles, the Gentile churches could not have been seen as standing in continuity with the promises of God to Israel.[34] Paul's description of the decision reached at Jerusalem in Gal 2:6–10 gives the appearance of being a decision handed down by the Jerusalem authorities. The equality between Paul's mission and that of Peter may not have been as equal as Paul would have liked. Only Peter is referred to as having an apostleship (v. 8). Paul continues to be defensive about the "pillars." No titles are given Paul and Barnabas in this passage. Indeed, Barnabas is associated with Paul in the agreement, though Paul tries to make it appear that the decision applies to his own, independent mission. Finally, the collection appears to represent some form of mandate laid on Paul by the "pillars."[35] Whatever the later history of Paul's relationships with Jerusalem, this passage acknowledges Peter's leadership in the Jerusalem group that had the authority to oversee missionary activity.

Our sources suggest that Peter is associated with missionary activity among Jews and possibly among those Gentiles who were converted through their associations with the Jewish synagogues. At least in the initial period that activity seems to have been centered in Jerusalem. It is possible that Peter later moved away from Jerusalem to some form of traveling mission, but that activity is difficult to recover. S. Brown suggests that there could not have been any clear tradition that Peter engaged in missionary activity among the Gentiles, or Matthew would have used it. Therefore, he concludes, Peter's role was ambiguous. His example could have been invoked on either side in the dispute that was going on in the Matthean community. Perhaps Peter left Jerusalem (Ac 12:17; 21:18) as a result of differences between himself and James. It appears that differences between himself and Paul had led the latter to leave Antioch and engage in an independent mission.[36]

All of these examples show that the nature and extent of missionary activity in the early community is hardly as clear-cut as the Lukan schema might have us believe. There were quite different understandings of the mission to the Gentiles, and there may even have been some about the call to renewal and repentance issued to Israel itself. For example, "to the peoples," now a reference to the Gentile mission in Mt 28, might have originated in a command to go beyond Galilee and Judaea to the Diaspora. The question of the Diaspora appears briefly in Jn 7:35. These examples all show that the association between resurrection and various forms of apostolic mission to the Gentiles was a development that could be used in various ways.

Behind such appeals to resurrection one always finds the concern to defend the mission against charges of merely human origin or rejection of the fundamental continuity between Christianity and the traditions of Israel. The impulse toward evangelization most closely linked with resurrection would have to have been an urgent appeal to Israel to repent in the name of Jesus, the Messiah. Such a mission would have been closely related to that of Jesus and his disciples in the period before Easter.

RESURRECTION AND THE FOUNDATION OF THE CHURCH

We have seen that the relationship between resurrection and apostolic commission was not an invariable one in the early period. It must always be situated within the particular community from which a tradition comes. The understanding of apostleship and mission appears to have varied from one group to another within the New Testament church. The strains and perplexities of the Gentile mission were addressed by appropriating resurrection symbolism as the basis for claiming divine legitimacy. However, the Pauline and Matthean materials show that this development could take a very different course in different communities. They also show that Peter's role is more complex and more difficult to discover than one might think solely on the basis of Acts.

An earlier use of resurrection to legitimate authority within the Christian community appears to be attached to the leaders of the Jerusalem community. But even here we may have secondary developments. A resurrection appearance may have played a special role in legitimating the authority of James, the brother of the Lord, since he had not been a disciple of the earthly Jesus. He was also not included among the group of disciples to whom Jesus was said to have appeared at Easter.[37] By the second century the popular traditions embedded in the apocryphal acts show that the explicit commissioning and activity of the risen Jesus is tied to the missionary efforts of the twelve. Thus, the connection between resurrection and a missionary apostleship was established in the popular imagination.

NOTES

1. B. Holmberg, *Paul and Power. The Structure of Authority in the Primitive Church as Reflected in the Pauline Epistles* (Philadelphia: Fortress, 1980), 181. Antioch and the other churches in the earliest period were tied to Jerusalem. See the discussion of claims to have seen the risen Lord as the basis of authority in H. von Campenhausen, *Ecclesiastical Authority and Spiritual Power in the Church of the First Three Centuries* (Stanford: Stanford University, 1969), 13–23. E. Haenchen *(The Acts of the Apostles* [Philadelphia: Westminster, 1971], 143, note 8) understands the use of "witness" in the commissioning of Ac 1:8 to mean that the apostle is to witness Jesus' resurrection before Israel and the Gentile authorities.
2. W. O. Walker ("Post Crucifixion Appearances and Christian Origins," *Journal of Biblical Literature* 88 [1969], 165) suggests that the appearance to five hundred was intended to serve a democratizing effect by countering exclusivist claims to visions of the Lord.
3. E. S. Fiorenza ("Word, Spirit and Power: Women in Early Christian Communities," *Women of Spirit* [eds. R. Ruether and E. McLaughlin; New York: Simon & Schuster, 1979], 52–55) thinks that Luke has underplayed the role of the women disciples in chapter 24 because their testimony was not accepted. She points to later Gnostic writings in which Mary Magdalene is the prototype of the enlightened Gnostic. E. Schillebeeckx *(Jesus* [New York: Seabury, 1979], 345) avoids claiming that the importance of the appearances to the women has been suppressed by arguing that the superiority of the apostles' testimony is only being grounded in what was tradition for Luke. Mary plays a crucial role in getting the disciples to see that death has not shattered their communication with Jesus.
4. See the discussion of the situation in Galatian in H. D. Betz, *Galatians* (Philadelphia: Fortress, 1979), 3–9.
5. See H. Schlier, *Der Brief an die Galater* (MK VII; Göttingen: Vandenhoeck & Ruprecht, 1964, 4th ed.), 27f.; A. Oepke, *Der*

Brief des Paulus an die Galater (THKNT 9; Berlin: Evangelische, 1964), 17f.

6. Betz, op. cit., 38f.
7. J. Schutz, *Paul and the Anatomy of Apostolic Authority* (Cambridge: Cambridge University, 1975), 152–255.
8. Betz, op. cit., 70f.
9. G. Theissen, *The Social Setting of Pauline Christianity. Essays on Corinth* (Philadelphia: Fortress, 1982), 27–67.
10. H. Conzelmann *(1 Corinthians* [Philadelphia: Fortress, 1975], 152) notes that the argument about having seen the Lord is a necessary one for a person claiming apostolic authority but is not a sufficient condition for such a claim, since not all appearances carried that implication.
11. K. Lehmann, *Auferweckt am dritten Tag nach der Schrift* (Quaestiones Disputatae 38; Freiburg: Herder, 1968), 31.
12. J. Murphy-O'Connor, "Tradition and Redaction in 1 Cor. 15:3–7," *CBQ* 43 (1981) 587–89. Murphy-O'Conner suggests that the passage has the following structure: (a) traditional creed (vv. 3–5); (b) proof that the resurrection could be verified (v. 6); (c) tradition used to emphasize the expansion of the apostolate beyond the "twelve" (v. 7); (d) Paul's apostleship (vv. 8–10); (e) common agreement on the creed (v. 11).
13. If Christophany served to legitimate leadership in the earliest community, then one might accept Walker's suggestion (op. cit., 164) that the James tradition was formulated when James replaced Peter as the head of the Jerusalem community.
14. On Luke's responsibility for composing the conversion stories, see G. Lohfink, *The Conversion of St. Paul* (Chicago: Franciscan Herald Press, 1976); for a summary of the theories about the genre of the passage, see C. Hedrick, "Paul's Conversion/Call: A Comparative Analysis of the Three Reports in Acts," *Journal of Biblical Literature* 100 (1981), 415f.
15. Hedrick, op. cit., 417–19.
16. Ibid., 420–23.
17. Ibid., 424–26.
18. Ibid., 426f. Hedrick attributes the discrepancies in the Acts accounts to Luke's literary technique of clarifying a narrative through repeating it in another (op. cit., 427–32).
19. Holmberg, op. cit., 160f. One need not accept all of the details of this reconstruction of Paul's relationship to Jerusalem to see that there is difficulty in drawing a clean distinction between the different types of authentication in the early community.
20. J. D. G. Dunn, "The Relationship between Paul and Jerusalem

according to Galatians 1 & 2," *New Testament Studies* 28 (1982), 28.

21. Ibid., 470–74.

22. Ibid., 470.

23. S. Brown, "The Matthean Community and the Gentile Mission," *NovT* 22 (1980), 194–98. Brown thinks that Paul's persecution of Christianity was based on its disregard for the Law, a position that can be traced back to Jesus even if the more radical rejection of the ritual law is to be attributed to the later community. Criticism of the temple and its cult could exist alongside strict obedience to the Law, as in the case of Essene writings and Diaspora Judaism. Brown argues that a mission to the Samaritans did not necessarily imply mission to the Gentiles (op. cit., 200–203).

24. Ibid., 207–12.

25. Ibid., 214, 219–21.

26. R. E. Brown *(The Community of the Beloved Disciple* [New York: Paulist, 1979], 29, 55–58); the way for a more universal approach had been paved in the mission to the Samaritans. See the discussion of Jn 15:18–16:4a by B. Lindars, "The Persecution of Christians in Jn 15:18–16:4a," *Suffering and Martyrdom in the New Testament. Studies Presented to G. M. Styler* (eds. W. Horbury and B. McNeil; Cambridge: Cambridge University, 1981), 48–69. R. Brown (op. cit., 63) suggests that the turn in the gospel from opposition to the Jews toward opposition to the world indicates the opposition of Gentiles to the mission undertaken by the community. F. F. Segovia ("John 15:18–16:4a: A First Addition to the Original Farewell Discourse?" *Catholic Biblical Quarterly* 45 [1983], 225–30) thinks that this early addition is concerned with persecution by the synagogue.

27. Schnackenburg has been particularly wary of presuming that evangelization was a primary interest of the Johannine community. Thus, his reconstruction of the Johannine sources is quite different from R. Brown's, which accepts the implicit missionary significance of Johannine parallels to explicit missionary language elsewhere in the New Testament.

28. Haenchen, op. cit., 139–43.

29. H. Conzelmann, *Die Apostelgeschichte* (HNT 7; Tübingen: J. C. B. Mohr, 1963) 22f.

30. Luke also uses "witness" for Stephen in Ac 22:20. On the development of the use of the term *apostolos,* see Haenchen, op. cit., 164f. Luke's usage differs from Paul's in 1 Cor 15:7–8. Paul customarily uses *apostolos* for a group of missionaries wider than

the circle of the twelve; see C. K. Barrett, *The First Epistle to the Corinthians* (New York: Harper & Row, 1968), 293f.

31. Haenchen, op. cit., 143; 163.

32. Ibid., 219. Paul testifies to resurrection as the dividing line between Christians and their Jewish accusers in Ac 23:6, 8; 24:15, 21; 26:23.

33. Dunn, op. cit., 463–66. Dunn notes that the visit to Peter has the explicit purpose of gaining information from Peter, while James is only described as someone to be seen, presumably representing a courtesy visit. Dunn points out that Paul's "lest somehow I should be running or had run in vain" (Gal 2:2c) uses an expression that always refers to actual and not hypothetical possibilities (1 Cor 8:9; 2 Cor 2:7; 9:4; 11:3; 12:20; Gal 4:11; 1 Thess 3:5). An adverse judgment would render his work ineffective and useless (cf. 2 Cor 6:1; Phil 2:16; 1 Thess 3:5).

34. Ibid., 467–71.

35. Betz, op. cit., 98–100; Dunn (op. cit., 473) thinks that the collection may have been viewed as an indication of Paul's subordination to Jerusalem. Paul presents it as a corollary to his understanding that his Gentile converts are included in Israel.

36. S. Brown, op. cit., 219.

37. Dunn (op. cit., 469–71) suggests, for example, that Paul had visited Peter the first time because he sought information about Jesus' teaching that Peter as one of Jesus' disciples would be able to provide. James would not be in that position.

SEVEN

Resurrection as Kerygma

Our earliest evidence for the resurrection is in kerygmatic formulae. The formula in 1 Cor 15:3b–5 connects the resurrection to the death of Jesus for sin on one side and to the affirmation that the Lord was seen by his disciples on the other. Even the short affirmations of the early formula can hardly be described as an immediate report of the encounter with the risen Lord. Both "death for sins" and "according to the Scriptures" imply a period of reflection on the meaning of the passion and resurrection of Jesus. Though kerygmatic formulae are older than resurrection narratives, they are still products of developing Christian reflection.[1]

1 Cor 15:1–10 reminds us of another important characteristic of the early kerygmatic formulae. We do not see them in the original context in which early Christians heard and used them. The formulaic character of the passages in question suggests that they originated in a liturgical setting. We only see them in larger contexts in which the associations that the audience had with this formulae enabled the authors to use them for new purposes. The formula affirmations fall into two general classes. One type is based on the

antithesis of death and resurrection. The second type refers to Christ as having been raised without any mention of the death of Jesus. The second type often appears in short clauses that are attached to a word in a longer sentence. J. Schmitt thinks that the "clause type" originated in liturgical acclamations of Christ as Lord.[2] Such a connection appears to be implied by the formula in Rom 10:9.

Other examples of this formula appear in 1 Thess 1:9f.; Rom 4:24 (where it introduces the antithetical type in 4:25); Gal 1:1; Rom 8:11; 2 Cor 4:14a; 2 Cor 1:9; Col 2:12b, and 1 Pt 1:21. It is frequently an epithet that marks God as the one who raised Jesus. In some instances, it serves as an introduction to God's life-giving power that effects salvation. It has been shown to be effective in the resurrection of Christ and will also bring about the future resurrection of the believer (Rom 8:11; 4:17; 2 Cor 4:14). The passion and resurrection type often consists of a short contrast between the two states: "he died and was raised," as in 1 Thess 4:14a, ". . . if we believe that Jesus died and was raised . . . ," or Rom 14:9, ". . . Christ died and lived again . . ." Such short statements cannot be distinguished from simple statements of fact that Christians believe that Christ died and rose.[3]

The connection between such formulae and the acclamation of Jesus as Lord poses a further question about the development of the early resurrection traditions: what is the relationship between resurrection and the christological titles attributed to Jesus? We have seen that some interpreters think that the tradition behind Mt 28:16–20 saw resurrection as Jesus' entry into the glory of the Son of Man. Early acclamations like "Lord Jesus" (1 Cor 13:3) or *"Marana tha"* ("Come, Lord") suggest that prayer provided the context in which Jesus was acclaimed as exalted Lord. Exaltation language is not attached to the kerygmatic formulae. But, as we shall see, it does appear in passages like Phil 2:6–11 and 1 Tim 3:16, which appear to be hymnic in origin.[4]

Thus, the preaching and liturgical practice of the early church appear to have shaped resurrection traditions in three areas: in kerygmatic formulae, in linking them with the development of christological titles for Jesus, and in hymnic expressions of Jesus' exaltation. Each of these areas makes an important contribution to the central place that resurrection occupies in the early Christian confession of Jesus.

KERYGMATIC FORMULAE IN THE PAULINE TRADITION

The large number of kerygmatic formulae and related expressions in the Pauline corpus suggests that resurrection was probably a prominent feature in the apostle's preaching. Here we will be concerned with passages from the Pauline tradition that appear to reflect pre-Pauline resurrection formulae (Rom 1:3f.; 4:24f.; 8:34; 10:9; 1 Thess 1:10; 1 Cor 15:3–11; 2 Tim 2:8). Hymnic traditions from the Pauline corpus will be treated in the concluding section of this chapter. The next two chapters on resurrection as presence and resurrection and the future of the Christian will provide further opportunities to explore the Pauline preaching of resurrection.

1 Thessalonians 1:9–10

1 Thess 1:9–10 may be the earliest formula in the Pauline corpus. This formula would be derived from the Gentile mission. The Jewish appeal to pagans is reflected in the first phrase, turning from idols to serve the true, living God. The second phrase places the resurrection in the context of Jesus' coming at the parousia. God has raised Jesus so that he is the One who comes from heaven in judgment and salvation. Thus, the message of salvation is firmly rooted in the parousia expectation. This formula shows no traces of the later developments in which salvation is described in terms of the death of Jesus.[5] This image links Jesus' title "Son of God" to his exaltation and his function as savior in the judgment.

Romans 1:3f.

Paul introduces a formula into the greeting of Romans, which shows further development of the connection between Jesus' resurrection and his position as Son of God:

> concerning his Son, who was seed of David according to the flesh, and was designated Son of God in power according to the spirit of holiness, from the resurrection of the dead, our Lord, Jesus Christ.

This formula is presented as the content of Paul's apostolic message. Paul speaks of it as the gospel, "preached beforehand" through the prophets in Scripture (vv. 1c–2). The theme of the previous embodiment of the gospel in Scripture was an important development in the early kerygmatic formulae. The parallel structure of this expression makes its formulaic background evident.

The Christology presupposed in this formula presents the resurrection as Jesus' exaltation to be Son of God. Its non-Pauline character is evident in a number of unusual expressions that it contains: from the seed of David; spirit of holiness; designated; from the resurrection of the dead. It is not constructed around the death and resurrection pair but around the Son of David/Son of God pair.[6]

Exegetes are divided over the question of whether or not Paul has made additions to an earlier formula. The contrast, according to the flesh/according to the Spirit, appears so frequently in Pauline paraenesis that some interpreters think it is a Pauline addition.[7] However, the contrast in this passage contains the peculiar expression "spirit of holiness," which is not characteristic of Paul. To remove it from the passage weakens the parallelism. According to the flesh and according to the Spirit are not being used here to contrast two ways of life as they are in ethical exhortation. They are being used to describe two different modes of Jesus' existence. Therefore, we would presume that the contrast was in the formula prior to Paul's use of it.[8] Unlike the contrasts found in some of the materials from christological hymns, the formula does not presume that "according to the flesh" means a mode of life in which Jesus was humiliated. Son of David is used as a messianic title in the infancy narratives and in Mk 12:35 and 2 Tim 2:8. Thus, both parts of the formula seek to describe Jesus' messianic role.[9]

Exegetes are also divided over whether or not the expression "in power" was a Pauline addition. It appears to be superfluous in a formula that is already too long. In addition, it is attached to Son of God rather than to the verb "designated." Both K. Wengst and H. Schlier point to other places in which Paul uses the word *dynamis* of Jesus' resurrection as evidence that he added the phrase. In 1 Cor 6:14 it refers to the power that Jesus has to raise the believer. 1 Cor 5:14 also uses the word for power that is possessed by Jesus. Phil 3:10 speaks of the "power of his resurrection." Thus, for Paul, Son of God in power would appear to be equivalent to calling the risen Jesus Lord. Paul may have added "in power" to Son of God because he no longer holds the view that Jesus becomes Son of God through his exaltation at the resurrection. Jesus is God's Son throughout his life (e.g., 1 Cor 8:6; Phil 2:6; Gal 4:4; Rom 8:3).[10] Wengst suggests that the formula originated in a baptismal context that celebrated the adoption of Christians as "sons of God." It points to the reception of the spirit of holiness by the newly baptized.[11] Perhaps in the baptismal context it also represented the transformation of those who were sons of David in the human sense into "sons of God," members of the messianic kingdom.

J. Murphy-O'Connor asks what we should understand Jesus to have "gained" at the resurrection. He points to Knox's claim that Jesus "became the new man at the resurrection"[12] as an unfortunate way of answering the question. Paul would not agree that Jesus did not exhibit the perfection that God intended for human persons during his lifetime. He does agree, however, that resurrection represents something new for Jesus. Consequently, Paul has added the "in power" to the traditional phrase "designated Son of God" as a way of expressing what that gain is. One can find a parallel concept in Paul's "become a life-giving Spirit" in 1 Cor 15:54.[13] There the "gain" is more clearly represented as Christ's role in the salvation of the believer.

Romans 4:24–25

This passage contains both types of formula, the short predication in v. 24 and the two-membered contrast between the One who died and was raised in v. 25. In v. 24, Paul attaches to the word God the epithet "who raised Jesus, the Lord, from the dead." The passage as a whole is designed to bring to its conclusion the argument that Abraham shows the coming of justification by faith. The same God who spoke to Abraham is the one who has raised Jesus. Unlike the previous example, this formula is perfectly balanced. The word "handed over" *(paredothē)* is traditional in formulas that refer to the passion (cf. 1 Cor 11:23; Rom 8:32; Gal 2:20; Eph 5:2). Verse 24 introduced the resurrection into the discussion of the chapter by describing God as the one who raised Jesus from the dead. That addition paves the way for the resurrection half of this formula. Unlike the pre-Pauline formula in Rom 3:24–26 in which both atonement for sin and justification are attached to the death of Jesus, this formula associates resurrection and justification. However, one cannot conclude that the death and resurrection of Jesus are thereby given two different functions with regard to salvation.[14]

The short clause in v. 24c reflects an earlier description of God in 4:17. The God in whom Abraham put his faith is the one who "gives life to the dead." In raising Jesus, God acts as he had with Abraham.

At the same time, the justification received by the believer follows
from the power established in Christ's resurrection. The formula
may be based on the parallel use of sin and justification in Is 53:11.[15]
This passage makes resurrection God's activity. It looks to the justification of those who believe in the God who has demonstrated his
power to give life and salvation to those who believe in him. E.
Kaesemann attempts to describe the dynamic behind Paul's use of
the formula by contrasting death and resurrection. Christ's death on
the cross for sin occurred once for all. Christian faith only has access
to that saving death through the resurrection. Thus, resurrection is
both a real victory of the crucified One and the foundation of the
event of justification that "constantly wins new ground in the encounter with the risen Lord."[16]

Romans 8:34

The dynamic character of the relationship between the Christian
and the risen and exalted Lord appears in Paul's description of the
confidence that the Christian has in God's "for us" (Rom 8:31–39).
This confidence is grounded in the offering of his Son on our behalf.
The passage is constructed around a series of diatribe questions.

> *Who will bring a charge against God's elect? God is the one who
> justifies. Who will condemn? Christ is the one who died and was
> raised, who is at the right hand of God, who intercedes for us.*

Once again v. 34 appears to be overloaded. The association between resurrection and Christ's exaltation at God's right hand in a
context that uses judgment metaphors suggests the exaltation and
parousia tradition of 1 Thess 1:10. The final clause, which presents
Christ as heavenly intercessor, is a tradition found elsewhere in the
New Testament, as in 1 Jn 2:1. Since neither of the concluding clauses
is particularly Pauline, their phrasing may derive from independent
hymnic or liturgical traditions.[17] They fit the apocalyptic patterns
that underlie the section.[18] This section is concerned with the theme
of the vindication of the righteous (cf. 8:1). The Christian is encouraged to stand firm. The victory of Christ is present, through his
position as risen and exalted, and future in that there will be no
charge that can be brought against the faithful in the judgment.

Romans 10:9

Paul has begun an argument from Scripture for justification by faith in Rom 10:5. The formula in Rom 10:9 is identified as the message of faith that Paul preaches.

He has attached the formula to the citation of Deut 30:14. It is the interpretation of the Word that is near in the Deuteronomy passage. The Word of faith is near in the mouth and heart. The two parallel confessions about Jesus—Jesus is Lord and God raised him from the dead—may have had independent origins. Paul may have added the framework of mouth and heart to bring the two formulas together and apply them to the passage from Deuteronomy. Since both formulae are traditional, Paul would appear to be using the traditional confession in association with Scripture to justify his message. Paul is not concerned with defining the relationship between the two affirmations about Jesus. His interest is in soteriology. Hence, the formula belongs to the same pattern that we observed in Rom 4:25. Paul links resurrection and the justification of the believer.[19]

This passage belongs to Paul's reflection on the relationship between the Christian community and Israel. The confession that the risen Jesus is Lord establishes a community that represents the eschatological people of God, the righteous, over against Israel. The community is the place in which the message of righteousness through faith is heard. It is the place where the Word is near. Its life is linked to the presence of the Lord, since it is the place of that lordship.[20]

1 Corinthians 15:1–34

The other formulae in the Pauline corpus are short sentences and appear as parts of ongoing arguments. We have already seen that the formula in 1 Cor 15:3b–5 represents a tradition that Paul insists (v. 11) is preached by all the apostles. We have seen that the apostle has worked together a collection of resurrection traditions in order to defend his equality as an apostle to the Jerusalem authorities.

Verse 12 initiates a lengthy defense of resurrection against some who are claiming that there is no resurrection of the dead. The chapter is divided into two sections by the diatribe question in v. 35. That verse introduces a substantively new mode of arguing the case. The arguments in vv. 12–34 are of three types: (a) appeal to the traditions of eschatology and confession of the resurrection inherited by Christians (vv. 12–19); (b) appeal to Scripture (vv. 20–28); (c) a series of ad hominem arguments (vv. 29–34). Such a combination of tradition, Scripture, and ad hominem argument in a diatribe framework is a typically Pauline mode of argument.[21] The diatribe question in v. 35 opens a section in which Paul suddenly engages the question of resurrection on a theoretical level. He employs exegetical traditions that we can also trace in Philo. This second mode of argument defends the possibility of there being a resurrected body. Verses 50–58 integrate that perspective into the apocalyptic patterns of Christian eschatology. We will leave the discussion of the second half of the chapter until chapter nine when we discuss resurrection and the future of the Christian. It goes beyond reuse of material that represents common Christian preaching.[22] The arguments in vv. 12–34 are less specific to the Corinthian situation. They may well reflect Paul's customary way of preaching resurrection. Thus, the arguments in this chapter have diverse origins. Some probably reflect stock topics of early Christian preaching.

1 Corinthians 15:1–11

The opening of the chapter, vv. 1–3a, makes it clear that what follows is tradition held by all churches. While there is disagreement over the exact extent of the traditional material, the formula represents a primitive gospel: Jesus died, was buried, was raised, and appeared, all "according to Scripture."[23] Though some interpreters think that "according to Scripture" was a later addition, it represents a fundamental element in a number of kerygmatic interpretations of the events of Jesus' death and resurrection. Thus, we would argue that it is a necessary element in proclaiming those events as salvific.[24]

C. K. Barrett contrasts the paratactic style of the list of appearances with the earlier clauses in the formula. However, he thinks that Paul would not have created the expression Peter and "the twelve," since he never speaks about "the twelve." Therefore, even if it was not part of the original formula, it was probably part of the tradition as Paul received it.[25] Lk 24:34 suggests that there were formulae that combined resurrection kerygma and appearance traditions. The verb ōphthē, which we find here and in Lk 24:34 (also Ac 9:17; 26:16; 13:13), is not the one Paul uses when he is simply referring to his own experience of seeing the Lord (Gal 1:15; 1 Cor 9:1). Therefore, it would appear to be dependent on the tradition of such a formula. The formula that linked an appearance of the Lord to Peter and the twelve would appear to have been one that legitimated their position in the community.[26]

In this formula, *etaphē* (he was buried) emphasizes the first clause. The first and third clauses are balanced with the "according to the Scriptures" traditions. Finally, the reference to the witnesses vindicates the claim that Jesus was raised. As a formula, this example appears to reflect a unique stage in the development of the resurrection traditions. Its foundation in the two-membered death and resurrection formulae is still evident. But it is developing away from such a simple affirmation of the saving events to a summary of those events, toward a listing of "what happened." Such a concern would find its full expression in the development of narrative accounts that included the death, burial, resurrection (empty tomb), and appearance traditions.[27]

1 Corinthians 15:12–19

Verse 12 introduces the claim that underlies the lengthy treatment of resurrection in this chapter: some were denying that there is a resurrection of the dead. Many of the older commentators presumed that the Corinthians held some view like the "baptismal resurrection" attacked in 2 Tim 2:18. Others hypothesize that the situation is similar to that in 1 Thess 4:13ff. The Corinthians are convinced that those who have died cannot participate in the parousia.[28] Paul appears to be quoting a Corinthian slogan in v. 12b: "there is no resurrection of the dead."[29] This slogan does not itself suggest that the resurrection has occurred in the baptismal experience or that the Corinthians are concerned about the ability of those who have died to participate in the parousia.

More recent commentators have sought to link denial of resurrection to views found elsewhere in 1 Cor. R. A. Horsley has used parallels from Philo of Alexandria to reconstruct the type of spirituality held by Paul's Corinthian opponents. He suggests that they understood salvation as identification with the wisdom of God, which was seen as an immortalizing transformation of the soul.[30] Wedderburn thinks that the Corinthians derive their sloganizing of theological positions from Cynic/Stoic preaching.[31]

A. J. M. Wedderburn suggests that part of the sloganizing wisdom of the Corinthian opponents affirmed the inferior nature of the body. Paul has to correct such a view in 1 Cor 6:13–14. He cites and corrects a Corinthian slogan in v. 12. In vv. 13a and b–14 he first uses an expression that he presumes the Corinthians accept: the body (= stomach) is destined for destruction. Paul then draws a distinction between the transitory body that passes away and the body as des-

tined for resurrection. Paul presumes that the Corinthians accept
several features of traditional Christian eschatology. The present age
is coming to an end (7:29, 31; 10:11; 13:8, 10, 12; 15:24ff., 50ff.), Christ
is going to return (11:26; 15:23; 16:22), and the world will be judged
(3:13ff.; 4:5ff.; 6:2f.; 11:32). The combination of such eschatological
expectations and the Corinthian conviction that Christians are endowed with the Spirit shows that their denial of resurrection is not
based simply on a philosophic view that the soul is immortal. They
must have presumed that endowment with the Spirit meant that the
person had a new spiritual self that survives death.[32]

Verses 13–19 are constructed to demonstrate the absurdity of the
Corinthian slogan. The basis of the *reductio ad absurdum* is that the
slogan implies denial of the message that Christ has been raised. That
move makes it clear that the issue is not that the Corinthians denied
an element of the creedal affirmation that Christ had been raised.
They are denying the view that resurrection applies to the fate of
Christians.[33] The formula as such does not draw any implications
about the fate of Christians from the proclamation of Christ's resurrection. Paul intends the reader to conclude that all of the elements
in the list are obviously false: denial of Christ's resurrection makes
the Corinthians' faith or salvation empty; their sins are not forgiven
(v. 17); all the apostles and even God are liars. The rhetorical conclusion to the section in v. 19 appears to draw upon a popular proverb in
first-century apocalyptic preaching:

> *For if there were this life only, which belongs to all men, nothing
> would be more bitter than this.* [2 Bar. 21.13; Charles, *Pseud-
> epigrapha* 2.494]
> *If for this life only we have hoped in Christ, we are of all men
> most to be pitied.* [1 Cor 15:19]

The apocalyptic proverb contrasts the present life, which belongs
to all human beings, with the future, which belongs to the elect.[34]
Paul may have used such a slogan as part of his preaching. He is
reminding the Corinthians of something familiar to them.

1 Corinthians 15:20–28

The arguments that are initiated in these verses form the backbone
of the doctrinal section in vv. 35–58. Verses 20–22 introduce the
parallel figures of Christ and Adam, which will be fundamental to
that section. Here they serve as the foundation for an apocalyptic
argument in vv. 23–28.[35] J. Lambrecht points out that each section
begins with a thesis followed by an explanation. Each explanation

employs a midrash on Scripture.[36] The first thesis (v. 20) holds that Christ has been raised as the "first fruits" of those who have died. The explanation is given in terms of the parallelism between Christ and Adam. Though the doctrinal explanation of the parallel is deferred until the next section, the simpler form of the parallel as we find it in vv. 21–22 may have formed an independent element of Paul's preaching. All that is required is the simple parallel: death comes into the world through one person, Adam; life comes into the world through one person, Christ. The Corinthians may even have agreed with that affirmation.

Verses 23–28 locate the coming of that life within an apocalyptic timetable. Christ is raised, then those who belong to him, and finally the end of the world comes. Paul may have Christianized a typical apocalyptic scheme in this section.[37] He is using this scheme in order to establish the fact that the time in which the Christians now live is not yet the time of fulfillment. The final consummation of all things comes with Christ's handing the kingdom over to the Father. The proper understanding of the time in which the Christian lives is linked to the interpretation of two Old Testament passages. Ps 8:7 is used to describe humanity in the time before the end; Ps 110:1, to describe the messianic task as completed when all is handed over to God. The argument for the eschatological order is introduced with *dei* (it is necessary) in v. 25. Paul is insisting upon the necessity of the present interval in which Christ is ruling. Elsewhere in the New Testament Ps 110:1 is a familiar proof text for the exaltation of Christ.[38] T. Callan's study of the use of Ps 110:1 and its relationship to the expectation that Christ will come again concludes that it is frequently understood to imply a period in which Christ rules as enthroned Messiah before the final subjection of his enemies. The use of the psalm in 1 Cor 15:25 is unusual in that it stresses the active role of Christ in subduing his enemies—though the ultimate victory is still reserved to God's power (v. 27). Callan thinks that his passage represents a development in the understanding of Christ's messianic exaltation. Jesus is presented as presently enthroned as Messiah and as ruling. His reign does not begin with the parousia.[39]

The passage emphasizes the subjection of all things. The "all" in the citation of Ps 8:7 refers back to the list of enemies in vv. 26–27a, a list that culminates in the destruction of death. The passage also departs from the usual apocalyptic traditions of a final battle between God (or his angelic agent) and his enemies. Presenting death as the final enemy demythologizes the passage. No battle is required. Death is vanquished by the life-giving power of Christ. Thus, the passage looks back to v. 22.[40] This shift is also evident in another departure from the usual apocalyptic scenario. There one would presume that the rule of the Messiah is to take place between the defeat of Satan and the handing over of the kingdom. Here death is destroyed with the resurrection of those over whom the Messiah might be said to reign now—the Christians.[41]

Paul is using these traditions to insist that denial of resurrection cannot be maintained in the face of two elements of the traditional preaching: (a) the parallelism of Adam and Christ and (b) the eschatological expectation of the subjection of all things. Verses 35–38 will be directed against the exegetical base on which Paul's opponents constructed their view of salvation. The eschatological timetable that Paul constructs in this section envisages Jesus' resurrection as the beginning of a process that reaches its completion at the parousia. The parousia is no longer seen as the beginning of the defeat of God's enemies. Jesus is not enthroned in heaven waiting for the parousia to begin his reign. Rather, the passage exploits the eschatological implications of resurrection imagery to show that Jesus is already reigning.

1 Corinthians 15:29–34

The final verses in this section contain a series of ad hominem arguments for the resurrection. Paul returns to the type of argument used in vv. 13–19. He insists that without "resurrection of the dead" actions that Christians take for granted would be meaningless.

The obscure practice of baptism on behalf of the dead has led to much debate. Paul does not provide information about what is entailed in the practice. He is only concerned with arguing that such a practice is inconsistent with denial of the resurrection. Verses 30–32a make the experience of the apostle evidence for the absurdity of the Corinthian slogan. Paul regularly uses the catalog of apostolic hardships as grounds for his "boasting" before God (1 Cor 4:9–13; 2 Cor 6:4–10; 11:23–29).

Verses 32b–34 string together a series of proverbial sayings taken from the paraenetic tradition. This string of sayings rounds out the ad hominem section of the argument. Verse 32b contains a saying that appears in a number of Greek epigrams; on drinking cups and on gravestones. Its original meaning was simply, given the shortness of life, it should be enjoyed while possible.[42] A. J. M. Wedderburn notes that it was used against the Epicureans.[43] The second quotation in the string is equally well known. It was derived from Menander. Some exegetes think that Paul means this quotation to be applied directly to the Corinthian problem: they are not to associate with

people who hold such views about the resurrection.[44] The final injunction, "be sober," also had an established place in the conventions
of moral exhortation. It is addressed to those who pursue life in
ignorance of virtue. Paul's opponents may have claimed that they
had "become sober" as part of the ideology by which they described
their view of perfection.[45] Paul is thus equating them with those
actually living in ignorance and whose behavior was probably rou-
tinely condemned in early Christian preaching with the type of slogans that Paul uses here. The traditional material assembled here
reinforces Paul's assertion that denial of resurrection renders meaningless both beliefs that the Corinthians hold and practices in which
they engage. They may as well return to the futile way of life condemned in the popular sayings.

Most of the traditions used in this argument have nothing to say
about resurrection itself. Only the apocalyptic traditions of vv. 23–27
and the proof texts in Ps 110:1 and Ps 8:7 may be directly tied to the
early Christian understanding of the resurrection. Resurrection appears to have been first understood as exaltation. It has now been
expanded to imply that that exaltation means the beginning of
Christ's messianic reign. Verse 19 and the sayings in vv. 32b–34
represent a form of popular wisdom about the futility of this life. It is
possible that such pieces of popular wisdom were used to preach
resurrection. Christians are thus distinguished from those who have
no hope and are thus condemned to lives of futility. Verses 20–22
suggest that the "life-giving power" of Christ was presented as the
antithesis of Adam's fall into death. It was attached to the resurrection and heavenly exaltation of Christ. But it is not limited to the
future events of the parousia. It is the power that believers experience as effective in their lives. The combination of that image with an
eschatological timetable provides an indication of the messianic rule
of Christ. These associations make it clear that the resurrection of
Jesus had been understood from an early time as the eschatological
turning point of the ages and not merely as the reward for Jesus as a
righteous individual. Those promises that are expected for the *eschaton* are in the process of being realized. Thus, there is an incipient
sense that the resurrection has cosmic significance. Something has
changed in the world's relationship to God. We have seen that the
Matthean narrative dramatized the eschatological shift in the ages
with the apocalyptic signs of earthquake, angelic visitation, and a
proleptic resurrection of the righteous.

2 Timothy 2:8–13

The style of Pauline resurrection paraenesis reappears in 2 Tim 2:8–13. This passage is a recollection of the Pauline kerygma. It is directed toward those who live in the generation after the apostle. 2 Timothy seeks to present the tradition as it should be taught in the community.[46]

Verse 8, "Remember Jesus Christ risen from the dead, from the seed of David, according to my gospel," presupposes a two-membered formula of the type found in Rom 1:3f. That formula is designated here Paul's gospel. This tradition subsumes the two-part structure under the announcement that Christ was raised from the dead.[47] Verses 9–10 employ a common Pauline theme: preaching the gospel is tied to apostolic suffering (see Phil 1:7, 8 (bonds), 14–17). Verse 10a adds a motivation for that suffering, "on account of the elect."

The series of parallel phrases that conclude this section (vv. 11–13) are sometimes described as a hymn. However, the structure and content of the lines suggests that it is a formulaic piece designed for instruction rather than liturgical use. The author has introduced it with the saying about the "secure *(pistos)* word," which occurs several times in the pastorals (1 Tim 1:15; 3:1; 4:9; 2 Tim 2:11; Tit 3:8). This introduction appears to have been attached to affirmations about salvation, which the author intends to be applied to the present.[48]

The language in which this passage speaks about the future of the Christian emphasizes ruling and reigning with Christ. Unlike Eph 2:4–6, this passage does not turn the Christian experience into being raised with Christ into the heavens.[49] Rather, it appears to prefer a more general set of images of eternal life for salvation. This passage shows how the formulae of Pauline paraenesis were carried into the Pauline churches. They form a pattern of traditional apostolic kerygma that is to be taught and handed on. The resurrection of Jesus is presented as a central article of belief in that context.

ACTS

Acts uses kerygmatic formulae as part of the sermons in which the apostles announce that the age of fulfillment has dawned. Acts frequently pairs resurrection and crucifixion in the pattern of human rejection met by divine affirmation (2:24–31; 3:15; 4:10).[50] The risen Jesus sits at God's right hand as the messianic leader of the new Israel (2:33–36; 3:13; 4:11; 5:31). The presence of the Spirit in the community is a sign of Christ's glory and power (2:33; 5:32). One also finds in these sermons the older eschatological timetable in which the messianic age is soon to be consummated with the return of Christ (3:32; 10:42).[51] Luke presents resurrection as that to which the apostles are to give testimony.

The pattern of human rejection and divine affirmation presents resurrection as the point at which Jesus receives messianic titles (2:36; 5:31; 13:33; 17:31).

J. A. T. Robinson detects an even more primitive Christology behind Ac 3:12–26. Jesus is presented as the servant and Mosaic prophet sent to Israel. Though the people rejected him, as had been prophesied, they still have the opportunity to repent. Their repentance will bring Jesus back to Israel as her Messiah.[52] The mission is viewed as a call for Israel's repentance. Jesus' messianic coming still lies in the future. That formulation requires only a slight expansion of Jesus' own teaching, since he saw the Kingdom of God breaking in with his ministry. The transition to heaven does not exploit the eschatological associations of resurrection as a change in the ages. Resurrection vindicates Jesus and establishes him as Messiah-designate in heaven.

Though Robinson may be right in identifying the process by which the earliest affirmations of Jesus' messiahship emerged in association with resurrection, it is unlikely that Luke understands this passage to say anything different from the others. He has picked up the tradition of Jesus as prophet like Moses in the gospel. Lk 13:33 links Jesus' destiny in Jerusalem to his role as prophet. Echoes of Deut 18:15–18 also appear in the expression "Listen to him" (Lk 9:35; Ac 7:7).[53] Ac 3:14–15 presented the fundamental paradox: the Jews denied the Holy and Righteous One, the author of Life, but God raised him up. This speech provokes the same response as the others. The apostles are arrested for preaching "resurrection of the dead" (4:2).[54] Ac 17:30–31 picks up a theme from Jewish apocalyptic preaching: God is overlooking the sins of the Gentiles rather than punishing them as he does Israel. The Gentiles will receive the punishment due their sins at the judgment. Acts proclaims that the resurrection of Jesus has summoned all people to judgment. It is proof of his election as judge (cf. Ac 10:42). The original Christology behind such affirmations may have been that of resurrection as Jesus' exaltation to the glory of the heavenly Son of Man. Coming in judgment is regularly associated with Son of Man imagery in the earliest synoptic traditions.[55]

Acts 2:24–36

This section of Peter's Pentecost sermon makes extensive use of scriptural proof to demonstrate that resurrection is part of the divine plan. Verse 24 uses the typically Lukan formulation that makes God the subject of the active verb to raise and Jesus the object of that divine activity.[56] The Septuagint of the Old Testament prophetic texts (Ps 18 [17]:5f.; 116 [114]:3; 2 Sam 22:6) interprets the "birth pangs" as the pangs of death. Luke uses this tradition to lead into the proof text that follows.

Verses 25–31 provide the first scriptural proof for the resurrection. Ps 16:8–11 (also in 13:35), "You will not abandon my soul to Hades, nor let your Holy One see corruption," is taken as a prophecy of resurrection. Christ was not abandoned to Hades. His flesh did not see corruption. Thus, the Lukan understanding of the bodily character of resurrection can be interpreted as the fulfillment of these prophecies. Luke argues that David's death and the presence of his body in the tomb proves that he could not have been speaking about himself. He must have been speaking about God's promise to one of his descendants. Verse 33 makes it clear that resurrection is understood as exaltation to the right hand of God. This exaltation corresponds to David's prophecy (v. 30) that God would set one of his (= David's) descendants on his throne. Luke has interpreted the throne to which the prophecy refers to be the heavenly throne of God.[57] The earlier traditions (Rom 1:4; 1 Tim 3:6) simply spoke of the exalted One as endowed with the Spirit of God. Luke transforms that tradition by having the endowment with the Spirit make it possible for Jesus to confer that Spirit on his followers (Lk 24:49; Ac 1:4). Once again, the scriptural proof is introduced with the argument that David could not have been speaking about himself (v. 34a). Such a qualification would appear to reflect an early Christian defense of the christological interpretation of Scripture.[58] Here Ps 110:1 is used in its most common apologetic form, as proof that Christ is exalted to the right hand of God.

Luke's argument in this speech provides three elements of the resurrection tradition with a foundation in Scripture. Thus, the speech also serves to demonstrate that christological interpretation of Scripture, which his resurrection narratives traced back to Easter. Jesus is shown to have fulfilled three prophecies: (a) Jesus did not remain in Hades; (b) his body did not experience corruption; and (c) he was exalted to the right hand of God. Verse 33b appeals to the outpouring of the Spirit on the community as evidence for the exaltation of Christ. Luke also includes the motif of the apostles as witnesses to the resurrection in his argument (v. 32).

The final verse of the section presents a fourth feature of the resurrection imagery. Jesus is given titles of messianic glory at the resurrection. "Lord" can be derived from the psalm quotation. "Christ" appears to be derived from the application of Ps 2 to Jesus. In Ac 4:26, Ps 2:2 is used to explain the hostility shown against Jesus. The christological tradition behind this image of Jesus' entry into messianic glory is sometimes described as adoptionistic. However, Luke appears to use this tradition simply as the divine counter to the human rejection of Jesus that culminated in his death. Luke is not asserting that Jesus became Lord and Christ at his resurrection in a way that he had not been during his life.[59]

The Titles Kyrios and Christos

Luke has employed a tradition that linked the christological titles Lord and Messiah to the proclamation that Jesus is exalted at the right hand of God. The connection between these titles and the psalm texts was pre-Lukan. Scholars have debated over the origins of early Christian use of the title "Lord" for Jesus. Some, pointing to its rarity outside the Septuagint, had insisted that Greek-speaking Jews did not commonly use *Kyrios* for God. They presume that its use reflects the influence of the pagan practice of speaking of the gods as "lords," such as we find in 1 Cor 8:6. If that were the only possible origin for the title, then the interpretation of the resurrection as Jesus' exaltation to the status of "Lord" could not be any earlier than the development of a mission to the Gentiles independent of Judaism. Other scholars point to the early Aramaic prayer "Come, Lord" *("Marana tha")* of 1 Cor 16:22. This prayer suggests that Aramaic-speaking Christians addressed Jesus as Lord *(mar').*[60] The Aramaic evidence from Qumran now makes it possible to show that the absolute form *mar'* was used for God, though it is not yet shown to have been a rendering of the Tetragrammaton (11 QTgJob 24.6–7; 1 QApGen 20.12–13, 15; 4 QEn b.1.4.5).[61] Thus, it is possible to argue that the title Lord was used to indicate that the exalted Jesus is on a level with God, though early Jewish Christianity would be careful not to identify him directly with God. The Aramaic prayer *"Marana tha,"* "Our Lord, come," suggests that the title was first used for Jesus as the One who is to come in the judgment (see also 1 Cor 11:26).[62] The saying about the future coming of the Lord that Paul quotes in 1 Thess 4:16–17 reflects this understanding of Lord as applied to the coming of Christ at the parousia.[63] Thus, the traditions behind this passage associate Jesus' exaltation to lordship with the resurrection, as does the kerygmatic formula in Lk 24:34. The connection between resurrection and use of the *Kyrios* title in acclamation appears in other formulae, such as 1 Cor 12:3 and Phil 2:10–11. It is part of Paul's affirmation when he says that he has "seen the Lord" (1 Cor 9:1).[64] It also appears in Jn 20:28, where Thomas acclaims Jesus "Lord and God." This acclamation makes explicit the divinity implied in the title Lord. That transition is characteristic of the Christology of the Fourth Gospel, which goes well beyond other New Testament traditions in speaking of Jesus as God. Most of the New Testament does not make such an identity explicit. The title Lord is understood to imply that the exalted Jesus has an equality with God in power or in rule.

The Davidic psalm text suggests that *Kyrios* carried regal overtones. These overtones appear in the synoptic stories that use Davidic traditions as well (Mk 12:36/Mt 22:41/Lk 20:39). Such overtones are attached to another motif that was associated with resurrection, Jesus' kingship over the believers. Fitzmyer points to the contrast between Lord and slave in Phil 2:6–11. There the contrast represents two conditions assumed by the earthly and exalted Jesus, respectively. However, Paul frequently takes slave as a description for the Christian disciple in relationship to Jesus as Lord (Phil 1:11; Rom 1:1; Gal 1:10; Col 4:12; 2 Cor 4:5; 1 Cor 6:20, the Christian has been "bought by the Lord").[65] Thus, Paul translates the image of Jesus as Lord into the everyday life of the Christian believer.

The kerygmatic formula in Rom 10:9 provided another example in which belief that Jesus has been raised is the grounds for the affirmation that he is Lord. This belief is described as the faith that brings Christians salvation. Though Lord is the most frequently used title for Jesus in Luke-Acts, it does not appear in connection with the parousia. Ac 3:19 speaks of God as the one to send the appointed Messiah, Jesus, as Lord. Luke uses Lord for the earthly Jesus in his gospel. In doing so, he departs from Mark, who has only one example of Lord applied to the earthly Jesus (Mk 11:3). It would appear that by the time Luke wrote, it had become customary to refer to the earthly Jesus as Lord.[66] Thus, for Luke, resurrection represents God's confirmation of the lordship that Jesus has always possessed. It does not imply any change in his status.

H. Conzelmann claims that Luke does not make any distinction between the title Lord and the title Messiah, while J. Fitzmyer insists that the way in which Luke correlates the two titles should warn us against interpreting one in terms of the other.[67] In Paul and in some Lukan texts *"Christos"* has lost its technical meaning, "Messiah," and is simply taken as part of Jesus' name (e.g., Lk 4:10; 8:12; Ac 2:38; 3:6; 4:33; 9:34; 10:36, 48; 11:17; 15:26; 16:18; 20:21; 24:24; 28:31). However, Luke continues to use *"Christos"* as a title for Jesus (Lk 2:11, 26; 3:15; 4:41; 9:20; 20:41; 22:67; 23:2, 35, 39; 24:26, 36; Ac 2:31, 36; 3:18; 4:26; 5:42; 8:5; 9:22; 17:3; 18:5, 28; 26:23). The term Messiah was clearly associated with the expectation for a kingly or political leader of the Davidic line in the first century.[68] The pre-Lukan gospel tradition attributed "Messiah" to Peter's recognition of Jesus' identity (Mk 8:30–31). But the gospels also show a reluctance on Jesus' part to use the title of himself. The evident concern to correct possible misunderstanding of the use of the title Messiah for Jesus appears to be rooted in an awareness of the political overtones of the title. Luke's sensitivity to this point is evident in his revision of Jesus' answer to the High Priest's question about his messiahship. Mark has him give an unequivocal "I Am" (Mk 14:62). Luke has Jesus evade the issue (22:67–68).[69] Luke uses Messiah as a title to show that Jesus is the One who brings salvation to humanity (Lk 2:26, 29–32; 9:20; 23:35). He cast Jesus's suffering at Jerusalem as a fundamental part of that messianic task (24:26, 46). Though the awkward formula in Ac 3:19–21 might presume that resurrection is only a prelude to Jesus' coming as Messiah, that understanding is not typical of the New Testament.[70] Lord appears to be the title that refers to Jesus' future coming and rule. Thus, Luke has recovered the titular use of Messiah because he is able to articulate a nonpolitical understanding of the term in Jesus' suffering. The title Messiah, unlike the title Lord, did not have an inherent connection with resurrection or exaltation language and was easily used for Jesus in the nominal sense.

Son of God and Resurrection

The Lukan tradition in Ac 2 linked Jesus' designation as Messiah and Lord at the resurrection with the expectations attached to a descendant of the Davidic line. We have seen that the early kerygmatic formula in Rom 1:3f. is based on a parallelism between Son of David and Son of God. The formula also suggested an equivalence between Son of God and Lord. The Son of David expectations, on the other hand, are applied to the earthly Jesus. As was the case with the title "Lord," scholars have found a rich field of hellenistic parallels for the title "Son of God." It was once thought to imply that Christians had taken over categories from hellenistic myths or stories of "divine men" to apply them to Jesus.[71]

M. Hengel has pointed out, however, that the expression Son of God has a much more precise distribution in the Pauline writings. While Paul uses Lord some 184 times, Son of God only appears fifteen times, eleven of them (Rom, seven times; Gal, four times) in those letters in which Paul is concerned about the relationship between Christianity and Judaism. Further, these passages fall into two groups. The first consists of passages in which Jesus as Son of God is associated with the gospel Paul is commissioned to preach; that is, they fall into passages in which Paul is defending his apostleship (Rom 1:3f., 9; Gal 1:15f.). The second group is soteriological. As Son of God, Jesus makes it possible for Christians to participate in the glory of God or to be sons of God (Rom 8:3, 29, 32; Gal 4:4f.). 1 Cor 1:9 has Son of God at the beginning of the letter; it reappears in the parousia tradition of 1 Cor 15:28. The soteriological implications of the title are also evident in the parallel use of the expression "Son" in 1 Thess 1:10.[72] Within the context of Pauline theology the connection between Son of God as the source of Paul's gospel and the soteriological use of Son of God is grounded in Paul's conviction that salvation now comes to those who have faith outside the Law. Paul has founded his special apostleship to the Gentiles on that gospel. He has defended his claim to apostolic authority on his vision of the risen Lord. In Gal 2:20 the culmination of an argument that one no longer lives under the Law comes when he contrasts his former life "in the flesh" (= as a Jew under the Law) with the life he now has through faith in the Son of God, "who loved me and gave himself up for me." Thus, Paul attaches the salvific significance of Son of God to Jesus' death on behalf of humanity. It is not a new state into which Jesus enters at his resurrection.[73]

Rom 1:3f. preserves an older tradition in which Jesus was designated Son of God at the resurrection. Similar associations are preserved in Ac 13:33. There God's raising Jesus is said to fulfill Ps 2:7. For Luke this section represents the decisive turn toward the Gentiles. Paul's sermon summarizes the Lukan picture of salvation history. Verses 30–37 provide another defense of the early Christian preaching of resurrection. The defense begins with the tradition that the apostles are witnesses to the resurrection. It continues with a series of quotations introduced by Ps 2:7. Verses 34–37 pursue the theme of the Davidic promises. The incorruptibility of the risen Jesus is evidence that he has fulfilled those promises. This theme was part of an apologetic argument in Ac 2:24–32. The connection between Ps

2:7 and Jesus' appointment as Son is traditional. It appears in Mk 1:11, Heb 1:5, and 5:5.

Though early Christian apologetic fastened on Old Testament passages that used Son of God for the adoption of the king, there is no evidence that Son of God was a messianic title. The Essene midrash on the opening verses of Ps 1 and 2 (4 Q Flor 1–2.1.10) use 2 Sam 7:14 for an individual spoken of as the "shoot of David" (Jer 23:5). Other examples in which the Essenes use the titles Son of God and Sons of the Most High are clearly not messianic. They may simply refer to the king. Thus, it is not possible to attribute the messianic use of Son of God to Palestinian Jewish speculation. Nor can we presume that Son of God is equivalent to Messiah. Yet its appearance in pre-Pauline formulae shows that the title developed as part of the early kerygma.[74] Rom 1:3f. links the sonship of the risen Lord with the Spirit. Ac 2:33 has recast an earlier tradition in which resurrection and Spirit are associated. The earliest tradition may have pictured the resurrection as Jesus' installation into divine sonship. At the same time, the development of the title Son of God appears to have been dependent on Jesus' own language, especially his description of God as Abba, which rapidly became a distinguishing mark of early Christian prayer (e.g., Rom 8:14; Gal 4:6).[75] The use of the Son of God title appears to require both the hints from Jesus' own language and the understanding that Jesus fulfills promises attached to the Davidic Messiah. The confession of Jesus as Son of God appears to have originated in the confession of resurrection as his divine exaltation.[76] 1 Thess 1:10 and Ac 3:19ff. indicate that the earliest tie between resurrection and the messianic activity of Jesus lay in the expectation of his return in judgment (see also 1 Thess 4:14ff.). Ac 3:19ff. ties the parousia expectation to the Christology of Jesus as Mosaic prophet; it is tied to Jesus' position as Son of God in 1 Thess 1:10 and to the confession that Jesus is Lord in 1 Thess 4:14ff. Son of God also appears in connection with Son of Man in Ac 7:56, though Son of Man does not appear as a title in the resurrection kerygma of the New Testament.[77] As a vision of Jesus' exaltation at the right hand of God, Ac 7:56 appears to refer to the resurrection. It reflects the early development of Son of Man traditions out of the application of Dan 7:13 to the parousia of Jesus. Rev 1:13 and 14:14 also use the Daniel imagery of the Son of Man to describe Jesus' exaltation in heaven.[78] These images are the result of early Christian exegetical elaboration, since there is no strong evidence for pre-Christian Jewish expectations of the "Son of Man" as a messianic figure. Use of Daniel in formulating the resurrection/parousia images led to application of the title to Jesus. Ac 7:56 reflects a Lukan tendency to add Son of Man to passages in which the other gospels do not have it. Luke has taken a Son of Man saying and put it on the lips of a speaker other than Jesus.[79] He may have formulated the saying as a judgment oracle against those who have condemned Stephen based on the model in Mk 14:62. Or the verse may represent a primitive tradition. If it is a kerygmatic tradition, then one might presume that some other title, perhaps Lord or Son of God, stood in the original.

CHRISTOLOGICAL HYMNS

A number of kerygmatic formulae describe resurrection as Jesus' exaltation (Rom 10:9; 1 Thess 1:10; see also the connection between resurrection and exaltation in 1 Pt 1:21; Ac 3:13; 5:30f.; Eph 1:19). The imagery of the exaltation of the suffering righteous was developed in connection with the wisdom traditions of Judaism. The hymnic patterns in the New Testament use a similar contrast in which the pattern of humiliation and exaltation is used to describe the earthly destiny and heavenly glory of Jesus.

Interpreters have always found the compressed language of these hymns in need of further elaboration. Consequently, various attempts have been made to associate them with a mythical story, which they are said to summarize. Such stories tell of a heavenly redeemer who comes into the world of evil and darkness in order to call the true believers back to their true home in the heavenly light world. Or the story might be that of the righteous sufferer in Wis 2–5 who is put to death by his enemies but triumphs over them in the heavenly divine court. Or the story might be the myth of Adam's fall completed by his eventual restoration.[80] None of the stories that have been reconstructed in this way has succeeded in accounting for the christological hymns in the New Testament. E. Fiorenza has suggested that we understand such hymns as "reflective mythology." Their early Christian authors have used terminology and symbols from the surrounding milieu in order to reflect upon the significance of Jesus. However, their use of such material does not necessarily presuppose a single background. The mythic overtones of these hymns are a necessary part of their attempt to present the cosmic lordship of Christ as the foundation of their soteriology.[81]

Philippians 2:6–11

Phil 2:6–11 provides the earliest example of such a hymn.[82]

Who being in the form (morphē) of God
did not consider being like (isa) God an opportunity to be seized,
but emptied himself,
taking the form (morphē) of a slave.

Being in the likeness (homoiōma) of humans,
and being found in the shape (schēma) like a human,
he humbled himself,
being obedient unto death—[add: death on a cross]

Therefore God "hyper-exalted" him,
and bestowed on him the name above every name,
so that at the name of Jesus every knee would bend

and every tongue confess [add: in heaven, on earth and under the
  earth]
"Jesus Christ is Lord" [add: to the glory of God, the Father]

Paul appears to have made three additions to the hymn: death on a cross; in heaven, on earth, and under the earth; and the concluding doxology. These additions do not change the structure of the hymn. The expression "in heaven, on earth, and under the earth" may belong to a pre-Pauline stage in which the emphasis lay on Christ's exaltation as Lord over the powers of the cosmos. The final doxology with the move from acclamation of Jesus' soteriological power to the glory of the Father is typical of Paul (Gal 1:1; 1 Thess 1:1; 1 Cor 8:6).[83] Paul's addition of "death on a cross" is a reflection of the apostle's own theological orientation. Paul looks at the death of Christ in soteriological terms. He always thinks of it in terms of its benefit for the believer. Paul's additions make it clear that the hymn describes the eschatological act in which God brings salvation to his people.[84]

Commentators disagree about the extent to which the likeness of Christ to God in the opening verse presupposes a doctrine of preexistence.[85] Murphy-O'Connor has proposed that it means no more than Wis 2 does when Wisdom asserts that immortality, which was considered likeness to God, would belong to any human who did not share the sin of Adam.[86] If the hymn does presuppose a more developed doctrine of preexistence than that in Murphy-O'Connor, then exaltation becomes Jesus' return to the glory that he had before. However, the explicit development of that type of Christology appears to belong to the later reflections of the Fourth Gospel rather than to the early period represented by this pre-Pauline hymn.[87] Consequently, whether in terms of the suffering righteous person or in terms of the Pauline parallel between Adam and Christ, most exegetes see the hymn as focusing on the contrast between Christ's earthly life and the exaltation that he now enjoys with God. The one who had obediently taken up the role of humiliated slave now reigns over the whole cosmos as its exalted Lord.

The paradox inherent in this hymn depends on the recognition that it is not telling a mythical story but is speaking about a particular life. The distinctiveness of its picture of exaltation emerges when one contrasts it with the alternative images that are found in the contexts from which the author of the hymn has taken its symbols. Though the exaltation of the righteous sufferer appears to have provided the basic pattern for this type of hymn, we find that this hymn does without any presentation of the triumph over the enemies responsible for Jesus' death. Instead, it focuses entirely on the contrast between the lowliest state, that of the slave, and the most exalted, that of cosmic Lord. The contrast presents what would be almost unthinkable: one who is like God can accept being like a slave, can accept suffering and death. This paradox is said to lie at the heart of Christ's exaltation to cosmic lordship. As we have seen elsewhere, this hymn presumes that the lordship of Christ over the cosmos is already effective. It is not something for which one must wait until the parousia. In singing the hymn, the congregation joins the hidden praise of the whole cosmos.[88] Paul's additions have only heightened the paradox of Jesus' lordship. This vision goes well beyond any picture of individual vindication. It claims that what is at stake is nothing less than the subjection of all levels of the universe to the rule of God.

Colossians 1:1–15

The Philippians hymn did not specify the nature of Christ's likeness to God. Col 1:15–20 does so explicitly. It identifies Christ with the wisdom of God that is active in creation. Each of the four names given him at the beginning of the hymn have ties with the philosophic picture of divine wisdom found in Philo. As with the previous chapter it is easier to recognize the hymnic character of the passage than to agree on the division into strophes. Verse 18a appears to introduce the second half, Christ's activity in salvation. However, many exegetes see it as the conclusion to the first half of the hymn. They understand "body" to have been used by the author of the hymn in the philosophical sense of cosmos. They think that "church" is an exegetical addition to the term body.[89] J. Gnilka's solution, which is the one followed here, is to take vv. 17–18a as the middle strophe between two longer strophes.[90]

He is the image of the invisible God, the first born of all creation,
for in him all things were created
in heaven and on earth,
visible and invisible;
whether thrones, dominions, powers or principalities,
all things were created through him and for him.

He is before all things,
and in him all things hold together.
He is the head of the body, [add: the church].

He is the beginning, the first-born from the dead,
in order that he might be first in all things,
for in him all the fulness was pleased to dwell,
and through him to reconcile to himself all things,
making peace [add: through the blood of his cross]
whether on earth or in the heavens.

Commentators agree that the author of the letter has added the reference to "blood of his cross" in v. 20. That expression performs the same function as the addition of "church" to body. It takes an expression that was originally cosmological and gives it an interpretation that relates it to the church.[91] Cosmological images are much more pronounced in this hymn than they were in the Philippians hymn. But the ecclesial interpretation that the author has given to the cosmological language makes it clear that the community of believers is the place in which Christ exercises his cosmic rule. We do not need to untangle the cosmological background behind the various images for the creative activity of God that are used of Christ here. The parallels between the images of creation and salvation set in a cosmological context make the universal significance of salvation evident.[92] The cosmological images of creation dominate the first strophe, so that any hints of humiliation are eradicated. Yet the soteriological perspective of the cross and resurrection of Christ as the reconciliation of humanity with God is retained. The cosmological background might make it seem difficult to see why such reconciliation would be required if the Christ is the foundation of the entire cosmos, holding it all together as the first part asserts. E. Schweizer resolves this dilemma by referring to the liturgical imagery that allows the community to see that it participates in both orders: the divine order of creation and the order of redemption. Thus, the creative, sustaining presence of divine wisdom and the life-giving presence of the exalted Christ, which was derived from the resurrection kerygma, have been merged. The concentration of these two powerful images of God's presence have left no room for the "on earth" part of the life of Christ. At best, it may be presupposed in the expression "first born of the dead" (v. 18b).[93] Thus, this hymn is different from the expression of Jesus' life as "taking the form of a slave" in Phil 2:7f. or the "was manifested in the flesh" of 1 Tim 3:16. The additions made by the author of the letter strengthen the connection between the cosmological imagery of the hymn and the salvific death and resurrection of Christ. The church is the body of which Christ is the head. The cross is the place of reconciliation. Thus, the cosmological vision of the hymn is ultimately founded in the events of salvation. The key to that interpretation is found in the only allusion to resurrection in this hymn (v. 18b). This verse deliberately parallels the creation image of v. 15. "Beginning" is a cosmological term used of Wisdom in Prov 8:22. The connection between Wisdom and the image of God is evident in Philo (Leg. All. 1.43; see also Wis 7:26). Wisdom is described in these traditions as the firstborn of creation (Prov 8:22, 25; Philo, Ebr. 30–31; QGen 4.97). "First born from the dead" parallels that expression but also shows that we have moved out of the realm of the creative activity of divine wisdom. It is necessary to look to the traditions of Christian preaching to find parallels for these expressions. The traditions of the resurrection kerygma provide several suggestive parallels for the origin of this expression: Christ is "first fruits" (1 Cor 15:20, 23), originator of life (Ac 3:15), first to rise from the dead (Ac 26:33). Rev 1:5 uses the expression "first born from the dead." The expression "first born of many brethren" appears in Rom 8:29, where it is clearly used in the context of new creation. The explanatory phrase attached to "first born from the dead" shows that the Colossians hymn pictures resurrection as the culmination of the cosmological presence of divine wisdom. The words "in all" refer to "all things" (vv. 16, twice; 17 and 20). The expression "be the first" uses the epithet "first born" (vv. 15 and 18b) and the "he is before all things" (v. 17). Thus, "first born from the dead" corresponds to the cosmological "first place" occupied by divine wisdom. J. D. G. Dunn has pointed out that the resurrection and exaltation tradition is what has made it possible to use the language of divine wisdom for Christ. It is the resurrected Christ in whom Christians have come to recognize the embodiment of divine wisdom and power.[94]

This perspective on the hymn shows that it is not primarily about preexistence. Rather, it demonstrates that the creative activity of God has been fulfilled in Christ. Resurrection as exaltation has made possible the link between divine wisdom and the salvation found in Christ.

Hymnic Fragments

The other hymnic passages in the New Testament, which draw upon the language of resurrection and exaltation, appear to be only fragments that the authors have woven into their writing. They are sometimes difficult to interpret, given their fragmentary character, but they confirm the importance of these hymnic traditions in filling out the proclamation of the risen Christ in early Christian communities.

Hebrews 1:2b–4

The opening verse of Hebrews contains hymnic language that parallels both the wisdom Christology of Colossians and the picture of the risen Christ as the One exalted over all the cosmic powers of the Philippians hymn.[95] The author of the epistle has taken the proof text for Christ's exaltation, Ps 110:1, from the hymn (v. 3) and used it as the conclusion to a section of psalm quotations (vv. 5–13). This collection of quotations demonstrates the truth of Christ's exaltation (v. 4). Since Hebrews is seeking to demonstrate that Christ has ascended into the heavens, he adds *"en hypsiliois"* (in the heavens; v. 3) to the psalm reference, just as he adds *"en ouraniosis"* (in the heavens) in 8:1.[96]

The hymnic fragment in vv. 2b–3 deals with the cosmological activity of wisdom:

whom (= the Son) he appointed heir of all things,
through whom he also made the universe (tous aionas);
who is the radiance (apaugasma) of his glory
and the stamp (charakter) of his being (hypostasis),
sustaining all things through his powerful word,
when he had made purification for sin, was seated at the right hand
    of the greatness on high.

This description of the cosmological activity of the Son as divine wisdom is contained between the assertion that these are the "last days" in which God has spoken through his Son rather than the prophets and the concluding reference to the soteriological activity of the Son making purification for sin. Purification will be the guiding image for salvation as Jesus' entry into the heavenly sanctuary through death. This entry into the true sanctuary makes the perfect, unrepeatable sacrifice for sin (4:14–5:10).[97] Several characteristics of divine wisdom are applied to the Son: "reflection of God's glory" (Wis 7:26); "stamp of his nature" (Philo, Plant. 18, where the stamp is the divine Word); sustaining all things by his powerful Word (Philo, Heres 36; Mut 256). At the same time, we also find in Philo use of these terms in a soteriological context. They refer to the activity by which wisdom perfects the soul.[98] The "heir of all things" is the soul, which has received the "stamp" of virtue, its likeness to the divine. Hebrews understands "heir" to refer only to the Son. Perfection can come to the believer only through the Son's purification. The ambiguity of the cosmological and soteriological images of divine salvation is evident in the introduction to the hymn. To be appointed heir could refer to an eternal cosmological status, or it could mean "appointed beforehand" as part of the eschatological plan of salvation.[99] Hebrews has singled out the concluding exaltation to provide the basis for his application of the hymn. He draws that implication from the hymn in v. 4: "In this way he has become as much greater than the angels as the name he has inherited is superior to theirs." We have seen that Phil 2:10f. also associated Christ's "hyperexaltation" above the powers of the cosmos to the name he has received. For Philippians, that name is Lord, the name that he receives when he is exalted to the divine throne. Hebrews knows the same pattern of exaltation and superior name. However, for Hebrews the name associated with Christ's heavenly exaltation is Son.

The psalm quotations that follow make this understanding of the exaltation clear. Verse 5 brings forward two traditions to prove that "Son" is the name that has been given to the exalted Christ.[100] Both citations belong to the tradition of exegesis that represents the resurrection as Jesus' gaining a new status, a status that is acknowledged in the act of christological affirmation. Thus, resurrection is Jesus' heavenly exaltation. The second argument that the author gives for the exaltation of Christ picks up the term "firstborn." We have seen that the cosmological overtones of that term were used in Col 1:18 to speak of Christ as "first born from the dead." Hebrews evokes an image of God conducting the Son into the heavens, where he is then worshiped by the angels. The angelic worship serves to demonstrate the superiority of the Son to the angels.

The following psalm texts about the angels (v. 7) and the Son (vv. 8–9; 10–12) establish the superiority of the Son on metaphysical grounds. Unlike that of the angels, the existence of the exalted Son is immutable and unchanging. J. W. Thompson argues that we can only understand the significance of this affirmation if we presume that the author is writing against a background of middle Platonic philosophy. Philo applied that philosophy to the Old Testament. Angels correspond to the intermediate beings, the *daimones*. Philo says that since they share human characteristics of passion and change, they were able to fall (Gig. 17). The angels, then, belong to the intermediate world. The exaltation of Christ places him in the eternal, heavenly world. Thus, Hebrews has translated the eschatological category of the Messiah's eternal rule into a metaphysical one.[101]

Ephesians 1:20-23

The conclusion to the thanksgiving in Ephesians expands upon the images of exaltation that are characteristic of the hymnic traditions. These verses focus entirely upon the resurrection and exaltation. This passage follows the lead of Colossians and makes the body of the exalted Christ the church. Verse 23 substitutes the word "church" for the pronoun "we," which had been used to designate the people of God. The same passage also picks up the imagery of "fullness" from the Colossians tradition. It transforms that cosmological term into an ecclesial one.[102] Gnilka points out that it is not possible to reconstruct a hymn behind these verses. Rather, an extended, periodic sentence appears to have been constructed out of creedal affirmations that had become common in the early Christian communities.[103] In vv. 20–22 God is the subject. Verse 23 suddenly switches the subject to the church. Thus, v. 23 appears to be the author's application of the traditional material. The clauses can be divided into two paired sets: the two aorist participles "he has raised" and "he has enthroned" and the two aorist verbs "he put under" and "he appointed." These descriptions of what God did for the Messiah are entwined with others that emphasize the divine power that is active in these events.

The cosmological and metaphysical patterns of the Colossians and Hebrews hymns are missing from this fragment. Ephesians focuses on resurrection as exaltation to lordship over all things. It gives that exaltation a striking ecclesiological interpretation, since the fullness of Christ is identified with the church as his body. Since the author understands the church as the body over which Christ rules, he will also describe the new life of Christians in terms that parallel the exaltation of Christ. Having been made alive with Christ, the Christian sits in the heavenly places with Christ (2:5f.).

Ps 110:1 continues to provide the foundation for the image of

Christ's exaltation. This passage picks up the image of God subjecting all things to Christ that we saw attached to the exaltation kerygma in 1 Cor 15:25–28.[104] Verse 21 recalls the "naming" that is also part of the exaltation image. With the hint of the superior divine name, we find the familiar list of powers to which the exalted Christ is superior (cf. 1 Cor 15:24; Col 1:16; Phil 2:9–11). However, as in the Hebrews example, this superior name is never stated.[105] The tradition of the subjection of all things in v. 22 (cf. 1 Cor 15:27) prepares the way for the author's introduction of the church as the place in which the fullness of the exalted Christ is realized.[106]

1 Timothy 3:16

Our final example of the hymnic affirmation of resurrection occurs in a passage that is introduced as "the mystery of piety" (cf. 3:9, "mystery of faith"). The image of mystery suits the Christology of the passage that speaks of Christ's "manifestation." The image of Christ as the manifestation of what has been hidden since the foundation of the world also appears in 1 Pt 1:20, where "was made manifest" parallels "predestined." Heb 9:26 uses this image of Christ appearing at the end of the age in the heavenly sanctuary. The pastoral epistles use appear or become manifest for both the First and Second Coming of Christ. Here it refers to the earthly life of Jesus in contrast to the resurrection as exaltation.[107] The content of this section can hardly be treated as a chronological list. If the list were in chronological order, "lifted up in glory" would have to come before the reference to Christ as preached among the nations. The passage is built upon contrasting pairs: flesh, spirit; world, glory; angels (= heavenly realm), nations (= earthly). It does not directly use the language of the other hymnic examples. Yet it has clearly been assembled out of traditions that are related to them. "Vindicated in the Spirit" appears to depend on an exaltation tradition like that of Rom 1:4. "Made manifest to the angels" is closest to Hebrews, where we found the image of God introducing the Son into the presence of the angels. This passage treats Jesus' earthly life as an epiphany in the flesh. It evokes the image of manifestation in the ascent to the throne.

The hymnic traditions have considerably expanded the kerygmatic affirmations of resurrection by situating the events of salvation or resurrection as exaltation in a cosmic context. The confession that God has raised Jesus from the dead has come to mean much more than a simple affirmation that Jesus' preaching and life have been vindicated by God. The risen One is the enthroned Lord of the cosmos. Resurrection is presented as Jesus' entry into messianic dignity. He becomes Lord, Son of God; and perhaps at an earlier stage Prophet or Messiah were also titles linked to the resurrection tradition. However, we have seen that these Christian titles were not simply well-established messianic affirmations taken over from Judaism. Their development appears to have required the resurrection as a catalyst. They enabled the Christians to attach a share in the sovereignty of God to the exalted Lord. They perceived Jesus' rule to have begun, to be effective in the Christian community. They are not simply awaiting Christ's entry into his messianic office with his Second Coming.

The hymnic traditions seek to take the relationship betweeen Jesus and God that has become evident in the exaltation traditions and ground it in images of the creative activity of divine wisdom. Hebrews, for example, understands the Son of the exaltation tradition to be the Son who is the divine Word or wisdom of creation. At the same time, the resurrection as exaltation is the crucial point in the story of salvation. That is the point at which Jesus enters heaven as the Son who makes atonement for sin. These cosmological images also suggest that salvation is more than the conversion of individuals. As in the older apocalyptic imagery the death and resurrection or the exaltation of Jesus stands at a turning point in the relationship between God and the world.

At the same time, the developments of the resurrection traditions appear to have moved away from the affirmation of resurrection as such. Wisdom Christology provides quite a different set of images for understanding the relationships among God, Jesus, and the world. These new images will take on a life of their own. We also see a theology of divine epiphany in the pastoral epistles that is different from the older Pauline emphasis on the cross and resurrection. Heb 6:2 even goes so far as to list resurrection among those topics that are for beginners in the faith. The author's presentation of Christ as the heavenly High Priest goes beyond such elementary topics.

We have also seen that early Christian preaching defended its understanding of resurrection as Christ's heavenly exaltation through appeal to the Scriptures. Such appeals initially developed out of the necessity to show that Jesus' death and resurrection were part of the divine plan for salvation. However, as the tradition developed, the same psalm passages are invoked to provide evidence for other elements in the proclamation that Jesus has been exalted as Lord. He is superior to all the powers of the cosmos. He bears the

name that only he can have, "Son." These traditions show that while
the affirmation of Jesus' resurrection is a fixed element in the kerygma from the earliest times, it can still be the catalyst for the
shaping of new images.

NOTES

1. See E. Schillebeeckx *(Jesus* [New York: Seabury, 1979], 391f.) on
   the reflective nature of kerygmatic formulae. Schillebeeckx hy-
   pothesizes a period of reflection on the part of the disciples who
   had been reassembled by Peter. He thinks that they experienced Jesus' resurrection as an offer of forgiveness. However,
   Schillebeeckx's own methodological criteria make such an extrapolation problematic. We must admit that we cannot extrap-
   olate back from formulae that have been developed to express
   the belief of a community into the experiences of the apostles as
   a group and to describe those experiences as we might the
   experiences of persons known to us.
2. J. Schmitt, "Le 'Milieu' littéraire de la 'Tradition' citée dans 1
   Cor., XV, 3b–5," *Resurrexit. Actes du symposium international
   sur la résurrection de Jésus* (ed. E. Dhanis; Rome: Libreria Editrice Vaticana, 1974), 171f.
3. Also Ac 17:3; Rev 2:8; Ignatius *Smyrneans* 2. Similar passages
   occur in Phil 3:10f.; Gal 2:19b–20c; 2 Cor 1:5, 7; 5:10–12; Rom
   8:17b; 14:7–8; Col 3:3; Heb 2:9; 1 Pt 1:11; 4:13; 5:1; Mk 16:6; Lk
   24:6; Ignatius *Ephesians* 20.1; *Magnesians* 5.1; *Trallians, superscriptio; Philadelphians, superscriptio;* 8.2; *Smyrneans* 5.3;
   7.1b, 2; 12.2; *Polycarp* 7.1; *Epistle of Barnabas* 15.9. Schmitt
   (op. cit., 172) thinks that the short formula may have originated
   in an apologetic scheme directed at a Jewish audience similar to
   that in Ac 3:15, 4:10, and 5:30.
4. Ibid., 176. Schmitt points to the reinterpretation of elevation in
   Ac 2:33–35 and 5:31 as evidence that exaltation was not originally part of the kerygmatic formulae. Acclamations such as the
   Aramaic *"Marana tha"* would appear to belong to the earliest
   Palestinian traditions.
5. D. M. Stanley, *Christ's Resurrection in Pauline Soteriology*
   (Rome: Biblical Institute Press, 1961), 84. This parousia perspec-

tive may have originated in the Jerusalem community. To become a Christian meant to hope for salvation at Christ's return on the basis of his resurrection. The emphasis on the soteriological effects of the death of Jesus may have developed out of the Gentile mission. The "sins" of those who had not been part of Israel, which God had been going to punish at the judgment, have been taken away by Jesus. See S. K. Williams on Rom 3:24–26 (*Jesus' Death as a Saving Event. The Background and Origin of a Concept* [Missoula, Mont.: Scholars, 1975], 19–56). Paul has generalized the earlier formula to place both Jew and Gentile on the same footing in their need for justification through faith.

6. O. Michel, *Der Brief an die Römer* (Göttingen: Vandenhoeck & Ruprecht, 1966, 4th ed.), 38–40. Some interpreters speak of such Christology as adoptionist; see J. D. G. Dunn, *Christology in the Making* (Philadelphia: Westminster, 1980), 45f. Others (see J. Fitzmyer, "Romans," in R. Brown, J. Fitzmyer, and R. Murphy, eds., *Jerome Biblical Commentary* [Englewood Cliffs: Prentice-Hall, 1967], 294) are more cautious. They see the focus to be on stages in the process of salvation. These stages are spoken about as changes in Jesus' relationship to God. Through the resurrection, Christ is endowed with power (Phil 3:10; 1 Cor 15:45). The salvific role that Christ plays as a result of that gift of power is reflected in the use of Ps 2:7 to speak of Jesus as the one who has become Lord and Messiah at the resurrection (see Ac 2:34–36). However, the resurrection is not being understood as making Jesus Son of God in a causal sense. H. Schlier, *Der Römerbrief* (HTKNT 6; Freiburg: Herder, 1979), 23f.

7. R. Bultmann, *Theology of the New Testament. Vol. I* (New York: Scribners, 1951), 49; K. Wengst, *Christologishe Formeln und Lieder des Urchristentums* (Gütersloh: Gerd Mohn, 1972), 112f.

8. Schlier, op. cit., 24; E. Kaesemann, *Commentary on Romans,* (Grand Rapids: Eerdmans, 1980), i0f. The usage here is also different from the example of Jn 6:63. The Johannine passage is closer to the paraenetic contrast in Paul, since "flesh" designates reality opposed to the Spirit. 1 Pt 3:18 is closer to those passages, though "flesh" refers directly to what has died and Spirit to the realm in which Christ has been made alive.

9. Kaesemann, op. cit., 11; Wengst, op. cit., 115. For Davidic expectations, see Ps. Sol. 17.21ff., 4Q Flor, and 2 Sam 7:11ff.

10. Wengst, op. cit., 114; Schlier, op. cit., 24f. Kaesemann (op. cit., 12) argues against excising the *dynamis* phrase. He thinks that it is equivalent to "in glory" in 1 Tim 3:16 or "at the right hand

of the greatness on high" of Heb 1:3 and is a designation of the place of Christ's enthronement.

11. Wengst, op. cit., 116; Kaesemann, op. cit., 13.
12. J. L. Knox, *The Humanity and Divinity of Christ* (Cambridge: Cambridge University, 1967), 84.
13. J. Murphy-O'Connor, *Becoming Human Together* (Wilmington, Del.: Glazier, 1982, 2nd ed.), 80. Murphy-O'Connor notes that resurrection is also described as augmentation as well as loss in the martyrdom traditions like 2 Macc 7:23. A person who thought in the humiliation and exaltation patterns of the christological hymns would naturally think of augmentation in terms of life-giving power (p. 81).
14. Stanley, op. cit., 171–73; Fitzmyer, *JBC*, 305; J. Reumann, *Righteousness in the New Testament* (Philadelphia: Fortress/Ramsey, N.J.: Paulist, 1982), 39f., 78.
15. Ibid., 305; Kaesemann, op. cit., 128f.; Reumann, op. cit., 39.
16. Kaesemann, op. cit., 129.
17. Kaesemann, op. cit., 248.
18. P. V. D. Osten-Sacken, *Römer 8 als Beispiel paulinischer Soteriologie* (Göttingen: Vandenhoeck & Ruprecht, 1975), 14–50.
19. Wengst (op. cit., 28) suggests that the two traditions were combined before Paul took them over. Paul would hardly have omitted any elements of a reference to Jesus. He thinks (op. cit., 37; 46f.) that the formula probably developed in the setting of baptismal liturgy in a Gentile Christian community. Fitzmyer (*JBC*, 321) suggests the baptismal liturgy of an early baptismal community.
20. Kaesemann, op. cit., 291f.
21. See, for example, the detailed outline of the Galatians argument in H. D. Betz, *Galatians* (Philadelphia: Fortress, 1979), 16–23.
22. This verse also begins the section in which Paul is directly countering a spirituality of immortality through identification with the divine whose roots lie in Philonic tradition (see P. Perkins, "'An Ailment of Childhood': Spiritual Pediatrics for Adults," *Dimensions of Contemporary Spirituality* [ed. F. Eigo; Villanova: Villanova University, 1982], 99–108).
23. J. Kloppenborg ("An Analysis of the Pre-Pauline Formula 1 Cor 15:3b–5 in Light of Some Recent Literature," *Catholic Biblical Quarterly* 40 [1978], 351–57) concludes that the formula originated in the Palestinian church but had been mediated to Paul by way of the hellenistic mission. See the similar conclusion of H. Conzelmann, *1 Corinthians* (Philadelphia: Fortress, 1975), 251–54.

24. For the addition of "according to the Scriptures," see Kloppenborg, op. cit., 364. R. H. Fuller *(The Formation of the Resurrection Narratives* [New York: Macmillan, 1971], 15) traces the image of atoning death to that of the Maccabean martyrs. That image antedates the use of passages such as Is 53:11 to explain the death of Jesus. Conzelmann (op. cit., 252) notes that the addition of "according to the Scriptures" marks the two verbs "he died" and "he was raised" as the fundmental ones in the formula.

25. Fuller, op. cit., 28. C. K. Barrett *(The Gospel According to St. John* [Philadelphia: Westminster, 1978 rev. ed.], 341f.) admits that the primitive tradition may have contained the expression. Kloppenborg (op. cit., 358f.) argues that "was seen" requires some dative of witness and is likely to have introduced the pre-Pauline expression "Peter and the twelve."

26. H.-W. Bartsch ("Inhalt und Funktion des Urchristlichen Osterglaubens," *NTS* 26 [1979/80], 183–91) constructs an elaborate argument to link *ōphthē* to apocalyptic traditions. He concludes that it implies fulfillment of prophetic promises of the saving presence of God. Bartsch agrees (ibid., 193–94) that Luke sees these promises to have been fulfilled with the activity of God, which places the crucifixion and resurrection at the midpoint of a salvation history that is then continued with the mission charge. Conzelmann (op. cit., 256f.) argues that the simplest understanding of the origin of the *ōphthē* formula is that it refers to a founding appearance to Peter, which apparently was associated with Jerusalem.

27. Bartsch, op. cit., 181f.; Schmitt, "Milieu," 179–80.

28. G. Wagner, ". . . encore 1 Corinthiens 15. Si les chrétiens refusent d'agir alors Christ n'est pas ressuscité," *Études Théol Rel* 56 (1981), 599–607; A. J. M. Wedderburn, "The Problem of the Denial of the Resurrection in 1 Corinthians XV," *NovT* 23 (1981), 229–33; Barrett, op. cit., 347–49.

29. Wedderburn, op. cit., 237f.

30. R. A. Horsley, "How Can Some of You Say That There Is No Resurrection of the Dead? Spiritual Elitism in Corinth," *Novum Testamentum* 20 (1978), 203–31. Spiritual elitism is correlated with the disputes that divided the community. G. Theissen *(The Social Setting of Pauline Christianity. Essays on Corinth* [Philadelphia: Fortress, 1982], 69–119) sees the elitism at Corinth as based on the socioeconomic divisions within the Corinthian church. The wealthy expect special privilege and claim special insight.

31. Such materials are part of Paul's own preaching, as Malherbe has argued for 1 Thessalonians ("Gentle as a Nurse: The Cynic Background to 1 Thess ii," *Novum Testamentum* 12 [1970], 203–17). Wedderburn (op. cit., 234–35), pointing to similar passages in Philo, thinks that the Corinthians have adopted images of living without dependence on possessions as proof that their mortal life was at an end—as in Philo's description of the Therapeutae (Vit. Contemp. 13). He argues that they interpreted Jesus' sayings about the satisfaction of human needs (Mt 5:6; 6:33) and the promise of riches (Mt 10:21; Lk 18:30) and rule (Mt 19:28) in light of that hellenistic philosophy. References to the Kingdom of God are rare in other Pauline letters but appear several times in 1 Cor (4:20; 6:9f.; 15:24, 50) and may indicate a preoccupation with interpreting Jesus' sayings.

32. Wedderburn, op. cit., 236–39.

33. Conzelmann, op. cit., 265.

34. Ibid., 267.

35. Barrett, op. cit., 353.

36. J. Lambrecht, "Paul's Christological Use of Scripture in 1 Cor 15:20–28," *New Testament Studies* 28 (1982), 504.

37. Conzelmann, op. cit., 270.

38. See Mk 12:36 par.; Ac 2:34; Heb 1:13; Conzelmann (op. cit., 272 note 88) warns against drawing the conclusion that "exaltation" was derived from this passage. The image of exaltation belongs to Jewish resurrection tradition and is older than any particular Scripture text used to support it.

39. T. Callan, "Psalm 110:1 and the Origin of the Expectation that Jesus Will Come Again," *Catholic Biblical Quarterly* 44 (1982), 633–35.

40. Conzelmann, op. cit., 273f. Lambrecht (op. cit., 511–14) emphasizes the fact that the argument is not completed until the development of the Adam typology in vv. 44b–49.

41. Barrett, op. cit., 354–57. This passage does not say anything about resurrection and the future of those who are not Christians.

42. Conzelmann (op. cit., 278) points to the proverbs: "Know the end of life. Wherefore sport and revel on earth." *Epigr. Graec.* 344.3; "Eat, drink and sport with love; all else is nought." Plutarch, *Alex. Fort. Virt., Moralia,* 336c.

43. Wedderburn (op. cit., 241) points to the wide use, though inappropriate, of such arguments against Epicureans in polemic. Christians are frequently treated as "Epicureans" for the purposes of later polemic.

44. Conzelmann (op. cit., 278f.) suggests that v. 34f. implies nonassociation with such persons, although he admits that one cannot exclude the possibility that Paul had general nonconformity with the world along the lines of Rom 12:2 in mind.

45. J. Murphy-O'Connor, *1 Corinthians* (Wilmington: Glazier, 1979), 145.

46. P. Trummer, *Die Paulustradition der Pastoralbriefe* (Frankfort: Lang, 1978), 204.

47. M. Dibelius and H. Conzelmann, *The Pastoral Epistles* (Philadelphia: Fortress, 1972), 108; Trummer (op. cit., 203) sees the dangling clause "from the seed of David" as evidence that that Jewish messianic title was no longer understood.

48. Dibelius and Conzelmann, op. cit., 28f.

49. Trummer, op. cit., 205.

50. C. F. Evans, *Resurrection and the New Testament* (SBT ser. 2, no. 12; London: SCM, 1970), 132f. This is the primary approach of the sermons in Acts. Evans argues (op. cit., 135) that Acts does not have its own, new doctrine of resurrection. Resurrection is simply views as the announcement that Jesus is Lord. Israel is called to accept this announcement.

51. Fitzmyer, op. cit., 160.

52. J. A. T. Robinson, "The Most Primitive Christology of All?" *Twelve New Testament Essays* (London: SCM, 1962), 140f.

53. Fitzmyer, op. cit., 213.

54. E. Haenchen, *The Acts of the Apostles* (Philadelphia: Westminster, 1971), 208–12. Preaching the resurrection is the crime of which Paul is accused in Ac 23:8. Luke associates that accusation with the Sadducees (Ac 5:17), so that a single group within Judaism is the only one held responsible for the opposition to Christianity (op. cit., 214f.).

55. Ibid., 353.

56. Fitzmyer, op. cit., 195; Haenchen, op. cit., 180.

57. Haenchen, op. cit., 183.

58. Conzelmann (op. cit., 30) points to Rom 10:6f. as a parallel to this usage.

59. In Ac 10:38 and Lk 4:18 Jesus is clearly designated Messiah during his lifetime. Haenchen (op. cit., 187) argues that Luke is using older formulae that are at odds with his own Christology. Luke understands the earthly Jesus to have been endowed with the Spirit and to have been Son of God (Lk 2:40ff.; 3:22; 4:18; 9:35). However, Luke consistently uses older traditions that he interprets in light of his own understanding. Here, for example, the exalted one receives the Spirit not because he is being

endowed with it for the first time but so that he can pour it out
upon his followers (op. cit., 187–88).

60. See J. A. Fitzmyer, "To Know Him and to Know the Power of
His Resurrection," *To Advance the Gospel* (New York: Cross-
road, 1981), 218–35; idem, "The Semitic Background of the
New Testament Kyrios Title," *A Wandering Aramean. Aramaic
Essays* (Missoula, Mont.: Scholars, 1979), 114–24.

61. Fitzmyer, *Aramean,* 124–27. Fitzmyer also points to the evidence in the Hebrew of the Qumran psalter for the use of *'adon*
in the absolute to refer to God. Thus, it is possible to find a
Palestinian milieu in which Jesus would be addressed as Lord.
Kyrios represents translation of the Semitic title into Greek by
the earliest Greek-speaking converts.

62. J. Fitzmyer, *The Gospel According to Luke I–IX* (AnBi 28; Garden City, N.Y.: Doubleday, 1981), 202.

63. See also 1 Cor 16:22; Rev 22:20; 1 Cor 11:23–26. Fitzmyer,
Aramean, 129.

64. Ibid., 128.

65. Ibid., 132.

66. Fitzmyer, *Luke* 1, 203.

67. Conzelmann, op. cit., 30. Haenchen (op. cit., 208) suggests that
"at the right hand," which applies to the Messiah, must have
been added to the *"Kyrios"* in the psalm text by Luke. See also
Lk 2:11. Fitzmyer, *Luke* 1, 203f. If the formula is pre-Lukan
(which is possible; Fitzmyer, op. cit., 202), the combination of
the two titles may not be an indication of how Luke understood
them. However, Fitzmyer is correct in questioning the tendency to interpret all christological titles in the New Testament
as though they contained the same range of meanings.

68. The title Messiah is not used of the expectations centered on the
Davidic king in the Old Testament. Dan 9:25 is the first use of
mashiah for a future, anointed agent of Yahweh in the Davidic
line. The Essene writings speak of anointed figures from Israel
and Aaron as well as following the Danielic usage (1 QS 9.11; 1
Q Sa 2.14, 20; CD 20.1; 4 QPBless 2.4; 4 QFlor 1.11–13; 4
QpIsaa 8–10, 11–17). This usage is not clearly titular. A Pharisaic
background is probably to be presumed for the use of *mashiah*
in Ps. Sol. 17.23, 36; 18.6, 8 (Fitzmyer, *Luke* 1, 471f.).

69. Fitzmyer, *Luke* 1, 298f.

70. Ibid., 200.

71. M. Hengel, *The Son of God* (Philadelphia: Fortress, 1976), 17–
56; Dunn, *Christology,* 12–22. Dunn points out the weakness in

the older theories that held that the title Son of God implied preexistence as a divine being descended to earth.

72. Hengel, op. cit., 7–10. Son of God appears in 2 Cor 1:18f. as shorthand for Paul's gospel. Hengel (op. cit., 12) recognizes the relationship between Pauline soteriology and Son of God implied in Gal 2:20 but does not treat the issue of living under the Law or under faith in this connection. He presumes (op. cit., 12–15) that Son of God is closely related to *Kyrios.*

73. Dunn (op. cit., 36–46) points out that Paul retains the eschatological orientation of the title Son of God from older sources and uses it in contexts in which he is concerned to emphasize the soteriological effect of the believer's relationship with the exalted Christ. But the more characteristic Pauline understanding is the connection between Son of God and the crucifixion as the key to salvation (also implied in the sending language of Gal 4:4f.).

74. Fitzmyer, *Luke* 1, 206f.

75. Dunn, op. cit., 35.

76. M. Hengel, *The Son of God* (Philadelphia: Fortress, 1976), 63–66. H. Merklein ("Die Auferweckung Jesu und die Anfänge der Christologie (Messias bzw. Sohn Gottes und Menschensohn)," *Zeitschrift für Neutestamentliche Wissenschaft* 72 [1981], 1–16) emphasizes the necessity of resurrection as the grounding of Jesus' messianic authority in order for one to be able to speak about a messianic Christology.

77. Though one might presume that Son of Man would be closely tied to resurrection as exaltation, the title itself is not part of the resurrection kerygma; Hengel, op. cit., 65; Merklein, op. cit., 25; Fitzmyer, *Luke* 1, 210.

78. Dunn (op. cit., 91) suggests that for Revelation the image has the advantage of expressing the close relationship between the Son of Man figure and God. This relationship appears in the Ancient of Days image in Dan 7:9f. and in the use of the Alpha and Omega formula in Rev 1:17.

79. Fitzmyer, *Luke* 1, 210.

80. See the survey in Dunn, op. cit., 98–128. Dunn attempts to synthesize a number of Pauline texts in order to arrive at an Adam myth as the foundation for the hymnic tradition.

81. E. S. Fiorenza, "Wisdom Mythology and the Christological Hymns of the New Testament," *Aspects of Wisdom in Judaism and Early Christianity* (ed. R. Wilken; Notre Dame: Notre Dame, 1975), 17–41.

82. J. Gnilka *(Der Philipperbrief* [HTKNT; Freiburg: Herder,

1968], 131–37) surveys the various reconstructions proposed for the hymn. He prefers a bipartite division, which follows the humiliation-exaltation division of the hymn (p. 111). We think that the tripartite division provides a more even division into strophes.

83. Ibid., 130.
84. Gnilka, op. cit., 130f.; J. Murphy-O'Connor, "Christological Anthropology in Phil II, 6–11," *Revue Biblique* 83 (1976), 45–49.
85. Gnilka, op. cit., 144–47; Dunn (op. cit., 114–25) argues that the hymn is dependent on early Christian Adam speculation. Presented with the same choice that Adam had, Christ avoided Adam's sin. "Image" and "glory" refer to Adam, as they do in 1 Cor 15. Christ undid Adam's sin by freely choosing the death that Adam experienced as a punishment. Thus, the hymn is a description of the character of Christ's life.
86. Murphy-O'Connor, "Anthropology," 41–44.
87. Gnilka, op. cit., 144f.; Dunn, op. cit., 239–50. Dunn (p. 249) sees the Fourth Gospel as making the decisive combination of the Logos hymn in the prologue with the Father/Son Christology. Without that combination preexistence and incarnation Christology could never have been developed.
88. G. Bornkamm, *Early Christian Experience* (New York: Harper, 1969), 121.
89. See the discussion of the hymnic structure in E. Lohse, *Colossians and Philemon* (Philadelphia: Fortress, 1971), 41–46. Lohse holds that the author of Colossians made the additions referring to the church in v. 18a and similarly in v. 24. E. Schweizer *(The Letter to the Colossians* [Minneapolis: Augsburg, 1982], 56–63) surveys the various theories about the origin and development of the hymn. The first strophe extols Christ as the Creator through whom everything has come about; the connecting strophe says the permanence of the cosmos has been secured by Christ, who is preordained and set at its head. In the concluding strophe the risen Christ is celebrated as the One in whom divine fullness and the reconciliation of the world have come about.
90. J. Gnilka, *Der Kolosserbrief* (Freiburg: Herder, 1980), 51–59.
91. Ibid., 59; 74–77; Schweizer, op. cit., 59, note 10. Schweizer points to an analogous tendency in Paul. Rom 4:17 interprets the cosmic formula, the one who calls the dead to life, and calls into existence what does not exist, in soteriological terms. For Paul, it refers to the justification of the sinner. See also Lohse, op. cit., 60.

92. Lohse, op. cit., 50; Gnilka (op. cit., 71–73) points to the parallelism between vv. 16a and 19. Schweizer (op. cit., 72f.) points out that while the New Testament presupposes a doctrine of divine creation, it rarely achieves the thematic shape that we find here. Colossians insists that even the creative activity of God is known in Christ.
93. Schweizer, op. cit., 84f.
94. Dunn, op. cit., 191–93.
95. Ibid., 206–208; J. W. Thompson, *The Beginnings of Christian Philosophy: The Epistle to the Hebrews* (Washington: Catholic Biblical Association, 1982), 128f.; O. Michel, *Der Brief an die Hebräer* (Göttingen: Vandenhoeck & Ruprecht, 1966, 6th ed.), 94–106.
96. Thompson, op. cit., 129. *"En hypsiliois"* could have been part of the hymnic tradition and inspired the change to the citation in Heb 8:1 (Michel, op. cit., 105).
97. Michel (op. cit., 94f.) sees this pattern as an accommodation of the hellenistic understanding of the mediator of creation to the apocalyptic view of a correspondence between the end time and the time of creation.
98. On "reflection of divine glory" and "stamp of divine nature" as characteristics of the soul, see Philo Opif. 146; Spec. Leg. 4.23; Heres 38.181, 294; Deut 83; Leg. All. 3.95–97.
99. See Dunn, 207f. Michel (op. cit., 94) points to the eschatological use of "heir" in Rom 4:13.
100. Ps 2:7 (also in Heb 5:5) appears in Luke's collection of proof texts for resurrection as exaltation in Ac 13:33. Though Hebrews' second text 2 Sam 7:14 (also Heb 12:7) is not cited in the Acts collection, 2 Sam 7:12 appears in Ac 13:23 (and Ac 2:30). Therefore, the two texts were probably combined in the tradition prior to Hebrews. Michel (op. cit., 109f.) suggests that the combination may have originated in a Jewish florilegium tradition.
101. Thompson, op. cit., 131–37. Hebrews continually contrasts the unchangeable divine world with the transitory nature of this world. Thompson argues that vv. 10–11 belong to that contrast and are not an announcement of judgment as Michel (op. cit., 120f.) thinks.
102. M. Barth *(Ephesians 1–3*, [AnBi 34; Garden City, N.Y.: Doubleday, 1974], 153–210) provides an extensive analysis of this passage and parallels to it in the Pauline corpus, although he is unwilling to accept the view that a disciple of Paul's wrote Ephesians and used Colossians as a model in doing so. On the

latter view, see J. Gnilka, *Der Epheserbrief* (Freiburg: Herder, 1971), 7–33.

103. Gnilka, op. cit., 93f.

104. Gnilka, op. cit., 94.

105. Gnilka (op. cit., 95) suggests that Ephesians associates names with the powers. By giving no name for Christ, the author shows that he is above the powers.

106. Gnilka (op. cit., 99–111) surveys the traditions behind the imagery used for the church here. While "body of Christ" can be traced to Pauline tradition (1 Cor 12:12–28; Rom 12:3ff.), its cosmic connotations belong to philosophic traditions of the cosmos as a body (Plato, Tim 30b, 47c–e; Seneca Ep. 95.52; Philo, Haer. 155f.; Plant 7). Ephesians has apparently combined these traditions with another in which the Church is the fullness of Christ (cf. 4:13). The cosmological sense of the word fullness *(pleroma)* is often linked to its use in second-century Gnostic writings. However, Ephesians and later Gnostics are probably both dependent on popular philosophy for the term. Ephesians is likely to have taken it from Col 1:18.

107. Dibelius-Conzelmann, op. cit., 61; Dunn, op. cit., 236f.

EIGHT

Resurrection as Jesus' Presence

The early community felt itself to be in contact with the active presence of the risen Lord. Different traditions have given different forms of expression to that sense of presence. The Lukan narrative, which set a temporal limit to resurrection appearances after forty days, comes the closest of any tradition to situating resurrection in the past. This chronological scheme sorts out experiences that were initially all connected with Easter: Jesus' resurrection, exaltation, and the gift of the Spirit to his followers. A perception of the presence of the risen Lord informs the christological affirmations "Lord" and "Son of God." The risen Lord is not merely the One expected to deliver the righteous at the parousia. He is the One who provides the salvation out of which the community lives now (cf. 1 Cor 12:3; Phil 2:11). This strong sense of presence overcomes the general feeling that death and exaltation separate the believer from the Lord. Even Hebrews, which has translated that distance into metaphysical categories and has the intermediate world of angels between this world and the heavenly sanctuary, provides a sense of presence. Hebrews insists that the High Priest who has entered the sanctuary is a compassionate intercessor (4:14–15; 5:10).

This sense of presence had sociological consequences for the life of early Christian communities. One of the most striking consequences is that no disciple steps forward and becomes the successor of Jesus. Yet that would have seemed the most normal mode for the transfer of authority in a religious sect or a philosophical school. That departure from the common response of such a group to death or separation has been directly linked to the early Christian conviction that resurrection enabled Jesus' presence to remain with the community.[1]

The most elaborate development of resurrection symbolism in connection with the present life and experience of the Christian occurs in the Pauline tradition. On the one hand, resurrection belongs to the formal eschatology that the apostle preached as God's plan of salvation. On the other hand, resurrection is closely tied to the Christian experience of life in the Spirit, which is the first fruit of the glory to come (2 Cor 1:22; Rom 8:23).[2] Though Paul's letters make expansive use of resurrection images in describing the present life of the believer, Paul does not integrate the two ways of speaking about resurrection: resurrection as an eschatological event and resurrection as qualifying the present experience of the believer.[3]

The implications of the resurrection symbolism for the community life of believers goes beyond the question of authority and its legitimation. W. Meeks has argued that in the Pauline tradition the message of cross and resurrection carried a persuasive power because it correlated with the social experience of Paul's converts. They represent the middle range of society, neither the destitute poor nor the aristocratic leaders of the city. One finds in the Pauline congregations wealthy, independent women; Jews; proselytes; members of the imperial household; artisans; traders; freedmen; and women and their descendants. Such persons experienced a conflict between the status that society attributed to them in terms of their social origins and the power, wealth, and status they had achieved. Meeks holds that such persons would find a strong experiential component in the paradox of the Pauline gospel or the Philippians hymn. The resurrection and exaltation of the one who had been slave—hidden, humiliated, crucified—would speak directly to the tension in their own experience.[4] The claims that are made for such "hidden status" are not open to logical argument or verification. They are elaborated in complex metaphors and analogies. Baptism dramatized and the eucharist recalled these experiences in antithetic parallels. Over and over again we find the experience of dying and rising providing the pattern of

Pauline paraenesis. The apostolic weakness is true apostolic greatness (2 Cor 4:10). The resurrection endows sexuality and the body with religious importance (1 Cor 6:14).[5] The poverty of Christ is the motivation for contributing to the collection (2 Cor 8:9).[6]

Clearly, we cannot hope to provide a comprehensive analysis of all uses of resurrection language in Pauline soteriology and their possible sociological correlates, let alone do the same for all of the other images of presence associated with resurrection. In this chapter we can only hope to look at selected examples of resurrection and presence in the New Testament in order to lay out the basic patterns that emerge in different traditions. The first section deals with the presence of Jesus behind the teaching and/or authority of leaders in the community according to the Matthean and Johannine traditions. The second section treats resurrection and paraenesis in the Pauline epistles, and the third section deals with the cultic embodiment of Jesus' presence in the baptismal and eucharistic traditions. These explorations make it clear that the language of soteriology stands or falls with the resurrection kerygma in much of the New Testament.

PRESENCE, TEACHING, AND AUTHORITY

The resurrection commission at the conclusion of Matthew's gospel combined mission to the nations and the command to baptize and teach Jesus' commandments with the promise of Jesus' presence until the end of the age. The promise of Jesus' presence is tied to the injunction that the disciples are to teach their converts to "keep all things which I have commanded you." The Fourth Gospel contains a parallel tradition in 14:23: "if someone loves me, he will keep my word, and my Father will love him, and we will come and make our dwelling with him." This saying is used as the response to a disciple's question about Jesus' promise to return. How can he return in such a way that he manifests himself to the disciples but not to the world? This exchange also implies a question of why Jesus did not manifest himself to the world. The Fourth Evangelist provides an answer to that implied question in 14:24a: "the one who does not love me, does not keep my words." In other words, the "world" cannot experience Jesus' return, since it is the place that rejects Jesus and the disciples who are now commissioned to represent him (15:18–16a).[7] The abiding presence of Jesus is tied to the keeping of Jesus' words in the community of believers. The Johannine tradition has provided a new image for that presence, the indwelling of the Father and Son with the believer.

We may have evidence of a further link between these traditions in Mt 20:18 and Jn 14:24b. We have seen that the Matthean image has developed out of a tradition that understands resurrection as Jesus' exaltation to be Lord or Son, a prominent part of the resurrection kerygma. The authority by which Jesus' teaching will be expanded to the nations is the authority that he has as *Kyrios*. The issue of Jesus' authority dominates the Fourth Gospel. Jesus' words and works, which are from the Father, stand opposed to the interpretation and counterclaims of his unbelieving opponents. John always concludes his defense of Jesus' authority by appealing to the special identity between the Son and the Father. The Son is the perfect representation of the Father's will and activity. The conclusion in Jn 14:24b summarizes this Johannine argument: "the word which you hear is not mine, but that of the Father who sent me" (cf. Jn 7:16; 8:26, 28; 12:49f.; 3:11, 32; 15:22f.). Its Christology enables the Johannine community to identify the authority of the risen *Kyrios* with the Word of the earthly Jesus. The social setting of these two sayings is quite different. The Matthean community was struggling over the question of expanding its mission to the Gentiles. The Johannine community, on the other hand, appears to have drawn sharp boundaries around itself as a result of its experiences of hostility. Those who believe in Jesus are "from above"; they no longer belong to "the world" (e.g., 17:16).[8] The Christology deemed blasphemous by the Jewish authorities throughout the gospel may have been the precipitating cause of the expulsion of Johannine Christians from the synagogue (5:16–18; 9:22; 16:2). The concern with persecution in the discourse traditions (15:18–16:4b) indicates that after the expulsion from the synagogue, there may have been a new round of hostility experienced by those engaged in the Gentile mission. It had two results for those who remained[9] within the Johannine community. Theologically, the Johannine community shaped its identity in terms of allegiance to the Christology of Jesus' identification with the Father. Sociologically, the Johannine group drew sharp boundaries between the circle of believers who walked in the light of the Word they had heard from Jesus and those who did not. The community is perceived as the place in which Father and Son dwell. It stands over against a hostile world that does not hear the voice of Jesus in those he has left in the world as his representatives. Thus, the presence of Jesus in the community is a fundamental symbol of its identity.

These passages show that the role of resurrection as presence can be quite different when one asks about the experience of the Christian community that is making that assertion. They also show that early Christian communities linked the presence of Jesus and the teaching of Jesus as it is lived out within the community. Such assertions of presence could have very concrete social embodiment. The rules for dealing with an erring member in Mt 18:15–17 are legitimated by a power "of the keys" possessed by the Christian community assembled in judgment. That authoritative power is grounded in the presence of Christ to the assembly (v. 18). In John 20:23, a similar power is attached to the gift of the Spirit at Easter. 1 Jn 5:16–17 shows how such powers to forgive were exercised in a somewhat later period. Forgiveness is tied to prayer for the person who has erred.[10] 1 John makes this specific application depend on the more general tradition of confidence in prayer. We find a similar association in Mt 18:19–20. In short, there appears to have been a widespread tradition in the New Testament churches that saw the presence of the exalted Lord as the guarantee behind the community's application of his teaching in such instances. It was attached to specific proceedings within the community and was not merely a detached piece of symbolism or theological abstraction.

THE JOHANNINE DISCOURSES

The Johannine discourse traditions have interpreted the promises of return in light of the perception that the Father and Son dwell with the community. This return is rooted in the community's obedience to Jesus' Word. The Fourth Gospel always summarizes that Word in the commandment to "love one another." Hence, the presence of Jesus and the paraenesis of the Johannine community are closely linked.[11]

The Johannine discourses also have a second, unique way of expressing this sense of divine presence. It is embodied in a collection of five sayings about the Paraclete. Interpreters are divided over the relationship between these sayings and the rest of the discourse material. Some think that they were added to the discourses at a later time.[12] We cannot presume that the Paraclete sayings all come from the same context or that they are the Johannine equivalent to the Holy Spirit. The identification of the Paraclete with the Holy Spirit appears to have been secondarily added to the Paraclete saying in Jn 14:26.[13]

The first Paraclete saying in Jn 14:16f. follows the assertion that the one who loves Jesus will keep his commandments. Jesus promises to send the Paraclete from the Father. This promise is thus located in the same context as the promise of the return of Father and Son to the believer. Jn 14:16–17 promises that this "other Paraclete" will remain with the disciples forever. Like the returning Son, the Paraclete cannot be seen or received by the world. The parallel between this promise and that of the return of the Father and Son is striking. It embodies the same contrast between the disciples who receive the Paraclete (or Father and Son) and the world, which does not. In characterizing the Paraclete as "another" Paraclete, the passage presumes Jesus to have been the first. 1 Jn 2:1 presents Jesus as the heavenly Paraclete and intercessor. Such a tradition may be behind the use of the word "another," though the present use of the saying requires that Jesus be seen as Paraclete during his earthly life rather than after his exaltation.[14]

This passage also identifies the Paraclete as the Spirit of Truth. A similar expression is used in the Dead Sea Scrolls for the angel of light who is the guide and protector of the members of the sect (1 QS 3.6,18f.; 4.21, 23; 1 QM 13.10).[15] The other four sayings in the collection attribute specific functions to the Paraclete figure. Two of them are in forensic contexts. The Paraclete, Spirit of Truth, is promised disciples who must defend themselves (15:26). This tradition resembles the promise that the Holy Spirit will aid persecuted disciples in the synoptic tradition (Mk 13:11). Mt 10:32 includes that promise in his missionary charge. John is using it in commissioning the disciples to represent Jesus before a hostile world.

The Paraclete saying in Jn 16:7–11 shows a similar division between the community and the world. The function of the Paraclete is shifted from defending the disciple to convicting the world of its failure to believe in Jesus. Thus, the Paraclete vindicates the community's understanding of Jesus and demonstrates that the world that persecutes those who testify to Jesus stands condemned. The presence of the Paraclete thus lessens the tension that such rejection might cause, since it reassures the Christians that the Word that they have heard is from God. The sharp division between the community and the world that runs through the discourses makes the Paraclete imagery equally inner-directed.

The remaining Paraclete sayings concern the function of the Paraclete in assuring the teaching and understanding of Jesus by the community (14:26; 16:13–15). Jn 16:13–15 ascribes functions to the Paraclete that are much like those of the Johannine Jesus. He will guide the disciples into "all truth." This guidance appears to imply truth that had not been explicitly said by Jesus. Verse 12 leaves the

Paraclete the task of completing what had been left unsaid by Jesus. Verses 13b–15 justify the activity of the Paraclete in the same terms that the controversy stories had used for Jesus' teaching in relationship to the Father. He does not act on his own but takes his teaching from Jesus (and ultimately the Father) in order to declare it to the disciples. In so doing, the Paraclete glorifies Jesus, just as Jesus' ministry glorified the Father (17:1).

The saying about the Paraclete's teaching in Jn 14:24f. presents the "all things" of the Paraclete as a teaching that is parallel to the process of remembering what Jesus had said. "Remembering" in the Fourth Gospel is the postresurrection understanding of Jesus' words and actions. This understanding is often associated with the fulfillment of Scripture. Here the Paraclete is responsible for the process of remembering as it is experienced within the Johannine community. We have seen that the Lukan tradition made the process of christological interpretation of Scripture dependent on the Easter instruction of the risen Lord. This image of the community's instruction through the ongoing divine presence that is linked to the risen Lord was continued in the later history of the community. 1 Jn 2:20–27 appeals to an anointing that is present in the community. That anointing is to serve as proof against the lies told by the author's opponents. The author of the epistles insists that the community does not require anyone to teach it, since the tradition that has been possessed from the beginning and the anointing of the community are sufficient.[16] At this point the implications of the Johannine vision for ecclesiology become clear. No human teacher or leader can stand in the place of Jesus. It is the Paraclete, not a human teacher or church official, who is charged with providing the proper interpretation of Jesus' teaching for the community.

Johannine Christians stand in sharp contrast to the apostolic churches like that of Matthew. The Johannine church did not seek to institutionalize its teaching in officials who could succeed to the authority of the apostles. The abiding presence of the Paraclete is the answer to the question of Jesus' departure and the death of the apostolic witnesses. R. E. Brown argues that the crisis over false claims to interpret the Johannine tradition that we witness in the Johannine letters may have led those who remained faithful to the elder's vision to seek to establish a more Petrine type of church authority in their communities.[17] The Matthean use of traditions that were also found among Johannine Christians indicates that they may have been able to make such a move without losing the sense of a dynamic presence of the risen Lord.

PRESENCE AND PAULINE PARAENESIS

The Pauline tradition makes the most exhaustive use of resurrection symbolism in the New Testament. The lordship of Christ proclaimed by the kerygma is to be extended to the life of Christians. Paul finds a variety of ways to present the death and resurrection of Christ as the pattern that determines the shape of Christian life in the Spirit. Christ's resurrection shows to whom the Christian now belongs.[18]

The Apostolic Example

One of the central images by which the paradox of the death and resurrection of Christ is made evident is the suffering of the apostle. 2 Cor 1:9 shows that Paul applies the formula "God who raises the dead" directly to his own sufferings in Asia. The power of God evident in the resurrection proves to be a source of encouragement to the suffering apostle. Such a God can be trusted. This consolation follows upon the perception that apostolic suffering reflects the suffering of Christ. Paul's understanding of this situation goes even further: the community that the apostle has founded also participates in that apostolic suffering and consolation. This participation is possible because, for Paul, the powers of the new age are present in this age.[19]

The picture of the death and life of Jesus as powers now at work emerges even more strongly in 2 Cor 4:10–11. The paradox of life and death is manifest in the apostle. The body in which he carries around the dying of Jesus is also the one in which Jesus' life is manifest. The weakness and suffering of the apostle thus prove the life-giving power evident in Jesus' resurrection. Paul's defense of his apostleship combined his claim to have seen the Lord with the evidence of the fruitfulness of his apostleship. A similar pattern is evident in Paul's perception of his apostolic suffering. The "life" that is manifest in the apostle is not simply the power of an individual to survive hardship because he is committed to a cause. Rather, it also bestows life insofar as the apostle's preaching becomes the source of life and salvation for others. Consequently, Paul turns immediately from the example of the death and life paradox in the apostle to the life that is manifested in the Corinthians (2 Cor 4:12–13). He reminds the Corinthians, however, that the "life" that they now experience as believers awaits the future resurrection.[20]

Paul continues to discuss the relationship between the future resurrection of the believer and the present suffering of the apostle in 2 Cor 4:16–5:10. Part of the "groaning and suffering" of the present life can be seen as evidence that we are not yet transformed into what we shall be. The mortality and transitory nature of our present existence is contrasted with the eternal glory of being with the Lord. But even this reflection is more than speculation. The apostle does not lose heart in affliction. 2 Cor 5:6–10 makes the importance of the present life in the body clear. It is the area of faith and obedience to Christ. Each person will be judged according to the obedience rendered in the body. In this description, the expression "away from the Lord" characterizes the difference between the present and future existence of the Christian. The Spirit mediates between the two as the "down payment" on that future (2 Cor 5:5).

Paul applies this vision of the paradox of apostolic suffering to the Corinthian community, which is in danger of abandoning his vision for that of an apostolate characterized by manifestations of divine power. 2 Cor 13:4 speaks of the possibility that Paul will have to visit Corinth and mount a formal defense of his apostolate. Just as Christ was crucified in weakness but now lives by the power of God, so the apostle will find himself living by the power of God when he comes to deal with the community. Thus, the power of God evident in the risen Lord can even be invoked in legal or quasi-legal proceedings between the apostle and the community.[21] Though it is cast in the typical, Pauline antithesis of weakness and power, this appeal to the power of the risen Lord in a quasi-legal setting resembles the invocation of Jesus' presence in Mt 18. 1 Cor 5:1–5 is a more direct example. The apostle has pronounced judgment against the incestuous person. He will be present "in the spirit" when the community exercises that judgment against the individual. In removing the individual from the community, Christians are said to be exercising "the power of our Lord Jesus." The parallel with 2 Cor 13:4 leaves no doubt that it is the power of the risen Lord that is invoked in these legal settings.[22]

These examples represent concrete ways in which the power of the risen Lord might be brought to bear within the early Christian community. For the apostle, the experience of the power of the risen Lord comes in the flourishing life of the communities that have come into being through his preaching of the gospel. But the same power may be invoked in disciplinary action against those communities whose response does not conform to the gospel as it was preached by the apostle. Just as the resurrection of Christ is ascribed to the life-giving power of God (1 Thess 1:10; 1 Cor 15:15), so the power of that resurrection also has its origin in God (2 Cor 13:4; Rom 1:4).[23]

Our final example of the apostle's application of the "power of the resurrection" to his own life appears in Phil 3:9–11. The passage retains the dual pattern that was evident in 2 Cor 4: knowledge of the risen Lord now and hope for the future in which the Christian is to be associated with him. This passage follows a sharp attack against the influence of Judaizers in the community.[24] Paul presents his own life as evidence that righteousness is not won through obedience to the Law. Paul now considers all of his past achievements worthless in comparison to the righteousness that comes through faith (vv. 3–9). Paul describes this new situation as "knowing Christ Jesus my Lord" (v. 8) or as "knowing him and the power of his resurrection" (v. 10). This knowledge is manifest in the apostle's sharing the sufferings of Christ, in becoming like him in death so that he may attain resurrection from the dead (v. 11). Gal 2:19–20 makes a similar point. The apostle has died to the Law in order to live to God; to be crucified with Christ; to live by faith in the Son of God, who was handed over to death. Paul argues in Gal 2:21 that to set aside the grace of God would be to make the death of Christ empty.[25] The expression "knowledge of Christ" represents knowledge of Christ as the risen *Kyrios.* It is equivalent to "knowing the power of his resurrection," a formula that is unique to the Pauline traditions.[26] For Paul, the power of Jesus' resurrection is the effective action of the exalted Lord in the life of the apostle. At the same time, Paul never loses sight of the transitory character of this life, which still awaits its fulfillment in judgment and the resurrection of the death. Paul's hypothetical formulation in v. 11, "that if possible I may attain resurrection from the dead," should not be understood as an expression of doubt on Paul's part about either his own resurrection or that of the believer. The hypothetical clause is derived from the polemic character of the passage. It is directed against Paul's opponents and their insistence that obedience to the Law is the only way to righteousness.[27]

Paul wants the community to imitate him. He warns them against imitating the opponents, who are earthly people bent on destroying the cross of Christ (vv. 17–19). Paul uses a collection of stock epithets to describe the opponents: they are headed toward destruction; they glory in their shame; they make their god their belly; they have minds set on earthly things. These epithets provide the contrast between the earthly type of person and the heavenly person, the Christian.[28] The goal of living in such a way as to attain a heavenly commonwealth appears in Philo (Conf. Ling. 78). It represents the orientation of the wise person. The heavenly commonwealth is the true home of the virtuous person. Such people live in this world and in the body as strangers. However, Paul does not follow Philo in attaching the image of the heavenly commonwealth to the progress of the soul. He does not exploit the dualism of bodily nature over against the soul. For Paul, the heavenly commonwealth means expecting the return of the exalted Lord as judge (1 Thess 1:10). The final manifestation of the power of Christ's resurrection will be the transformation of the earthly body into the glorious body like that of the risen Lord. This transformation is the second member of a pair. It answers to the experience of the apostle in this life, which is "being conformed to Christ's death" (v. 10; cf. Rom 8:29).

Exhorting the Community

We have seen that the apostle frequently used his own example as evidence for the power of the resurrection. Paul characteristically employs this pattern: the apostle is the imitator of the Lord; the community is to respond by imitating the apostle.[29] In Phil 3, they must imitate the apostle by counting all "earthly things," that is, righteousness gained through the Law, as worthless over against "knowing Christ." Thus, the power of the risen Lord is reflected in the change from attempting to attain salvation through the Law to becoming righteous through faith.

Other examples of the paraenetic use of resurrection imagery could be derived from the Pauline injunctions to Christians to walk in the Spirit (e.g., Gal 5:24–25; Rom 7:6) or to live for Christ and not oneself (2 Cor 5:15). These examples follow the same patterns of exhortation that we have seen in Paul's use of his apostolic example.

1 Corinthians 6:12–20

The Corinthian situation brings out one further element in Paul's use of resurrection paraenesis that is only alluded to in our other examples: the importance of Christian evaluation of what is done in the body. In connection with Phil 3:19–21 we saw that Paul did not adopt the common hellenistic distinction between what belongs to the bodily, perishable realm and what belongs to the soul, to the immortal realm. Instead, he contrasts the earthly body with the glorious transformed body that awaits the Christian in the resurrection. In 2 Cor 5:10, Paul concludes a similar passage on the transformation of the body into the glory of the resurrection with the reminder that all persons are to be judged according to what they have done in the body.

This passage shows the apostle using that teaching about the body to counter opposing views held by some Christians in Corinth. The passage contains a series of quotations by which Paul attacks slogans that were being bandied about by the Corinthians. Each slogan is corrected by the apostle. The general position held in the slogans is that what a person does with the body, in this case a person's sexual conduct, is irrelevant. Paul advances a number of arguments against the Corinthian slogans. Verse 13 depends directly on an application of the belief in the future resurrection of the believer's body.

The slogans in v. 12 are most closely paralleled by the philosophic preaching of the Stoic/Cynic school. They argued for radical freedom from the false conventions, prejudices, and restraints of society. The first slogan, "I am free to do anything," is met by Paul's "but not everything is for the best." Later, it will become clear that what is for the best in Paul's mind is what will build up the community (1 Cor 10:23f.). The slogan is repeated and met with Paul's "I will not let myself be dominated by anything." This answer points to the philosophic understanding of freedom: the wandering Cynic is free because he is not bound by the passions and ties of other humans. Paul's view will not be that of the Stoic, though he is able to use their language. In 1 Cor 3:21f., we find Paul Christianizing a Stoic formula, "all things are yours (= Stoic) . . . ," with the addition of the assertion "and you are Christ's." Once again, we are confronted with the risen Christ's lordship over the believer. The second half of the argument in this section elaborates on that conviction that the believer is Christ's. The consequence of that fundamental relationship is that the Christian cannot acquire freedom except in the service of Christ.

Murphy-O'Connor finds a similar slogan and answer pattern in vv. 13–14. Verse 13a contains the Corinthian slogans. Verses 13b–14 give Paul's responses[30]:

food is meant for the belly	*the body . . . for the Lord*
and the belly for food	*and the Lord for the body*
God	*God*
will destroy both one and the other	*and the Lord will raise us through his power*

The same power by which God raised Christ is to be exercised on behalf of the Christian. Therefore, Paul argues, what is done in and with the body does have significance for the Christian. Unlike the Corinthian view—which may also be behind the denial of the resurrection—that the body is merely a perishable entity, Paul sees in the resurrection evidence that the body, too, is the realm of divine action.[31] Thus, in this instance, Paul draws direct conclusions from his understanding of the resurrection as the bodily transformation of Jesus. Paul's ability to draw such a conclusion should remind exegetes not to take an overly spiritualized view of the arguments about the difference between earthly and resurrected body elsewhere in Paul. Paul does think of resurrection as a transformation that allows us to draw conclusions about the nature of bodily existence.[32]

THE NEW CREATION

One of the fundamental patterns of Pauline paraenesis takes the death and resurrection kerygma as an exhortation to die to the Law or to the old life and live in the Spirit under the lordship of the risen *Kyrios*. Rom 7:4–6 summarizes this pattern: the freedom from the Law (and sin) won by the death of Christ is given to the believers so that they serve the risen Lord by bearing fruit.[33] Rom 8 treats the life of walking in the Spirit as one in which the Christian awaits the new creation. The activity of the Spirit makes it possible for Christians to be free from the Law by living in the Spirit. Thus, the Spirit bridges the gulf between the presence of new life in the Spirit and the reality of a world that is not yet transformed.

While the activity of the Spirit is the dominant theme, each section of Rom 8 contains an indication of the relationship between the theme of that section and the resurrection. E. Kaesemann has observed that Paul's understanding of the Spirit is shaped by his cross and resurrection Christology. The risen Lord manifests his presence and lordship through the Spirit. The task of the Spirit is to keep the community in discipleship to the Lord.[34]

Verses 1–11

The contrast between life in the Spirit and life in the flesh dominates the first section. This dualistic contrast has its origins in two-ways paraenesis. For the elect, the Spirit of God would root out the falsehood and sinfulness of the flesh, which worked against perfect obedience to the Law.[35] But Paul's view is not an intensification of this type of Jewish preaching, since he puts the Law along with sin as one of those things from which the gift of the Spirit has freed humanity.

The first section of the chapter comes to its conclusion by tying the Spirit operative in Christian life to the risen Lord. Verse 11 begins with the description of the Spirit dwelling in the Christian according to the kerygmatic formula, God is the one who raised Christ from the dead (Rom 4:24f.). The Spirit "makes alive our mortal bodies." At this point in the paraenesis the "making alive" is that which enables the Christian to walk in the life of the Spirit. Later, the "new life" will refer to the future. This reservation is typical of Pauline paraenesis. The Christian manifests the lordship of Jesus by walking in the Spirit now.

Verses 12–17

This section expands the christological focus of the previous section. The indwelling Spirit is the spirit of sonship. The concluding verse makes it clear that this relationship is grounded in the relationship between Christ and the Father. The expression "heir" and the reference to future glorification (v. 17) point toward the glorious eschatological future.[36] The Christians will be heirs with the risen Lord. But they can already be spoken of as "sons," since the Spirit enables the community to address God as Father. In this world, that sonship is manifested in the Christians' sharing the sufferings of Christ, a well-established Pauline theme. The "fellow heirs" look forward to the "first born of many brothers" in 8:29. Thus, suffering with Christ can be applied to all the sufferings of a world that has not yet been transformed into the new creation.

Verses 18–30

Verse 18 makes the eschatological implications of the previous sections evident. It introduces "glory" from v. 17, and the section concludes with a reference to glory as well (vv. 29f.). In that conclusion, the implications of the exaltation of Christ are once again introduced into the argument. The intervening verses consist of a network of traditional apocalyptic images. They have been reshaped by the apostle to provide a threefold testimony to Christian hope.[37] Once again, the sufferings of the present are reevaluated. They are an indication that those who are sons will achieve the destiny for which they hope because they participate in the "way of thinking of the Spirit." Thus, these sufferings are no longer the torments of an evil age that the righteous must endure.[38] They bear positive testimony to the glorious destiny that awaits the Christian, since the Christian share in the groanings of creation proves that Christians possess the "first fruits" of redemption.

At the same time, the Christian is tied to the world by a body that is not yet glorified. Hence, even the adoption of the Christian is not complete.[39] It retains its future dimension in awaiting the redemption of the body (v. 23). Verses 29–30 turn to speak of the full adoption as sons. Paul expands upon the kerygmatic traditions of Rom 4:25. He invokes the hymnic traditions that spoke of Jesus as not only Son but image of God (Col 1:15; 2 Cor 4:4; Heb 1:3, 6). Here the picture of "being conformed to Christ" derived from the passion and resurrection paraenesis is combined with the understanding of Christ as image. Salvation will be completed when Christ's image becomes that of the believer. The allusion to the creation of humanity in the image of God (Gen 1:27) would immediately lead the reader to the picture of Christ's death as the life-giving action of the new Adam in Rom 5:12–21.[40]

Colossians shows that "first born" (1:18) presented the relationship between the risen Christ and the believers who were to come after him. Here "first born" also suggests the eschatological adoption of Christians rather than their present status as sons. Therefore, "being conformed to the image of the Son" must also be an eschatological reality. It is not completed in the present activity of the Spirit. This expression is a parallel to Phil 3:21; the Savior will "change our lowly body to be like his glorious body by the power which enables him to subject all things to himself."

Other commentators see this passage as a reflection of baptismal traditions, which may have been the setting for the hymnic language that is employed. However, the carefully structured reservation, present conformity to the crucified and future conformity to the risen Lord, typical of Pauline paraenesis, is not characteristic of the baptismal traditions. The pre-Pauline baptismal formula in Gal 3:27–28, for example, proclaimed the "putting on of Christ" as the obliteration of all the distinctions characteristic of this world, male and female; slave and free; Jew and Gentile.[41] In Gal 3:29, Paul immediately translates that formula into the affirmation that all who belong to Christ are now heirs of the promises to Abraham. Here the eschatological reservation dominates the presentation of the Christians as heirs. Now they are heirs by suffering with Christ so that they will later be glorified with him (v. 17).

The baptismal connotations of the passage seem to be intensified in v. 30, since "he glorified" is in the past tense and not the future. Glory also contains overtones of the restoration of the lost image in which humanity returns to the heavenly glory that had been lost by Adam (Rom 3:23).[42] A baptismal setting might see that "glorification" as accomplished when the Spirit of God is received in baptism. The post-Pauline baptismal traditions clearly move beyond the eschatological reservation (see Eph 2:5f.).

However, Paul speaks of the Christian being changed into the glory of the son through the Spirit in 2 Cor 3:18. Therefore, he appears to have thought of glory as partially present and partially future.

Verses 31–39

The final section of the chapter is often described as a "hymn of victory" even though one cannot reconstruct a hymn from the passage. Paul has taken over a number of expressions from traditional preaching and woven them together to summarize the whole section.[43] Paul's gospel of righteousness through faith is vindicated in the triumphant conclusion that no power in the cosmos can separate the believer from the love of God in Jesus.[44] The section focuses on the cross as the manifestation of God's love and as the source of righteousness for the believer. The God who is behind this victory, who is "for us," is known in the death and resurrection of Jesus (cf. 1 Cor 1:21).

Verse 34 uses a liturgical tradition in which the resurrection was described as exaltation at God's right hand in a forensic context. The forensic metaphors of condemnation and intercession keep the passage rooted in the tension of Christian life in this world. Paul does not conclude that Christians are not condemned because they are already remade in the image of the Son of God. Rather, this freedom from condemnation remains rooted in the salvation that is found in the cross and resurrection of Jesus.

LITURGICAL TRADITIONS

Both the hymnic and kerygmatic traditions appear to have developed in liturgical contexts. The acclamation of God as "Abba" and the adoption of Christians as "sons" are part of the baptismal tradition. Though the hymnic traditions must have had a liturgical setting, their setting is more difficult to determine.[45] Since the Christian comes under the rule of the exalted Lord in baptism, the presence of the Lord to the believer may also be tied to this setting.[46]

Romans 6:1-11

The baptismal allusions in Rom 8 remind the reader of Paul's earlier use of baptismal material in Rom 6. Paul is not concerned with presenting a theological analysis of baptism in either section. The diatribe question in Rom 6:1-2 presents the question that Paul must answer: What is the relationship between the Christian and sin? Does Paul's understanding of righteousness through faith provide a free reign to sin? The same question recurs in v. 15.[47] The expression "do you not know" in v. 3a indicates that Paul is about to introduce something the reader should know. The parallel between baptism and entering into the death of Christ was probably traditional. For Paul, the key to the passage is the transition from life under sin to new life that is free from sin. He presents this view in v. 4 and then in two parallel sections, vv. 5-7 and 8-10. Christ's resurrection is paralleled by the new life in which the believer walks. The affirmation about the death and resurrection of Christ follows the two-membered resurrection kerygma. "By the glory of God" is equivalent to speaking of Christ's being raised by the power of God.[48]

Does the parallel between Christ's resurrection and the Christian walking in newness of life represent traditional paraenesis? Or has Paul modified a formula that originally spoke more directly of the believer rising with Christ? Rom 8:29f. suggests that "being conformed to the image of the Son" might have stood in parallel to the resurrection of Christ. Verses 5 and 8 speak of the Christian participation in the resurrection as future.

The parallels are clearly death and resurrection. Paul may have introduced "walk in newness of life" into the formula in v. 4. Verses 12 and 13 will pick up the theme of walking as a life that is free from the dominion of sin. Paul presents that new obedience as the way in which Christians manifest their identification with the risen Lord.[49] Verse 9 makes the resurrection of Christ evidence of the power over death that will make it possible for the believer to live with Christ. Death has no hold over Christ. This affirmation provides the transition to the next parallel between Christ and the believer. This parallel exploits the possibility of speaking of both Christ and the believer as "alive to God":

Verse 10 (Christ):   Verse 11 (Christian):
                                             So also you must consider
                                             yourselves,

The death he died,
he died to sin, once for all,   *dead to sin*
the life he lives, he lives to God   *and alive to God in Christ*
                                             Jesus.

Sin is to have no more dominion over the Christian than death has
over the risen Christ.

Colossians 2:11–12 and Ephesians 2:5–6

These formulae speak more directly about the baptized participating
in the resurrection of Christ. Though taken from later writings, the
parallelism may have been part of the tradition that Paul has refined
in Rom 6:1–11. Colossians and Ephesians contain other elements that
appear to have developed the type of paraenesis in Romans. Col 3:1
bases its imperative on the past sharing in the resurrection and Christian concern for the things above. Thus, the "life to God" of Rom 6:11
has become a life whose reality is hidden in heaven.[50] Colossians
retains something of the Pauline reservation in speaking of the hid-
denness of the Christian's life with God (3:3). Col 3:4 looks toward the
future. When Christ, who is the life of believers, is revealed, they,
too, will be revealed with him in glory. This reference to the parousia
is unique in Colossians.[51] Colossians has translated Paul's usual contrast between this age and the new one (Gal 4:25f.; Phil 3:13) into
spatial metaphors. The exaltation of Christ reflects the tradition developed out of Ps 110:1. The exalted Lord represents the reality of
the heavenly world to which the believer belongs.[52]

Although this paraenesis does not mention baptism directly, it
opens with a reference to the believers as "having been raised" (3:1).
That reference recalls the baptismal tradition in Col 2:11–12. The
paraenesis on the "hidden life" of the Christian may have been
developed in connection with such baptismal instruction. The connection between the two passages has been broken by Colossians' use
of the baptismal formula in a section directed against an opposing
teaching about the heavenly destiny of the Christian.[53] Most exegetes agree that the passage suggests a syncretistic philosophy composed of a mixture of Jewish, philosophic, and cultic practices. The
hints given in the section indicate that the opponents claimed:

a. to provide knowledge and probably superiority to the elemental beings of the cosmos.

b. to tie this knowledge to a heavenly ascent of the soul. If astrological or magical beliefs were involved, then the ascent of the soul would require means to get beyond the demons that guarded the lunar and planetary sphere ruling this world.

c. that if this philosophy had integrated Christ into its scheme, then the ascent may have been treated as the way to the Christ, who is enthroned above the heavens and powers.

d. that this ascent also involved some form of worship of or with the angelic powers.

e. that this worship required certain ascetic practices: foregoing certain foods (vv. 16 and 21); sexual abstinence and severe treatment of the body ("putting off the body of flesh," v. 11; v. 23); meticulous observance of special sacred days and seasons (v. 16).

f. that some sort of initiatory rite, whether baptism or circumcision, was part of this cult.

g. that the devotee was said to receive divine "fullness" as a result of these practices.

Throughout Colossians, the author insists that Christianity is superior to this philosophy and provides the true access to the heavenly reality that the opponents claimed.[54]

Verse 11 refers to baptism as "circumcision not made by hands." Since baptism and circumcision are not paralleled elsewhere in the New Testament, the author has probably directed this understanding against his opponents.[55] Verse 12 shows that the author is using a baptismal formula that originated with the type of death and resurrection tradition one finds in Rom 6:4f.[56] When one sees this passage as a counter to the Colossian heresy, it is easy to understand why the author emphasizes the fact that the Christian "has been raised with him through faith in the working of God, who raised him from the dead." The opponents thought that the powers of the universe stood between them and the divine world in which Christ is enthroned. We have seen that the imagery of Christ's exaltation over the powers could easily carry such overtones. Colossians insists that Christians belong to the heavenly world of the risen Christ from the time they are baptized. They have no need of the techniques for ascent being put forward by this false philosophy. Verse 12 also echoes the traditional resurrection formula in insisting that the power of God was active in raising Christ from the dead. Verses 13–15 pick up the theme of baptismal deliverance from the powers of sin, death, and the Law. In the forgiveness of sins God bestows life on the believer. Traditional material in vv. 13c–15 emphasizes that the cosmic victory is won by the crucified. It is based in the power of God that is active in the resurrection of Jesus. Thus, in the triumphal exaltation of Christ, God has made the cosmic powers his captives, just as though they were captives in an imperial triumph.[57] Not only is the believer already "resurrected with Christ" and thus quite above the heavenly powers, but the powers themselves are disarmed. They can neither help nor hinder a person's quest for the divine.

Ephesians 2:5–6

Colossians has reformulated the traditions of baptism as participation in the death and resurrection of the exalted Lord to meet the challenge of a false spirituality. Eph 2:5–6 contains a similar baptismal tradition. The author was probably familiar with Colossians, and 2:1–6 could reflect a nonpolemic use of that tradition. We have seen that Eph 1:20–23 emphasized the subjection of all cosmic powers to Christ. This section celebrates the power and graciousness of God, who has taken those who were following the "prince of the power of the air," condemned to judgment, and made them alive together with Christ (v. 5b). Instead of being subject to cosmic powers God has "made us sit with him in the heavenly places in Christ Jesus" (v. 6). Thus, the Christian shares the exaltation that the Jewish tradition had pictured for the righteous. As in Colossians and the other resurrection traditions, the emphasis remains on the active power of God. The exaltation of Christ follows from that power.[58]

2 Timothy 2:18

The sure saying in 2 Tim 2:11–13 presented the death and resurrection pattern of the baptismal tradition without any overtones of present resurrection or exaltation. The Christian has died with Christ and now "endures," while hoping to live with or reign with Christ. This formula may have been directly influenced by Rom 6:8. The third "sure saying" appears to be out of context in the chapter. Like the first two sayings, it appears to be a quotation. God is faithful to his covenant irrespective of the human response (cf. Rom 3:2f.).[59]

This saying is directed against those who would engage in disputes. Much of the section is typical polemic. 2 Tim 2:18 suddenly introduces a specific charge, "holding that the resurrection is past already." Its connection with a baptismal formula suggests that the author's opponents held some form of baptismal resurrection.[60] If one takes all the references to false views in the pastorals as referring to the same group, then the opponents may be similar to the Colossian heresy. However, they show no evidence of concern with cosmic powers or with the ascent of the soul. They preach an asceticism that prohibited marriage (1 Tim 4:1–10, countered by the emphasis on marriage; 1 Tim 2:15; 5:14; Tit 2:4) and insisted on abstinence from certain foods (1 Tim 5:13; and indirectly, Tit 1:15). They claimed to teach secret knowledge (2 Tim 2:13; 1 Tim 6:20) and may have adopted some Jewish practices (Tit 1:10, 14).[61] The opponents may have supported their view on the basis of baptismal traditions that spoke of "being raised with Christ." 2 Timothy has reached back to a version of the tradition in 2:11–13, which makes having life and reigning future expectations of the Christian. The Christian must now persevere in the life of Christian service.

1 Peter 3:18–22

1 Peter is directed to those in the rural areas of Asia Minor. These Christians were resident aliens in their communities and subject to suspicion and persecution. They were known to be a separate group (1 Pt 4:16) and were suspect as members of a strange religious cult (3:13). 1 Peter seeks to instruct Christians about their relationships to such a world. They must demonstrate their distinctiveness by separating themselves from pre-Christian associations and patterns of behavior (1:14, 18; 2:11; 4:1–4). But they must also demonstrate by their loyalty and civic obedience that they are not a threat to the community (2:13–17).[62]

The baptismal allusion in 1 Pt 3:18–22 is set in the instruction about how to deal with persecution. Christians must maintain a clear conscience so that they will never provide grounds for the charges brought by their enemies (vv. 16–17). The baptismal section leads to the traditional exhortation: the Christian leads a life free from the sins and passions that characterized pre-Christian behavior. Anyone who suffers in the same way that Christ did is free from sin (4:1). No one can escape judgment. After his death Christ preached to "the spirits in prison" (3:19). They, too, "might live according to God."[63] This tradition is used to assure those who have followed Christ as innocent sufferers that they will be vindicated. God will punish those whose way of life is opposed to him. At the same time, he is the God who vindicates the innocent sufferers (2:20–25; 3:14, 18–22; 4:6, 13–19; 5:6–11). Thus, the exhortation in this section has recovered one of the earliest foundations of the exaltation traditions: to assure the righteous that God does vindicate innocent suffering.[64]

1 Pt 3:18–22 is the third christological section in the letter. 1 Pt 1:18–21 presents the death of Christ as part of preordained plan: the innocent Lamb has been "made manifest" at the end of time to ransom Christians from the futile ways of their ancestors. The resurrection and exaltation of Jesus is the basis of Christian confidence in God. 1 Pt 2:22–25 presents the sinless suffering and death of Christ as a model for Christians. Christians do not return insults but suffer in the confidence that God judges justly (v. 23). The death to sin, which Christ has made possible by his death (v. 24), is embodied in this form of Christian suffering.[65]

1 Pt 3:18–22 continues this type of paraenesis. Verse 18 takes traditional material as the basis for the author's central theme: the suffering of the righteous One is the source of salvation for the sinful and unrighteous.[66] The pattern of death, resurrection, and exaltation over the powers in vv. 18 and 22 has been filled with materials that appear to have had a different origin. Verses 19–20a speak of the risen Christ preaching to the spirits in Hades. These spirits are identified with those from the days of Noah. The concern with Noah, concern with the "sons of God," and the image of storage places for the spirits all reflect developments of the Enoch traditions. Elaboration of the stories of the fallen angels and their descendants' role in the postflood sinfulness of humanity were staples of this tradition. This passage appears to reflect a Christian tradition that had appropriated these Jewish mythological traditions.[67]

Verses 20b–21 continue the Noah theme. The flood is taken as a type of baptism. Such a typology resembles the comparison between baptism and passing through the sea in 1 Cor 10:1–13. The interpretation of this tradition in v. 21b does not attach divine salvation to baptism as such but attaches it to the power of the risen Christ. The expression "appeal to God for a clear conscience" is unique in the New Testament. Heb 10:22 is the closest parallel. Jesus, the heavenly High Priest, makes it possible for the Christian to draw near in faith, "with our hearts sprinkled clean from an evil conscience and our bodies washed with pure water." 1 Peter does speak of Jesus as a sacrificial lamb. It would appear that the tradition behind both writings had developed an image of the sacrificial death of Jesus, providing the cleansed conscience that accompanied the baptismal washing. 1 Pt 3:21b now contrasts the clear conscience attained through the resurrection of Jesus to the washing of baptism. The parallel structure of Hebrews is more likely to have been the original tradition.[68] But 1 Peter wishes to exhort the reader to continue to have such a "clear conscience" by remaining innocent victims. The conclusion to the verse, "through the resurrection of Jesus Christ," also points forward to Christ's heavenly exaltation in v. 22. The elements of exaltation in this verse are typical of the tradition: exaltation to the right hand of God; subjection of the angels and powers. The paraenesis that follows this passage centers on judgment and vindication. Hence, the image of the enthroned Christ is probably intended to convey the exaltation of Christ as judge. Verse 22b also contains the motif of exaltation as entering into heaven. This motif is also similar to the traditions in Hebrews (cf. Heb 4:14; 8:1; 9:24; 10:12). But while Hebrews considers resurrection and exaltation to be equivalent, 1 Peter distinguishes them as separate events.

J. H. Elliott suggests that the exalted Christ played an important role for the Christians to whom 1 Peter is addressed. It assured them that they had not further lowered themselves by identifying with a despised group, the Christians. Instead, by being united with Jesus, they have a share in his exaltation—a share won by also sharing his innocent suffering.[69] Christians also identify with Jesus' subordination. God has rewarded Jesus' subordination by subjecting the powers to him.[70] The clear conscience is the key to the Christian life being advocated by the author (2:19; 3:16). Those who follow the pattern of innocent suffering set by Christ can expect a vindication like his. Thus, the images of Christ's death and resurrection taken from the baptismal tradition are directed at the concrete problems of Christians in Asia Minor. They are to guide the Christian's behavior in response to persecution. They will also teach Christians to be proud of what distinguishes their life and behavior from that of their neighbors.

MEAL TRADITIONS

The baptismal traditions appear to have been the primary locus for resurrection imagery. The meal scenes in the Johannine and Lukan resurrection stories often lead to the presumption that early Christians experienced the presence of the risen Lord in the eucharistic assembly. But the stories themselves do not support the elaborate theologies of presence attached to them. Luke is primarily concerned with the new understanding of Scripture gained from the risen Lord. Recognition of the Lord takes a secondary place. Recognition may have been attached simply to the fact that Jesus carries out the central rite of the Christian community and not to any special sense of presence. The supper tradition in Mk 14:25/Mt 26:29 separates Jesus' eating at that supper from any meal until the coming of the kingdom. Matthew makes it clear that the messianic banquet will renew the Last Supper by adding "with you" to the "drink it new" in Mk 14:25. Luke's version attaches such a reservation to both the eating and drinking: "I shall not eat it until it is fulfilled in the Kingdom of God," and "I tell you that from now on I shall not drink of the fruit of the vine until the Kingdom of God comes" (Lk 22:16, 18). Luke may have intended to show these prophecies to have been fulfilled in the meals between the risen Jesus and his disciples. However, those meals with the risen Lord are decisively ended with the ascension in Luke-Acts. They are now only part of the early Christian witness (10:41). The only connection the Lukan tradition can make between the postresurrection meals and the later Christian traditions is to provide an additional etiology beyond the Last Supper tradition for the Christian practice.

1 Corinthians 11:23–26

The picture painted by Paul in 1 Cor 11:23–26 is fundamentally the same. Verses 23b–25 report a traditional formula. The body, which is "for you" in the word bread is identified with the body that Jesus handed over to be crucified. The cup represents the new covenant made possible by the shedding of Christ's blood. This formula gives no indication of interpreting the representation of the crucified in the words spoken over the bread and the cup as presence. The community celebrates the death of the One who is now exalted as Lord.[71] Paul ties the eucharist to proclamation of the death of Christ in v. 26. That proclamation is limited by the parousia. The eucharist belongs to the time between the death of Christ and his return. That orientation is also evident in the prayer for the coming of the Lord, *"Marana tha"* (1 Cor 16:22; cf. Didache 10:5).[72]

C. K. Barrett suggests that the resurrection was not associated with the eucharist in the pre-Pauline tradition because the supper was understood as an anticipation of the messianic banquet in the shadow of the cross. The resurrection had not altered the fact that the messianic banquet lies in the future, though it confirmed Christian hopes for the future. Paul sees resurrection as Christ's exaltation in heaven as *Kyrios.* The power of the *Kyrios* is effective in the life of the believer, but the Lord does not return in some form of earthly presence.[73]

R. A. Horsley suggests that the Corinthians may have seen the eucharist as an opportunity for identification with divine wisdom, since both Wisdom and Philo identify wisdom with the water from the rock and the manna, a typology for the eucharist (1 Cor 10:3–4).[74] This soteriology of identification with divine wisdom does not presuppose identification with the risen and exalted Christ.

John 6:51b–58

This section of John makes an explicit link between the eucharist and the resurrection of the believer on the last day. Many exegetes think that this passage represents a later addition to the gospel.[75] We have seen that the evangelist reinterprets "resurrection on the last day" in light of the saving presence of Jesus as "the resurrection and the life" (11:24–27). Jn 6:35–50 makes a similar correction in the story of the manna in the wilderness. The living bread is the life-giving Word spoken by Jesus. Whoever believes in him will be raised up by Jesus on the Last Day (vv. 40 and 44). These claims attribute God's power to Jesus in a way that is characteristic of the Fourth Gospel but quite different from the other New Testament traditions. We have seen that most of the New Testament resurrection traditions keep the power of Jesus' resurrection closely tied to God's activity. God's power raised Jesus and will raise the believer. But the Johannine tradition shows Jesus to be the One who exercises God's powers of giving life and judging (e.g., 5:21). This christological perception can be seen to inform even statements that speak of resurrection on the "Last Day" rather than using the more uniquely Johannine language about the believer's having eternal life. Jn 6:51b–58 appears to represent the eucharistic tradition of the Johannine community. By juxtaposing the eucharistic tradition with the interpretation of the manna as Jesus' life-giving Word, the Evangelist brings the eucharist under the same soteriological perspective that he has maintained throughout the gospel. Salvation is found in receiving Jesus as the Word and revelation of the Father.[76]

Verse 56 links this formulation of the eucharistic tradition to the indwelling language of the discourses: "he who eats my flesh and drinks my blood abides in me and I in him." This is the same principle of abiding in the community that was promised in the discourses (14:20–22). The discourse imagery continues in v. 57. Jesus has been sent by the Father to confer life: "As the living Father sent me, and I

live because of the Father, so he who eats me will live because of
me." This passage does not yet extend that "sending" to the disciples,
as the discourses do, since it is set during the earthly ministry of Jesus.
Commissioning can only take place when the divinely appointed
agent departs. This phrase may represent another Johannine reformulation of traditional language about the risen Jesus. Other traditions consistently attribute resurrection to the life-giving power of
God. The life that Jesus enjoys with the Father is the life that believers expect to be their future. Thus, the Johannine understanding of
Jesus' relationship to the Father and its understanding of the presence of Jesus to the community appear to have transformed this
tradition. The earlier tradition has probably linked participation in
the eucharist with the expectation of sharing the life that the risen
and exalted Jesus has received from the Father.

RESURRECTION, PRESENCE, AND SOTERIOLOGY

The most important developments in the early Christian resurrection language are grounded in the hymnic and kerygmatic traditions.
They provided the starting point for the resurrection language that is
used in early Christian exhortation. Christians are encouraged to live
in conformity with the conviction that Jesus is the crucified and risen
Lord. The presence or power of the risen Lord served to guarantee
the authority of the community in interpreting Jesus' teaching. It was
invoked in disciplinary actions of the community.

In the Pauline churches the kerygma of the cross and resurrection
formed a fundamental element in the preaching of salvation. The
death and resurrection of Jesus are not only the turning point in
God's plan of salvation; they are the model for the life of the believer.
Discipleship requires conformity to the image of the crucified and
risen Lord. It demands that one see the life one leads in the body as
the key to future salvation. It looks forward to sharing the life and
transformation of the risen Lord. This conviction about salvation also
served to "weed out" claims to salvation that came from competing
visions of divine and human reality at Corinth, Colossae, and in the
pastoral epistles. The baptismal traditions of the early Christian community served as the primary place for the liturgical representation
of participation in the death and resurrection of the Lord. The power
of the resurrection is experienced by the Christian in baptism. Chris-

tians are no longer under the dominion of whatever power best describes their past life, the Law, sin, the passions, "the prince of the air," or that to which all these lead according to the paraenetic tradition, death. Instead, one is "alive to God," able to walk in the Spirit. This change to the lordship of Christ represents the effective presence of the power of salvation in a world that still awaits eschatological transformation. It is the manifestation of the change given humanity through the life-giving and saving power of God, the power that raised Jesus from the dead. Thus, resurrection extends well beyond the story of an individual righteous sufferer. It reflects God's fulfillment of the saving promise to creation.

NOTES

1. A. Dulles *(A Church to Believe In* [New York: Crossroad, 1982], 9); this sense of presence means that Jesus alone remains master and Lord. The Johannine community carried this perception to the point of resisting all forms of institutionalized leadership long after they had been adopted in other communities (see R. E. Brown, *The Community of the Beloved Disciple* [New York: Paulist, 1979], 86–88).

2. C. F. Evans, *Resurrection and the New Testament* (SBT ser. 2, no. 12; London: SCM, 1970), 155–68. R. Tannehill *(Dying and Rising with Christ* [Berlin: Töpelmann, 1967], 126–28) stresses the importance of the cross and resurrection pattern in shaping the Christian life. Dying with Christ always refers to the new situation in which the Christian lives afterward. It serves to qualify the present.

3. Evans, op. cit., 161. This lack of reflective integration can be seen in Paul's description of righteousness through faith as well. On the one hand, the believer is righteous. On the other, Paul directs the process of sanctification toward the future. For an attempt to reconcile the various strands in Paul's soteriology by making a distinction between righteousness and sanctification, see K. Donfried, "Justification and Last Judgment in Paul," *Interpretation* 30 (1976), 140–52.

4. W. Meeks, *The First Urban Christians. The Social World of the Apostle Paul* (New Haven: Yale University, 1983), 22–23; 191.

Meeks also observes that this status inconsistency plays an important role in apocalyptic (p. 174). The Jewish community makes a claim to greatness that is not borne out in the order of the world. At a still deeper level, the paradox expresses the archetypal pattern of human hopes and fears.

5. J. Murphy-O'Connor, "Corinthian Slogans in 1 Cor 6:12–20," *Catholic Biblical Quarterly* 40 (1978), 391–96. Paul has established a pattern of correlation. He answers the Corinthian devaluation of the body by using the resurrection to establish the value of the body because it is the object of divine action.

6. W. Meeks, "The Social Context of Pauline Theology," *Interpretation* 36 (1982), 271–73.

7. R. Schnackenburg, *Das Johannesevangelium III. Kap. 13–21* (HTKNT IV/3; Freiburg: Herder, 1975), 92. Schnackenburg also sees apologetic significance in the question as an expression of concern over the fact that appearances of the risen One were limited to the apostles as witnesses. A similar question is implicit in Ac 10:40f., "But God raised him on the third day and made him manifest; not to all the people but to us who were chosen by God as witnesses, who ate and drank with him after he rose from the dead." Celsus would later (c. Cel. 2.63–67) criticize Christians by insisting that Jesus should have appeared to his enemies. The Johannine tradition may be answering a similar objection when the Paraclete is presented as the One who convicts the world of sin (16:8–11).

8. See the pioneering analysis of the sociological consequences of Johannine symbolism by W. Meeks, "The Man from Heaven in Johannine Sectarianism," *Journal of Biblical Literature* 91 (1972), 44–72. The use of dualistic symbols both reflects the experience of the community and leads the community to perceive the world in ways that reinforce that experience. Brown (op. cit., 88–91) tries to avoid concluding that the Johannine community had become a sect by emphasizing those elements in the Johannine tradition that remained open to the outside. He also uses sect in purely religious terms as a group hostile to a larger orthodox consensus. But he admits that over against some of the other groups the Johannine community may have appeared to be a religious sect.

9. "Remain" is a central expression for solidarity and loyalty within the Johannine tradition: it is used to describe discipleship (1:32f., 38f.); it describes loyalty in a conflict in which some desert Jesus (8:31, 35); and the vine image in Jn 15:1–10 makes "remaining" in Jesus the foundation of the community's identity. This im-

agery persisted into a later period and is applied against the schismatics by the author of the Epistles (1 Jn 2:6, 24; 3:9, 24; 4:13).

10. This practice is not to be applied to the "sin unto death," apparently that of the secessionists. (See the discussion of this passage in R. E. Brown, *The Epistles of John* [AnBi 30; Garden City, N.Y.: Doubleday, 1982], 611–19; 635–38.) Jas 5:15 also attests to an early Christian practice of prayer for the sinner.

11. P. Perkins, *Love Commands in the New Testament* (Ramsey, N.J.: Paulist, 1982), 107–11.

12. See the survey of opinions about the Paraclete sayings in R. E. Brown, *The Gospel According to John XIII–XXI* (AnBi 29A; Garden City, N.Y.: Doubleday, 1970), 699–700; 1135–42; Schnackenburg, op. cit., 156–73. I have argued *(John,* 189–95) that the five sayings represent different stages in the development of the Johannine image of the Paraclete.

13. J. T. Forestell, *The Word of the Cross: Salvation as Revelation in the Fourth Gospel* (Rome: Biblical Institute Press, 1974), 134–37. Forestell traces the description of the activity of the Spirit in John to three contexts: (a) eschatological, the Spirit associated with the coming of the Messiah (1:32f.; 3:34b); (b) the Spirit as representing the contrast between the human world and the divine one (3:5–8; 4:23f.; 6:63); and (c) as the source of eternal life (4:10; 7:29; 20:22–23).

14. Forestell, ibid., 136; Schnackenburg, op. cit., 84.

15. Forestell, op. cit., 137; Schnackenburg, op. cit., 85. Schnackenburg thinks that the title Spirit of Truth for John referred simply to the function of the Spirit in leading the community into truth (as in 16:13; for truth as an attribute of the Johannine community, see 1 Jn 4:6; 5:6). Brown, *John* II, 644.

16. Brown, *Epistles,* 368–75.

17. Brown, *Epistles,* 106–12. Brown finds in the role of shepherd given Peter in Jn 21 a later generation's accommodation to the authority of the presbyter-bishop.

18. V. Furnish, *Theology and Ethics in Paul* (Nashville: Abingdon, 1968), 169–81.

19. Tannehill, op. cit., 90–98.

20. Ibid., 87f.

21. Tannehill (op. cit., 98–100) notes the irony in Paul's threat to exercise power against his opponents. Even this claim is moderated by the insistence that weakness and power of Christ must guide the life of the apostle even in response to such opposition.

22. H. Conzelmann *(1 Corinthians* [Philadelphia: Fortress, 1975],

97f.) emphasizes that this use of "power" represents an archaic sense of the dynamistic rite. The archaism of the ritual has been shifted somewhat, since the power of the Lord does not automatically cause the man's destruction; that is seen to be the result of his exclusion from the community.

23. J. A. Fitzmyer, "To Know Him and to Know the Power of His Resurrection (Phil 3:10)," *To Advance the Gospel* (New York: Crossroad, 1981), 204–207. Fitzmyer points to the significance of *"en dynamei"* in Rom 1:4 for this perception of power granted to the risen *Kyrios* by the Father. 1 Cor 1:24 calls Christ the power of God. Fitzmyer links this concept of power with the language of divine glory that is associated with the resurrection in Rom 6:4; 2 Thess 1:9; Phil 3:21; Rom 5:2; Col 3:4; and with the image of Jesus as the glory of God in 1 Cor 2:8. Both the Old Testament and the Dead Sea Scrolls parallel the glory and power of God (ibid., 210–13).

24. The abrupt beginning and sharp tone of this section of the letter are so unlike the rest of Philippians that many commentators think that they represent a fragment of a letter that Paul had written to the Philippian community at a different time from the rest. See the discussion of the literary problems of this section in J. Gnilka, *Der Philipperbrief* (HTKNT; Freiburg: Herder, 1968), 5–18. Gnilka thinks that the controversy letter consists of 3:1a–4:1, 8–9.

25. Gnilka, op. cit., 192–97.

26. Ibid., 192 note 45. Outside of Paul only in 2 Pt 3:18; see 1 Cor 1:5; 12:8; 13:2; 14:6; 2 Cor 2:14; Col 2:3; Eph 4:13.

27. Ibid., 196f.

28. Ibid., 205f. We have seen that such *topoi* were also part of Paul's preaching of resurrection in 1 Cor 15:23–28. Those who have their hopes set on this life only are the most miserable of people.

29. J. Schutz, *Paul and the Anatomy of Apostolic Authority* (Cambridge: Cambridge University, 1975), 266f.

30. Murphy-O'Connor, op. cit., 392–94; other commentators think that 13a is Paul's concession to the Corinthians that food is indifferent.

31. Ibid., 395f.; Conzelmann, op. cit., 111.

32. Murphy-O'Connor (op. cit., 394) insists correctly that the possibility of treating the body as a person elsewhere in Paul does not mean that this passage is not using body in the physical sense.

33. Though this chapter does not explicitly state how the Christian comes to die to the Law, it would apparently refer to the exposition of baptism in Rom 6. "Body of Christ" may be used in the

double sense of the physical body of Christ that died on the cross and the body as the community into which the Christian is baptized. Tannehill (op. cit., 45f.) points out that Paul conceives the believer's "dying with Christ" in terms of God's action, what happens to humans rather than as something they do. The immediate cause of the believer's death here must be the body of Christ as the crucified (J. Fitzmyer, "Romans," in R. Brown, J. Fitzmyer, and R. Murphy, eds., *Jerome Biblical Commentary* [Englewood Cliffs: Prentice-Hall, 1967], 312). E. Kaesemann *(Commentary on Romans* [trans. E. Bromily; Grand Rapids: Eerdmans, 1980], 188); what is said about the power of sin in 6:4ff. has been transferred to the Law here.

34. Kaesemann (op. cit., 212) proposes the following outline for the chapter: vv. 1–11, Christian lives in the Spirit, not the flesh; vv. 12–17, Christian life as sonship; vv. 18–30, eschatological hope as the foundation of Christian life; vv. 31–39, the victory being won in the Christian life.

35. Ibid., 212; parallels to the expression "sinful flesh" occur in the Dead Sea Scrolls, 1 QS 11.9; 1 QM 4.3; 12.12.

36. The argument about sonship in this passage reflects Paul's earlier argument in Gal 4:1–10. As in Gal 4:6, the acclamation "Abba, Father" uttered in the Spirit attests to the sonship of believers (Kaesemann, op. cit., 229).

37. P. V. D. Osten-Sacken, *Römer 8 als Beispiel paulinischer Soteriologie* (Göttingen: Vandenhoeck & Ruprecht, 1975), 78–123.

38. Kaesemann (op. cit., 234) observes that creation should not be misunderstood as referring to the natural world over against the human world. In apocalyptic contexts, creation always includes humans and their projects. They must be included in the reference to creation here in order for the language of subjection of creation in v. 20 to be appropriate. Kaesemann (p. 232f.) suggests that "all creation" in v. 22 focuses attention on nonhuman nature and thus sharpens the contrast with v. 23.

39. Ibid., 112f. Thus, the Christian does not short-circuit the paradox of life in the present. Life in the Spirit is not identified with the life of eschatological glory.

40. Tannehill, op. cit., 26f.

41. H. D. Betz, *Galatians* (Philadelphia: Fortress, 1979), 181–201. Betz insists that such a formula had its social correlate. Christians could see themselves as among the "free" not merely in some abstract theological sense but also in the sense of freedom from the bonds and restraints of the ancient social world.

42. O. Michel, *Der Brief an die Römer* (Göttingen: Vandenhoeck & Ruprecht, 1966, 4th ed.), 212.
43. Osten-Sacken (op. cit., 14–50) reconstructs an apocalyptic Jewish Christian catechism on righteousness behind this passage. Kaesemann (op. cit., 245f.) makes a more plausible case for a variety of apocalyptic expressions woven into this passage.
44. Kaesemann (op. cit., 246f.) sees the tendency to read the passage as hymnic as obscuring the diatribe argument. The initial question "If God is for us, who is against us?" raises the question of the whole message of Rom 5–8. "Being for us" refers to the whole plan of salvation history.
45. E. Schweizer, *The Letter to the Colossians* (Minneapolis: Augsburg, 1982), 47–55; E. Lohse, *Colossians and Philemon* (Philadelphia: Fortress, 1971), 40f. The cultic setting of the material in Eph 1:20–23 is difficult to determine (see Barth, op. cit., 210). J. Gnilka *(Der Epheserbrief* [HTKNT; Freiburg: Herder, 1971], 93) thinks that v. 19 implies a baptismal setting. Gnilka *(Philipperbrief,* 147) cannot decide between a baptismal or a eucharistic setting for the Philippians hymn.
46. Tannehill, op. cit., 7f.
47. Tannehill (op. cit., 7–9) thinks that the argument extends to the whole chapter; also Michel (op. cit., 148). Kaesemann (op. cit., 163) finds a major shift in v. 12. He points out that several Pauline baptismal themes are not contained in Rom 6: there is no mention of the conferring of the Spirit or of the incorporation of the baptized into the body of Christ.
48. Michel (op. cit., 153) finds in the died, buried, raised, a three-membered formula like that of 1 Cor 15:3–4.
49. Kaesemann, op. cit., 166f. Tannehill (op. cit., 24f.) insists that the passage is speaking of a corporate change, not of a singular event applied to each individual. At baptism the Christian becomes part of the "new Adam" (pp. 28–30).
50. Tannehill, op. cit., 47f.; Lohse (op. cit., 132f.) agrees that this passage has gone beyond Romans but warns against the conclusion that its view of sharing the resurrection implies some sort of turn toward an immortalizing transformation of the soul at baptism that would result in denial of resurrection or a Gnostic spirituality.
51. Gnilka, op. cit., 175; Schweizer (op. cit., 172) points to the concern with hope (1:5, 23) and the concealment of the believer's new life as evidence that the eschatological reservation and the associated need for exhortation is retained.
52. Gnilka (op. cit., 172f.) emphasizes the importance of Colossians'

understanding of the exalted Lord as a reinterpretation of the hellenistic view of the heavenly world.

53. See the reconstructions of the Colossian heresy in Schweizer, op. cit., 125–34 (Jewish appropriation of Pythagorean themes); and Lohse, op. cit., 127–31 (syncretistic mystery initiation that had taken on Jewish elements); Gnilka, op. cit., 163–70 (as Jewish shell filled with pagan religious practices, especially magic and astrological lore from Asia Minor). Gnilka emphasizes the sectarian nature of this heresy, which would foster a sense of elitism in members of the group.

54. Gnilka (op. cit., 167f.) emphasizes the necessity to see the refutation of the heretics behind other passages in the letter, as in the references to wisdom and knowledge (1:9, 28; 2:3; 3:16; 4:5).

55. Lohse, op. cit., 102. Schweizer (loc. cit.) argues that the spiritualizing interpretations of circumcision in Philo and among the Essenes (= conversion to obedience to the Torah; 1 QS 5.5; cf. Rom 2:29) are the background to this view. Phil 3:3 uses a spiritual sense of circumcision against Jewish legalism. Consequently, the ethical interpretation of circumcision as "putting off the body of the flesh" was part of Colossians' tradition.

56. Lohse, op. cit., 103; Gnilka, op. cit., 133–35; Schweizer, op. cit., 143–45.

57. Lohse, op. cit., 106, 112; Schweizer, op. cit., 148–52; Gnilka, op. cit., 142. God is the active subject from v. 13 on.

58. Gnilka, *Epheserbrief,* 113, 119f.

59. M. Dibelius and H. Conzelmann, *The Pastoral Epistles* (Philadelphia: Fortress, 1972), 109. The Qumran rule (1 QS 11.11f.) speaks of God's fidelity overcoming the sinfulness of the sectary.

60. Ibid., 110.

61. See the reconstruction in Dibelius-Conzelmann, op. cit., 65–67. It presumes that the heresy is a gnosticizing group with ties to Judaism. The author has been deliberately vague in describing the opponents because he wishes the letters to serve as a general handbook for any situation that might arise.

62. J. H. Elliott, *A Home for the Homeless: A Sociological Exegesis of 1 Peter* (Philadelphia: Fortress, 1981), 21–100.

63. L. Goppelt, *Der Erste Petrusbrief* (MK XII/1; Göttingen: Vandenhoeck & Ruprecht, 1978), 227.

64. Goppelt (ibid., 276f.) suggests that the formulation of the kerygmatic tradition here has been cast in the past tense because the judgment of the dead is no longer expected in the near future.

65. Goppelt (ibid., 204–207) notes that the author's use of traditional formulae gives the passage its hymnic character. The earlier

examples in 1 Cor 15:3 and Rom 4:25 do not show any influence
of the Is 53 traditions such as one finds here. This section may
have been influenced by a developing eucharistic tradition.

66. Goppelt (ibid., 240–42) surveys the attempts to reconstruct a
single hymn behind this passage. He thinks that the elaborations
of the formulae in vv. 19–20a and 20b–21 occurred in the catechetical tradition.

67. Ibid., 246–55.

68. Similar interpretations of the cleansing rituals occur at Qumran
(1 QS 5.8–10; CD 15.8; 16.7; 1 QH 14.17). Goppelt, op. cit., 260.

69. Elliott, op. cit., 127.

70. Elliott, op. cit., 159, note 117. The passive verb in v. 22 implies
that God is the ultimate agent (cf. 2:23; entrusted himself to
God), as is also the case in 1 Cor 15:27f.; Eph 1:22; Heb 1:13; 2:5–
9.

71. Conzelmann (op. cit., 196–201) notes the various attempts to find
the presence of Christ in the eucharistic act. It is often asserted
that "remembrance" means a sacramental presence. To a Jewish
reader, it might suggest the Passover remembrance; to a pagan
reader, the memorial feasts on behalf of the dead. C. K. Barrett
(*The First Epistle to the Corinthians* [New York: Harper & Row,
1968], 266–67) points out that the eucharistic meal draws on
both of those traditions. It commemorates a divine act of salvation, and it does commemorate the death of an individual.

72. Barrett, op. cit., 270f. Conzelmann (op. cit., 201f.) thinks that the
eucharist belongs in a period defined as between resurrection
and parousia rather than passion and parousia. Paul, he argues,
does not consider the eucharist an anticipation of the messianic
banquet but a celebration that belongs to the period in which
Christ reigns as Lord.

73. Consequently, one should not read back into Paul the incorporation of resurrection into the eucharist that one finds in later
liturgies like the Church Order of Hippolytus, 4.11: *memores
igitur mortis et resurrectionis* (Barrett, op. cit., 271). The misunderstanding at Corinth does not depend on a presumption of
identification with the risen Lord present in the eucharist (pace
Conzelmann, op. cit., 198, note 52; 202).

74. R. A. Horsley, "How Can Some of You Say That There Is No
Resurrection of the Dead? Spiritual Elitism in Corinth," *NovT* 20
(1978), 226–29. Horsley suggests that Paul has focused on the
exalted Christ in order to replace the Corinthian fascination
with Wisdom.

75. Forestell (op. cit., 140–45) argues that chapter six should be taken

as a whole. Brown *(Community,* 51f.) points out that the Fourth Gospel locates traditional views alongside the reinterpretation of those traditions. Consequently, one cannot attribute all sacramentalism or final eschatology to the hand of a redactor.

76. J. T. Forestell *(The Word of the Cross: Salvation as Revelation in the Fourth Gospel* [Rome: Biblical Institute Press, 1974], 140–45) observes that John treats all sacraments from the perspective of Jesus as saving revelation (see 3:5 on baptism).

NINE

Resurrection and the Future of the Christian

Resurrection in paraenetic contexts often refers to a future in which the believer will share the life that Jesus now enjoys.[1] The importance of resurrection in early Christian ethical exhortation is often grounded in the double understanding of Jesus' exaltation as Lord. Jesus is now "at the right hand of God," separate from this world, and destined to be its judge. But the same Jesus who is "in heaven" is also available to the believer in the Spirit. Or, in the more striking metaphors of Colossians and Ephesians, the believer lives a life hidden in heaven with Christ.

W. Meeks's interpretation of the social function of cross and resurrection symbolism in the Pauline churches provides a way in which Christians might adopt the language of resurrection as a description of their present experience. Their own sense of disparity between the status attributed to them by the community and that earned through their achievement made a language of paradoxical humiliation and exaltation (2 Cor 4:14) a natural reading of experience. It may also have explained to the potential convert the real gain in taking what might otherwise appear to be a step down in converting to Christianity.[2]

Given the amorphous character of such speculation about the post-mortem fate of the individual in antiquity, one cannot presume that the Christian preaching about resurrection or future judgment answered existing questions. The resurrection of Jesus played an important role in solidifying the Christian use of eschatological language. A. T. Lincoln has pointed out that this commitment did not take the form of a concern with heaven as the future "residence" of the believer. Rather, it was shaped in the much broader context of understanding salvation to be centered on the Christ, who is exalted in heaven.[3] Paraenesis anchored the lordship of Christ in the present. The Spirit manifested in the resurrection of Christ is the same power of God that is to triumph in the future.[4]

The interaction between the lordship of the risen Christ expressed in paraenesis and the conviction that the future of the Christian is somehow with or like that of the Lord provides the experiential base for resurrection symbols. First-century Christians appear to have had less difficulty seeing that the exalted Lord could influence the lives of believers here and now than they did in drawing out the implications for the fate of the righteous from the symbols that expressed resurrection beliefs. Such implications had to be developed through the outward growth of the symbolic language of the Christian community.

R. Kieffer's survey of resurrection in Pauline thought comes to a similar conclusion. Resurrection speaks of two stages in the eschatological consummation of all things being brought about by God. First, the resurrection of Jesus; then that of the believer at the parousia (2 Cor 4:13f.; 1 Thess 4:14; 1 Cor 6:13). Between the two events, the Spirit, the power of the resurrection, is active. That activity manifests the exaltation of Christ, who is the firstborn or the image to which the Christian is to be conformed. This pattern makes it possible for resurrection language to provide an all-embracing context for the life of the Christian. But, Kieffer observes, Paul has not integrated all the dimensions of resurrection symbolism that he uses. His language about the day of judgment is traditional, rather naive imagery. Paul did not rethink the judgment metaphors to the same extent that he recast resurrection symbols.[5] This tendency to function at different levels of cognitive elaboration cannot be overlooked in dealing with the resurrection material in the New Testament. Not everything affirmed by a particular author is affirmed with the same degree of reflective consciousness. Paul clearly insists that the believer's resurrection is tied to that of Christ. His images of how that link is to be described show great variability.

RESURRECTION AND JUDGMENT

Paul is most dependent on traditional imagery when he is speaking about the future judgment. R. Tannehill suggests that he finds the modes by which the believer participates in the life of the risen Christ significantly more important than judgment. They are certainly better integrated into Paul's thought.[6] The simplest way of connecting the resurrection of Christ and that of the believer is to attribute both to the power of God. 2 Cor 4:14 contains a formulaic expression of that belief: "knowing that He who raised the Lord will bring us with you into His presence." This conviction is integrated into Paul's understanding of the weakness of the apostle. That apostolic weakness is the foundation of salvation for his converts: "so that life is at work in you" (4:12). Paul makes this affirmation out of his confidence that he possesses the same spirit of faith as the psalmist. The power of the resurrection is made manifest in the ministry of the weak and suffering apostle, who makes life possible for others.

The integration is provided by the larger context of Pauline language in which the formula is found. The phrase itself presupposes a rather simple pattern: God has raised and exalted Jesus into his presence; he will do the same for the believer. Rom 8:11 takes this pattern and transposes it so that the presence of the Spirit in the Christian now is linked to the future resurrection. This passage concludes the first section of a major reworking of apocalyptic themes in light of the presence of the Spirit. V. Furnish concludes that Paul is not concerned about resurrection as an event in "world history." His interest lies in resurrection as the manifestation of God's victory over the powers of death.[7]

Many exegetes would point to Rom 11:15 as an example of the Pauline appropriation of the event character of resurrection. Resurrection represents the culmination of God's promises of salvation. The conversion of Israel is the last event in the history of salvation.[8] However, this passage does not speak of the resurrection but of a parallel: conversion of the Gentiles and reconciliation of the world followed by conversion of the Jews and life from the dead. Both phrases are probably traditional. Reconciliation of the world is used in 2 Cor 5:19 to describe the result of apostolic labors in bringing the

Gentiles to God. Should life from the dead be given a similar interpretation? If so, it would not refer to the general resurrection or the
parousia but to the renewal of Israel.[9] Others argue that the passage
has no temporal implications at all. The metaphor "life from the
dead" simply describes the change in Israel. She passes from "hard-
ness of heart," her present rejection of God's messianic plan of salvation, to life. This interpretation insists that the parallel to the ministry
to the Gentiles as reconciliation of the world requires a nonparousia
reading of both passages.[10] Thus, even Rom 11:15 reflects Paul's
tendency to apply resurrection language to the present experiences
of the Christian. The power of the resurrection, which is presently
manifest in the mission to the Gentiles, will also be shown in the
divine conversion of Israel. The orientation of Paul's use of resurrection language toward the present experience of the Christian, coupled with the general tendency of religious language in this period to
be directed toward present experiences of divine salvation, may
explain the confusion about resurrection and the future of the Christians that appears in Thessalonika and Corinth. While the Corinthian
difficulties may have been generated by a competing vision of salvation, the example in 1 Thess 4:13ff. is formulated in terms of a rather
naive reading of apocalyptic metaphors.

1 Thessalonians 4:14 and 5:10

1 Thess 4:14 points to the resurrection of Christians who have died. It
will occur as with the coming of the Lord. As is generally the case,
God is the power responsible for that resurrection. At this point, Paul
is dependent on traditional material. He gives this hope its present
application in the paraenesis of 5:9–10. The Christian is not destined
for judgment. Rather, Jesus' death "for us" means that "whether we
wake or sleep we might live with him." These two verses define the
Christian "hope of salvation," which is the theme that Paul is addressing in 1 Thessalonians.[11]

Paul begins the exposition of the Christian hope of salvation with
the question about the fate of Christians who have died (vv. 13–14).
Verses 15–17 contain a saying of the Lord about the parousia. The
second half of the saying (vv. 16b–17) shows that the faithful will
participate in the parousia through resurrection, if they have died, or
through being "caught up with the Lord." Verse 18 applies the saying about the parousia as exhortation to the community.[12] Verse 14
uses a creedal affirmation of the two-membered type, "since we
believe that Jesus died and rose again." This summary is unusual in

that the name "Jesus" is used. However, 1 Thess 1:10 also has "Jesus."
Therefore, it is possible that both expressions reflect an early stage in
which death and resurrection were predicated of Jesus. The more
usual formulation would be to include some christological title along
with the affirmation of the resurrection such as the "his Son" in 1
Thess 1:10.[13]

Such formulas were certainly part of Paul's preaching in Thessalonika. The question about resurrection did not arise because the
Thessalonians had not heard about resurrection. Verse 13 begins with
the "we do not wish you to be ignorant" that is typical of passages
that Paul wishes to emphasize. Verse 13b reflects another characteristic of Pauline preaching of resurrection, the contrast between the
Christian and the life of the outsider, "those who have no hope." We
have seen a similar *topos* in 1 Cor 15:19: "if we have hope in this life
only." It appears to represent a *topos* in Pauline preaching.[14] The
conclusion to v. 14 draws the conclusion from this affirmation based
on the parallel between Christ and the believer (cf. Rom 6:4): "even
so, through Jesus, God will bring with him those who have fallen
asleep."[15] It appears to be based on a tradition of Christ's return at
the parousia. The implications of "with Christ" in Paul's own
paraenesis are directed toward the present, as is the case in 1 Thess
5:10. This Pauline sense of the present dependence of the believer on
the exalted Christ is also part of the formulation of the parousia
tradition in v. 17b: "and so we shall always be with the Lord."[16]
Scholars are divided in their analysis of the saying about the parousia.
Paul may have reformulated the saying. The saying itself may have
originated as a word of the exalted Lord spoken through a Christian
prophet.[17] Paul does not appear to have composed the logion. The
apocalyptic elements in vv. 16–17a are not typical of the apostle.
However, v. 15b could have been Paul's own expansion: "we who are
alive, who are left until the coming of the Lord shall not precede
those who have fallen asleep." It applies the saying to the situation
about which the Thessalonians appear to be concerned, the relationship between those who are alive and those who have died at the
parousia. The resurrection of the Christian dead will make it possible
for them to come with the Lord (v. 16b).

Attempts have been made to distinguish two stages in the formation of the material in vv. 16–17a. The original saying, it is suggested,
was concerned with the coming of the Son of Man. The inclusion of
resurrection in a saying about the coming Son of Man suggests further development in the understanding of Jesus' exaltation.[18] Paul
concentrates on the relationship between the living and deceased
Christians at the time of the parousia. His own formulation of the

relationship in v. 15b lacks the apocalyptic imagery of the traditional logion.[19] Scholars have often supposed that while Paul initially thought that he would be alive at the parousia, as in the "we" here, he changed his mind as he faced experiences of imprisonment and persecution (Phil 1:21–24; 2:17; 2 Cor 1:8f.; 5:8). Yet 1 Cor 15:51 again has Paul speak as though he were to be among the living. E. Best suggests that Paul felt either possibility to be an acceptable form of expression. 1 Thess 5:10, with its "whether we wake or sleep," expresses that sentiment.[20]

This apocalyptic logion envisages a great gathering of the righteous with the Lord. Resurrection is the mode in which the deceased are gathered to be with the Messiah. It recalls Jewish images of the gathering of the righteous. As a prophecy of the parousia, the saying is unfinished. We do not see what transpires. Do the Lord and the righteous ascend into heaven? Do they come to earth for a great gathering of the nations in judgment? Paul's own sayings about the parousia as the culmination of the subjection of all things to Christ and through him to God suggests that there must be more to the story. 1 Thess 1:10 presumes a scene of judgment at the parousia.

Paul's addition in v. 17b suggests that he has reminded the Thessalonians of enough to make his point. He presumes that they know what he means when he speaks of "being with the Lord." Best thinks that the expression originally had apocalyptic overtones. It would have referred to the life of the righteous with the Messiah after the resurrection (as in 1 En. 62.1f.; 71.16). This expression has been further developed in Lk 23:43; Mt 28:20; Jn 17:24; and Rev 3:4, 20f.[21] Paul uses a number of expressions for suffering, dying, rising, and living with Christ (Rom 6:3–11; Gal 2:19; Rom 8:17). These expressions all move from the future possibility of the life of the righteous with the Lord to the present experience of living with Christ. This development is grounded in Paul's understanding of conversion or baptism as the beginning of that eschatological life with Christ that is perfected at the parousia.[22] 1 Thess 5:10 instructs the living that they have died with Christ in order to live with him. That relationship makes it immaterial whether they are alive or dead at the parousia. But this relativizing of the difference between the living and the dead Christians does not make the present life with Christ a simple reflection of the future. The distinction is preserved by Paul's insistence that Christian salvation is grounded in participation in the death of Christ. Thus, resurrection as the future of the Christian is the occasion for instructing the living. They must not mourn like "those who have no hope." Whether alive or dead, they "live with the Lord."

1 CORINTHIANS 15:35–58

Paul drew upon a number of traditions and common arguments in the first half of 1 Cor 15. Two rhetorical questions introduce the shift from that traditional material to a sustained presentation of resurrection and the future of the Christian. "How are the dead raised? What sort of body do they come in?" (v. 35). Though these questions do not have the form of the slogans of his Corinthian opponents elsewhere in the letter, they may reflect the type of objection raised by those who denied the resurrection. 1 Cor 6:13 shows that Paul presumes that the body is involved in resurrection. That conviction was very likely strengthened for Christians by the conviction that the risen Lord was the crucified. However, in order to defend that claim, Paul must move beyond the metaphorical use of bodily language for living humans to speak of the righteous in terms appropriate to embodied persons. The objections that Paul formulates during the argument show that he is aware of the problem. The question is whether or not he is able to formulate a coherent argument for his conviction. N. Frye sees this argument as an example of the commitment to the older mode of metaphoric discourse over the abstract, rational formulations of the philosophic traditions. The metaphoric code saw the psyche as a bundle of conflicting forces. In describing the bodily character of resurrection, Paul has identified "spirit" with body to present the image of "spiritual body" entering resurrection (1 Cor 15:44). Paul is not concerned about distinctions between spirit and body. He is interested in the distinction between spirit and soul, as 1 Cor 2:14 indicates.[23]

This spirit/soul division may be detected throughout the argument in this section. Paul presumes from the outset that the human, earthly body is a psychic one. It belongs to the realm of human life. What is gained in resurrection, then, is "spiritual body."[24] The Corinthian objections appear to be aimed at the distinction between spiritual and material reality. Paul appears to begin to answer out of a commitment to the metaphoric structure of apocalyptic, even though he often modifies apocalyptic images, as he has done in describing the role of the Spirit and the present sufferings of the righteous in Rom 8:18–25.[25] The Corinthians may well have interpreted the resurrection of Jesus in such a way that it had nothing to do with the fate of the body or of creation as a whole. Paul's own preaching, as we have seen, makes the Spirit, the power of the resurrection, directly present to Christian life. But Paul thinks in bodily images. When he speaks of the Lord's "body of glory" in Phil 3:21, he ties the image of the crucified and exalted together by using transformed body as the description for resurrection. The only other reference to "spiritual body" in Paul occurs in 1 Cor 15:44. 1 Cor 15:45 immediately turns to a picture of the risen Christ as "life-giving Spirit" and thus quite dispenses with the language of body. Paul frequently presupposes that one thinks of "spiritual body" as the reality of resurrection. Thus, one may even wonder if he is able to consider seriously an alternate reading of human reality in terms of mind or soul as the central reality of the person.

Background and Terminology of the Argument

The major difficulty in interpreting the argument in 1 Cor 15:35–50 lies in reconstructing the position that gave rise to the Corinthian denial of resurrection. Unlike 1 Thess 4:13ff., which was concerned only with the fate of those who had died prior to the parousia, this argument addresses the issue of resurrection as the fate of all Christians. Verses 51–58 make the transition, which is not explicit in 1 Thessalonians, to the understanding that the resurrection transformation will apply to those who are living at the parousia as well as to those who have died.

Paul presents the argument in this section as an argument about bodies. He does not set the terms of the argument as resurrection over against immortality of the soul or bodily transformation over against an ascent of the soul out of the bodily, material world into the divine one. Yet such presuppositions represent the most coherent alternatives to the Pauline language of salvation that were available to the Corinthians. Since Paul does not provide any clue that the opponents were using such commonplaces, some exegetes presume that there was no coherent doctrine of the soul or salvation behind the Corinthian position. The Corinthians were simply unable to draw any connection between the resurrection of Christ and the future of the believer.[26]

Many of the slogans in 1 Corinthians have parallels in popular Cynic/Stoic preaching. Paul uses such *topoi* in 1 Cor 15:12–19, 32–34. They appear to have originated in anti-Epicurean polemic and have been part of Paul's own way of preaching.[27] Some interpreters presume that misappropriation of popular philosophical concepts by the Corinthians is responsible for the problems at Corinth, including the denial of the resurrection.[28] Given the "indifference" toward the body at Corinth, one must presume that denial of the resurrection is dependent on devaluation of the material world over against the spiritual one.[29] Aiding the development of such views among the Corinthians, we find the experiences of endowment with the Spirit of God. Paul's innovation lies in supposing that body can be used with the description "spiritual" to point to some reality quite different from the earthly, material body of our daily experience. One need not presume much philosophical sophistication among the Corinthians to suggest that they would presume that something of the new, spiritual self did survive death. The question of how well Paul understood the Corinthian views still remains. Many interpreters presume that he was unable to think of salvation in the terms that the Corinthians used to frame the question. The convictions that he derived from seeing resurrection as the final state of the righteous in the renewed creation make it inconceivable that the survival of some immortal part of the person could properly reflect the final destiny of the believer.[30]

Scholars have found additional parallels to the line of argument pursued in 1 Cor 15, especially in the treatment of Adam, in Philo.[31] B. Pearson's study about the language of the spiritual and psychic in 1 Corinthians suggests that there must be a background of Philonic tradition to the controversy, since the type of distinctions presupposed are only found in this letter in the Pauline corpus. Paul would not have taken over such an uncharacteristic set of anthropological categories if he had not had reason to do so on the basis of the situation to which he was addressing himself. "Psychic" *(psychikos)* is limited to 1 Cor (2:14; 15:44, 46). "Earthly" *(choikos)* only occurs in 1 Cor 15:47–49 in the entire New Testament. "Fleshly" *(sarkikos)* only occurs as an anthropological category in 1 Corinthians, although its cognate *sarkinos* does appear in Rom 7:14. Finally, "spiritual persons" *(pneumatikoi)* only occurs coordinated with other anthropological categories here. Paul can use the term *pneumatikoi* in paraenesis (see Gal 5:16–6:10). But the anthropological context is lacking there. Consequently, the combination of categories is probably derived from the specific polemic at Corinth.[32] The philosophic grounding for such anthropological categories has nothing to do with the physical body in itself. The question concerns the destructive function of the passions in the soul over against the control of the divine part of the human person, the mind. Some persons may be said to be so dominated by the passions that they are bereft of mind altogether (see Plutarch, *Daim. Soc.* 591D–F.).

This dualism between what is subject to the passions and what is

subject to reason or divine control appears to be the one that concerned the Corinthians. The lowest category, the "fleshly," only appears in 1 Cor 3:1. It has been introduced by Paul in order to attack
the behavior of the Corinthians, who think that they are spiritual.[33]
The distinction being used by the Corinthians, along with its correlate claim to divine wisdom, is clearly evident in the psychic/spiritual
distinctions that Paul reformulates in 2:14–15. Paul argues that if the
Corinthians cannot understand the wisdom of the cross, they prove
themselves to be psychic and not spiritual persons.[34] Combination of
such hellenistic anthropological categories and Christian preaching
about the presence of the Spirit in the life of the believer was made
easier by the use of these categories in the Jewish interpretation of
Gen 2:7. "Mind" is consistently replaced with the "spirit" of the
Genesis story as the highest category in the human spirit. Further,
the *psychē/pneuma* combination is unique to Jewish and Christian
writers. Therefore, the Corinthians would appear to have appropriated a form of hellenistic philosophy that had been mediated through
Jewish exegesis of Genesis.[35]

This background in Genesis exegesis is further indicated by the
importance given to Adam in the argument. Philo provides an elaborate exegesis of Genesis in which he defends the view that the material body is naturally corruptible. That natural body is not what is
subject to the divine punishment of death. The divine punishment is
applied to the soul when it does not strip off the passions and acquire
true virtue and union with divine wisdom. Philo's exposition makes it
clear that immortality is predicated of the mind because the mind is
the divine image. No one, he insists, should think that the image
referred to in Gen 1:26f. has anything to do with "bodily form."
There is nothing godlike about the human body (Philo, Opif. 69–71).
The earthly and perishable mind requires commandments and exhortation. The imperishable mind is in the image of God, the heavenly Adam. Paul appeals to Gen 2:7. Like Philo, he will distinguish
two types of human. Paul does more than reverse Philonic patterns
of argument. He insists that priority is to be rooted in the order of
salvation, not is cosmology. Consequently, Paul speaks of "first" and
"second" Adam. Such terminology is of no concern to Philo, who
establishes priority in the ontological order. The ontological order
reflects the superiority of the heavenly mind over the earthly, body-
loving one. For Philo, the heavenly mind is what partakes in the
divine Spirit.

With this background in mind, we may turn to Paul's argument in
the second half of 1 Cor 15. It falls into three parts: (a) the seed
analogy, with its reflection on the glory appropriate to different types

of flesh (vv. 36–41); (b) application to the resurrection of the Christian through the use of Adam exegesis (vv. 42–50); (c) the revelation of the apocalyptic mystery of the culmination of all things (vv. 51–58).

1 Corinthians 15:35–41

The first section uses a nature analogy to argue for the possibility of transformed body. Paul begins with a question about body *(sōma)* and then switches to talking about different types of flesh *(sarx)*. He appears to use the two words interchangeably, since v. 40 again returns to distinctions of body. That shift also enables Paul to speak of the distinctions between the various heavenly bodies, which could not be spoken of as "flesh."[36]

By speaking of heavenly bodies, Paul is able to introduce the concept of glory. It is first introduced as a cosmological category, but in v. 42 it will be applied to the resurrected body. The pattern behind this section is cosmological. Philo's account of creation (Opif. 65–71) contains an elaborate treatment of differences on animal life based on the differences in perception possessed by the soul *(psychē)* of each time. In fish, bodily substance *(ousia somatika)* predominates over psychic substance. Consequently, fish are to be considered both living beings and nonliving beings, as they only have enough *psychē* to maintain their bodies. Birds and land animals have more perception. They manifest more of the properties of ensouled being. Finally, humans go beyond even the category of soul. They possess mind, a sort of "soul of the soul." Philo thinks that the human embryo passes through all of the earlier stages of being. However, some divine act of creation bestows the mind on the human. Thus, there is a radical discontinuity between the structure of body and soul that humans possess in the most exalted degree in the animal kingdom and the "divine image," the mind.

Paul agrees that there is a radical discontinuity. But his argument retains a distinctive eschatological cast that is not met with in the cosmological sources for his discussion. Verse 38 makes it clear that the power by which the transformation from one type of body to the next takes place is a new act of the creative power of God.[37]

Paul grounds the possibility of transformation in the differences between created entities. He locates in the flesh or body distinctions that the more technical account of Philo would locate in the degree of perception or the *psychē.* The image of the glory of the heavenly beings could well be derived from apocalyptic (cf. Dan 12:1–3). Apocalyptic images of the glory of the stars were not without their cosmological side. They picture the righteous as exalted like the stars. Of course, in Philo's cosmology the stars are created of eternal, immutable matter and are quite above the realm of change. A similar immutability is implied in the apocalyptic visions of astral immortality. That vision contrasts with other apocalyptic images of the stars' being cast from the sky at the parousia. Pearson thinks that Paul's opponents would probably have spoken of *psychē* and *pneuma*. Paul, who cannot think of expressing the fate of the individual person except in terms of *sōma*, has shifted to the categories of flesh and body.[38] Thus, the opening question "What kind of *sōma*?" means something different to Paul and to his opponents. For them, "what kind of *sōma*" would be answered with "no kind of *sōma*." It is mere folly to think that *sōma* has anything to do with divine reality. For Paul, the question represents the folly of presuming that the glorious *sōma* of the resurrection has anything to do with the perishable, limited, and corruptible body of our present experience. God has shown the ability to give to each type of being the appropriate *sōma*. God will do no less in the resurrection.

1 Corinthians 15:42–50

Comparison of this discussion of Christ and Adam with Rom 5 quickly reveals that Paul is operating on foreign territory here. Romans uses the familiar terms of salvation history: trespass and death came through the first Adam; the free gift, the grace of God and life, came through the other. We have also seen that this "life" that became available in Christ was more than forgiveness of sin. It is the life that the Christian lives and that will be perfected in the resurrection. That eschatological understanding of Christ as the antitype of Adam never requires that Christ be spoken of as Adam. It is the risen Christ who became the life-giving spirit, as in 1 Cor 15:22.[39]

Verses 42–44a set up a pattern of antitheses that provides the transition from the argument about the types of body in the created order to the transformation of the human body in the resurrection. The human body is the only one that attains its glory through resurrection. The opening, "thus also the resurrection of the dead," looks back to the denial of the resurrection in v. 12b. Paul is picking up that argument as well as concluding the argument that had begun with the question How? when he presents the pairs that apply to the resurrected human body: sown in corruption/raised in incorruption; sown in dishonor/raised in glory; sown in weakness/raised in power; sown a psychic body/raised a spiritual body.

The first and last pairs reflect the anthropological vocabulary of the Corinthians. The middle two appear to be Paul's own formulation. He has shifted from glory as the brightness of heavenly bodies to glory as equivalent to honor. The third antithesis, weakness and power, is typically Pauline.[40] Verse 44b introduces a thesis that would be somewhat surprising to anyone familiar with the hellenistic Jewish exegesis of Philo. Within that context, Paul's expression "spiritual body" is a contradiction in terms. Verse 45 continues the argument with a glossed citation of Gen 2:7 also aimed at establishing the difference between Paul's position and that of his opponents. The Septuagint of Gen 2:7 has "God formed earthly *(choun)* man from the earth; and breathed into his face a breath of life and the man became a living soul *(psychē zōsan)."* Philo presumes that the earthly man of Gen 2:7 has only *psychē.* Spirit belongs to the heavenly Adam of Gen 1:26f. Paul writes, "It is written, the first man Adam became a living soul *(psychē zōsan),"* and then adds, "the last Adam a life-giving Spirit."

Pearson thinks that the "last Adam" must come from the apocalyptic treatment of Adam. Gen 2:7 is rarely quoted in Jewish materials. In 1 QH 11.20f., it is the first part of a verse that emphasizes the earthly origins of humanity. Paul has created an eschatological targum on Gen 2:7. He has introduced the first/last distinction and reversed the two clauses. As a result, prior to the eschaton, the only Adam in whom the Christian participates is the first or earthly Adam. This reversal makes the comparison fall into line with the antitype form of the comparison in Rom 5.[41]

Verses 46–47 underline the reversal that has been carried out in the citation: the first and not the second man is the man of earth. The second and not the first man is the heavenly one. In addition, Paul makes it clear that the heavenly Adam does not represent any part of humans as they are now.[42] Jewish apocalyptic sources speak of Adam being restored to the glory that he had before the fall (Apoc. Mos. 37.5; Life of Adam and Eve 25.3). They refer to an image of Adam kept in heaven until the last days (2 Bar. 4.2–6; 4 Ez 8:52). The Essenes spoke of the "glory of Adam" being promised to the sons of light (1 QS 4.23; CD 3.20; 1 QH 17.15). "Earthly" *(choikos)* in v. 47 refers to earthly *(choun)* in Gen 2:7.

R. A. Horsley points out that v. 48 could easily be a slogan of Paul's opponents. They would have held that there were two types of people: those who take after the second (in Genesis' order) Adam, who was shaped out of earth and was psychic, and those who take after the heavenly, spiritual Adam.[43] Verse 49 then applies the final modification to the tradition of the two Adams: we now bear the image of the earthly one; we shall bear the image of the heavenly. Thus, the divine image of Gen 1:27 is irrevocably tied to the risen Christ. Phil 3:21 reflects a similar view: "the Lord will change our lowly body to the form of his glorious body through the power which enables him to subject all things to himself."

Verse 50 serves to move from the Adam argument to the apocalyptic conclusion that the pattern of Paul's thought leads us to expect. The antithesis of corruptible and incorruptible, which lies behind Philo's insistence that body has nothing at all to do with a divine image, remains to be described. The second half of v. 50 could well be another of the Corinthian slogans: the corruptible will not inherit incorruptibility. Paul has introduced it with the comment "flesh and blood will not inherit the kingdom of God." This slogan hardly seems to have been formulated as part of this debate. "Flesh and blood" is a Semitic expression for human being (as in Gal 1:16). It oftens appears in contexts that stress creatureliness and mortality. Paul used the expression "inherit the kingdom of God" in 1 Cor 6:9f. as part of a catalog of vices that he is applying to the injustice of Corinthians who take each other to court. The connection made between "inherit the kingdom of God" and the traditional vice list in 6:9-10 suggests that the phrase belonged to early Christian paraenesis. 1 Cor 6:11 contrasts the state of the Corinthians prior to their conversion, when they were the type of people described by the vice catalog, with their position as persons who now possess the Spirit of God. Thus, the first half of the verse appears to be a traditional paraenetic formula. The combination of the two clauses would still appear to require explanation, since it introduces precisely the type of duality that Paul would seem to resist: that the corruptible (body) and the incorruptible (spirit) have nothing in common. For Paul, the radical difference lies in the gift of salvation. Spirit is not an anthropological category but a gift of God.[44]

1 Corinthians 15:51-58

Paul shifts to a new mode of discourse when he comes to explain the antithesis of the previous verse. He is now speaking with the wisdom of the eschatological prophet, the one who knows the mysteries of the end time. His readers are allowed to participate in the eschatological mystery, which he reveals to them.[45] We also find out what happens to the living at the parousia. They are not only snatched up as in 1 Thessalonians, but they are "changed." Resurrection is an image applied to the righteous dead who proved to be incorruptible.

Paul speaks of the living as changed in the twinkling of an eye. 2 Bar. 50.2 contains a similar tradition. But 2 Bar. is concerned about a quite different issue: how to make sure that the dead are recognizable by the living. It is preliminary to the judgment and the subsequent transformation of the righteous into angelic glory (2 Bar. 51.1–6). Paul's mystery would appear to represent an apocalyptic tradition of this type: at the parousia, the dead are raised, and all the righteous are transformed into angelic glory.

For Paul, the glory that the righteous attain at the resurrection is not simply that of the angels or of the stars. It is the glory of the risen Christ, as is evident in Phil 3:21 and Col 3:4. A variant of that tradition appears in 1 Jn 3:2: "and it has not yet been revealed what we shall be, but we know that if he is revealed, we shall be like him for we shall see him as he is." R. Brown thinks that this tradition is grounded in transformation into God's image through a vision of the divine rather than transformation into the image of the risen Christ.[46] If one reads it in terms of the hellenistic "like by like," then it would come closer to the position of Paul's opponents. Paul rejects such an understanding of the transformation of the Christian by insisting that it refers to the image of the risen Christ, which the believer will receive at the end of all things. Verse 53 brings the argument back to the question of how what is perishable might inherit the kingdom and to the seed images of v. 42. Paul uses the language of "putting on" to guarantee the continuity between the believer and this future existence.[47] Horsley thinks that the language of "putting on" may represent one final correction of the opponents. The ideal in the Philonic pattern was to strip the divine essence of the person naked by leaving behind the body, the passions, and everything that belonged to the corruptible world (Gig. 53ff.; Ebr. 99–101; Fug. 58ff.).[48] Paul completes his argument by demonstrating the necessity of such transformation on the basis of Scripture with a combination of two prophetic passages about the divine victory over death, Is 25:8 and Hos 13:14.[49]

Thus, the establishment of incorruptibility is seen in apocalyptic categories as the divine conquest of death. It is not grounded in an anthropology that calls for the separation of the immortal from the mortal and from the material world. Paul then breaks into the argument at v. 56 with a set of associations that are more characteristic of his own thought: the relationship between death, sin, and the Law. Death has its hold over human beings through the operation of sin, which thus perverts the Law. These themes will reappear in Rom 5 and 7. Yet they are so unusual in 1 Corinthians that some exegetes consider the verse a gloss. However, the continuation in v. 57 follows the pattern set in Rom 7, where a lengthy meditation on the perversion of the Law through sin and death leads to the thanksgiving for the power of God in Christ that has ended their dominion.[50]

Verse 58 concludes the section with a stock piece of paraenesis. Knowing that the perseverance of the community in the work of the Lord will not be in vain recalls the opening of the argument in v. 14. Paul had argued there that without the truth of resurrection all his apostolic labor and the faith won by it would be in vain. Even this final injunction may represent one final transformation of the Corinthian categories into an apocalyptic perspective. H. Conzelmann notes that "increasing in the work of the Lord" has taken a common *topos* of ethical preaching (cf. 2 Cor 9:8; 16:10) in a nonphilosophic sense.[51] The passage contains another term, immovable *(ametakinētos)*, which only occurs here in the New Testament. The terminology of "immovability" reflects a spirituality influenced by popular Platonism. The soul of the wise person has retreated from the changeable realm of the senses to the domain of stability, union with the divine. This vision of stability of the soul united with the divine may have been part of the Corinthian sloganizing.[52] Such a view could only seek freedom from the body, not the return of the body in any form. Paul has gone out of his way to show that one only enters the realm of the immortal and incorruptible through resurrection. Then one participates in the final victory over death won by God's power in the risen Lord. Paul now hints that immovability must be obtained through perseverance in the Christian life. Once again, we are back to the Christian life as the place in which the power of the resurrection is made manifest.

2 CORINTHIANS 5:1–10

This passage of 2 Corinthians provides one further attempt by Paul to express the relationship between resurrection and the body. Some exegetes see it as Paul's capitulation to the type of language used by his opponents.

This section is part of a meditation on the ministry of the apostle. Verses 4:17–18 appear to have reformulated an objection that the body is a weight that holds the person back from the ecstasy of divine vision.

Paul follows a pattern similar to his treatment of the Spirit and the present afflictions of the righteous in Rom 8. The "weight" is the eternal glory, the eternal and unseen reality, that is being prepared in the present afflictions of the apostle.

2 Cor 5:1–10 continues this meditation on the body. Paul agrees that in the present we are separated from God. But he persists in reminding his readers that it does not matter whether one is with or away from the Lord. What counts is living so as to please him. Paul also continues to create images that emphasize the coming transformation of the body as "putting on" rather than as taking off or becoming naked. He would not appear to have shifted his view from that in 1 Corinthians. Instead of speaking of stripping off the bodily tent or garment in order to enter the heavenly dwelling, Paul speaks of the heavenly dwelling as one that is given by God. Paul admits that the corruptible earthly dwelling is destroyed or swallowed up in the process. But his awkward concern with putting on rather than being unclothed can only be seen as a direct rejection of the alternative view of the soul's entry into heaven by shedding the body.

The passage comes to a sudden apocalyptic conclusion. Each person is to be judged according to what the person has done in the body. This apocalyptic conclusion suggests that Paul is still talking about a transformation that is to take place at the judgment. He has not shifted into the image of a postmortem transformation or putting on immortality. The Spirit works through the sufferings of the apostle. In Paul's view, the apostle, like all other Christians, must then await the culmination of all things. Apostolic suffering is the beginning of the future "weight of glory" and the true mark of the apostle.[53]

RESURRECTION AND ETERNAL LIFE

The language of eternal life occurs as frequently as that about resurrection in the Jewish writings of this period. It does not of itself imply any speculation about an immortal soul, since a text may speak of "life" simply as the reward of the righteous. Texts that speak of resurrection can also speak of life with Christ or with God as images of future expectation. Such language may occur in an apocalyptic scenario with such life as the reward for judgment. Or one may find the language of eternal life used as a transformation of resurrection language out of its apocalyptic context. The first option appears in Revelation, which emphasizes the contrast between death and heavenly life. The second is fundamental to the eschatological perspective of the Fourth Gospel.

Revelation 20:11-15

The life and death polarity that runs through Revelation culminates in this brief vision of judgment (20:11–15), which precedes the description of the new heaven and earth. The eschatology of Rev 20 is complicated by the vision of the "first resurrection" in which those who had been martyred for their refusal to worship the beast share a thousand-year reign with Christ (20:4–6). Their coming to life and reigning with the Messiah represents one of the oldest uses of resurrection imagery in Judaism, the resurrection as vindication of the martyr.[54] Revelation has combined that image with another form of eschatology: the dead are all brought to life for a great judgment. They do not come to life until after the thousand-year reign. Hence, the resurrection of the martyrs bears the unusual label "first resurrection." The condemnation of the wicked at the final judgment is said to represent the real death, "the second death" (vv. 6 and 14), not the death of the martyr. The judgment scene is rather sparse, especially in contrast to the expanded description of the divine plagues and catastrophes to be visited on the world that makes up the body of the work. R. Kraft observes that in speaking of the dead coming to judgment, Revelation does not speak of resurrection, even though the reference to "first resurrection" in vv. 5b and 6 certainly leads the reader to presume that this one is the second. Instead, the author has piled up images of death. The word occurs four times in two verses (vv. 12–13). The books of judgment (life) appear in Dan 7:10. They are opened before God, enthroned in the heavenly court. Unlike 2 Bar. 50, the author of Revelation shows no concern for the bodily character of those brought to life for judgment. All that is at stake is the everlasting death that they will now suffer. That death stands in contrast to the life of the faithful in the new Jerusalem with God and the Lamb. Thus, resurrection itself plays a minor role in the visions of Revelation. It belongs to the traditional language of the vindication of the martyr and is introduced in that context. Otherwise, the contrast between death and life rules the apocalypse. The future of the faithful is eternal life in the glorious presence of God and the Lamb.

Eternal Life in the Fourth Gospel

John presents the power of the risen Lord as present in Jesus, the Son of God. Apocalyptic language about judgment and the return of Jesus has been reinterpreted in light of this overriding sense of Jesus as divine presence. This transformation leads E. Becker to ask whether or not such an eschatology can be adequately combined with the cross. Does it not bypass the questions of historical and cosmological salvation raised by the apocalyptic visions of human destiny in a created order under the rule of God?[55]

John knows the traditions about resurrection as the future of the believer. However, eternal life is the gospel's central metaphor for salvation. Both resurrection and the cross belong to a pattern of salvation as revelation that runs throughout the gospel. Those who hear and receive Jesus' Word possess eternal life. J. T. Forestell compares this pattern to salvation in the wisdom traditions. He notes that even John's baptismal language about "birth from above" can be paralleled in the wisdom tradition (Jn 3:3–8; Wis 9:16–18).[56]

Just as we saw in Paul's reformulation of the Corinthian perspective, John does not suppose that life is an inherent property of the human mind or spirit. The divine Word is described as "life of the world" in Jn 1:4. However, the gospel makes it clear that this life is not seen as a cosmological endowment of the human species with an immortal soul. Rather, life has the character of a divine quality that is possessed by God and Jesus (5:26; 6:57; 11:25; 14:6). That life is the salvation communicated to the believer by Jesus. In the apocalyptic scenario of Revelation, "eternal life" is presented as following upon cosmic judgment. The Fourth Gospel, on the other hand, presents the cosmic judgment of the world as present in Jesus (e.g., 3:19–21; 9:39; 12:31). At the same time, the evangelist preserves the tradition of future judgment alongside his realized eschatology (e.g., 7:33f.; 14:1–3; 17:24).

John 5:19–30

Jn 5 contains an extensive reformulation of judgment language. This reformulation centers on Jesus by attributing the life-giving and judging powers of God to the Son. Jn 5:21 interprets resurrection as giving life.

This affirmation appears to reapply the type of resurrection tradition in which the life-giving power of God that has been manifest in

Jesus is to be used on behalf of the believer. The Son is the One to whom the Father has given this power. This passage was prefaced with the assertion that the Father will show the Son "greater works than these . . . that you may marvel." This promise is double-edged. On the one hand, "marvel" indicates the reaction of an unbelieving crowd (Jn 7:21, which refers to this passage). The expression may refer to the further condemnation that will be attached to the two remaining miracles in the gospel: the healing of the blind man and the raising of Lazarus. The first miracle shows that Jesus' presence separates those who can see (= the believers) from those who cannot. The second demonstrates Jesus' life-giving power but is also the precipitating cause of Jesus' death. On the other hand, within this passage, "greater works" does not refer to the miracles of Jesus but to his giving life and judging.

"Giving life" has priority over judgment in Johannine language. Jn 3:16–19 insists that the sending of the Son was not for the purpose of judgment but so that the believer might have eternal life (3:14–15). Judgment is the consequence of disbelief. Similarly, Jn 12:46–47 argues that the light came so that the believer would not remain in darkness. It came to save and not to condemn.[57] Since judgment is the consequence of disbelief, John can also speak of the believer as one who has passed from death to life; as one who does not come into judgment but has eternal life (v. 24). Jn 5:25 proclaims that the hour has now arrived when the dead will hear the voice of the Son of God and live. This formulation recalls apocalyptic images of the dead rising at the trumpet call of the last day. The eschatological awakening of the dead was a standard element in early Christian catechesis (1 Thess 4:13–18; Heb 6:2; Apoc 17:18, 32). Verse 26 makes it clear that John is attaching this saying to his understanding of the life-giving power of Jesus.[58]

This understanding of Jesus' life-giving power is clearly linked to Jesus' equality with the Father (v. 18). Jn 5:27–29 presents a separate fragment of the type of apocalyptic judgment tradition that the evangelist appears to have used as the basis for these sayings.[59]

The realization of these hopes is symbolically represented in the Johannine story of Lazarus. He is called forth into life by the life-giving power of Jesus (5:25; 11:24, 43). The one who believes in Jesus, even though he dies, will never die (11:25f.). The bread of life discourse (Jn 6:39f.) and the eucharistic sayings (Jn 6:54, 57f.) also associate the promise of eternal life with Jesus (see also 3:15; 6:53; 14:19; 20:31). The gospel is pervaded by the belief that eternal life is gained through belief in Jesus.

John 14:1–7

John uses this perspective of the presence of eternal life in Jesus to reinterpret the apocalyptic traditions that he has inherited. This section takes on a tradition about the "mansions" in the Father's house. The seer sees such mansions in 1 En. 39.4f.; 41.2; IV Ez 7:80, 100.[60] Schnackenburg suggests that this tradition was originally close to that in 1 Thess 4:16ff.:

(a) *he will come down from heaven*   *I am coming again*
(b) *we will be snatched up . . .*   *I will take you*
(c) *we will always be with the*   *where I am you will be*
     Lord

However, John sets this promise in a discourse that finds Jesus' return in the indwelling of the Father and Son with the community and not in the parousia.[61]

John 17:1–5

Jn 17:1–5 provides a final example of this Johannine transformation of traditional language. The hour of Jesus' glorification is proclaimed as present. Verses 4 and 11 show Jesus speaking from the vantage point of one who is no longer in this world. Jesus' return to glory means life for those who believe (v. 2). The gift of power over "all flesh" appears to be part of the exaltation tradition (e.g., Dan 7:14; Mt 28:18). The power of the exalted or glorified Jesus to give life to the righteous reflects the early kerygma, which associated such life with the exaltation of the Lord in power.[62] Jesus' gift of eternal life is the final manifestation of his unity with the Father. Thus, it represents the completion of the work that he was sent to accomplish (v. 4). The explanatory gloss in v. 3 expands on this life-giving activity.[63] Verse 3b belongs to the language of early Christian preaching to the Gentiles: "that they know you, the one, true God and Jesus Christ whom you have sent." Knowledge of the one true God and of Jesus Christ appears in the early formula of 1 Thess 1:9f. The background to the Johannine expression probably referred to the awaiting the return of the exalted Son at the parousia. John sees that "sending" to be the Father's sending of Jesus into the world.[64] The Jewish Wisdom tradition connects knowledge of God with eternal life. Thus, the explanatory gloss has translated the missionary language of the Johannine tradition into the perspectives of Johannine Christology and eschatology. Eternal life consists in knowing that Jesus is the one sent by the Father. This knowledge is no longer attached to the expectation that Jesus is to be sent from heaven as judge. It acknowledges the divine name that Jesus bears and is manifest in his exaltation on the cross (vv. 6–8, 11–12; cf. Jn 8:24–29). For John, the crucifixion is the moment of Jesus' exaltation.

The theme of Jesus' reception of the divine name (vv. 11–12) also represents a theme from the earlier traditions of exaltation. Phil 2:6–11 presented the crucified as the one exalted over the cosmos. In this exaltation, he receives the divine name *Kyrios*. John sees the Son as making the divine name known to the disciples (v. 6) as part of his earthly message. Thus, we have another example of John's taking a postresurrection tradition into the presentation of the life of Jesus.[65] However, the gospel acknowledges that the believer remains "in the world." There remains a future dimension to this knowledge of God as possession of eternal life. The use of the more traditional images of future eschatology are one way in which the Fourth Gospel presents that dimension. The conclusion to Jn 17 also speaks of a future in which those who belong to Jesus will see the glory that he has had since before the foundation of the world (v. 24). The surrounding verses describe the ways in which Jesus has made the Father known: they know that Jesus is from the Father; they know the divine name; they know—that is, have in them—the love shared by the Father and the Son (vv. 25–26). Thus, this vision of Jesus' eternal glory is the culmination of the knowledge that the disciples have already received. Forestell suggests that had one asked what this passage meant to a Johannine Christian's understanding of the future, one would have been told that the death of the believer (who does not pass through judgment) would be like that of Jesus. It would be a passage to the Father.[66]

The realized eschatology of the Johannine tradition, with its insistence on the presence of divine life-giving power in Jesus, could hardly come to any other conclusion. The divine life that has been shared with believers cannot be "turned off" by physical death (e.g., 11:25f.). Though the Johannine resurrection narrative does present a physical image of the bodily return of the crucified, the translation of resurrection language into the language of eternal life in the gospel does not present us with a clear picture of the relationship of the body to that future. Certainly the Lazarus story and the tradition of the dead emerging from the tombs would suggest some vaguely bodily image of the individual who enters this eternal life. The pattern of reinterpretation that we find in the gospel does not presuppose any philosophical anthropology. There is no suggestion of an immortal soul over against a mortal body—though such an image could later be easily read out of the statements in the gospel. But as far as the Fourth Gospel is concerned, the Son is exercising the life-giving power of God.

The apocalyptic images and traditions that have been incorporated into the gospel suggest that some bodily images might have been associated with the Johannine belief in resurrection. Apocalyptic traditions continued to play an important role in the religious language of the Johannine communities, as the Johannine epistles show. They are preoccupied with the fate of the believers in the judgment.[67] The perfectionism of the author's opponents may have taken the realized eschatology of the gospel and transformed it into a doctrine of an assured salvation.[68] But even as the author recovers older traditions of judgment, resurrection does not emerge as the primary language of salvation. The promise to the believer in 1 Jn 2:23–25 is much as we find it in the gospel. Belief in the Son and keeping his word shows that the Christian abides in the Father and Son. The promise that follows is the promise of eternal life. 1 Jn 3:2, as we have seen, promised transformation into the divine image. Thus, both traditions of judgment, of future transformation and of salvation as eternal life for those who believe in Jesus, continued to be taught in the Johannine communities.

We should not jump to the conclusion that the Johannine tradition associated eternal life with a doctrine of an immortal soul. The Gnostic interpreters of the Johannine traditions in the second century would find that transition an easy one to make. But the Johannine teachers do not see immortality or eternal life as a topic of anthropological speculation. They understand it to be a reality grounded in the salvation that comes with the sending of the Son. Jesus has actualized the promises of life that were part of the Biblical tradition. As in some of the earlier Jewish traditions the language of resurrection, which belonged to the early kerygmatic traditions shared by Johannine and other Christians, could continue to exist alongside the traditions of eternal life. Nor was it necessary for this tradition to define the connection between that life and the bodily nature of the believer. It was sufficient to speak of the believer's transition from judgment into life through faith in Jesus as Son. The hints that we are given about the future of the Johannine believer suggest living in the presence of the glorified Lord to have been the primary image of that future that was operative among Johannine Christians.

SUMMARY

The centrality of resurrection images and traditions in the New Testament distinguishes it from the Jewish origins out of which the Christian movement emerged. This difference cannot be explained as a simple reflection of some wider cultural preoccupation with immortality. Even the resurrection traditions themselves look more to the present experience of the believer than they do to the future. There is surprisingly little speculation about that future even though it is clearly an object of established belief that the future of the Christian is determined by the present exaltation of Jesus. Indeed, one can only understand the central place that resurrection occupies in the language of the New Testament by pointing to its significance in understanding Jesus as the decisive point of divine salvation. Resurrection is always associated with a divine act of salvation. Often the life-giving power of God manifest in the resurrection of Jesus underlies the salvation experienced by the believer. This perception stems from the associations between resurrection and the fate of the righteous, which are also part of its Jewish context. Thus, resurrection is not an anthropological category. It does not represent a statement about humans in general, though it is occasionally generalized in images of universal judgment. Much of the New Testament has moved away from the eschatological parameters of Jewish resurrection traditions. The New Testament continues to agree with those traditions that link resurrection and the expectation that God's justice will prevail in the universe, but it also holds the paradoxical view that that future victory has already begun. Of course the resurrection kerygma never places resurrection on the same level as other events in the human story or even in Jesus' story. Though resurrection manifests the life-giving power of God, this exercise of divine power does not represent some facet of the created order as such. Rather, it is tied to judgment as the vindication of divine justice. It belongs to the culmination of the divine purpose that is expected at the end of the world.

The experiences of the presence of the Spirit within the early Christian communities might be said to confirm the view that God's power had raised Jesus from the dead. We have seen that the paraenetic tradition exhorts the Christian to manifest the power of the resurrection in life, while looking forward to sharing the glory of the risen One. Consequently, the resurrection may be said to shape the life of the believer directly insofar as it reorients behavior from the pre-Christian life of the individual to those patterns of life that represented "walking in the Spirit." The Pauline traditions are the ones in which resurrection symbolism appears to have been the most expansively developed. Some of these developments have been important factors in a symbolism of crucifixion and resurrection that "fit," perhaps even explained, the life of the Christians to whom Paul preached his gospel. This match between resurrection symbolism and the life of the believer not only served to orient the life of the believer toward the risen and exalted Lord. It also supported the conviction that the powers that appear to govern the world are not really its rulers. The obedience that the Christian owes God is paid to the true power in the cosmos, the exalted Lord. Full manifestation of Jesus' exaltation as Lord is awaited for the parousia. Like the resurrection itself, Jesus' rule over the cosmos represents the presence of God's power, which is both real and not yet fully realized in the world as humans know it. Without the believing community, which lives from the power of the resurrection, the eschatological event of Jesus' resurrection would not leave a trace in the world to which its message was addressed. The Johannine tradition saw clearly that Jesus' return had been to "his own" and not to the world. When divorced from the supporting experiences of a believing community and the persistent exhortation to reorder one's life in view of resurrection, resurrection easily retreats to the amorphous lines that it enjoys in Jewish writings of the period. It represents either a projection of future hopes for vindication of the order that one believes God has established in the world, or it becomes a mere item of belief. We have seen that that item of belief could even be attached to the fate of Jesus, simply. It might not be felt to have any implications for the fate of the believer.

Resurrection's metamorphic significance in the language of New Testament Christianity lay in the possibility of expanding the symbol to embrace various dimensions of Christian life. However, the expansion of the symbol was not always the same or always transparent to all Christians. Paul's arguments with the Corinthians show how far apart the apostle and his community were in understanding what resurrection meant. The apocalyptic and parousia imagery associated with resurrection, which includes resurrection as anticipation of a new creation, makes it clear that the symbol points to ontological and historical dimensions that are not captured by a simple story of an individual's assumption into heaven. Nor was resurrection felt to be simply the renewal of fellowship between Jesus and the disciples.

Resurrection is the exaltation of the one who died to heavenly lordship. The power of God to give life brings about the resurrection (Rom 4:17; 2 Cor 1:9). Seen as the eschatological power of God, resurrection is not a miracle by which God merely intervenes on behalf of Jesus but is the beginning of God's renewal of all things.

Without the larger metaphoric context provided by the eschatological expectations that surrounded resurrection, the symbol quickly becomes indistinguishable from the return of the divine soul to its heavenly source, though one might suppose that the body is somehow attached. Or it is translated into some modern variation on individual eschatology such as an intrapsychic event, like the conversion of the disciples or their move to a new level of insight, consciousness, or self-understanding. Becker rightly speaks of such translations of resurrection as "docetic." Resurrection is an event that is claimed to have occurred and yet is quite without effect except as it is subjectively appropriated by individuals. He considers the Johannine translation of resurrection to eternal life for the person who "knows" Jesus' identity with the Father to be such a docetic understanding of resurrection. There are a number of other nonapocalyptic readings of resurrection: closure of Jesus' life; confirmation of Jesus' divine status; or, in antidocetic polemic, proof that Jesus is the one who is the Christ; confirmation of Jesus' divine preexistence; the basis for the claim that grace is mediated through the sacraments; or an image of individualized postmortem survival or judgment.[69] Unlike these translations, Becker argues that the Pauline images are forged in a dynamic tension. On the one hand, the believer participates in the decisive event of the saving death and resurrection of Jesus. On the other, that participation is shaped by the consciousness that one awaits the culmination of all things at the parousia. Elsewhere in the New Testament, the tension dissolves. The parousia no longer impinges on the present, and the believer's participation in the resurrection is internalized and spiritualized.[70]

Clearly, resurrection does not have a well-defined conceptual structure. M. E. Dahl points out that it does not belong to the systematic order of well-articulated concepts. It belongs to the imaginative order of aesthetic and intuitive insights. On the one hand, transmission of such insights to the present demands more than the mere repetition of the words and images of the New Testament. It requires some explication and perhaps even systematization. On the other hand, resurrection as "event" can only be understood in metaphoric and mythic categories. Critical analysis may be required to make sure that they are the "right myths," but the myth itself is always greater than any possible conceptual systematization.[71]

1 Cor 15 provides a point of departure from which some of the central convictions underlying resurrection come into view.

1. Resurrection implies some unity in the person that does not divide somatic and spiritual. Paul, like other writers who attend to the apocalyptic images in which resurrection emerges, is hard put to describe the connection. Hence, one finds expressions like transformed, glorious body, body like that of the risen Lord, or even angelic body (Mk 12:25).

2. This bodily continuity ensures the identity of the exalted Lord with Jesus, who died on the cross. It also can be seen to have significance for the way in which Christians are to understand their bodies (1 Cor 6:13).

3. Resurrection depends on the perception that the world is not as it appears. God's purposes are being accomplished even in the midst of those evils that appear to thwart them.

4. Resurrection requires some expression of the presence of the power of God in the experience or lives of the believers. The ways in which that presence is expressed are quite varied. But without them resurrection takes on the empty or docetic ring to which Becker has pointed.

5. The experience of presence may take the form of ecstatic spiritual experiences. It may be given shape in the ritual of the community, particularly the baptismal participation in the death and resurrection of Christ. But it also receives powerful expression in the paraenesis that calls the Christian to walk in the new life of the Spirit.

6. Resurrection is still a communal symbol, which speaks of the new life of the righteous with the Lord. Application of resurrection to those outside the community of the faithful, usually as a mode to render judgment possible, remains secondary. Even less articulated is any connection between resurrection and philosophic questions about the immortality of individual souls or about the immediate postmortem fate of individuals. One finds that the faithful continue to live out of the power of the resurrection. They expect to be "with the Lord," but it is often not clear whether that expectation is fulfilled after the individual's death or at the consummation of all things.

This brief survey hardly exhausts every image of resurrection that is drawn in the New Testament. However, it does indicate some of the shapes that the symbol takes. It suggests that not every transformation one might care to make reflects what the New Testament understands of resurrection. One must continue to question the adequacy of a particular view to the Christian experience of salvation and discipleship. The Johannine tradition raises the possibility of transforming resurrection language into the related images of bestowing eternal life. This transformation perceives the life-giving power of God in the Word of Jesus experienced by the believer as divine revelation.

The problem of recovering significant speech about resurrection for our own day is acute. Many Christians find themselves in the position of a believing docetism. They hold resurrection as an item in a creed, but it has no revelatory power and certainly no ordering relevance to their lives. Unless reminded of resurrection in some ritual context, many would not even include it on a list of things that they believe. Faced with the death of other Christians, many are like the Thessalonians—lamenting like those who have no hope.

This loss of resurrection as an effective symbol has its epistemological correlation. We cease to perceive the world of time and history as having a meaning beyond that which we are able to assign it in the ordinary dimensions of human experience. Indeed, within the linguistic horizons of modernity, it is much more difficult to speak about such a dimension of meaning than it was in the first century. We live out of a three-way conflict between the facticity of our everyday language, the conceptual language of the metaphysical traditions that gave shape to most Christian systematization of belief, and the language of metaphoric consciousness in which the Bible operates.

Resurrection lies strongly in the metaphoric tradition, though 1 Cor 15 suggests that it is already being pushed by philosophic traditions. But Christians now find themselves working through patterns and images that are sedimented in all three language codes. Resurrection cannot be expressed in the ordinary language of modernity; such language has no need for a realm of transcendent meaning. And it certainly has no place for the metaphoric images of divine power and activity in the world on which resurrection is founded. But the dilemma of speech about resurrection at this point is no different from the dilemma about faith generally. Its explanatory necessity for the world is no longer self-evident. Religion has complied by retreating into the intrapsychic dimension, which it thought could provide refuge for its symbols. But modernity lies within as well as without. It has chased religion into the psyche with its own therapies and strategies for self-realization, for well-being, and even for ecstatic experience of the world. Resurrection, like the other symbols of the religious traditions, can be transformed and shaped by the changing situations of a believing community, but it has little power to illuminate a person's life when fragmented and disincarnated.

NOTES

1. J. G. Gager, "Functional Diversity in Paul's Use of End-Time Language," *Journal of Biblical Literature* 89 (1970), 325–37. A. T. Lincoln *(Paradise Now and Not Yet. Studies in the Role of the Heavenly Dimension in Paul's Thought with Special Reference to His Eschatology* [SNTSMS 43; Cambridge: Cambridge University, 1981]) comes to similar conclusions from studying Paul's language about heaven. In Galatians, the "heavenly Jerusalem" serves to negate the dominant role of the earthly Jerusalem (and the Law). The death and resurrection of Christ have made that move to the heavenly pole possible. At the same time, "heavenly Jerusalem" ensures the continuity of salvation history (op. cit., 9–32). 1 Corinthians links resurrection to both bodily and heavenly reality. One must be transformed into the heavenly reality (pp. 45–54). 2 Cor 4:16ff. assures the Corinthians that even if the suffering apostle were to die, he would receive a glorious body at the parousia (pp. 69–71). When Paul emphasizes realized eschatology, he does so in paraenetic contexts. The key is the Christian's belonging to the exalted Christ. Throughout the Pauline corpus, resurrection is worked out in terms of the impact that it has on the present (pp. 174–80).
2. W. Meeks, *The First Urban Christians. The Social World of the Apostle Paul* (New Haven: Yale University, 1983), 277.
3. Lincoln, op. cit., 184–89.
4. V. Furnish, *Theology and Ethics in Paul* (Nashville: Abingdon, 1968), 169; Lincoln, op. cit., 191–95. Like much of the Jewish material of the time, the New Testament deals with resurrection only as it relates to the righteous. How judgment of nonbelievers was envisaged is often unstated.
5. R. Kieffer, "Résurrection du Christ et résurrection générale," *Nouvelle Revue Théologique* 103 (1981), 332–41.
6. R. Tannehill *(Dying and Rising with Christ* [BZNW 32; Berlin:

Töpelmann, 1967], 130f.) insists that Paul presumes "rising with Christ" as part of his own thought.

7. Furnish, op. cit., 168.

8. E. Kaesemann, *Commentary on Romans* (trans. E. Bromily; Grand Rapids: Eerdmans, 1980), 307. For the view that this passage refers to resurrection, see Stanley, op. cit., 197.

9. Kaesemann (op. cit., 307) favors the parousia interpretation, since the parousia would bring the apocalyptic hopes of Israel to their conclusion.

10. J. Fitzmyer, "Romans," in R. Brown, J. Fitzmyer, and R. Murphy, eds., *Jerome Biblical Commentary* (Englewood Cliffs: Prentice-Hall, 1967), 323.

11. K. Donfried, in an unpublished paper presented to the New England regional meeting of the SBL/CBA on April 6, 1982, argued that the basic structure of faith, hope, and love forms the pattern of the letter. 1 Thess 5:9–10 follows upon the passage about the armor of salvation. Hope is the helmet of salvation. Hence, vv. 9–10 serve as the definition of hope.

12. See the discussion of the literary structure of 1 Thess 4:13–5:11 in W. Harnisch, *Eschatologische Existenz. Ein exegetischer Beitrag zum Sachanliegen von 1 Thessalonischen 4,13–5,11* (Göttingen: Vandenhoeck & Ruprecht, 1973), 16–28.

13. E. Best, *A Commentary on the First and Second Epistles to the Thessalonians* (London: Black, 1972), 187.

14. See Harnisch, op. cit., 29f.; Best (op. cit., 185) points to a similar *topos* in 1 Pt 1:3f., 21. This *topos* is not (pace Best) concerned with other expressions of hope in antiquity. It probably was part of the Cynic/Stoic repertoire of anti-Epicurean slogans.

15. Best, op. cit., 187.

16. Harnisch, op. cit., 38.

17. Harnisch, op. cit., 39–47; Best, op. cit., 189–95. For early Christian prophets, see Ac 11:27f.; 13:1; 15:32; 21:9ff.; 1 Cor 12:10, 28. Best (op. cit., 191) points out that consolation is one of the functions of the early Christian prophet in 1 Cor 14:31. Paul does not distinguish sayings of the Lord from those of the earthly Jesus. 1 Cor 7:10 and 9:14 attribute sayings of the earthly Jesus to the Lord. Consequently, whatever the origin of the logion, Paul presumes that it has binding authority as divine revelation (Best, op. cit., 193).

18. Harnisch, op. cit., 42–46. Best (op. cit., 194) thinks that had the saying come from an early Christian prophet, the *Kyrios* form of the saying would have been used. As we have seen, *Kyrios* does belong to the resurrection kerygma, while the Son of Man tradi-

tions have developed in the context of interpretations of Jesus' exaltation. However, this logion appears to have combined the two traditions.

19. Harnisch, op. cit., 47–49. Harnisch's discussion is marred by the presumption that the problem in 1 Thessalonians is the same as that in 1 Corinthians. Consequently, he thinks that v. 15b is an actual slogan being advanced by some people in Thessalonika.

20. Best, op. cit., 195, 197.

21. Best, op. cit., 200. Best's examples move out of the realm of parousia sayings. Both Matthew and John, as we have seen, refer to presence of the Lord with the community.

22. Ibid., 201f. Harnisch treats all of 5:1–11 as a description of the eschatological existence of the baptised. It has been suggested that a pre-Pauline baptismal tradition underlies 5:4–10 (op. cit., 117–25). However, we do not see evidence of the gnosticizing enthusiasm that Harnisch (pp. 131–42) thinks that Paul's baptismal paraenesis is said to counter.

23. N. Frye, *The Great Code. The Bible and Literature* (New York: Harcourt Brace Jovanovich, 1982), 20f.

24. Lincoln, op. cit., 39.

25. 1 Cor 15 raises the question of why Christianity needs apocalyptic. Recent studies of apocalyptic have tended to focus on the mythic and dualistic elements in apocalyptic visions and to obscure the components of cosmic universalism inherent in apocalyptic metaphors. J. C. Beker insists that the latter are essential to Paul. His dualism is limited to the vision of salvation history and of Israel's place in it *(Paul the Apostle: The Triumph of God in Life and Thought* [Philadelphia: Fortress, 1980], 108f.). Paul never uses "two ages" to intensify the sense that the present age is one of increasing evil. Most "day of the Lord" language in Paul occurs in contexts in which traditional formulae and expressions are being used. Paul is concerned about the two realms that determine human life within God's created order.

26. See M. E. Dahl, *The Resurrection of the Body* (SBT 36; London, SCM, 1962), 76; for a survey of typical reconstructions and the objections to them, see Dahl, ibid., 7–35; and G. Wagner, ". . . encore 1 Corinthiens 15. Si les chrétiens refusent d'agir alors Christ n'est pas ressuscité," *Études Théol Rel* 56 (1981), 599–607. C. K. Barrett *(The First Epistle to the Corinthians* [New York: Harper & Row, 1968], 347) observes that the early kerygma itself did not contain any comment on the fate of believers. He opts for a "gnosticizing" vision of present resurrection, which could have been based on Paul's own preaching of the power of the resur-

rection in the lives of believers (p. 348). H. Conzelmann (*1 Corinthians* [Philadelphia: Fortress, 1975], 261–63) argues that Paul has misunderstood his opponents and that one cannot reconstruct their views with any certainty if Paul has misunderstood them. Lincoln (op. cit., 35) points to the explanation for why some have died in 1 Cor 11:30 as evidence for the similarity between this problem and that in Thessalonika. He thinks that the Corinthians thought that, like angels, they would simply continue to reign with Christ. Consequently, Paul insists that "flesh and blood" cannot inherit the kingdom (p. 35f.). Their interpretation may have been used at Corinth and may be reflected in the Corinthian preoccupation with reigning. Sayings that could have given rise to some of the Corinthian views are satisfaction for the hungry (Mt 5:6 par.); supplying needs (Mt 6:33 par.); in full measure (Lk 6:38); promised riches (Mk 10:21 par.); not just in heaven (Lk 18:30); rule and judge the world (Mt 19:28 par.). The Corinthians probably assimilated these traditions to ideas taken from hellenistic culture. On the sayings of Jesus at Corinth, see H.-W. Kuhn, "Der Irdische Jesus bei Paulus als traditionsgeschichtliches un theologisches Problem, *Zeitschrift für Theologie und Kirche* 67 (1970), 295–320.

27. A. J. M. Wedderburn, "The Problem of the Denial of the Resurrection in 1 Corinthian XV," *NovT* 23 (1981), 241.

28. G. Theissen, *The Social Setting of Pauline Christianity. Essays on Corinth* (Philadelphia: Fortress, 1982), 132–37.

29. Wedderburn, op. cit., 236. Wedderburn (p. 230) agrees that it is implausible to presume that the Corinthians denied resurrection because they held an Epicurean view. The conventional character of such anti-Epicurean *topoi* meant that they migrated from one setting to another.

30. Wedderburn (op. cit., 240, note 39) observes that Cavallin has shown that inconsistent images of the afterlife can be found within the same document. However, the Corinthians do not appear to have been willing to assimilate all views of the afterlife. They have explicitly rejected resurrection. Further, this rejection can best be understood in connection with convictions about the inferiority and the indifferent status of the body elsewhere in the letter.

31. See the detailed survey of the terminology of spiritual status in Philo and 1 Corinthians by R. A. Horsley, "How Can Some of You Say That There Is No Resurrection of the Dead? Spiritual Elitism in Corinth," *NovT* 20 (1978), 207–16; 226–29. Horsley shows that such a context implies that baptism was understood as being

about union with Wisdom, not with the risen Christ. Consequently, the situation presupposed in Corinth is different from that in 2 Timothy or Colossians and Ephesians.

32. B. Pearson, *The Pneumatikos-Psychikos Terminology in 1 Corinthians. A Study in the Theology of the Corinthian Opponents of Paul and Its Relationship to Gnosticism* (SBLDS 12; Missoula, Mont.: Scholars, 1973), 1–6. R. Jewett *(Paul's Anthropological Terms: A Study of Their Use in Conflict Settings,* [Leiden: Brill, 1971], 340–54) thinks that Paul is using Gnostic terminology. He argues that *psychē* (soul) and *pneuma* (spirit) represented the basic duality of the Corinthians. Pearson's study suggests that Gnostics of the second century were dependent on the same traditions of hellenistic Jewish exegesis that are being used by the Corinthian opponents. Gnosticism was more creative in reinterpreting older traditions than in formulating new ones (op. cit., 2–4; 82–85).

33. Conzelmann (op. cit., 71) notes that Paul is shifting from the language of "mysteries" to pedagogical terminology. "Fleshly people" is not directed at the Corinthians fundamentally because they are sinners but because they are "babes," uninstructed. Thus, Conzelmann points out (loc. cit., note 23) the dualism in the passage is not Gnostic.

34. Conzelmann (op. cit., 67–69). Pearson (op. cit., 28) thinks it likely that the spiritual Corinthians thought that the cross applied only to the spiritually immature, those who still required milk. Philo uses this type of terminology in his description of the moral pedagogy appropriate to each type of soul (Agr. 8f.; Leg. All. 3.196; Pearson, op. cit., 29f.).

35. Pearson, op. cit., 11f.; Lincoln (op. cit., 40f.) objects that Philo never contrasts spirit and *psychē* as two parts of the soul. But we have seen that he does distinguish two minds: an immortal, heavenly one and an earthly, perishable one. Pearson is not claiming that the Corinthians—or the later Gnostics who use these distinctions—took them directly from Philo. Rather, Philo is the witness to a common tradition of hellenistic Jewish speculation.

36. Conzelmann, op. cit., 281f.

37. Dahl (op. cit., 31) points out that the creative activity of God is seen as continuous. The past is referred to as "has pleased," the present "gives," and an implied "will give" refers to the future. The eschatological renewal of creation is already in process in the present.

38. Pearson, op. cit., 25.

39. J. D. G. Dunn *(Christology in the Making* [Philadelphia: West-

minster, 1980], 125–27) protests against using parallels from Philo to describe Paul's vision of Adam, since Paul sees in Adam the restoration of the divine image through sharing the resurrected life of Christ. Dunn's objection is based on the picture of Adam in Romans 5, which we would agree was formulated independently of the traditions that have forced the argument in 1 Cor 15.

40. Conzelmann, op. cit., 283. For weakness and power, see 1 Cor 1:24f.; 4:10; 2 Cor 12:10; 13:3, 9.

41. Pearson, op. cit., 22–26.

42. Pearson, op. cit., 24; Lincoln, op. cit., 42–49.

43. Horsley, op. cit., 222. Since the Corinthians probably used the terminology of psychic and spiritual, Paul has probably introduced "earthly" here as well.

44. Pearson, op. cit., 41. Thus, Dahl (op. cit., 75) has observed that Paul is not arguing for any natural immortality of the human person. He is insisting upon God's power. Resurrection (p. 84) is not simply the outcome of creation or the immortality of the soul that it was given in the creation.

45. H. C. Kee, *Christian Origins in Sociological Perspective* (Philadelphia: Westminster, 1980), 59. Conzelmann (op. cit., 290) argues that Paul is revealing himself as a teacher of mysteries, as he has done elsewhere in the letter (2:6; 13:2; 14:2). He thinks (pp. 57–60) that Paul had presented himself in Corinth as a teacher of apocalyptic wisdom.

46. R. E. Brown, *The Epistles of John* (AnBi; Garden City, N.Y.: Doubleday, 1982), 392–96.

47. Conzelmann, op. cit., 291f.

48. Horsley, op. cit., 224f.

49. Conzelmann, op. cit., 291. Paul's quotation does not follow any of the common LXX text traditions. The Theodotian text comes close to "swallowed up" and "in victory," so Paul may have known a variant of that tradition. Paul has treated both clauses in Hosea as referring to death rather than preserving the death and Hades parallel. He has replaced the "penalty" *(dikē)* in the first part of the citation with the "victory" from the Isaiah passage (Conzelmann, op. cit., 292f.).

50. Conzelmann, op. cit., 293.

51. Loc. cit.

52. M. Williams, "Stability as a Soteriological Theme in Gnosticism," *The Rediscovery of Gnosticism. Vol. 2: Sethian Gnosticism* (ed. B. Layton; Leiden: E. J. Brill, 1981), 826–28.

53. R. E. Brown *(The Virginal Conception and Bodily Resurrection*

of Jesus [New York: Paulist, 1973], 86, note 147) comments that though this passage might seem to imply exchange of one body for another rather than transformation, Paul is not really concerned with that issue. He is concerned with how Christians ought to live in the interim, as in Phil 1:21–23. F. Fallon *(2 Corinthians* [Wilmington: Glazier, 1980], 42–47) notes that it would be quite unlike Paul to speculate about some state of postmortem transformation. He has simply shifted the mystic language of his opponents to the parousia.

54. H. Kraft, *Die Offenbarung des Johannes* (HNT 16a; Tübingen: J. C. B. Mohr, 1974), 255–57.

55. J. C. Beker, *Paul the Apostle: The Triumph of God in Life and Thought* (Philadelphia: Fortress, 1980), 180.

56. J. T. Forestell, *The Word of the Cross: Salvation as Revelation in the Fourth Gospel* (Rome: Biblical Institute Press, 1974), 113–15, 123–25.

57. R. E. Brown, *The Gospel According to John I–XII* (AnBi 29; Garden City, N.Y.: Doubleday, 1966), 147–49; R. Schnackenburg, *The Gospel According to St. John. Vol. 1: Chaps. 1–4* (New York: Herder, 1968), 398–404. We agree with Schnackenburg that this section of Jn 3 is the evangelist's commentary on the images of crucifixion and eternal life that conclude the Nicodemus discourse. Schnackenburg observes that eternal life through belief in the crucified and exalted One is not the central metaphor of this interpretation. Instead, the evangelist has shifted to the perspective of Jesus' mission, which is presented by reinterpreting judgment language (op. cit., 399f.). We would add that the present construction of Jn 12 follows a similar pattern. Jn 12:32–34 presents Jesus' coming exaltation on the cross as a Son of Man saying. The chapter concludes with a presentation of Jesus' mission to the world.

58. R. Schnackenburg, *The Gospel According to St. John. Vol. II: Chaps. 5–12* (New York: Seabury, 1980), 133f. Schnackenburg *(John II,* 135) notes that most Jewish writings except the Septuagint of Dan 7:22 reserve judgment to God. Though the later Son of Man material in 1 Enoch (49:4; 61:9; 62:2f.; 63:11; 69:27) uses the image of judgment being turned over to another figure, the Johannine tradition is unique in its clear assertion that the powers of God are being exercised by Jesus. Even the other Christian traditions that present Jesus as judge usually reserve the life-giving power of resurrection to the Father.

59. Ibid., 145–59. He considers this passage a redactional addition that incorporated earlier traditions. The rest of the chapter

shows no concern with a dual judgment. The passage is the only one in the gospel that speaks of judgment and the last day (cf. 12:48). He observes (p. 148) that the connection between Son of Man, resurrection, and judgment represents early Christian apocalyptic traditions like those preserved in Heb 6:2 and Rev 10:42.

60. R. Schnackenburg, *Das Johannesevangelium III. Kap. 13–21* (HTKNT IV/3; Freiburg: Herder, 1975), 67f.; R. E. Brown, *The Gospel According to John XIII–XXI* (AnBi 29A; Garden City, N.Y.: Doubleday, 1970), 625f. Philo can also refer to the place to which the immortal soul goes in heaven as the house or mansion of God (Som 1.256; Conf. Ling. 78).

61. Schnackenburg, *Johannesevangelium III*, 69–71; cf. Jn 14:18f.

62. Schnackenburg, *Johannesevangelium III*, 194. Schnackenburg suggests that the point of the soteriological exaltation of Jesus here in John is universality (6:37f.; 10:28). John is not thinking only of a limited group of disciples.

63. Schnackenburg, *Johannesevangelium III*, 191, 195. This verse is cast in a different rhetorical form from the rest of the prayer. It is the only place in the gospel (except 1:17, another comment) in which the name Jesus Christ is used.

64. Brown *(John II,* 753) sees the connection between knowledge of God and life as a reflection of the covenant themes that are invoked by the Last Supper discourses, since the Old Testament tradition connects knowledge of God and life (Jer 24:7; 31:33–34; and see the connection between knowledge and life in the Dead Sea Scrolls, e.g., 1 QS 11.3–4).

65. Ibid., 752. Brown observes that while later Gnostic commentators will exploit the Johannine understanding of knowledge as salvation, John remains rooted within the Biblical understanding of knowledge of God. It depends on a historical revelation, the death and resurrection of Jesus, and remains tied to keeping the commandments of God/Jesus. The clear use of kerygmatic and earlier Christian traditions in the gospel makes it quite unnecessary to attribute its language of Jesus' descent and exaltation to the appropriation of some myth of a descending/ascending redeemer.

66. Forestell, op. cit., 127.

67. See Perkins, *The Johannine Epistles* (Wilmington: Glazier, 1979), 3–7.

68. Brown, *Epistles,* 54–55; 81–85.
69. Becker, op. cit., 153–58.
70. Ibid., 158–60.
71. Dahl, op. cit., 85f.; 94f.

TEN

Resurrection and Second-Century Christianity

INTRODUCTION

Resurrection is a pervasive feature of the symbolism of the New Testament. Since Christians did not take over resurrection as a clear, well-defined symbol, resurrection was easily filled out with the content of other stories, symbols, or interpretations. The dispute between Paul and the Corinthians reflects confusion over the relationship between the relatively undifferentiated resurrection symbolism and the more sharply differentiated understanding of the soul and its position in the material and divine world.[1]

W. C. van Unnik has argued that the available evidence suggests that the second century was preoccupied with debates over the significance of resurrection to a degree that has not been paralleled since.[2] These debates were not about resurrection as the conclusion to the life of Jesus. They were concerned with the question of resurrection as the fate of believers or of humanity as a whole. These arguments required evaluation of the place of the body in Christian soteriology. The reformulations that would be required were not always clear. It was easy for all parties to presume the Platonic view of matter. Neither Platonism nor Stoicism would sponsor the conviction that the kind of immortality predicated of spiritual substance could be attributed to the material body. The apologists generally found themselves arguing on two fronts. In order to defend Christian soteriology, they insisted that the soul was not naturally immortal. Against the Gnostics, who often appealed to the more common view that flesh could not participate in immortality, they argued that the body did participate in immortality.[3]

When it is addressed to outsiders, Christian apologetic must make the case for the plausibility of resurrection language. When it is addressed to fellow Christians or to Gnostics, who claimed a superior interpretation of resurrection as the illumination of the soul or as the soul's ascent to its heavenly home, the apologetic argument had to make the case for resurrection as a better understanding of soteriology than that held by the opposition. Certain arguments became common property. Arguments from the cyclic patterns of nature and from the omnipotence of God form the background of the assertion that resurrection is not inherently impossible. The suitability of the body's share in resurrection is defended on the grounds that the body shared in the deeds by which the soul either gained or lost its salvation. Of course, these stock arguments have their weak points. No Platonist would grant that the body deserves a share in salvation based on its association with the soul in deeds done in life, since the soul is the responsible agent in any deeds done by the body. The mind is responsible for governing human passions. What is material does not have any responsibility for the passions that arise merely because of the changeable nature of the body.

The argument that the body deserves a share in salvation is more appropriate in contexts that attributed an active role to the body's passions in the deeds of a person. We find such an active evaluation in the Gnostic opponents of Christianity, who attribute evil to matter rather than simply disorder, as the Platonic tradition does.[4] The Gnostics take over Platonic images of the body as a prison with a seriousness that would never be acceptable in their original philosophic context. Much of the second-century Christian argument is directed against the Gnostic interpretations of resurrection.

Origen attempted to resolve the remaining conflict between the Christian language of resurrection and what would appear to be the "scientific" view of matter by speaking of two levels of understanding. A more literal understanding of resurrection of the body is directed toward uneducated Christians. But there is also a more philosophically nuanced understanding. The material body, like all matter, is subject to change. But, Origen argued, there must be a principle of continuity underlying that change. That is the principle of identity that serves the resurrected body. It is quite different in quality from what we speak of as body. Thus, it would be wrong to presume that the body that is raised is the same, in the sense of having the same material components, as the body that we have now. Origen has pointed to one of the key spots in the confession of resurrection. On the one hand, it appears to have the strength of preserving the individuality that is fundamental to our separate identities. Preservation of identity was originally necessitated by the emergence of resurrection in the context of individual judgment or vindication. This view emerges naturally in the narrative language that speaks of humans and their activities in the world and has little need to distinguish spiritual and material principles like soul and body. On the other hand, no scientific understanding of matter whether in the second century or the twentieth permits such a peculiar form of individualization. Matter never appears with a permanence appropriate to immortality or to the spiritual world. Thus, resurrection as a symbol functions quite adequately within the realm of myth, symbol, or narrative—just as the characters seen in Hades in Homer or Plato are described as having bodies and being punished. But if one is to seek to answer the question about resurrection on the same level on which the philosopher speaks about the immortality of the soul or its likeness to the divine, then one cannot simply repeat the language of narrative or myth. One must make some answer in terms appropriate to the principles that are understood to structure the world.

The orthodox tradition, which will emerge from the debate, will not be conducive to Origen's attempt to integrate resurrection into an understanding of the physics of matter and of spiritual transformation. Rather, it will represent the more conservative traditions that contented themselves with assertions that are drawn simply from the level of narrative. The physical body one now possesses is to be restored completely to all humans. The good will enjoy perfect happiness; the wicked, eternal punishment. The fourth Lateran Council defined this belief as *de fide.*[5]

We can distinguish three levels of involvement with resurrection traditions in second-century writings. At the imaginative level, we find portrayals of the risen Lord as a luminous and polymorphous divine being. This portrait reflects the Lord who is worshiped and known as the reflection of God. However, that same imagery of the

divine Lord provided the Gnostic teachers with a setting for their
own interpretations of Jesus' teaching. They regularly composed dialogues that claimed to contain secret instruction given by the risen
Lord. Thus, speculation about the risen Lord is transformed into
speculation about an esoteric level of Christian teaching.

In quite a different vein, both orthodox and Gnostic teachers found
themselves pressed to explain what resurrection meant for the salvation of the believer. The Jewish matrix of judgment and vindication,
which had carried the original resurrection traditions, did not translate easily into the hellenistic world. For those with some education
in the popular philosophical trends of the time, resurrection as transformation of the body to a state of incorruptibility also seemed implausible. Individual salvation and immortality would have to lie with
the soul, if they were to lie anywhere. Exaltation could be attached to
that same soul's journey to astral immortality.

The conflicts and debates of the second century led to specification
of how the doctrine of resurrection applied to the future of the
believer. Even those Christian writers most in sympathy with Platonic speculation have to introduce important qualifications. The
process of divinization is not natural. It does not represent the human
person brought to perfection through reason or philosophy. It can
only come to a person as gift of the Creator, as reward for obedience
to the virtue revealed by God.

THE APOSTOLIC FATHERS

Many of the references to resurrection in the Apostolic Fathers continue the traditions of the first century. Resurrection appears to be
part of the traditional Christian language, which does not require
much argument or debate. One reason for this position may have
been the large number of Jewish Christian traditions that appear in
these writings. Within that larger context, resurrection is easily seen
as an operative symbol for vindication and judgment. It is not presented with a serious competing soteriology.[6]

Ignatius of Antioch

Ignatius of Antioch presumes that Christ's resurrection is the prototype for that of the believer (Tral. 9.1–2). The opening half of the Tral.
9.1–2 formula is paralleled in Ignatius' *Ephesians* (18.2). That section

concludes with the affirmation that the passion underlies the cleansing from sin that Christians receive in baptism. *Smyrneans* 1.1–2 concludes its reference to the passion with resurrection.

Ignatius's primary focus is on the polemic against opponents who deny the reality of Jesus' incarnation and suffering death on our behalf.[7] Ignatius considers resurrection a stage of the passion. Ignatius implies that his docetic opponents will find themselves without bodily reality, just as they suppose the true Christ to have been. Like the docetic explanations of the crucifixion that we find in second-century Gnostic writers, the opponents were probably able to understand resurrection as the triumphant return of the Lord to his heavenly home. What they would not accept was any suggestion that the divine had suffered and died. Because the opposition has not yet formulated an interpretation of resurrection, Ignatius is able to use that belief against them. The Gnostic thinkers of the second century will be quite willing to grant Ignatius's premise. They do expect to attain "bodies" of the same type that they think the risen Lord possesses.[8]

Polycarp of Smyrna

Polycarp also warns against those who deny the incarnation. But unlike those castigated by Ignatius, these people are said to deny judgment and resurrection.[9] Their views appear to be closer to those we find in later second-century writers; none of the apocalyptic elements are maintained. Phil. 7.1 contains another feature that we find more prominently later in the second century: the connection between resurrection and interpretation of the sayings of the Lord. Other details about Polycarp's opponents suggest a more comprehensive opposition to Christian preaching about Jesus grounded in sayings interpretation.

Phil 1.2–3 treats resurrection as an attribute of God, as was the case in kerygmatic formulae from the New Testament.

Phil 2.1 contains an outline of the traditional teaching.[10]

Polycarp presumes that the resurrection of Christ is proof that those who believe in him will also be raised.

Phil 2.2 reflects one of the oldest resurrection traditions. Resurrection is the reward for the righteous who have been faithful to the commandments of God.

Barnabas and Didache

The paraenetic traditions in *Barnabas* and *Didache* are closely related. They both have used a tradition of "two ways" exhortation, and both preserve other Jewish and Jewish Christian traditions.[11] The only reference to resurrection in *Didache* appears in its apocalyptic conclusion (16.6–8).[12] *Barnabas* shares Jewish traditions with *Didache*, but it also contains several references to resurrection. We have already seen that resurrection appears in paraenetic traditions as a reward that is to motivate obedience. *Barnabas* makes use of resurrection in the conclusion to its version of the two-ways exhortation (21.1c).[13]

After showing that the two ways lead to life and death, respectively, resurrection is placed in parallel with the promise of a recompense. The underlying tradition may indeed have intended that resurrection is reward for the righteous, since that is the understanding of resurrection in *Didache* 16.6f. However, *Barnabas* 5.6 makes resurrection "in the body" a means for judgment.

This tradition also makes Christ rather than God the one who raises the dead. A similar transition from God's to Christ's power of giving life was already evident in the Fourth Gospel. Here it is connected with the theme of Christ's victory over death.[14] This theme was a popular one in the Christian apocalyptic traditions of the second century.[15]

Barnabas 15 contains an extensive discussion of the Jewish Sabbath legislation and Christian freedom from that obligation. Resurrection is tied to the Christian observance of Sunday as the replacement for the Jewish Sabbath. This is the true rest intended by the Creator.

Shepherd of Hermas

The *Shepherd of Hermas* preserves a melange of Jewish Christian traditions from the Roman community. It exhorts its readers to repentance even though the "end is not yet."[16]

Sim 5.6.5–7 takes the incarnation of the preexistent Holy Spirit in the flesh of Jesus as an indication that all flesh that has been obedient and had the Spirit dwelling within will be rewarded.

The adoptionist language of this Christology provides the author with the parallel between Christ and the believer. The believer can expect the same triumph of the Spirit and the same reward for obedience.[17]

1 Clement

1 Clement provides one type of argument for resurrection that will become standard, the analogy between resurrection and transformations that occur in the natural order. Although the argument is introduced with the Pauline expression that Christ is the "first fruits" of those raised from the dead (34.1), 1 Clement does not cite Paul's argument. Instead, he gives a fourfold argument: (a) from seasons and grains of seed (24); (b) from the story of the Phoenix (24–26); (c) from prophecies in Scripture (Pss 28:7; 3:6; 23:4; Job 19:6), and (d) from divine omnipotence and providence. Both the seed argument and the cycles of day and night represent the providential ordering of creation that guarantees that everything takes place in its proper season.[18] 1 Clement is not concerned with the possibility of the resurrected body being spiritual as Paul is.

The Phoenix story was a popular item of natural history. It occurs in Pliny the Elder *(Natural History* 10.2) as well as in apocryphal Jewish writings (2 En. 12.1; 19.6; 3 Bar. 6.3–13). The Phoenix passage in 2 En. 12.1–3 links the birds with the passage of the sun through the sky. It is part of the divine order that they attend the sun bearing heat and dew. Thus, the sequence of arguments in 1 Clement, transition from day to night, divine providence, and phoenix, may well have been derived from a stock piece of cosmological lore. 1 Clement has shifted the tradition from the order of creation to resurrection. 1 Clement also presents resurrection as the reward for the righteous (26.1).

2 Clement

Shepherd of Hermas tied resurrection to a paraenetic tradition that emphasized purity of flesh. 2 Clement has a similar view of repentance and purity (8.4, 6).

In response to the objection that the flesh does not participate in resurrection and judgment, 2 Clement emphasizes the fact that this flesh is the one in which we receive a reward. The parallelism of flesh and spirit also shows a shift toward incarnation as the central image of salvation. 2 Clement is not primarily interested in defending the teaching of resurrection. Resurrection of the body is presumed as part of the ethical exhortation to the purity and holiness that comes with reception of the Spirit.

Diognetus

Diognetus claims to answer questions about Christianity for the pagan inquirer. Thus, it belongs with writings of the apologetic type. It seeks to distinguish Christianity from the follies of Judaism and of paganism. *Diognetus* does not expound a doctrine of resurrection as such. Its author argues that humanity had no chance of achieving immortal life until God revealed his Son (9.2–4). The person who lives a life of virtue as defined by Christianity becomes like God. That person escapes the only death that a person must fear, the punishment due sinners (10.4–7). The only route to immortality is Christianity.

These authors show a developing conviction that the body that is resurrected is, indeed, the body that a person bears in this life. But resurrection is not yet the subject of much reflective interpretation. Only 1 Clement provides the beginning of a sustained apologetic argument for the plausibility of resurrection that goes beyond what was commonly taught.

APOCRYPHAL GOSPELS AND ACTS

Apocryphal gospels and acts are the best source for imaginative images of resurrection in the second and third centuries. They often portray Jesus as larger than life or as appearing in different forms. Some describe Jesus on or after Easter. Others are visionary appearances of the Lord from heaven. Such appearances reinforce the conviction that Jesus is alive and present to his followers in a concrete way.

Gospel of Peter

The *Gospel of Peter* expands the gospel stories of the events at Jesus' tomb into a full-fledged description of the resurrection event. The reader is shown Christ emerging from the tomb:

> *Now in the night, when the Lord's day dawned, when the soldiers two by two in every watch, were keeping guard, there rang out a loud voice in the heaven, and they saw the heavens opened and two men come down from there in a great brightness*

and approach the sepulchre. That stone which had been laid
against the entrance to the sepulchre started by itself to roll and
gave way to the side, and the sepulchre was opened, and both the
young men went in . . . they saw again three men come out
from the sepulchre, and two of them sustaining the other, and a
cross following them, and the heads of the two reaching to
heaven, but that of the one who was being led by the hand
reached beyond the heavens.   [Gospel of Peter 9–10; Hen-
necke-Schneemelcher, vol. 1, 185f.]

These events are witnessed by the guard as well as by crowds of
others who have come to the tomb. The author goes on to elaborate
on the legend of the guard's report to Pilate, who commands them to
remain silent, the women's visit to the tomb, a combination of elements from the canonical tomb stories, and an appearance to Peter,
Andrew, and Levi while they are fishing (chaps. 11–14).

Ascension of Isaiah

This work presents the story of Jesus as it is revealed to Isaiah during
his ascent into heaven. As in the *Gospel of Peter,* Jesus emerges from
the tomb on the shoulders of angels. However, the grave is opened
by Michael and the Holy Spirit (3.16–18). Isaiah foresees that the
risen Lord will send out his disciples to preach.

Christ's ascension to the seventh heaven is to occur after Christ has
spent 545 days with his disciples on earth. A similar period of postresurrection revelation will appear in Gnostic accounts as well.[19] Some
of the righteous ascend with Christ and receive garments, thrones,
and crowns (9.17). Thus, readers can imagine their own fate as similar
to the glorious ascent of the righteous in the company of the risen
Lord.

This tradition of ascension through the spheres appears to have
originated in Jewish Christian circles. A late second- or early third-
century Gnostic writing, the *Apocryphon of James,* contains the extended period of postresurrection teaching that culminates in the
ascent of Jesus through the spheres.[20] James and Peter receive the
Lord's final teaching and try to follow his ascent, but they fail to go
beyond the lower regions of angelic rejoicing (CG 1.15.8–29; NHLE:
36).[21]

The resurrection that *Ascension of Isaiah* refers to as the first item
in the apostolic kerygma must be the glorious ascension to heaven
around which the rest of the work is structured. However, unlike
other second-century authors, he does not identify the garments of

the resurrected with the fleshly body. Instead, in language much closer to Jewish apocalyptic traditions, the author speaks of the righteous receiving garments of glory and entering into an angelic state of existence.

Epistula Apostolorum

Gnostic writers exploited the period of postresurrection appearances to claim that Christ taught all or some of his disciples the Gnostic interpretations of his teaching. They frequently cast Gnostic teaching in the form of a dialogue between the risen Lord and the disciples.[22] The *Epistula Apostolorum* appears to have been composed as an orthodox response to such Gnostic dialogues.[23] When the Lord appears to the disciples, they think he is a ghost. However, three of the disciples touch Jesus, thereby proving that he is risen in the flesh (chap. 11). Then, much as in Gnostic dialogues, the Lord promises to tell the disciples, "What is above the heaven, what is in heaven, and your rest that is in the kingdom of heaven" (chap. 12). The initial revelation recalls the traditions of *Ascension of Isaiah*. Jesus describes his descent through the heavenly powers assuming the angelic forms. He even assumes the form of Gabriel at the Annunciation, when, as Logos, he becomes incarnate in the Virgin. Jesus answers questions from his disciples. Emphasis on the fleshly incarnation, the suffering, and the resurrection represents an attack on the docetic forms of descent and ascent Christology that are typical of Gnostic writings. The disciples are being assured that Jesus' own "wearing the flesh," his being "begotten though unbegotten," implies that they will be raised in the same manner that the Father awakened Jesus from the dead (chap. 21). The disciples are told, "In regeneration you obtain the resurrection in your flesh."

Epistula Apostolorum contains several comments about the relationship between flesh, soul, and spirit in resurrection. It insists that all three are involved. This emphasis is directed against claims that only the soul or only the mind (or spirit in the *Apocryphon of James*) can ascend into the heavenly realm. Jesus asserts that the resurrection will happen while the soul and spirit are in the flesh (chaps. 24–26). The reader learns that the confusion being generated by false teachers was predicted. However, such teaching is to be rejected on the basis of the teaching of the risen Lord himself, teaching given to all the apostles. Further, the Christian is to hold to the view that the flesh is the subject of resurrection at the judgment.

The Apocryphal Acts

The apocryphal acts contain both elements of preaching about the resurrection and of visions of the Lord. In the *Acts of Thomas* the twin relationship between Thomas and the Lord makes it possible for Jesus to appear as though he were the apostle.[24] He appears to a bridal couple in their chamber and persuades them to "abandon this filthy intercourse" and "become holy temples, pure and free from afflictions and pains both manifest and hidden," so that they will "not be girt with the cares for life and for children, the end of which is destruction" (chap. 12). The image of the soul's union with its heavenly counterpart in the bride chamber is common in Gnostic writings.

In the second of the acts Thomas builds a miraculous heavenly city and converts the Indian king Gundaphorus. As Thomas is sealing his converts with oil, they receive a revelation of the exalted Lord through his voice (chap. 27).

The apostle prays for the coming of the Spirit on the new converts, which will reveal the hidden mysteries to them, purify them, and make it possible for them to rest in the heavenly regions of the eighth (= above the seven planetary spheres). At this point, they have a further vision of the Lord as a being of great light.

Thus, the *Acts of Thomas* envisage the Lord as a great, luminous being who can appear in the human world. The pattern of attaining rest in the eighth presupposes the ascent of the soul through the heavenly spheres. There it attains immortality, perhaps union with a celestial counterpart in the bride chamber, and garments appropriate to its new location. Thomas's speech to a group of potential converts in the third act makes it clear that this ascent has nothing to do with the material body. The audience is exhorted to raise themselves above the earthly level in order to find salvation (chap. 37).

Chapters 108–113 (E. Hennecke and W. Schneemelcher, vol. 2, 498–504) contain a lengthy allegory of the soul's fall from its heavenly home. It wanders, lost and forgetful, in the lower world until a heavenly decree summons it back to its Father's kingly home. The soul is clothed in the garments that it had left in heaven and restored to its primordial unity. This "Hymn of the Pearl" easily fits into the stories of the descent, forgetfulness, and ascent of the soul in Gnostic mythology. However, this hymn does not use language that appears elsewhere in the *Acts of Thomas*. It can easily be separated from the context in which it is located. Therefore, many interpreters think that it was a later addition to the text.[25] As an addition, it fills out the details of the soteriological pattern that are left unspecified in the narrative.

The soteriology of the *Acts of Thomas* is predominantly one in which the believer now dwells in a hostile land, a place of struggle against the demons. But he or she knows that victory is assured by the powerful Savior, who is able to come to the believer's aid in the conflict. The resolution of the conflict can only be found in the immortality and joyous life with the Lord that awaits the faithful ones in heaven. Resurrection as such does not appear as a metaphor in this soteriology. What is crucial is the availability of the hidden, divine power to aid the disciple while living in this world.

A similar soteriological pattern informs the *Acts of Peter and the Twelve Apostles* (CG 6.1).[26] As is the case with the *Acts of Thomas*, this writing does not contain peculiarly Gnostic theological themes. The story describes a meeting between the disciples and a mysterious pearl merchant.[27] The merchant is rejected by the rich, since they think that he has nothing to sell. The poor are curious to see his pearls.

Peter asks the way to the stranger's city, since the apostles have been commissioned to spread the word of God everywhere (5.8–14; NHLE 266). The stranger warns that one must renounce everything in order to make the journey. He responds to Peter's comment that he hopes Jesus will enable them to make that journey with, "He is a great power for giving strength. For I too believe in the power of the Father who sent him" (6.17–19; NHLE: 268). When they reach the city, Jesus appears as a physician (8.14–20; NHLE: 268). Jesus reveals his identity, and the disciples worship him (9.2–21; NHLE: 269). They are to go forth as physicians of the soul. Their healing miracles are the occasion to introduce people to the real healing, that of the soul, "so that through the real powers of healing for their bodies, without the medicine of this world, they may believe in you, that you have the power to heal the illnesses of the heart also" (11.16–26; NHLE: 270). The disciples are warned to avoid partiality toward the wealthy, which the author claims has corrupted some churches. As in the other apocryphal acts traditions, Jesus is able to appear in various forms, which leave him unrecognized by those who see him. The motif of Jesus, the physician, was a prominent part of apocryphal acts, since they emphasized the healing powers of Jesus active in the apostles.[28] The *Acts of Peter and the Twelve Apostles* is also typical of many of the apocryphal acts in its emphasis on encratite renunciation of the world as the only foundation for true piety. However, the emphasis on true, spiritual healing over against the physical healing of the miracle tradition is uncharacteristic of the genre. It may be that claims to miraculous healing powers had become problematic in the community from which this writing comes. The patterns established in these writings reappear in other apocryphal material from the second and third centuries. Those concerned with bodily resurrection often emphasize the necessity of ascetic practices such as continence in order to make it a worthy vehicle for such salvation. Others speak of immortality as achieved by the soul, which follows the path of victorious ascent into the heavens that was marked out by the Lord. Such imaginative stories provide the hearer with a powerful conviction that the risen Lord lives in the heavens, that he might appear at any time, and that the believer will share a similar, glorious destiny.

GNOSTIC REVELATION DIALOGUES

Gnostic writers deliberately use the narrative line of an appearance of the risen Lord to a chosen group of disciples to advance the claim that Gnosticism is the true, esoteric interpretation of Christianity.[29] The content of the revelations runs the gamut of Gnostic teaching about cosmology and soteriology. The docetic Christology of the appearance traditions in Gnosticism correlates with the claim to manifest the hidden, esoteric teaching of Christ. This Christology insists that the resurrection appearances show forth the inner reality of the Christ. The survey of this theme in Chart Four indicates its importance for Gnostic traditions.

Chart Four
Resurrection Appearances: The Inner Reality

ApocryJn	SJC	PetPhil
[vision] creation trembled and shone multiple forms: youth, old man, servant	"great angel of light" not in his first form; in invisible spirit	great light appeared; mount shone [prayer to Father in holy child Jesus; Son/Christ of immortality; redeemer]
[fear] afraid why doubt? afraid?	wondered and afraid Savior laughed; why perplexed?	[fear persecution] why asking me?

ApocryJn	SJC	PetPhil
[interpretation; "I Am"] you are not unfamiliar with this likeness are you?	no mortal flesh can endure it; only pure and perfect flesh like that he taught us about on Mt. Olives in Galilee	you are witnesses I spoke all these things to you
I am one with you (pl) forever I am Father, Mother, Son. I am unpolluted, incorruptible One.	[peace be with you]	I am Jesus Christ who is with you forever

ApocPet	AcPet12	2ApocJas
[vision] like one laughing on tree with Holy Spirit; the Savior, great ineffable light around them ineffable, invisible angels blessing him.	Lithargoel, physician	I (Jas) stretched out my hands and I did not find him as I thought he would be
[fear] vision crucifixion; asks to flee	calls "Peter"; P. afraid	
[interpretation; I Am] of crucifixion scene released incorporeal body I am the intellectual Spirit filled with radiant light. One coming = our intellectual pleroma, which unites perfect light with my Holy Spirit.	loosens garment in which clothed self for our sake; It is I! Recognize me!	Understand! [James' hymn: he is the one creator did not see; is life; light; will come to be; Holy Spirit, Invisible One, did not descend on earth; naked; no garment clothing him.

The loose connection between setting and content suggests that the Gnostic appearance traditions were formulated independently of the content of the dialogues. Those that reflect a postresurrection appearance use much of the common second-century imagery for the appearance of the Lord.[30] Some of them may have originated in narrative traditions that filled in the gaps that had been lacking in the first-century traditions. We have seen, for example, that neither appearances to Peter nor to James are given as such in the first century despite the fact that our earliest traditions refer to such appearances. The Gnostic writings include appearances to both Peter and James.

We have already met a Gnostic "acts of the apostles" in the *Acts of Peter and the Twelve Apostles.* The Gnostic *Apocalypse of Peter* recounts a dialogue between Jesus and Peter that may have been set prior to the crucifixion. However, its genre and content are closer to the postresurrection dialogue tradition. The author is also concerned with the attempts of the orthodox bishops to repress Gnostic teaching. Consequently, he may have placed the revelation prior to the crucifixion in order to answer the argument that nothing in Jesus' teaching during his lifetime substantiates the Gnostic claims. A similar concern emerges in the postresurrection revelations of the *Letter of Peter to Philip.* Jesus chides his disciples, reminding them that what he is about to teach he had already taught during his life (CG 8.135.2f.; NHLE: 395–97).[31]

Two postresurrection dialogues are attached to James. The *Apocryphon of James* concludes with an ascent of the soul similar to that in the *Ascension of Isaiah.* The *First Apocalypse of James* combines a precrucifixion revelation of Gnostic teaching with a postresurrection appearance to the brother of the Lord.[32] The first-century traditions associate Mary Magdalene with the empty tomb; some of them also connect her with an appearance of the Lord near the tomb. The *Gospel of Mary* from the Berlin Codex presents an account of revelation that she had received privately from the Lord. The revelation forms part of a dialogue among the apostles prior to their setting out to preach according to the commission that they had received from the Lord. The opening of the work and a major part of Mary's revelation are missing. The work may have opened with some form of postresurrection revelation, since the first section concludes with a repetition of the commission to preach, the "peace" greeting, and a promise of the eternal presence of the Son of Man (8.14–9.6; NHLE: 472). Mary's revelation, possibly an independent piece of tradition,[33] says that she saw the Lord in a vision. This vision becomes an account of the soul's ascent through the hostile spheres to its place of rest. We cannot tell from what survives whether this vision was set before or after the crucifixion.

Other Gnostic dialogues are associated either with individual disciples or with the group of disciples (see *Dialogue of the Savior, Sophia of Jesus Christ, Letter of Peter to Philip*).[34] The elements of recognition of the Lord are not as prominent in these Gnostic writings as they are in the first-century stories. The apocryphal acts preserve the theme of recognition in the stories of the different forms that the Savior assumes: twin of the apostle, mysterious pearl merchant, physician. However, second-century stories, in general, are not pervaded by the miraculous discovery that the Lord has been raised in the way that the first-century traditions are. Whether Gnostic or not, second-century writers take the Lord's resurrection as a matter of course. But the Gnostic settings do concern themselves with the commissioning of apostles by the risen Lord. The commissioning, for them, provides an opportunity to advance the claim that true apostolic teaching is Gnostic.

The revelation dialogues often associate the Savior with light.[35] The *Apocryphon of John* adds polymorphous appearance and cosmic signs to its description.[36] The revealer appears as an old man, a child, and a servant (CG 2.1.32–2.9; NHLE: 99). This account could easily represent a more general tradition about the polymorphous image of the risen One. It emphasizes the unity of the various forms. However, the revealer immediately identifies himself with the Gnostic god, Father, Mother, and Son, in the I Am section of the revelation (2.9–15; NHLE: 99). The *Apocryphon of John* shows its readers that the risen Christ, the Gnostic revealer, and the Gnostic divine triad are identical. This identification is crucial to the author's apologetic intent, to show that all true Christians are Gnostic Christians.[37]

The long version of the *Apocryphon of John* from Codex II includes a hymnic passage in which the Savior identifies himself with the Gnostic Pronoia, the divine wisdom, who descends into the lower world to bring revelation (30.11–31.25; NHLE: 115f.). On the final descent, the Pronoia/revealer even enters the prison of the body in order to awaken the slumbering Gnostic souls.

This image of the call to awakening being delivered to the Gnostic or to the slumbering Adam as the prototype of the Gnostic presupposes a soteriology of baptism, enlightenment, and ascent of the soul that is typical of a broad spectrum of writings in the Nag Hammadi collection. In the cultic tradition, earthly baptism is identified with a heavenly one in which darkness is put off and light is put on. The Gnostic thus quits the "body of flesh," just as the ascending Savior does.[38]

The luminous appearance of the revealer is emphasized in Gnostic revelation dialogues. However, the Gnostics did not create luminous imagery for the risen One. Light is an index of heavenly reality and divine glory in the apocalyptic traditions of the first century. 1 Cor 15:43, 50 combine glory and incorruptibility, the two attributes that are most emphasized in the Gnostic discriptions of the revealer. Christ appears as a luminous, heavenly figure in Rev 1:12–16. Similarly, Acts describes the appearances to Paul as taking place in blinding light and as auditions of a heavenly voice (9:1–9; 22:9–18; 26:9–19). These features are emphasized by the *Letter of Peter to Philip*, which draws upon the opening chapters of Acts as well as Jesus' resurrection appearances for its narrative framework. The Transfiguration stories also use similar motifs for the heavenly glory of Jesus (Mt 17:2; 1 Pt 1:16–19).[39] Peter to Philip has drawn upon established traditions to formulate a powerful imagery of Jesus' appearance and his divine presence from heaven. In both *Sophia of Jesus Christ* and in the *Letter of Peter to Philip,* the promises in Mt 28:19f. play an important role. Jesus' authority and continued presence are passed on to the Gnostics.[40]

A number of the formulae in the *Letter of Peter to Philip* reflect primitive Christian traditions. The opening prayers may well represent the type of prayer formula that was common among second-century Christians. God is described as incorruptible in both Rom 1:23 and 1 Tim 1:27. Incorruptibility also represents the future state of the believer in 1 Cor 15:42–51. 2 Clem 20.5 describes Jesus as the "pioneer of incorruptibility." Of course, Gnostic writers use this theme to contrast the heavenly world with the lower, material one in order to sponsor rejection of all that is material. The description of Jesus as "your holy child, Jesus Christ" recalls Ac 4:27, 30 and *Didache* 9.2 and 10.2. The Father is, of course, "well pleased" with Jesus in both the baptism and Transfiguration stories. However, the Christology of this writing is not simply built up out of traditional phrases. Its favorite designation, "Illuminator," is typically Gnostic. The Gnostic writings show little concern with the bodily elements of the resurrection stories. What counts is the luminous appearance of the risen Lord. That appearance is well suited to the Gnostic image of a savior who descends to enlighten those lost in the darkness of the world. The second element in the resurrection stories that place an important role for the Gnostics is the commissioning of witnesses to the true teaching of the Lord. The New Testament traditions were silent about any content to Jesus' postresurrection discourse with his disciples and were ambiguous about the period between Easter and the ending of resurrection appearances. These ambiguities provided open ground for elaboration in the second century. Similarly, uncertainties about who were recipients of the original visions—was there one or more than one appearance, to individuals as well as to the twelve, and the like—provided another place for the development of new traditions. The Gnostics need not have invented all of the traditions that they used. Some of their stories may be based on apocryphal material that was already circulating among Christians in general. The vision of the risen Lord as polymorphous, as luminous divine figure who appears from heaven, had a broad appeal across various segments of second-century Christianity. These images probably represent the description that second-century Christians would give if they were asked what was meant by belief that Jesus had been raised.

APOLOGISTS

Before we turn to the debates between Gnostic and Christian teachers on resurrection, we will look at those arguments aimed at those who stood outside Christian circles. Second-century apologists sought to explain resurrection or to defend the reasonableness of such belief in the face of non-Christian objections. This type of apologetic is necessary to present resurrection in a context that treats the material world as transitory and corruptible over against the divine eternal world. The true reality of the divine world, so it was commonly held, was only mediated to humans through the soul.

Justin Martyr

Justin Martyr's *Dialogue with Trypho* develops traditional associations between resurrection and judgment. Chapter 45 raises the issue in the context of the question about what happens to those persons who lived their life righteously according to the Law. Those who did what was pleasing to God before Christ's coming are to be saved. Justin links resurrection with the millenarian tradition of a thousand-year rule of the Messiah on earth. Justin condemns as heretics and atheistic those who "venture to blaspheme the God of Abraham, Isaac and Jacob, who say that there is no resurrection of the dead, and that when they die their souls are taken to heaven." In the next section of the *Dialogue,* Justin provides proof for his view of the millennium from prophecies of Isaiah and on the basis of Rev 20:4–5. The passage from Revelation is understood as the prelude to the general resurrection and judgment of all people. Justin associates that view with Jesus' saying about resurrected existence as like that of angels from Lk 20:35–36.

Justin also argues that when Christians claim to be "sons of God" they are claiming the immortality that God had intended humans to have from the beginning *(Dialogue* 124).[41] He invokes the Psalms as evidence. Since the Psalms refer to humans as "sons of God," they must have the power to become such. Some of the same traditions reappear in Justin's *Apology,* where they take on a new guise. For example, Plato is invoked to prove that eternal punishment involves body as well as soul (1 Apol. 8).

Justin also addresses the question of the delay of the parousia. It springs, he says, from God's concern for those who might yet be saved through repentance (1 Apol. 28). It is part of the divine providence, which includes the powerful spread of Christianity as preached by the apostles.

Justin also makes it clear that the postresurrection instruction of the Lord concerned prophecies of the passion (1 Apol. 1). Thus, the tradition that we saw embodied in the Lukan resurrection narrative had been continued in the second century.

Justin goes beyond these traditional materials in 1 Apol. 18–19. He is well aware that the Christian views about judgment and resurrection conflict with other beliefs about immortality. Justin's argument begins by rejecting the view held by most second-century Platonists that the world is eternal. But, Justin argues, if the world is begotten, the same thing should apply to the soul. What, then, prevents the soul from simply dying? Justin argues that natural immortality is not what keeps the soul from dying but a divine justice that will not permit the wicked the consolation of thinking that they simply die.

Justin follows good Platonic tradition in linking this unusual view of the soul to the question of the eternity of the world. Justin's argument insists that God is the only naturally incorruptible and unbegotten one. Whatever is not God is created and therefore corruptible. Further, were the soul naturally immortal, it would not fall into vice, ignorance, or any other folly. Finally, Justin argues, there could not be more than one unbegotten principle, since it would be impossible to differentiate one from another. Consequently, there must be a single, unbegotten cause of all things. Although this argument about creation does not take up the question of resurrection directly, it lays a foundation for rejecting the major competing vision of salvation, the natural immortality of the soul and its knowledge of God. The argument establishes the sovereignty of God as Creator over against everything else in the universe. Only God is unbegotten and incorruptible. Consequently, both body and soul are equally dependent on His divine power if they are to continue in existence. It is no more difficult for God to maintain souls in existence than it is for Him to maintain material creation.

1 Apol. 18–19 draws out the significance of Justin's argument over creation. In chapter 18, Justin acknowledges the widespread skepticism about any survival after death. He begins the chapter by refuting the view that death ends in insensibility.[42] That view only benefits the wicked. Justin then invokes a number of popular practices

and superstitions to prove that people do not in fact hold that death is the end of all things. Justin points to necromancy, to calling up the spirits of the departed, belief in possession by the spirits of the dead, belief in familiar spirits, and belief in oracles.[43] In addition, Justin points to the indications of an afterlife to be found in the teachings of Homer, Empedocles, Pythagoras, Plato, and Socrates. Justin argues that while the pagan has only an ill-defined conviction that one survives death, Christians have a certain conviction that they will receive the body back. This certainty is grounded in the belief that God is Creator, one for whom anything is possible (1 Apol. 18).

1 Apol. 18 argues that nature proves the reasonableness of this belief in resurrection. Instead of using seed analogies such as we found in 1 Corinthians and 1 Clement, Justin points to the origin of the human being from sperm as proof that God has power sufficient to bring people back from the dead.[44] He argues that the view that everything dissolves into its elements is unworthy of the power of God.[45] This view limits God's power within the bounds of human imagination.

Justin concludes the argument with two sayings of Jesus that authenticate Christian belief in what might seem to be impossible (Mt 10:28; 19:26).

Justin begins to collect pagan analogies for the Christian belief in judgment in 1 Apol. 20. He contrasts the Christian view of a final "conflagration" with the Stoic understanding of the return of all things, even God, to the primordial fire. Once again, Justin understands the debate to be grounded in cosmological perceptions about the world. Unlike the Stoic God, the Christian Creator is superior to the world of change.[46] Justin's emphasis on the ability of both the condemned and the blessed to experience sensation appears to be an implicit defense of the preaching of resurrected body.

Justin's defense of Christian eschatology depends on the claim that it encapsulates the hints about eschatology that are embedded in the philosophic and poetic traditions. The only one that he cannot accommodate is the Epicurean view that death represents dissolution back into the original elements. This view was widely condemned by opponents of the Epicureans as "atheistic." Justin repeats the standard anti-Epicurean argument: the Epicurean view destroys the foundations of morality. What is new in Justin's Christian argument is the combination of transcendent God, all-powerful Creator, and the possibility of a new act of creation, the resurrection of the body.

Tatian

Tatian's *Oratio* makes two of Justin's themes, the nature of the soul and the power of the Creator, central. Bodily resurrection is a manifestation of divine power in a new act of creation that has nothing to do with the Stoic view of conflagration. With regard to the soul, Christian apologists were forced to distinguish immortality as divine gift from the natural immortality of Platonism. Tatian's exposition of the Christian doctrine of creation appears to have been derived from a lost work of Justin's that had used Stoic material to prove Christian teachings much as we have seen him do in 1 Apology.[47] Tatian bases his argument for resurrection as a new creation by arguing that matter is not a principle that was coexistent with God.[48] Matter was brought into being by the Creator (Or. 5.3). This same creative power implies that there will be a bodily resurrection at the end of all things. Tatian distinguishes the Christian view that all things come to an end from Stoic views of conflagration and cyclic recurrence. Resurrection is not the complete repetition of the cosmic process because it culminates in the judgment of humanity (Or. 6.1).

Prior to being born, the individual is merely a potentiality of substance and matter. After death, one returns to the same state. Whether the individual is burned, drowned, or eaten by wild beasts, the matter of which the body was composed remains in the world. Therefore, Tatian concludes, "God, the ruler, when he wishes, will restore to its original state the substance that is visible only to him" (Or. 6.2). This argument does not address the question of whether it is appropriate to the nature of the relationship between soul and body that the body be restored. Tatian argues against the view that the soul is naturally immortal. He distinguishes between souls that are ignorant of the truth and those that have knowledge of God. Those ignorant of the truth died with the body, while those with knowledge of God are animated by the Spirit of God. Thus, Tatian has adapted the tripartite body, soul, spirit division to his argument by equating the highest principle, spirit, with God's Spirit.[49]

Tatian presumes that the spirit in humans was lost with the fall (Or. 7).[50] He argues against the Stoics that the created soul, and not the divine Spirit, is what is active in humans (Or. 16.2–3). In order for humans to have knowledge of God, they must receive revelation.[51] This anthropology treats spirit and soul as an original syzygy, which has been fractured. It enables him to argue against the natural immortality of souls as they exist. However, Tatian is then forced to graft resurrection onto a doctrine of spirit that does not require resurrection language (Or. 13.1).

Thus, one has the peculiar image of resurrecting the soul. The only way out of the natural darkness of the soul is union with the divine Spirit. The soul in its natural state has only a "spark" of the Spirit's power. That spark is not sufficient to give the soul knowledge of the divine realm. Instead, the soul's search for God miscarries into idolatry (Or. 13.2). Tatian goes on to argue that the judgment that brings each human either pleasure or pain will apply to the immortal spirits, the demons, as well (Or. 14.2). By linking the soul to the divine Spirit, the soul's lost unity can be restored. Tatian insists that the union of soul and body is found in the composite nature of the soul. However, unlike his Platonist contemporaries, who would also agree that union of soul and body implied that the soul was composite,[52] Tatian concludes from the conjunction of soul and body that it is never possible for the soul to exist without the body (Or. 15.1).

Tatian goes on to deny that the human being can be defined as a "rational being capable of intelligence and understanding." Instead, those who practice virtue are said to be in the image of God. But this image can only be attained by those believers who receive the divine Spirit (Or. 15.2–3).

Tatian has not been able to link the salvation of the soul with the defense of bodily resurrection in a way that would counter the Platonic objection that resurrection is unnecessary. While the conjunction between body and soul as the locus of sense perception fits well with the view of judgment as eternal experience of pleasure and pain, Tatian's own example of the punishment of the nonbodily demons proves the opposite. It is possible to afflict the soul as the seat of sense perception with pleasure or pain quite without any bodily vehicle.[53] It appears that Tatian has incorporated resurrection of the body into an anthropology and understanding of salvation that was formulated without any concern for resurrection.

Athenagoras

Athenagoras's *Legatio* is composed as a forensic speech addressed to the emperor, which was to be circulated among the general public. Athenagoras emphasizes the complete power of God over the world (Leg. 13.2). Christians are uncompromising in their insistence that this God is the only one to be worshiped (Leg. 16.1–3). The emphasis on radical monotheism is combined with an equally strong emphasis on the moral character of Christian behavior.

Athenagoras introduces the doctrine of resurrection as part of the defense against the suspicion that Christians practice cannibalism. He says that those who do not believe in any afterlife would be more likely to commit such an outrage (Leg. 36.2). Resurrection permits punishment for the body, which has contributed the impulses that cause humans to do evil.[54] The concluding section of the chapter acknowledges the possibility that people will reject the doctrine of resurrection. Athenagoras says that he is dispensing with proof from the authority of philosophers, who might also be shown to teach such a doctrine, lest he be accused of diverting the reader from the purpose of the argument. He insists that both Plato and Pythagoras can be shown to be compatible with a doctrine of resurrection, since it is possible for bodies to be reconstituted out of the elements from which they arose.[55]

The assertion that he will not talk about the philosophers and the claim that Plato's and Pythagoras's teaching about the elements supports resurrection frame a difficult argument about the relationship between the intelligible and sensible worlds. This argument attempts to explain how bodies can be reconstituted. Their reassembly appears to be based on the survival of the "form" of these bodies in the intelligible realm. One might have expected the soul to have been presented as the necessary form. However, that view is clearly not entertained. We have seen that Tatian presumed to reconstruct the body out of its elements on the basis of a substance visible to God alone. Perhaps there was a typical argument in Christian circles that held that God reconstituted elements of the body on the basis of His knowledge of the required "form" of each individual.[56] The Athenagoras text presumes a double compounding: first the intelligibles are compounded into corporeals and then into physical bodies. This process may reflect an attempt to explain the relationship of intelligible forms to a world of compound bodies.[57] Philo's description of creation also presupposes a dual process. God must first fashion an intelligible world before creating the visible one "in order that . . . He might be able to use an immaterial and most god-like model, producing from this elder model a younger imitation which would contain within itself as many sensible classes of being as there were intelligible ones" (Opif. 16).[58] Leg. 31.4 contains an argument that is more simplistic than the later one. It presumes that the body is the locus of feeling but that it will cease to afflict the "changeless and impassible soul" when it is possessed of the heavenly Spirit. A theme from Tatian's argument against natural immortality appears to lie behind this argument as well. The Spirit makes it possible for those who are saved to lead a changeless and impassible life in God's presence. Those who are condemned, on the other hand, will be able to suffer all the torments of the fire to which they are condemned.

Athenagoras may have used earlier Christian apologetic traditions in this defense of Christian virtue. Those traditions would have claimed that only Christians attained the impassibility claimed by the Stoic philosophers.

Theophilus

Ad Autoc. 1.5 provides a striking example of Christian adaptation of eschatological traditions to meet the counterclaims of popular Platonism. In treating God's invisibility, Theophilus argues that the vision of God is made complete at the resurrection. However, God becomes somewhat visible in this life through the effects of divine providence. The argument from providence is typical of Stoic philosophers. For Theophilus, the claim about seeing God in the providential ordering of the world is based in the fact that the Spirit of God surrounds and guides the cosmos.[59] But lest the reader presume that all that is intended is transformation of the soul, Theophilus uses 1 Cor 15:53f. to prove the claim that the vision of God is only attained with the resurrection (1.7). A list of evidence is provided to convince the skeptic that resurrection is believable. The list is prefaced by what appears to be a proverbial expression: "Faith leads the way in all actions."[60] Thus, it encourages the believer to "trust God" just as the farmer trusts seed to the earth, a person trusts the ship to the pilot, the sick person trusts the doctor, and the student trusts the doctor.

God has already demonstrated divine power by bringing the individual into existence out of nonexistence, out of "moist matter and a tiny drop." Having made the person out of what did not exist, God can do so again. This argument is a traditional one in second-century resurrection apologetic. Theophilus also aims a barb at his audience when he suggests that the popular belief in statues of the gods working miracles is surely more incredible than the Christian belief in resurrection (1.8). Ad Autoc. 1.13 resumes the argument about resurrection. Theophilus claims that consideration of these matters is sufficient to enable a person to gain that belief in God that is necessary for salvation (1.14). The section opens with the hypothetical demand that the author show at least one instance of a person who has been raised. First, Theophilus answers that belief would have no importance if a person witnessed an event of resurrection. Second, he points to myths in which both Hercules and Asclepius are said to have been raised after death. Third, he remarks that even if one could bring a dead person back to life, people would still not believe.

Theophilus then turns to the actual evidence of resurrection that God has provided in nature: the change of seasons; the cycle of day and night; the "resurrection" of grains and fruits from seeds that have died—even from seeds that have been eaten by birds. Such arguments from the natural order are conventional. However, Theophilus ties them directly to the theme of an all-powerful divine providence that is operative in these natural occurrences. He then draws the standard conclusion that they show God to be capable of resurrection.

Theophilus singles out as particularly marvelous demonstrations of this divine power the monthly cycles of the moon and the recovery of flesh by a person who has suffered a severe illness. He acknowledges that a person might say that the patient gained flesh back through the food eaten. But, he claims, even that process testifies to divine creative activity, since God created the required relationship between the body and food.

Theophilus's arguments are largely conventional. What appears different in the work is the clarity with which resurrection is presented as the foundation of the vision of God. Theophilus also shows us a doctrine of creation that derived from Jewish Christian sources that had been reformulated according to the Stoic vision of a pervasive, providential divine Word. For the second-century debate with outsiders, the doctrines of monotheism, of God's creative providence, and of the cycles of nature were a large part of the presentation of resurrection. We have often found the language of future judgment presented as the distinguishing characteristic of Christian eschatology. When resurrection is tied to judgment, it is presumed that the bodily character of resurrection makes appropriate punishment of the body possible. The body plays less of a role in the reward of the righteous, since it is difficult to square with the language of vision of God as the goal of human life. We have also found in Justin, Athenagoras, and Tatian signs of traditions in which Christians had given a more philosophical defense of their belief. This tradition of argumentation appears to have focused on providing a doctrine of the elements that would explain how resurrection is possible. Throughout these arguments, resurrection is assumed to mean restoration of the physical body. The question of the appropriate body for resurrection becomes explicit in the debates between Gnostic teachers and their orthodox opponents.

GNOSTIC TEACHERS

The most striking examples of Gnostic understanding of the resurrection of the believer come from passages in which the author expounds 1 Cor 15. Theodotus describes Paul the "apostle of the resurrection" as a type of the Paraclete whom Jesus had predicted (Excerpta 23.2). Excerpta 22 provides a Valentinian exegesis of 1 Cor 15:29. The living are the angelic counterparts of the Gnostics. They have not descended into this world, that is, into death. The angels were baptized when the dove descended on Jesus (Excerpta 22.6). That baptism makes it possible for the Gnostic, who has been baptized in the same manner as his or her angelic counterpart, to ascend through the spheres into the Pleroma (22.4–5). The ascent into the Pleroma is the resurrection. The Gnostic soul is raised "equal to angels, restored to the males, member to member, to form a unity" (22.3). Excerpta 80 describes the translation of the soul into the Ogdoad as a second birth. This birth takes place at the time of death. It represents "the destruction of death by death, and of corruption by resurrection." Thus, the Gnostic fulfills the words of 1 Cor 15:49: "Having born the image of the earthly man, he will then bear the image of the heavenly one" (80.3; Foerster, vol. 1:230). These accounts reflect a standard Valentinian interpretation of resurrection language. Origen provides yet another example of Valentinian exegesis in his report of Heracleon's exegesis of Jn 4:46–53 (Com. In Jo. 13.60; Foerster, vol. 1:177). Heracleon used the words "He was about to die" to refute the view that the soul is naturally immortal. His argument apparently included proof of the destruction of the soul based on the saying in Mt 10:28. We have seen that Christian apologists also found themselves compelled to reject the philosophic view of the soul as naturally immortal. Heracleon understood the soul as having a tendency toward immortality that had to be realized in the coming of true immortality. He argued that Paul was speaking about the soul in 1 Cor 15:54. Origen claims that he does not understand Heracleon's argument at this point. He proceeds to give another interpretation of the story that treated it as an indication of the different types of person in the world.[61] This section of Heracleon's commentary appears to have been concerned with conversion. That concern may have been responsible for his insistence on the natural mortality of the soul over against those who claimed it to be immortal.

On the Resurrection

The fourth treatise in Codex I contains a tract devoted to the subject of resurrection. The treatise is cast as a didactic letter from a Gnostic teacher to a disciple.[62] The author tells his disciple, Rheginos, that he should not think *merikos*, "according to particulars,"[63] nor should he live in conformity with the flesh. Instead, he is to perceive himself as one who is already risen and brought to life (CG 1.49.9–24; NHLE: 53). The pupil is one who still lacks the exercise or practice necessary for persons who are to be released from this element, the material body, and to return to their primordial unity (49.25–35). The text also presents images of resurrection that imply the destruction of the body and a regeneration of inward, spiritual members in association with interpreting Biblical passages.[64]

The author says that his opponents seek to exalt themselves by answering questions to which they have no answer. They go beyond the "word of truth." He also contrasts the masses who have no faith in resurrection with the few who find it. The author begins with difficulties that must be eradicated before the reader can gain a proper understanding of his teaching. First, what is the nature of the Lord? The author explains that the earthly teaching of the Lord included the topic of humanity's inevitable immortality.[65] The human and divine aspects of the Lord, his revelation as Son of Man and Son of God, form the foundation of a dual victory over death.[66] The Lord conquered death as Son of God. As Son of Man, he restored what had been lost to the Pleroma (44.26–36; NHLE: 61).[67]

The next section expounds the double destruction of death that is implied by the opening argument. The Savior "swallowed up" death by putting aside this perishable world and transforming himself into an imperishable aeon (45.14–18; NHLE: 51). This language has appeared in other writings. The *Apocryphon of John* begins by referring back to the Lord's prediction that the aeon to which the disciples would go is the type of the imperishable aeon (CG 2.1.12–19; NHLE: 99). The vision of the Lord in the *Apocalypse of Peter* shows his transformation into the imperishable aeon as a merger with the intellectual pleroma (7.83.10–15; NHLE: 344). The reference in *On the Resurrection* to the Savior's having "swallowed up" death and the visible world (45.14–20; NHLE: 51) may be a reference to 1 Cor 15:54.[68] However, the author goes on to quote as evidence of the apostle's teaching a passage that conflates Rom 8:17 and Eph 2:5–6 (45.24–28). In raising himself up, the Savior has shown the Gnostic the way of immortality.[69] The Pauline allusion shows that the present existence of believers is one in which they have suffered, risen, and gone to heaven with the Lord. However, the explanation does not present a completely realized eschatology. Instead, the author speaks of the Gnostic as "wearing him (= the Savior) in this world." The Gnostic is like a sunbeam and will be drawn up to heaven at death without any obstacle (45.28–39). B. Layton points to a similar use of the image of the Lord as the sun and his ray as lifting up the believer in the *Odes of Solomon* (15.1b–9a).[70] However, this image probably came to the author from Platonic traditions. Plutarch's treatment of the decline of oracles includes a description of those rational beings—demigods, heroes, and men—that are below the level of gods. Hesiod is credited with teaching that there are four classes of rational beings. The golden race was transmuted into good divinities, and the demigods were turned into heroes (Def. Or. 415B). Souls are said to be transmuted just like matter (Def. Or. 415BC).

Purified, divine souls belong to the realm of the sun. Plutarch would agree with the tripartite anthropology that appears in *On the Resurrection:* "this is the spiritual resurrection which swallows up the psychic in the same way as the fleshly" (45.39–46.2). He would not, of course, use resurrection language and would speak of the noetic part or the mind instead of the pneumatic or spiritual. A favored few may be able to separate the mind from the soul. The separation is accomplished out of love for the image (of the good), which is the sun. They leave the vestiges of the soul on the moon (944EF). The moon is described as an element into which the soul dissolves. For those who have led a philosophical life, the dissolution happens quickly, since the mind has abandoned her and the soul no longer has passions (945A). Plutarch's correlation of the ascent and descent of the soul with the elements and the planetary regions suggests that *On the Resurrection* may be repeating an argument for resurrection that Christians had developed on the basis of a similar stoicized Platonism. All the Gnostic has to do is shift from ascent to the stars to return to the Pleroma. This argument probably originated in a Christian context in which its intent was to defend Christian views of immortality against those of the philosophic tradition. The Christian asserts that the righteous attain immortality; the Platonist opponent, that only a very few souls, after a long period of time, achieve immortality with the gods. *On the Resurrection* hints at this context when it follows the argument with the contrast between those who believe that "the dead shall rise" and the worldly philosopher who does not

(46.3–21; NHLE: 51f.).[71] Faith, not philosophy, is the only route to the saving knowledge that gives immortality.

Philosophic debate also appears in the affirmation about faith that follows. The thought or mind of those who have known the Savior will not perish (46.12–24; NHLE: 52). This knowledge is a wisdom or truth for which the Gnostic is predestined. The author grounds the certainty of that truth in its origins, that is, the Pleroma (46.35–47.1).[72] The Pleroma is eternal, all-encompassing, and much greater than the small, material creation that it surrounds.[73] The epithets given the Pleroma are reminiscent of those used for God—powerful, all-encompassing, *agenētos* (did not come into being), always existing. Thus, this Gnostic affirmation about the Pleroma occupies the same place in the argument that other second-century Christian writers give to affirmation of the omnipotence of God as Creator.

The treatise then turns to the question of whether or not the resurrected will have bodies in the immortal aeon. It is apparently answering an objection that proposed that if the soul had received a body upon descent into the world, the body would coexist with the soul in the next (47.4–24; NHLE: 52). Orthodox writers raised similar arguments in defending bodily resurrection. They also attached claims about bodily resurrection to affirmations of divine omnipotence. *On the Resurrection* holds that the soul uses the flesh here. However, the cause of life is far superior to the body. The soul loses nothing by departing from the world and from the corruptible flesh. The author apparently intends to formulate a *reductio ad absurdum* that presents those who claim resurrection for the body seeking to exist "as corruption."[74]

This rejection of bodily resurrection leads to the final section. There resurrection is the identification of the Gnostic soul with the Pleroma (47.24–48.19; NHLE: 52f.). The various parts of the argument are not altogether clear. Apparently, the reference to the one who leaves the body behind being saved immediately (47.31–48.3) is directed against those who suggest that salvation must await the general resurrection. The author immediately asserts that the visible members of the body do not rise. Only that which is within does so.[75]

The final question appeals to the Transfiguration story as evidence for the truth of resurrection. Layton thinks that the reference to the Transfiguration is part of an objection: the resurrection is an illusion or a sensible manifestation that requires the continuity of the body. M. L. Peel insists that the Transfiguration is a positive demonstration of the inner or spiritual body that is raised.[76] Both interpretations somewhat expand the text. The author clearly presumes that the Transfiguration is evidence of his view of resurrection. He is probably

repeating what he knows to be a conventional argument. But he may
also have considered it a congenial proof, since it indicates that resurrection can be immediate transformation. It does not have to await
any future transformation of the body. The author tacks on several
examples of the changeable character of the material world in order
to show that if anything is illusory, it is that world in which the living
die, the rich become poor, and kings are overthrown (48.20–30).
Resurrection, on the other hand, is a truth that "stands firm" (48.33).
The contrast between the changeable, material world and the stability of the divine world is a *topos* that Gnostic soteriology has derived
from Platonism. This soteriological assertion is followed by a list that
the author calls "symbols and images" of the resurrection.[77] It says
resurrection is "revelation of what is; transformation of things; transition to newness; imperishability [which descends] upon the perishable; light which flows down upon darkness, swallowing it; the Pleroma which fills the deficiency" (48.34–49.5; NHLE: 53). This chain
of images moves from the individualized process of transformation to
the cosmic transformation of all that belongs to the Pleroma.

The author clearly holds that the teaching on resurrection that he
gives represents the truth of the Christian revelation and to salvation
by Christ, the divine and human Savior. But he just as clearly holds
that Christians who think that resurrection refers to flesh as well as
soul and that it will only occur at the judgment are also in error. His
soteriology fits the Gnostic understanding of the restoration of the
divine to the Pleroma. At the same time, the author rejects the claim
that immortality comes through philosophy. He insists that it comes
through Gnosis, since Jesus' ascent makes it possible for the believer
to be similarly clothed and to follow the Savior like a ray of the sun.
Like most second-century Christians, the author sees Christ as the
One who has destroyed death.

Gospel of Philip

A more elaborate teaching on resurrection lies behind sections of the
Gospel of Philip.[78] The author addresses the question of the "naked-
ness" of spiritual bodies in light of traditions from 1 Cor 15. Some are
said to fear that they will rise naked. They are shown the inferiority
of the fleshly body in contrast to the heavenly body that they will
wear in the next world.[79] The *Gospel of Philip* holds that the believer
must be transformed into divinity while on earth through the sacrament of the bridal chamber. This secret ritual is described as the

necessary "image of resurrection" through which the Gnostic attains identity with the divine.[80] We cannot describe the entire sacramental theology of the *Gospel of Philip*. However, it is necessary to remember its cultic orientation when evaluating claims made by the author. *Gospel of Philip* insists that the resurrection is not attained after death. It must be attained in this life (56.15–20; NHLE: 134).

After a parable comparing the soul to a precious object that is hidden from thieves in something of no value, the exposition of resurrection continues with specific references to 1 Cor 15:50 and Jn 6:53. The section is a series of questions and answers about bodily resurrection. The questions and answers go beyond the simple denial of bodily resurrection. They explain that it is necessary to put on the appropriate garments, apparently through the sacramental rituals of the sect.[81] The author answers two types of objections: (a) those who hold that a person rises in the body of flesh, and (b) those who object that there is no connection at all between what happens in the flesh (presumably during the sacraments) and the resurrection (56.27–58.22; NHLE: 134–35).

The author's sacramental theology is dictated by the conviction that truth is mediated to those in this world through the body. Consequently, bodily sacraments are a necessary part of resurrection.[82] The various levels at which the truth is operative underlie *Gospel of Philip*'s description of Jesus as the one who enters the world in diverse forms. Jesus is said to have shown himself to his disciples in his greatness on the mountain. This may be a reference to the Gnostic images of the risen Jesus. He transforms the disciples and utters a prayer of thanksgiving (58.5–14; NHLE: 135).

The resurrection vision provides an etiology for a Gnostic prayer of union with the divine angels. The Thanksgiving refers to the epiclesis of a Gnostic eucharist, which may have been understood to have been instituted by the risen Lord. The eucharistic context is strengthened by the concluding exhortation, "Do not despise the Lamb, for without it, it is not possible to see the king. No one will be able to go in to see the king if that person is naked" (58.14–17; NHLE: 135).

Gospel of Philip links resurrection to eucharist, to baptism, and to the reunion of the image with its angel in the bridal chamber (69.25f.; NHLE: 142). Thus, one cannot speak of *Gospel of Philip* as simply teaching baptismal resurrection. The author rejects the sacraments of other groups, claiming that their baptism does not confer the Spirit. He insists that unless resurrection is attained sacramentally in this world, it cannot be attained in the next (66.8; 66.16–20; NHLE: 140; 86.6–14; NHLE: 151). He explains the ascent of the soul past the powers as made possible by its invisibility. Since it has been clothed with the perfect light, "the powers do not see those who are clothed in the perfect light, and consequently are not able to detain them. One will clothe himself in this light sacramentally in the union" (70.5–9; NHLE: 142). Once again, the future destiny of the Gnostic must be established through the sacramental realities of the present. Thus, the author comments, "What is the resurrection? The image must rise again through the image" (67:14–18; NHLE: 140).

Gospel of Philip acknowledges the difference between the present body in which these sacraments are received and the one that is our garment at the resurrection. The latter is linked to the true reality of the risen Lord. Thus, the Lord does not rise in the body that is buried but in the true flesh (68.31–37; NHLE: 141).

Gospel of Philip has gone further than any of the other Gnostic writers in linking together the resurrection appearances of Jesus, the soteriology of the ascent and reunification of the soul, and sacramental practice. It argues that sacramental praxis is necessary, since one must attain in this life the salvation that one expects for the future. The author is claiming a basis for extending this concept to resurrection in the New Testament itself. He persistently repeats the injunction that the person must gain resurrection here (73.1–5; NHLE: 143). Not all Gnostic teachers would accept this emphasis on the real mediation of salvation through ritual. The author has acknowledged this difficulty when he counters both those who think that they must rise in the flesh and those who teach that the soul will rise naked. This Gnostic group is not concerned with speculation about the nature of resurrection or its foundation in a particular anthropology or soteriology. It is concerned with the cultic experience of the reality of resurrection. Once the Gnostic has passed through the sacramental order of this sect, he or she has come to know him or herself as one "who is risen already."

CHRISTIAN TEACHERS

We now turn to three Christian writers whose treatment of resurrection is at least partly directed against the objections and reformulations of the Gnostic teachers: Irenaeus, Tertullian, and Origen.

Irenaeus

Irenaeus addresses the central themes of the Gnostic treatment of resurrection along lines that will become established Christian teaching. His central contribution to the development of Christian understanding of resurrection is his insistence that both body and soul are necessary to have a human person (Adv. Haer. 5.6.1). They are both part of God's intention for humans in the creation. Consequently, they must both be involved in salvation, which brings that divine purpose to its fulfillment. Irenaeus follows the traditional pattern of Christian apologetic when he argues that God's power as Creator enables him to transform the human body (Adv. Haer. 5.3.2). He uses the narrative elements of the gospels and Acts to counter Gnostic views. He points to Jesus' healing miracles (Adv. Haer. 5.12.5; 13.1) and to the debate about resurrection between Jesus and the Sadducees (Adv. Haer. 4.5.2). Irenaeus also knows that his Gnostic opponents frequently appeal to 1 Cor 15:50. He counters with 1 Cor 15:53 as evidence that the apostle did not teach a spiritual resurrection but a transformation of the mortal body that renders it immortal.[83]

Like *On the Resurrection*, Irenaeus can start with the evidence for the divinity and humanity of Christ in the two titles Son of God and Son of Man. But, for Irenaeus, the incarnation is not simply descent from a heavenly realm. The incarnation is the means by which the clothing of the mortal with immortality is possible. Like the Gnostics, Irenaeus will speak of the corruptible being swallowed up, but he will mean something quite different by it (Adv. Haer. 3.19.1).

Like *Gospel of Philip*, Irenaeus emphasizes the significance of the sacraments. He uses the traditional understanding of the eucharist against his Gnostic opponents (Adv. Haer. 5.2.2–3). If it is not possible for God to save the flesh, he argues, then it is not possible for God to transmit salvation through the eucharistic sacrifice, either. Our bodily nature receives the sacraments and is transformed. Throughout Irenaeus's treatment one finds a new emphasis on the transforming power of the Spirit in bringing about salvation.[84] The dying and rising of a grain of wheat, which becomes the eucharist, exemplifies the ordering of the whole world toward the salvation that has become available in Christ.[85]

At the same time, Irenaeus warns that humans should not mistake salvation received through the power of God for their own accomplishment. They cannot lay claim to being endowed with natural immortality. Just as the elements of the eucharist are transformed by divine power, so the Christian is transformed (Adv. Haer. 5.2.3).

Irenaeus accuses the Gnostics of denying the power of God as Creator when they deny the resurrection. If God created humans out of dust, he can even more easily reintegrate what had been created. Further, if it is so impossible for the flesh to receive life from God, then Irenaeus's supposedly live opponents must be walking "dead men" (Adv. Haer. 5.3.2–3). Thus, he turns back at the Gnostics their own epithet "dead men," a term they had directed at those Christians who did not have gnosis.

The heart of Irenaeus's refutation comes in the discussion of the created image of God in the human being (Adv. Haer. 5.6–13). Irenaeus rejects the whole tradition of a Platonic reading of Genesis that goes back to Philo. That tradition held that the image of God in the human being is the soul or mind, simply. Instead, Irenaeus argues that the body is part of the image fashioned by the Creator. Consequently, the body must also have been created with the capability of being transformed into the life that is brought about by the Spirit of God.[86] The incarnation is central to this transformation, since it is the perfect image of God. The transforming work of the Holy Spirit makes the believer a temple of God. Irenaeus has taken Paul's metaphor from the paraenesis of 1 Cor 6:13 to show his opponents that the body was created as temple and as "members of Christ." He includes in this demonstration the sayings about Jesus' raising the temple in three days, that is, the temple of his body from Jn 2:19f. (Adv. Haer. 5.6.1–12).

Irenaeus insists that the clear sense of the resurrection of Jesus in the New Testament and of the New Testament promises of resurrection for the believer is that resurrection refers to the body. He points to the resurrection stories in which the body that the risen Jesus shows the disciples is the body that was crucified (Adv. Haer. 5.7.1). Irenaeus insists that 1 Cor 15:36, 42–44 refers to the body. They cannot refer to the life-giving spirit, since it makes no sense to speak of the spirit as subject to mortality (Adv. Haer. 5.7.2). However, Irenaeus does not suppose that the transformation of the believer by the Spirit is entirely in the future. He suggests that the activity of the Spirit in the present is the beginning of that transformation. Thus, he is willing to say that the activity of the Holy Spirit makes the believer "spiritual even now, and the mortal is swallowed up by immortality." Irenaeus will not leave his Gnostic opponents as the only ones to claim experience of the transforming activity of the Spirit. But we are still only partially transformed. We have not yet attained the vision of God. Irenaeus warns that one cannot expect to attain future glory by casting aside the flesh. If anything, our present life in the Spirit proves that the future will include the body (Adv. Haer. 5.8.1). God will make the believer like Christ through the Spirit. The completely transformed person is made "after the image and likeness of God."

Irenaeus would also agree with those Gnostic teachers who took the doctrine of resurrection to imply that humans have a certain freedom from the flesh in the ascetic life. He acknowledges that the Christian must walk according to the Spirit and not according to the desires of the flesh (Adv. Haer. 5.8.2). Irenaeus is able to use ethical categories from Paul against the Gnostic interpretation of 1 Cor 15:50. He argues that by "flesh and blood" Paul is referring to those who do not have the Spirit. Their soul simply cooperates with the passions of the body. Consequently, such persons cannot hope to inherit the kingdom (Adv. Haer. 9.1). Irenaeus applies Paul's ethical dualism to the contrast between the image of the earthly Adam that we once bore and that of the heavenly one that we will bear in 1 Cor 15:48f. The former applies to the time in which we were without the Spirit and did not obey God. But now we must obey God in the Spirit in order to make the flesh suitable for the kingdom (Adv. Haer. 5.9.3).

Irenaeus may also have had his Gnostic opponents in mind when he compares the bridegroom taking the bride to the Spirit taking the body and thus transforming flesh and blood (Adv. Haer. 5.9.4). He concludes that 1 Cor 15:50 is the apostle's exhortation not to lose the Spirit. Without the Spirit of God, flesh and blood cannot inherit the kingdom. Irenaeus devotes several chapters to proofs that the Spirit is God's agent in making the believer heir to the kingdom. He insists on the ethical interpretation of the saying about "flesh and blood not inheriting the kingdom" and pointing to passages in which Paul uses the language of flesh and spirit in an ethical sense (Adv. Haer. 5.10–11). However, Irenaeus's anthropology requires further qualifications. The animating breath of life is not to be identified with the life-giving Spirit of God (Adv. Haer. 5.12.2). The former is common to all living beings, while the latter can only come to those who please God. He finds this distinction in Paul's treatment of the two Adams in 1 Cor 15:45. God first made the human alive, that is, a living soul. Then God provided his life-giving Spirit. But humanity lost that life when it turned to sin. It is regained when humans turn to the good and receive the Spirit.

Other passages from Paul show that the person who is saved is the same person who was lost. The ethical contrast between those who follow the desires of the flesh and those who resist them provides Irenaeus an opportunity to mock his opponents' understanding of casting off the body. Paul must have meant subjection of the desires when he told his readers to "cast off the old person." Paul cannot have meant that one should cast off the physical body, or else the apostle would have been advising his readers to commit suicide (Adv. Haer. 5.12.3).

Miracles like the raising of Lazarus are also evidence that resurrection concerns the body (Adv. Haer. 5.13.1). Irenaeus strengthens this argument with an appeal to incarnation. It would have been ridiculous, he argues, for the Lord to take on flesh if he did not intend to save what had been molded out of dust by God (Adv. Haer. 5.14.1–2). Irenaeus rejects the view that Jesus' flesh was somehow different from that of other humans because Jesus was sinless. Indeed, if that were true, then one could not speak of Christ as having reconciled humanity to God (Adv. Haer. 5.14.3). Prophecies from Isaiah and the vision of the dry bones of Ezekiel round out the proof of resurrection by showing that it was part of God's promise to humanity (Adv. Haer. 5.15.1).

Irenaeus acknowledges the fact that his argument depends on an understanding of creation that is foreign to that in Gnostic mythology. Against their view that the material world and the body had been created by lower powers, even by an evil god, Irenaeus points to both the Genesis narrative and to passages in the Old Testament prophets in which God is said to breathe life into humanity. While the Gnostic myth describes humanity as originating from a watery substance, Genesis says that Adam was fashioned out of earth in the image and likeness of the same God who fashioned him (Adv. Haer. 5.15.3–4). When the body dies, it returns to the substance from which it came (Adv. Haer. 5.16.1). The same divine Word that was active in creation is assimilating humanity to God through incarnation (Adv. Haer. 5.16.2). While Irenaeus knows that the Gnostics have their own interpretation of Genesis and Paul, he argues from his own perspective that resurrection is the culmination of a continuous process of salvation. That process has been oriented toward fashioning humanity in the image of God. This divine image was perfectly realized in the incarnation, since the incarnate Word is the perfect, obedient image of God. Thus, Irenaeus has answered the soteriology of his Gnostic opponents by creating a different account of the divine image in relation to humanity. This image does not exclude the body, since the entire cosmos is subject to the divine Word. Salvation is directed toward human persons as both body and soul (Adv. Haer. 5.20.1).

Tertullian

Tertullian wrote his treatise *On the Resurrection of the Dead* near the beginning of the third century.[87] His opponents seem to have been Valentinians. They understand resurrection as the reception of saving gnosis in baptism.[88] Tertullian insists that resurrection is a promise directed toward the body. Those who hold a contrary view only do so because they do not properly understand creation. Such people also refuse to acknowledge the flesh of Christ in constructing their systems. They either reject the reality of the flesh of Christ or hold that it has some peculiar qualities that are not shared by other bodies. Consequently, Gnostics do not have to conclude from the resurrection of Jesus that the flesh is raised (Res. Car. 2). If the Gnostics had held a true understanding of God as creator and of Christ as redeemer of the flesh, they would not have been in error about resurrection.

Tertullian accuses his opponents of holding the flesh in contempt. He devotes a large section of the treatise to a panegyric on the dignity of the flesh (Res. Car. 5–18). Several arguments directed against the Gnostics are included. Even if one entertains the Gnostic view of creation, Tertullian argues, that God would have stopped the creation of the flesh if it had not been according to divine will. Christians acknowledge that both the flesh and the soul take their existence from the divine Word. But the Bible emphasizes the creation of the flesh by saying that when he comes to create it, God does so with his own hand. Only after forming the flesh did God breathe life into it. Thus, God intended the human to be both flesh and soul (Res. Mort. 5). In addition, the soul requires the flesh. Without the flesh, nothing would be subject to the soul (Res. Mort. 7). But Tertullian does not wish to simply collect reasons for praising the flesh that might be available to anyone. He opened the treatise with a collection of intimations of immortality in paganism. But even the vague hope for resurrection found in the tombs that line the roads out of Carthage and the practice of funeral meals for the dead does not represent the new hope that has come through Christianity (Res. Mort. 1; 3). Christianity shows that God has conferred special dignity on the flesh. A person must come to saving faith while in the body. The sacraments are bodily realities that make the cleansing of the soul possible. It is the flesh that is washed, anointed, signed with the cross, has hands imposed on it, and eats the eucharist. Each of these bodily actions aids the soul's salvation. Consequently, the body cannot be separated from the soul in receiving a reward (Res. Mort. 8). *Gospel of Philip* might agree about the importance of the sacraments. Yet it would never conclude, as Tertullian does, that the body that receives those sacraments is the one that shares the final salvation of the person.

Other elements in the panegyric are traditional pieces of Christian apologetic. The Creator who produced everything out of nothing can restore the flesh that had been buried. God has endowed creation with an instinct for renewal that is evident in the cycles of day and night, of the seasons, and of the mysterious Phoenix, which is also mentioned in Scripture (Ps 92.12, LXX; Res. Mort. 11–13). Since flesh and soul are linked in their deeds, it is only just that they be linked in judgment (Res. Mort. 14–15). Tertullian uses this argument about the judgment to deal with the objection that it is not sufficient to say that the Creator has the power to restore the flesh. One must also show cause why he should exercise that power. Tertullian points to those passages in Scripture that link thoughts to the heart, speak of the flesh as sinful, and exhort one to glorify God in the body as proof that the body and soul were intended to be linked together in salvation (Res. Mort. 15–16). Finally, Tertullian argues that since the body is the location of feelings, the soul would not attain either reward or punishment without it (Res. Mort. 17).

Following the panegyric, Tertullian analyzes phrases that his opponents have misinterpreted. He argues that the word *resurrectio* implies that something that has fallen is to be restored. But the soul does not fall into death. Therefore, the body is the only possible subject of resurrection. When the words "of the dead" are added to "resurrection," then that conclusion is inescapable. The body is the only thing that could be described as dead (Res. Mort. 18). Tertullian knows that the Gnostics will claim that they understand "death" to refer to the soul that is ignorant of God. Tertullian rejects this interpretation as mere sophistry designed to hide from others the Gnostic intention to deny resurrection altogether (Res. Mort. 19).

There is more at stake than merely accusing his opponents of deceptive behavior. Tertullian's method treats Scripture in the same "literal sense" as a legal document. The Gnostics, on the other hand, claim that Scripture is to be interpreted allegorically. Tertullian acknowledges this fundamental difference when he begins to argue that the predominant sense in the Bible is literal and not figurative (Res. Mort. 20). Statements that are uncertain are to be interpreted in light of those that are certain (Res. Mort. 21). Tertullian applies these distinctions to analyzing passages about resurrection. Those in which Paul speaks figuratively, like Col 1:21 or 2:12–13, must be set alongside those in which he makes it clear that the Christian awaits bodily resurrection in the future (Res. Mort. 23–24). In fact, Tertullian argues, we would never be able to understand that a word is used allegorically without referring it to its literal sense (Res. Mort. 16). One can show from the prophets, especially Ezekiel, that God always intended resurrection (Res. Mort. 28–31). Tertullian accuses his opponents of being inconsistent. They never interpret statements about the soul to be about something else (Res. Mort. 32).

Once he has established the principle for interpreting Scripture, Tertullian inquires into the passages that treat resurrection in the New Testament. Christ's words, his controversy with the Sadducees, and his miracles are all evidence that he taught a bodily resurrection (Res. Mort. 34–38). Tertullian devotes most of his time to the Pauline passages that were the most popular among Gnostics. Like Irenaeus, Tertullian uses the context to reject the Gnostic interpretation of 1 Cor 15:50. The Gnostics cannot claim to teach a resurrection of Christ if they reject resurrection of the body. Tertullian points to the burial of Christ as clear evidence that resurrection referred to the flesh that was buried (Res. Mort. 48). Since the punishment that humanity suffered as a result of Adam's sin was death in the flesh, Christ as second Adam must be raised in the flesh if he is to reverse Adam's sin.

This emphasis on the flesh of Christ leads Tertullian to conclude that the images of exaltation and enthronement at God's right hand mean that resurrected flesh has been placed in heaven. The claim that flesh and blood will not inherit the kingdom has to be interpreted as a promise that death will end. Corruption cannot enter heaven (Res. Mort. 51). Tertullian agrees that this change represents something new. It requires the Spirit to make it possible for humans to enter the kingdom (Res. Mort. 50). Tertullian insists that when Paul speaks about what is mortal putting on immortality, he is referring to the mortal body and not to some other part of the person (Res. Mort. 51). Paul's argument about the seed can only make sense if it presumes that what is raised is the body that is buried (Res. Mort. 52). As he makes his case, Tertullian accuses his opponents of confusing the issue by attributing the grammatical opposition between the abstract nouns mortality and immortality to the substances that possess such qualities. The opponents speak as though a mortal body were identical with the abstraction mortality. Thus, it becomes easy for them to conclude that the body can have nothing to do with immortality or incorruptibility (Res. Mort. 51). Another favorite element in the argument between orthodox and Gnostic teachers was the contrast between the earthly and heavenly Adam. Tertullian acknowledges the claim of Gnostic exegetes that psychic body represents the soul and that it is condemned to death. Tertullian argues that the Gnostic creation stories present events in the wrong order.[89] They presume that the psychic was created before the earthly. However, Scripture describes the creation of the flesh first. Then it is given life-giving soul (Res. Mort. 53). Since it was the bodily substance that came alive, it must become spiritual body when it recovers the animating soul. Christ can only be a second Adam if he is also flesh like the first Adam (Res. Mort. 53).

The Gnostics are also fascinated with the image of the swallowing up of mortality. Tertullian argues that his opponents create difficulties by isolating terms from the contexts in which they occur (Res. Mort. 54).[90] They make it appear that "swallowed up" applies to the flesh rather than to death. Death cannot be changed. However, nothing makes it impossible for mortality to be transformed into immortality (Res. Mort. 54). The opponents' arguments falter on an improper understanding of substance and attributes. They think that the great difference between earthly and resurrected body requires that the former cease to exist and something else takes over (Res. Mort. 55). Tertullian presses the issue: what is required to enable us to identify some thing that has changed as the same thing? He presents a number of instances in which we are willing to speak of something as the same even though it has undergone radical change. Human beings may change and become almost the opposite of what they were before, and yet we still speak of the same person. The Bible contains even more remarkable stories of transformation: Moses' hand changes from normal to leprous (Exod 4:6–7); Moses' face is transfigured when he sees God (Exod 34:29); the Lord is transfigured, and Moses and Elijah appear with him (Mt 17:2–4). Tertullian finds the Transfiguration story particularly significant. It shows the transformation of Moses, who has not yet received back the body that was buried; the transformation of Elijah, whose body never was buried, along with that of the Lord. Elijah and Elisha show that it is possible to experience resurrection without experiencing death (Res. Mort. 58). Paul also hopes that the present body will be transformed into a glorious body like that of Christ (Phil 3:21; Res. Mort. 55). All of these changes show that the substance of the flesh can be preserved while it undergoes transformation.

Tertullian claims that his opponents are arguing from constraints upon humanity that are set by the way in which the world appears to them. However, Tertullian admits that arguments from the simple power to do something are not sufficient. God's power to provide a human destiny beyond the constraints of the material world still requires a cause to show why he might do so. Tertullian presents an opposing argument that is the inverse of this one. An opponent might claim that there is good reason to assume that God would not bother to transform the body. The body, so the opposition argues, is designed to enable the soul to interact with the material world. To eat, to move, to manipulate objects, to propagate the species, and the like. However, all these functions presuppose a world of change and decay. None of them would be necessary in heaven. Therefore, why would God maintain something that was no longer needed? (Res. Mort. 60). Tertullian admits that the body will not be required to perform these functions in heaven. He falls back on the argument that judgment must be applied to the entire person. He also attempts to disarm the argument that use is the only sufficient cause for preserving something. He points to the restoration of an old ship that is no longer in service (Res. Mort. 60). Or, more appropriately, given his opponents, to the deliberate failure to use certain bodily functions in ascetic traditions in fasting, celibacy, and the like. He charges his opponents with thinking of bodily functions as disgraceful animal passions rather than as natural and necessary. They should see that the mouth has its uses in speech and prophecy, not merely for eating (Res. Mort. 61). Useless only refers to the fact that the restored body has "nothing to do." If it did not exist at all, it would not be called useless. Besides, Tertullian comments, "it may possibly have something to do; for in the presence of God there will be no idleness" (Res. Mort. 60).

Tertullian concludes the treatise with a return to the christological insight that dominates his understanding of salvation. The joining of God and humanity in Jesus means the unity of flesh and spirit in salvation. The two are fitted together as bride and groom. If—as the Valentinians did—one claims that the bride is the soul rather than the flesh, then the flesh belongs to the soul as its dowry (Res. Mort. 63). However, Tertullian prefers that the "bride" be the flesh that, through the covenant in Christ's blood, receives the spirit as bridegroom (Res. Mort. 63). He exhorts the soul to love the flesh almost as much as the Lord, since it is like a brother, and to pray for its redemption, since any sins the flesh may have committed are due to the soul. Those who deny the resurrection hate the flesh because they hate the Creator; they deny the existence of Christ as Word made flesh, and they pervert the Scriptures by misinterpreting them or introducing other myths into them.

Tertullian's treatise on resurrection contains many of the traditional second-century arguments. But it has also introduced new emphases and insights that point to the debates that are emerging in the third century: Jesus' status as human and divine and the authority of Scripture. Tertullian has also raised the issue of the relationship between Christian reflection and philosophy in a new way. For Tertullian, the "givens" of Christian soteriology and anthropology must be read out of Scripture. The literal sense of the Biblical text is, Tertullian argues, resurrection of the flesh, the transformation of the body that is buried. Tertullian acknowledges that this doctrine cannot be defended on the grounds of natural philosophy. It can only depend on revelation about the created order, the destiny of humanity, and the fulfillment of that destiny in the incarnate Word who has taken body with him into heaven.

Origen

Our uncertainty about the presuppositions of second-century Alexandrian Christianity makes it difficult to evaluate what survives of Origen's teaching on resurrection. However, his refutation of the second-century, anti-Christian polemicist Celsus provides a valuable look at the type of argument that second-century Christians faced. Celsus may have learned much of what he takes to be Christianity from Gnostic thinkers. Consequently, Origen's refutation of Celsus is also, in part at least, a refutation of Gnostic views.[91]

Origen holds the view that one comes to a vision of God through the purified intelligence (Com. In Jo. 32.27.338; 19.4.23f.). Origen's own account of the material world would make it impossible for him to accept Tertullian's view that the body is part of the "essence" of the human being. Body, for Origen, is not part of the nature of any being. Origen's account of creation presupposes a gradation between God, pure spirit, and pure matter. Consequently, Origen would have no difficulty in using a category spiritual body as appropriate to the redemption of the soul. He is not constrained by the dualism of spirit and matter that afflicts his Gnostic opponents.[92]

Origen's first answer to pagans who mock Christian preaching about resurrection repeats established polemic. He refers to the myth of Er in the Republic and the legend about a woman preserved by Empedocles. If such wonders can be attributed to ancient heroes, then certainly Jesus, who had performed so many miracles, can be raised (c. Cel. 2.16). Celsus objects that Christians have simply taken stories about Jesus from the tales of wonder-workers and from pagan myths (c. Cel. 2.55–56). Origen replies that Celsus's Jewish source could hardly have placed any trust in pagan myths. Besides, the difference between the Christian story and the pagan myth is easily

established. Jesus' death was not a trick but an event that was witnessed. Celsus's informant cannot deny the resurrection of Jesus
without also denying his own belief in the miracles of Elijah and
Elisha. Christians claim that an even greater power than the intervention of a prophet was at work in Jesus, namely, the power of God
(c. Cel. 2.56–58).

These arguments are followed by a series of objections to the
Christian accounts of resurrection. They show that resurrection narratives were being used by Christians to advance their claims about
the resurrection of Jesus. The first objection is that the testimony of a
hysterical woman, Mary Magdalene, cannot be accepted as evidence.
Origen replies that she was not the only witness to Jesus' resurrection
(c. Cel. 2.59). Then the objection is raised that the visions of the
resurrection are hallucinatory wish fulfillment similar to the type of
dream that Epicurean philosophers posit as the basis of visions of the
gods. Origen replies that Plato would grant that shadowy apparitions
of the gods and of others who have died are a proof of immortality.
But, more to the point, the encounters with the risen Lord took place
during the day and show no signs of hysteria (c. Cel. 2.60). The next
objection to the appearance accounts is that the wounds were merely
mentally induced impressions. Origen insists that they were real (c.
Cel. 2.61). This last exchange shows that Origen does not subscribe to
a docetic account of the risen Lord typical of Gnostic writings.

Origen appears to hold that the body of Jesus was always different
from the bodies of other humans. He argues that the resurrection
accounts show that Jesus possessed a type of intermediate material
body. The risen One is neither "naked soul" nor material body,
simply. Thus, Jesus was not recognized by Simon and Cleopas on the
road. He could be touched but at the same time was able to enter a
room through closed doors and to vanish out of the sight of his
disciples (c. Cel. 2.62). Though one might presume that this intermediate body only applies to the risen Jesus, Origen's answer to the next
set of objections provides a more complex picture.

The essential objection is that Jesus should have appeared in public
after the resurrection (c. Cel. 2.63). Origen uses the appearances of
Jesus during his life as part of his defense for the nonpublic character
of the resurrection appearances. He argues that Jesus appeared to
different groups according to their ability to perceive him. Origen is
adopting the traditions of the polymorphous Christ to this argument.
Judas had to kiss Jesus in order to show the arresting party who Jesus
was since he could appear in many different forms. The Transfiguration story shows that even the disciples differed in their ability to
perceive Jesus. Finally, after the resurrection, there was nothing

about Jesus that could have been seen by the multitudes (c. Cel. 2.64). If Jesus had shown himself to his tormentors, they might have been blinded like the men of Sodom (c. Cel. 2.67). Origen uses Paul's remark that some of the Corinthians are still carnal to prove that Jesus could not even have appeared to all of those who had believed in him during his lifetime, since not all believers have the necessary insight. Besides, he points out, God did not show himself to all the people in the Old Testament visions (c. Cel. 2.66). The final objection is the converse of the challenge to public appearances. Jesus ought, Celsus argued, to have disappeared suddenly from the cross. Origen's reply shows the distance between his own view and a docetic interpretation of the resurrection. He says that for Jesus to have done so would have destroyed the entire purpose of the incarnation (c. Cel. 2.68–69).

The objections in *Contra Celsum* Book II are attributed to a Jewish informant whom Origen accuses of bad faith, since he in fact believed resurrection of the dead to be possible (c. Cel. 2.77). The next set of objections in Book IV deal with problems about the relationship between body and soul. Origen's answers are not always clear. They appear to draw on a theory of matter and its qualities that has been formulated in response to the theory of matter held by Origen's opponents. Origen says that Celsus held that all bodies are made of the same corruptible matter (c. Cel. 4.56). He counters by arguing that Christians hold that there are different types of bodies. In resurrection, the qualities of bodies change so that they are no longer natural but spiritual. Divine providence means that bodies receive the qualities given them by the Creator. Thus, the divine Word can also change the qualities of matter (c. Cel. 4.57).

Celsus is also reported to hold—possibly on the basis of a popular exegesis of the *Timeus*—that only the rational soul is God's creation. The body has a different origin (c. Cel. 4.58). Origen's answer does not address the cosmological underpinnings of such a claim. He merely points to the honors that humans pay the bodies of good people as evidence to the contrary (c. Cel. 4.59). The similarity between this argument and Tertullian's opening remarks about burial suggests that the argument was a piece of established apologetic.

The final argument in the series appears to depend on a misrepresentation of second-century cosmological discussions. Celsus is reported to have argued that nothing produced from matter is immortal. Origen counters that such a claim leads to absurd conclusions. The world is produced from matter and is immortal. Origen assumes, as he does elsewhere, that Celsus is really a Platonist and holds that the world is eternal. If the world is not immortal, then it is subject to destruction and thus must be produced by God (c. Cel. 4.61). As it stands, this argument is hardly satisfactory. It may have originated in second-century apologetic circles as a means to show that the world is created over against Platonists who hold that the world is eternal.

Book V contains an extensive quotation of Celsus' objections (c. Cel. 5.14). The series moves from cosmology and the nature of matter to eschatological claims made by Christians. As Origen represents it, Celsus's argument has five headings:

1. The idea that God is going to destroy the world in a great fire that only Christians will survive is absurd.

2. The claim that the dead will rise from the earth in the same bodies in which they were buried is a "hope for worms."

3. The soul would not want a rotted body. Besides, there are even Christians who do not believe that the body is raised.

4. Christians have no answer to the question, What sort of body will they return with? They merely retreat behind the power of God as Creator. But God cannot do what is shameful or contrary to nature.

5. God can confer immortality on the soul. But to raise the flesh would be contrary to divine reason and character. Nothing could bring God to do something of that sort.

The last two objections contain an important philosophical point that Tertullian's rhetorical training led him to emphasize. The claim that God has the power to do something does not prove that he has the will to do it or has actually done it. One must still provide a reason for God to do what is claimed. Celsus objects that God never will do what Christians say he has done and will do, since it is contrary to nature.

Origen's initial response to the first argument is to invoke the Stoic theories of conflagration. This is the conventional defense. But he then goes on to introduce a distinction that will be crucial to his argument. Much of what the Bible says about judgment is addressed to the simple, to souls that cannot be deterred from evil except by fear of punishment (c. Cel. 5.16). When Celsus accuses Christians of having a "hope for worms" or of presenting the soul with a rotted body, he has misunderstood what Christians really believe. Paul shows that the body we receive in the resurrection is not the same one in which we lived but one that has been changed for the better (c. Cel. 5.17–18). At this point, Origen hints that there are secret parts of the Christian teaching on resurrection that are not known by all. Paul's sayings prove this distinction. We are told to seek to bear the image of the heavenly Adam and that flesh and blood will not inherit the kingdom. (Here Origen is drawing upon two favorite Gnostic texts, as we have seen.) Anyone who studies wisdom knows that the soul does not wish to have a rotted body but one that is incorruptible (c. Cel. 5.19). Origen points to the Stoics, Plato, and the Pythagoreans as evidence that resurrection is not a doctrine that can be understood by the simple (c. Cel. 5.20–21). However, Origen appears to acknowledge that this sudden shift in position might make him appear like the Gnostic teachers whom Celsus has read. It might suggest that he is one of those who secretly denies the resurrection. Origen affirms that he follows Paul (1 Cor 15:36–44) in saying that the body is to be transformed (c. Cel. 5.22).

Since the body is transformed, Origen can answer the objection that God would not raise the body, as it would be shameful to do so. Origen agrees that it would be unworthy of God to raise up untransformed matter. But it is quite different to transform matter. In doing so, God is not acting contrary to the laws of nature but is lifting humanity up above nature, making humans more divine and preserving them in that state. Thus, God is acting in accord with divine nature and not contrary to it (c. Cel. 5.23).

Origen's final references to resurrection suggest the lines along which his own spiritual interpretation might have proceeded. He speaks of the tabernacle of the soul as having a "spermatic logos" that the righteous seek to put on rather than seeking to put something off. Origen appears to have thought of the relationship between soul and body in such a way as to make the necessity of body intelligible. He comments that since the soul is naturally incorporeal and invisible, it requires a body suited to the place in which it exists. He appeals to the view that there is a diversity of types of body between the divine and pure matter. The resurrected body is the appropriate vehicle for the soul, which would otherwise not be distinguishable. Origen may also have presumed that there was a natural tendency for souls to embody themselves in the material appropriate to their location in the universe (c. Cel. 7.32).

Finally, Origen turns to an objection that appears to have denied that the body could have anything to do with the created image of God. We have seen that Philo carefully excluded the human body from the divine image. Origen insists that Christians do not consider the body to be the image of God. Nor do they consider God to be material. Presumably, the accusation behind this passage had said that Christians had an unworthy, material concept of God, which was evidenced in their claims about the body. Origen follows established traditions of Alexandrian interpretation when he asserts that the image of God in the human being is the rational soul, which is thereby superior to the body (c. Cel. 7.49). The reply to Celsus shows that by the late second century Christian teaching could be challenged on three fronts. First, there were challenges to Christian claims about the resurrection of Jesus. That testimony was presented as embodied in the gospel narratives. Second, resurrection could be challenged on cosmological grounds. Matter and soul are two quite different entities with different origins. The soul's destiny might lie in the heavenly world as befits its divine origin, but the body could never be located there. Finally, the entire complex of symbols that Christians use to describe their view of the end of the world and judgment could be perceived as mythological and as quite unworthy of the divine origin of all things. We also see in both Origen and Tertullian an acknowledgment that the controversies that the early third century had inherited from the second century could not be resolved without a more explicit understanding of the methods appropriate to the interpretation of Scripture. Tertullian takes the route of legal hermeneutics that relies on semantic analysis to determine the binding, literal meaning of the text. Origen, on the other hand, finds himself pushed to insist that some parts of Scripture are metaphors for those who can see no further, while other passages can only be understood by those with the appropriate learning and insight. The language of fiery judgment and punishment belongs to the former category; that of resurrection, to the latter.

NOTES

1. A. J. M. Wedderburn ("The Problem of the Denial of the Resurrection in 1 Corinthians XV," *NovT* 23 [1981], 236) argues that there is no concept of resurrection that would make sense in a hellenistic milieu. Philo never mentions such a view; nor is there anything in the language used about the soul in pre-Christian Greek writers that would translate what is meant by resurrection.
2. W. C. van Unnik, "The Newly Discovered Gnostic 'Epistle to Rheginos' on the Resurrection," *Journal of Ecclesiastical History* 15 (1964), 141–43, 153–55.
3. J. N. D. Kelly, *Early Christian Doctrines* (New York: Harper &

Row, 1975, 3rd ed.), 466–67; A. Grillmeier *(Christ in Christian Tradition. Vol. 1* [Atlanta: John Knox, 1975], 58) notes that as Gnostic opposition to bodily resurrection grows, Christian authors find themselves using the incarnation as the dogmatic point for reinterpretation of human nature to strengthen the argument that the body shares salvation.

4. J. Dillon, *The Middle Platonists* (London: Duckworth, 1977), 384–92. Not even Plutarch, who comes closest to the Gnostics in his evaluation of matter, will make it an active principle of evil capable of overwhelming the mind. On the relationship between Plutarch and Gnostic mythological themes, see H. D. Betz, "Observations on Some Gnosticizing Passages in Plutarch," *Proceedings of the International Colloquium on Gnosticism* (ed. G. Widengren; Stockholm: Almqvist/Leiden: Brill 1977), 169–78. Plutarch comes close to the Gnostics in finding that the soul is not imprisoned in the body by her own ignorance (p. 174), since if the soul really knew what awaited her after death, relief from the body, nothing could keep her prisoner (Plutarch Frag. 178; Loeb *Moralia* xv 1969, 316–25). Plutarch also insists against Stoic opponents that God is radically transcendent. However, he will not take the final plunge characteristic of Gnostic dualism and divorce the divine from any association with or reflection in this world (pp. 177–78).

5. M. E. Dahl, *The Resurrection of the Body* (SBT 36; London: SCM, 1962), 37. Aquinas is more attentive to the difficulties of making such an assertion than many theologians. Christ's conquest of sin overcomes the dissolution of body and soul that we experience as death (S.T. Suppl. Qu 75.art 3; Dahl (p. 39) also points to Clement of Alexandria Strom. 8.9: the death of Christ cures the disease that has infected the human race. Dahl (p. 49) points out that Aquinas's use of "supernatural" allows him a way out of the dilemma faced by Origen. The risen body is a supernatural substance created by divine act. This substance represents the most natural condition for human beings.

6. See J. Daniélou *(The Theology of Jewish Christianity* [Chicago: Regnery, 1964], 237) on Ignatius *Magnesians* 9.2, for example. Daniélou traces the influence of the descent into hell and victory over the powers motif in the second century to the development of Jewish Christian apocalyptic traditions (ibid., 179f.; 234–36); T. H. C. van Eijk *(La Résurrection des Morts chez les Pères Apostoliques* [Paris: Beauchesne, 1974], 143–93) agrees that the Apostolic Fathers represent the transition between the first cen-

tury and the explicit doctrinal reflections of the treatises on resurrection later in the second and third centuries.

7. J. N. D. Kelly, *Early Christian Creeds* (New York: McKay, 1972, 3rd ed.), 70; R. M. Grant, *Ignatius of Antioch and Polycarp of Smyrna* (New York: Nelson, 1966), 78; van Eijk, op. cit., 108–12.

8. For a summary of the Valentinian explanations of the body of Jesus and the Savior, see J.-D. Kaesteli, "Valentinianisme italien et valentinianisme oriental: leurs divergence à propos de la nature du corps de Jesus," *The Rediscovery of Gnosticism. Vol. 1: The School of Valentinus* (ed. B. Layton; Leiden: Brill, 1980), 391–403.

9. Kelly *(Doctrines,* 463) suggests that the opponents are either docetists like those attacked by Ignatius or that they are closer to the followers of Marcion (so Irenaeus Adv. Haer. 3.3.4). Van Eijk (op. cit., 128–32) argues against any connection with Marcion's teaching. He thinks that Polycarp is responding to a crisis in the credibility of traditional eschatology brought about by the delay of the parousia.

10. Kelly *(Creeds,* 70) observes that the basic structure of this creed is bimembered; the longer christological section is subordinated to the assertion about God. He thinks that it probably is a fragment of the routine instruction of converts in the church at Smyrna. It contains a number of allusions to material in 1 Peter (1:21; 3:22; 4:5).

11. See the discussion of this common tradition in R. Kraft, *The Didache and Barnabas* (New York: Nelson, 1965), 5–14; J.-P. Audet, *La Didache. Instructions des Apôtres* (Paris: Gabalda, 1958), 122–63.

12. Kraft, op. cit., 68, 178; van Eijk, op. cit., 18–28.

13. Kraft, op. cit., 161; van Eijk, op. cit., 29–32.

14. In the *Odes of Solomon* 17, Christ, the prisoner of death has broken the power of hell and liberated all the dead by his resurrection (see Daniélou, op. cit., 245).

15. Daniélou, ibid., 234–36. The motif originates out of concern for the fate of the righteous of Israel.

16. G. F. Snyder, *The Shepherd of Hermas* (New York: Nelson, 1965), 8–18. Snyder points out that the Jewish-Christian character of the work does not keep its author from using other materials of a non-Jewish provenance. The work appears to have been composed in stages: Vision 1–4 sometime in the reign of Trajan; Vision 5—Similitudes 8 and 10, shortly afterward to describe the nature of repentance; and Similitude 9 to bring the whole to-

gether and to threaten those who had left the church (pp. 22–24).

17. Snyder, ibid., 109. Snyder sees a parallel between this view and the Johannine picture of redemption as participation in the existence of Jesus (p. 108).

18. Daniélou (op. cit., 24) and van Eijk (op. cit., 49–51) think that the alteration of the seasons was an argument derived from the Stoics. Evidence of divine providence in the natural order is a common Stoic theme in the first and second centuries.

19. See Daniélou, op. cit., 382. Irenaeus claims that the Valentinians (Adv. Haer. 1.3.2) and the Sethian-Ophites (Adv. Haer. 1.30.40) held to such a period. The Apocryphon of James (CG 1.2) has a 550-day period. The latter draws upon Jewish Christian traditions. The peculiar time period may merely reflect a Jewish Christian tradition (P. Perkins, *The Gnostic Dialogue* [New York: Paulist, 1980], 48). The Apocryphon of James also presents a positive assessment of Jesus' suffering and of martyrdom in imitation of Jesus (Perkins, ibid., 145f.). The writing as a whole, however, appears to have been an answer to arguments against the Gnostics similar to those of Irenaeus (ibid., 150–54; and Perkins, "Johannine Traditions in *Ap. Jas.* (NHC 1, 2)," *Journal of Biblical Literature* 101 [1982], 411–14).

20. Perkins, *Dialogue*, 145–55.

21. The passage hints that the disciples fail to ascend higher because the other disciples call them back (and thus keep them from attaining knowledge of the heavenly realms?); see Perkins, *Dialogue*, 152.

22. The resurrection dialogue framework is often a secondary addition to materials that can be found elsewhere in similar or almost identical form without that framework. Such a setting suggests that the genre was directed as apologetic against orthodox Christians (Perkins, *Dialogue*, 91–98; 157–62).

23. Simon Magus and Cerinthus are explicitly named as opponents (chap. 7; E. Hennecke and W. Schneemelcher, *New Testament Apocrypha* [2 vols.; trans. R. McL. Wilson; Philadelphia: Westminster, 1963], vol. 1, 194). On the second-century origin of its anti-Gnostic polemic, see Duensing, in E. Hennecke and W. Schneemelcher, ibid., 190f.; W. Hornschuch, *Studien zur Epistula Apostolorum* (Berlin: de Gruyter, 1965), 4–7; 92–97.

24. See A. F. J. Klijn, *The Acts of Thomas* (Leiden: Brill, 1962), 30–33, 38–53; W. Foerster *(Gnosis. Vol. 1: Patristic Evidence* [Oxford: Oxford University, 1972], 337–42) sees in the Acts of Thomas a link between Gnosticism and Manichaeism. G. Bornkamm (Hen-

necke-Schneemelcher, *New Testament Apocrypha,* vol. 2, 429–41) points out that the Acts provide mythological material for the development of Manichaeism. Klijn has consistently argued that the Acts of Thomas are not peculiarly Gnostic but reflect the syncretistic form of Christianity typical of eastern Syria in this period. The Acts of Thomas do not contain the unique elements of Gnostic hermeneutics and mythology. Foerster (op. cit., 342) argues that the narrative style of the Acts makes it impossible to construct a Gnostic system from them but thinks that they contain enough allusions to lead to the presumption that they were written by Gnostics. A similar debate surrounds the *Acts of Peter and the Twelve* from the Nag Hammadi collection.

25. Foerster, op. cit., 340.
26. NHLE: 265–70; D. M. Parrott, ed., *Nag Hammadi Codices V, 2–5 and VI with Papyrus Berolinensis 8502, 1 and 4* (NHS XI; Leiden: Brill, 1979), 198–229. M. Krause, "Die Petrusakten in Codex VI von Nag Hammadi," *Essays on the Nag Hammadi Texts in Honour of Alexander Böhlig* (NHS III; Leiden: Brill, 1972), 36–58; Perkins (op. cit., 125–28) does not agree with Krause's suggestion that this is the lost beginning of the *Acts of Peter,* part of which is preserved in the Berlin codex (NHLE: 478–93; *Nag Hammadi Codices 5.2–5 and 6.475–77*). Parrott (op. cit., 202) argues that the *Acts of Peter and the Twelve* is not Gnostic.
27. Parrott (op. cit., 198) thinks that the mention of the "eleven" and the fact that the disciples are taking this journey on their own initiative means that this meeting is being presented as the first encounter between the risen Lord and the disciples (also Krause, op. cit., 38). Perkins (op. cit., 125) thinks that it is unlikely that an apocryphal storyteller can be pushed for such consistency. Rather, one should consider the story an example of the appearance of the polymorphous Christ. In the world of the apocrypha Jesus could appear at any time.
28. See P. Achtemeier, "Jesus and the Disciples as Miracle Workers in the Apocryphal New Testament," *Aspects of Religious Propaganda in Judaism and Early Christianity* (ed. E. Fiorenza; Notre Dame: Notre Dame University, 1976), 164–75.
29. See the survey of the setting of the resurrection dialogues in Perkins, *Dialogue,* 37–58.
30. The *Apocalypse of Peter* is a revelation dialogue between Peter and Jesus before the crucifixion. It reveals the docetic truth about the crucifixion and predicts the hostility of orthodox church leaders to Gnostic teaching (Perkins, *Dialogue,* 116–22). The *First Apocalypse of James* contains both revelation right

before the crucifixion and after the resurrection. In the earlier revelation, Jesus teaches James about the ascent of the soul through the spheres. In the postresurrection revelation, he teaches a docetic interpretation of the crucifixion, tells James the formula for the ascent of the soul, and commissions him to pass the revelation on through a secret chain (ibid., 141–44).

31. Perkins, *Dialogue,* 121f.

32. Ibid., 141–45.

33. See MacRae, in D. M. Parrott, ed., *Nag Hammadi Codices V, 2–5 and VI with Papyrus Berolinensis 8502, 1 and 4* (NHS XI; Leiden: Brill, 1979), 454f.

34. A Gnostic writing from a later period, the *Pistis Sophia,* makes extensive use of the genre of a revelation dialogue with the twelve plus women disciples, Mary, the mother of the Lord, Mary Magdalene, and Salome. Book I, chapters 1–6, have an elaborate description of the light power coming down on Jesus on the Mount of Olives after eleven years of postresurrection instruction of the disciples. Book IV contains another revelation dialogue tradition. See C. Schmidt and V. MacDermot, *Pistis Sophia* (NHS IX; Leiden: Brill, 1978), 137–41. *Pistis Sophia* is clearly derived from a period in which much of the original coherence of the Gnostic traditions that it exploits has been lost. They are all pieces of esoteric lore.

35. Perkins, *Dialogue,* 43; 49.

36. Similar elements appear in association with the angelic revealer in the *Zostrianos* (CG 8.*1*) and in the *Pistis Sophia* (ibid., 43).

37. Perkins, ibid., 91–94.

38. See H.-M. Schenke, "The Phenomenon and Significance of Gnostic Sethianism," *Rediscovering Gnosticism vol. 2: Sethian Gnosticism* (ed. B. Layton; Leiden: Brill, 1981), 602–10. Though one may not be able to speak of a specific form of Sethian Gnosticism as a separate sociological sect, the pattern of baptism and enlightenment as part of a cultic pattern that is presupposed over a broad segment of the Nag Hammadi writings is correct.

39. See the text and commentary by M. Meyer, *The Letter of Peter to Philip* (SBL Diss. Ser. 53; Chicago: Scholars, 1981); and K. Koschorke, "Eine gnostische Pfingstpredigt zur Auseinandersetzung zwischen gnostischem und kirchlichem Christentum am Beispiel der Epistula Petri ad Philippum (NHC VIII, 2)," *Zeitschrift für Theologie und Kirche,* 74 (1977), 323–43. Koschorke argues that the focus of the document lies in the Pentecost speech and not in the revelation dialogue. See Meyer, op.

cit., 105–110. Meyer thinks that 2 Pt 1:16–19 refers to a resurrection appearance rather than to the Transfiguration.

40. Meyer (op. cit., 112) notes that the apocalyptic reference at the end of Matthew, "until the end of the world," has been dropped because it is inappropriate to a Gnostic context.

41. Also see 1 Apol. 10; 52. Kelly, *Doctrine*, 469.

42. This view was popularly defended by Epicureans, who also claimed that if most people believed it, they would not fear the Gods; see Epicurus (Diogenes Laertius, *Lives*, x).

43. For a Platonist discussion of the relationship between oracles and the *daimones*, which seems to be required by Justin's argument, see Plutarch, *Defectu Or.*, 944CD.

44. This analogy had cosmological overtones. Stoic cosmologies used the analogy of human reproduction in describing the origins of the world.

45. The dissolution of all things into their elements is an Epicurean view opposed to the Stoic conflagration.

46. Though Justin does not admit it, the Platonists also argued that the Stoic view of conflagration was unworthy of the transcendence of the divine.

47. Daniélou, op. cit., 27.

48. Tatian's presumption that matter is a formless substrate is standard Platonic interpretation of the Timeus. Antiochus of Aschalon carefully indicates that it cannot be dissolved into nothingness, though it may be dissolved into infinitely divisible parts (Dillon, op. cit., 82). However, there was an interpretation of Plato that originated with Eudorus that held that as the ground of all existence the One also had to be the causal principle of matter (ibid., 128). This view reappears in Philo's account of creation. Philo is not entirely consistent, since he can also speak of preexistent matter (ibid., 158).

49. The connection between spirit and divine spirit derives from the Stoic view of the divine spirit as spread throughout the cosmos and identified with the human mind (W. D. Hauschild, *Gottes Geist und der Mensch* [BEvT 63; Munich: Kaiser, 1972], 22). This view is hinted at in Philo. However, Philo wishes to avoid directly identifying the mind with the Spirit of God (Opif. 135; Spec. Leg. 4.123; Rer. Div. Haer. 55). The divine Spirit in the human is the basis of natural knowledge of God—as Tatian also claims—(Leg. All. 1.37f.; Plant. 20). But knowledge of God beyond this natural knowledge, ecstatic knowledge through the Spirit, is the condition of the perfection of the human and of the

saving knowledge of God (Plant. 23; Praem. Poem. 36ff.; Decal. 175; Hauschild, op. cit., 20; 24; 57f.).

50. Hauschild (op. cit., 198f.) finds parallels between Tatian and the treatment of the spirit in Gnostic writings like *Gospel of Philip* and *Nature of the Archons,* in which the Spirit breathed into humans is lost with the fall.

51. In order to combine Stoic and Judeo-Christian images, Tatian speaks of the spirit and soul in the human as syzygy. Hauschild (ibid., 201f.) thinks that the lack of a role for Christ in this presentation indicates that Tatian has derived it from another source. His exegesis of Gen 2:7 can be paralleled in Jewish sources. His images of the soteriological activity of the divine Spirit in providing knowledge of God come close to the traditions of Gnostic writings (op. cit., 205f.), though a Gnostic writer would never feel compelled to combine this doctrine with resurrection. Tatian's treatment of the demons remains Christian in insisting that the demons are evil. Yet his parallel between the fate of the demons and that of the human soul in punishment may be influenced by Platonic speculation about the *daimones.* Plutarch has a theory that the *daimones* differ in virtue (Def. Or. 417B). It is difficult to determine whether these are human souls that have not been sufficiently purified to escape reincarnation or *daimones* who have been sent to the earthly realm for punishment (Dillon, op. cit., 223–24).

52. The composite nature of the soul is a central element in Plutarch (Dillon, op. cit., 211–13). What Plutarch's Stoic opponents miss is that the "higher" rational element is independent of the body. Plutarch argues that to treat the soul as unitary would involve it completely in the irrationality of bodily passions (Daem. Soc. 591D–F). Other parallels can be found between Plutarch and Tatian. Plutarch claims that the mind is external to the body. It represents a presiding *daimon.* However, it is not clear that all souls have such a *daimon.* Some are said to sink entirely into matter. This image of the separable mind as a celestial counterpart fits Tatian's presumption that the soul has lost its companion spirit and that the process of salvation must restore that spirit.

53. Tatian has further muddled the issue by identifying matter and evil. He says of the demons, who—unlike humans—cannot repent and be saved, "They are reflections of matter and evil" (Or. 15.3). This view would serve to counter the idea of a resurrected body, since it appears to saddle the soul with evil matter. As such, it is apposition that is closely reflected in the "underworld of

Platonism," which flourishes in Gnostic traditions (Dillon, op. cit., 213; Hauschild, op. cit., 202–205).

54. One may still wonder how appropriate this presentation of the body as the source of evil impulses is, since it fits more comfortably into the anti-body ascetic traditions of Christianity and Gnosticism than it does into the views of pagans in general. The ascetic traditions intensified the stoicized Platonism of the period in which freedom from all the body's concerns was represented as passionlessness *(apatheia)* and turning the mind to its eternal home (Dillon, op. cit., 392). The general philosophic view was that the passions could be made allies of the soul (ibid., 189).

55. W. Schoedel, *Athenagoras Legatio and De Resurrectione* (Oxford: Oxford University, 1972), xxvii. The view that Plato and Pythagoras taught resurrection is repeated in Tertullian (Res. Carn. 1; ibid., 87, note 3). The doxographers held that both Pythagoras and Plato taught that elements could be changed into one another. Daniélou (op. cit., 26) notes that this doctrine as it is enunciated appears more appropriate to a Stoic theory of the elements—both Justin and Tatian make such an adaptation of the Stoic theory. Athenagoras may have taken the *topos* and simply attached it to Pythagoras and Plato.

56. Daniélou (op. cit., 27) presumes that the argument presumes a permanent form for the body, which permits its reconstruction. See also Schoedel, op. cit., 87, note 2.

57. Generally, Platonists avoided the problem of relating forms to the multiplicity of the material world. Dillon (op. cit., 48f.) observes that the handbooks summarize the Timeus without further reflection. Seneca (Ep. 59) lists grades of being that distinguish "ideas" as eternal exemplars of the things brought into being from "forms" or immanent ideas. The former are the thoughts of God (Dillon, op. cit., 136–38).

58. The peculiar emphasis on compounding in Athenagoras's argument may be understood if the tradition on which he draws, like that in Philo, treated ideas as numbers (on Philo, see Dillon, op. cit., 159). The combination of Plato and Pythagoras, which Athenagoras presumes, may have been based on a doxographical summary.

59. Daniélou (op. cit., 334) observes that the passage combines two different presuppositions about the vision of God: (1) a transformation of the Platonic view that the soul must be purified and detached from the earthly realm in order to view God; (2) the Stoic view that the providential ordering of the cosmos provides knowledge of God. Platonists often attacked the Stoic vision of

providence for its determinism. They argued that it did not provide for human free will (Dillon, op. cit., 208–10). Theophilus's appeal to the reader to remove the cataracts created in the eyes of the soul by evil deeds (1.2) presumes the Platonist view of human freedom.

60. So R. M. Grant, *Theophilus of Antioch. Ad Autolycum* (Oxford: Clarendon Press, 1970), 11, note 1.

61. E. Pagels *(The Johannine Gospel in Gnostic Exegesis* [SBLMS 17; Nashville: Abingdon, 1973], 83–85) argues that this story represents a Gnostic account of the conversion of psychic Christians rather than the conversion of pneumatic (Gnostic) Christians.

62. Though the work was originally thought to be by Valentinus, exegetes generally agree that such an attribution cannot be defended (see M. L. Peel, *The Epistle to Rheginos. A Valentinian Letter on the Resurrection* [Philadelphia: Westminster, 1969], 156–80). This work has no trace of the bridal chamber imagery that is typical of Valentinian treatises. Peel thinks that the lack of such terminology indicates that the writing is a late one whose author no longer understood those themes. For a collection of parallels to various Gnostic traditions, see the commentary in the *editio princeps,* M. Malinine et al., *Epistula ad Rheginum* (Zurich and Stuttgart: Rascher, 1963). B. Layton *(The Gnostic Treatise on Resurrection from Nag Hammadi* [HDR 12; Missoula, Mont.: Scholars, 1979) takes quite a different approach. Rather than look at Valentinian parallels, as the *editio princeps* does, or at Biblical allusions, as Peel does, Layton looks to the parallels between this writing and the popular Platonism of its time.

63. See the discussion of the philosophic use of the expression *kata meros,* "in part," in Layton, op. cit., 103–4. The expression is used to designate fruitless speculation in contrast to true knowledge.

64. Such divergences lead some commentators to question the coherence of the doctrine in the treatise. J. E. Ménard ("La notion de résurrection dans l'Épître à Rheginos," *Proceedings of the International Colloquium on Gnosticism. Stockholm, August 20–25, 1973* [Stockholm: Almqvist & Wiksell/Leiden: Brill, 1977], 123–31) argues that one must distinguish between the sources of a text of this type and the elements that give it an impression of orthodoxy. He traces this image of an "inner body" to Iranian and Jewish Christian sources that have been transformed when combined with a quite different view of the Spirit and of knowledge as the vision of God. The diverse origins of the elements of the writing makes it impossible to fit them into a

philosophic whole. Peel (op. cit., 49f.) finds the doctrine of spiritual resurrection incompatible with the teaching about spiritual body. Layton (op. cit., 122) claims that the author's own philosophical position cannot be reconstructed from this treatise, since little space is devoted to doctrinal exposition. The author presents himself as one who knows more than he is telling. He spends much of his time answering real or supposed difficulties. However, even the promises of deeper explanations are so typical of this genre of literature that the treatise itself may reflect all that the author knows about resurrection.

65. *On the Resurrection,* 44.13–21; NHLE: 51. Layton correctly points out that the "law of nature" about which Jesus is said to speak is simply the conventional expression for the inevitability of human mortality (op. cit., 51).

66. *On the Resurrection,* 44.21–26; NHLE: 51. We disagree with Layton's attempt to remove the overtones of christological titles from the expressions Son of Man and Son of God (op. cit., 52). He admits that by the second century the two titles were seen as expressing two sides of the Savior's nature. It is also typical of the second century to speak of the Savior conquering death.

67. Layton (op. cit., 53) does no more than provide a suggestive sketch of the possibilities. He argues that the required elements come together in Clement of Alexandria (Stromata 4.158.4ff.; 7.57.1f.). Stromata 6.73.3 speaks of the *apokatastasis* of the Gnostic. However, Plutarch, who contains many parallels to the gnosticizing Platonism of this tradition, seems more to the point. He interprets the myth of the Republic (269C–E) as a cyclic process of sleeping and awakening on the part of the cosmic world soul (De Proc. in An. 1026EF), though he does not do much with this interpretation (see Dillon, op. cit., 205f.). Plutarch apparently presumes that the processes of creation in the cosmos are reflected in the creation of humans (Dillon, op. cit., 213f.). His view of those few who died "the second death" and go to the realm of the sun suggests that some from there are also sown in the realm of the moon. Consequently, it is never clear whether any souls that were once on earth attain permanent immortality (see Dillon, op. cit., 223f.).

68. Layton, op. cit., 58.

69. Layton (op. cit., 59) presumes that the author is thinking of the mind in humans as immortal and is arguing that what has to be shown is how to shed the body. This presumption is based on the view that the author thinks that Gnostic souls preexist as immortal entities. However, we have seen that some Gnostic teachers

apparently followed their orthodox counterparts in denying any natural immortality of the soul.

70. Layton (op. cit., 63) points to the Platonic image of the sun as linked to the soul's perception of the world of ideas, not to its preservation.

71. Layton (op. cit., 67) sees this passage as the beginning of the argument proper. The author will turn from traditional images to an essentially philosophical exposition of salvation. During the exposition it becomes clear that any notion of the body's participation in resurrection or of resurrection as a future event will be dropped. The immortal mind merely has to throw off the body.

72. Layton (op. cit., 71f.) gives an exposition of the classical theory of mind that ignores the parallels in Plutarch. He asks whether it is possible for there to be some souls without mind and hence souls predestined to be without wisdom. This possibility is explicitly presented in Plutarch (De Gen. Soc. 591D–F). Some souls have become so submerged in matter that they are not receptive to guidance from a guardian *daimon* (see Dillon, op. cit., 212).

73. Literally, "the Pleroma is that which is surrounded." I suspect, along the lines of debates reported in Adv. Haer. 2.1.3, that the original reference was either to the fact that the Pleroma would have to contain all things or be contained by something beyond itself. Otherwise, the original reference must have meant the created world by "the All" rather than the Pleroma.

74. Layton's reconstruction of the argument (op. cit., 77–85), as initiated with an objection that presumes the body is to be retained, is to be preferred over the awkward renderings of other commentators. He observes that the imaginary questioner is committing the same fallacy that Plutarch attributes to the masses, failing to distinguish the mind from the soul.

75. Layton (op. cit., 91f.) argues against Peel (op. cit., 143–49) that this passage does not indicate a Valentinian view of an inner, spiritual person. Layton observes that On the Resurrection is unclear about the distinction—if indeed there is one—between soul and mind in the order of salvation.

76. Layton, op. cit., 94–96. M. L. Peel, *The Epistle to Rheginos. A Valentinian Letter on the Resurrection* (Philadelphia: Westminster, 1969), 143–49; Peel, "Eschatology," 160. Hence, in Peel's view, On the Resurrection is a close exegete of Paul but differs from the apostle in holding that the transition to a spiritual body occurs immediately after death rather than at some future end of the world.

77. Layton (op. cit., 99) suggests that the author is using images and

symbols here because the list refers to those things that he has used to turn the mind from the material to the divine world.

78. Peel ("Eschatology," 160f.) argues that some of the apparent contradictions in *Gospel of Philip* can be resolved if one assumes that the author holds a doctrine of spiritualized resurrection similar to that in *On the Resurrection.*

79. CG *2* 56, 32–34; 57, 19–22; NHLE: 134f. See Meyer, op. cit., 138.

80. J. Buckley, "A Cult Mystery in the Gospel of Philip," *Journal of Biblical Literature* 99 (1980), 571. Buckley (ibid., 572f.; 575–78) argues against those who do not think that the *Gospel of Philip* is referring to an actual rite.

81. J. Ménard, *L'Évangile selon Philippe* (Paris: Letouzey & Ane, 1967), 140–43. The contrast is between the earthly garment of flesh and the heavenly garment. Ménard argues that all references to garments in the *Gospel of Philip* are to Gnostic sacraments. He suggests that in all of the sacraments referred to, baptism, anointing, eucharist, and bridal chamber, there was allusion to this putting on of the spiritual vestment (op. cit., 144). Buckley (op. cit., 572) points to the hints that the bridal chamber is above the other sacraments to support her view that it represents the union of the soul with its celestial counterpart. She argues that the sacrament was represented by earthly marriage. A radically ascetic group like that represented in *Testimony of Truth* has no place for such sacraments. The author condemns groups that practice baptism and apparently another group that permits marriage (see Pearson in B. Pearson, ed., *Nag Hammadi Codices IX and X*, [NHS XV; Leiden: Brill, 1981], 107–9).

82. See the explanation of the author's doctrine of the necessity of images, names, and types in relation to this sacramental theology in Buckley (op. cit., 572f.; 580). Buckley suggests that the tendency to deny that Gnostics experienced salvation in this world has led commentators to underestimate the sacramental theology of Gospel of Philip. The author insists that full salvation is attained through the mediation of the sacraments (op. cit., 575; 581).

83. W. C. van Unnik, "A Document of Second Century Theological Discussion (Irenaeus A.H. I.10.3)," *VC* 31 (1977), 218.

84. Evans, op. cit., 6; Kelly, op. cit., 470; Hauschild, op. cit., 207; Daniélou, op. cit., 400–401.

85. On the sweep of the plan of salvation in Irenaeus, see Grillmeier, op. cit., 101. Irenaeus has expanded the idea of a plan of salvation to counter the Gnostic separation of God and the world. The plan for the fulfillment of all things in Christ that is concluded at

the parousia embraces both the creation and the end of all things. Creation, incarnation, redemption, and resurrection are all part of a single, saving work of God.

86. Hauschild, op. cit., 209f.; Daniélou, op. cit., 398–99. The possession of the divine Spirit confers immortality in Irenaeus.

87. On the relative chronology of Tertullian's writings, see T. D. Barnes, *Tertullian. A Historical and Literary Study* (Oxford: Oxford University, 1971), 44–48. Barnes suggests a date of 206/207 for Res. Mort., just after Tertullian had composed *De Anima* and the *Adversus Valentinianos* and just before his lengthy refutation of Marcion.

88. Peel, *Rheginos,* 129; Koschorke, op. cit., 143.

89. Arguments as to the order of events are another standard of legal reasoning; Sider, op. cit., 21.

90. Debate about the context of a term was another standard element in legal dispute about documents; Sider, op. cit., 85f.

91. See H. Chadwick *(Origen. Contra Celsum* [Cambridge: Cambridge University, 1965], xxiv–xxix) for a survey of the opinions about the date of Celsus. Chadwick concludes that on balance we should assign him to A.D. 177–80. He suggests that Alexandria is more likely than Rome, since he doubts that Celsus would have confused Gnosticism and orthodox Christianity had he been living in Rome during his period. However, one must be cautious about presuming that the dividing line was so clearly drawn in Rome. Certainly that was not the case earlier in the century when Justin, Marcion, Valentinus, and Ptolemy were all teachers there. Irenaeus, who had been in Rome during the period that Chadwick assigns to Celsus, presumes that many people are still convinced that the Gnostics are Christians.

92. J. Daniélou, *The Origins of Latin Christianity* (Philadelphia: Westminster, 1977), 420–24; Kelly, op. cit., 471.

ELEVEN

Resurrection and the Foundations of Christian Faith

In the course of the second century, resurrection moved from the center of Christian discourse. Resurrection and associated themes no longer formed the organizing center of the way in which Christians spoke about themselves. Instead, the saving power of Christ is linked with incarnation rather than with the proclamation of his resurrection. At the same time, resurrection has come to be a firmly established part of the tradition both as referred to Christ and as a statement about the future of the believer. Yet as K. Rahner has observed, resurrection is often an incidental element in the experiential pattern of Christian belief.[1] He suggests that it is a normal part of response to divine revelation that even beliefs that are central can become marginal in the lives of the faithful. Revelation always overtaxes the human being. People may accept an item of official belief that is not at all part of the "unwritten catechism" by which they

conduct their lives. We have seen that in the New Testament resurrection was an integral part of paraenesis. In subsequent centuries,
however, resurrection ceased to be integrated into the daily lives of
Christians. It became, as R. MacMullen put it, about immortality of
the soul for many pagans, a belief that it is easy to forget that one
holds.[2] Rahner points out that this situation is not based on the difficulty of understanding the doctrine. Theologians, too, have found
resurrection incidental to their systems.[3] He suggests that the reason
for this situation lies in the theological developments in soteriology.
The development of incarnation as the principle expression of soteriology shifted resurrection out of the center of thought. Rahner points
out that the doctrines of soteriology that were developed out of
incarnation tended to look upon salvation as some form of judicial
transaction, as satisfaction. In that context the cross is no longer
immediately connected with resurrection.[4] Further, the salvation of
the righteous came to be understood entirely in terms of the vision of
God. Resurrection, as we have seen, is not easily integrated into that
soteriology. It is difficult to feel the existential significance of Paul's
concern for the saints coming with Christ at the parousia from that
perspective, for example. The saints are, after all, felt to be in heaven
already enjoying the vision of God.[5] Or, to take the perspective of
systematic theology, it becomes difficult to express the permanent
salvific function of the risen Lord. Satisfaction is accomplished on the
cross, and the reward for the righteous is in the vision of God.[6] The
elements of divinizing presence that had been part of the New Testament experience of resurrection came to be expressed in the piety of
the Catholic West as devotion to the presence of Christ in the Blessed
Sacrament.[7]

Rahner's observations may still be said to describe the piety of
many Christians. However, we also find a resurgence of resurrection
language among theologians. This theological recovery of resurrection language has been fueled by the increased attention to exegetical work. Since the New Testament elaborates the implications of
resurrection symbolism in a number of directions, one is not surprised to find an equal diversity in the appropriation of resurrection
by the theological community.[8]

One of the most basic questions hounding modern debates is that
of what sort of event, if indeed event is the proper word, could be
meant by resurrection.[9] The question is most frequently raised in
connection with Jesus' resurrection. The death of Jesus is clearly a
public, and hence historical, event. The resurrection, by contrast, is
never public. No one witnesses the actual resurrection. We have only
stories of visits to a tomb that had been found to be empty and of

experiences of Jesus' disciples, who discover that God has raised the crucified.[10] While not doubting that first-century Christians held that the body of Jesus was no longer on earth, some twentieth-century theologians have wondered whether conclusions about Jesus' body are implied in resurrection language. Certainly the removal of a body from the world might be considered an event from the standpoint of those who wish to treat as event a phenomenon that is in principle open to public witness.[11] But we have seen that even in the first century resurrection language did not carry with it a well-defined set of expectations about the body. The identity of the body of Jesus with the crucified in the New Testament narratives performs a different function from that of providing information about Jesus' physical remains. That identity makes it clear that the one who appears is the same as the one who died. The risen Lord is the crucified and not some "inner essence," as the Gnostics thought, or some ghost or hallucination, as many opponents of Christianity have argued.

The question of the identity of the risen and crucified Jesus has several implications. Clearly, the problem of the personal identity of the individual and the relationship between such identity and bodily continuity is not solved by observing that resurrection never simply meant the resuscitation of a corpse. Thus, the questions of anthropology continue to be an issue. J. A. T. Robinson, for example, protests that resurrection should not be used to put Jesus in a class by himself —a conclusion that might easily be drawn from the exaltation traditions. Similarly, he argues, one should not envisage resurrection as the manifestation that Jesus is a supreme Yogi, able to separate the eternal self from the body—a modern equivalent of some of the second-century Gnostic views. Rather, resurrection is a pledge of a new creation and not an isolated event. Robinson suggests that we might employ the resources of other religious traditions in order to find ways of expressing the bodily component of resurrection belief.[12]

However, the concern for the implications of resurrection as an anthropological category appears to run counter to another important element in the symbolism. Resurrection was intended to express something about the uniqueness of Jesus. This special status was reflected in the exaltation traditions by presenting Christ as the Lord, the ruler of the cosmic powers, the embodiment of the divine wisdom, and the like. This perception is not derived from the symbolism of resurrection as the fate of the righteous person, simply. Rather, it was associated with the singularity of the resurrection of Jesus as an eschatological event that occurred prior to the eschaton. The wisdom traditions had spoken of the righteous person's exaltation into the presence of God in a timeless dimension. But the apocalyptic traditions felt that the resurrection of the righteous was tied to the final manifestation of God's justice at the parousia. Thus, proclamation of Jesus as the crucified and risen One implied that there was something about his being with God that was not like that of other righteous people. This particularity is expressed in Paul's description of the risen Lord as the second Adam. C. F. D. Moule takes this christological perception itself as a challenge to the "bones of Jesus" ways of thinking about resurrection. He argues that the postresurrection confession of the universality of Jesus requires some perception, however imprecisely formulated, that the God manifested in Jesus was preexistent. Since the preexistent One is not the less a person for lacking flesh and blood, the postexistent Christ does not require them, either. The body language of the New Testament should be understood as a way of establishing the personal identity of the crucified and risen One.[13]

These observations show that there is an underlying conflict between the attempt to elucidate resurrection in terms of anthropology and the attempt to do so in terms of Christology. This conflict is particularly evident when the Christology seeks to elucidate the claims of universality inherent in the vision of the risen Christ as exalted Lord. Shifting the christological question to the incarnation makes resurrection secondary in the description of Jesus' mediation of salvation. It is hardly surprising that much of the twentieth-century interest in recovering resurrection language comes from theologians who wish to ground Christology "from below," from affirmations about Jesus' life and ministry.[14]

However, the question about resurrection and Christology is only part of a larger question about the vision of God implied in the Christian tradition.[15] The initial resurrection symbolism was tied to the problem of theodicy, the manifestation of God's righteousness in judgment. Resurrection proclaims that some part of that divine purpose has been accomplished in and through Jesus. But the question of God might also be raised somewhat differently in the contemporary context. D. Tracy has suggested that the radically theocentric character of theological reflection is necessary to its public dimension. Theology has the task of reflecting on those pressing questions that confront humanity as a whole. It is not merely the expansion of a symbol system peculiar to a particular group.[16]

The quest for a theocentric and public hearing for theological reflection appears in two different forms. One represents the recovery of resurrection and apocalyptic symbolism in the theologies of liberation. There the connection between resurrection and justice for the oppressed is explored in connection with the contemporary struggle for liberation. The vision of God as the one who determines the goal of liberation for all humans is also opposed to secular ideologies of social transformation. The other quest for a theocentric and public hearing is found in the search for the cosmological significance of Christian language about resurrection and soteriology. The best-known example is the theological cosmology of Teilhard de Chardin. Like the liberation theologians, Teilhard was also concerned to put a human face on the process of a changing world. This human face would stand in opposition to the dehumanizing effects of Marxist ideology and/or technological development.[17] Both the cosmological and liberation approaches seek to answer another pressing question, How is the Christian vision of salvation universal?

These efforts to recover resurrection symbolism are seeking a way beyond the private isolation of religious belief as a matter of detached individuals or communities that have little to say about the fate of humanity or the concerns of the world in which they live. This desire to recover the public and universal message of Christianity can be seen in the theological appropriation of the Christ hymn in Col 1:15–20. In his commentary, J. Gnilka traces the history of these developments. The question is raised whether the modern theological endeavor should move beyond the vision of the exalted Christ as "with God" or as Lord simply of the believing community to make explicit the relationship between the exalted One and creation. Admittedly, such an expansion cannot be described as what is meant by the first-century author directly. Yet it might be argued that it is the appropriate response of the twentieth-century Christian to the proclamation of the risen Lord.[18]

RESURRECTION AS KERYGMA

Search for a Christology that begins with the life of Jesus necessarily reopens the question of resurrection. The resurrection kerygma expressed a new awareness of Jesus' relationship with God.[19] The exaltation traditions presented Jesus as the Lord of the cosmos. That perception was an essential ingredient in the development of Christologies that spoke of Jesus as preexistent divine Wisdom and Word.[20] Students often put the question directly: Why resurrection? Isn't the saving death of Jesus enough for salvation? Such questions are a good illustration of the contemporary setting of resurrection language. Most people who ask these questions are not presuming to reduce Jesus to the status of a great person like Gandhi or M. L. King. They presume that the death of Jesus is the key element in the Christian language about salvation. Since Jesus is God incarnate, they argue, his return to God after death is assured, and hence not a reward for righteousness. Resurrection, ascension, and exaltation are merely alternative ways of speaking about that return. How one chooses to speak of it is quite incidental.

R. Haughton has observed that Christians often talk as though it were obvious that resurrection made a difference, but that talk has no content. One cannot find out what kind of difference resurrection either did make or could have made. She observes that resurrection usually claims to be about bodies. But if it is about bodies, it must be treated in the context of one's view of incarnation. The question that goes unanswered is, "What happened to bodies with the resurrection of Jesus?"[21]

Some theologians would argue that this concentration on body is a reification of what was originally simply a feature of narrative. The genesis of resurrection faith is set forward in a story, which required that the crucified be bodily present. By using bodily presence, the narrator also provides us with the conviction that resurrection is about something that happened to Jesus. It is not simply a description of experiences of the disciples finding their fellowship renewed in the Lord. Schillebeeckx's conversion model of the resurrection experience does attempt to avoid this reduction. E. Schillebeeckx distinguishes two phases in the resurrection kerygma: (a) the perception that Jesus belongs to God in a special sense, and (b) God's fidelity to Jesus. If the death of Jesus reflects human rejection of a divine offer of salvation, the resurrection shows that offer both renewed and extended in the lordship of Jesus. Thus, resurrection is not merely an endorsement of the mission of Jesus, as some accounts suggest when they speak of resurrection as the continuation of Jesus' cause. Schillebeeckx points out that resurrection is incomplete, since it is not accompanied by the parousia.[22] Nor is resurrection simply a miracle that affirms Jesus' special status with God, though it did serve that function in the early kerygma. Resurrection belongs to the larger story of God's dealing with Israel. A. Wilder points out that resurrection is always linked with the expectation of immanent renewal of creation. Though it may be difficult to recapture the experience to which the apocalyptic symbolism of the New Testament points, one can, he suggests, look to other artistic expressions of that sense of cosmic renovation in which the world has been transfigured.[23]

We seek to revive the illuminating power of a symbol. Such a process cannot consist in mere explanation or exegesis. The symbol must also emerge in the depths of artistic experience in the larger community. The theological explorations with the language of resurrection may point to directions in which its power of expression can be heard. The pressing desire to recapture an experience of meaning in resurrection language should not tempt one to short-circuit the reflective process or to hurry the gestation of new images at the artistic level. Such a "quick route to relevance" is often attempted by theologians who claim that the worshiping community has immediate access to the experience of the risen Lord. The close tie between resurrection and the liturgical symbols of the New Testament community might seem to support such a tactic. However, as W. Pannenberg has cautioned, there is always a serious danger of self-delusion whenever a group presumes that its experience as a community or the experience of individuals provides an immediate access to divine perfection. Paul's difficulty with the Corinthian community is a clear warning against that view.[24]

One can find other elements in the New Testament that would make one suspicious of laying too heavy a burden on the liturgical presence of the risen Lord. The New Testament speaks of that presence as "hidden" in the period between the conclusion of the appearances and the parousia. Exaltation does imply lordship over creation, but that lordship is a paradoxical one in that it is removed from direct presence to the world.[25] The Johannine traditions speak of both a new presence of God to the community and of the irrevocable departure of Jesus from his disciples. We often think about the paradoxical return of Jesus to his own in Johannine discourses as though it were like returns as we experience them: the person who had departed is now present, that is, no longer absent. This type of experience cannot be what is intended in the Fourth Gospel, which is structured around a pattern of Jesus' descent from and return to heaven.[26] The importance of that pattern in the narrative suggests that it represents an ongoing reality in the life of the Johannine Christians. The Lord is present while absent. Indeed, the very awakening of faith in the Lord as risen and alive with God may intensify the experience of absence. For the earliest believers the experience of absence and of the imminent parousia complement each other. But, as Pannenberg points out, we cannot let our desire for experience cut out the reality of faith, which is directed toward what Jesus was. Through discovering that Jesus, we find out what Jesus is for us today.[27] The conviction that the risen Lord lives and works through the community does not justify the claim that the experience of

God's empowering presence provides direct access to the resurrection, though resurrection may be said to be a precondition of that experience. Without it, Jesus would remain "among the dead." Whatever else death may mean for the human, it clearly separates the dead from presence to this world.[28]

W. Kasper surveys the areas in which resurrection language is being used in contemporary theology.[29] Each of these areas is a point of departure from which to recover the resurrection kerygma as an illuminating symbol of Christian faith. On the most basic level, one finds the recovery of resurrection as "sign." It points to the events of Jesus' life and death as incomplete without expression of their significance. That significance requires that Jesus' life and death be seen as part of that larger order in which God's saving activity is directed toward the creation. The bodily character of resurrection language may function at this level as a counter to all those forms of docetism that seem to be the easiest mode for imagining Jesus' relationship with God. The confession of Jesus' unique relationship with God is quickly put in patterns of descent and ascent, of the separation of an "untouched" divine reality from its bodily appearance. Or if we take the burial story as our starting point, it is all too easy to imagine that resurrection is nothing more than the resuscitation of a corpse, though one avoids asking where such a revived corpse resides. Resurrection constantly seems to stretch our imaginative powers. We may have more difficulty in this department than our first-century ancestors who had "angelic existence" as a mediating category between the human and the divine.

Some of these difficulties are created by the transposition of resurrection out of its original apocalyptic context. There resurrection was part of the renewal of all things. Therefore, it did not stand over against a world of untransformed bodies, of presence, of space and time that would continue untouched. It did not stand over against the apparent continuation of the rule of evil and death, either. But as soon as one proclaims resurrection in a world where nothing appears to have been transformed except Jesus, it raises all of these questions. What is the "reality" to be attached to resurrection in, or with reference to, a world where nothing appears to have changed? The angel or "light-being" categories of the first century easily divorced resurrection from the question about the transformation of this world by making it appear that salvation could be described as the transfer from this world to some other. The crucial question became how to negotiate that transfer and not what is the destiny of this world itself. Leave it behind and one need not care about such a question. The twentieth-century recovery of resurrection language recognizes the false "two worlds" image of salvation that has resulted from the general assimilation of this model. Resurrection is acknowledged to be about the saving transformation of the world, bodies, and persons and not about a transfer out of the world to some realm projected by the human imagination. If none of the attempts to formulate this insight appears adequate, that inadequacy attests to the difficulty of breaking out of the dualistic way of conceiving the problem. We have seen in the first chapter that our language tradition embodies three ways of speaking about the real. The discovery of abstraction in Greek philosophy moved away from the narrative perceptions of reality in the deeds of gods and heroes. But it left us with a transcendent, divine world of reason that was real in contrast to the shifting world of sense perception and mortality. The modern era, on the other hand, is overwhelmingly utilitarian. What is real is what humans can manipulate. This view leaves us with the uneasy feeling that all language about the reality of the divine is only fairy tale. It does not feel real. Thus, we tend to think of resurrection as something like the near-death experiences that we set the medical and psychological professions to cataloging. We are looking for some material proof that we, the same persons who "died," continue to have the same sort of experience after death that we now associate with our identity as persons. And we imagine that the life of the crucified and risen Christ is the same sort of continuation. Such imagining merely extends our sense of reality to make of the unknown a continuum of the same mode of existence. Such an imaginative projection cannot be adequate to proclaiming resurrection, since resurrection presupposes the transformation of creation beyond the limitations, imperfections, and evil that shape our present experience.

Theologians have attempted to overcome the dualism inherent in our understanding of resurrection by recovering the category of God's relationship to creation. They acknowledge that dualism has isolated God from the real world so that whatever is relevant to God or to salvation is simply the transaction between individual believers and their experience of the divine. This divorce requires some perception that the world is the object of divine action if it is to be overcome. This initiative must also be related to the real situation of the world. It cannot be separated out as a "salvation history," which is without connection to the world.[30]

In addition to claiming that God has a special relationship to the world, Christians are also claiming that a specific person within that human history plays a critical role in determining God's relationship to the world. Theologians use different models to describe that significance. For some, the only way to speak of such a transition is to speak of Christ as the one who opens up a new possibility for humanity. However, that possibility must still be effected in the world by the transformation of humans and of their societies. Other theologians maintain that a real transformation takes place in and with Jesus. After the crucifixion and resurrection the relationship between God and the world is ontologically different.[31]

This ontological difference may be described on an anthropological level as a definitive act that changes the relationship of humanity to God for all time. This act, picking up the Adam parallels, is sometimes described as the definitive response of human freedom in obedience to God. Or it may be described in cosmological terms as the decisive breakthrough of the final stage of development of human consciousness. This breakthrough will become complete when the world itself witnesses the decisive change in spiritual reality toward which the dynamics of life and freedom are pushing. Or it may be described historically as a revelation about the purpose of the human quest for liberation and justice. The human search for such a purpose in its historical activity cannot be answered from within the world and human history as we know them. The answer must be given from a perspective that can claim to stand over against that ongoing process.[32]

These examples make it clear that the recovery of speech about resurrection cannot proceed without similar developments in other areas of Christian thought and symbolism. Theologians are seeking nothing less than a public expression of faith, a language that is not to be the private code of a group of initiates, who speak about things with no relation to the world or lives of other humans—or perhaps even to their own lives apart from interactions with other members of the group. At the same time, theologians are not trying to translate unused (or unusable?) symbols and expressions into the common speech of modernity. We have seen that some of the most fundamental insights of Christian soteriology simply will not translate into the limits of utilitarian realism and its language.

Our commitment to the parameters of space and time that define our experience makes it difficult for us to orient our imagination toward that redefinition of reality that appears to be required by our theological perceptions of the world. Theologians have pointed out that we cannot continue to think of heaven in spatial terms. Rather, we must think of a dimension in which the creature is fully taken up into God.[33] We may even label the spatial imagery of the Bible "mythological," since it does not correspond to place in the world as we know it. Yet we often continue to imagine ourselves "with God" in a future life that is as like that of humans in this world as possible.

We perhaps imagine ourselves continued in space and time with all of the psychic dimensions attached to those concepts. As long as we pursue such forms of imagination, resurrection fades from view. The search for a voice in which the kerygma may be spoken is a complex task. Theologians who have pursued one line have often criticized others who were exploring a different mode of expression.[34] We should rather acknowledge that progress in our understanding of any reality is advanced as much by the limited and partial analyses of that reality as by systems that claim to give a final, overarching explanation. The rest of this chapter will take some soundings in the contemporary exploration of resurrection in its relevance to this world and to the Christian's life and action in it.

RESURRECTION AND THE UNIVERSALITY OF CHRISTIANITY

The risen and exalted Christ was presented as Lord of the cosmos. One concrete expression of that universality was found in the mission of preaching associated with the commission of the risen Jesus. We have also seen that resurrection implied a positive judgment about Jesus' messianic status. He did indeed represent God's intended salvation for Israel. Israel's failure to flock to Jesus as her Messiah created as many questions for the first-century Christian mission as it does for Jewish and Christian relationships today.[35] But Christians in the twentieth century have become increasingly uncomfortable with the religious and cultural imperialism that accompanied evangelization in the name of the universal lordship of Christ. They are seeking ways of expressing the universality of Christ that will not do violence to the religious truth and salvation that comes to expression in other religious traditions.[36]

The dialogue with Judaism is mandated on the Christian side by the undeniable fact that the Jesus, whom Christians worship as Lord, belongs to the story of Judaism. The Christian God is also the God of Abraham, Isaac, and Jacob. But the Christian sense of that common heritage need not be reciprocated from the Jewish side. H. Küng has observed that Judaism's historical rejection of the Christian claims for Jesus makes dialogue unnecessary from their side. Jesus is not part of the significant history of Israel and her prophets for that community. A certain "good will" or interest in self-explanation to a predominantly Christian community may lead some Jews to engage in dialogue for pragmatic reasons.[37] The real dividing line is in the person of Jesus. Jesus both unites the Christian tradition with Judaism and forces what may appear to be an unbridgeable gulf between the two groups. The problem does not lie in appreciating the cultural significance of Jesus in the history of the West or his significance as founder of a major world religion through which a large number of non-Jews adopt the God of the Hebrew Scriptures. The problem, as Küng has quite accurately observed, lies in Jesus' religious significance as a member of the Jewish community. Can one even begin to engage in a dialogue on the basis of the real claim that Christians advance for Jesus: that he is more than a prophetic figure; more than the Torah; that he is a Messiah, crucified in the name of the Law. One might suppose that at this point discussion must come to an end.[38] The resurrection implies that Jesus has religious significance for Judaism. It implies that the life and ministry of Jesus reveal something about the God of Israel that is to be heard by those who are heirs to the traditions of Moses and the prophets—not simply by those of us who are "adopted children," thanks to our belief in Jesus. Theologians cannot dictate a solution to this question from the outside as though they could compel the Jewish community to attend to an unfinished piece of business in its religious history. However, as Küng suggests, our attempts to understand and present Jesus and his ministry within the Judaism of the first century can remove obstacles to the question.[39]

Theologians acknowledge similar challenges from the other religious traditions of the world. The Christian confession of the universality of Christ and of his unique relationship to the divine makes it difficult to accept the view that there is a pluralism of religious adepts who have shown different groups the paths to salvation.[40]

Once again, the pressure for dialogue seems to be unequal. The non-Christian religions may feel that they should enter a dialogue with Christianity out of politeness or out of self-interest if they live in a community where the presence of Christianity forces itself upon one's consciousness. Christians, on the other hand, are compelled to enter such a dialogue on the basis of their understanding of the universality of Christ. Yet the basis for such a dialogue scarcely exists. Beyond the academic study of religion, many of these traditions barely have the language in which to pursue global questions of salvation and human meaning in the contemporary world that shapes Christian experience and reflection.[41] Christianity and the other religions both have to pursue the quest for truth in a modern world that none of the religious traditions had anticipated. Nor can one honestly say that any of the religious traditions has yet found a way to represent adequately that world so that they can provide the spiritual orientation in it that is so badly needed by humanity. They might, as Küng suggests, engage in dialogue out of a common recognition of the critical situation facing humanity in our world.[42]

It was often thought to be a sufficient expression of Christian universality to see in Christ the complete revelation of the human relationship to God. Other traditions might have attained some measure of that insight, but they were held to be inferior ways of salvation simply waiting for the spiritual corrective of a Christian transformation in order to reach their full potential. The non-Christian traditions, like Judaism, were viewed as premessianic. With the preaching of the gospel, those traditions should be converted to Christ. However, Christianity's experience with Judaism should raise a cautionary note. On the one hand, there would be no Christianity without Jews who found Jesus to be Messiah and Son of God. On the other, Israel as a whole did not acclaim the Messiah. This failure seemed contrary to what one expected of the appearance of the Messiah at the time. Consequently, Christianity remains in dialogue with Judaism on two fronts: (a) as a separate religious tradition and (b) as part of its own religious heritage. Similar processes might be supposed for the Christian mission to other religious traditions. For those who find in Christ the fulfillment of their religious hopes or expectations, one might expect to discover the authentic, "unknown Christ," as R. Panikkar has suggested.[43]

J. Metz has warned against the implicit elitism of generalizing from Christian experience to a universal anthropology of the human encounter with the divine.[44] He proposes that one begin with the recognition that religions are embodied in narrative and practice, not in a transcendental realm of identical humans confronting a world that is equally the same for all observers. He argues that the "knowledge" that belongs to faith is not on the level of abstract universals but is practical knowledge.[45] The universality of the Christian mission is grounded in God's will to save humanity. This offer of salvation is an invitation tendered through the stories of the tradition. This narrative calls humans to freedom and liberation.[46] In approaching the question of universality through narrative and practice, Metz hopes to resolve the dilemma of combining the social particularity of Christian communities with the conviction that the church has a universal mission that is grounded in the saving will of God. What is lacking in this construction is any suggestion of real dialogue between the stories and associated praxis of the different traditions. The Christian story may indeed be a universal call to liberation based on the conviction that the crucified is Lord, but is it the only story in town? Might there not be other stories of liberation that call into question elements of the Christian story as it is told or the conclusions for praxis that Christians draw from it? Metz's insistence that the liberation theologies of the various minority groups and Third World cultures have a message for all Christian theology is an approach to such dialogue. His concern that we not permit theology to degenerate into regional or other brands of theology acknowledges the problems posed by our pluralistic situation.[47]

J. Cobb has tried to describe what interreligious dialogue might look like if one could break out of our feelings of superiority and cultural isolation. He takes Buddhism as a starting point by attending to those issues of Buddhist thought that seem to provide the strongest challenge to the Christian view of reality. These elements are particularly at odds with the Christian account of the relationship between God and human persons. Buddhism challenges all forms of attachment, even attachment to God or Nirvana. Consequently, Christian forms of attachment such as devotion to God or to Jesus could be seen to reflect a clinging to the deceptive reality that humans fashion for themselves.[48] Even more to the point, Buddhism suggests that the Christian preoccupation with the self is an illusory reification. Christian attachment to self is reflected in the reification of time and history as the ultimate theater of human activity, ethical action, and personal meaning.[49] Christians become preoccupied with past and future as though these had some reality, since reified past and future alone can provide this self with its support. Within this context, the Christian vision of resurrection, of restoration of the personal identity of the individual, can only appear to be the greatest form of illusion. Cobb insists that genuine dialogue requires learning on both sides. The negative side of Christian selfhood is not its hope for future transformation but its immersion in a sense that a person's present action is not genuinely new but is determined by past history. It might also be necessary to perceive love along lines sketched by Buddhist compassion, that is, love without the problems inherent in love as attachment to a limited and imperfect self. In both respects the dialogue with Buddhist criticism may unleash new possibilities given in Christ.[50] On the other hand, the Christian concern for the personal structure of existence may be a necessary clarification over against Buddhism. Christianity insists that the move toward the transcendent does not dissolve the personal structure of existence. In addition, certain questions of socioethical and global concern require rootedness in concern for our historical destiny, a concern that can appear all too illusory in the Buddhist view.[51] This brief example indicates the long road that still must be traveled if Christianity and the other religions of the world are to move beyond the polite exchange of information about each other's beliefs to a real dialogue and mutual enrichment. In the particular case of Buddhism, resurrection might call Christians to break out of the false limitations that they set on their understanding of self and for Buddhists to see that the personal lies at the very heart of transcendent reality.

At the same time, we cannot lose sight of the orientation of resurrection toward the future. The ongoing process of the human community is not entirely completed with the exaltation of Jesus. Thus, part of the religious venture of humanity also lies in the future. Some twentieth-century Christians have suggested that the religious divisions of humanity require a transcultural image of Christ. Such a vision must call the human community from its self-absorption in the particulars of separate cultures and religions to a concern and love for all on the planet. Without such a universal religious symbolism, the spiritual traditions of humanity will have no voice in the global problems confronting the race.[52]

The desire to find such a vision of the whole is reflected in the widespread adoption of the scientific term "evolution" outside its biological context. It provides a "scientific myth" by which the whole process may be encompassed. S. Toulmin has shown that the adoption of this mythology was founded in a desire to show that a human ethic will indeed prevail in the universe.[53]

Teilhard de Chardin represents the most forceful adaptation of the evolution myth within Catholic circles. His adaptation depends on the conviction that the resurrection of Jesus is historical in a special sense. It stands at that special nodal point in the process marked by the other genuine mutations from one form of being to another. Just as the transition to consciousness represented a crucial mutation out of the materially complex world, so the resurrection marks a decisive reversal of the relationship between the human and the bodily. With Jesus, there emerges the existence of a life that is forever and without death. Our relationship to the cosmos has depended on having a body. The new "mutant" in Jesus can only mean that the cosmos is transformed. Therefore, it implies the end of time as we experience it. This transformation cannot be said to be contained within the structures of this world.[54]

Toulmin has pointed out that in Teilhard's view this mutation represents a cosmic drive toward the emergence of a hyperpersonal order.[55] Therefore, we cannot conclude that the expansion of Christ's resurrection to believers or to humans generally can be described in any way that is simply continuous with the persons and experiences that we presently associate with ourselves and others as individuals.[56] Toulmin has traced the roots of Teilhard's speculation about evolution to philosophical convictions about natural theology and directed vital forces. He observes that Teilhard has been criticized for presuming that the cosmos proceeds toward a Christic culmination by theologians. They protest that this vision is inadequate to the soteriological necessity that human perfection be grounded in another order altogether. Since Teilhard's synthesis is neither good science nor good theology as these are commonly understood, one might presume that they have little value for the future of human inquiry. However, Toulmin suggests that Teilhard's attempt to forge a synthetic picture may reflect the shape of future reflection. He points out that Christian theology grew up in a world with quite different, static perceptions of cosmic history, with a much smaller scale of time and space. The myths and images were drawn against that scale. Whatever the weaknesses of the Teilhardian vision, especially in maintaining a causal picture of evolution proceeding directly toward a Christic culmination, it does point to the necessity for Christian thought to establish its natural theology within a contemporary view of nature. However, that necessity should not presume that it will be possible to demonstrate that there is a single, unambiguous intentionality that informs the whole of cosmic history.[57]

Theologians may well agree that such an intention cannot be demonstrated. Yet they may continue to raise the question of whether such an intention has been revealed. Such conviction is attached to many of the contemporary interpretations of resurrection. The problem, of course, lies in making the shift from kerygma and narrative to ontology. The New Testament speaks as narrative. Christ as the new Adam brings to perfection what had been left unfinished in the story of the old Adam and the human community, for example. The question is whether or not one can conclude that this new Christian narrative could emerge without reflecting a real change in the ontological order of the cosmos, whether at the level of a "new mutant" in some Teilhardian sense or at the level of a direction to the human struggle for liberation, as liberation theologians suggest. It is not appropriate to criticize either group for implying an innate, necessary causality behind the process of human development. Teilhard's understanding of evolution is not that of a continuous process but one that is seen to have critical points such as the emergence of consciousness and the incarnation and the future recapitulation of all things in Christ at the parousia. Teilhard's writings do not clearly explain the process of the spiritual maturation of human consciousness that would seem to be required of the present stage in evolution.[58] But it would be fair to say that at each of the critical junctures one could not foresee the new stage "from below," from the previous level of complexification. Thus, the account given of the cosmic difference made by the incarnation and resurrection of Christ can only be understood as a descriptive one. It is not a deduction from some unalterable theorems of the evolutionary process.

Certainly Teilhard does envisage this Christ event as having established humanity irrevocably in the center of the cosmic processes. He speaks of the incarnation as the culmination of divine creative activity and the foundation for divine involvement in raising the world to God. Without the dualism of the second-century Gnostic, Teilhard has adopted the expression "pleromization" to describe the fullness of being in which God and the completed world exist together.[59]

J. A. Lyons has shown that the motivating image behind this vision is Col 1:17b, which Teilhard translated from the ecclesial context in Paul into a cosmic context. This vision was seen to imply that Christ is Lord even over a plurality of inhabited worlds.[60] At the same time, Teilhard seeks to avoid the pantheistic conclusions that might be drawn from his monistic vision. He insists that the unification of all things does not destroy their differentiation. 1 Cor 15:28c provides him with a scriptural basis for the differentiating union of all things in Christ.[61]

For Teilhard, the resurrection represents the point at which Christ assumes his cosmic role. The ontological reality of the resurrection transformation led him to formulate a doctrine of three natures in Christ: (1) the divine, that is, as Word of God; (2) the human, that is, Jesus; and (3) the cosmic, that is, as the resurrected One in whom the cosmos is corporeally organized. Not surprisingly, this view has been subject to severe criticism as being without any foundation in Christian Scripture or tradition.[62] The resurrection as the point of transition between the human and cosmic natures of Christ makes it clear that the latter is not possible without the former. In that respect, Teilhard avoids the problem of the classical incarnation Christologies. Resurrection is not reduced to an unnecessary appendage. He also avoids the problem of the Logos Christologies in which everything is already given in the creative activity of the Logos. Teilhard has grasped the dynamics of the resurrection symbolism whether or not his ontological conclusions can be defended. The risen Christ represents the transformation of creation, not a mere continuity of creation. Further, the identity of the crucified and risen One suggests that the humanity of Jesus is in some way a precondition for his exaltation as Lord. He does not, contrary to the early Christian de-

scent and ascent stories, simply return to a former state as divine
Logos when he is raised. Finally, resurrection does imply statements
about the whole of things. Such statements cannot be static descriptions of the world but must be claims about that toward which the
cosmos is heading. Teilhard has taken up the challenge of making
that statement about the whole in terms of what he understood to be
a description appropriate to the twentieth-century cosmos rather
than one derived from the first or second century.

As in the case with the attempts to speak of the universality of
Christianity in the context of world religions, so, too, in the dialogue
with contemporary scientific myths and symbols, Christians have
barely begun. Dialogue is not a one-way street in which the Christians twist and turn the symbolic language of the tradition to new
symbolic representations of modern culture. Teilhard clearly expected that his theological reflections on biology would influence
scientific circles as well as theological ones. He is accutely conscious
of what Toulmin has categorized as the other dominant scientific
myth of our time, the extrapolation of the second law of thermody-
namics into an apocalyptic scenario of the final demise of the cosmos.[63] Teilhard interpreted this thermodynamic myth to imply that
the processes of the universe would lead back to homogeneity and to
the end of freedom. Life and evolution, he argued, run counter to
that principle, since they tend toward increasing complexity and
differentiation. This increasing complexity and differentiation create
more freedom. "Energy" is transformed into spirit when one reaches
the level of human beings.[64]

Teilhard's vision could, of course, be taken as grounds for asserting
that Christ represents the fulfillment of human religious aspirations.
Such a claim presumes that the spiritual mutation toward which the
development of the cosmos is tending is not an automatic result of
some natural process but that it requires a further act of spiritual
freedom from humanity. While Teilhard thinks that Christian
ecumenism converges on the risen Christ, he apparently holds that
the convergence of Christianity and non-Christian religions requires
two major shifts of the non-Christian party. Non-Christians must
discover the incarnational and personal nature of the divine, and
they must acknowledge the future-oriented character of salvation
with its call to human activity in and for the world.[65] Thus, what
underlies the quest for a perception of the universality of Christ in
both the cosmological and "encounter of religions" approaches is
fundamentally a question about the suitable spiritual orientation of
the human being toward the world of the twentieth century.

RESURRECTION AND CHRISTIAN PRAXIS

In the New Testament, resurrection often accompanies exhortation about how to lead a Christian life. The theological approaches to understanding the universality of Christ seek to ground Christian life in a spirituality that will adequately deal with the complexities of the twentieth-century world. The New Testament resurrection imagery suggested a renewed presence of the divine in the world. Some twentieth-century thinkers perceive this presence of the divine as a movement toward universalization that is continuing on the evolutionary and religious level in the processes of our time.

Another way of approaching the question of resurrection and Christian spirituality is to ask about its significance for Christian understanding of the individual's relationship to God and the world. Rahner observes that Christian piety has often missed the meaning of resurrection as Jesus' exaltation. On the one hand, Christians may simply imagine themselves to engage in loving participation in the life of Jesus. Such a spirituality makes Jesus' life a challenging and inspiring symbol like that of any other great religious leader. Or Christians may address themselves to the risen Lord in a way that does not differ at all from their approach to the transcendent God as such. The story of Jesus recedes from view into "past history."[66] Rahner argues that Easter postulates a unity between the transcendent and history such that the history of God's saving activity is brought to its completion in the history that is actually ours and not in some other dimension. The exalted Lord is the crucified in such a way that the earthly life of Jesus is not over and done with but is completed and eternally valid. That eternal validity grounds the continued activity of the risen Lord on behalf of humanity. Consequently, his intercession with the Father, for example, is not some new occupation provoked by the prayers of the faithful but is part of the eternal validity of Jesus' life.[67]

This spirituality also assumes a distinction between the hope embodied in resurrection of the righteous and the expectation of divine judgment. The righteous hope for perfection in all elements of their being. That perfection is not psychic regression to satisfaction of infantile desire but the perfection of the story of human freedom that has been written in that person's acts. As expectation of divine judgment, on the other hand, resurrection points to the failure of human freedom.[68] The association of divine judgment with resurrection recalls the collective, historical reality of human life. The crucial development of human freedom does not take place in isolation. Human freedom belongs to the larger world, which requires transformation. There is always the danger of reading salvation or eschatology as the story of the fate of particular individuals. The individual, then, might be taken up into God, while the world as a whole would continue indefinitely to whatever biological or cosmic fate unfolds out of the expansion of its material processes.[69] At this point, Rahner's eschatology finds itself in agreement with the Teilhardian vision. We know matter as the seedbed of human consciousness and freedom that move to fulfill their end in history. One might, Rahner suggests, conclude that if matter has also transcended itself into freedom and subjectivity elsewhere in the cosmos, then a similar experience of divine self-communication in grace will bring it to its perfection.[70]

The transcendental understanding of the world as ordered toward divine judgment does not, of itself, explain the insistence on resurrection as a symbolic representation of that expectation. The appeal of resurrection as the language of Christian hope lies in its double-sided character. One hopes for a future, but the reality of that future has already been demonstrated in the resurrection of Jesus.[71] Judgment is also an activity of divine grace. It is false to perceive judgment as nothing more than the final, strict application of the Law to all of humanity. Expiation Christologies often carry with them the implication that the demands of the Law remain. But the resurrection of the crucified shows that God is "in on" the death of Jesus in a more radical way. God's presence to the world takes the shape of the cross.[72]

Resurrection, then, raises the question about the appropriate language of redemption. It proclaims that Jesus became the world's salvation so that the future of the world with God is not completely open but has been determined in some way.[73] This determination of salvation is to be reflected in the life of the Christian. Since believers have been freed from sin, they are not the victims of its internal power to enslave. Having been freed from death, they do not fear death as the end of the person, as some cruel joke played against our human activity and striving. Having been freed from self-will and selfishness, they can risk that self on a vision of the rule of God. This salvation is not presented as some quick transformation of all the negative elements in our lives or psyches. Nor is it primarily a matter of individual vocation. Easter is imagined as calling into being a new gathering, a community in which this reality is to be lived out. Nor can we expect that any human community will be the perfect embodiment of its originating vision.

The calling of such a community into being reflects an important element in the Biblical view of salvation. The reconciliation that occurs in Jesus is embodied in the imperatives that the Christian lives out through divine grace. These imperatives are not merely a matter of individual morality, since salvation is directed toward humans in their communal existence as people of God.[74] Just as liberation must embrace a person's bodily and psychic nature, so it must also embrace the social dimensions of one's life with others, since an individual's freedom depends on the existence of a larger order of freedom. The construction of human solidarity does not reify society as the sole factor that determines individual consciousness and freedom. Indeed, as Pannenberg points out, resurrection only emerges when we find a distinction between the individual and the group. As long as the fate of the individual was entirely submerged in that of the nation, the question of the destiny of the righteous among the people was not even posed. This distinction between the individual and the community within which he or she lives makes the question about the meaning of individual lives inevitable. It points forward to a hope that human destiny is fulfilled beyond death, since it is often not fulfilled in the present.[75] This double-sided perspective, the liberation of human community and the fulfillment of an individual destiny that is not encompassed by the fate of the particular community to which one belongs, represents one of the most important correctives that Christian theology has to make to the modern ideologies of liberation. Secular ideologies of liberation submerge the individual in the communal destiny. Wilder has pointed out that powerful mythologies of return to a primal innocence often fuel the rhetoric of liberation.[76] This innocence is purchased at the expense of a colossal act of forgetting, one that the Christian story of crucifixion and resurrection can never permit. One "forgets" all the victims of the revolution. Or one justifies their suffering in the name of a justice and freedom that can only belong to a future generation.[77] A further qualification demanded by the Christian vision of liberation is aimed at materialist presumptions of modern society. Political and economic progress will not of themselves solve the spiritual problems of the twentieth century. Even the developed countries experience the poisoning effects of fear, apathy, uncertainty, and despair.[78]

However, these caveats do not absolve Christians from concern for justice and freedom in the concrete circumstances in which they live. Liberation theologians from all parts of the globe have called for a reordering of priorities. For too long doctrinal norms rather than

Christian life and praxis have held sway.[79] Consequently, "that one believes in resurrection" has been felt to be more important than "how one acts out of the resurrection kerygma." But the original expressions of Christian theology were immediately bound to Christian practice. Their rhetorical focus lay in mutual encouragement to engage in mutual activity. This general orientation does not, of course, solve the problem of particular actions to be undertaken by Christians in particular situations. Such matters of practical action can never be derived as theoretical conclusions from general principles. The question of "what to do" has to be resolved through an articulated consensus of the community involved.[80] But it does impose a particular shape on the pattern of Christian activity. The universalism of the offer of salvation implies that concern is to be extended to all. It also keeps in view the failure of merely human claims to create salvation, since redemption is, finally, a gift and not a feat of social engineering. Just as salvation is offered to all, all must be reminded that they bear the burden of human guilt for the evils that they struggle to overcome. The myth of an innocent, self-righteous liberator ranged against an evil oppressor has no place in the Christian account of liberation. Though it is possible to see all cries for freedom as evidence of God's identification with the suffering, which will continue until the parousia, Christians must seek to avoid the dangers of destruction inherent in revolution. Hatred for exploitation cannot be permitted to exclude hope for conversion of those who are exploiters. Nor is the vision of freedom dominated by the resurrected and crucified Lord overly optimistic about freedom as a human creation.[81] Freedom often takes the shape of false promises and plays on the same dynamics that are used by the oppressors. The yearning of all people for freedom is grounded in God's own promise. It is not to be gained for one group at the expense of another. J. Moltmann points out that one of the most potent weapons of social control and oppression is "fear of death," subtle manipulation of the psychodynamics of the death instinct. This tactic is not limited to situations in which individuals are in fear of actual execution. It includes all manipulation of people on the basis of this deep-seated fear.[82] Christians can find other grounds for being concerned about the destructive potential of nuclear proliferation or the ecological demise of areas of the planet. They need not accept the manipulative rhetoric of fear so often exploited by those whose identification with the cause thrives on evoking mass hysteria. Nor is this eschatological call to freedom complete when persons have been freed from some evil. They must be free for the new activity that flows from God's salvation. The task of justice and freedom in the community that is called into being by the risen Lord will always remain incomplete.[83]

The modes in which contemporary theologians seek to recover resurrection symbolism are as diverse as the use of that symbolism in the first century. The approaches surveyed in this chapter look to the resurrection as a symbolic way of orienting the believer's life and understanding of the world. This concern is motivated by the desire to find a more comprehensive expression for Christian faith than that of an isolated, private experience. It seeks a universal vision for Christianity, one that is potentially transcultural and—in some cases —could be extended to the emergence of conscious life anywhere in the universe. It is hoped that a transcultural Christ could aid us in overcoming the boundaries that have isolated people within the particularity of their cultural and religious traditions, an isolation whose devastating political effects are evident everywhere in the world. A cosmic Christ integrates the bewildering processes of the living universe into a vision with a human face and a transhuman goal. The crucified and risen Christ affirms God's solidarity with the cry of the oppressed for liberation and justice. It commits the Christian community to solidarity with the suffering of humans throughout the globe. The call to community with the risen Christ reminds the church of its essential vocation as charismatic witness and fellow traveler in the human struggle.

One can suggest, as Metz does, that the apocalyptic overtones in resurrection symbolism answer to a pressing question in human consciousness.[84] Are we to imagine time as an infinite, impersonal, and homogeneous expanse, or are we to imagine it as the locus of expectation and grace. Or, supposing we adopt the evolution story, are those individuals who perish in the long course of development toward the "next stage" simply gone? In short, the symbolic myths born of the scientism of the modern world have a dangerous emptiness. There is no reason for any activity beyond the private pursuit of what the individual finds pleasant and convenient in this life. Yet the most pressing social and political issues of our day require both a long view and a global one. An apocalyptic symbolism may be a more appropriate way for humans to find the hope and commitment necessary to envisage something beyond the imprisoning facticity of things as they are. What is required is not the ability to calculate some short time period between the present and the culmination of all things. Rather, what is required is the perception of the empowering presence of the risen Lord as the divine gift and promise for humanity.

NOTES

1. K. Rahner, "The Resurrection of the Body," *Theological Investigations. Vol. 2* (Baltimore: Helicon, 1963), 203–16.
2. R. MacMullen, *Paganism in the Roman Empire* (New Haven: Yale University, 1981), 56.
3. Rahner, op. cit., 207.
4. K. Rahner, "Dogmatic Questions on Easter," *Theological Investigations. Vol. 4* (Baltimore: Helicon, 1966), 123f. Rahner sees this process beginning with Tertullian, who combined incarnation with the judicial transaction by which humanity is reconciled to God.
5. Rahner, "Resurrection of the Body," 206.
6. Rahner, "Dogmatic Questions," 124.
7. Ibid., 125.
8. The pluralism of the New Testament language is often not reflected in the theological systematization of resurrection symbolism. Each theologian tends to claim to present the theology of resurrection. No single New Testament author can be said to have incorporated all the elements of resurrection symbolism. J. L. Houlden *(Patterns of Faith* [Philadelphia: Fortress, 1977], 35) cautions that one cannot find what would be described as a theology of the death and resurrection of Jesus anywhere in the New Testament.
9. See W. Loewe ("Appearances of the Risen Lord: Faith, Fact and Objectivity," *Horizons* 6 [1979], 177–92) for a discussion of the implicit assumptions about objectivity behind the views of Easter in contemporary theologians.
10. Consequently, E. Schillebeeckx *(Jesus* [New York: Seabury, 1979], 331) can say that the resurrection of Jesus is never an event.
11. Some theologians insist that event can only refer to something that is in principle like others in our experience, that is, something repeatable. Hence, the resurrection as a singularity would not qualify (see W. Kasper, *Jesus, The Christ* [New York: Paulist, 1976], 33).
12. J. A. T. Robinson *(The Truth Is Two-Eyed* [Philadelphia: West-

minster, 1979], 127) suggests that the "subtle body" of Indian thought or the image of the absorbed saint in Buddhism might provide suitable categories. The former is much like what is intended by Gnostic speculation on spiritual body. It would not preserve the connection between resurrection and what has happened in this world that is an important part of resurrection symbolism.

13. C. F. D. Moule, *The Origins of Christology* (Cambridge: Cambridge University, 1977), 139.

14. For a general discussion of the problem, see R. H. Fuller and P. Perkins, *Who Is This Christ? Gospel Christology and Contemporary Faith* (Philadelphia: Fortress, 1983), 1–27. This shift is presented by its exponents as an alternative to the Christology "from above," from reflection in the incarnation of the Logos or the second person of the Trinity of classical Christology and counciler decrees. See H. Küng, *On Being a Christian* (Garden City, N.Y.: Doubleday, 1976), 436–56; 129–33; E. Schillebeeckx, *Interim Report on the Books Jesus and Christ* (New York: Crossroad, 1981), 123–43. G. Rupp's analysis of Karl Rahner's Christology, *(Christologies and Cultures* [The Hague: Mouton, 1974], 203–15), shows that it turns on incarnation, not resurrection. Incarnation and not resurrection represents the novum in which the final and decisive change in the relationship between humanity and God occurs.

15. Houlden (op. cit., 56) points out that the significance of resurrection turns on one's belief in God.

16. D. Tracy, *The Analogical Imagination* (New York: Crossroad, 1981), 52.

17. See J. A. Lyons, *The Cosmic Christ in Origen and Teilhard de Chardin* (Oxford: Oxford University, 1982), 205.

18. Gnilka, *Der Kolosserbrief* (HTKNT; Freiburg: Herder, 1980), 86–87.

19. This is not to deny that other Christologies may have developed in connection with the various types of Jesus tradition, but even those Christologies had to come to grips with the resurrection kerygma. The resurrection and the "divine man," miracle-working Christ are combined in the apocryphal acts. The "wise sayings" are attributed to the risen One.

20. See Fuller and Perkins, op. cit., 121–28.

21. R. Haughton, *The Passionate God* (Ramsey, N.J.: Paulist, 1982), 1. We are not persuaded that her hermeneutic of romantic love overcomes the problems she poses, however.

22. Schillebeeckx, *Jesus*, 641–43.

23. A. Wilder, *Theopoetic* (Philadelphia: Fortress, 1976), 95–97.

24. W. Pannenberg, *Jesus—God and Man* (Philadelphia: Westminster, 1968), 114. Pannenberg notes that the notion of experience in many modern theologies is quite ambiguous. Though believers know that the risen Lord lives, they do not attain such knowledge through an experience of association with the Lord (ibid., 27). Kasper (op. cit., 140) points out that the Easter experience as a factor in the faith of later Christians is only available in the community of believers.

25. Pannenberg, op. cit., 28; 113.

26. See the ground-breaking analysis of this symbolism by W. Meeks, "The Man from Heaven in Johannine Sectarianism," *Journal of Biblical Literature* 91 (1972), 44–72. Meeks locates the absence of Jesus in the community's experience of isolations from the larger world, which had been reinforced by negative experiences of that world.

27. Pannenberg, op. cit., 28; Schillebeeckx, *Report.* 78f. Schillebeeckx is careful to dissociate himself from those who would dissolve the objective character of resurrection into the "experience of faith" of the disciples. This type of dissolution is often implied by those who then wish to identify the experience of the worshiping community with the experience of the risen Lord.

28. K. Rahner ("The Life of the Dead," *Theological Investigations IV* [Baltimore: Helicon, 1966], 353f.) argues that it is not reasonable to suppose that the dead can be met in this world as various spiritualists assert.

29. Kasper, op. cit., 135–40.

30. Ibid., 145–47.

31. See the typology of Christologies in Rupp (op. cit., 38–47). Rupp notes that Roman Catholic theology is committed to a realist account of the effect of Jesus' death and resurrection. Salvation is brought about in such a way that the world is ontologically different. The transformation inherent in salvation is not dependent on the human response of appropriation.

32. See Kasper, op. cit., 136. S. Toulmin *(Return to Cosmology* [Berkeley: University of California, 1982]) has observed that a similar problem besets the question of cosmology in the modern period. It was realized that the extrapolation of laws and processes that operate within the whole cannot be used to make a statement about the whole (pp. 1–85). However, the cosmological question was not banished from the world by the strict bounds of scientific skepticism; nor should it be. Toulmin argues that we cannot answer the questions about the purpose of the

whole of things that are so vital to our decisions about how to proceed into the future until scientists, philosophers, and theologians again pursue the cosmological question (pp. 255–75).

33. Kasper, op. cit., 150.

34. W. P. Loewe ("Encountering the Crucified God: The Soteriology of Sebastian Moore," *Horizons* 9 [1982], 232–34) has seen such a tendency in Moore's attack on Schillebeeckx's understanding of resurrection for not being an adequate account of the psychodynamics of guilt in the transaction between the disciples and the events of crucifixion and resurrection (see S. Moore, *The Fire and the Rose Are One* [New York: Seabury, 1980], 142f.).

35. K. Stendahl *(Paul Among Jews and Gentiles* [Philadelphia: Fortress, 1976] 4f.; 28f.) argues, for example, that Paul's understanding of the place of Israel in salvation history (Rom 11:25–32) implies that God will provide salvation for Israel without presuming that Israel accepts the messianic ministry of Jesus. Jesus appears as the Messiah who makes possible the eschatological conversion of non-Jews to faith in the God of Abraham, Isaac, and Jacob.

36. See Fuller and Perkins, op. cit., 149–61.

37. Küng, op. cit., 166–72.

38. Ibid., 173f. A related issue that comes up in such discussion is whether or not God has chosen those beyond Israel to be "people of God" as he has chosen Israel.

39. Küng, op. cit., 174.

40. Ibid., 89–104.

41. Küng (op. cit., 104–12) speaks of the lack of reflective, theological articulation in the other religious traditions. While one can easily argue that the path of knowledge pursued by religious traditions in the West is quite different from the path of discipleship pursued in the East, one might hesitate to endorse Küng's negative understanding of the stagnation of thought in Eastern traditions, since they, too, have been changing under the impact of modernization.

42. Ibid., 112–16. Küng observes (op. cit., 114f.) that when we speak about this type of dialogue between religious traditions, we must be careful not to imprison them within the reconstructions that scholars have made on the basis of their classical texts.

43. R. Panikkar, *The Unknown Christ of Hinduism* (London: Darton, Longman & Todd, 1964). Panikkar would caution that the dialogue between religions cannot be the creation of academic theologians. It must proceed at the deeper level of spiri-

tual awakening—as, for example, in the encounter of monastic and ascetic traditions.

44. J. Metz, *Faith in History and Society* (New York: Seabury, 1980), 160–62. Metz is explicitly critical of the transcendental anthropology of Rahner with its emphasis on the anonymous Christian. However, the same question can be addressed to any theological position that generalizes from its experience of salvation to an understanding of humanity as a whole.

45. Ibid., 158f.

46. Ibid., 165.

47. Ibid., 136–44.

48. J. Cobb, *Beyond Dialogue. Toward a Mutual Transformation of Christianity and Buddhism* (Philadelphia: Fortress, 1982), 79f.

49. Ibid., 90–92.

50. Ibid., 105–108.

51. Ibid., 110; 132f.

52. W. M. Thompson, *Jesus, Lord and Savior: A Theopathic Christology and Soteriology* (New York: Paulist, 1980), 12.

53. Toulmin, op. cit., 53–71. Metz (op. cit., 5f.) agrees that evolution functions as an ideological meta-theory that is not subject to verification or scientific clarification when it is used as a vision of the whole. He criticizes it as a quasi-religious symbol that has been generated by scientific knowledge and that is antithetical to a human identity, since it presumes an anonymous process in control of the world. Toulmin's suggestion that the real appeal of evolution as myth lies in its grounding confidence in a universe directed toward the human as its goal and hence by moral purpose seems a better understanding of the phenomenon than Metz's view. Toulmin has anchored his claims by looking at the use of evolution in specific thinkers, while Metz merely generalizes from what he apparently understands the myth to mean.

54. G. Martelet, *The Risen Christ and the Eucharistic World* (London: Collins, 1976), 77–92.

55. Toulmin, op. cit., 117.

56. Martelet (op. cit., 28) picks up Teilhard's images of the risen Christ as the goal of the universe and emphasizes the symbolic presence of that reality in the "body of the Lord." In so doing, he has sidestepped the theological challenge of Teilhard's expressions about hyperpersonalism.

57. Toulmin, op. cit., 113–24.

58. Lyons, op. cit., 208f.

59. Ibid., 156, 184.

60. Ibid., 149.

61. Ibid., 168–71.
62. Ibid., 187, 193–97. Lyons points out that Teilhard considered himself to be carrying out a much-needed theological task within the limits set by the tradition.
63. Toulmin, op. cit., 124.
64. Martelet (op. cit., 48–53) observes that Teilhard's opposition to the "entropy myth" is paralleled in his opposition to the Freudian theory of the death instinct.
65. R. Faricy, *The Spirituality of Teilhard de Chardin* (Minneapolis: Winston, 1981), 100–104; Lyons, op. cit., 187.
66. K. Rahner, "On the Spirituality of the Easter Faith," *Theological Investigations. Vol. 17* (New York: Crossroad, 1981), 8–11.
67. Ibid., 12–15; Thompson (op. cit., 199) emphasizes the transformation of the Platonic image of the passionless God into that of the exalted Christ as the one who continues in pathos with his followers as the crucial transformation that the Christian story brings to the image of God.
68. K. Rahner, "Jesus' Resurrection," *Theological Investigations. Vol. 17* (New York: Crossroad, 1981), 16–18. Rahner grounds the hope of resurrection in the transcendental orientation of human persons toward freedom and their expectation that such free acts have a validity beyond the significance that they gain in this life. But he agrees that, strictly speaking, resurrection is a gift of divine grace that can only be given in revelation.
69. K. Rahner, *Foundations of Christian Faith* (New York: Crossroad, 1978), 444–46.
70. Ibid., 446–47.
71. J. Moltmann, *The Crucified God* (New York: Harper & Row, 1974), 170–78.
72. Ibid., 176–92.
73. Kasper, op. cit., 154–56; Rahner, "Dogmatic Questions on Easter," *Theological Investigations. Vol. 4* (Baltimore: Helicon, 1966), 128f. Both theologians insist that salvation is an ontological reality and not merely a judicial one. The exalted Lord is the permanent mediator of salvation (Rahner, op. cit., 131).
74. Kasper, op. cit., 16–17; Metz, op. cit., 63.
75. Pannenberg, op. cit., 83f.
76. Wilder, op. cit., 38. Wilder also cautions against the ambiguity of cults of eros and ecstasy (ibid., 60).
77. Metz, op. cit., 74f.
78. J. Moltmann, "The Hope of the Resurrection and the Practice of Liberation," *The Future of Creation* (Philadelphia: Fortress, 1979), 112f.

79. C. Davis, *Theology and Political Society* (Cambridge: Cambridge University, 1980), 2–5.

80. Ibid., 16–49. Davis sees the development of a Christian critical theory as a pressing need for such discussions. He also suggests that much of our confusion stems from the lack of an effective functional relationship between church and society as well as from an unwillingness to break with the authoritarian character of the Christian mind-set that feels that only what is imposed by an appropriate authority requires our attention.

81. Moltmann, *Crucified God,* 97–101.

82. Ibid., 103f.

83. Moltmann *(Future,* 107–109) points out that the church is always an exodus community. It is always called to be a witness and not a mere reflection of the society in which it exists.

84. Metz, op. cit., 169–76.

TWELVE

Resurrection and the Contemporary Encounter with Death

No one can escape the preoccupation with death in our society. We are assaulted with images of those killed in revolutionary violence, criminal assault, and the accidents of ordinary life on every news broadcast. Even the "style of dying" for persons who have lived out their lives has been eroded. Where we once possessed a culturally developed style for those final hours that made them a summation of a person's life, we now expect the medical community to erase the problem.[1] P. Aries has cataloged the cultural changes in the art of dying in the West. Once the primary eschatological vision had been of the righteous in triumph with the exalted, enthroned Christ. In the Middle Ages, it became the torments of the damned. Then one finds a further shift from judgment as a universal, cosmic event to judgment at the hour of an individual's death as the crucial moment of reckoning.[2] Thus, we can see that resurrection as the triumphant victory over death, which is shared with the enthroned Lord, had lost its hold on the Christian imagination.

Further developments in the iconography of death reflect a shift in the collective unconscious.[3] By the sixteenth century the focus shifts away from the moment of death as the point of conversion. Both Catholic and Protestant spiritual writers encourage their readers to meditate on human mortality and the fragile passage of time.[4] By the nineteenth century death has been hidden behind the romantic myth of the "beautiful death." Most people no longer believe in hell, and a new quest for information about life after death arises in spiritualist circles.[5] It becomes customary to remove all signs of death from the sick room until the person is clearly about to die. Aries notes that Vatican II attempted to counter this process by renaming Extreme Unction the Sacrament of the Sick. However, in doing so, it inadvertently gave way to the same cultural aversion to the moment of death.[6] Even our contemporary "death and dying" craze has not reversed the trend. It reflects the desire to consign the whole process to the hospital or hostel; a more humane hospital, perhaps, but still one away from the family and in the hands of professionals who are to deal with it.[7]

The materials that Aries has surveyed do not suggest that the sensibilities of believers in the traditional Christian doctrines are any different from those of the society at large. In earlier periods, popular piety and clerical practice facilitated the shifts in the perception of death. Having turned the practice and meaning of death over to the medical professionals, we can hardly be surprised when psychologists and doctors emerge as the new spiritualists of our time, with a whole flood of books to reassure us about the process of dying and even of our postmortem survival.

One may easily detect strains of piety that reach back to earlier stages when one reads what theologians say about death. H. Küng, for example, tells the reader that it is more important to shape one's life around the effective power of the life of Jesus in the Easter stories than to explain them, since Jesus is the criterion of mortal life and finite death.[8] What does such an expression mean? It could mean that one should embody the ideals of the earthly Jesus with the confidence that such a form of life is the most meaningful. Such a view is far removed from the dying of the believer as well as the public death of Jesus. Or is the expression "mortal life and finite death" a reflection of the sixteenth-century piety of contemplating the finite character of life as the key to living as a Christian? Küng defines death as a transition out of the conditions that surround and control the individual to God. Although those persons who have died are not unrelated to the world, they enjoy a new relationship to God within God's imperishable reality. However, this transition is not a natural process that is simply given with being human. Küng quickly introduces the soteriological aspect of resurrection language by speaking of it as God's new act of creation based on faith.[9]

One might argue that our process of dying has always been a matter of faith at the most fundamental level. Humans have constructed complex cultural representations of death and its relationship to life to tell them about what is unseen and unknown. Küng's description captures one of the most pressing experiences of our dying—we are not related to the world of the living. This isolation may occur in the hospital long before a person has died. Yet believers are to be assured that they are related to God in a new way. The question that needs to be put to such an attempt to deal with contemporary anxieties is simple. Can anyone reasonably and actively believe in a relationship to God that belongs to such a transcendental realm? Can the isolation of contemporary death be overcome by assertions of that sort without an integration into our consciousness of the sense that the dead are, after all, related to the living in God?[10]

The resurrection stories and traditions of Jesus' resurrection as presence do, in fact, express a conviction that this point of discontinuity has been overcome. However, the view that Jesus' resurrection remains a unique instance until the parousia makes it difficult to move from that story to a conclusion about the dead in general.[11] 1 Thess 4:13–18 reflects a more comprehensive attempt to deal with the first-century version of this question. Paul contrasts the Christian dead and the consequent results for Christian mourning with those who have died without hope. The Christian dead are described as coming "with Jesus." This consolation is grounded in the conviction that the Lord will come with those who have died with him and thus restore that living community of the faithful. Symbolically at least, the image of the risen Lord as the One who would return at the parousia established a conviction that the great separation that appears to occur at death need not dominate the experience of believers.

However, Paul's great, transforming vision of the risen Christ with the faithful has been gone from our cultural imagination for several centuries. Death itself has become even more individualized and isolated. If the social, public, and corporate dimensions of dying are lost, one finds it difficult to speak a language of rising that clearly affirms the transformation and eternal validity of those facets of our human existence. Further, there is a question of the relationship between resurrection and alternative perceptions of the human person. Is immortality of the soul, for example, a more natural expression of the human psyche than resurrection? Christian apologists often try to make an appeal for resurrection on the grounds that its bodily character is more appropriate to our contemporary understanding of the human person. The embodied character of our human life is the foundation of our identity, our transactions with what we define as world, and our relationships with other selves in that world.[12] However, the use of "body" in such contexts is philosophically ambiguous. G. Martelet observes that "body" can symbolize what ties us to nature and to the species. The question of immortality is then precisely the demand to be more. It is grounded in the conviction that the human is not reducible to nature or to what appears to lie under the dominion of death.[13] While the theologian may assert that resurrection stands against such a reduction, mere assertions do not constitute an adequate anthropology.[14] Other theologians quickly identify body with person. They argue that resurrection implies continuity of the self with its history. Whatever is bodily in the constitution of self would presumably be part of the spiritualized corporeality of resurrection. On the other hand, resurrection cannot be about anything that we commonly refer to as body, since it must refer to a dimension beyond space and time.[15]

The contemporary acknowledgment of resurrection as beyond space and time could easily create a further distance between the religious symbols and the experiences of persons being told to use them to interpret life. How are we to imagine anything about such a mode of existence? And, without images, do we simply operate off the images of the wider culture whatever they happen to be? Theologians can hardly be the only ones to address this issue, since the images of human persons and their connections to the larger world are quite fragmented and contradictory. Exploration of this question requires a dialogue between theology and the different human sciences.

PSYCHOLOGY AND THE SYMBOLISM OF IMMORTALITY

From its inception psychology has intended to offer more than therapy. Freud's later papers expanded clinical observations from the realm of therapy to a hermeneutic of culture. The death instinct originates in the perplexities of analysis. Why does the adult persistently repeat infantile situations of stress and failure? Freud first generalizes at the level of instinct. The living being seeks its own death in seeking to restore an earlier state of unity. While Eros may overcome this urge, it, too, is only finite and depends on being with another. Of itself, the living substance has only an urge toward death. Death, then, is not a harsh reality from without but the internal aim of life itself.[16] On the cultural level, the death instinct leads to that destructiveness that threatens everything that Eros might bind together. P. Ricoeur suggests that the various manifestations of the death instinct are part of a collective term that is grounded in negativity. The forms taken by this negativity, compulsion to repeat, the inertia of life, and destructiveness are not identical. Freud has also understood the negativity enacted in play and symbol as the underlying foundation of human consciousness.[17]

Faced with the manifold sources of human suffering, Freud apparently holds that humans have only one recourse: resignation to the inevitable excess of suffering over pleasure. This conviction underlies the Freudian struggle against illusion, especially the illusion fostered by religious symbols. Freud is convinced that religion has exhausted its resources for both instinctual constraint and consolation. Humans fail to acknowledge death not only because the unconscious cannot believe its own demise but out of a deep-rooted fear of death that is the by-product of our sense of guilt.[18] In the end, Freud recaptures that sense of the inevitable resignation to death born of the love of life, which Aries has described as the cultural attitude of the later Middle Ages. Freud is trying to hold together two different meanings of death: (a) death is a necessity of nature that I can only accept, and (b) death is a destructive instinct against which Eros bids me struggle.[19]

Ricoeur protests that Freud's theory of religion and symbol only attends to the archaic and regressive and not to the transformative power of symbol as a summons beyond the present. In the latter case, symbol aids in the consolidation of the person through the conversion of desire and fear. Freud excludes the possibility of faith as participation in the source of Eros. He does not see that such participation is not necessarily the consolation of the child. It may equally well be the empowering of the adult.[20] Similar criticisms have been raised by others within the psychoanalytic community. Jungian analysts have found in religious symbols like resurrection the proclamation of the victory of love and reconciliation as fundament psychic realities, contrary to the Freudian image of the psyche seeking an inorganic and undifferentiated unity in the pleasure principle.[21] However, even in Jung's reconstruction, the appropriation of such symbols of transformation can no longer be mediated through the church. The church depends on a level of "mass-minded" consciousness, which operates directly and often dangerously on the unconscious level. Today humans must undertake the individual quest for psychic integration through analysis.[22]

P. Homans points to the fundamental features of modern consciousness as threefold. First, the rationality and instrumentality of our technological culture are evident in a degree of self-analysis and abstraction that has never before been reached on such a widespread basis. Consequently, people are separated from their traditional sources of meaning. Reaction to that situation takes two forms. On the one hand, nostalgia for the integrative symbols of the past leads to countermodernization in traditionalist movements that seek to reassert those ancient symbols. On the other, demodernization produces new attempts to create values and community that reject modernity's emphasis on anonymity and rationalistic individuality.[23] Freud's analysis represents the clear establishment of the first characteristic of modernity in the realm of understanding the human psyche. The various post-Freudian attempts to recover the positive role of symbol, of intuition, of community, and the like are committed to the third. They have been joined in that pursuit by those religious groups that have managed to overcome the impulse to join the second drive, countermodernization.

R. J. Lifton characterizes the human as a "symbol-mongering" animal. Emergence into humanity involved the ability to transcend oneself in the realm of the symbolic. One can, he argues, trace the progress of our culture by the shifting modes in which we symbolize immortality. The cultural effort to maintain the collective sense of immortality not only requires available symbols of immortality; it requires that they connect with experience and provide an ultimate pattern of continuity. Thus, a viable biosocial symbolism includes intense emotional experience as well as a sense of unending continuity. A religious mode must include direct involvement in prayer, service, or some other form of ritual as well as imagery of ultimate transcendence or rebirth.[24] The trauma of the nuclear age represents a radical destruction of the modes of continuity that we as a species have been able to use to symbolize our immortality.[25]

Lifton has constructed a typology of five modes of immortality: biological, theological, through achievements, through nature, and experiential. The nuclear world, with its threat of total extinction, has broken a fundamental connection in our psychic life. None of our symbols carry that exhilarating sense of illumination or truth. Yet we need symbols to construct our experience, to be able to perceive, know, and feel. We know death when we can explore it and relate it to the continuity of life through our cultural symbols.[26]

For the human being, biological immortality is never simply the continuation of the species. In its most fundamental sense, it is mediated through identification with a family and its ancestors. It also underlies the dangerous violence of nationalism, which can emerge from love of country. Theologies like that of Teilhard de Chardin play an important role in connection with this first mode of immortality. They represent genuine attempts to extend biosocial immortality to identification with humanity as a whole.[27] We can suggest other examples of this endeavor within the New Testament. It is fundamental to the language of the earliest Christian communities that they constitute a new family. The language of familial ties, the ethics of the household code, and the intensely personal character of relationships in the early Christian communities all point to family and household as the fundamental model of community understanding. Paul's apocalyptic imagery of the unity of all believers with Christ provides a fundamental biosocial model of immortality for this new community. A basic theological image for immortality is that of a hero who transcends death and provides a model for future believers to do the same. The symbolism of death and rebirth is deeply rooted in the human psyche. It can fuel religious immortality even in the absence of specific doctrines about the afterlife. The believer is "reborn into the timeless realm of ultimate, death transcending truths." Thus, Lifton suggests that in Christianity the spiritual achievement symbolized in the Christ story is more important than any doctrine of immortality. What is fundamental for any religious vision is its sense of contact with power, a power that is life-giving and transcends death.[28]

The third mode of immortality is the creative. In this mode, one survives through what one has created, whether it be works of art or achievements in some other endeavor. The modern world has made this mode of experience available through scientific and technological achievement in a powerful new way. Because these achievements are no longer the work of an individual genius, they provide participatory feelings of immortality for a large group of persons linked to them. Professions like teaching, psychology, and medicine may also provide sentiments of immortality in the conviction that one's work changes the lives of others.[29] The industrialization of society threatens the identification with nature as a mode of immortality. People have responded with the various cults of the "great outdoors"—even the popularity of "outdoor clothes" worn by those who will never engage in any of the activities for which they were designed represents the deep-seated anxiety over our relationship with nature.[30] Neither creativity nor communion with nature appear as modes of immortality in the New Testament. One might suggest that the apocalyptic framework of much New Testament writing makes them implausible. Nature as such is passing away. It is to be renewed by a divine act of new creation. If it gives testimony to anything, it is to its own transitory character. Similarly, the expectation that individual or collective achievements will provide immortality cannot stand in the face of a divine judgment that is to bring all human history and accomplishments to an end. Lifton's final mode of immortality is unlike the others. It is not mediated by cultural institutions and activities but is an experiential transcendence. This is achieved in an inner experience so intense that time and death disappear. Lifton rejects the Freudian claim that all such states are regressive. The self feels integrated, alive, connected with reality. Such an experience eliminates the destructive side of the death symbol: separation, stagnation, disintegration, and meaninglessness. Consequently, it is possible that such an experience will lead to profound inner change. However, in our culture those who seek such experiences usually do so on the margins of our society. As a result, they are left without any of the connecting imagery of transcendent meaning by which the experience can be converted into ongoing meaningful activity.[31]

The powerful experiences of the Spirit in early Christian communities also carried with them the possibility of ecstasy without integration. The frequent use of resurrection imagery in connection with ethical exhortation is one way of overcoming this danger. The cult is not to be turned into a vehicle for experienced immortality and transcendence.

Lifton's analysis of symbolism leads him to reject post-Freudian analyses like that of Becker, which make the effort to repress the terror of death, that is, of annihilation, the foundation of all human culture.[32] E. Becker argues that humans cannot live without limiting their perception of reality. Character formation provides us with the necessary shell of defense against the overwhelming anxieties of the human condition. As we learn the use of words and clichés that go with the roles we may play in our particular society, we also learn to cover over the root feelings of being at a loss in the world and the terror of death.[33] Lifton insists that this preoccupation with the "death side" of the fundamental human polarities has missed the symbolization of the life process that accompanies them.[34]

The positive side of these polarities makes it possible for one to ask what it would mean for a human being to die well. Dying well would require that one felt a sense of completion, of integrity and movement in one's life that makes dying part of a larger immortalizing current. Though many thanatologists have emphasized the transition from anger and anxiety to claim acceptance in the dying, they have not appreciated the necessity for the dying to make some final assertion of their ties to the imagery of continuing life. Most cultures provide anticipations of the death process that include both termination and continuity. The funeral is both rite of passage and period of mourning for the survivors. The practice of cosmetic embalming creates severe confusion of literal and symbolic modes, since the body, which should decay, becomes the symbol for the continuity that is envisaged in immortality.[35] Lifton argues that the integrity with which one approaches death is realized on three levels: (a) one's judgment about one's past; (b) one's ability to leave some honorable trace of oneself for the future; and (c) the immediate experience in the process of dying.[36] Perhaps because it is least tied to the symbolic representations of death and immortality, we have as a culture been devoting most of our attention to the process of dying. There we can hold the medical profession responsible for our social and religious embarrassment.

Though there are many psychoanalytic theories about death and its function in the formation of human culture, they all warn that the symbolism of death and immortality cannot be disregarded. If reality is essentially a world that must be accepted without mediation of meaning through religious symbolism as Freud argued, then some other pattern must fill the gap. Stoic resignation in the face of what appears to be a surplus of suffering in the human condition can itself be felt as a mode of heroic transcendence. This feeling is intensified when that resignation lifts those persons who find themselves "without illusion" above the masses who persist in their delusions. From the psychoanalytic point of view, the particular symbols by which a culture mediates the integrity of life and the continuity of immortality are not inherently different from each other. They may perhaps reflect shifting pressure points within a culture, as in the emergence of resurrection symbolism.

The integral connection between psychic symbols of immortality and continuity with the larger community appears to be particularly important in the New Testament. There resurrection, a relatively ill-defined symbol, proves to be a structural element in the symbolic world of a newly emerging community. Its perceptions of continuity and immortality correspond to the newness of its sociocultural position. The convert's life has been restructured in the new Christian family.[37] The baptismal symbolism of this group provided a powerful representation of death to the old self and its world, and rising into the life of the new self, with a new community as a new human being.[38] This ritual enactment embodies all of the elements of immortality symbolism that have been emphasized in the psychoanalytic accounts. Even under the classical Freudian description of the death instinct and its embodiment in the superego, we find a powerful enactment of the process of shedding the guilt, the relationships, the vices, and even the gods of the past in order to acquire a new Father, the one whom this community is given the power to address directly as "Abba" (father) in the Spirit.[39]

With that powerful ritual expression of what is reflected in the language about resurrection, the first Christians were not simply reconstructing their sense of reality through affirmation, though the affirmation of cosmological symbols is one of the most enduring facets of mental activity.[40] Christianity's new imaginative powers were given scope in the ritual life of the community. We can only partially recover that life from textual evidence. Ritual is an even more archaic form of human expression than narrative. Acts and gestures are addressed to the divine with the result that one feels the powerful reality of the divine in the enactment of the peoples' attitude toward that unseen divine presence.[41]

Formula, creed, and hymn are the most fundamental categories in which the resurrection experience is articulated. This ritual and figurative language appears to have emerged from the depths of the human psyche. The new relationships that constituted the world into which the first Christians were reborn reached down into the depths of our human involvement with mortality, the roots that we require for our perceptions of the continuity of life. These needs are not, as Freud sometimes claims, part of the unavoidable psychopathology of human life. Rather, their symbolic exploration and expression represent the springs of significant human action and creativity.

From this standpoint, we should not presume that the contemporary difficulty with resurrection as an element in the Christian kerygma is a reflection of the implausibility of the symbol. Instead, one must ask about the modes of our symbolic participation with reality in general. Do many of our rites and symbols communicate enlightenment to the psyche? Or has it become necessary for such enlightenment to be mediated through understanding? Through what Ricoeur has called a "second naïveté"? By learning to think about the content of our symbolic heritage, we are able to appropriate its truth. We need not be reductionist about the recovery of the symbol. We need not presume that it tells us only about the inner workings of the human psyche. The language of religious symbolism and myth also reveals the larger structures of existence within which human beings live.[42] Here we glimpse an even more disturbing question behind the search for understanding our mortality, the fate of wisdom itself. Nor should we presume that religious rites and symbols provide an easy "shortcut" that allows the individual to dispense with wisdom in the pursuit of salvation. The devastating effects of that dichotomy are all too evident in the fractured life of the mind and heart in our time.

THE PHILOSOPHER AND IMMORTALITY

With the transition from the question of the psyche to the question of wisdom, we have entered the realm traditionally dealt with in philosophy. Once again, we can only sketch out some of the questions that either illuminate or raise problems for belief in resurrection. First, is it possible to provide a better understanding of what might be meant by "body" in resurrection language? What is the involvement of persons with the bodily realm? Second, is there a message about reality behind the widespread philosophic and religious symbols of immortality? Do such symbols and reflections carry an ontological truth to which philosophical reflection ought to attend? Third, what is the character of human involvement with mortality itself? Is the acknowledged finiteness of human life, or even unacknowledged anxiety about death, the source of what is best in human achievement?

The Body and the Person

Theologians often seek to prove the suitability of resurrection by appealing to the "embodied" character of the human person. J. Hick has criticized the contemporary atheistic humanists for being all too ready to adopt the theory that consciousness is an epiphenomenon of the brain. This conclusion is not as well established in brain research as they presume. But having adopted it, it follows that the structures of reflective consciousness cannot provide any information about its future beyond the death of the brain, since there can be no such future.[43] Hick's own approach is to point to the widespread research in parapsychology to indicate that such an account of consciousness is not adequate to reality.[44] Other biologists and philosophers are equally divided over the question of the relationship between consciousness and brain.[45]

At the very least, one must be able to make a real distinction between mind and body in order to even speak meaningfully about resurrection of the body. Philosophic reflection shows that the relationship between our sense of person and body is ambiguous. While changes in the body can be registered by consciousness, not all such changes are relevant to or even conscious factors in the ongoing identity of the person. We sometimes suppose that what "having a body" means is found in that sense of connection between conscious intent and subsequent bodily action.[46] Philosophers have sought to circumvent the problems of giving a "scientific account" of the relationship between mind and body by giving a phenomenological description of our experience of the bodily. J. N. Findlay proposes the following survey of the bodily elements of our experience. The most striking feature of bodies is their persistence. What is bodily provides for regularity and almost exact recurrence over time. In addition to this primordial experience of permanence and continuity, what is bodily has the power to elicit imagination, conviction, and expectation even when it is not present. Another feature of the regularity of bodily reality is its aloofness from human desires. Consequently, the sense of reality associated with what is bodily becomes a paradigm for what is believable and knowable. What is bodily must be accepted as it presents itself. However, bodily reality is also public. We experience what is bodily as the mode through which we communicate with others and in which we exist in a world.[47] It is possible, of course, to develop an extensive set of antinomies when one attempts to describe what we mean by bodily continuity through space and time.[48] Substantial permanence is more than mere continuous presence. It also requires a framework against which it is possible to specify changes as determinate specifications of what persists. Findlay derives four categorical requirements for body from Kant: (1) It must represent a discoverable, persistent, and substantial identity in time. (2) At any point in the development of what is bodily, it must be possible to draw lines of causal or originative development. (3) In order to give meaning to the coexistence of bodies in a common world, a body must effect and be effected by other bodies. (4) Bodies must fall into a limited number of recognizable kinds.[49] This description already suggests difficulties with some of the sentences theologians use about resurrected body. Whatever is bodily is tightly integrated in the spatiotemporal order. The possibility of incoherence arises with the attempt to affirm resurrection of a body that is not connected to "space/time" but to some other dimension that is obscurely labeled "God."

One could argue that this phenomenological description of body is well suited to the early Christian perceptions about the risen Jesus. We have seen that the New Testament symbolizes the significance of Jesus' resurrection in terms of ongoing presence and activity with regard to this world. This presence and activity culminates in the parousia and the resurrection of the righteous. However different Jesus' presence "with God" may be from our ordinary experience of presence, belief in resurrection asserts a continuity between that state and human experience in the spatiotemporal world. It is not surprising, then, that the Gnostics, who were most concerned to defend the radical discontinuity between the material, bodily world and that of the spirit, became the most vigorous opponents of the proclamation of bodily resurrection. The Gnostic rejection of the material world is not a psychic oddity. It focuses on one of the antinomies associated with the spatiotemporal orientation of what is bodily. Instead of being impressed with the continuity behind the changing features of what is bodily, the Gnostic is impressed by the fact that what is supposedly so permanent really does decay and disappear. We find that there is little we can do about the tendency of the material to change, especially when it most effects us through our own bodies. The same facticity that so impressed us with its permanence can also confront us with the most frightening experience of fragility. One is forced to turn away from the bodily toward another pole of existence, the spiritual one.

Findlay has argued that as one progresses toward the mystical pole of the world, both corporeality and temporality are liquidated. If space and time are thus transcended, then so, too, any individuality that is dependent on association with the spatiotemporal body. Even if there is at the higher level something that can be described as "body," an instrument for the ego, that body is quite different from ours. One might not use "body" for such an entity at all. However, Findlay suggests that transcendence of spatiotemporal individuality cannot be taken to imply complete eradication of separateness. He argues that the idea of personal separateness is so intertwined with all of the higher values that it cannot be constructed as simply a phenomenon of the lowest level of spiritual reality.[50]

Theologians often leap to the slogan "personal individuality" as the root experience of what is meant by resurrection. Again, one must be careful about what is being presumed by such affirmations.[51] Findlay has argued that it is the peculiar pathology of the Semitic religions to generate antinomies based on their inability to part with the contin-

gency of the concrete. These traditions are not afraid to impute the
contingencies through which it is manifest to the religious absolute.
As a result, disjunctive possibilities are treated as categorical actuali-
ties. In the more evolved types of Semitic thought the arbitrary
elements fill in the realm of necessity. The particularities and contingencies of the revelation of the divine are treated with a dignity and
authority that can only belong to impersonal values.[52]

These objections can also be directed against Christian claims for
resurrection, as they generalize from a contingent experience and
unique claim about an individual to a revelation about the character
of the postmortem fate of humanity. The resurrection of the body
could only be generalized by showing that it represented an insight
of universal significance quite apart from the claim that it has occurred in the unique instance of an individual life. Theologians may
quickly retort that resurrection is not subject to philosophic analysis
because it is grounded in revelation. It is an act of God, which is
appropriate to the situation of righteousness under a God who requires his justice of humanity. Other theologians may beat a hastier
retreat by simply repeating arguments against the continuance of
the body. Some insist that there is no way to reconcile resurrection of
the body with the traditions of "beatific vision," an all-encompassing,
direct experience of God. J. Morrell argues, for example, that continuity is the only way in which one can speak of the "same person"
receiving the reward of the divine vision. But the Christian tradition
has always presumed that the soul exists independently of the body.
What, then, is contributed by postulating the reassembling of the
person and the body at some later time? There are logical problems
with the claim that the reassembled person is the "same person"
responsible for good or bad actions on earth. Consequently, the claim
that resurrection guarantees that the "same person" is rewarded or
punished is not as coherent as it might appear. Further, there is no
conceivable place for an embodied self in heaven. The awareness of
divine presence does not require mediation through any bodily reality. Indeed, such a vision would leave the person quite unaware of
being embodied. Therefore, Morrell challenges Christians to choose.
Either heaven means total realization of oneself in relationship to
God, which Christians have traditionally called "beatific vision," or
the significance of resurrection as the center of Christian eschatology
implies that one must construct an eschatology that is different from
divine vision.[53]

Lack of a coherent doctrine of creation and re-creation renders
contemporary arguments about resurrection more inconsistent than
their first- and second-century counterparts. Within the phenome-

nology of body sketched by Findlay, this earlier conviction can be related to the sense of being in a world. That world embraces both our experiences of external objects, of space and time, and our experiences of the presence of other persons. That experience of others is mediated through bodily reality. Bodily reality is responsible for a special quality of expected presence even when a person or thing is not immediately present in our environment. St. Augustine's description of mourning for his dead friend links this experience of expected and failed presence to the reality of our perception of death. The reality and torture of grief is experienced in the temporal and physical expectations of his friend's presence. Augustine writes, "My eyes looked for him everywhere, but he was not given to them; and I hated all places, for they did not contain him. Nor could they say to me, 'He is coming,' as they had done when he was alive and absent" *(Confessions* 4.4.9). The initial images of resurrection in the New Testament were all concerned with reconstituting community, a presence to each other and to the Lord. For them, the fate of the believer is to be part of that community that is not broken apart by death.

The Truth of Immortality

The problems associated with resurrection as a claim about the continuity of some form of bodily reality beyond death do not invalidate all suggestions of immortality. From the first century to the twentieth, many people have found immortality credible even though resurrection does not seem to be plausible. For example, if it is plausible to hold that human life here and now is constituted by a relationship to the divine, then it is plausible to assume that such a relationship may continue even in the absence of many of the other relations that partially construct the human person.[54] The primary condition for a philosophically coherent account of immortality is the possibility of an existential relationship between the human and transcendent reality.

Findlay has suggested that such a relationship to the "mystical pole" of reality is as much part of the human experience as our relationship to the material pole of reality. The crucial point in acknowledging that relationship is found to be a conversion of human awareness. Conversion appears at the point in the life of the human spirit when the higher-order, impersonal interests, which had previously served as a framework for strengthening our personal attachments, take over and make those personal attachments quite subor-

dinate. This conversion also represents an increase in love for that
transcendent pole of reality.[55] Given this human experience of the
transcendent, the goal of human life can only be described as unity
with that pole of reality. Hence, the *parinirvana* of Buddhist tradition or the *apotheosis* of Platonic mysticism are the most likely representation of the final state of human beings.[56] However, most people
either never experience such a conversion toward the absolute or do
so in ways that are only partial and incomplete in this life. Therefore,
Findlay suggests that one must also conceive of an afterlife that is
parasitic upon this one. The task of that life would be assimilation and
spiritual digestion of the activities and experiences of this life.[57]

At this point in the argument the reader may well wonder if it
would not be necessary to use body language to describe such survival. What else could the expression "assimilation of the experiences" be except some form of mediation of experience through a
form of bodily reality. While Findlay does not put the problem in
these terms, Hick's construction of a global theology of death based
on the insights of the philosophic and religious traditions of humanity
does pursue this hypothesis. He argues that any doctrine that held
that the process of conversion was instantly perfected at the moment
of death faces serious objections. It makes the slow and difficult process of personal growth through our own free reactions in the contingencies of our human life pointless.[58]

Hick's method of exploring the problem is to look for central affirmations behind the diversity of mythic and poetic expressions in the
religious traditions of humanity. These central affirmations are to
form the basis of a global theology. All religious traditions require
some eschatology to render their claims coherent. Hick proposes to
clarify the confusion that emerges in dealing with diverse eschatologies by distinguishing two types of statement about postmortem existence, those that refer to the final state of the human being and those
that refer to some intermediate state between death and that final
one. Statements about *parinirvana* or *apotheosis* belong to the first
type. Statements about resurrection belong to the second.[59] Hick
reconciles resurrection and visionary traditions by presuming that
resurrection is not about the final state but about the intermediate
stage. He speaks of this sort of statement as "pareschatology." The
function of pareschatology is to make it possible for the person to
continue progress toward perfection.[60] Since any description of after-death existence that supposes passing out of this existence and
resynthesis in another dimension of space and time presents difficulties of synchronizing the two dimensions, the simplest hypothesis is

to presume an immediate continuity between the deceased and the resurrection life. Whatever transformations the person later undergoes, the immediate postdeath state represents a continuation of the psychophysical entity that just died.[61] Hick points to difficulties with the image of an immortal ego continuing through a series of lives. As self-conscious egos, we are embedded in our culture and in a long series of projects and opportunities. Such projects, and with them much of our humanity, are bound up with the finitude of death. Consequently, one must presume breaks in the duration of existence in order to have pareschatology. Personal identity must be conceptualized in a way that does not limit it to the boundaries of a particular physical body. Vedanta speaks of continuing threads of consciousness, intention, and hope passing from one existence to another. The Tibetans describe existence in a plurality of worlds. Both provide for a coherent pareschatology.[62]

Resurrection applies only to the endeavor to describe human existence in this intermediate condition. The mystical pole of the great religious and philosophical traditions is always understood as the stage at which the ego state has been transcended. Though the Western traditions might appear to insist on a personalism of God and an individuality of the creature that would make such a view impossible, the mystical writing of the West has found ways to describe the relationship to God that overcomes separation. The West properly insists on the corporate nature of the individual and of salvation, since the development of human civilization has led us through the transformation of the individual. Trinitarian theology provides a clue to the final transformation. It presents the ultimate state of the divinity as the harmonious unity of a single corporate person.[63]

One might point out that Christianity has been down this route before. A number of the Gnostic systems of the second century incorporate either reincarnation or an intermediate after-death state prior to the final reunification of the soul with its pleromatic counterpart that reproduces such a structure of pareschatology. Further, the Gnostic pleroma into which the enlightened pass is represented as a harmonious community of the elect; sometimes it is described as the heavenly or spiritual church. At the same time, most Gnostic systems preserve differentiation within the heavenly world by using the epithets of negative theology like "unbegotten" and "unknowable" to separate the divine from the pleroma that owes its origin to the highest God. Though Hick's examples may be more familiar to the Western reader than that of Gnostic myth and cosmology and though Hick presumes that transformation takes place through a knowledge that does not have to be brought by a heavenly revealer, the structure of his soteriology is not significantly different from that of the Gnostics. This similarity can be traced to the method Hick has used to solve his problem. The sources upon which he draws have a religious structure similar to that found in Gnostic writers. Both presume that the truth of other religious systems is to be gleaned through an overarching construction of a system or myth. Both proceed from a philosophical mysticism that finally cannot do anything but reject embodiment at the highest stage.

Naturally, the Christian theologian (and perhaps exponents of the other religious traditions as well) will protest. The New Testament, as we have seen, insists that resurrection cannot be construed as anything but the ultimate state of the human being. The intermediate state is left rather vague. The New Testament does not commit itself to a description of what the spiritual body will be like beyond the sense that it has some connection with the body that was buried. But that spiritual body is clearly not a vehicle for learning in the intermediate state. Some theologians have suggested that after the death and resurrection of Jesus, God was different. Jesus had, as it were, taken bodily reality into God. Thus, we find ourselves faced once again with the central dilemma of revelation and particularity over against the universalizing and general statements appropriate to the philosophical tradition. Resurrection cannot be made philosophically coherent without distorting some of its fundamental commitments. Philosophical clarification may illuminate and even correct much of what is at stake in the religious language of resurrection, but in the end the two must part company.

Mortality and the Meaning of Life

The final challenge posed by the philosophical tradition may be directed at the desirability of belief in any form of immortality. Some would point out that mortality and finiteness are defining factors of human life. Its beauty, urgency, and seriousness are grounded in our awareness of mortality. Similarly, the profound sense of the tragic, the failed possibility, even frustration at the misuse of life, all require a real perception of our fragile and temporally limited existence.[64] This argument is sometimes posed as a challenge to humanity. The great mask covering the reality of death should be stripped away. Then humans will not be able to evade the question of the significance of their life by projecting it into the framework of another world or a different existence. They will learn to love their finitude as it is at the same time as they learn to assume adult responsibility for the completion or failure that accompanies life.[65]

Sometimes the challenge sounds much like the sixteenth-century piety of meditating on mortality and death in life. It gains its force from the widespread and obvious strategies for avoiding the reality of death that often attach themselves to religious belief. Similar strategies are equally adaptable for avoiding the problems of evil and human responsibility. One might point, for example, to the view often expressed by pious Christians that they do not have to worry about nuclear or ecological extinction. The end of the world brings the coming of God's kingdom. One can hardly blame the philosopher who finds such views humanly and morally repulsive from charging them to Christian eschatology. Hick argues that the strength of the Christian position was in its insistence that the time of grace and repentance is bounded by death. However, he thinks that Christians were wrong in concluding that the process of perfection is limited to a single life.[66]

The tension created by the challenge to confront our mortality in a realistic way can be a catalyst to transform our foundational convictions about immortality and resurrection.[67] The problem of the meaning of our life is closely tied to the question of its finitude. Noble enlightenment and courage in the face of death proposed by the philosophic vision of mortality is as limited as the Stoic courage of Freudian resignation. So, too, perhaps is that sense of a life that has fulfilled its purpose in a way that enables one to view it with a sense of closure. Religious traditions have always sought to address the larger human community in their hopes for salvation.

R. Nozick has observed that for most people a sense of meaning requires some form of "continuing forever." They may wish to leave traces in the world. Or they may choose to see their lives as incorporated into a larger divine plan. The sense of continuing takes on other peculiar features as one begins to question it. The person does not, for example, wish to be transformed into a universal, say, a number, that continues forever. There is a sense, difficult to uproot, that holds that what is eternal is better than what is finite.[68] The "better" brings us closer to the question of value that lies at the heart of our human concern with death and with the transcendent. The desire to overcome the finiteness of a single human life in order to integrate that life into a structure of meaning is the desire to forge a connection to what is really good. There are, of course, great variations in individual awareness of and strategies for satisfying the demand for such integration. Limits pose the question of meaning. We seek to answer that question by asking about our relationship to the unlimited as the ground of our commitment to meaning and value.[69]

The question still remains as to whether or not the conviction of human immortality is the only way to describe our connection to such a transcendent source of meaning. One might suggest, for example, that the sense of participation in the life of God can break through into the present life of a human being. One might even insist that only such a breakthrough in the finiteness of human life can really endow it with the meaning that we seek in our projections of immortality.[70]

These reflections on the confrontation with immortality and the question of meaning have led us back to another of the convictions that we found at the origins of resurrection symbolism: the necessity to affirm the meaning of righteousness in concrete situations and finite human lives. The persecution of the righteous and the prosperity of the wicked, let alone the crucifixion of a Messiah, seemed to make a mockery of those values of justice proclaimed by the tradition. To allow the righteous to vanish as though they hadn't mattered was intolerable. This difficulty is not just the result of the narrative commitment to divine activity and justice in the Biblical stories. It is equally well grounded in our expectations of the transcendent pole of reality.[71] While accepting the humanist critique of the false uses of immortality, the theologian may still argue that the conviction of participation in a process that is more encompassing than the limits of our world and finite life will itself require realization of that goal in a new life. And one may insist with at least equal plausibility that such hope and transcendent purpose have given human life as much depth, scope, and vitality as the heroic creation of meaning in the face of mortality proposed by the existentialist philosopher.

THEOLOGICAL RESPONSES TO THE ENCOUNTER WITH DEATH

The questions raised by the twentieth-century encounter with death have not gone unnoticed in the theological community, though it is difficult to find a comprehensive treatment of the problem in any single theologian. For some, the challenge to ethical engagement in the world is primary. For others, the development of an anthropology of human relationship to the transcendent is the key. For yet others, the primary questions are psychological. How does the Christian understanding of death and resurrection contribute to the formation of an adult rather than an infantile personality? The first approach is exemplified in liberation theology: the second, in the transcendental anthropology of Karl Rahner; and the third, by Sebastian Moore's psychological exploration of Christology.

Death and the Task of Liberation

For the liberation theologian, the false consciousness of modernity is exemplified in the privatization of death and in the resistance to encounter with death. This false consciousness creates the vision of an undifferentiated time that extends well beyond any human purposes. It cannot imagine that foreshortening of time in the presence of divine judgment, which lies at the heart of Biblical eschatology. Liberation theologians point to the economic underpinnings of our failure to relate to the dead. For the citizen of the industrialized world, persons are primarily viewed as those with whom one enters into relationships of exchange. The exchange may not be monetary. It may also be described in terms of satisfaction of needs. The dead are not capable of such relationships. This pervasive environment of personal value as exchange reduces the sense of other primary human relationships—friendship, thankfulness, attention to the dead. Mourning has been written out of our culture because it does not bring a return.[72]

The denial of death's destructive power and the powerful expressions of hope and confidence in the human future as part of a greater order in the cosmos are the most important liberating elements in religious eschatologies. People cannot engage in the struggle for justice and transformation if they remain in psychological bondage to powers of death. Such powers can be embodied in traditions of government, law, religious observance, or any other institution that holds people tied to reality as fixed.[73] Both the personal and political powers that claim to govern human life can use the psychodynamics of death to imprison. Cynical resignation in the face of death is as threatening to human well-being as is the desperate attempt to cover up the reality of death. Oppression establishes itself on death and manipulates people through their fear of death. Consequently, only those who are neither cynical nor afraid can be counted on to persist in the quest for a truly just and human world.[74] Since for the liberation theologians, as we have seen, resurrection is a symbol of the triumph of justice for the human community, one can never say that eschatology distracts people from moral commitment to this world and to universal human good. Further, it might be argued that only such a cosmic image of hope will enable groups of people to shake off the exploitation of death by the powers of the world. In contrast to the domineering sociopolitical powers, one finds the exalted Christ as Lord of the cosmos. Individual courage in the face of death is not enough. There must be a community empowered to stand against death-dealing tactics of the larger society. Philosophy addresses individuals in the name of universal truths. Religious tradition calls forth a community of the righteous in the name of a concrete revelation.

Gathering a Life in the Encounter with Death

Rahner's anthropology focuses on the significance of the free moral decisions of the individual as the fundamental factor in constituting the human self. The profound significance of human freedom calls for a completion that is greater than the individual events that go into making up a life.[75] Death cannot be adequately described as the separation of two entities called soul and body. It does appear as the climax of the weakening of human powers, a helpless collapse about which we can finally do nothing. But there is another side. This side shows death as the final, supreme act of human freedom in which a person's life is gathered up and "ripens for eternity."[76] Both of these themes recapture earlier views of death that were once widespread in our culture.

Resurrection picks up that primordial affirmation that wills the eternal validity and the absolute value of free moral decisions. This validity must be maintained in the face of experiences of a finite world that appear to disconfirm it. At this point, Rahner's transcendental anthropology and the concern of liberation theology to affirm the absolute validity of the moral claims upon the activity of human persons come together, though Rahner speaks about individual decision, whereas the liberation theologian speaks about socioeconomic structures and a new community. This primordial hope, Rahner argues, belongs to every human person as person. It is grounded in the quest for meaning in one's life, in the conviction that the single human existence has validity. Again, the liberation theologian would agree that the religious perspective sees each human person as having absolute value, since that person is the object of divine love. Unlike the secular ideologies, a liberation theology will not forget "the enemies" and those persons who appear to have been sacrificed in the human struggle for justice. Rahner insists that from a transcendental perspective moral choice requires this commitment to the value of each individual person.

But resurrection hope is more than an affirmation of the moral order of the world. Rahner suggests that an implicit hope for bodily resurrection also belongs to the human person as such. This hope is reflected in the experience of concreteness. This person, not some abstract part of the person, and this life in the sum of its free acts are what counts. Of course, this transcendental hope is expressed differently by different people. But, Rahner insists, it is part of the phenomenology of human experience, quite apart from any philosophical elaboration.[77]

Rahner is not claiming that such transcendental analysis demonstrates the truth of the specific revelation that those hopes have been fulfilled in Christ. Or that transcendental analysis can show that the powers of death, finiteness, and guilt have been overcome. Or that in the presence of God human history now has an abiding and real validity. These convictions are all grounded only in revelation. The transcendental hope of immortality and resurrection provides the horizon within which it is possible to understand the experience of Jesus' resurrection in faith. Since human awareness of death is part of death, we cannot ignore the question of whether or not there is something more for the person we experience as the subject of love, responsibility, freedom, pain, fidelity, and the like. Nor, contrary to the philosophic tendency to interpret immortality as the desire to go on forever, do we really perceive the type of human life we know as something that could be stretched out forever. There is that demand for completion. It is not satisfied by more of the same. If life simply went on forever, then that question about the definitive validity of our human free choices of the good would never be resolved.[78]

This phenomenology of human experience cannot prove the existence of immortality or resurrection, but it reveals the sources from which such beliefs draw their illuminating power. For the believer, the revelation of resurrection as the culmination of human destiny is experienced as the gracious answer of God to these questions and longings of our humanity. Rahner argues that faith in this revelation does not presume some special, mystical relationship to the absolute, since this faith is mediated through concrete testimony about the fate of Jesus. This mediation of faith is not the same thing as crediting the gospels or the apostles with a historicity that would be accepted as proof by all rational persons. Judgments about "historicity" require that the witnesses to an event testify to an event that we accept as like other events in human experience. Consequently, while our transcendental hope in resurrection provides a foundation for "hearing in faith," we must say that our faith is in contact with the reality of resurrection only in the experience the believer has that Jesus lives as the resurrected One. For those who seek historical evidence, we can only reconstruct the convictions that the first witnesses had about their experiences.[79]

Since the dimension in which resurrection occurs is not spatiotemporal, the "body" about which one speaks must refer to the whole person. Rahner suggests that there are a number of elements of the "resurrection dimension" that are implied by the expression "of the body." Perhaps the most important is that nearness to God does not imply distance or separation from the world any more than eternity is simply an unbroken string of temporal instants.[80] Further, Christianity cannot be reduced to any form of idealism. The survival of the person has meaning only if the whole reality of the world is embraced. One cannot set the biophysical world over against the realm of the spirit and proclaim that the former is indifferent to the spirit. For Rahner, the resurrection of Jesus points to the story of spiritual person. It indicates that there is some respect in which the material world, too, enters into the finality that we envisage for the human person.[81]

Rahner has not attempted to resolve all the perplexities about space, time, body, and person raised by the philosophical discussion. He sees the purpose of philosophical reflection to be the illumination of that horizon of human understanding and questioning in which the symbols and doctrines of faith can speak in an insightful way. But those symbols also speak as an answer, which could not have been predicted no matter how intense our hope that something of the sort might be the case. In the end, the answer depends on faith in a very particular divine revelation. This revelation also throws up new questions. What, for example, do we mean if we speak about the finality of the material? What does the conviction that being in God does not separate a person from the world and its fate mean? How does the transforming completion of the person in death become part of the life of those who confront death? To what extent might the Christian response to the experienced questions of death and meaning contribute to the larger concerns about death in our world? Does the Christian have anything to say that speaks to those humans who do not find a living presence of Jesus in their lives about our shared human concerns?

Christianity and the Psychology of Death

S. Moore's explorations of the psychodynamics of Christian belief in the crucified and risen One approaches some of these questions.[82] His reflections begin to answer the challenge of recent phenomenologies of hope. W. Lynch argued, for example, that human imagination must have a true image of its journey through life to death. Without such an image, in which it is "all right" to die, the repressed anxiety about death will be expressed in violence or sadistic images.[83]

Moore proposes that one of the most difficult projects facing the human imagination is to overcome the ego-oriented view of death. From the perspective of the human ego, death always appears to be the destruction of meaning, of all the projects that the ego has constructed. We are terrified of losing the illusions with which we have lived. We can only imagine immortality as dissolution or as a special chance to continue. Though we speak about the resurrection of Christ, we often picture him among the dead. That picture may include a special place for the "great dead," a place that none of us expect to share despite the New Testament claim that believers are "with Christ." In this imagining, we miss that central affirmation that Christ has changed the face of death. Death is not as our fragile ego imagines it.[84]

Moore has suggested that the perception of the risen Christ reverses a problem of the human psyche that lies even deeper than our anxiety about death. It is our anxiety in the face of the Other, of the transcendent, of God, of the eternal.[85] Humans naturally desire to be a self before the Other, but that desire to be with God, to love and be loved by God, is haunted by our own knowledge of our failures. It is haunted by a primordial human envy of the gods that imagination projects as immortal and by all-powerful beings for whom humans are slaves and puppets. It is haunted by the shadow God, the Freudian superego, who knows and demands all. In the crucifixion, the disciples are confronted with the sham of human claims to innocence. The one who is truly without sin or guilt dies. But the same event also confronts them with the death of God. The God of power and judgment does not come forth against his enemies.[86]

The resurrection of Jesus brings forth a new affirmation of God purged of these false constructions of the human psyche. As a therapy of the spirit, it provides a vision in which the ego's suspicion that death and divine love are incompatible is overthrown. Whatever our

suspicions, whatever our involvement with guilt in all its forms—
even that most adult form of failed responsibility—we cannot attribute these suspicions to God. We cannot allow these suspicions to
obscure the friendship that God has shown for us.[87]

The crucifixion and resurrection raise a question about our understanding of the heroic. We cannot accept heroism as the final human
posture in the face of death. Jesus is not a hero. He comes to crucifixion out of a determination to embrace both humanity and God. He
does not seek, welcome, or glory in death but accepts it as "from
God." In this distinction, another archaic human image falls to the
ground, the image of the heroic death. Thus, Moore suggests, we
should be careful not to "enthrone" death. True, my death shows that
I am not God. But death should not be permitted to undercut the
value of any human person. Death is wrongly perceived if it fuels
empty heroics and is perhaps most wrongly described when it is
represented as the ultimate factor in human life and culture.[88]

Moore's meditations suggest that a Christian psychodynamics has
yet to be glimpsed in its full power. If such a task were followed
through, it would raise questions about the roots of our cultural
involvement with death. Like the other theological approaches, this
approach would insist that popular secular solutions to the question
of the meaning of human life in the face of death must enter into
dialogue with the Christian stories of justice, death, and life. But
Moore has also uncovered another level of questioning that is even
more radically repressed. Indeed, both psychology and philosophy
can be used to keep it repressed. Findlay has uncovered it as the
"mystic pole" of life. The most deeply repressed question in the
modern world is the question about God. The affirmation about the
resurrection has been from the beginning an affirmation about God.
And one may at least suspect that the fear of death serves to mask this
more radical fear, the fear of God. To find that God is not "feared," is
not omniscient superego, requires a transformation of the psyche as
radical as the image of cross and resurrection planted at the heart of
the Christian message. The Gnostics split off the God who was feared
from the transcendent and established the Creator as hostile ruler of
the material world. This extreme solution is of the same order as the
proclamation of Nietzsche's Zarathustra that "God is dead." There is
no connection at all between the human and the divine; all the gods
are idols. Moore's analysis suggests that only some gods are idols, idols
created by a psyche that finds fear of death less frightening than the
suspicion of divine love.

NOTES

1. P. Aries, *The Hour of Our Death* (New York: Knopf, 1981). The thirteenth century reflects the transition from death as the summing up of life to death as failure, as cutting life off (pp. 123–29); the moment of death loses its significance in the sixteenth century, when death becomes a model of human mortality (pp. 297–315); romantic imagery created the "beautiful death" (pp. 409–54), which, until the mid-twentieth century, emphasized the dialogue between the dying person and those gathered around him or her (pp. 562–93).

2. Ibid., 95–110.

3. Ibid., 299, 314.

4. Ibid., 298–315.

5. Ibid., 455–74.

6. Ibid., 563f. This comment only refers to the psychodynamics of the change within our culture. It is not intended as a reflection on the theological reasons given for making the change, which brings the sacrament back to its earliest intent.

7. Ibid., 592–93.

8. H. Küng, *On Being a Christian* (Garden City, N.Y.: Doubleday, 1976), 380.

9. Ibid., 358–60.

10. K. Rahner ("The Life of the Dead," *Theological Investigations. Vol. 4* [Baltimore: Helicon, 1966], 353) tries to distinguish the sense in which the dead are separated from this spatiotemporal world and the sense in which they continue to be related to the world in God.

11. Rahner (ibid.) speaks of the resurrection as a special miracle in the case of Jesus, which permits such contact. We find that formulation too restrictive.

12. W. Kasper (*Jesus the Christ* [New York: Paulist, 1976], 201f.) points to the ambiguities of embodiment in that it enables us to hide ourselves.

13. See also G. Martelet, *The Risen Christ and the Eucharistic World* (London: Collins, 1976), 55–59. For a philosophical discussion of the problem of self-identity and continuity in relationship to

bodies, see R. Nozick, *Philosophical Explanations* (Cambridge: Harvard University, 1981), 29–110. Nozick defends a theory of self-identity as closest continuer, which neither excludes nor gives any special priority to embodiment. What is important is the persistent, reflexive activity of self-synthesizing.

14. Martelet, op. cit., 55–59.
15. Küng, op. cit., 351.
16. P. Ricoeur, *Freud and Philosophy* (New Haven: Yale University, 1970), 281–93.
17. Ibid., 313–18.
18. Ibid., 318–24.
19. Ibid., 338.
20. Ibid., 524–39. Ricoeur observes that Freud often held on to concepts that he had reformulated in other parts of his system when he dealt with problems of religion.
21. See W. B. Clift, *Jung and Christianity. The Challenge of Reconciliation* (New York: Crossroad, 1982), 140–49. Clift admits that the Christian symbols of cross and resurrection are not adequately treated in the account of evil and the shadow in Jung. Jung equates resurrection with rebirth as a material symbol of the emergence of the Self.
22. Ibid., 118–23; P. Homans, *Jung in Context: Modernity and the Making of a Psychology* (Chicago: University of Chicago, 1979), 170–92.
23. Homans, op. cit., 202–204.
24. R. J. Lifton, *The Broken Connection. On Death and the Continuity of Life* (New York: Simon & Schuster, 1979), 283–92.
25. Ibid., 335–87. J. Schell *(The Fate of the Earth* [New York: Knopf, 1982], 116–19) speaks of the nuclear peril as the most violent form of the wider ecological crisis by which the living can stop the future generations from entering into life and in so doing cut off that public, common world that surrounds us at both ends of our life and which is the foundation of our immortality.
26. R. J. Lifton, "The Sense of Immortality: On Death and the Continuity of Life," *The Philosophy of Order* (eds. P. Opitz and G. Sebba; Stuttgart: Klett-Cotta, 1981), 137–52; *Connection,* 3–20.
27. Lifton suggests *(Connection,* 18–20) that the search for life on other planets is another embodiment of the modern desire to extend the community with which one identifies in this cosmic sense.
28. Lifton, *Connection,* 20f.
29. Ibid., 21f.
30. Ibid., 22f.

31. Ibid., 24–35.
32. Lifton, *Connection*, 50–52; See E. Becker, *The Denial of Death* (New York: Free Press, 1973), ix, 1–12. Becker argues that most societies are able to express their urge to transcend death in meaningful patterns of heroism.
33. Becker, op. cit., 51–60.
34. Lifton, *Connection*, 53.
35. Ibid., 92–99.
36. Ibid., 105.
37. See W. Meeks's discussion of conversion to Christianity as resocialization *(The First Urban Christians. The Social World of the Apostle Paul* [New Haven: Yale University, 1983], 88–90).
38. Ibid., 150–57.
39. Ricoeur (op. cit., 536–43) criticizes Freud's failure to perceive the sublimation of the father in religious traditions.
40. S. K. Langer *(Mind: An Essay on Human Feeling. Vol. 3* [Baltimore: Johns Hopkins, 1982], 20–25) argues that assertion is one of the most primordial mental acts. The mind affirms itself as a whole in making assertions about the world as a whole. Langer suggests that at the emergent stages of the human mind, world building was embodied in a proliferation of imaginative images. In the contemporary world, however, most people, whether they are members of modern or primitive societies, no longer engage in such activity. They limit their categorical, religious assertions to affirmation of formally stated beliefs. Conceptions that have not emerged spontaneously from the minds of those who employ them have to be supported by self-affirmation (op. cit., 21f.).
41. Ibid., 32f.
42. P. Ricoeur, *The Symbolism of Evil* (Boston: Beacon, 1967), 3–24, 347–57.
43. J. Hick, *Death and Eternal Life* (New York: Harper & Row, 1976), 112–28.
44. Ibid., 121–46.
45. See, for example, the defense of the separateness of mind and brain by R. Sperry, *Science and Moral Priority: Merging Mind, Brain and Human Values* (New York: Columbia University, 1983). Without insisting that there is an airtight case against explanations of mind from the neurobiological level, we would prefer to speak of the problems with such research as indicative of the necessity to move from neurobiology to an understanding of the human as critically involved with the symbolic. Hick ad-

mits that Soviet scientists use parapsychological research to reach a thesis opposite to his own.

46. B. Williams, *Descartes: The Project of Pure Inquiry* (New York: Penguin, 1978), 278; 293. Williams (pp. 70–73; 118) argues that the Cartesian understanding of person implies circumstances in which it is possible to make a real distinction between body and soul and to envisage the possibility of disembodied soul.

47. J. N. Findlay, *The Discipline of the Cave* (London: George Allen & Unwin, 1966), 26–27.

48. Ibid., 123–63.

49. Ibid., 113–15.

50. J. N. Findlay, *The Transcendence of the Cave* (New York: Humanities Press, 1967), 127–34.

51. Findlay's observation that it is difficult to hold together a great philosophical synthesis like that of Hegel or a great theological one like that of Aquinas is amply demonstrated in this type of apologetic. Findlay observes that while the objects of religion may have the most to offer by way of explanation and justification in the human cave, they are also the most blemished. Except when held together by unusual and strong pressures, they fly apart into various components. Great syntheses always dissolve into simplifications *(Transcendence,* 106).

52. Ibid., 107; 111–13.

53. J. Morrell, "Perfect Happiness and the Resurrection of the Body," *Religious Studies* 16 (1980), 29–35.

54. E. Fontinell, "Immortality: Hope or Hindrance?" *Cross Currents* 31 (1981), 167.

55. Findlay, *Transcendence,* 136, 176.

56. Ibid., 178.

57. Ibid., 167.

58. J. Hick, "Present and Future Life," *Harvard Theological Review* 71 (1978), 1–15.

59. Hick, *Death,* 15–28.

60. Ibid., 399–408.

61. Ibid., 286–95.

62. Ibid., 410–22.

63. Ibid., 425–60.

64. J. P. Fell, *Heidegger and Sartre. An Essay on Being and Place* (New York: Columbia University, 1979), 227–33; Nozick, op. cit., 579f.; Hick, op. cit., 97–104.

65. Fell, op. cit., 235.

66. Hick, *Death,* 455.

67. Fontinell, op. cit., 170–75.

68. Nozick, op. cit., 580–94.

69. Ibid., 600–619.

70. Hick, *Death*, 104–109.

71. Findlay *(Transcendence*, 136) observes that as one moves toward the mystical pole of reality, the apparent tension between fact and value is overcome.

72. J. Metz, *Faith in History and Society* (New York: Seabury, 1980), 174.

73. T. F. Driver, *Christ in a Changing World. Toward an Ethical Christology* (New York: Crossroad, 1981), 18.

74. J. Moltmann, "The Hope of the Resurrection and the Practice of Liberation," *The Future of Creation* (Philadelphia: Fortress, 1979), 104.

75. Rahner, op. cit., 349f.

76. Ibid., 127f.

77. Ibid., 350; *Foundations of Christian Faith* (New York: Crossroad/ Seabury, 1978), 368f.

78. *Foundations*, 271–73.

79. Ibid., 273–77.

80. K. Rahner, "The Resurrection of the Body," *Theological Investigations Vol. 2* (Baltimore: Helicon, 1963), 211f.

81. Ibid., 213f.

82. W. P. Loewe ("Encountering the Crucified God: The Soteriology of Sebastian Moore," *Horizons* 9 [1982], 225–30) parallels Moore's explorations and those of Martin Luther. Moore has set himself the task of formulating a Christian critique and elaboration of the Jungian understanding of the Self by emphasizing the transcendent finality of the human subject. He rejects Becker's reliance on a dualism of self-worth and absolute dependence. Moore holds that this dichotomy is overcome in the experience that the graciousness of the Other promotes my life-affirming autonomy (see Loewe, 224).

83. W. Lynch, *Images of Hope* (New York: New American Library, 1965), 210–13.

84. S. Moore, *The Crucified God Is No Stranger* (New York: Seabury, 1977), 56–70.

85. S. Moore, *The Fire and the Rose Are One* (New York: Seabury, 1980), 138f.

86. Ibid., 77–81; Loewe, op. cit., 219–21. Loewe observes that Moore claims to have reconstructed the psychic experience of the disciples with Jesus and out of those experiences the origins of belief in Jesus' divinity. This claim goes well beyond the actual accomplishment of the meditations, which have provided a powerful

interpretation of some of the symbols of Pauline theology (p. 232).

87. Moore, *Fire and Rose*, 115.
88. Ibid., 122–25.

Works Consulted

Achtemeier, P. J. "He Taught Them Many Things: Reflections on Markan Christology," *CBQ* 42 (1980), 465–81.

——. "Jesus and the Disciples as Miracle Workers in the Apocryphal New Testament," *Aspects of Religious Propaganda in Judaism and Early Christianity* (ed. E. Fiorenza; Notre Dame: Notre Dame University, 1976), 164–75.

——. "The Lucan Perspective on the Miracles of Jesus: A Preliminary Sketch," *JBL* 94 (1975), 547–62.

——. "Toward the Isolation of Pre-Markan Miracle Catenae," *JBL* 89 (1970), 276–79.

Albertz, M. "Zur Formgeschichte der Auferstehungsberichte," *ZNW* 21 (1922), 259–69.

Aletti, J.-N. *Colossiens 1, 15–20. Genre et exégèse du texte: Fonction de la thématique sapientielle* (Rome: Biblical Institute Press, 1981).

Alsup, J. E. *The Post-Resurrection Appearance Stories of the Gospel Tradition. A History-of-Tradition Analysis* (Calwer theologische Monographien 5; London: SPCK, 1975).

Arai, S. "Zur Christologie des Apokryphon Johannes," *NTS* 15 (1968/69), 302–18.

Aries, P. *The Hour of Our Death* (New York: Knopf, 1981).

Attridge, H. "Greek and Latin Apocalypses," *Apocalypse: The Morphology of a Genre, Semeia* 14 (1979), 159–86.

Audet, J.-P. *La Didache. Instructions des Apôtres* (Études Bibliques; Paris: Gabalda, 1958).

Bammel, E. "Herkunft und Function der Traditions-elemente in 1 Kor 15, 1–11," *ThZ* 11 (1955), 401–19.

Barnes, T. D. *Tertullian. A Historical and Literary Study* (Oxford: Oxford University, 1971).

Barrett, C. K. *The First Epistle to the Corinthians* (New York: Harper & Row, 1968).

———. *The Gospel According to St. John* (Philadelphia: Westminster, 1978, rev. ed.).

Barth, M. *Ephesians 1–3* (AnBi 34; Garden City, N.Y.: Doubleday, 1974).

Bartsch, H.-W. "Die Argumentation des Paulus in 1 Cor 15, 3–11," *ZNW* 55 (1964), 261–74.

———. *Das Auferstehungszeugnis. Sein historisches und sein theologishes Problem* (Hamburg: Herbert Reich, 1965).

———. "Inhalt und Funktion des Urchristlichen Osterglaubens," *NTS* 26 (1979/80), 180–96.

———. "Der Schluss des Markus-Evangeliums," *ThZ* 27 (1971), 241–54.

Becker, E. *The Denial of Death* (New York: Free Press, 1973).

Becker, J. "Testamente der zwölf Patriarchen," *Jüdische Schriften aus hellenistisch-römischer Zeit* (ed. W. G. Kummel; Gütersloh: Mohn, 1974), 679–82.

———. *Untersuchungen zur Entstehungsgeschichte der Testamente der zwölf Patriarchen* (Leiden: Brill, 1970).

Beker, J. C. *Paul the Apostle: The Triumph of God in Life and Thought* (Philadelphia: Fortress, 1980).

Benoit, P. "Marie Madeleine et les disciples au tombeau selon Jean 20, 1–18," *Judentum, Urchristentum, Kirche* (BZNW 26; ed. W. Eltester; Festschrift für J. Jeremias; Berlin: Töpelmann, 1964, 2nd ed.), 141–52.

———. *The Passion and Resurrection of Jesus Christ* (New York: Sheed & Ward, 1969).

Berger, K. *Die Auferstehung des Propheten und die Erhöhung des Menschensohnes. Traditionsgeschichtliche Untersuchungen zur*

Deutung des Geschickes Jesu in frühchristlichen Texten (Göttingen: Vandenhoeck & Ruprecht, 1976).

Bertram, G. "Die Himmelfahrt Jesu vom Kreuz aus und der Glaube an seine Auferstehung," *Festgabe für Adolf Diessmann zum 60. Geburtstag* (Tübingen: J. C. B. Mohr, 1927), 187–217.

Best, E. *A Commentary on the First and Second Epistles to the Thessalonians* (London: Black, 1972).

Betz, H. D. *Galatians* (Philadelphia: Fortress, 1979).

———. "Observations on Some Gnosticizing Passages in Plutarch," *Proceedings of the International Colloquium on Gnosticism* (ed. G. Widengren; Stockholm: Almqvist/Leiden: Brill, 1977), 169–78.

———. "Ursprung und Wesen des christlichen Glaubens nach der Emmauslegende (Lk 24, 13–32)," *ZTK* 66 (1969), 7–21.

Blank, J. *Krisis* (Freiburg: Herder, 1964).

Blenkinsopp, J. "Interpretation and the Tendency to Sectarianism: An Aspect of Second Temple History," *Jewish and Christian Self-Definition. Vol. 2: Aspects of Judaism in the Graeco-Roman Period* (Philadelphia: Fortress, 1981), 1–26.

Blinzler, J. "Die Grablegung Jesu in historischer Sicht," *Resurrexit. Actes du symposium international sur la résurrection de Jésus* (ed. E. Dhanis; Rome: Libreria Editrice Vaticana, 1974), 56–102.

Bode, E. L. *The First Easter Morning: The Gospel Accounts of the Women's Visit to the Tomb of Jesus* (Rome: Biblical Institute Press, 1970).

Boers, H. W. "Apocalyptic Eschatology in 1 Cor 15," *Int* 22 (1967), 50–65.

Bogaert, P. *Apocalypse de Baruch* (SC 144; Paris: Éditions du Cerf, 1969).

Boimard, M.-É., and Benoit, P. *Synopse des quatre évangiles au français. Commentaire* (Paris: Éditions du Cerf, 1972).

Boomershine, T. E. "Mark 16:8 and the Apostolic Commission," *JBL* 100 (1981), 225–39.

———, and Bartholomew, G. L. "The Narrative Technique of Mk 16:8," *JBL* 100 (1981), 213–23.

Boring, M. E. *Sayings of the Risen Jesus* (SNTSMS 46; Cambridge: Cambridge University, 1982).

Bornkamm, G. "Der Auferstandene und der Irdische. Mt 28, 16–20," *Zeit und Geschichte* (ed. E. Dinkler; Tübingen: J. C. B. Mohr, 1964), 171–91.

———. *Early Christian Experience* (New York: Harper, 1969).

Bousset, W., and Gressmann, H. *Die Religion des Judentums im späthellenistischen Zeitalter* (Tübingen: J. C. B. Mohr, 1926, reprinted 1966).

Brann, E. *The Paradoxes of Education in a Republic* (Chicago: University of Chicago, 1979).

Braun, R. "Nouvelles observations linguistiques sur le rédacteur de la 'Passio Perpetuae'," *VC* 38 (1979), 105–17.

Breech, E. "These Fragments I Have Shored Against My Ruins: The Form and Function of 4 Ezra," *JBL* 92 (1973), 267–74.

———. *The Silence of Jesus. The Voice of the Authentic Man* (Philadelphia: Fortress, 1983).

Broer, I. *Die Urgemeinde und das Grab Jesu. Eine Analyse der Grablegungsgeschichte im Neuen Testament* (StANT 31; Munich: Kösel, 1972).

Brown, P. *The Making of Late Antiquity* (Cambridge: Harvard University, 1978).

Brown, R. E. *The Community of the Beloved Disciple* (New York: Paulist, 1979).

———. *The Critical Meaning of the Bible* (Ramsey, N.J.: Paulist, 1981).

———. *The Epistles of John* (AnBi 30; Garden City, N.Y.: Doubleday, 1982).

———. *The Gospel According to John I–XII* (AnBi 29; Garden City, N.Y.: Doubleday, 1966).

———. *The Gospel According to John XIII–XXI* (AnBi 29A; Garden City, N.Y.: Doubleday, 1970).

———. "Not Jewish Christianity and Gentile Christianity but Types of Jewish/Gentile Christianity," *CBQ* 45 (1983), 74–79.

———. *The Virginal Conception and Bodily Resurrection of Jesus* (New York: Paulist, 1973).

Brown, S. "The Matthean Community and the Gentile Mission," *NovT* 22 (1980), 193–221.

Buckley, J. J. "A Cult Mystery in the Gospel of Philip," *JBL* 99 (1980), 569–81.

Bultmann, R. *Theology of the New Testament. Vol. I* (New York: Scribners, 1951).

Callan, T. "Psalm 110:1 and the Origin of the Expectation that Jesus Will Come Again," *CBQ* 44 (1982), 622–36.

Camelot, P.-Th. *Ignace d'Antioche, Polycarpe de Smyrne, Lettres. Martyre de Polycarpe* (SC; Paris: Éditions du Cerf, 1958).

Cameron, J. M. "The Idea of Christendom," *The Autonomy of Religious Belief* (ed. F. Crossan; Notre Dame: Notre Dame University, 1981), 8–37.

von Campenhausen, H. F. *Der Ablauf der Osterereignisse und das leere Grab* (Heidelberg: C. Winter, 1966, 3rd ed.).

———. *Ecclesiastical Authority and Spiritual Power in the Church of the First Three Centuries* (Stanford: Stanford University, 1969).

Cantinat, J. *Réflexions sur la résurrection de Jesus (d'après saint Paul et saint Marc)* (Paris: Gabalda, 1978).

Carlson, D. C. "Vengeance and Angelic Mediation in *Testament of Moses* 9 and 10," *JBL* 101 (1982), 85–95.

Carlston, C. E. "Transfiguration and Resurrection," *JBL* 80 (1961), 233–40.

Carr, W. *Angels and Principalities. The Background, Meaning and Development of the Pauline Phrase hai archai kai hai exousiai* (Cambridge: Cambridge University, 1981).

Cavallin, H. C. C. *Life After Death: Paul's Argument for the Resurrection of the Dead in 1 Cor 15. Part I: An Enquiry into the Jewish Background* (Lund: Gleerup, 1974).

Chadwick, H. *Origen. Contra Celsum* (Cambridge: Cambridge University, 1965).

Christ, F. "Das Leben nach dem Tode bei Pseudo-Phokylides," *ThZ* 31 (1975), 140–49.

Clift, W. B. *Jung and Christianity. The Challenge of Reconciliation* (New York: Crossroad, 1982).

Cobb, J. *Beyond Dialogue. Toward a Mutual Transformation of Christianity and Buddhism* (Philadelphia: Fortress, 1982).

Collins, J. J. "Apocalyptic Eschatology and the Transcendence of Death," *CBQ* 36 (1974), 21–43.

———. *The Apocalyptic Vision of the Book of Daniel* (HSM 16; Missoula, Mont.: Scholars, 1977).

———. *Between Athens and Jerusalem. Jewish Identity in the Hellenistic Diaspora* (New York: Crossroad, 1983).

———. "Cosmos and Salvation. Jewish Wisdom and Apocalyptic in the Hellenistic Age," *HR* 17 (1977), 121–42.

———. "Jewish Apocalypses," *Semeia* 14 (1979), 21–59.

Conzelmann, H. "Zur Analyse der Bekentnisformel 1 Kor 15, 3–5," *EvT* 25 (1965) 1–11 [ET: "On the Analysis of the Confessional Formula in 1 Cor 15:3–5," *Int* 20 (1966), 15–25].

———. *Die Apostelgeschichte* (HNT 7; Tübingen: J. C. B. Mohr, 1963).

———. *1 Corinthians* (Philadelphia: Fortress, 1975).

Coppens, J. "La glorification céleste du Christ dans la théologie néotestamentaire et l'attente de Jésus," *Resurrexit. Actes du symposium international sur la résurrection de Jésus* (ed. E. Dhanis; Rome: Libreria Editrice Vaticana, 1974), 31–51.

Crossan, J. D. "Empty Tomb and Absent Lord (Mark 16:1–8)," *The Passion in Mark* (ed. W. Kelber; Philadelphia: Fortress, 1976), 135–52.

Culler, J. *The Pursuit of Signs. Semiotics, Literature, Deconstruction* (Ithaca: Cornell University, 1981).

Curtis, K. P. G. "Luke 23:12 and Jn 20:3–10," *JTS* 22 (1971), 512–15.

———. "Three Points of Contact Between Matthew and John in the Burial and Resurrection Narratives," *JTS* 23 (1972), 440–44.

Dahl, M. E. *The Resurrection of the Body* (SBT 36; London: SCM, 1962).

Daniélou, J. "The Empty Tomb," *Month* n.s. 39 (1968), 215–22.

———. *Gospel Message and Hellenistic Culture* (Philadelphia: Westminster, 1973).

———. *The Origins of Latin Christianity* (Philadelphia: Westminster, 1977).

———. *The Theology of Jewish Christianity* (Chicago: Regnery, 1964).

Davies, S. L. *The Gospel of Thomas and Christian Wisdom* (New York: Seabury, 1983).

Davis, C. *Theology and Political Society* (Cambridge: Cambridge University, 1980).

Delling, G. "Speranda Futura. Jüdische Grabinschriften Italiens über das Geschick nach dem Tode," *Studien am Neuen Testament und Hellenistichen Judentum* (Göttingen: Vandenhoeck & Ruprecht, 1970), 39–44.

Delorme, J. "The Resurrection and Jesus' Tomb: Mark 16, 1–8 in the Gospel Tradition," *The Resurrection and Modern Biblical Thought* (ed. P. De Surgy; New York/Cleveland: Corpus, 1970), 74–106.

Derrett, J. D. M. *The Anastasis: The Resurrection of Jesus as an Historical Event* (Shipston-on-Stour: Drinkwater, 1982).

Deschamps, A. "La structure des récits évangéliques de la résurrection," *Bib* 40 (1959), 726–41.

Dhanis, E. "L'ensevelissement de Jésus et la visite au tombeau dans l'évangile de saint Marc (Mc., xv, 40–xvi, 8)," *Greg* 39 (1958), 367–410.

———, ed. *Resurrexit. Actes du symposium international sur la résurrection de Jésus.* (Rome: Libreria Editrice Vaticana, 1974).

Dibelius, M., and Conzelmann, H. *The Pastoral Epistles* (Philadelphia: Fortress, 1972).

Dillon, J. *The Middle Platonists* (London: Duckworth, 1977).

Dillon, R. J. *From Eye-Witnesses to Ministers of the Word: Tradition and Composition in Luke 24* (Rome: Biblical Institute Press, 1978).

Dodd, C. H. "The Appearances of the Risen Christ: An Essay in Form Criticism of the Gospels," *Studies in the Gospels* (ed. D. E. Nineham; Oxford: Oxford University, 1957), 9–35.

———. *Historical Tradition in the Fourth Gospel* (Cambridge: Cambridge University, 1963).

Dodds, E. R. *Pagan and Christian in an Age of Anxiety* (Cambridge: Cambridge University, 1965).

Donahue, J. R. "A Neglected Factor in the Theology of Mark," *JBL* 101 (1982), 563–94.

Donfried, K. "Justification and Last Judgment in Paul," *Int* 30 (1976), 140–52.

Driver, T. F. *Christ in a Changing World: Toward an Ethical Christology* (New York: Crossroad, 1981).

Dunn, J. D. G. *Christology in the Making* (Philadelphia: Westminster, 1980).

———. "The Relationship between Paul and Jerusalem according to Galatians 1 and 2," *NTS* 28 (1982), 461–78.

———. *Unity and Diversity in the New Testament* (Philadelphia: Westminster, 1977).

Dupont, J. "Ressuscité le troisième jour," *Bib* 40 (1959), 724–61.

Edwards, R. A. *A Theology of Q* (Philadelphia: Fortress, 1976).

Ehrardt, A. "The Disciples of Emmaus," *NTS* 10 (1963/64), 182–201.

———. "Emmaus, Romulus und Apuleius," *Mullus. Festschrift für Theodor Klauser* (Jahrbuch für Antike und Christentum, Ergänzungsband 1; eds. A. Stuiber and A. Hermann; Münster: Aschendorff, 1964), 93–99.

Eijk, T. H. C. van *La Résurrection des Morts chez les Pères Apostoliques* (Théologie Historique 25; Paris: Beauchesne, 1974).

Elliott, J. H. *A Home for the Homeless. A Sociological Exegesis of 1 Peter* (Philadelphia: Fortress, 1981).

Elliott, J. K. "The Text and Language of the Endings to Mark's Gospel," *TZ* 27 (1971), 255–62.

Ellis, P. "But Some Doubted," *NTS* 14 (1967/68), 574–80.

Ernst, J. "Schriftauslegung und Auferstehungsglaube bei Lukas," *Schriftauslegung. Beiträge zur Hermeneutik des Neuen Testaments und im Neuen Testament* (ed. J. Ernst; Paderborn: Ferdinand Schöningh, 1972), 177–92.

Evans, C. F. *Resurrection and the New Testament* (SBT ser. 2, no. 12; London: SCM, 1970).

Fallon, F. *2 Corinthians* (Wilmington: Glazier, 1980).

Faricy, R. *The Spirituality of Teilhard de Chardin* (Minneapolis: Winston, 1981).

Fascher, E. "Die Auferstehung Jesu und ihr Verhältnis zur urchristlichen Verkündigung," *ZNW* 26 (1927), 1–26.

Fell, J. P. *Heidegger and Sartre. An Essay on Being and Place* (New York: Columbia University, 1979).

Festorazzi, F. "Speranza e risurrezione nell'Antico Testamento," *Resurrexit. Actes du symposium international sur la résurrection de Jésus* (ed. E. Dhanis; Rome: Libreria Editrice Vaticana, 1974), 5–25.

Findlay, J. N. *The Discipline of the Cave* (London: George Allen & Unwin, 1966).

———. *The Transcendence of the Cave* (New York: Humanities Press, 1967).

Fiorenza, E. S. *In Memory of Her. A Feminist Theological Reconstruction of Christian Origins* (New York: Crossroad, 1983).

———. "Wisdom Mythology and the Christological Hymns of the New Testament," *Aspects of Wisdom in Judaism and Early Christianity* (ed. R. Wilken; Notre Dame: Notre Dame University, 1975), 17–41.

———. "Word, Spirit and Power: Women in Early Christian Communities," *Women of Spirit* (eds. R. Ruether and E. McLaughlin; New York: Simon & Schuster, 1979), 30–70.

Fischer, U. *Eschatologie und Jenseitserwartung im Hellenistischen Diasporajudentum* (BZNW 44; Berlin: de Gruyter, 1978).

Fitzmyer, J. "The Contribution of Qumran Aramaic to the Study of the New Testament IV. Addendum: Implications of the 4Q 'Son of God' Text," *A Wandering Aramean. Aramaic Essays* (Missoula, Mont.: Scholars, 1979), 102–14.

———. *The Gospel According to Luke (I–IX)* (AnBi 28; Garden City, N.Y.: Doubleday, 1981).

———. "The New Testament Title 'Son of Man' Philologically Considered," *A Wandering Aramean; Aramaic Essays* (Missoula, Mont.: Scholars, 1979), 143–60.

———. "Nouveau Testament et Christologie. Questions actuelles," *NRT* 103 (1981), 18–47; 187–221 [expanded ET: *A Christological Catechism* (Ramsey, N.J.: Paulist, 1982)].

———. "The Semitic Background of the New Testament Kyrios Title," *A Wandering Aramean; Aramaic Essays* (Missoula, Mont.: Scholars, 1979), 115–42.

———. "To Know Him and to Know the Power of His Resurrection," *To Advance the Gospel* (New York: Crossroad, 1981), 203–13.

Floyd, W. E. G. *Clement of Alexandria's Treatment of the Problem of Evil* (Oxford: Oxford University, 1971).

Foerster, W. *Gnosis 1. Patristic Evidence* (Oxford: Oxford University, 1972).

———. *Gnosis 2. Coptic and Mandaic Sources* (Oxford: Oxford University, 1974).

Fontinell, E. "Immortality: Hope or Hindrance?" *Cross Currents* 31 (1981), 163–84.

Forestell, J. T. *The Word of the Cross: Salvation as Revelation in the Fourth Gospel* (Rome: Biblical Institute Press, 1974).

Frei, H. W. *The Eclipse of Biblical Narrative. A Study in Eighteenth and Nineteenth Century Hermeneutics* (New Haven: Yale University, 1974).

Frend, W. C. H. *Martyrdom and Persecution in the Early Church. A Study of a Conflict from the Maccabees to Donatus* (Garden City, N.Y.: Doubleday/Anchor, 1967).

Friedrich, G. "Die Bedeutung der Auferweckung Jesu nach Aussagen des Neuen Testaments," *TZ* 27 (1971), 305–24.

Frye, N. *The Great Code. The Bible and Literature* (New York: Harcourt Brace Jovanovich, 1982).

Fuller, R. H. *The Formation of the Resurrection Narratives* (New York: Macmillan, 1971).

———, and Perkins, P. *Who Is This Christ? Gospel Christology and Contemporary Faith* (Philadelphia: Fortress, 1983).

Funk, R. *Parables and Presence* (Philadelphia: Fortress, 1982).

Furnish, V. *Theology and Ethics in Paul* (Nashville: Abingdon, 1968).

Gaechter, P. "Die Engelerscheinungen in der Auferstehung Jesu," *ZKT* 89 (1967), 191–202.

Gager, J. G. "Functional Diversity in Paul's Use of End-Time Language," *JBL* 89 (1970), 325–37.

George, A. "The Accounts of the Appearances to the Eleven from Luke 24, 36–53," *The Resurrection and Modern Biblical Thought* (ed. P. De Surgy; New York/Cleveland: Corpus, 1970), 49–73.

Ghiberti, G. "Repertoire Bibliographique. Bibliografia sulla Risurrezione di Gesu," *Resurrexit. Actes du symposium international sur la résurrection de Jésus* (ed. E. Dhanis; Rome: Libreria Editrice Vaticana, 1974), 645–745.

Giblin, C. H. "A Note on Doubt and Reassurance in Mt 28:16–20," *CBQ* 37 (1975), 68–75.

———. "Structural and Thematic Correlations in the Matthean Burial and Resurrection Narratives," *NTS* 21 (1974/75), 406–20.

Glombitza, O. "Gnade—das entscheidende Wort. Erwängungen zu 1 Cor 15, 1–11. Eine exegetische Studie," *NovT* 2 (1957/58), 281–90.

Gnilka, J. *Der Epheserbrief* (HTKNT; Freiburg: Herder, 1971).

———. *Der Kolosserbrief* (HTKNT; Freiburg: Herder, 1980).

———. *Der Philipperbrief* (HTKNT; Freiburg: Herder, 1968).

Goppelt, L. *Der Erste Petrusbrief* (MK XII/1; Göttingen: Vandenhoeck & Ruprecht, 1978).

———. *Theology of the New Testament. Vol. 1: The Ministry of Jesus in its Theological Significance* (Grand Rapids: Eerdmans, 1981).

———. *Theology of the New Testament. Vol. 2: The Variety and Unity of the Apostolic Witness* (Grand Rapids: Eerdmans, 1982).

Goulder, M. D. "Mk SVI.108 and Parallels," *NTS* 24 (1977/78), 235–40.

Gourgues, M. *À la droite de Dieu. Résurrection de Jésus et actualisation du Psaume 110:1 dans le Nouveau Testament* (Paris: Gabalda, 1978).

———. "A propos du symbolisme christologique et baptismal de Marc 16.5," *NTS* 27 (1980/81), 672–78.

Grant, M. *From Alexander to Cleopatra: The Hellenistic World* (New York: Scribners, 1982).

Grant, R. M. and Graham, H. H. *First and Second Clement* (New York: Nelson, 1965).

Grant, R. M. *Ignatius of Antioch and Polycarp of Smyrna* (Camden, N.J.: Nelson, 1966).

———. *Theophilus of Antioch. Ad Autolycum* (Oxford: Clarendon Press, 1970).

Grass, H. *Ostergeschehen und Osterberichte* (Göttingen: Vandenhoeck & Ruprecht, 1964, 3rd ed.).

Greenfield, J. C., and Stone, M. "The Enochic Pentateuch and the Date of the Similitudes," *HTR* 70 (1977), 51–65.

Grelot, P. "The Resurrection of Jesus: Its Biblical and Jewish Background," *The Resurrection and Modern Biblical Thought* (ed. P. De Surgy; New York/Cleveland: Corpus, 1970), 1–29.

Grillmeier, A. *Christ in Christian Tradition. Vol. 1* (Atlanta: John Knox, 1975, rev. ed.).

Grundman, W. *Das Evangelium nach Matthaus* (THKNT I; Berlin: Evangelische, 1971).

Guillaume, J.-M. *Luc interprète des anciennes traditions sur la résurrection de Jésus* (EBib; Paris: Gabalda, 1979).

Guitton, "Épistémologie de la résurrection. Concepts préalables et programme de recherches," *Resurrexit. Actes du symposium in-*

ternational sur la résurrection de Jésus (ed. E. Dhanis; Rome: Libreria Editrice Vaticana, 1974), 108–30.

Haenchen, E. *The Acts of the Apostles* (Philadelphia: Westminster, 1971).

———. *Der Weg Jesu. Eine Erklarung des Markus-Evangeliums und der kanonischen Parallelen* (Berlin: de Gruyter, 1968, 2nd ed.).

Hamilton, N. Q. "Resurrection Tradition and the Composition of Mark," *JBL* 84 (1965), 415–21.

Hanson, P. "Old Testament Apocalyptic Reexamined," *Int* 25 (1971), 454–79.

Hare, D. A., and Harrington, D. J. "Make Disciples of All the Gentiles (Matthew 28:19)," *CBQ* 37 (1975), 359–69.

Harnisch, W. *Eschatologische Existenz. Ein Exegetischer Beitrag zum Sachanliegen von 1 Thessalonischen 4, 13–5, 11* (Göttingen: Vandenhoeck & Ruprecht, 1973).

Hartmann, G. "Die Vorlage der Osterberichte in Joh 20," *ZNW* 55 (1964), 197–220.

Harvey, A. E. *Jesus and the Constraints of History* (Philadelphia: Westminster, 1982).

Haughton, R. *The Passionate God* (Ramsey, N.J.: Paulist, 1982).

Hauschild, W. D. *Gottes Geist und der Mensch* (BEvT 63; Munich: Kaiser, 1972).

Hedrick, C. "Gnostic Proclivities in the Greek Life of Pachomius and the Sitz im Leben of the Nag Hammadi Library," *NovT* 22 (1980), 78–94.

———. "Paul's Conversion/Call: A Comparative Analysis of the Three Reports in Acts," *JBL* 100 (1981), 415–32.

Hengel, M. *Judaism and Hellenism* (Philadelphia: Fortress, 1974).

———. "Maria Magdalena und die Frauen als Zeugen," *Abraham unser Vater* (ed. O. Betz; Leiden: Brill, 1963), 243–56.

———. *The Son of God* (Philadelphia: Fortress, 1976).

Hennecke, E., and Schneemelcher, W. *New Testament Apocrypha. Vol. 1: Gospels and Related Writings. Vol. 2: Writings Relating to the Apostles, Apocalypses and Other Subjects* (tr. R. McL. Wilson; Philadelphia: Westminster, 1963).

Hick, J. *Death and Eternal Life* (New York: Harper & Row, 1976).

———. "Present and Future Life," *HTR* 71 (1978), 1–15.

Holmberg, B. *Paul and Power. The Structure of Authority in the Primitive Church as Reflected in the Pauline Epistles* (Philadelphia: Fortress, 1980).

Homans, P. *Jung in Context. Modernity and the Making of a Psychology* (Chicago: University of Chicago, 1979).

Hooke, S. H. "Life after Death: The Extra-Canonical Literature," *ExpTim* 76 (1964/65), 273–76.

Hopkins, K. *Conquerors and Slaves* (Cambridge: Cambridge University, 1978).

Hornschuch, W. *Studien zur Epistula Apostolorum* (PTS 5; Berlin: de Gruyter, 1965).

Horsley, R. A. "How Can Some of You Say That There Is No Resurrection of the Dead? Spiritual Elitism in Corinth," *NovT* 20 (1978), 203–31.

Houlden, J. L. *Patterns of Faith* (Philadelphia: Fortress, 1977).

Hubbard, B. *The Matthean Redaction of a Primitive Apostolic Commissioning* (Missoula, Mont.: Scholars, 1974).

Hultgård, A. *L'eschatologie des Testaments des Douze Patriarches* (Acta Universitatis Upsalensis. Historia Religionum 6; Stockholm: Almqvist & Wiksell, 1977).

Iersel, B. van "The Resurrection of Jesus," *Concilium* 60 (1970), 54–67.

Jeremias, J. "Flesh and Blood Cannot Inherit the Kingdom of God," *NTS* 3 (1955/56), 151–59.

——. *New Testament Theology. Vol. 1: The Proclamation of Jesus* (New York: Scribners, 1971).

Jewett, R. *Paul's Anthropological Terms: A Study of Their Use in Conflict Settings* (Leiden: Brill, 1971).

Johnson, B. A. "Empty Tomb Tradition in the Gospel of Peter," *HTR* 59 (1966), 447–48.

de Jonge, M. *The Testaments of the Twelve Patriarchs: A Study of Their Text, Composition and Origin* (Assen: Van Gorcum, 1953).

——. "The Use of the Word Anointed in the Time of Jesus," *NovT* 8 (1966), 132–48.

Kaesemann, E. *Commentary on Romans* (trans. E. Bromily; Grand Rapids: Eerdmans, 1980).

Kaesteli, J.-D. "Valentinianisme italien et valentinianisme oriental: Leurs divergence à propos de la nature du corps de Jesus," *The Rediscovery of Gnosticism. Vol. 1: The School of Valentinus* (ed. B. Layton; Leiden: Brill, 1980), 391–403.

Kasper, W. *Jesus the Christ* (New York: Paulist, 1976).

Kearney, P. J. "He Appeared to 500 Brothers (1 Cor XV, 6)," *NovT* 22 (1980), 264–84.

Keck, L. *Paul and His Letters* (Philadelphia: Fortress, 1979).

Kee, H. C. *Christian Origins in Sociological Perspective* (Philadelphia: Westminster, 1980).

———. *Community of the New Age* (Philadelphia: Westminster, 1977).

Kegel, G. *Auferstehung Jesu—Auferstehung der Toten. Eine Traditionsgeschichtliche Untersuchung zum Neuen Testament* (Gütersloh: Mohn, 1970).

Kelber, W. *The Oral and the Written Gospel* (Philadelphia: Fortress, 1983).

Kelly, J. N. D. *Early Christian Creeds* (New York: McKay, 1972, 3rd ed.).

———. *Early Christian Doctrines* (New York: Harper & Row, 1975, 3rd ed.).

Kieffer, R. "Résurrection du Christ et résurrection générale," *NRT* 103 (1981), 330–44.

Kingsbury, J. D. "The Composition and Christology of Mt 28:16–20," *JBL* 93 (1974), 573–84.

———. "The Figure of Peter in Matthew's Gospel as a Theological Problem," *JBL* 98 (1979), 67–83.

Kirk, G. S. *Myth: Its Meaning and Function in Ancient and Other Cultures* (Berkeley: University of California, 1970).

Klijn, A. F. J. *The Acts of Thomas* (Leiden: Brill, 1962).

———. *Seth. In Jewish, Christian and Gnostic Literature* (Leiden: Brill, 1977).

Kloppenborg, J. "An Analysis of the Pre-Pauline Formula 1 Cor 15:3b–5 in Light of Some Recent Literature," *CBQ* 40 (1978), 351–67.

Knox, J. L. *The Humanity and Divinity of Christ* (Cambridge: Cambridge University, 1967).

Kobelski, P. J. *Melchizedek and Melchresa* (CBQMS 10; Washington: Catholic Biblical Association, 1981).

Koester, H. "Gnostic Writings as Witnesses for the Development of the Sayings Tradition," *Rediscovery of Gnosticism. Vol. 1: The School of Valentinus* (ed. B. Layton; Leiden: Brill, 1980), 238–56.

———, and J. M. Robinson, *Trajectories Through Early Christianity* (Philadelphia: Fortress, 1971).

Koschorke, K. "Eine gnostische Pfingstpredigt zur Auseinandersetzung zwischen gnostische und kirchliche Christentum am Beispiel der Epistula Petri ad Philippum (NHC VIII, 2)," *ZTK* 74 (1977), 323–43.

———. *Die Polemik der Gnostiker gegen das kirchliche Christentum* (NHS XII; Leiden: Brill, 1978).

Kraft, H. *Die Offenbarung des Johannes* (HNT 16a; Tübingen: J. C. B. Mohr, 1974).

Kraft, R. *The Didache and Barnabas* (New York: Nelson, 1965).

———. "Philo on Seth: Was Philo Aware of Traditions Which Exalted Seth and His Progeny," *Rediscovery of Gnosticism. Vol. 2: Sethian Gnosticism* (ed. B. Layton; Leiden: Brill, 1981), 457–58.

Kramer, W. R. *Christ, Lord, Son of God* (SBT 50; London: SCM, 1966).

Krause, M. "Die Petrusakten in Codex VI von Nag Hammadi," *Essays on the Nag Hammadi Texts in Honour of Alexander Böhlig* (NHS III; Leiden: Brill, 1972), 36–58.

———. "Die Sakramente in der Exegese über die Seele," *Les Testes de Nag Hammadi* (NHS VII; ed. J. Ménard; Leiden: Brill, 1975), 47–55.

Kremer, J. *Das älteste Zeugnis von der Auferstehung Christi: Eine bibeltheologische Studie zur Aussage und Bedeutung von 1 Kor 15, 1–11.* (SBS 17; Stuttgart: Katholisches Bibelwerk, 1967).

———. "Zur Diskussion über 'das leere Grab,'" *Resurrexit. Actes du symposium international sur la résurrection de Jésus* (ed. E. Dhanis; Rome: Libreria Editrice Vaticana, 1974), 137–59.

———. *Die Osterbotschaft der vier Evangelien* (Stuttgart: Katholisches Bibelwerk, 1968).

Kuhn, H.-W. "Der Irdische Jesus bei Paulus als traditionsgeschichtliches und theologisches Problem," *ZTK* 67 (1970), 295–320.

Küng, H. *On Being a Christian* (Garden City, N.Y.: Doubleday, 1976).

Lambrecht, J. "Paul's Christological Use of Scripture in 1 Cor 15, 20–28," *NTS* 28 (1982), 502–27.

Lange, J. *Das Erscheinen des Auferstandenen im Evangelium nach Matthäus. Eine traditions- und redactionsgeschichtliche Untersuchung zu Mt 28, 16–20* (Würzburg: Echter, 1973).

Langer, S. K. *Mind: An Essay in Human Feeling. Vol. iii* (Baltimore: Johns Hopkins University, 1982).

Layton, B. *The Gnostic Treatise on Resurrection from Nag Hammadi* (HDR 12; Missoula, Mont.: Scholars, 1979).

Leaney, A. R. C. "Theophany, Resurrection and History," *Studia Evangelica* (ed. F. L. Cross; Berlin: Akademie, 1968).

———. "The Resurrection Narratives in Luke XXIV, 12–53," *NTS* 2 (1955/56), 110–14.

Lehmann, K. *Auferweckt am dritten Tag nach der Schrift* (QD 38; Freiburg: Herder, 1968).

Leon-Dufour, X. "Bulletin d'exégèse du Nouveau Testament. Sur la résurrection de Jésus," *RSR* 57 (1969), 583–622.

———. "The Appearances of the Risen Lord and Hermeneutics," *The Resurrection and Modern Biblical Thought* (ed. P. De Surgy; New York/Cleveland: Corpus, 1970), 107–28.

Lifton, R. J. *The Broken Connection. On Death and the Continuity of Life* (New York: Simon & Schuster, 1979).

———. "The Sense of Immortality. On Death and the Continuity of Life," *The Philosophy of Order* (eds. P. Opitz and G. Sebba; Stuttgart: Klett-Cotta, 1981), 137–52.

Lightfoot, R. H. *The Gospel Message of St. Mark* (Oxford: Oxford University, 1950).

Lilla, S. R. C. *Clement of Alexandria. A Study in Christian Platonism and Gnosticism* (Oxford: Oxford University, 1971).

Lincoln, A. T. *Paradise Now and Not Yet. Studies in the Role of the Heavenly Dimension in Paul's Thought with Special Reference to His Eschatology* (SNTSMS 43; Cambridge: Cambridge University, 1981).

Lindars, B. "The Persecution of Christians in Jn 15:18–16:4a," *Suffering and Martyrdom in the New Testament. Studies Presented to G. M. Styler* (eds. W. Horbury and B. McNeil; Cambridge: Cambridge University, 1981), 48–69.

Lindemann, "Die Osterbotschaft des Markus. Zur Theologischen Interpretation von Mk 16.1–8," *NTS* 26 (1979/80), 298–317.

Loewe, W. P. "Appearances of the Risen Lord: Faith, Fact and Objectivity," *Horizons* 6 (1979), 177–92.

———. "Encountering the Crucified God: The Soteriology of Sebastian Moore," *Horizons* 9 (1982), 216–36.

Lohfink, G. "Die Auferstehung Jesu und die historische Kritik," *BLit* 9 (1968), 37–53.

———. *The Conversion of St. Paul* (Chicago: Franciscan Herald Press, 1976).

———. *Die Himmelfahrt Jesu. Untersuchungen zu den Himmelfahrts- und Erhöhungstexten bei Lukas* (StANT 26; Munich: Kösel, 1971).

Lohse, E. *Colossians and Philemon* (Philadelphia: Fortress, 1971).

———. *Die Auferstehung Jesu Christi im Zeugnis des Lukasevangeliums* (Biblische Studien 31; Neukirchen: Neukirchener, 1961).

Lonergan, B. *Insight. A Study of Human Understanding* (New York: Philosophical Library, 1957).

———. *Method in Theology* (New York: Herder, 1972).

Longstaff, T. R. W. "The Women at the Tomb: Matthew 28:1 Reexamined," *NTS* 27 (1980/81), 277–82.

Ludemann, G. "Zur Geschichte des ältesten Christentums im Rom I. Valentin und Marcion II. Ptolemäus und Justin," *ZNW* 70 (1979), 86–114.

Lynch, W. *Images of Hope* (New York: New American Library, 1965).

Lyons, J. A. *The Cosmic Christ in Origen and Teilhard de Chardin* (Oxford: Oxford University, 1982).

McArthur, H. K. "On the Third Day," *NTS* 18 (1970/71), 81–86.

MacCormack, S. G. *Art and Ceremony in Late Antiquity* (Berkeley: University of California, 1981).

MacDonald, D. "A Conjectural Emmendation of 1 Cor 15:32: Or the Case of the Misplaced Lion Fight," *HTR* 73 (1980), 265–76.

MacMullen, R. *Paganism in the Roman Empire* (New Haven: Yale University, 1981).

MacRae, G. W. "Whom Heaven Must Receive Until the Time. Reflections on the Christology of Acts," *Int* 27 (1973), 151–65.

Mahoney, R. *Two Disciples at the Tomb. The Background and Message of Jn 20.1–10* (Theologie und Wirklichkeit 6; Frankfort: Peter Lang, 1974).

Malherbe, A. J. "The Beasts at Ephesus," *JBL* 87 (1968), 71–80.

———. "Gentle as a Nurse: The Cynic Background to 1 Thess ii," *NovT* 12 (1970), 203–17.

Malinine, M., et al. *Epistula ad Rheginum* (Zurich and Stuttgart: Rascher, 1963).

Manek, J. "The Apostle Paul and the Empty Tomb," *NovT* 2 (1957), 276–80.

Marcovich, M. "On the Text of Athenagoras, *De Resurrectione*," *VC* 33 (1979), 375–82.

Martelet, G. *The Risen Christ and the Eucharistic World* (London: Collins, 1976).

Martin, D. *The Breaking of the Image: A Sociology of Christian Theory and Practice* (New York: St Martin's, 1979).

Martini, C. *Il problema storico della resurrezione negli studi recenti* (Rome: Gregorian, 1959).

Marxsen, W. *The Resurrection of Jesus of Nazareth* (Philadelphia: Fortress, 1970).

Meeks, W. *The First Urban Christians. The Social World of the Apostle Paul* (New Haven: Yale University, 1983).

———. "The Man from Heaven in Johannine Sectarianism," *JBL* 91 (1972), 44–72.

———. "The Social Context of Pauline Theology," *Int* 36 (1982), 268–77.

Meier, J. *Matthew* (Wilmington: Glazier, 1980).

————. "Nations or Gentiles in Matthew 28:19?" *CBQ* 39 (1977), 94–102.

————. "Two Disputed Questions in Matt 28:16–20," *JBL* 96 (1977), 407–24.

————. *The Vision of Matthew* (New York: Paulist, 1979).

Ménard, J. E. *L'Évangile selon Philippe* (Paris: Letouzey & Ane, 1967).

————. "L'Évangile selon Philippe et l'Exégèse de l'Âme," *Les Textes de Nag Hammadi* (NHS 7; Leiden: Brill, 1975), 56–77.

————. "La Notion de résurrection dans l'Épître à Rheginos," *Essays on the Nag Hammadi Texts In Honour of Pahor Labib* (NHS VI; ed. M. Krause; Leiden: Brill, 1975), 110–24.

————. "La Notion de Résurrection dans l'Épître a Rheginos," *Proceedings of the International Colloquium on Gnosticism* (ed. G. Widengren; Stockholm: Almqvist & Wiksell, 1977), 123–31.

Merklein, H. "Die Auferweckung Jesu und die Anfänge der Christologie (Messias bzw. Sohn Gottes und Menschensohn)," *ZNW* 72 (1981), 1–26.

Metz, J. *Faith in History and Society* (New York: Seabury, 1980).

Meyer, M. *The Letter of Peter to Philip* (SBLDS 53; Chicago: Scholars, 1981).

Meyers, E. M., and Strange, J. F. *Archaeology, the Rabbis and Early Christianity* (Nashville: Abingdon, 1981).

Michel, O. *Der Brief an die Hebräer* (MK XIII; Göttingen: Vandenhoeck & Ruprecht, 1966, 6th ed.).

————. *Der Brief an die Römer* (MK; Göttingen: Vandenhoeck & Ruprecht, 1966, 4th ed.).

Minear, P. "We Don't Know Where . . . Jn 20:2," *Int* 30 (1976), 125–39.

Moltmann, J. *The Crucified God* (New York: Harper & Row, 1974).

————. "The Hope of the Resurrection and the Practice of Liberation," *The Future of Creation* (Philadelphia: Fortress, 1979), 97–114.

Moore, S. *The Fire and the Rose Are One* (New York: Seabury, 1980).

————. *The Crucified God Is No Stranger* (New York: Seabury, 1977).

Morrell, J. "Perfect Happiness and the Resurrection of the Body," *Religious Studies* 16 (1980), 29–35.

Moule, C. F. D. *The Origins of Christology* (Cambridge: Cambridge University, 1977).

————. "The Post-Resurrection Appearances in the Light of Festival Pilgrimages," *NTS* 4 (1957/58), 58–61.

————. "St. Paul and Dualism: The Pauline Concept of Resurrection," *NTS* 12 (1965/66), 106–23.

Murphy-O'Connor, J. *Becoming Human Together* (Wilmington: Glazier, 1982, 2nd ed.).

——. "Christological Anthropology in Phil II, 6–11," *RB* 83 (1976), 25–50.

——. *1 Corinthians* (Wilmington: Glazier, 1979).

——. "Corinthian Slogans in 1 Cor 6:12–20," *CBQ* 40 (1978), 391–96.

——. "Tradition and Redaction in 1 Cor 15:3–7," *CBQ* 43 (1981), 582–89.

Mursillo, H. *The Acts of the Christian Martyrs* (Oxford: Oxford University, 1972).

Mussner, F. *Die Auferstehung Jesu* (Munich: Kösel, 1969).

——. "Schichten in der paulinischen Theologie, dargetan an 1 Kor 15," *BZ* 9 (1965), 59–70.

Myers, J. M. *I and II Esdras* (AnBi 42; Garden City, N.Y.: Doubleday, 1974).

Nauck, W. "Die Bedeutung des leeren Grabes für den Glauben an den Auferstanden," *ZNW* 47 (1956), 243–67.

Neirynck, F. "ΑΝΑΤΕΙΛΑΝΤΟΣ ΤΟΥ ΗΛΙΟΥ (Mc 16, 2)," *EvT* 54 (1978), 70–103.

——. "Les femmes au tombeau," *NTS* 15 (1968/69), 168–90.

——. "Marc 16, 1–8 tradition et rédaction," *ETL* 56 (1980), 56–88.

Neyrey, J. "The Apologetic Use of the Transfiguration in 2 Peter 1:16–21," *CBQ* 42 (1980), 504–19.

Nickelsburg, G. W. E. "The Apocalyptic Message of *1 Enoch* 92–105," *CBQ* 39 (1977), 309–28.

——. "Enoch, Levi and Peter: Recipients of Revelation in Upper Galilee," *JBL* 100 (1981), 575–600.

——. "The Genre and Function of the Markan Passion Narrative," *HTR* 73 (1980), 153–84.

——. *Jewish Literature between the Bible and the Mishnah. A Historical and Literary Introduction* (Philadelphia: Fortress, 1981).

——. *Resurrection, Immortality, and Eternal Life in Intertestamental Judaism* (HTS xxvi; Cambridge: Harvard University, 1972).

——. "Riches, the Rich and God's Judgment in 1 En. 92–105 and the Gospel According to Luke," *NTS* 25 (1979), 324–44.

——. "Some Related Traditions in the Apocalypse of Adam, the Books of Adam and Eve, and 1 Enoch," *Rediscovery of Gnosticism. Vol. 2: Sethian Gnosticism* (ed. B. Layton; Leiden: Brill, 1981), 515–39.

Nicol, W. *The Semeia in the Fourth Gospel* (Leiden: Brill, 1972).

Nineham, D. E. *The Gospel of St. Mark* (Baltimore: Penguin, 1967).

Nozick, R. *Philosophical Explanations* (Cambridge: Harvard University, 1981).

O'Collins, G. G. "Is the Resurrection an Historical Event," *HeyJ* 8 (1967), 381–87.

Oepke, A. "Auferstehung (des Menschen)," *RAC* I (1950), 930–38.

———. *Der Brief des Paulus an die Galater* (THKNT 9; Berlin: Evangelische, 1964).

Ogilvie, R. M. *The Romans and Their Gods in the Age of Augustus* (New York: Norton, 1969).

Olafson, F. *The Dialectic of Action. A Philosophical Interpretation of History and the Humanities* (Chicago: University of Chicago, 1979).

O'Neill, J. C. "Did Jesus Teach that His Death Would Be Vicarious as Well as Typical," *Suffering and Martyrdom in the New Testament, Studies Presented to G. M. Styler* (eds. W. Horbury and B. McNeil; Cambridge: Cambridge University, 1981), 9–27.

Ong, W. *Interfaces of the Word* (Ithaca: Cornell, 1977).

———. *Presence of the Word* (New Haven: Yale University, 1967).

Osten-Sacken, P. V. D. *Römer 8 als Beispiel paulinischer Soteriologie* (Göttingen: Vandenhoeck & Ruprecht, 1975).

O'Toole, R. "Christ's Resurrection in Acts 13.13–52," *Bib* 60 (1979), 361–72.

Pagels, E. *The Johannine Gospel in Gnostic Exegesis* (Nashville: Abingdon, 1973).

———. *The Gnostic Paul* (Philadelphia: Fortress, 1975).

Panikkar, R. *The Unknown Christ of Hinduism* (London: Darton, Longman & Todd, 1964).

Pannenberg, W. *Jesus—God and Man* (Philadelphia: Westminster, 1968).

Parrott, D. M., ed. *Nag Hammadi Codices V, 2–5 and VI with Papyrus Berolinensis 8502, 1 and 4* (NHS XI; Leiden: Brill, 1979).

Pearson, B. "The Figure of Seth in Gnostic Literature," *Rediscovery of Gnosticism. Vol. 2: Sethian Gnosticism* (B. Layton, ed.; Leiden: Brill, 1981), 472–504.

———, ed. *Nag Hammadi Codices IX and X* (NHS XV; Leiden: Brill, 1981).

———. *The Pneumatikos-Psychikos Terminology in 1 Corinthians. A Study in the Theology of the Corinthian Opponents of Paul and*

Its Relation to Gnosticism (SBLDS 12; Missoula, Mont.: Scholars, 1973).

Peel, M. L. *The Epistle to Rheginos. A Valentinian Letter on the Resurrection* (Philadelphia: Westminster, 1969).

———. "Gnostic Eschatology and the New Testament," *NovT* 12 (1970), 141–65.

Pelikan, J. *The Emergence of the Catholic Tradition (100–600 A.D.)* (Chicago: University of Chicago, 1971).

Perkins, P. "An Ailment of Childhood: Spiritual Pediatrics for Adults," *Dimensions of Contemporary Spirituality* (ed. F. Eigo; Villanova: Villanova University, 1982), 79–115.

———. "The Apocalypse of Adam: Genre and Function of a Gnostic Apocalypse," *CBQ* 39 (1977), 382–95.

———. *The Gnostic Dialogue* (New York: Paulist, 1980).

———. *The Gospel According to John* (Chicago: Franciscan Herald, 1978).

———. *Hearing the Parables of Jesus* (Ramsey, N.J.: Paulist, 1981).

———. *The Johannine Epistles* (Wilmington: Glazier, 1979).

———. *Love Commands in the New Testament* (Ramsey, N.J.: Paulist, 1982).

Perrin, N. *Jesus and the Language of the Kingdom* (Philadelphia: Fortress, 1976).

———. *Rediscovering the Teaching of Jesus* (New York: Harper & Row, 1967).

Pesch, R. *Das Markusevangelium. II Teil. Kommentar zu Kap. 8, 27–16, 20* (HTKNT II/2; Freiburg: Herder, 1977).

———. "Zur Entstehung des Glaubens an die Auferstehung Jesu," *TQ* 153 (1973), 201–28.

Philonenko, M. *Joseph et Aseneth* (SPVS 13; Leiden: Brill, 1968).

Potscher, W. "Die Auferstehung in der klassichen Antike," *Kairos* 7 (1965), 208–15.

Pousset, E. "Croie en la résurrection," *NRT* 96 (1974), 366–88.

———. "La résurrection," *NRT* 91 (1969), 1009–44.

Rahner, K. "Dogmatic Questions on Easter," *Theological Investigations. Vol. 4* (Baltimore: Helicon, 1966), 121–33.

———. *Foundations of Christian Faith* (New York: Crossroad/Seabury, 1978).

———. "Jesus' Resurrection," *Theological Investigations. Vol. 17* (New York: Crossroad, 1981), 16–23.

———. "The Life of the Dead," *Theological Investigations. Vol. 4* (Baltimore: Helicon, 1966), 347–54.

————. "The Resurrection of the Body," *Theological Investigations.* *Vol. 2* (Baltimore: Helicon, 1963), 203–16.

————. "On the Spirituality of the Easter Faith," *Theological Investigations. Vol. 17* (New York: Crossroad, 1981), 8–15.

Reumann, J. *Righteousness in the New Testament* (Philadelphia: Fortress/Ramsey, N.J.: Paulist, 1982).

Rhoads, D., and Michie, D. *Mark as Story* (Philadelphia: Fortress, 1982).

Ricoeur, P. *Freud and Philosophy* (New Haven: Yale University, 1970).

————. *Hermeneutics and the Human Sciences* (Cambridge: Cambridge University, 1981).

————. *The Rule of Metaphor* (Toronto: University of Toronto, 1977).

————. *The Symbolism of Evil* (Boston: Beacon, 1967).

Riedl, J. "Wirklich der Herr ist auferweckt geworden und dem Simon erschienen (Lk 24, 34. Entstehung und Inhalt des neutestamentlichen Osterglaubnis)," *BLit* 40 (1967), 81–110.

Rigaux, B. *Dieu l'a réssuscité. Exégèse théologie biblique.* (Gembloux: Duculot, 1973).

Ritt, H. "Die Frauen und die Osterbotschaft. Synopse der Grabgeschichten (Mk 16, 1–8; Mt 27, 62–28, 15; Lk 24, 1–12; Joh 20, 1–18)," *Die Frau im Urchristentum* (QD 95; eds. G. Dautzenberg, H. Merklein, and K. Muller; Freiburg: Herder, 1983), 117–33.

Robinson, J. A. T. "The Most Primitive Christology of All?" *Twelve New Testament Essays* (SBT 34; London: SCM, 1962), 139–53.

————. *The Truth Is Two-Eyed* (Philadelphia: Westminster, 1979).

Robinson, J. M. "Jesus: From Easter to Valentinus (or to the Apostles' Creed)," *JBL* 101 (1982), 5–37.

————, ed. *The Nag Hammadi Library in English* (San Francisco: Harper & Row, 1977).

Rochais, G. *Les Récits de résurrection des morts* (SNTSMS 40; Cambridge: Cambridge University, 1980).

Rollins, W. G. *Jung and the Bible* (Atlanta: John Knox, 1983).

Rousseau, A., and Doutreleau, J. *Irenée de Lyon. Contre les hérésies* (SC; Paris: Editions du Cerf, 1965–82).

Rowland, C. *The Open Heaven. A Study of Apocalyptic in Judaism and Early Christianity* (New York: Crossroad, 1982).

Rudolph, K. "Die 'Sethianische' Gnosis. Eine Häresiologische Fiction," *Rediscovery of Gnosticism. Vol. 2: Sethian Gnosticism* (ed. B. Layton; Leiden: Brill, 1981), 577–78.

Rupp, G. *Christologies and Cultures* (The Hague: Mouton, 1974).

Russell, D. S. *The Method and Message of Jewish Apocalyptic* (Philadelphia: Westminster, 1964).

Sagnard, F. *Clément d'Alexandrie: Extraits de Théodote* (SC; Paris: Éditions du Cerf, 1948).

Sampley, P. *Pauline Partnership in Christ* (Philadelphia: Fortress, 1980).

Schell, J. *The Fate of the Earth* (New York: Knopf, 1982).

Schenk, W. "Textlinguistische Aspekte der Structuranalyse, dargestellt am Beispiel von 1 Kor xv.1–11," *NTS* 23 (1976/77), 469–77.

Schenke, H.-M. "The Phenomenon and Significance of Gnostic Sethianism," *Rediscovery of Gnosticism. Vol. 2: Sethian Gnosticism* (ed. B. Layton; Leiden: Brill, 1981), 588–616.

———. "Auferstehungsglaube und Gnosis," *ZNW* 59 (1968), 123–26.

Schenke, L. *Auferstehungsverkundigung und leeres Grab. Eine traditionsgeschichtliche Untersuchung von Mk 16, 1–8* (SBS 33; Stuttgart: Katholisches Bibelwerk, 1969, 2nd ed.).

Schieber, H. "Konzentrik im Matthäusschluss. Ein form und gattungskritischer Versuch zu Mt 28, 16–20," *Kairos* 19 (1977), 286–307.

Schille, G. "Das Leiden des Herrn: Die evangelische Passionstradition und ihr Sitz im Leben," *ZTK* 52 (1955), 161–205.

Schillebeeckx, E. *Christ* (New York: Crossroad, 1981).

———. *Interim Report on the Books Jesus and Christ* (New York: Crossroad, 1981).

———. *Jesus* (New York: Seabury, 1979).

Schlier, H. *Der Brief an die Galater* (MK VII; Göttingen: Vandenhoeck & Ruprecht, 1964, 4th ed.).

———. *Der Römerbrief* (HTKNT 6: Freiburg: Herder, 1979).

Schmidt, C., and MacDermot, V. *Pistis Sophia* (NHS IX; Leiden: Brill, 1978).

Schmitt, J. "La Résurrection de Jésus: des formules kérygmatiques aux récits évangeliques," *Parole de Dieu et sacerdoce* (Mélanges Msgr. Weber) (Paris: Gabalda, 1962), 93–105.

———. "Le 'Milieu' littéraire de la 'Tradition' citée dans 1 Cor., XV, 3b–5," *Resurrexit. Actes du symposium international sur la résurrection de Jésus* (ed. E. Dhanis; Rome: Libreria Editrice Vaticana, 1974), 169–80.

Schnackenburg, R. "Zur Aussageweise 'Jesus ist (von dem Toten) Auferstanden,'" *BZ* 13 (1969), 1–17.

———. *The Gospel According to St. John. Vol. 1: Chaps. 1–4* (New York: Herder, 1968).

———. *Das Johannesevangelium II. Kap. 5–12* (HTKNT IV/2; Freiburg: Herder, 1971) [ET: *The Gospel According to St. John. Vol. II: Chaps. 5–12* (New York: Seabury, 1980)].

———. *Das Johannesevangelium III. Kap. 13–21* (HTKNT IV/3;

Freiburg: Herder, 1975) [ET: *The Gospel According to St. John. Vol. 3: Chaps. 13–21* (New York: Crossroad, 1982)].

Schnider, F., and Sterner, W. *Die Ostergeschichten der Evangelien* (Schriften zur Katechetik 13; Munich: Kösel, 1970).

Schoedel, W. *Polycarp, Martyrdom of Polycarp, Fragments of Papias* (New York: Nelson, 1967).

―――. *Athenagoras Legatio and De Resurrectione* (Oxford: Oxford University, 1972).

Schubert, K. "Auferstehung Jesu im Lichte der Religionsgeschichte des Judentums," *Resurrexit. Actes du symposium international sur la résurrection de Jésus* (ed. E. Dhanis; Rome: Libreria Editrice Vaticana, 1974), 207–23.

―――. "Die Entwicklung der Auferstehungslehre von der nachexilischen bis zur frührabbinische Zeit," *BZ* 6 (1962), 177–214.

Schutz, J. *Paul and the Anatomy of Apostolic Authority* (Cambridge: Cambridge University, 1975).

Schweizer, E. *The Letter to the Colossians* (Minneapolis: Augsburg, 1982).

Scroggs, R., and Groff, K. J. "Baptism in Mark: Dying and Rising with Christ," *JBL* 92 (1973), 531–48.

Segovia, F. F. "John 15:18–16:4a: A First Addition to the Original Farewell Discourse?" *CBQ* 45 (1983), 210–30.

Seiensticker, P. "Das Antiochenische Glaubensbekenntnis 1 Kor. 15, 3–7 im Lichte seiner Traditionsgeschichte," *Theologie und Glaube* 57 (1967), 286–323.

―――. *Die Auferstehung Jesu in der Botschaft der Evangelisten* (SBS 26; Stuttgart: Katholisches Bibelwerke, 1967).

Senior, D. "The Death of Jesus and the Resurrection of the Holy Ones (Mt 27:51–53)," *CBQ* 38 (1976), 312–29.

Sevrin, J. M. "Les Noces Spirituelles dans l'évangile selon Philippe," *Muséon* 87 (1974), 143–93.

Sider, L. *Ancient Rhetoric and the Art of Tertullian* (Oxford: Oxford University, 1971).

―――. "Structure and Design in the 'De Resurrectione Mortuorum' of Tertullian," *VC* 23 (1969), 177–96.

Smith, J. Z. *Imagining Religion. From Babylon to Jonestown* (Chicago: University of Chicago, 1982).

Smith, M. *Clement of Alexandria and a Secret Gospel of Mark* (Cambridge: Harvard, 1973).

Snyder, G. F. *The Shepherd of Hermas* (Camden, N.J.: Nelson, 1968).

Sperry, R. *Science and Moral Priority: Merging Mind, Brain and Human Values* (New York: Columbia University, 1983).

Sporlein, B. *Die Leugnung der Auferstehung. Eine historische-*

kritische Untersuchung au 1 Kor. 15 (Regensburg: F. Pustet, 1971).

Stanley, D. M. *Christ's Resurrection in Pauline Soteriology* (Rome: Biblical Institute Press, 1961).

Stegner, W. *Der Christushymnus 1 Tim 3,16: Ein Struktur-analytische Untersuchung* (Frankfort: Lang, 1977).

Stein, R. H. "Is the Transfiguration (Mk 9:2–8) a Misplaced Resurrection Account?" *JBL* 95 (1976), 79–96.

———. "A Short Note on Mk xiv.28 and xvi.7," *NTS* 20 (1974/75), 445–52.

Steinseifer, B. "Der Ort der Erscheinungen des Auferstandenen. Zur Frage alter galiläischer Ostertraditionen," *ZNW* 62 (1971), 232–65.

Stemberger, G. *Der Leib der Auferstehung* (AnBi 36; Rome: Biblical Institute Press, 1972).

Stendahl, K., ed. *Immortality and Resurrection* (New York: Macmillan, 1971).

———. *Paul Among Jews and Gentiles* (Philadelphia: Fortress, 1976).

Strecker, G. *Der Weg der Gerechtigkeit. Untersuchung zur Theologie des Matthäus* (Göttingen: Vandenhoeck & Ruprecht, 1971).

Stroumsa, G. "Polymorphie divine et transformations d'un mythologème: l'Apocryphon de Jean et ses sources," *VC* 35 (1981), 412–34.

Stuhlmacher, P. "Das Bekenntnis zur Auferweckung Jesu von den Toten und die biblische Theologie," *ZTK* 70 (1973), 365–405.

Sullivan, J. P. *Petronius, The Satyricon and Seneca, The Apocolocyntosis* (New York: Penguin, 1977).

Tannehill, R. *Dying and Rising with Christ* (BZNW 32; Berlin: Töpelmann, 1967).

———. "The Gospel of Mark as Narrative Christology," *Semeia* 16 (1979), 57–93.

Taylor, V. *The Gospel According to St. Mark* (New York: St. Martin's, 1952).

Theissen, G. *The Social Setting of Pauline Christianity. Essays on Corinth* (Philadelphia: Fortress, 1982).

Thompson, A. L. *Responsibility for Evil in the Theodicy of IV Ezra: A Study Illustrating the Significance of Form and Structure for the Meaning of the Book* (SBLDS 29; Missoula, Mont.: Scholars, 1977).

Thompson, J. W. *The Beginnings of Christian Philosophy: The Epistle to the Hebrews* (CBQMS 13; Washington, D.C.: Catholic Biblical Association, 1982).

Thompson, W. M. *Jesus, Lord and Savior: A Theopathic Christology and Soteriology* (New York: Paulist, 1980).

Thüsing, W. *Erhöhungsvorstellung und Parusieerwartung in der ältesten nachösterlichen Christologie* (SBS 42; Stuttgart: Katholisches Bibelwerk, 1969).

Toulmin, S. *The Return to Cosmology. Postmodern Science and the Theology of Nature* (Berkeley: University of California, 1982).

Toynbee, A., ed. *The Crucible of Christianity* (New York: World, 1969).

Tracy, D. *The Analogical Imagination* (New York: Crossroad, 1981).

————. *Blessed Rage for Order* (New York: Seabury, 1975).

Trilling, W. *Das Wahre Israel. Studien zur Theologie des Matthäus-Evangeliums* (Munich: Kösel, 1964).

Trompf, G. W. "The First Resurrection Appearances and the Ending of Mark's Gospel," *NTS* 18 (1971/72), 308–30.

Trummer, P. *Die Paulustradition der Pastoralbriefe* (BEvT 8; Frankfort: Lang, 1978).

Turner, J. *The Book of Thomas the Contender* (SBLDS 23; Missoula, Mont.: Scholars, 1975).

van Unnik, W. C. "A Document of Second Century Theological Discussion (Irenaeus A.H. I.10.3)," *VC* 31 (1977), 196–228.

————. "The Newly Discovered Gnostic 'Epistle to Rheginos' on the Resurrection," *JEH* 15 (1964), 141–67.

Van der Horst, P. W. *The Sentences of Pseudo-Phocylides* (SVTP iv; Leiden: Brill, 1978).

VanderKam, J. C. *Textual and Historical Studies in the Book of Jubilees* (Missoula, Mont.: Scholars, 1977).

Vermule, E. *Aspects of Death in Early Greek Art* (Berkeley: University of California, 1979).

Voeglin, E. *The Ecumenic Age* (Baton Rouge: Louisiana State University, 1974).

Wagner, G. ". . . encore 1 Corinthiens 15. Si les chrétiens refusent d'agir alors Christ n'est pas ressuscité," ETR 56 (1981), 599–607.

Wahle, H. "Die Lehren des rabbinischen Judentums über das Leben nach dem Tod," *Kairos* 14 (1972), 291–309.

Walker, N. "After Three Days," *NovT* 4 (1960), 261–62.

Walker, W. O. "Post Crucifixion Appearances and Christian Origins," *JBL* 88 (1969), 157–65.

————. "Christian Origins and Resurrection Faith," *JR* 52 (1972), 41–55.

Walter, N. "Eine vormatthäische Schilderung der Auferstehung Jesu," *NTS* 19 (1972/73), 415–29.

Wanke, J. " '. . . wie Sie ihn beim Brotbrechen erkannten'. Zur Auslegung der Emmauserzählung Lk 24.13–35," *BZ* 18 (1974), 180–92.

Wedderburn, A. J. M. "The Problem of the Denial of the Resurrection in 1 Corinthians XV," *NovT* 23 (1981), 229–41.

Weeden, T. *Mark. Traditions in Conflict* (Philadelphia: Fortress, 1971).

Weiser, A. "Die Rolle der Frau in der urchristlichen Mission," *Die Frau im Urchristentum* (G. Dautzenberg, H. Merklein, K. Müller, eds.; Quaestiones Disputatae 95; Freiburg: Herder, 1983), 158–81.

Wengst, K. *Christologische Formeln und Lieder des Urchristentums* (Gütersloh: Gerd Mohn, 1972).

Whittaker, M. *Tatian Oratio ad Graecos* (Oxford: Oxford University, 1982).

Wilckens, U. *Auferstehung. Das biblische Auferstehungszeugnis untersucht und erklärt* (Themen der Theologie 4; Stuttgart/Berlin: Kreuz, 1970) [ET: *Resurrection. Biblical Testimony to the Resurrection: An Historical Examination and Explication* (Atlanta: John Knox, 1978)].

———. *Die Missionsreden der Apostelgeschichte: Form- und traditionsgeschichtliche Untersuchungen* (WMANT 5; Neukirchen: Neukirchener, 1961).

———. "The Tradition History of the Resurrection of Jesus," *The Significance of the Message of Resurrection for Faith in Jesus Christ* (ed. C. F. D. Moule; SBT ser. 2, no. 8; London: SCM, 1968), 51–76.

Wilder, A. *Jesus' Parables and the War of Myths. Essays on Imagination in the Scriptures* (Philadelphia: Fortress, 1982).

———. *Theopoetic. Theology and the Religious Imagination* (Philadelphia: Fortress, 1976).

Williams, B. *Descartes. The Project of Pure Inquiry* (New York: Penguin, 1978).

Williams, M. "Stability as a Soteriological Theme in Gnosticism," *The Rediscovery of Gnosticism. Vol. 2: Sethian Gnosticism* (ed. B. Layton; Leiden: Brill, 1981), 819–29.

Williams, S. K. *Jesus' Death as a Saving Event. The Background and Origin of a Concept* (HDR 2; Missoula, Mont.: Scholars, 1975).

Wilson, J. H. "The Corinthians Who Say There Is No Resurrection of the Dead," *ZNW* 59 (1968), 94–96.

Wilson, S. G. "The Ascension: A Critique and an Interpretation,"
    ZNW 59 (1968), 269–81.
Winston, D. *The Wisdom of Solomon* (AnBi 43; Garden City, N.Y.:
    Doubleday, 1979).
Winter, P. "1 Corinthians XV 3b–7," *NovT* 2 (1957/58), 142–50.
Wisse, F. "On Exegeting the Exegesis on the Soul," *Les Textes de Nag
    Hammadi* (NHS 7; ed. J. Ménard; Leiden: Brill, 1975), 68–81.
———. "Stalking those Elusive Sethians," *The Rediscovery of Gnosti-
    cism. Vol. 2: Sethian Gnosticism* (ed. B. Layton; Leiden: Brill,
    1981), 563–76.
Woll, D. B. *Johannine Christianity in Conflict: Authority, Rank and
    Succession in the First Farewell Discourse* (SBLDS 60; Chicago:
    Scholars, 1981).
Wong, D. W. F. "Natural and Divine Order in 1 Clement," *VC* 31
    (1977), 81–87.

Zanartu, S. "Les Concepts de vie et de mort chez Ignace d'Anti-
    oche," *VC* 33 (1979), 324–41.

Index